GEORGE MACDONALD
AND HIS WIFE . .

Photo by] GEORGE MACDONALD, LL.D., 1892 [Elliott & Fry

GEORGE MACDONALD AND HIS WIFE

BY
GREVILLE MACDONALD, M.D.

WITH AN INTRODUCTION
BY
G. K. CHESTERTON

TWENTY-EIGHT ILLUSTRATIONS

LONDON : GEORGE ALLEN & UNWIN LTD.
RUSKIN HOUSE, 40 MUSEUM STREET, W.C.

This edition of *George MacDonald and His Wife* (2025) is an independent production by
theroomtoroam.com

George MacDonald and His Wife was first published in 1924 by George Allen & Unwin Ltd, London
Cover art by Haleigh DeRocher
Back Cover Extract by CS Lewis © copyright CS Lewis Pte Ltd.
All rights reserved

ISBN: 978-1-917830-23-2

FOREWORD

THIS is the hundredth year since George MacDonald's birth, and the time is ripe for reminding the world of a spiritual genius whose art was so rare that, had he confined himself to poetry and purely imaginitive story-telling, he could not have been almost forgotten. His fairy-tales and allegorical fantasies were epoch-making in the lives of multitudes, children and parents alike, and still are widely read. His novels, not only those which, conceived in his native country, inaugurated a new school in Scottish literature, but his stories of English life also, stirred the religious world to its depths and left their impress direct or mediate on the deeper thought of the whole English-speaking world.

The story here given tells of a long struggle against prejudice and contumely, poverty, ill-health and bitter griefs, yet all endured triumphantly because of the man's love for truth and his wife's vigilant ministration. Apart altogether from their significance in the intellectual and religious history of the age, its events, now that they are set down, look as though they just had to be chronicled. They give so realistic a picture of domestic and widely shared happiness three generations back that, with present-day customs on all sides usurping the time-honoured instinct for family joys and responsibilities, they should set many asking, What then are the riches we have flung away? Indeed, so simple, faithful and happy were his father and mother, so full their lives of pathos and humour, that it seems right to give their history in full detail.

There was nothing to conceal, and nothing has been concealed. Some who have given the writer much help have thought certain points too intimate for publication. On the other hand, only those capable of loving this man and wife for their courage, their tenderness, and their wide hospitalities will be much interested; and it is to these only the book can lie open and reveal its sanctities. Were the story produced a hundred years hence, its method would never be questioned—even though no hand like the present compiler's, dutifully in love with its subjects, could be found for the task.

As matter of fact, George MacDonald had expressed a hope that his Life would not be written: his message was all in his books, and no biography could add to it. But against acquiescence in such hope, stands one fact that he could not have foreseen. To the astonishment of the family, there was published immediately after his death a life of George MacDonald, incorrect, imperfect, and with little understanding of his place in the literary world, notwithstanding the writer's evident love and admiration for his subject. Hence it seemed right that with the wonderful letters now available, the biography should be undertaken by one who, however limited his abilities, owed to George and Louisa MacDonald everything, shared so much of their joy and sorrow, and witnessed their victory over the common tragedy of life. There is not anything herein set down but facts and truths, criticisms and admirations, which he feels that his parents, were they now at his side, while yet inhabiting that larger life for which they lived and suffered, would approve: "If it is to help our grandchildren to live nobly and the world to love purely, then God be with your telling of our story!"

ACKNOWLEDGMENTS

THE opportunity must not pass without thanking the many friends of the writer and lovers of his parents for the help they have given. Without the material contributed from all parts of the globe, from all sects and grades of British, Irish and American lovers of George MacDonald, the book had never been written; without friends' encouragement over a work that has proved almost as heartrending as delightful, without their sympathetic criticism of the script, readers of its final form might have suffered much from its imperfections.

First among these friends must be named the late Sir William Robertson Nicoll, who, having read the first half of the book, believed it would prove "one of the fullest records of a victorious faith in the whole history of the Christian Church"; but he did not live to read the second half. The book is in the next place indebted to Mrs. Crawford Noble of Aberdeen, George MacDonald's youngest sister, for having rescued from threatened flames a long series of letters from him to their father, almost every one of which is included. The writer's cousin, Robert Troup, of The Farm, Huntly, has been very helpful in contributing local and family information, while a more distant relative, Dr. John MacDonald of Kildrummy and William Will of *The Graphic*, have lent descriptive documents. Mrs. Arthur Morley Francis, Mrs. George MacDonald's sister, had set down at the writer's request, and in view of this work, many and delightful particulars about her own family in the 'forties; but she died in 1910. The writer's sister, Mrs. Cecil Brewer, has been wise and helpful in many suggestions. To James A. Campbell of Barbreck, learned in Celtic lore and Scottish history, and to Ernest Rhys warm thanks are due for pointed and illuminating criticism. Sir Leonard Powell and Mrs. Henry Hett have contributed certain useful items, the latter lending some early unpublished verse. Miss Rose Goodwin, more intimate with George MacDonald's works than anyone the writer knows, has given him sympathetic aid; and the Rev. Cyril H. Valentine of Arundel has helped with some apposite details; while a fellow student of George MacDonald, the Rev. Charles Green's reminiscences of their theological college are full of point and atmosphere; and Mrs. W. Carey Davies has lent invaluable letters. Last, but not least, to Joseph King, the writer's cousin, and his wife, Maude Egerton King, thanks are rendered for their patient weighings and endorsement.

The list of those who have sent contributions, many of them referred to in the text, and who have given permission to publish letters, is a long one. Lady Lovelace and Lady Wentworth, have allowed the printing of Lady Byron's letters to George MacDonald; Mrs. Arthur Severn and Mr. Alexander Wedderburn, K.C., have sanctioned the inclusion of Ruskin's letters; Mr. and Mrs. C. Edmund Maurice have permitted the use of letters of Frederick Denison Maurice and Octavia Hill. The Hon. Wilfrid Ashley has approved the printing of a letter of Lord Mount-Temple and some extracts from his privately printed *Memorials*; Miss Rosamond Gilder, daughter of the late Richard Watson Gilder of New York, has granted the loan of her father's letters with full discretion in dealing with them. Albert Bigelow Paine, Mark Twain's biographer, has given permission to reprint a letter and certain words of appreciation. A few letters of other old friends of the family have been printed without their representatives' permission, it proving impossible to discover them. Messrs. G. Michelmore, of 5, Royal Opera Arcade, S.W., and Mr. C. Richardson, of 42*a*, Rosamond Street, Chorlton-on-Medlock, Manchester, both firms being booksellers, have generously given the writer access to certain autograph letters of George MacDonald; while Messrs. Elliott and Fry have disinterestedly allowed the reproduction of several copyright photographs.

Many other contributions, such as full notes of George MacDonald's lectures and sermons, personal incidents, declarations of his influence over people's lives and thoughts, have been sent, and should be included but for lack of space. The text is nevertheless indebted much to these kindnesses, for they give sense of his real spiritual dynamic.

Lastly, to Mr. Stanley Unwin, the publisher, more than formal thanks are due for his appreciation of George MacDonald's true place in literature, and his sympathy with the biographer in difficulties inseparable from a work of this nature.

CONTENTS

		PAGE
FOREWORD		1
ACKNOWLEDGMENTS		3
INTRODUCTION		9
PREFACE		16

BOOK I
BOYHOOD AND YOUTH

CHAPTER		
I.	THE PLACE OF BIRTH	19
II.	HIS PARENTS	25
III.	THE MACDONALD DESCENT	38
IV.	THE MACKAY DESCENT	46
V.	BOYHOOD	51
VI.	THE YOUNG PHILOSOPHER	67
VII.	THE YOUNG POET	74
VIII.	THE DISCIPLE	85

BOOK II
THE LOVER

I.	THE WOOL-WORK SLIPPERS	91
II.	THE FAMILY OF JAMES POWELL	96
III.	THE NEW OUTLOOK	107
IV.	BETROTHAL	110
V.	NEW FRIENDS AND DUTIES	118
VI.	FATHER AND SON	129

BOOK III
CALLED AND REJECTED

I.	THE CALL TO ARUNDEL	135
II.	MARRIAGE	143
III.	THE PASTOR	154
IV.	THE THREE BROTHERS	160
V.	THE HERESY HUNT	177

BOOK IV
MANCHESTER

I.	ALEXANDER JOHN SCOTT	191
II.	THE WILDERNESS	196
III.	A HOME AGAIN	206
IV.	THE PREACHING ROOM IN RENSHAW STREET	212
V.	WITHIN AND WITHOUT	220
VI.	THE PAINTED TABLE	228
VII.	LOOKING AT DEATH	241

CHAPTER

BOOK V
MIGRATIONS

| I. | KINGSWEAR AND HUNTLY | 259 |
| II. | ALGIERS | 266 |

BOOK VI
HASTINGS

I.	THE TACKLEWAY	277
II.	ADESTE FIDELES	285
III.	FATHER AND BROTHER FALL ASLEEP	290
IV.	PHANTASTES	294
V.	LADY BYRON	300

BOOK VII
THE NOVELIST

I.	DAVID ELGINBROD	317
II.	JOHN RUSKIN	328
III.	LEWIS CARROLL	342
IV.	SWITZERLAND	347
V.	THE EDINBURGH CHAIR	353
VI.	BUDE	359
VII.	VERBAL INSPIRATION	371
VIII.	THE RETREAT	379
IX.	THE BLUE BELL	389
X.	FREDERICK DENISON MAURICE	397

BOOK VIII
AMERICA

I.	THE INVITATION	409
II.	THE RECEPTION	419
III.	NEW FRIENDS	437
IV.	FAREWELL	450

BOOK IX
THE VALLEY OF THE SHADOW

| I. | PALAZZO CATTANEO | 465 |
| II. | PORTO FINO | 483 |

BOOK X
CORAGGIO

I.	MR. GREATHEART	501
II.	THE PASSING OF CHRISTIANA	516
III.	A SHEAF OF LETTERS	528
IV.	LAST WORDS	537
V.	THE LONG VIGIL	546

| BIBLIOGRAPHY | 563 |
| INDEX | 567 |

ILLUSTRATIONS

GEORGE MACDONALD (1892)	*Frontispiece*
	TO FACE PAGE
GEORGE MACDONALD'S FATHER AND MOTHER	25
HIS FATHER AND GRANDMOTHER	25
THE MISSES CHARLOTTE, ANGELA AND CAROLINE POWELL	97
JAMES POWELL AND MRS. HELEN POWELL	97
GEORGE MACDONALD AND HIS WIFE (1855)	161
ALEXANDER AND JOHN HILL MACDONALD	161
BRONZE MEDALLION OF GEORGE MACDONALD (1855)	305
GEORGE MACDONALD (1862)	321
MRS. GEORGE MACDONALD, HER FAMILY AND LEWIS CARROLL	345
GROUP OF CONTEMPORARY WRITERS	353
THE RETREAT, HAMMERSMITH	385
GEORGE MACDONALD AND RICHARD WATSON GILDER (1873)	425
FAMILY OF GEORGE MACDONALD (1876)	465
BIG ROOM AT CASA CORAGGIO	505
GEORGE MACDONALD (1884)	513
LILIA SCOTT MACDONALD AS *CHRISTIANA*	521
GEORGE MACDONALD (1890) AND HIS WIFE (1885)	537
THE GOLDEN WEDDING	553

GEORGE MACDONALD'S BOOK-PLATE AFTER WILLIAM BLAKE

Song

Hark, in the steeple, the dull bell swinging
Over the furrows ill ploughed by Death!
~~Hark Over his young ones~~ the loud lark singing
Pours out his soul in ~~triumphant~~ triumphant breath!

Wild in the pine wood, the wind complaining
Moaneth and murmureth: ~~Life is bare!~~
Caught in the organ, the wind ~~from the organ~~ out straining,
Bursteth ~~out~~ free, in a soaring prayer!

Sit on the ground, and hold fast thy sorrow
I will give ~~~~ freedom, to mine in song;
Haunt thou the tomb, and deny ~~~~ the morrow,
I will go watch in the dawning long!
~~~~ strong!

For I
Shall ~~~~ see them, and know their faces!
Look in the depth of the eyes of old!
Clasp the same self in the old embraces,
Tenderer, sweeter, by many a fold!
~~~~

Toll for the burying, Sexton tolling!
Sing for the second birth, angel lark!
Moan, ye poor pines, with the Past condoling!
Burst out, brave Organ, and kill the Dark!

George MacDonald.

Aosta.
Oct. 3, 1887.

INTRODUCTION

Certain magazines have symposiums (I will call them "symposia" if I am allowed to call the two separate South Kensington collections "musea") in which persons are asked to name "Books that Have Influenced Me", on the lines of "Hymns that Have Helped Me". It is not a very realistic process as a rule, for our minds are mostly a vast uncatalogued library; and for a man to be photographed with one of the books in his hand generally means at best that he has chosen at random, and at worst that he is posing for effect. But in a certain rather special sense I for one can really testify to a book that has made a difference to my whole existence, which helped me to see things in a certain way from the start; a vision of things which even so real a revolution as a change of religious allegiance has substantially only crowned and confirmed. Of all the stories I have read, including even all the novels of the same novelist, it remains the most real, the most realistic, in the exact sense of the phrase the most like life. It is called *The Princess and the Goblin,* and is by George MacDonald, the man who is the subject of this book.

When I say it is like life, what I mean is this. It describes a little princess living in a castle in the mountains which is perpetually undermined, so to speak, by subterranean demons who sometimes come up through the cellars. She climbs up the castle stairways to the nursery or the other rooms; but now and again the stairs do not lead to the usual landings, but to a new room she has never seen before, and cannot generally find again. Here a good great-grandmother, who is a sort of fairy godmother, is perpetually spinning and speaking words of understanding and encouragement. When I read it as a child, I felt that the whole thing was happening inside a real human house, not essentially unlike the house I was living in, which also had staircases and rooms and cellars. This is where the fairy-tale differed from many other fairy-tales; above all, this is where the philosophy differed from many other philosophies. I have always felt a certain insufficiency about the ideal of Progress, even of the best sort which is a Pilgrim's Progress. It hardly suggests how near both the best and the worst things are to us from the first; even perhaps especially at the first. And though like every other sane person I value and revere the ordinary fairy-tale of the miller's third son who set out to seek his fortune (a form which MacDonald himself followed in the sequel called *The Princess and Curdie*), the very suggestion of travelling to a far-off fairyland, which is the soul of it, prevents it from achieving this particular purpose of making all the ordinary staircases and doors and windows into magical things.

Dr. Greville MacDonald, in his intensely interesting memoir of his father which follows, has I think mentioned somewhere his sense of the strange symbolism of stairs. Another recurrent image in his romances was a great white horse; the father of the princess had one, and there was another in *The Back of the North Wind*. To this day I can never see a big white horse in the street without a sudden sense of indescribable things. But for the moment I am speaking of what may emphatically be called the presence of household gods—and household goblins. And the picture of life in this parable is not only truer than the image of a journey like that of the Pilgrim's Progress, it is even truer than the mere image of a siege like that of The Holy War. There is something not only imaginative but intimately true about the idea of the goblins being below the house and capable of besieging it from the cellars. When the evil things besieging us do appear, they do not appear outside but inside. Anyhow, that simple image of a house that is our home, that is rightly loved as our home, but of which we hardly know the best or the worst, and must always wait for the one and watch against the other, has always remained in my mind as something singularly solid and unanswerable; and was more corroborated than corrected when I came to give a more definite name to the lady watching over us from the turret, and perhaps to take a more practical view of the goblins under the floor. Since I first read that story some five alternative philosophies of the universe have come to our colleges out of Germany, blowing through the world like the east wind. But for me that castle is still standing in the mountains and the light in its tower is not put out.

All George MacDonald's other stories, interesting and suggestive in their several ways, seem to be illustrations and even disguises of that one. I say disguises, for this is the very important difference between his sort of mystery and mere allegory. The commonplace allegory takes what it regards as the commonplaces or conventions necessary to ordinary men and women, and tries to make them pleasant or picturesque by dressing them up as princesses or goblins or good fairies. But George MacDonald did really believe that people were princesses and goblins and good fairies, and he dressed them up as ordinary men and women. The fairy-tale was the inside of the ordinary story and not the outside. One result of this is that all the inanimate objects that are the stage properties of the story retain that nameless glamour which they have in a literal fairy-tale. The staircase in *Robert Falconer* is as much of a magic ladder as the staircase in the *Princess and the Goblin*; and when the boys are making the boat and the girl is reciting verses to them, in *Alec Forbes*, and some old gentleman says playfully that it will rise to song like a magic Scandinavian ship, it always seemed to me as if he were describing the reality, apart from the appearance, of the incident. The novels as novels are uneven, but as fairy-tales they are extraordinarily consistent. He never for a moment loses his own inner thread that runs through the patchwork, and it is the thread that the fairy great-grandmother put into the hands of Curdie to guide him out of the mazes of the goblins.

The originality of George MacDonald has also a historical significance, which perhaps can best be estimated by comparing him with his great countryman Carlyle. It is a measure of the very real power and even popularity of Puritanism in Scotland that Carlyle never lost the Puritan mood even when he lost the whole of the Puritan theology. If an escape from the bias of environment be the test of originality, Carlyle never completely escaped, and George MacDonald did. He evolved out of his own mystical meditations a complete alternative theology leading to a completely contrary mood. And in those mystical meditations he learned secrets far beyond the mere extension of Puritan indignation to ethics and politics. For in the real genius of Carlyle there was a touch of the bully, and wherever there is an element of bullying there is an element of platitude, of reiteration and repeated orders. Carlyle could never have said anything so subtle and simple as MacDonald's saying that God is easy to please and hard to satisfy. Carlyle was too obviously occupied with insisting that God was hard to satisfy; just as some optimists are doubtless too much occupied with insisting that He is easy to please. In other words, MacDonald had made for himself a sort of spiritual environment, a space and transparency of mystical light, which was quite exceptional in his national and denominational environment. He said things that were like the Cavalier mystics, like the Catholic saints, sometimes perhaps like the Platonists or the Swedenborgians, but not in the least like the Calvinists, even as Calvinism remained in a man like Carlyle. And when he comes to be more carefully studied as a mystic, as I think he will be when people discover the possibility of collecting jewels scattered in a rather irregular setting, it will be found, I fancy, that he stands for a rather important turning-point in the history of Christendom, as representing the particular Christian nation of the Scots. As Protestants speak of the morning stars of the Reformation, we may be allowed to note such names here and there as morning stars of the Reunion.

The spiritual colour of Scotland, like the local colour of so many Scottish moors, is a purple that in some lights can look like grey. The national character is in reality intensely romantic and passionate—indeed, excessively and dangerously romantic and passionate. Its emotional torrent has only too often been turned towards revenge, or lust, or cruelty, or witchcraft. There is no drunkenness like Scotch drunkenness; it has in it the ancient shriek and the wild shrillness of the Maenads on the mountains. And of course it is equally true on the good side, as in the great literature of the nation. Stopford Brooke and other critics have truly pointed out that a vivid sense of colour appears in the medieval Scottish poets before it really appears in any English poets. And it is absurd to be talking of the hard and shrewd sobriety of a national type that has made itself best known throughout the modern world by the prosaic literalism of *Treasure Island* and the humdrum realism of *Peter Pan*. Nevertheless, by a queer historical accident this vivid and coloured people have been forced to "wear their blacks" in a sort of endless funeral on an eternal Sabbath. In most plays and pictures, however, in which they are represented as wearing their blacks, some instinct makes the actor or the artist see that they fit very badly. And so they do.

The passionate and poetical Scots ought obviously, like the passionate and poetical Italians, to have had a religion which competed with the beauty and vividness of the passions, which did not let the devil have all the bright colours, which fought glory with glory and flame with flame. It should have balanced Leonardo with St. Francis; no young and lively person really thinks he can be balanced with John Knox. The consequence was that this power in Scottish letters, especially in the day (or night) of complete Calvinistic orthodoxy, was weakened and wasted in a hundred ways. In Burns it was driven out of its due course like a madness; in Scott it was only tolerated as a memory. Scott could only be a medievalist by becoming what he would call an antiquary, or what we should call an aesthete. He had to pretend his love was dead, that he might be allowed to love her. As Nicodemus came to Jesus by night, the aesthete only comes to church by moonlight.

Now, among the many men of genius Scotland produced in the nineteenth century, there was only one so original as to go back to this origin. There was only one who really represented what Scottish religion should have been, if it had continued the colour of the Scottish medieval poetry. In his particular type of literary work he did indeed realize the apparent paradox of a St. Francis of Aberdeen, seeing the same sort of halo round every flower and bird. It is not the same thing as any poet's appreciation of the beauty of the flower or bird. A heathen can feel that and remain heathen, or in other words remain sad. It is a certain special sense of significance, which the tradition that most values it calls sacramental. To have got back to it, or forward to it, at one bound of boyhood, out of the black Sabbath of a Calvinist town, was a miracle of imagination.

In noting that he may well have this place in history in the sense of religious and of national history, I make no attempt here to fix his place in literature. He is in any case one of the kind that it is most difficult to fix. He wrote nothing empty; but he wrote much that is rather too full, and of which the appreciation depends rather on a sympathy with the substance than on the first sight of the form. As a matter of fact, the mystics have not often been men of letters in the finished and almost professional sense. A thoughtful man will now find more to think about in Vaughan or Crashaw than in Milton, but he will also find more to criticize; and nobody need deny that in the ordinary sense a casual reader may wish there was less of Blake and more of Keats. But even this allowance must not be exaggerated; and it is in exactly the same sense in which we pity a man who has missed the whole of Keats or Milton, that we can feel compassion for the critic who has not walked in the forest of Phantastes or made the acquaintance of Mr. Cupples in the adventures of Alec Forbes.

G.K. CHESTERTON.

PREFACE

Had the author of this book so chosen, he might have said of it what Charlotte Brontë said of her masterpiece upon its re-issue in 1848: "A preface to the first edition being unnecessary, I gave none."[1] But in truth much has changed since 1924, when Greville MacDonald wrote the story of his parents' lives. Today's reader (in contrast with G. K. Chesterton and C. S. Lewis) is generally a stranger to the Scots tongue, and is thus debarred from the great works which contain it, and which are mentioned so frequently throughout this biography. Indeed it will become clearer the farther one delves into Greville's tribute how much a knowledge of the novels will help us, as undoubtedly it helped Lewis and Chesterton before us. Above all, we may say that the first three Scottish novels (*David Elginbrod*, *Alec Forbes of Howglen*, and *Robert Falconer*) are indispensable, for they throw many fascinating lights upon their author's life and faith. Linguistic incomprehension of these key texts need no longer be a hindrance, as they are all now available—unabridged, and fully translated—from the same website[2] which produced this 2025 edition of *George MacDonald and His Wife*.

DAVID JACK.

---

[1] For the connection between *Jane Eyre* and MacDonald's *Phantastes*, see p. 317.
[2] i.e. The Room to Roam, from which all the Scottish novels are available in translation, excepting *Heather and Snow*—scheduled for release by Christmas 2025.

BOOK I
BOYHOOD AND YOUTH

CHAPTER I

THE PLACE OF BIRTH

GEORGE MACDONALD was born at Huntly in Aberdeenshire on December 10, 1824. "The Little Grey Town,"[1] a name conforming rather with its terrible winters than its richly flowered summers, lies in the valley of the Bogie River, with a wide circle of hills standing around.

In the centre of its market-place, with thatched well-house at one end, gabled merchants' dwellings and stores around, and toll-booth, or jail, at the other, stood the famous "Stannin' Stanes of Strathbogie," whither in older days the people were summoned by the Fiery Cross to battle. Yet constant raids and risings, punitive massacres and disastrous loyalty to chief or king—together with, later, the terrors of John Knox's Calvinism, longer withstood here than in the South—sobered at last the Highlander's semi-barbarous freedom and compelled him to that sobriety of thought which is one characteristic of Strathbogie's sons, and indeed of all Aberdeenshire; which, few dare dispute, has more brains to the square mile than any other northern county. Porridge and milk—for the poor skimmed to the blue, or sour—had supplanted

---

1 The original title of *Alec Forbes of Howglen*, which publishers rejected as not conforming with the then fashionable nomenclature in Fiction. The town that had sprung up around the old Huntly Castle was originally known as the Raws of Strathbogie, that name including the valley watered by the Bogie and the surrounding country. The lordship of Strathbogie had been granted in 1318 by Robert Bruce to Sir Adam Gordon after Bannockburn: a border laird, he took with him to the North the name *Huntly*, belonging to a village on his property in Berwickshire.

game got by bow and gun, or beef by marauding. But though oatmeal and John Knox had changed the morals of Ossian and the religion of Rome, they could not spoil the people's courage and devotion.

The ancient River of Romance runs through the town silently for most part, but at times, as if in sympathy with the rebel blood in every true Celt's veins, defies its banks, flooding and even wrecking a homestead here and there.

The River Bogie flows east of the town to join the fuller, peat-gold Deveron beyond the stately ruin of Huntly-Castle. Both rivers come from poetic sources. The Bogie's contributory, Burn of Craig, rushes from storm-swept flanks of The Buck—the "old Cabrach King" [1]—through the rich-timbered, gloomy Den of Craig, with its battle-scarred castle aloft, its kelpies below in unfathomed pools, to join the Burn of Glennie. Thence loitering in still deeps, curling over flat green rocks or leaping into cascade, it joins the open Deveron, which, topaz-stained from the windswept peat-mosses around The Buck, swirls round the foothold of Huntly Castle.

The mystic beauty and fury of these waters had no small share in inspiring the lads of Strathbogie to their fearsome sports; and they fostered a passion for adventure in the world, and memories of the old home with its dear, if terrible, religion. Romance never dies in the Celt; and even in the lowland Scot, though his intellect, his success, his science may strangle his ancient faith, his imagination never quite gives up the ghost.

In spite of the Gordons' personal treacheries, scandals such as that related of "Lord Rothie" in *Robert Falconer*, and historic cruelties—witness the feeding of two hundred orphans of their butchered enemies in Huntly Castle from pig troughs[2]—they were in some sort popular if also feared: "Ne'er

---

1   Cabrach = a stag
2   Related by Sir Walter Scott in *Tales of a Grandfather*, and by George MacDonald in *Alec Forbes*, vol. ii, p. 181.

misca' a Gordon in the Raws of Strathbogie" is a grim local proverb. But when, after the first Duke had surrendered Edinburgh Castle to the Orange troops (1688), and the Gordons were excluded from the court and all public service, they devoted themselves to the prosperity of their people and the development of handicrafts. And almost within living memory a creditable story used to be told of Alexander, the fourth Duke. At the farm-letting, just three years before George MacDonald's birth, the Duke's factor proposed breaking up several small holdings and adding them to the larger farms: "What are you to do with the cottars?" asked the Duke. "They will seek a living elsewhere," said the factor. The Duke postponed his decision till he had lunched, and then declared he would have all the people taken to the Deveron and drowned. "Oh, you joke, your Grace!" was the reply of the factor. "No, Mr.—," said the Duke; "if we are to deprive them of the means of living, this would be the most humane course. No, Mr.—; they or their forbears were here before us, and they will be here after I am gone. They will retain their holdings."[1] But the Duke died five years later: George MacDonald remembered watching the funeral cortège as a little two-year-old child. Then the factor had his way. So that the frugal and hardy crofters that once had been freely scattered over the glens of Strathbogie and furnished fearless fighters for chief and faith, rapidly disappeared. That the life and character of such crofters made deep impression upon the young George, his books reveal.

The life of Huntly centred in the Square. Its prosperity still depended upon agriculture and handicrafts, and machinery had not yet enslaved the poor to build an empire; indeed, George MacDonald's life ran contemporaneously with the greater part of the industrial revolution, and all the changes in life and manners, wealth and poverty, knowledge and labour-

---
[1] Told by George Gray in *Recollections of Huntly*, Banff, 1892.

saving, thereby introduced. The houses of Huntly were two-storied and slated, except the inn and some others that were gabled and thatched. Many of them had their ground-floors sunk for weaving shops—such as one sees still remaining in Bolton, Lancashire. The number of looms must have been very large—many for linen, the MacDonald factory perhaps providing the thread, though the greater part of its output, so it is said, was exported to South America. The cultivation and manufacture of flax—or *lint*, as it was called—was also an important industry, and the landscape was brightened by patches of sky-blue flax undulating in the wind. Spinning of fine woollen yarn also, for which Huntly was famed, was universal in the cottages around. Indeed, every home had its one or two wheels, many of beautiful workmanship, and the *spinsters* earned better wages than by any other indoor work.

The busy "Squar" must have been a prettier sight in 1824 than now. Around the well, with its canopy roof, pulley, chain and bucket, gathered the country women in grey cloak and white mutches, and the bare-headed maids, all with baskets on their arms with butter, eggs, cheese and live fowls. Mingling with them were the town women and domestic servants, their haggling and chaffering silenced only when the *"Customer"* appeared to collect the statutory "Custom pence." Everything was taxed in those days. Since the disarming Act of 1747—which forbade all kilts and tartans—knee-breeches and tailed coats of hodden grey, with glengarry bonnets, were the common dress of the men.

On market days there were stalls for all manner of produce, sweeties, shoes, haberdashery, etc. But one more important article was the candle-fir, thin slips of the resinous bog-fir, from one to two feet long, which were either laid on the great hearth with its peat-fire, or fixed in a sort of candlestick called the *puir-man* or *puir-page* (beggar or beggar-boy)—a block

THE PLACE OF BIRTH

of stone with a hole in the centre into which was fixed a wooden upright three feet high with a piece of cleft iron a-top into which the resinous candle was fixed.[1] Side by side in the market-place would stand a score or so of little carts, of the most primitive make, loaded with the bog-fir for candles. Some had also bags of moss-berries (cranberries) or of aitnachs.[2] The small, shaggy, long-tailed horses were hitched with hair-ropes to the carts. Behind one of the carts one might watch a group of town *nickums*, keenly on the look-out for opportunity to pluck hairs from the horses' tails. Fishing-gut not being available, such hairs more than repaid the risk of flying hoof or the fierce maledictions of Gaelic dealers; and both Bogie and Deveron with their trout were free to all fishers.

The mere mention of peat-fire and fir-candle carries one's imagination beyond the town into the small farmer's home. On each side the hearth are father and mother, with a *luckieminnie* (granny) or *luckiedad* most likely, the little ones and a servant or two round about. A *quarterer* too, a news-vending beggar, might be enjoying his periodic welcome, and in exchange tinkering broken vessels, or treating rheumatic joints, or charming away the warts. There would be singing of songs and ballads, story-tellings too of fairy and Kelpie, witch and "Auld Nickie Ben." The women will be spinning, or weaving mittens with the *cleek* (crotchet), the men *cleavin' can'les*, or whittling *harrow-tynds* (teeth), or perhaps cobbling brogues. But if the children are not yet abed, there will be silence while they get their lessons. Hospitalities were free and frequent, and young women would bring their wheels on their backs, their arms full of carded wool or

---

[1] Tallow candles were heavily taxed and too expensive for daily use except in the richer homes. The fir was brought from the peat-bogs of Abernethy in Invernesshire, a distance of thirty or forty miles, renowned for its industry of *cleavin' can'les*. The fir-candle is mentioned in *Castle Warlock*, vol. iii, p. 267.

[2] Juniper berries used to flavour beer. In the Highlands juniper sprays took the place of rushes for floor-covering and added sweetness to the peaty-atmosphere.

lint, when the cottar and his wifie were *giein' a forenicht*.

George MacDonald's writings are redolent of these simple ways. With crofters, their religion and wisdom, their poverty and hospitalities, no less than with lairds, tacksmen and farmers, he was intimate; while we need but cite his love of the spinning-wheel—that peaceful tool of the hand, full of music and mystery—to realise how inseparable were the bygone crafts from his poetic imagination.

GEORGE MACDONALD, SENR., 1822

MRS. GEORGE MACDONALD, SENR., 1822

GEORGE MACDONALD, SENR.

MRS. CHARLES EDWARD MACDONALD, GEORGE MACDONALD'S GRANDMOTHER

CHAPTER II

HIS PARENTS

CHARLES EDWARD MACDONALD, the grandfather of George MacDonald, was born in January 1746, three months before the Culloden tragedy. He was educated at Fordyce, in Banffshire, whose school even then was famed for the scholars it produced. The Gaelic was his father's tongue and Romanism his religion. But many Highlanders turned Protestant after Culloden—whether for their bodies' or their souls' safety. The youngest of a large family, Charles Edward was apprenticed to the weaving business, but gave it up when he was offered a clerkship in the firm of McVeagh Brothers, owners of the largest bleach-fields in Huntly. He was taken into partnership and soon succeeded to the business, adding to it a thread or gimp-spinning industry. He built the factory described in *Robert Falconer*, where the machinery was still driven by hand-power, and was probably but little modified from Hargreaves' original spinning-jenny.[1]

In 1821 the Duke of Gordon granted a lease of Upper Pirriesmill, known as The Farm, to Charles Edward's three sons, who had to reclaim a large half of it, then a dry "scaup."[2] It was this farm[3] in which George MacDonald spent his

---
1 Patented in 1764, soon to be amplified by Arkwright in 1769, when first horse-power, then water, robbed the hand of its ancient rights.
2 They were the first to introduce bones for manure and subsoil ploughing: they offered a penny a pound for all bones brought to them, and for many months men, women and children would crowd the place with their collections of bones lying about the country generally. The bones were crushed and sold to the farmers.
3 The "Howglen" of *Alec Forbes*. It is now in the hands of Mr. Robert C. Troup, the grandson of my father's uncle, James MacDonald.

boyhood. Natural advantages fitted it admirably for bleaching-fields, its sunny, close-mown meadow running beside the River Bogie's soft waters, which became renowned far and wide for their bleaching properties. "The wind gave life to everything. It rippled the stream, and fluttered the long webs bleaching in the sun: they rose and fell like white waves on the bright green lake; and women, homely Nereids of the grassy sea, were besprinkling them with spray. There were dull sounds of wooden machinery near, but they made no discord with the sweetness of the hour." [1]

Dairy farming, moreover, became an adjunct to sun's and river's services. For in the days prior to the discovery that sulphuric acid was a cheaper and equally efficient substitute for lactic acid, whey was an absolute necessity. When this waste of milk was no longer profitable, the cows were retained for more normal uses.

Here I must write fully about George MacDonald's grandmother, if only because her passion for saving souls from the eternal burning was reproduced in him with a zeal no less urgent that it had other interpretation. She was Isabella Robertson of Huntly. The grandmother in *Robert Falconer* was recognized, by all who remembered the old lady, as a wonderful portrait of her,[2] many of old Mrs. Falconer's words being actual utterances. She was born in 1756, the daughter of a linen-weaver. She was married on December 10, 1778, to Charles Edward MacDonald. Her father would not allow his daughters to learn writing "lest they should be writing to the lads." But she taught herself penmanship after she was sixty, and a letter of hers with portions of her diary lie before me. There were four sons and five daughters, though only one of the latter survived, she marrying the Rev. James Spence. The eldest son William

---

1 *Donal Grant*, vol. i, p. 111.
2 *Vide Robert Falconer*, vol. i, p. 62.

HIS PARENTS

converted certain disused bleach-works on the west side of the Bogie into a brewery and prospered. He was twelve years older than George (my father's father), who was followed by Charles and James. These three sons inherited the business, though Charles, presumably the favourite, got the bulk of the property, and so assumed the position of senior partner in the firm.

Charles Edward MacDonald, Isabella Robertson's husband, added a bank-agency to his business and became an elder in the Parish Church of Huntly. But because of the minister's inefficiency—the whole of Strathbogie being called "The Dead Sea"—his wife betook herself to the *Missionar Kirk*, whose minister's zeal and eloquence spread far and wide. She took her family with her, making some of them eager Missionars. So strong indeed became the evangelical movement, even in the Established Church, that the "Strathbogie controversy" on the question of church patronage was the immediate occasion for the disruption of 1843, which ended in the formation of the Free Church. Soldiers, it is still remembered, were sent to Huntly to maintain the parish ministers in their pulpits.

But the good lady, though stuff of the old Covenanting martyrs, had as fine an instinct for the righteous care of the valuables deposited with her husband, the banker—so he was called—as she had for the salvation of souls. For this responsible function, Charles Edward MacDonald received a salary of £20 per annum, and this remuneration was to cover rent, taxes and all risk of bad debts. The rent, however, involved no additional outlay; for at the same counter at which orders for goods to be bleached were received, the firm handled their banking business. But money was scarce in those days, and the bank had not even a safe until Mrs. Charles Edward appropriated to this use the family *Chanter Kist*, the traditional receptacle of family records—which records, while the family were still Catholics, would be found in no parochial registers—and destroyed all these as snares and wiles of Satan.[1]

Mrs. Charles Edward was as benevolent as she was a fine business woman. She adopted a family of four beggar children of questionable parentage and placed three of them out in the world. One became a prosperous merchant in Aberdeen; the second went to Jamaica; a third enlisted and soon died. She subscribed to the London City Mission, and was the inspiration of the Huntly temperance movement. Her antagonism to Roman Catholics was of course intense, although she always entertained the gentlest hopes for individuals misled by the "Scarlet Woman." My eldest uncle used to tell of a visit he once paid her shortly before she died in 1848 at the age of ninety-two. She could still with her strong glasses read large type in spite of her short sight. The newspapers that year were full of revolutions and the trembling of thrones. "Laddie," she said, "the newspaper is telling that amang a' the changes takin' place i' the warld, they have gotten a guid Pope at Rome; an' I have been prayin' to the Lord a' nicht to gie him a new hert an' a guid wife!"

But Charles, who was solely responsible for the bank business, fell into difficulties, his kindness of heart and optimism, his desire to play the patron among friends with whom he was so popular, men and women alike, encouraging his lack of conscience. He advanced money to irresponsible customers and himself became responsible, and was soon involved in transactions which, but for a legal flaw in the indictment, would have landed him in prison. He fled to America. The bleaching business in which he was

---

[1] The chanter-kist or treasure chest was an important item in every Highland household, whether of chief or clansman, laird or crofter. It was a huge, carved-oak coffer; and besides the pipes' black chanter and mouldy old papers, it might hold a family brooch—a glimmering cairngorm with lesser garnets, amethysts and topazes set round in high relief—and also, very commonly, a divining crystal, or in catholic districts a rosary, and perhaps even a sacred relic.

a partner was held responsible for his debts—those to the bank being near £6,000—a huge sum in those days; and the two brothers, George MacDonald's father and uncle, paid them in full, though they had no part in the bank's affairs. The burden of the annual repayments lay heavy upon them all through their lives.¹

It was over the backslidings of this her son Charles that his mother nigh broke her heart. The occasion of his unexpected return one Sunday afternoon in July 1835, recorded in the old lady's diary and witnessed by her grandson George, who had conducted her home from the Kirk, is described in the opening chapter of *Robert Falconer*. The burning of his violin, as given in the novel, was also a fact.² She was determined it should lead no other lads beyond reach of the Divine Grace. We cannot but guess that the splendid old woman—"with a volcanic heart of love, her outside was always so still and cold" ³—would have wept bitter tears, had she known how largely responsible she was destined to be for her little grandson's future renown as a novelist.

In spite of the two remaining brothers' indefatigable enterprise, the business was more than once almost overwhelmed in disaster. Glasgow spinning-mills made

---

1   In one of my grandfather's letters to my father he refers to the great burdens put upon him in his old age. He had, in addition to his brother's debts, taken upon him the responsibilities of one who is best unnamed. When my great uncle James, my grandfather having predeceased him, died, he bequeathed a great part of his small property to the Bank, the sum representing money due from his brother Charles; and, after some hesitation, the Bank refused it. Nor, when Charles died in New York in 1836, age forty-one, had it claimed the sum for which he had insured his life, and which was duly paid to his widow in Aberdeen—this fact being the only intimation she ever received of his death.

2   In the Island of Lewis the ministers of the Secession Church had compelled the destruction of pipes and fiddles. "If there was a foolish man here and there who demurred, the good ministers and the good elders themselves broke and burnt their instruments, saying:

'Better is the small fire that warms on the little day of peace
Than the big fire that burns on the great day of wrath.' "

(*Carmina Gadelica*, by Alexander Carmichael, 1900, vol. i, p. 26.)

3   *Robert Falconer*, vol. i, p. 293.

the factory unprofitable. Then, thanks to the invention of chloride of lime by Charles MacIntosh, F.R.S., the great Glasgow chemist, and cousin of my grandmother, Mrs. George MacDonald senior, the bleaching was no longer in demand. Lastly, they started the manufacture of potato-flour and starch.[1] Here the water-mill again did the work, mashing the potatoes and separating the rind, which was used to make a dressing for coarse canvas bags. But this was in its turn ruined by the three successive years of the potato-blight, 1846, 1847, and 1848, which caused terrible suffering in the Highlands, and which Dr. MacIntosh MacKay, minister of Dunoon and brother to my grandmother, worked so strenuously to alleviate. Thereafter the water-mill, no longer used for washing the fabrics sent to them for bleaching, or for mashing potatoes, must turn millstones to grind oats, and this became their principal business.

George MacDonald senior married Helen MacKay in 1822. Of her parentage and relatives more will be told presently. He had built the house in which his two eldest sons were born, Charles in 1823 and George, the future poet and novelist, in 1824. This house was situated in Duke Street, but has long since been converted into two shops. The grandmother lived in the adjoining house, at the corner of Church Street and Duke Street—the house in fact described in the novel as Robert Falconer's home;[2] and only the garden separated it from the factory.

My grandfather was "as fine a man," so they used to say, "as might be seen in four parishes," of noble presence, well built and robust—a "wyss" (*wise*) man, moreover, to quote

---

1 It was advertised as "*Farina*, a substitute for arrowroot and suitable for invalids and children's diet"—the fact being endorsed by the renowned Sir John Sinclair of Ulbster, the first President of the Board of Agriculture.

2 The late Rev. Robert Troup, who married Margaret MacDonald, daughter of my father's uncle James, related that latterly during the rebuilding of a part of the grandmother's house to make a shop of it, the door by which Robert Falconer found his way into Mary St. John's house was exposed. It opened by a few steps from the first floor, and had originally been the communication for the two families between the adjoining houses.

the vernacular. He was brave, patient, and generous; finely humorous, of strong literary tastes and profound religious convictions. My father's reverence for him was absolute, one transcendent hope being to meet him again. The character of David Elginbrod was drawn from him, the relation of this father to his daughter corresponding with his father's to himself. He rarely caressed his boys: it was not the fashion in those days to do so. Nor could he make up to them for the loss of their mother, though as they grew older he won a perfect intimacy with at least his son George. We realize this in the latter's dedication to him of his first volume of *Poems* (1857):

> Thou hast been faithful to my highest need:
> And I, thy debtor, ever, evermore,
> Shall never feel the grateful burden sore.
> Yet most I thank thee, not for any deed,
> But for the sense thy living self did breed
> That fatherhood is at the world's great core.

Of Helen MacKay we know but little beyond what we may gather from a simple miniature done immediately after her marriage, and her son's adoration of her memory. My step-grandmother once told me that she had been her dearest friend, and that she and her husband were the most beautiful woman and man she had ever beheld. Like all her many brothers and sisters, she was well educated and had good brains. Her brother, MacIntosh MacKay, LL.D., was the greatest Gaelic scholar of the day and a friend of Sir Walter Scott, who expressed himself as much indebted to him.[1] My father had little to tell us of her, for she died when he was eight years old of the tuberculous disease which had invalided her for as long as he could remember. Her love for her boys need not be spoken of; yet I cannot refrain from quoting the one letter of hers my father had cherished. It personifies this

---

1 *Vide* note to *The Two Drovers*, vol. 41 of the *Waverley Novels*.

love and introduces to the world her infant George in such wise that already we perceive some real heroism in his facing of adversity. The letter is written from Huntly to her mother-in-law, then in Aberdeen. But being undated, it gives no clue to Baby George's age when he suffered with so much equanimity his mother's heartless decision.

My dear Mother,
   I hope you will not think that my silence till now is the want of *sincere and warm affection for you*. If you for one moment thought this, I would be very much hurt, for I can assure you it is anything but this. And if I know my own heart I think I can say that nearest to my own mother there is not another I *love* and *esteem* more than my second mother—for you have been a mother to me ever since I came with you—and I hope I will ever feel grateful to you for it.
   I hope you will not be angry tho' I do not write a long letter. I am going to tell you something that will show you how little *sense* I have. Do you know I was almost angry on Saturday when your letter came to my dear G. about weaning our dear little Boy—for I was very unwilling to do it—and I always thought I would have been able to give him three months at least. But O! my heart [was] *very* sore when I saw that you, my dear husband, and Mrs. Ross—and indeed all the rest—were so earnest about it—that I was forced to begin that very morning. And he has not got anything from me since. But I cannot help my heart being very much grieved for him yet, for he has not forgot it: poor little fellow he is behaving wonderfully well as yet. He cryed desperate a while the first night, but he has cryed very little since and I hope the worst is over now...[1]
   The cheeses are drying nicely at the farm, but the Lass is very ill off for meat to the hens.[2] Just if you could put us upon any plan to get meat to them we would be very glad. We are selling very little butter. O I wish you were home again to us. O mind and write me very soon—for I will be no less than proud of a letter from you.
   Good evening my ever dear Mother,
      I ever am your affectionate daughter,
         Helen McD.

---

1 In 1888 an old lady, a Mrs. Mackie, living at Fort Langley, British Columbia, once told Mrs. Julian Peacock, now of Manchester, that she was foster sister of the Baby George, whose mother not being strong enough to support her little son, sent him several times a day to her mother's cottage to be fed along with her infant self.
2 As every farm-wife will realize, this lack of "meat to the hens" suggests a fine economy in the kitchen.

HIS PARENTS

Nearly a century old is this letter with its pretty Highland English. It has lain in my father's cabinet with its secret nest of drawers, along with a golden brown lock of that mother's hair and her wedding gift to her husband, a little silver-set seal with his name *George* engraved on its red stone; together also with little trifles belonging to those of his own children who had followed her to the grave.[1]

When George was two years old the family removed to Upper Pirriesmill, his father and his uncle James having built a little house in which both families lived, though, judging from the above letter, they were already farming there. This sharing of a small dwelling must have been difficult, but was accomplished in great friendliness, thanks largely to the elder's tact and gentleness of temper. His unselfishness was such that, often in opposition to some hasty and unwise step in business proposed and vehemently defended by Mr. James, he would tactfully substitute in his brother's mind his own wiser views; only to be adopted and acted upon after a day or two by James, who in that short time had come to look upon them as his own. My step-grandmother told me that her husband would just smile, as if in entire approval, when his brother

---

1   Folded into the letter are some verses in the same handwriting, but more carefully penned two years approximately before my grandparents were married. I presume they are original and so transcribe them, though intrinsically they are of no great value:

"Gallow Hill,
[some dozen miles from Huntly],
29th May, 1820.

"We come, dear Jesus, to thy throne
   To open all our grief;
Now send thy promised mercy down,
   And grant us quick relief.

"Though Satan rage and flesh rebel,
   And unbelief arise,
We'll wait around his footstool still,
   For Jesus hears our cries.

"Alas! but I am very dull this night after parting with my dear sister! O Lord, make me resigned to thy will.—HELEN."

got all the credit. So the Scottish proverb, "Freen's agree best sindry," had no meaning at The Farm.

Bleachfield Cottage, as it was named for a while, is as plain as a puritanical taste could design, but surrounded with trees. It had so little accommodation, that while it made amity and forbearance essential to the inmates' happiness, it doubtless fostered the tuberculous disease which destroyed so many of them. It is preserved as much as possible in its original form by my cousin, Robert G. Troup.[1] Box-beds, each entirely enclosed by panelling and door, were built along the wall of more than one sitting-room. Young George slept in an attic with a skylight, from which I think it was either himself or his brother John who set his kite free in token of ended boyhood, as he describes Robert Falconer doing.

In this place I must put on record certain instances of my grandfather's fortitude, generosity and humour, although the two latter points—along with his wisdom and piety and touches of austerity proper to the Calvinistic understanding of parental obligation—constantly illumine the long series of letters between him and my father until death set the period to it in 1858.

In 1825 my grandfather's left leg was amputated above the knee for white swelling, as tuberculous disease of the joint was then named, two years' previous treatment with blisters and seton having proved unsuccessful. My father was told by the doctor who operated—it being before the days of chloroform—how the patient refused the customary stupefying dose of whisky, or even to have his face covered, preferring to watch the operation; and that only for one moment, when the knife first transfixed the flesh, did he turn his face away and ejaculate a faint, sibilant "whiff!"

My grandfather was always ready to make fun of his loss. He would declare, and in such a way that no little hearers

---

[1] Certain guide-books are wholly erroneous in their descriptions of George MacDonald's home.

could disbelieve him, that twice every day the Aberdeen coach *Defiance* and its four horses drove between his legs. My sisters and I had it only from our Uncle Charles, and no questioning could extort any sort of explanation. But at last our mother took pity upon our fear that the obdurate uncle might be deceiving us. The explanation was this, that though our grandfather had his right leg always with him, the other was buried in the graveyard far away on the other side of the high road.

I have little doubt that the racy conversation between Thomas Crann, the dour theological stonemason in *Alec Forbes*, and George MacWha, the reprobate, originated in George MacDonald senior's delight in making fun of his wooden leg. MacWha is baiting the Calvinist with questions concerning the resurrection of a body with a wooden leg: " 'Wad it be a glorified timmer leg he rose wi', gin he had been buried wi' a timmer leg?' asked he; 'his ain leg wad be buried some gait.' 'Ou, aye, nae doubt. An' it wad come hoppin' ower the Paceefic or the Atlantic to jine its oreeginal stump—wad it no?' "

My grandfather's indifference to mere possessions is illustrated by an incident told me by my father. One day a young Aberdeen friend engaged in business remarked, when visiting at The Farm, that "a chap was awkwardly situated in a big city wanting a watch." Instantly out from his fob came my grandfather's silver turnip as a free gift to the lad, saying the sun was a better time-keeper in Strathbogie than any merchant's watch in Aberdeen. Thereafter my grandfather never carried or possessed a watch.

But more important is the story told I believe to this day of the way my grandfather used his wooden leg to save Huntly from a riot.

On April 8, 1846, the youngest of his daughters was born, and her mother's state had been giving some anxiety. No sooner was she out of danger and at last getting some sleep, than a breathless messenger arrived at the cottage, saying that the town was in an uproar and its worst elements coming up to The Farm in a dangerously angry mood, intending to burn, right before the cottage, my grandfather's effigy. For this was towards the end of the worst year of the three years' potato famine, and an evil report, that Messrs. George and James MacDonald were holding a store of grain until prices had risen even higher than they were, had been fermenting. My grandfather had just taken off his artificial leg and set it beside the fire, as was his wont when tired. He quickly replaced it and hurried down to stop their entry into the garden.

They were so much taken aback that their anger was immediately silenced. He told them that absolute quiet was essential if his wife was to win through, and he begged them to go down to the market and tell him there what the trouble was all about. Without one word of protest, they departed somewhat shame-facedly, carrying the effigy with them.

By the time my grandfather reached them in the market-place, however, they were joined by others and their anger revived. They built a bonfire alongside the Stannin' Stanes, with the clumsy effigy sprawling on top, its wooden leg ridiculously in evidence. When at last they were ready to kindle the faggots and my grandfather appeared in his usual blue swallow-tail coat with gilt buttons, black and white check trousers, and soft loose collar, the crowd burst into indignant rage. Quite unperturbed, however, he began to address them, when their hootings were instantly stilled.

"Bide a wee, lads," he shouted, "afore ye set the corp alow (*aflame*). *Ye've fastened the timmer leg to the wrang hurdie* (*hip*)." And leaning on his stick, he gravely added: "Noo, ye's gang on wi' yer ploys wi' a guid conscience, an burn yer auld freen'!"

Thus were the hungry set laughing and presently cheering the man their hearts knew if their minds misjudged. Then, at his invitation, a few went with him back to The Farm to be convinced that its barn, like their own meal-tubs, was empty.

Such humour could not but endear him to all. When he died in 1858, at the age of sixty-six, the grief was universal. Writing to my mother the day after the funeral, my father, having arrived too late to bid him *goodbye,* says: "Charles and I went to see some poor people this afternoon. It is very pleasant to hear how they all talk about my father. You would almost fancy he had been a kind of chief of the clan...I am glad my father has got through. I love him more than ever..."

CHAPTER III

THE MACDONALD DESCENT

"SURELY it is one of the worst signs of a man to turn his back upon the rock whence he was hewn."[1] So once wrote George MacDonald regarding his Gaelic origin; and one may add it would be a poor sign of our love for him if we thought that rock, grand as it must have been to hold such potentiality in it, unworthy of our regard or unprofitable in helping us to understand him.

That rock was the clan-system, educative and inspiring as it was disciplinary and impregnable.

The bards' teaching of their history, memorized in long array of heroic deeds and lofty emotions, fostered the Celt's sense of freedom, his spirit of joyful submission to the chief and his inherent belief in the equality of man. "My foes are thy foes, thy griefs mine," was claimed equally by chief or clansman. It was no disparagement among lesser septs if the chief married the humblest maid of the clan.

Such inheritance of liberty and heroism, poverty and romance, we may look upon as a likely nursery of genius.

> As some savage element of a race (wrote George MacDonald) will reappear in an individual of it after ages of civilization, so may good old ways of thinking and feeling, modes long gone out of fashion and practice, survive and revive modified by circumstance, in an individual of a new age...When the operative force of such regards has been fostered by the teaching of a revered parent...there can be no bound set to their possible potency in a mind of high spiritual order.[2]

---

1   In a letter to *The Spectator*, July 1867, vide postea, p. 318.
2   *What's Mine's Mine*, 1886, vol. i, p. 66

THE MACDONALD DESCENT

No one may pretend to understand the Gael, his devotion to the soil, his love of liberty, his intolerance of injustice, his eloquence and love of learning—witnessed alike in Scottish Highlander, Irishman and Welshman—unless he realize the significance of Sennachie, of bagpipes and harp, of claymore and tartan, as the outward and visible correspondences with the spiritual clan-faith. George MacDonald inherited all the characteristic virtues; and the clan-system, a social law built upon Faith rather than Competition, may in large measure explain his rooted fidelity to God and man.

George MacDonald's grandfather, named Charles Edward[1] after the Young Pretender, was, as has already been said, born three months before Culloden, and his mother died on the day of its disaster when the news of the battle reached her. Charles Edward's father, William, was one of the few who escaped Cumberland's ruthless stalking of every fugitive. My father's grandmother remembered him well, and the description given of him in *Robert Falconer*, my father told us, was almost in her exact words:

> He was a gey (*considerably*) auld man than, but as straucht as an ellwand, and jist pooerfu' beyon' belief. His shackle-bane (*wrist*) was as thick as baith mine; and years and years efter that, whan he tuik his son, my husband and his grandson ane in ilka han', jist for the fun o' 't, he kneipit their heids thegither, as gin they had been twa carloddies (*stalks of rib-grass*).[2]

Tradition tells how when he and his eldest son were passing through Nairn in their flight from Culloden, they were pursued by the townspeople, the blacksmith flourishing a redhot iron, and how their long legs carried them to safety.

---

1 In the Huntly Parochial Registers—e.g. on the occasions of his marriage to Isobel Robertson in 1778 and the birth of his children—we find the name as "Charles" only. In those days a double name, unless in the case of peers, was almost unknown. My great-grandfather's birth appears never to have been registered. But his father was a Catholic, and like most of his co-religionists would never have consented to the parochial registers.
2 *Robert Falconer*, vol. i., p. 65.

They hid and were secretly fed for months among the caves of Portsoy in spite of the proximity of these to his narrowly watched home, until, perhaps because the loss of his eyesight was considered sufficient penalty, he was forgotten.[1] It was at Portsoy that William's father, after his escape with his father from Glencoe, had settled and started business as quarryman and polisher of Portsoy marble.

Before the final overthrow of the clan-system in 1846, the family had farmed their own land, as I understood from my father; but it was of course then confiscated. It was probably near Portsoy; in *Robert Falconer*, which in details treats so largely of actual circumstances, it is mentioned as a few houses only, a kailyard or two, "wi' a bit fairmy (*farm*) on the tap o' a cauld hill near the seashore." The story of the Highlander's escape is elaborated into fiction in *Malcolm*; but the Duncan MacPhail of the novel, with his implacable hatred of the Campbells for their treachery at Glencoe,[2] their massacre in Strathbogie in 1639—when they left the country, it was said, "manless and moneyless, horseless and armless," and their successful ruse at Culloden, where the Clan Ranald,

---

[1] Caves on the north coast of Aberdeen, Banff and Elgin had been always associated with pipers. Should they be sauntering on the shore in the twilight some fairy lure might tempt them into any deep and gloomy cavern; and they would wander, all unconscious of danger, for miles inland until beneath this or that farm-kitchen or heather-clad hill to which they had been led. But because of the spell put upon them they would never more return. Only, from time to time their weird music might be heard in such places on still, starry nights, making little children and lovers weep for they knew not what.

[2] My father claims that revenge is not a characteristic of the Gael. It may be found in individual, but not in the race; and their literature contains nothing to foster such feeling. (*Malcolm*, vol. i, p. 133.)

Retribution, according to my friend James A. Campbell of Barbreck, was rather a law of Nature than called for by any instinct of hatred; and he illustrates it by an incident occurring in his family at the beginning of the seventeenth century. The perpetrator of an accidental death was sought by a rival sept of Campbells to extort the inevitable penalty. His foster brother, Donald MacCallum, donned his clothes while the fugitive slept and got himself shot in his stead. The avenging sept showed every honour to the hero and settled a croft upon his family for all time.

to which sept our family belongs, fought to the death—though drawn from a well-known character, was no portrait of the author's ancestor.

Though most of the Portsoy men who fought for Prince Charlie followed Sir William Dunbar of Durn,[1] this grandfather of George MacDonald senior, being Town's Piper of Portsoy,[2] joined the Frasers, who were Catholics to a man, and contributed a large contingent to the insurrectionary forces.[3] The piper's office, it should be noted, was still one of high rank, and had been often hereditary. Even when no quarter was given, his life would be spared by any Highland victors, and if taken prisoner, would be treated with the utmost consideration and honour. The Hanoverian Lowland troops would have shown him no such respect, and our ancestor was too proud to yield to any Campbell. So he fled; and was spared for the honour of being great-grandfather to the greatest of all the MacDonald bards.

The grandfather of this piper, as doubtless the documents in the family chanter-chest, destroyed by George MacDonald's

---

1 He served as a volunteer, and his great-grandson was one of the Jameson Raiders in the Transvaal.

2 From "A list of Persons concerned in the Rebellion [1745-6] transmitted to the Commissioners of Excise by the several Supervisors in Scotland in obedience to a general letter of the 7th May, 1746," with preface by the Earl of Rosebery. Scottish History Society, 1890.

* * * * *

List of Persons concerned in the Rebellion transmitted to the Board by Mr. Tolm Stuart, Supervisor of Excise at Banff.

Names.	Designations.	Abode.	County.	Station amongst the Rebels and circumstances of Rebellion.	Where they are now.
— William McDonald —	— Piper —	— Portsoy —	— Banff —	— Piper —	— —

3 I hope he was not attendant upon Simon Fraser, Lord Lovat, of infamous repute.

grandmother, would have proved, was one of the few of his clan who escaped massacre at Glencoe.

And it is Glencoe that must be looked upon as the traditional home of Clan Donald, which thence traced its descent back to the Lord of the Isles. It is, one may well believe, of some import in the inheritance of George MacDonald. Most who visit it are oppressed with a feeling of awe, even of terror—so endless seems its narrow cleft, so gloomy its barren mountains, with their wind and mist and rain. But nearer intimacy tells another story. Its warmth and fertility, its woody, roe-haunted springs, and the sky-blue burn that races and loiters in circuitous whirl through the peaceful glen, its bird-song from sky or rowan-bower; these and its desolating storms combined to make fit stronghold for a brave and poetical people. For all the MacIains—that tribe of the Clan Donald who claimed Glencoe for their own—were poets. It used to be said that no man thereabouts, whatever blood and features he might boast, was a MacIain if he never expressed himself in rime.

The story of the fatal night is variously told; but there can be little doubt as to the main points. Only one tradition connecting it with George MacDonald is extant, and that, for reasons given, cannot be authenticated.

The MacDonalds, or rather the MacIains, after entertaining the Campbells for fifteen days with lavish hospitality, were butchered by their guests in the dead of night. Alastir MacAonghais, as he was called locally, the half-brother of the old chief, and but a year or two younger, was at Brecklet at the time and had some warning of the treachery. So, with his family and some live stock, he crossed the River Laroch to the Ballachulish side of the pass, thus escaping the doom of his brother. The story goes that at the Jacobite rising of 1715, this Alastir, then over ninety years, was still living. When the Glencoe men marched away for Sherriffmuir, he insisted on going with them in spite of his people's protest. To save him from being a burden to the contingent, they sent a messenger after him with the news that his wife was dying. He returned at once—only to find her in perfect health and to be laughed at by her for preferring her society to that of the camp. In the morning he rose early, harnessed an old horse and rode away, never to return, though the battle was fought ere he came up with his people. He was buried at Dunblane. If this old warrior was my father's ancestor, he must have been grandfather to the piper of Culloden. The piper is said to have had a large family, only two of whom can be accounted for, Charles Edward, George Mac-Donald's grandfather, and an older brother, William, who was great-grandfather to my cousin, Dr. John MacDonald of Kildrummy.

The traditions of bardic renown are perhaps of as much importance in George MacDonald's inheritance as ingrain valour and loyalty. Whether the Clan Donald poets excelled those of other clans I do not know; but their high reputation is undisputed. Indeed, the bard or sennachie was almost as essential as the chief himself. He represented the intellect and imaginative gifts of the race, and was in himself sufficient answer to those charges of barbarism in which the Anglo-Saxon would, before Culloden, sum up the Highland character.[1]

To judge from what is still extant of these utterances, the poetic mode of declamation long preceded the prosaic.

---

[1] Dr. MacIntosh MacKay had, when minister of Laggan, unique opportunity for intimacy with some of these Sennachies or traditional historians. "Not a few of those," he wrote in an unpublished record of his friendship with Sir Walter Scott, "were men of sound and excellent common sense, and very sound judgment, and of much more extensive information than a stranger might expect to find. From one individual of the class, who was at the same time of good education and remarkable memory, I had but little difficulty in a short time in being able to forward to Sir Walter *a full and particular account* of the Battle of Mulrog, which Sir Walter has transferred bodily into the *Tales of a Grandfather!*..."

Even the law-givers, or Brehons, seem to have promulgated their decrees in verse, and St. Columba, himself of the Bardic Order, wrote mostly in metre. Indeed, my father's claim that, so far from poetry being but elaborated prose, as is commonly held, prose should be regarded as broken-down poetry, is largely justified by historic evidence.

Yet the bard alone was not enough to give men touch with their deepest possibilities, without music; and the harp, later the bagpipes and violin, were his lieutenants. The bard, too, had other and more exacting duties with his chief; he was secretary, prime minister and aide-de-camp; and second only to him in the executive was the piper.[1]

A nation whose chief notion of discipline was military compulsion could hardly realize the sublimity of an obedience inspired by love and devotion. If a Celt fought well because he hated too well, he often sinned because he loved too well; and he forgave, when he did forgive, with open hand and purse. If his ethics were in need of Christian discipline, his spiritual understanding needed no clerical dogmas either to refine or support it. His vision made of the Gael a singer in battle and in love, on mountain-top and by the cradle-side; it made of him a staunch supporter of Rome, a cruel Covenanter, or a stern

---

1   It is related that after witnessing the Battle of Inverlochy from the turrets of its old castle (1644), the most notorious of the MacDonald bards, Iain Lom (*Brown John*), whose hatred of the Campbells may have suggested to my father the character of Duncan MacPhail in *Malcolm*, wrote his most splendid poem extolling his leader, Alastair MacDonald, and ridiculing the Campbells, or "Blackcocks," in satire only less bitter than their enemy's claymore. Thereupon Argyll, chafing under his lash, offered a big price for the poet's head. Iain Lom, knowing the Marquis's courtesy as a Highlander would outweigh his animus, repaired to Inverary, delivered himself up and demanded the reward. Argyll received him most courteously in a room where the poet's attention was arrested by the heads of blackcock hanging on the walls. "You have never seen so many blackcock heads before, I am thinking?" said his host. "Yes, that have I!" was the answer. "Where, then?" "At Inverlochy!" "Oh, John," exclaimed Argyll, will you never have done with gnawing at us Campbells?" "My only regret, mighty Chief," was the reply, "is that I cannot devour them!"

believer in the Shorter Catechism as the only guide to salvation.[1]

These references to George MacDonald's racial inheritance—one of romance, devotion and piety, of unlettered literature and song, of poverty and freedom—are of first importance in understanding his character and work. Every point in it stands out nobly in him—even the quality of anger. For though this aboriginal virtue was in him and for the most part submerged (as our latter-day psychologist would express it), it would upon occasion flame up in indignation against any denial of beauty and truth, any cruelty, any trimming of Christ's teaching.[2] Even then its incentive was love; and it gave one some understanding of what the wrath of God might have meant to old Mrs. Charles Edward MacDonald when she was driven to lay her son's fiddle upon the flames.

---

[1] "Old Scotland," wrote my father, "has the sweetest songs in its cottages, and the worst singing in its churches, of any country in the world." (*David Elginbrod*, vol. iii, p. 99.)
[2] For one instance, *vide* p. 557.

CHAPTER IV
THE MACKAY DESCENT

BEYOND the facts of her beauty, the tender letter already quoted and her four sons of unusual character, we know little of George MacDonald's mother. Her relatives and forbears, however, were renowned in science and travel, in adventure and arms, in piety and politics. Her elder brother, MacIntosh MacKay, was, as already mentioned, a Celtic scholar and a friend of Sir Walter Scott; but, though a stern Calvinist, he could rebel, and was one of the prime movers in the disruption of the Scottish Church. Her only other brother was an officer who fought at Waterloo, George MacKay, a man of considerable intellectual parts, and the father of the beautiful Helen, who figures significantly in her cousin, George MacDonald's earlier life. The sisters of my Grandmother MacDonald remained single (with one exception) and lived by teaching.[1] One of these sisters, my great-aunt Christina, took charge of my father and his brothers when their mother died.

The MacKay clan, Celtic no less than the Clan Donald, belonged to the north-west of Sutherlandshire, Lord Reay's

---

[1] But being indifferently trained in the arts of water-colour drawing, embroidering French-lawn collarettes, netting silk purses, and "touching the harp strings," not to mention deportment and languishing, they found it difficult to get employment. Their Highland origin, moreover, prejudiced the Glasgow mothers against them. So at least Mistress Anne Grant, the well-known writer of *Letters from the Mountains* and the constant correspondent with their brother MacIntosh, accounted for her difficulty in finding situations for them, in spite of their intimacy with the classics and French.

country. The spirit of enterprise was as strong in these men as, in a smaller way, in Charles Edward MacDonald, his sons and grandsons. Something in full must be related of MacIntosh MacKay, because of his intimacy with his nephew—of whose genius he was proud enough, though greatly disturbed over his heresies. He was born in 1793,[1] and died in 1873. He became a minister in the Established Church, but was a leader in its disruption in 1843, becoming Moderator of the General Assembly of the Free Church. His claim to distinction is his scholarship. He was editor of *The Gaelic Dictionary*, and himself wrote fully four-fifths, as my father was informed and made note of in his copy of that book.[2] He had been offered quite early in his career the Humanity or Latin Chair in Glasgow. Tempting though the offer was, and while knowing his competency to fill it, he declined it: "I would not reconcile myself to the step of forsaking the sacred office to which I knew revered parents had early sought to devote me, and to which I have hitherto been hoping that I had dedicated myself." I remember him in 1868 as a stern, smileless old man with a massive forehead, who evinced his affection for the shy great-nephew by reproving his bad penmanship.

Sir Walter Scott, to whom he introduced the poetry of Robert MacKay or Rob Donn, and whom he helped in research among the Highlands, describes him as "a simple, learned man and a Highlander, who weighs his own nation justly; a modest and estimable person." Sir Walter introduced to him William Forbes Skene, the subsequent historian of Celtic Scotland, in order

---

1 The *Dictionary of National Biography* incorrectly places his birth in the year 1800. He was buried in Duddingston Churchyard, where an elaborate tombstone gives the date of his death in his eightieth year as May 17, 1873.
2 "He [Sir Walter Scott] had a visit from the learned and pious Dr. M. MacKay, the minister of Laggan, but now of Dunoon, the chief author of *The Gaelic Dictionary*, then recently published under the auspices of the Highland Society...." (*Lockhart's Life of Sir Walter Scott*, vol. vii, p. 283.)

that, as a lad under the minister's roof at Laggan, he might study Gaelic.

Dr. MacKay's and my grandmother's father was captain Alexander MacKay of Duard Beg, in Sutherlandshire, and their mother was Helen Falconer, daughter of the Rev. Alexander Falconer who in 1764 entered on his ministry at Edderachillis in Lord Reay's country in succession to the Rev. George Brodie. Captain Alexander's father was John MacKay, of Auldanrinie, who married Christina Brodie, daughter of the Rev. George Brodie, minister of Edderachillis from 1715 to 1740: the Christina whose beauty was sung by Rob Donn, the Reay country bard, of whom a life was written by Dr. MacIntosh MacKay. The Rev. George Brodie's wife, Barbara MacKay, was a lineal descendant of John Abrach MacKay, founder of the Clan Abrach branch of the MacKays, who flourished about 1430. Thus my father's Sutherland descent may well be regarded as of some importance among the many contributory streams of his inheritance. Helen Falconer's mother was Mary MacIntosh, sister of George MacIntosh, an influential Glasgow spinner and aunt to Charles MacIntosh, F.R.S.[1]

Much might be said of the Reay country as the time-honoured home of the MacKays, to show how the future poet may have been indebted to it for some of their racial characteristics. A more forbidding yet grander environment

---

[1] These particulars are taken from Dr. H. Scott's *Fasti Ecclesiæ Scotianæ*, and are supplemented from the *History of the House and Clan of MacKay*, by Robert MacKay, 1829, and annotated by my father.

In a letter of Dr. MacIntosh MacKay to my mother's youngest sister, he says: "I was born November 18, 1793 at Duardbeg, parish of Edderachillis, county of Sutherland. My paternal great-grandfather [George Brodie], and my maternal grandfather [Alexander Falconer], were ministers of that Parish. My father's ancestors for generations were eminent in battle, one of them specially honoured by King William III at Battle of Stenkirk, 1692. My father served with distinction in the Irish Rebellion, 1798. Better honours are from above. Read my own poor character in Rom. vii, specially in verses 24 and first ½ of 25, and in chapter viii, last two verses.

"M. MacKay."

"September 14, 1870."

could hardly be found, with its great bare mountains swathed in mist or flaming in sunset glory, its bitter coastline with sky-blue lochs and roaring rivers, its poor patches of fertile soil and its craggy pasturage for stag and sheep. Life was a contest with Nature, yet full of her sublimest ministration, and the people of Lord Reay's country found the secret of her ways and throve upon them—"simple-hearted children of God," Dr. MacKay describes them; "but all this is now changed."[1]

But to continue. The MacIntosh collaterals are of some importance. Thus, among my grandmother's first cousins was Charles MacIntosh, who invented the hot-air blast and gave to the industrial revolution, then still in its infancy, its amazing possibilities. His brother John, Captain of an East Indiaman and an ardent player on the bagpipes, built for himself Longwood House, in St. Helena, where Napoleon died. Another, William, an indigo-planter, lost his money in the French Revolution, and married his daughter to a marquis de Colville, to whom Charles MacIntosh gave the French patent rights of the hot-air blast as a magnificent wedding-gift: to be gambled away in six months, when my lord, returning to Glasgow to ask for another patent, was kicked out for his pains.[2]

Concerning the MacKay pedigree, Dr. MacIntosh MacKay states that he is unable to go farther back than his great-grandfather, who fought at Killiecrankie under General Hugh MacKay, whom my father always believed was also akin. The great General's sons died without issue.

---

[1] "It was discontent with poverty that began the ruin of the Highlands! If the heads of the people had but lived pure, active, sober, unostentatious lives, satisfied to be poor, poverty would never have overwhelmed them! The Highlands would have made Scotland great with the greatness of men dignified by high-hearted contentment, and strong with the strength of men who could do without!"—a passage which illustrates the sort of toryism that was the very backbone of George MacDonald's belief in social and individual evolution. (*What's Mine's Mine*, vol. iii, p. 199.)

[2] The Marquis's three daughters were as beautiful as their mother, and married, the eldest Baron St. Machose, the second Baron de Rasac, the third a M. de Lamont.

My father's other maternal uncle, Lieutenant George MacKay, married a Miss Janet Paterson, apparently an heiress, and lived at Banff. He had been appointed to an ensigncy in the 82nd Regiment in October 1813, with orders to join the 1st Battalion in the Peninsular. After Waterloo he was gazetted Lieutenant and proceeded with his regiment to Canada, where he distinguished himself greatly, but was presently retired on half-pay along with so many officers at that time. Thereafter he adopted a commercial life, was a J.P., and studied painting, besides devoting himself to public affairs. His charming personality made him beloved by all classes and ages. Helen, his second daughter—as beautiful as she was clever, my mother always declared—was sent to a finishing school in London; and her father, having business relations with the firm of leather-factors in the City of London, T. J. & T. Powell, begged my grandfather, James Powell, to befriend her. This led to close friendship and the introduction of her cousin George MacDonald to the family of James Powell and my father's falling in love with Louisa Powell, my mother. Helen had already married Alexander Powell, my mother's elder brother.

CHAPTER V
BOYHOOD

IT may be said that the evolution of man has depended upon his creation of the world on which he thrives. His cereals, root-crops and fruits, if nothing else, are of his own evolving; and upon such foundations his mental upbuilding has become possible. What is true of the race is epitomized in the individual. He discovers and creates the world in which he lives and moves, though different initial equipment, among offspring even of the same parents, qualifies differently the world each inhabits. The child is creating his world none the less that it is throughout fashioning himself.

Consequently, if we would know the world of George MacDonald's nurture and growth, we must realize his environment as it looked to and was created by the boy's own eyes—not as a guide-book, or even his own brothers, would describe it. Indeed it was quite a different world from his playmates'; though the meadows and rivers, the bleaching linen and blue skies, the cruel snows and celestial flowers, ostensibly looked and gave the same to all. It was not that he coloured "The Little Grey Town" with pigments from his paint-box, but rather that his keener vision everywhere disclosed fairyland and bewitchment, chivalry and devotion. Whether mastering his Shorter Catechism, or playing his furious games or lying sick with the pleurisy, he was always surveying and tilling the land that fed him.

George MacDonald's "earliest definable memory," he tells us, was, when between two and three years old, the funeral of the Duke of Gordon, already mentioned.[1] The Duke had died in London, and the body was brought to Elgin via Huntly—a six-weeks' journey. And this is what the little child saw: Countless black carriages drawn by black horses with postillions, and all draped in black velvet and nodding plumes.[2]

Earlier impressions of happy omen had of course been busy at work, moulding the little boy's alert yet so far passive brain long before this; that the memory of these was blotted out while that of the terrible emblem of death remained indelible, makes us ask whether it accounted for some of that melancholy which all through his later boyhood dogged his innate gaiety. But happy influences were certainly and early at work also, and are often referred to in his writings. In his poem called *The Hills* he so describes some of his home's surroundings that one sees even in his early years his mystic interpretation of things.[3]

George and Helen MacDonald had in all six children—all boys. James, the third of them, died when he was eight, and John MacKay, born in 1829, died in infancy. The others were Charles, George, Alexander and John Hill, the last two being respectively three and six years younger than George. George was eight years old when their mother died in 1832. Then their aunt, Miss Christina MacKay, came to live with them, her love and devotion being always remembered by her nephews.

Seven years after the death of his first wife their father married Miss Margaret McColl. She was a sister to Alexander Stewart McColl of Edinburgh,[4] to whom my father

---

1 "A Sketch of Individual Development," appearing in the *British Quarterly Review* for January 1882, and reprinted in *A Dish of Orts*, 1893. Alexander, 4th Duke of Gordon, died on June 17, 1827; so that my father was just two and a half years old at the time of the funeral.
2 *Recollections of Huntly*, by George Gray, Banff, 1892.
3 *Poetical Works*, vol. ii, p. 3.
4 Thus she was aunt to Norman McColl, Fellow of Downing and Editor of the *Athenæum* from 1871 to 1900.

acknowledged his indebtedness for the elucidation of Hamlet's great soliloquy, and dedicated to him his book on *Hamlet*, naming him—"a little less than kin and *more* than kind." To an uncle of his stepmother, Dr. Duncan McColl, R.N., he dedicated *The Portent*.

The new wife took the place of mother in the hearts of both father and boys; indeed my father owed to her everything that the most devoted of mothers can give. My own intimacy with her—for she died only in 1910 in her 102nd year, all her faculties except hearing unimpaired—revealed a tenderness of heart, a patience in adversity, a penetrating wisdom, together with a power of sympathy that account for much of the Celt's characteristic charm. She was pure Highland. The boys' new mother found her task less onerous than usually befalls. She used to say that one of the first things that struck her in her new home was the fine manners and courtesy of all the boys. If one of their elders rose to leave the room, either George or Alec would be always beforehand to open the door. She could not drop a thimble or a ball of wool but it was instantly picked up for her. They never were allowed to speak broad Scotch at table or before their elders, though among themselves and social inferiors they would lapse into the vernacular.

But even before the advent of their second mother the MacDonald boys had a happy childhood. There was always plenty of fun among themselves and with their elders. It must have been a couple of years, I take it, before George's mother died—before, in fact, the Shorter Catechism had tackled the old Adam in his little heart, that George was strutting about in his first pair of trousers before his Uncle William, when the latter vowed he now needed only a watch and a wife to make a man of him. "I can do well enough wanting the watch," promptly answered the little fellow, "but—but, I would like that I had a wee wifie!"

Sufficient discipline ruled the home. A look of displeasure from the beloved father was punishment for any sin, while his rebuke was awful indeed. Any complaints against their wild escapades, unless involving disobedience, he would smile at, though he might warn and restrict. There was plenty for the hungriest boys of all that was necessary—except, to be sure, oxygen indoors; but clothes were mostly shabby, and money was always scarce. On the other hand there were cattle in the byre, horses in the stable, wild bees' nests in the stone dykes, whose honeycomb eaten like bread was a priceless joy; there were pools for swimming, and a river for boating. There was fishing with rod and net, the latter especially when the rivers were swollen and muddy and the trout unable to see their way, like "human mortals in a thick fog, whether of the atmosphere or of circumstance."[1] How the *nickums* got horsehair for their rods has already been told. Nor must it be forgotten that of high importance in an imaginative boy's education, even though pedagogues denied them, were Kelpies in the dark pots of mountain-burnies or the still blacker pools of peat-cuttings on the moor. To these boys the world was a constant invitation to adventure, for they read into its realistic sweetness and terror the trappings of imaginative romance.

My father's love of horses and intimacy with every creature he handled date from his earliest childhood. His father's tenderness towards all living things and pity for their sorrows was, I think, never hid from his boys.[2] Of one grey mare he used to tell us—and indeed told the world in his writings. Whose her sire or whence she came, he did not know. Her small head and broad chest, clean limbs, and quarters so supple and sinewy that, when the boy had half scrambled, half leaped upon her bare back, she would

---

1 *Alec Forbes*, vol. i, p.67.
2 I recall a letter of my grandfather's from the Cabrach concerning the cruelties of grouse-shooting.

rush away like the wind, as if possessed by her rider's very soul, convinced him that Arab blood was in her. She was "*Missy*"—alike at The Farm and in *Ranald Bannerman's Boyhood*. He would lie sometimes peacefully on her back reading his book, *The Pilgrim's Progress*, *Paradise Lost*, or Klopstock's *Messiah*, and possibly, omnivorous boy that he was, Young's *Night Thoughts*—while "she ground and mashed away at the grass as if nobody were near her."[1]

He tells how they first learned to ride the plough-horses at watering time; how they would drop

head and neck and shoulders like a certain toy-bird, causing the young riders a vague fear of falling over the height no longer defended by the uplifted crest; and then drink and drink till the riders' legs felt the horses' bodies swelling under them; then up and away again with quick refreshed stride or trot towards the paradise of their stalls. But for us came first the somewhat fearful pass of the stable-door, for they never stopped, like better educated horses, to let their riders dismount, but walked right in, and there was just room, by stooping low, to clear the top of the door. As we improved in equitation, we would go afield, to ride them home from the pasture, where they were fastened by chains to short stakes of iron driven into the earth. There was more of adventure here, for not only was the ride longer, but the horses were more frisky, and would sometimes set off at the gallop.[2]

But the boys' father would not allow them a saddle till they had a sure seat on the bare back; and thereafter they needed but little teaching.[3]

After his father's second marriage there came three little sisters to these lads, Isabella in 1841, Louisa in 1843 and Jane in 1846. Isabella died at the age of fourteen with acute tuberculosis of the lungs. When she was twelve years

---

1 *Ranald Bannerman's Boyhood*, p. 54.
2 Loc. cit.
3 In a letter dated August 15, 1855, from my grandfather to my mother he says: "...you express a wish that I had seen him mounted on a noble steed as you had done somewhere in the country. You may just ask himself whether on various occasions I was not most tempted to thrash the rogue's back for his feats at horsemanship..." In later years, whenever my father had the opportunity on a friend's mount of following the hounds, he was never other than at home.

old she had sent her brother George a present of a knitted silk purse, to which he replies:

> How much I should like to spend a winter at home again, a snowy winter, with great heaps and wreaths of snow; and sometimes the wild wind howling in the chimneys and against the windows and down at the kitchen door! And how much I should love to spend one long summer day in June, lying on the grass before the house, and looking up into the deep sky with large white clouds in it. And when I lifted my head I should see the dear old hills all round about; and the shining of the Bogie, whose rush I should hear far off and soft, making a noise hardly louder than a lot of midges...And then the warmer evening, with long grass in the field where the well is, and the corn-craik crying *craik-craik*—somewhere in it, though nobody knows where...

Again in a letter to his father he speaks of running with his brother "through the long grass of a certain field on a warm summer night trying to catch the corn scraich, till recalled by you and reprimanded for trampling down the grass"; and then of the well, from which "on hot noon days I so often fetched you a jug of cold water when you came into the house hot and thirsty."

It is only when the youthful imagination sees things in their full significance that they imprint themselves on the palimpsest of the brain in such wise that they will never be erased. As surely as Robert Burns's soul was translated into the mouse's when she lit upon her tragedy, so was George MacDonald's into the little hedgehog's:

> A gray hedghog ran
> With tangled mesh of bristling spikes, and face
> Helplessly innocent, across the field:
> He let it run, and blessed it as it ran. [1]

It was because of the boy's love for the plough-horse that, as he watched its kindly labour, he became that horse, felt as it felt, leaned against collar with its great weight, quick cropped at a tussock at the turn, and worked no less hard for that moment's

---

1 *A Hidden Life.*

lapse from duty. Only because of his magical gift could himself, unskilled in ploughing, have written of ploughman's love and horses' obedience as he sets them before us in *A Hidden Life*—the "Classic Epic of Student Life in Aberdeen," as Sir William Duguid Geddes, his fellow student and late Principal of the University, names this poem.

> With sure eye,
> He saw the horses keep the arrow-track;
> He saw the swift share cut the measured sod;
> He saw the furrow folding to the right,
> Ready with nimble foot to aid at need.
> And there the slain sod lay, patient for grain,
> Turning its secrets upward to the sun,
> And hiding in a grave green sun-born grass,
> And daisies dipped in carmine: all must die,
> That others live, and they arise again.[1]

In connection with my father's keen observation of nature, I may mention how on market-days he would, when quite a small boy, be the first out of school and rush off to the *Gordon Arms*, where shepherds and Highland drovers forgathered. Waiting behind a partition, he would collect all manner of information concerning shepherd and crofter life. Although most of the talk was in Gaelic, he picked up enough to follow the trend of their talk. In after life he made some attempt to master the tongue, but could not afford the time and patience it demanded.

Indeed, to know in what full way the child was father of the man, we must study all his Scottish stories; they are redolent of the soil, so ardently loved by the boy, in all its dealings with men and man's with it.

Nothing on the place was done by machinery, for the water-mill, "with its dull wooden sounds, made no discord with the sweetness of the hour." [2]

---

1   *Poems*, 1857, p. 5; and *Poetical Works*, 1893, vol. i, p. 136; see also Sir Wm. Geddes' critique in *Blackwood* 1891, and quoted *infra* on p. 536.
2   *Donal Grant*, vol. i, p. 111.

There may be great pleasure in watching machine-operations (my father writes), but surely none to equal the pleasure we had. If there had been a steam-engine to plough my father's fields, how could we have ridden home on its back in the evening? Had there been a thrashing machine, could its pleasure have been comparable to that of lying in the straw and watching the grain dance from the sheaves under the skilful flails of the two strong men who belaboured them? There was a winnowing machine, but quite a tame one, for its wheels I could drive myself—the handle now high as my head, now low as my knee—and watch at the same time the storm of chaff driven like drifting snow-flakes from its wide mouth...I think I see old Eppie now, filling her sack with what the wind blew her; not with the grain; Eppie did not covet that; she only wanted her bed filled with fresh springy chaff, on which she would sleep as sound as her rheumatism would let her, and as warm and dry and comfortable as any duchess in the land that happened to have the rheumatism too...What more machines are there now? Strange, wild-looking mad-like machines, as the Scotch would call them, are growling and snapping, and clinking and clattering over our fields, so that it seems to an old boy as if all the sweet poetic twilight of things were vanishing from the country.[1]

Though in winter the school work began in earnest, it soon provided fresh opportunities for adventure. George was, however, a delicate boy—once in bed for four months; so he was often kept from school, though but half a mile distant, because of the deep snow or the even more treacherous thaw; his susceptibility to pleurisy, for which he would be bled from the arm, made caution necessary. But in spite of such hardships, the winter had its joys, a favourite sport being the excavation of great caves in the snow and battles with the snowballs.

All the short day, the sun, though low, was brilliant, and the whole country shone with dazzling whiteness; but after sunset, which took place between three and four o'clock, anything more dreary can hardly be imagined, especially when the keenest of winds rushed in gusts from the north-east, and, lifting the snow-powder from untrodden shadows, blew it, like so many stings, in the face of the freezing traveller.[2]

It must have been on such winter evenings that the boy's ingenuity was exercised to find amusement.

---

1   *Ranald Bannerman*, p. 51   2   Loc cit., p. 248

Once with the young brothers and cousins at his heels, he rushed into the kitchen, jumped upon the clean-scrubbed table, and began a learned discourse, indicating Bell Mavor, the maid, as a reprobate past redemption. She flicked at him with her dish-clout, when he turned upon her in righteous anger, as he set straight the improvised bands about his neck: "Div ye no ken fan ye're speakin' til a meenister, Bell? Ye's no fleg (frighten) awa' the Rev. Geordie MacDonald as gin he war a buzzin' flee (fly)! Losh, woman, neist to Dr. Chaumers (Chalmers), he's the grandest preacher in a' Scotland!"[1]

The story is substantiated by an even more humorous incident of which my grandfather in a letter dated April 23, 1850, reminded his son, then temporarily preaching at Whitehaven:

> I hope you will be able to stop in Manchester on your way South and preach a sermon to your kindred [Charles and Alec were then living in Manchester] that they may be able to judge of your qualifications and to be otherwise gratified. By the bye, when I think of it, they have repeatedly heard you long ago, when the basin-stand was your pulpit, and when matters *purely local* and *domestic* formed the leading subjects of your prayers before your congregation. I believe you had to thank your own *slim form* that you were not overtaken by the same awkward kind of calamity which befel *one of the brotherhood*, who, having got by force and the impulse of his own greater gravitation into the aforesaid *pulpit*, found when he had occasion to slip out again, that to do so was no easy matter; nay, it was an impossibility until he had discharged his audience, and, having more privately peeled off his trousers, made a shift to crawl out of his involuntary imprisonment! Take care, man, and don't ever preach in too small a pulpit for fear of the consequences!

But the school was always over by three o'clock, and Saturday was a half-holiday, whose happy anticipation was somewhat qualified by its appropriation to the Shorter Catechism[2] and the certainty that some at least would get

---

1   I have the story from Miss Bessie Hobrow, whose nurse, Jean Mavor, a native of Huntly, was Bell's sister, and corresponds in name and description with the farmer's half-sister at The Mains in *Sir Gibbie*.

2   The opening phrase of this epitome of Calvinistic dogmas is this: "The chief end of man is to glorify God and enjoy Him for ever." "For my part," writes the

a "licking from the tawse or even the more hated alternative of being *kept in*."

The first teacher of Charles, George, and James was a certain Rev. C—— S——, a Highlander, "a hard man with a severe, not altogether cruel temper, and a quite savage sense of duty"—the original of the barbarous Murdoch Malison in *Alec Forbes*. The character, almost incredible to us, was not overdrawn, as a schoolfellow of my father's assured Mr. R. Troup, though the latter adds that when S—— emigrated to Australia he made so touching a farewell speech to his scholars, boys and girls, that one of them, Mr. Troup's informant, must run straight home for a good cry under his father's counter.[1]

Little James MacDonald, as already mentioned, died when eight years old, and his schoolfellows, if no others, believed his death was in large part due to S——'s cruelty. But the author of *Alec Forbes*, creates a divine repentance for the man.

But tawse and pleurisy notwithstanding, George[2] made good progress at school, where Latin and mathematics were the foundation of most children's education, whether their fees were paid by parents or by the parish. Laird's son and ploughman's were on equal footing—a fact that largely explained the Scot's liberalism in politics and that understanding of the fellowman which is the first essential for success in the world. But not only were his lessons easily learned—though even with the brightest boy or girl, any slip in grammar earned fearful punishment, just as the

---

author of *Alec Forbes*, "I wish the spiritual engineers who constructed it had, after laying the grandest foundation-stone that truth could afford them, glorified God by going no further. (*Alec Forbes*, vol. i, p. 85.)

1   See footnote, p. 30. When my uncle, Charles MacDonald, went to Sydney in 1857, the first face he knew was that of this schoolmaster, now married to a sister of Dr. MacIntosh MacKay. His immediate question to his one-time pupil was: "And are the boys of Huntly always attending to their Shorter Catechism?"

2   Should it in a reader's ear sound like disrespect that I speak of my father by his Christian name, will that reader please remember that I am old enough to be that little boy's grandfather.

BOYHOOD

Calvinist's God extorts justice irrespective of responsibility—but he read a good deal, lying on the sofa often for hours together. His father had grave doubts as to what work he was fit for:

> The neighbours asked what he would make his son:
> "I'll make a man of him," the old man said;
> "And for the rest, just what he likes himself." [1]

But a dreamer he must have been already, and when still a schoolboy he would read his poetry to favourite schoolfellows. Mr. Troup tells how once he repeated to them a free metrical version of the 14th chapter of Isaiah.

The MacDonald boys had many delights, among them visits to the sea at Portsoy or Banff, where lived their uncle George MacKay and their pretty cousin Helen. Among the long series of letters written to his father up till his death, the first was penned during a holiday at Portsoy. Even in this one, though only nine, he refers to his ill-health; and it pursued him more or less all through his life. The calligraphy is as admirable as the grammar and diction.

G.M.D to his Father.

PORTSOY,
15 *August*, 1833.

MY DEAR PAPA,

I return you many thanks for the kind letter I received on Wednesday. I am happy to hear that you are well. I have been unwell for two or three days, my throat was a little sore and my head very painful, but I am quite well now and have been in the sea today and like it very much. When I was down at the bathing I met a boy who was once a schoolfellow of mine at Mr. S——'s school, and he showed me the carcase of a whale which had been cast on the shore. Mrs. Morrison told me that the men at the green got a good deal of fat of it...Johnny[2] is very amusing. He seems to be more frightened at the tub than at the sea. We are all quite well. Would you be so good as come down and stay with

---

1 "A Hidden Life," *Poetical Works*, vol. i, p. 145.
2 His youngest brother, then aged nineteen months.

us till we go home. Aunt makes me drink the water,[1] but I am unwilling to do it. I am sorry that my writing is so bad, but my pen is very bad.

I remain, my dear Papa, Your affect. Son,

GEORGE MACDONALD.

The next letter is interesting in its reference to some temperance society to whose rules George had subscribed. It also indicates his love of the sea which later rose to almost passionate expression.

PORTSOY,

August 1, 1834.

MY DEAR PAPA,

As you desired me to write to you by the first opportunity I have complied with your request. I received your kind letter just as I was coming out of a boat in which I had been sailing and thank you for it...I have bathed every day since I came, and I drink the salt water every two days. I have been at Fordyce, I think it was on Wednesday. We were in a very old house with a castle attached. The woman in the house took us up to a room and brought out the gin bottle. Mr. Mortimer pretended to take some of it, and got off with a very good excuse. Jane pretended to take some too but did not taste it. Margaret and James did take some of it, but when it came to me (I had whispered to Mrs. M. that I wouldn't take it) I said I *can't* take it so I got away and did not break any of the Rules of the Temperance Society. There was a Prussian schooner in the harbour and William and I went out with it yesterday morning and came back in the pilot boat. We were far out of sight of land [because of a sea fog] and I did not think it very easy to get over the ship's side into the boat. I am very fond of the bathing and William will perhaps learn me to swim. You may tell Aunt to send down a shirt to me as she said she would do. Tell Alex and Johnny that I will bring up some marble stones to them.[2] I have not more to say at present but in the meantime I remain, my dear Papa,

Your affectionate son,

GEORGE MACDONALD.

Spirit drinking was then as now the curse of Scotland, and the children were familiar enough with its evils. Beer, however, was looked upon as beneficial, and the young people

---

1 A usual prescription of the faculty as an adjunct to sea-bathing.
2 The Portsoy serpentine is very beautiful and its marbles were greatly prized by the boys.

often drank it with their dinner. But even they were exposed to the temptation of spirits, as the letter shows.

In 1837 the Huntly Juvenile Temperance Society was formed with George as its first President, he then being thirteen years old. The school children held a meeting once a fortnight in the MacDonald thread-factory, with young George in the chair, who, in the words of one of the members, always "spoke like a book." But this is anticipating.

In 1835, I think it was, a beneficent change came to the "Adventure School," as it was named, in the appointment, in place of Mr. S——, of the Rev. Alexander Millar. He was the son of the minister of the United Secession Church. Under him George made such progress that he excelled all others in his expressive reading. At a certain examination, and at the request of one of the examining ministers, he read aloud a metrical composition of his own, sent in by way of essay, the subject being *Patriotism*. Millar, recognizing his ability, gave him much help. He was set to teach others, then a fairly common arrangement. Millar would hold a morning class before breakfast, and sometimes George, instead of going home, would go with a schoolfellow to his home, join the family standing round the table and share their porridge, each with his wooden bicker of milk. Such free hospitality was common all over Scotland: indeed it may be stated as a law of social life that, wherever the fare is simple and frugal, there hospitality is open and unceremonious. Mr. Millar would invite him after school to go home with him, and their readings at times filled the hours till the boy must partake of the master's supper—potatoes and milk, oatcake and butter.

The brief record of dates by my great-grandmother concerning chiefly her grandchildren contains little interest, her penmanship and spelling being laborious. But one important incident is the boys' energy in the temperance movement:

1837. The Huntly Juvenile Temperance Society was begun by four young persons on Tuesday evening the fourth of December. On that same night the gas was first introduced into Huntly for preventing darkness to the town. The Juvenile Temperance Society was begun for preventing darkness to the mind.

A fortnight later the Society numbered twenty-two.

Declaration of the Huntly Juvenile Temperance Society: "We agree to abstain from distilled spirits except for medicinal purposes and to discountenance the causes and practice of Intemperance."

A further entry suggests that the juvenile zeal was yielding great results:

February 24, 1841. A whisky shop known by the name of The Pit was this day closed! It was next door to the New Church. Thanks to the Lord!

Though the remaining entry does not bear directly upon temperance, I cannot refrain from quoting it. The stern old Calvinist could not overlook the opening of the new church nor a festive dinner occurring on the same forenoon, particularly as the latter was followed up with a "dancing ball."

26th February. The Non-Intrusion Church was opened when the Rev. Mr. Candlish preached upon Matthew 6th chapter and 9th verse, "Hallowed be Thy name." On the same forenoon there happened a Cattle Show and a great dinner. A dancing ball began at 9 o'clock and continued until between 3 and 4 o'clock in the morning.

This day being the anniversary of the Birthday of the Earl of March and exactly two years from the laying of the Foundation Stone of the Gordon Schools, a procession of children was formed and several hundreds walked up to the Lodge accompanied by a band of music, and received from her Grace[1] a cake and an orange each. LET HER GRACE NEVER WEARY IN WELL-DOING.

Nothing better shows the invulnerability of youth's spirit than the failure of the Shorter Catechism, driven in by the tawse, to spoil the boys' play—the Scottish intrepidity

---

1   The Dowager. The dukedom became extinct at her husband Alexander's death in 1837. He was succeeded in the marquisate by George, 9th Marquess of Huntly.

BOYHOOD

being built upon the rocks of oatmeal, education and poverty.

School games were heroic, if furious, almost as bitter and dangerous as such amusements used to be in Ireland—to judge from Will Carleton's famous stories. The two schools in Huntly were always at daggers drawn, their enmity being hard to account for; certainly it was not due to sectarian or social differences. The battle always began with missiles—"Stone-showers which descended upon us like hail." [1] My father had never been a good thrower—his chest-ailments easily accounting for this, I think; and his duties lay chiefly in collecting and bringing into the fighting ranks the ammunition. But his spirit soon got him acknowledged as the leader, and his charges at the head of his troop must have been full "of meikle micht." [2]

Even in the merry-makings of later life, I remember my father's spirits as often highest and gayest of all the company.

The boy's love of the sea evidently increased year by year, till we find another letter written apparently two years later, but whether from Cullen, Portsoy, or Banff is unknown. Unfortunately it is not dated, though from the improved penmanship and mode of expression we may assume he was about twelve. He claims to have reached a final decision as to his future life, and determines that nothing else could be contemplated by him than the career of a sailor. Possibly

---

[1] *Ranald Bannerman's Boyhood*, p. 233.
[2] His romantic spirit thus dominating even his games recalls a verse in that rare old ballad, *The Battle of Harlaw*, published first in 1549:

> "And then throw fair Strathbogie land,
> His purpose was for to pursew,
> And quhasoever durst gainstand
> That race they should full sairly rew;
> Then he bad all his men be trew,
> And him defend by forss and slicht,
> And promist them rewardis anew,
> And mak them men of meikle micht."

(*Scottish Ballads, Tales and Songs*, by John Gilchrist, Edinburgh, 1815 vol. i, p. 31.)

he knew of his father's uncertainty as to what he was fit for.

G.M.D to his Father.

My dear Father,

It is now time for me to be thinking of what I should betake myself to, and tho' I would be sorry to displease you in any way, yet I must tell you that the sea is my delight and that I wish to go to it as soon as possible, and I hope that you will not use your parental authority to prevent me, as you undoubtedly can. I feel I would be continually wishing and longing to be at sea. Though a dangerous, it is undoubtedly an honest and lawful employment, or I would scorn to be engaged in it. Whatever other things I may have intended were in my childhood days, [so] that you can hardly blame me for being flighty in this respect. O let me, dear father, for I could not be happy at anything else. And I am not altogether ignorant of sea affairs, tho' I have yet a great deal to learn, for I have been studying them for some time back. If it were not for putting you to too much trouble I would beg an answer from you in writing, but I can hardly expect it, though I much wish it.

Your affectionate son
George.

At sixteen this high-spirited, responsible boy's childhood ended; for in 1840 he entered King's College, Aberdeen, and his manhood began.

CHAPTER VI
THE YOUNG PHILOSOPHER

IF a lad intended to enter for the Bursary Competition in Aberdeen, he would be sent to a grammar school for a few months to be coached, in Latin particularly. So when George was sixteen he went to the Aulton (Old Town) Grammar School, Aberdeen,[1] for the months of August, September and October, 1840.

If the school work was dry it was thorough. If that Academy had no sweetly shadowing trees, beyond still was the sea and the sky; and that court, morning and afternoon, was filled with the shouts of eager boys, kicking the football with mad rushings to and fro, and sometimes with wounds and faintings...Shock-headed Highland colts, and rough Lowland steers, as many of them were, out of that group, out of the roughest of them would emerge in time a few gentlemen—large-hearted courteous gentlemen, for whom a man may thank God...

Though it is Robert Falconer's experiences thus described, we may be sure it was George MacDonald himself who

would rush into the thick of the football game, fight like a maniac for one short burst, and then retire and look on...But sometimes, looking up from his Virgil or his Latin version, he would fling down his dictionary or his pen, and fly in a straight line, like a sea-gull weary of lake and river, down to the waste shore of the great deep.[2]

In November he took the twelfth place in the competition, winning the Fullarton Bursary of £14 per annum. This would generally cover a student's fees and a great part of his expenses for the five months' session. He entered King's College

---

1 Where Byron was sent to school when seven. It is said to be the oldest school in the Kingdom, the records dating back to 1256. The low, one-floor building still stands, but was vacated in 1863, when the present school was built.
2 *Robert Falconer*, vol. ii, p. 53

and passed through the usual curriculum of four sessions: "Bajan," 1840-41; "Semi," 1841-42; "Tertian," 1843-44; and "Magistrand," 1844-45; missing, as will be explained presently, the session 1842-43. He worked hard, though fitfully. He won the third prize in Chemistry and the fourth in Natural Philosophy, and considered seriously going to Giessen for work under von Liebig, many of whose books were already available in English. But this could not be. Then a strong desire took hold of him to study medicine. But here again the want of money stood in the way; so he devoted himself more and more to modern literature and languages. German, attracting his philosophic and poetical tastes, was acquired easily and thoroughly.

The standard of education in Aberdeen in the early days of the century was not high, and the teaching was more like that of English schools; but it was intimate and thorough, qualities that account largely for the northern University's fine achievements. If, it is said, Aberdeen gave fewer scholars to the world than did the English Universities, the faculty of developing their own innate gifts by the men themselves was more evident, and a higher average of brain-power seems to have been reached.

The following letter, written when half-way through his first winter session, shows that George still accepted the conventional dogmas without questioning.

ABERDEEN,
5 January, 1841.

MY DEAR FATHER,

I am much obliged to you for the kind letter which you sent me some time ago. I hope I wish to serve God and to be delivered not only from the punishment of sin, but also from its power. Our potatoes and meal are both almost done. Be so good as to send a fresh supply as soon as convenient...Mr Kennedy was at our Sabbath school soiree in the Old Town. He preaches most excellent sermons, and he never closes without saying something to the unconverted.

I am, Your ever affectionate son,

GEO. MACDONALD

THE YOUNG PHILOSOPHER

The Rev. John Kennedy, D.D., was from 1836 to 1846 pastor of the Blackfriars Congregational Church, which George and his brother Charles attended. The former—possibly the latter also—took Sunday-school classes, and so came into close touch with the minister:[1] by whose zeal and faculty for organization hordes of beggar-children roaming the Aberdeen streets were swept into his embryo *School of Industry*, which gave over 800 children one meal every day and their schooling.

The next letter suggests that already the young student might be questioning the old standards.

G.M.D to his Father.

Aberdeen,
28th Oct. 1841.

...I found all our friends well, and our lodgings very comfortable, although the lad who lodges along with us is not so much of a gentleman as we could wish; yet I hope he will not be any the worse in that respect for lodging with us...

I saw a most splendid procession to-day of the Chartists going out to meet Fergus O'Connor. There were about two thousand of them in the procession, and there might have been fifteen thousand on the streets. There were several different bands of music and banners and mottoes innumerable. There was a coach and three open carriages which went out to meet O'Connor, two with four horses and one with six horses in which was the chap himself—a pretty good-looking man, but not a good figure—tall and stout. I was down at the links for a short time while he was addressing the people. The scene was really splendid.

I was delighted when I heard the first bursar's name called out for £30. He is a poor lad from Orkney who was at the Grammar School with me, and was then a good scholar. He competed last year, and got only five pounds, but wouldn't keep it because it wouldn't keep him...

I hope by this time your business is settled. I am in some doubts whether or not I should study Chemistry...

---

[1] He married a sister of Professor John Stuart Blackie and had seven children, the eldest being Sir Alexander Kennedy, F.R.S. Sir Alexander writes to me thus about his father: "I have never met or known anyone to whom the word 'saintly' could be applied so entirely as to my father. To some of us who loved him most, however little we shared his particular opinions, it was the man himself who gave the glory to a narrow and impossible theology." My father, a warm friend of John Stuart Blackie, kept up his friendship with Dr. Kennedy, though they differed widely in opinion.

The "business" probably concerned the difficult times ahead which threatened George's career at King's College. His father was suffering already from the low market prices incident to the changing corn-laws, while Dr. Kennedy and enlightened politicians in Aberdeen were loud in advocating their total repeal. So George was compelled to face the conflict between the conservatism of his upbringing and the new remedies that, as some believed, would cure all social ills.

The state of the poor in the city was terrible and must have wrung his young heart. Even if at home he believed that all poverty, such for instance, as that of his grandmother's adoptions, must be due to the just anger of an outraged God, in Aberdeen

> The crowds of men, in whom a starving soul
> Cries through the windows of their hollow eyes
> For bare humanity,[1]

might well have bidden him question his theology.

The study of Chemistry and Natural Philosophy was deferred till the winter of 1843-4. That he won distinction in both is not surprising, seeing that they became minor enthusiasms with him. When a student five years later at Highbury Theological College, it will be told how he instituted on his own responsibility lectures to his fellow students on these subjects. Then again, writing to his father in 1850—a year before he married—and speaking of the possibility of his failure as a preacher, he declares, if he can get someone to lend him a hundred pounds, he will go out to Baron Liebig: "I have little fear of making a good chemist," he adds. In the Manchester days, too (1853-56), among his many adventures to pay his way, in spite of the increasing family and his constant ill-health, he gave lectures on these subjects at a Ladies' College.

This love of so precise a science as Chemistry—rigid in laws appertaining to the invisible atom—is very interesting

---

1 "A Hidden Life," *Poetical Works*, vol. i, p. 150

when we compare his logical honesty regarding facts with his imaginative grasp of un-demonstrable truth.

Here some may recall his own words regarding the apparent conflict between Science and Poetry:

> In the first months of his college life a new phase of experience begins... For a time knowledge is pride...But ever the thing that is known sinks into insignificance, save as a step of the endless stair on which he is climbing—whither he knows not; the unknown draws him; the new fact touches his mind, flames up in the contact, and drops dark, a mere fact, on the heap below...At the entrance of Science, nobly and gracefully as she bears herself, young Poetry shrinks back startled, dismayed. Poetry is true as Science, and Science is holy as Poetry; but young Poetry is timid and Science is fearless, and bears with her a colder atmosphere than the other has yet learned to brave...The youth gazes on the face of Science, cold, clear, beautiful; then, turning, looks for his friend—but alas! Poetry has fled. With a great pang at the heart he rushes abroad to find her, but descries only the rainbow glimmer of her skirt on the far horizon... "What is the storm any more!" he cries; "it is but the clashing of countless water-drops!" He finds relief in the discovery that, the moment you place a man in the midst of it, the clashing of water-drops becomes a storm, terrible to heart and brain: human thought and feeling, hope, fear, love, sacrifice, make the motions of nature alive with mystery and the shadows of destiny... [1]

George MacDonald missed the session of 1842-43, because, I presume, his bursary was not sufficient to meet all expenses, and his father found it impossible to help him. How the difficulty arose is tolerably clear.

As I have already remarked, there was, and at the best of times, never much money at home, notwithstanding an abundance of the bare necessaries of life. But now increasing hardships were assailing all the lesser farmers and crofters, Aberdeenshire being pre-eminently a country of small holdings.[2] Cheap food from abroad was essential

---

1 "A Sketch of Individual Development," by George MacDonald, *British Quarterly Review*, January 1882; reprinted in *A Dish of Orts*, 1893.
2 By 1842 the threat of low prices was thoroughly frightening the corn-growers. Not only this: the industrial revolution was making violent assault upon agriculture, and the opposition of the Tories to Free Trade was largely due to the realization of a fact fully acknowledged by Sir Robert Peel before his conversion to Free Trade, that machinery would be the ruin of the land.

if the factory hands, increasing now at an alarming rate in order to meet the demands of machinery, were to be fed; and though removal of the protection had been gradual till the corn-duty was abolished in 1846, the small farmers never recovered.

But apart from this gradual straitening of means up till the year in question, 1842, my grandfather and his brother, Messrs. George and James MacDonald, perennially creditors to the Aberdeen Bank for their brother Charles's delinquencies, were now subject to additional pressure for the liquidation of the debt they had undertaken to meet; and it is probably to this that reference is made in the letter last quoted. So that my father's determination to find employment and earn some money before resuming his studies is amply accounted for; and he made his ill the advantage of his good.

As is commonly known, the Aberdeen student, so often of cottar-, ploughman-, or shepherd-parentage, would work on the land during the seven months of summer and earn enough for the five at college; and he would come on foot a hundred miles or more, the carrier bringing beforehand the sack of oatmeal that was to feed him during the winter. But George MacDonald was physically unfitted for such work, though he must often have wished it were possible. So he spent some summer months in a certain castle or mansion in the far North,[1] the locality of which I have failed to trace, in cataloguing a neglected library. That he did acquire intimate experience of this kind is obvious from his frequent use of such-like material in his fiction—notably in *The Portent, David Elginbrod, Wilfrid Cumbermede, There and Back, Donal Grant,* and *Lilith.* The library, wherever it was, and whatever its scope, added much to the materials upon which his imagination worked in future years.

---

1   The fact is recorded by the Rev. Robert Troup, who at one time set down many points he remembered about his wife's first cousin—all valuable. See also *Alec Forbes*, vol. iii, p. 66.

THE YOUNG PHILOSOPHER

...Now I was in my element (he writes). The very outside of a book had a charm to me. It was a kind of sacrament—an outward and visible sign of an inward and spiritual grace; as, indeed, what on God's earth is not?...I found a perfect set of our poets—although it omitted both Chaucer and George Herbert. I began to nibble at that portion of the collection which belonged to the sixteenth century...I found nothing, to my idea, but love-poems without any love in them, and so I soon became weary. But I found in the library what I liked far better—many romances of a very marvellous sort, and plentiful interruption they gave to the formation of the catalogue. I likewise came upon a whole nest of the German classics...Happening to be a tolerable reader of German, I found in these volumes a mine of wealth inexhaustible.[1]

If the schoolmaster Millar first made him look out of window, this library led him out of doors, and beyond the bounds of academic scholarship.[2]

---

1   *The Portent*, 1864, pp. 82 and 83. He may have first found A. E. T. Hoffman's works in the library. To them, as is suggested later, pp. 259 and 297, he was possibly much indebted.

2   It is curious that I can find no record of how the summer months of 1842 were spent. In *Alec Forbes* we find Cupples telling of some "grit leebrary i' the far North" where he was employed, and some of this I take to be autobiographical. I have been at considerable pains, both in correspondence and in travelling, to ascertain where this library was situated; for its importance in my father's eduction cannot be questioned. But I have not been successful, though I have a strong suspicion that it was Thurso Castle, now the property of Sir Archibald Sinclair, Bart., of Ulbster, M.P. It has a fine library, and its owner in 1842 was Sir George Sinclair, son of the first baronet, Sir John, the first President of the Board of Agriculture, a great linguist and collector of German literature, which fact tallies with the account of the library in *The Portent*. He died in 1835. The fact that my grandfather had some sort of intimacy with him is suggested by the use of his name on an advertisement as recommending the potato-flour or "Farina" manufactured by the MacDonald Brothers at Huntly. But Sir Archibald, who has been most kind in helping me to a conclusion, can find no corroboration of my surmise.

The only other possible place is Dunbeath Castle, the property of Rear-Admiral Sir Edwyn S. Alexander-Sinclair, R.N., M.V.O. Lady Alexander-Sinclair tells me there was formerly a "wonderful library" there; but that when her husband succeeded in 1892, everything was left to his cousin's widow, including the books, which, at her death in 1911, were sold. She further says that friends of hers think it very probable that this was the very library my father catalogued.

CHAPTER VII

THE YOUNG POET

GEORGE MACDONALD, his engagement in the great library done, resumed his studies in Aberdeen much strengthened, we may presume, in mind and imaginative outlook. If his life's adventure was no more than opened, to have bravely begun it was foretaste of victory. From February to November 1843 he taught arithmetic in the Aberdeen Central Academy "with great spirit and skill," as its head master, Mr. Thomas Merton, states in a testimonial; and he secured some private pupils. Dr. Kennedy had all along been a warm friend to this lad, as enthusiastic in teaching as learning, and with sense of responsibility remarkable in one of his years; and to his house he came thrice a week to coach a student. By such means social pleasures came also, and his popularity in academic society was assured. He was an ardent, if nervous, speaker in the Debating Society; and at times his Celtic fire would carry all before him. It is told that he figured strong in drawing-room charades—the taste for which in England, so Thackeray says, had arrived from France after Waterloo; and it had now penetrated to Aberdeen. In such pleasures he was noted for his ingenuity in devising fantastic habiliments. Some years ago Mr. John Christie, the archaeologist, to whom I was indebted for much valuable research work, wrote me that the student George MacDonald used often to

THE YOUNG POET

visit Mr. Christie's grandfather's house, and that his mother described the lad on one occasion as taking part in charades; how they rummaged out an old bottle-green coat for him; and how, it being buttonless, he cut a huge carrot into discs and sewed them on the coat—the effect being prodigious. Sir Wm. D. Geddes, my father's junior by two years at King's College, writing in 1896, says that George MacDonald was quickly recognized as "a youth of imaginative power, but, like the typical Celt, dreamily careless of fame and class-list positions," and incidentally remarks: "I remember the radiance of a tartan coat he wore—the most dazzling affair in dress I ever saw a student wear, but characteristic of the young Celtic minstrel."[1]

Most of my family prefer to discredit the tartan coat, and my father's cousin, Helen MacKay, who saw much of him in these days, told me she never saw it. But Sir William Geddes gives it as a fact, and I think we should accept it. We must remember too that, not only did the students all wear "the scarlet gown with the closed sleeves," but that the variety of dress among the students—ploughman's, cottar's and shepherd's sons, young lairds and even sprigs of the Scottish nobility, occasionally in their kilts, must have been remarkable and delightful. My father might have found an old tartan coat at home and worn it partly for economy, and yet because he liked it.[2]

It was on his return to Aberdeen in 1843—he being not yet twenty—that Robert Troup, having just entered

---

[1] "Poetic Ideals of Education," a lecture by Principal W. D. Geddes, 1896

[2] My friend, James A. Campbell of Barbreck, a first authority on such points, writes me that "the tartan coat was often worn in old days, but was driven out by tourists and strangers." Lockhart tells of a minister and a lawyer "rigged out in new jacket and trousers of the Macgregor tartan," coming from New England to call upon Sir Walter Scott in 1818. *Life*, vol. iv, p. 199.

In *Heather and Snow* (1893) my father describes a young laird as "dressed a little showily in a short coat of dark tartan and a Highland bonnet with a brooch and feather," vol. i, p. 30.

his first session, was introduced to him. He wrote thus of him in 1898:

> He was studious, quiet, sensitive, imaginative, frank, open, speaking freely what he thought. His love of truth was intense, only equalled by his scorn of meanness, his purity and his moral courage. So I found him when I became acquainted with him next session. So I have found him ever since.

In passing I may remark that my father's dress was generally more or less of a protest against the ugly and unreasonable—and, thanks to her own fine taste, my mother always encouraged it. Growing a beard when fashion looked with horror upon such ornament as "heathenish"—unless no more than a fringe below the chin, like his father's!—wearing throughout life his hair a little longer than was latterly usual, his waistcoats fastening up to the low shirt-collar by a close-set superfluity of small cloth or sometimes gilt buttons and worn open for the middle third, showing his unstarched white shirt-front and occasionally a scarlet cravat—he always had a look of bardic splendour about him. At the same time he was scrupulously tidy in his dress—just as in his study—and very particular about his shoes: "A fool," says a Celtic proverb, "is known in the morning; he breaks his shoe-latchet"—i.e. is clumsy and untidy. But so absolutely unselfconscious was he, that in late years when on one occasion he walked with me down Regent Street, London, with his tartan plaid worn in Highland fashion fastened to the left shoulder by the glimmering topaz in silver setting, he was utterly unaware that everyone turned to look at him, and some even to follow. Just as every word he spoke, or deed he did, or offer he refused, proclaimed the man; so to such a one it was inevitable that his clothing should express his taste, quite oblivious of the world's praise and censure. The romantic outlook upon the world could not but find correspondence in some romantic fashioning of his habiliments. If "of the soul the body form doth take," then the

THE YOUNG POET

very clothing must—in the person of artist, musician, poet, whose work is to portray in outward sign the inward truth—make protest against the slavishness of fashion.

I cannot but think that the common charge of vanity brought against the Highlander is grounded upon stupid observation. The Celt is imaginative above all things, and so tends towards extravagance: but always with restraint, and so with no vanity.[1] Instinctively an artist, he—to adopt this day's jargon—is no novice in self-expression. It was never vanity that made him devise his noble costume of tartan kilt and plaid—not the less magnificent that it was so often in rags. As his taste compelled the piper to adorn his pipes[2] with motley, in sympathy with the unuttered music (*unutterable* to the poor Sassenach!) stored within, so does the Celt tend to express in his person something of that which does not find speech or song. Certainly my father thought far less of his outward appearance than does the average well-groomed Englishman, whose modesty chooses that, there being perhaps little within him that need be expressed, he shall pass in the crowd unnoticed.

Anyhow, my father's spirits in these student-days were full of a romantic vitality, though perhaps he was not widely appreciated by his fellow students. Sir William Geddes,

---

1   The modern vulgar bedizenment and display is all a late invention of prosperous Glasgow.
2   This remark calls to mind a single sentence that, as well as any I remember in his writings, bears witness to my father's lively observation as a boy and his masterly word as a man. Describing the dress of wandering Willie, the imbecile piper in *Ranald Bannerman's Boyhood*, he says: "So incongruous was his costume that I could never tell whether kilt or trousers was the original foundation upon which it had been constructed. To his tatters add the bits of old ribbon, list, and coloured rag which he attached to his pipes wherever there was room, and you will see that he looked all flags and pennons—a moving grove of raggery out of which came the screaming chant and drone of his instrument. *When he danced he was like a whirlwind that had caught up the contents of an old clothes-shop.*" The italics are mine, of course. Celtic sense of art gone mad indeed, but still not unlovely! One could wish the new art of this day, in its repudiation of law and decency, had enough sanity left to merit description such as this.

afterwards Principal of the University, thus wrote in 1865 to my father when a candidate for the Chair of Rhetoric in Edinburgh:

> ...Though you did not mix much with the students at College, and indeed hardly cared to descend into the ordinary arena of emulation, your fellow students were not unaware of the talents which you possessed. I remember distinctly the universal impression regarding you, that you were *master of powers which you had not put to the full measure of proof, but which were touched to fine issues and destined to yield great things*...

But it must be understood that if my father did not mix much with other students, there was nothing of the social life belonging to Oxford and Cambridge, unless in the debating societies. Greater friendships, some say, were made, if only because the men, for economy's sake, went often in pairs, sharing the same lodging and potato, even the same bed, and there was small danger of stifling individuality beneath a veneer of polish. Anyhow, George MacDonald's gaiety of heart was alternated, not only by periods of anxious thought, but often by something akin to despondency.

> I have recollections of him (wrote Mr. Troup) sitting by himself after the meal was over, silent and thoughtful, sometimes apparently musing, and sometimes reading while the others were talking. At other times he took his part heartily in the conversation that was going on. His older friends were anxious about his spiritual state.

Here it will be interesting to put in a word concerning Aberdeen itself in matters spiritual. Its whole tendency had always been to conservatism leaning to moderatism, if not indifferentism, until the early days of last century. All over the county the people had only the Established Church to look to, and that in some instances had become such "a moral waste" that it drove old Mrs. Charles Edward MacDonald from the Parish Church. Notwithstanding the intellectual activity of Aberdeen itself, it had been the last city to grasp the meaning of the solemn League and Covenant. In a measure it was geographically isolated from other great centres of thought—perhaps also, because it was, until Culloden, so much under the influence of the House of Gordon.

But the gospel-news of freedom, long ago proclaimed in Scotland's wars of independence and sung to her peasantry by Burns, was now revived by Rousseau and the French Revolution in the shrewd, calculating heart of granitic Aberdeen; and at last she was asking in philosophic word the eternal questions—even if to fly off at tangents that led nowhere.[1] Anyhow, her evangelical fervour was awakened, and no better evidence of its vitality could be found than in Dr. Kennedy's ministry, following on the heels of that redoubtable Presbyterian Irishman, Dr. Kidd. From 1840 to 1844 a veritable storm began to rage over the whole congregational body of Scotland. In Glasgow, students were expelled from the Congregational Theological Academy for adhering to Dr. Ralph Wardlaw's doctrine of Universal Redemption, and a number of Congregational Churches were disendowed for holding like views.[2] These and the excitement engendered by the offer of release from some of their mental chains took strong hold of certain young men attached to the Blackfriars Congregational Church in Aberdeen, greatly to Dr. Kennedy's concern. Among these black sheep most certainly was George MacDonald. Hence arose the anxiety of some of his best friends, not the least disturbed being his brother Charles, then in business in Aberdeen, who felt accountable for his junior's doctrinal respectability. But vigorous brain-work was going on all round about him. Other great minds as well as his were in the making. Thus socially, if not academically, he may

---

[1] "I like a rumbling and a roaring devil best," said Samuel Rutherford, *a propros* of Aberdeen's coldness.

[2] Even earlier than this the Rev. John MacLeod Campbell had in 1831 been driven from the Established Church for his views on the Atonement. The great split in the Church leading to the formation of the Free Church had nothing to do with doctrine, though evangelicalism had some share in its inspiration. It was in 1843 that nearly five hundred clergy seceded, led by Chalmers, Guthrie, MacIntosh, MacKay and Hugh Millar, on account of lay patronage being sustained in the courts.

have come in contact with Alexander Bain, that hard-headed supporter of J. S. Mill and opponent to the idealism of Reid, Dugald Stewart and the German philosophers. Among my father's juniors also was Sir William Geddes. A class-mate of his own was the Rev. Malcolm MacLennan, who wrote more than one book of Scottish stories, which, the *Edinburgh Quarterly* once said, were "nearly as good as George MacDonald's, though they lacked his rainbow hope." But in spite of close touch with fellow-men in study and social pleasures, George MacDonald lived in much real loneliness, his poetic longings taking him far afield. The sea particularly called him to share its turmoil and its peace, its mystic solace in rhythmic beat, its kindred protest in evasion of control.

Of all his fellow students at Aberdeen, the Rev. Robert Troup was the last remaining. George MacDonald, he tells us, and one James Maconochie, would sometimes take walks together. One wild night, about ten o'clock, they went to the Links and the seashore to watch the storm.

> When Maconochie returned about midnight to his sister's, he looked anxious and disturbed, and said: "I hope George MacDonald is not going out of his mind...When we got to the shore, he walked backwards and forwards on the sands amid the howling winds and the beating spray, with the waves coming up to our feet; and all the time he went on addressing the sea and the waves and the storm."

He appears to have written poetry more or less throughout these Aberdeen years. Some was copied into a book for his cousin Helen MacKay, along with *The Rhyme of the Ancient Mariner*, portions of Shelley's *Wandering Jew*, and extracts especially from such poets as Mrs. Hemans, James Hogg, Tom Moore and Stoddart. His free running, yet conventional lines are generally imitative, though occasionally holding a gem of his own cutting and polishing. This is natural to youthful poetic fervour, and their prevailing melancholy and introspection are almost proper to immaturity. Occasionally he gets free from his self-consciousness, although often his effusions are so weird and obscure that it is difficult to detect their motive. I quote one verse illustrative of the dominant mood and one poem of real power. Yet I am convinced my father could never have approved their publication unless for the light they throw upon an earnest undergraduate's attempts to express thought and feeling.

> Bury me, bury me deep
> In some lonely cove on the wild sea's shore.
> There none o'er my grave will come and weep:
> But the maddened waves' tempest-roar
> Will soothe this spirit when, shrouded in gloom,
> It visits its rough and unlettered tomb!

That the second was inspired by Shelley's *Cloud* is obvious enough, but it is something more than imitative.

SONG OF THE SPIRIT OF HAVOC

> I rise by night in the stormy light
>   Of the Northern streamers' play;
> I leave them behind in the gathering wind
>   That drives to the South away.
>
> Adown we sweep on the ocean deep,
>   And the waves begin their fray;
> Along we rush, and their tops we brush
>   Till they're crested with foaming spray.
>
> On old Norway's shore I seek the roar
>   Of the Maelstrom's whirlpool vast,
> When, moored hard by, a vessel I spy,
>   That rocks with uneasy mast:
>
> I dive below beneath the prow,
>   And the straining cable clasp,
> Then the creaking chain I snap in twain
>   And the slippery keel I grasp.
>
> Aloft I sail on a cloud of hail,
>   That drifts o'er the whitened land;
> Till on Aetna's height, 'mid the ruddy light
>   Of the crater's lip, I stand.

Down, down I go; the fierce flames glow,
  And I stir their smouldering ire,
Then up I spring, nor need my wing,
  In a column of roaring fire.

And the lava's glow, cast up from below,
  Lights over the sea my path,
While my smoking plumes taint with Aetna's fumes
  The Simoom with its withering wrath.

And the rush of my flight, in the dead of night,
  Thro' Arabia's heated air,
O'erwhelms in one grave the tyrant and slave,
  And the Moslem at his prayer.

In my homeward rush a village I crush
  With an avalanche of snow;
I hurl it down from its rocky throne
  To the ravenous gorge below.

And a sparkling train of fiery rain
  From the shaken stars I cast;
And the meteor's glare through the troubled air
  Tells where my wing hath past.

To the North away, ere yet it be day!
  For there is the home that I love:
I lay me to sleep in a cave of the deep,
  With the war of the waves above!

One other poem I found in this manuscript book gave him his first opportunity in publication. It is in blank verse and called *David*. Considerably improved it appeared, unsigned, in the *Congregational Magazine* for January 1846. It is above the quality of other verse in that journal, though it shows little sign of its writer's subsequent power.

But my father found one great solace to his moods, whether exalted or depressed, in the sympathy of his beautiful and accomplished cousin Helen MacKay.

She was born in February 3, 1822, and so was nearly three years his senior. She died in 1911, six years after him, the last of the MacKays of her line. Throughout his life the

THE YOUNG POET

intimacy of their childhood was never broken, and I do not doubt that, brilliant and highly educated as she was, with a beautiful voice and well-trained piano-playing—my mother thought her the most lovely and fascinating girl she had ever met—she did something to shape her Cousin George's mind and showed sympathy with his spiritual anxieties. In 1840, as I have said, she went to a finishing school in London, the year indeed that her cousin won his bursary; and she was married in 1844 to Alexander Powell,[1] the brother of her Cousin George's future wife. Between 1840 and 1844 she must have been much in London, and yet was making some visits to Aberdeen, thus, and probably with regular epistolary exchanges, keeping intimate touch with him. But she could not have been often in the North. Even now it is a long way from London to Aberdeen, and then the journey was always by sea.

That my father was thinking much of the possibility of studying medicine is shown by her reference to it in later years. She once told me she would amuse him by prophesying that somehow he would get his heart's desire, and "as a stout, elderly M.D. would be driving a good horse on his rounds visiting his patients." This is pleasant to remember in view of a joke between them in 1868, just after the honorary degree of LL.D. was conferred upon him by his *alma mater*. She addressed a letter to him as "*Doctor* MacDonald." To which he replied, *inter alia*, and in a postscript, "Quhat the muckle de'il gars ye pit the Doachter afore my name? Lat it come ahint it gin it likes!" Whereupon his cousin replied: "I thocht ye wad raither hae a Doctor afore ye than a *Lang-Leggit-De'il* (i.e. LL.D.) rinnin' aifter ye!" And my father's reply kept the ball rolling: "'Deed, lassie, ye hae the best o't aboot the doctor an' the deil."

The two would, in their many letters to one another

---

1   Concerning whose romantic and humorous courtship, *vide postea*, p. 100.

in after life, often use the broadest tongue, for a sentence or two, particularly when humorous, even though it is perhaps the most unmusical dialect in all Scotland.

But, fun and high spirits notwithstanding, young George MacDonald would have been, I think, very lonely, but for this loving friend. "I was able to help him when he was puzzled and undecided as to what life he was fit for," she wrote me a year after his death. She told me that already in Aberdeen he began to feel that one day he would be a poet, and that "he wrote many beautiful little things," she said, "as the lovely light began its dawn." She told me also that he was often much depressed in spirits—a quite usual characteristic, indeed, of the high-spirited Gael—and that she knew she was of use to him. She said a favourite saying of his then was, "I wis we war a' deid!" and that he often repeated it in after life. I never heard it, though I surmise that whenever he uttered it, it must have been in the sense that, only when we are dead shall we be alive enough to understand. His depression of spirits was physical rather than spiritual, for his vision was always lit by faith. Thus in 1869, on a yachting trip, he endured terrible suffering from an abscess in the knee, and wrote this to my mother: "Oh, I have gone through some of the folds of the shadow of death since I saw you, but the light has never ceased to shine"; [1] and again in 1877, one of the most troubled years, he wrote to my mother: "My windows are all darkened—all save the sky-light." [2]

---

1 See p. 394.   2 See p. 472.

CHAPTER VIII
THE DISCIPLE

THERE is good reason for assuming that even in his first year in Aberdeen, the revolutionary yeast of George MacDonald's genius was at work. The Chartist movement, after Fergus O'Connor's eloquent appeal to the hard-headed Aberdonians, must have been widely discussed in lodging and debating societies. So that when little more than seventeen he was in some form or other asking himself the general question, What need for the Gospel if the elect and no others are predestined to be saved? But probably it was during his sojourn in the far North that his Calvinistic chains became intolerable. Such a view seems to have been general at home, and his Uncle James, who adhered to the old teaching with quiet satisfaction, expressed it as his opinion. But my father, conscious that the awakening began long before his eyes were open, would ascribe no such definite period to his conversion.

> I well remember (he wrote forty years later) feeling as a child that I did not care for God to love me if he did not love everybody: the kind of love I needed was the love that all men needed, the love that belonged to their nature as the children of the Father, a love he could not give me except he gave it to all men. [1]

His poem *The Disciple*,[2] though not actually written till many years later, makes it clear that his fearless perception in student-days of the poetic gospel-story's supremacy to scholastic doctrine was the incentive to his soul's growth. This clarity of vision needed only strengthening by his logical intellect to

---
1 *Weighed and Wanting* (1882) vol. i, p.47
2 *The Disciple and Other Poems*, 1868.

give it indomitable fortitude. To see the things of his childhood as he saw them implied this germinal faculty; to justify it in manhood's years accounted for his power of presenting to others in true form and colour the things beheld. The new intimacy with a wider literature, which the great library made his, was, I repeat, food to his powers—"*doctrina sed vim promovet insitam*"—even if he must suffer much before he could write the final words of that pageant of spiritual moods *The Disciple*:

> The man that feareth, Lord, to doubt,
> In that fear doubteth thee.

So distinctly does this poem belong to the final year at King's College that some of its treasures must be quoted as autobiographical.

Quite boy-like he opens with regret, almost shame, that he cannot love the cold saintly heaven proclaimed in pulpit and hymns, though he tries so very hard.

> I do not care for singing psalms;
>   I tire of good men's talk;
> To me there is no joy in palms
>   Or white robed, solemn walk.
>
> I love to hear the wild winds meet,
>   The wild old winds at night;
> To watch the star-light flash and beat,
>   To wait the thunder-light.
>
> I love all tales of valiant men,
>   Of women good and fair;
> If I were rich and strong, ah! then
>   I would do something rare.
>   * * * *
> For as a bird against the pane,
>   I strike, deceived sore;
> I know no reason, yet remain
>   Outside it as before.
>   * * * *
> I sit and gaze from window high
>   Upon the noisy street:
> No part in this great coil have I,
>   No fate to go and meet.

THE DISCIPLE

> My books long days have untouched lain;
>   The lecture hour is slow;
> Far other thoughts go through my brain,
>   Than those gowned bosoms know.
>
> *   *   *   *
>
> Old books, new facts, they preach aloud—
>   Their tones like wisdom fall:
> I see a face amid the crowd
>   Whose smile were worth them all.

Then comes conviction as to the validity of his own revolt, while yet imprisoned for it:

> It is not fear of broken laws,
>   Or judge's damning word;
> It is a lonely pain, because
>   I call and am not heard!

Then at last, when the longing of his heart after God—whose love and beauty the learned dared hardly believe in—is in a measure answered, he rises again in protest, as in Robert Falconer's memorable speech to his horrified grandmother, and refuses God's love if he is singled out from the many:

> Nor claim I thus a place above
>   Thy table's very foot;
> 'Tis only that I love no love
>   That springs not from the root;
>
> That gives me not my being's claim;
>   That says not *child* to me;
> That calls not all men by the name
>   Of children to His knee.

Then once more from this universality of God's love, the youth protests that he cannot live without the direct personal tenderness of his creator:

> No; thou must be a God to me,
>   As if I stood alone;
> I such a perfect child to thee
>   As if thou hadst but one.
>
> *   *   *   *

> My story, too, thou knowest, God,
>   Is different from the rest;
> Thou knowest—none but thee—the load
>   With which my heart is pressed.

And the whole argument ends with an appeal that gives us clue to the writer's mission, whether imaginative, or critical, or didactic:

> My soul with truth clothe all about,
>   And I shall question free:
> The man that feareth, Lord, to doubt,
>   In that fear doubteth thee. [1]

The poem's piety and mysticism stand in no disagreement with the mental vigour, the dreaminess and poetic lassitude of its writer's undergraduate days. Yet that it was actually written much later is proved in one section by his speaking of his little daughter, "moaning and sore dismayed" in her sleep, and of how she becomes lost in rest when he lays his hand upon her. The eternal problem expressed in the poem was, I repeat, largely worked out for himself in undergraduate days long before he discovered his power in poetic utterance.

A Scottish critic wrote of *The Disciple and Other Poems* ten years after its first publication in 1868:

> He seems to see into the very soul of the matter and to see it with the eyes of his soul. He does not give us the vigorous flesh and blood reality as Browning would do, showing us its veins like the flesh of the pomegranate when divided, as his wife so beautifully puts it; nor does he give the sentiment of it, in all its delicate shades, as Tennyson would do. He does something quite different from either. He neither intellectualizes nor sentimentalizes. The exquisite beauty of the poem will suffice to justify the claims of George MacDonald not only to a high, but to the very highest rank as a poet...He is a great poet, because he is not like Tennyson or Browning or any other poet in the very least...The region from whence the pure and lovely light of Mr. MacDonald's poetry comes to us is almost wholly supersensual, and therefore it is most rare and precious. (*Scotsman*, April 12, 1878.)

---

[1] This final stanza is as amended in the collected *Poetical Works*, 1893.

BOOK II
THE LOVER

CHAPTER I

THE WOOL-WORK SLIPPERS

IN April 1845 George MacDonald took his degree of M.A., but found himself no nearer the choice of a profession. Failing a medical career, the ministry must have been constantly in his mind. His veneration and love for the Rev. John Hill, the minister at Huntly and his father's greatest friend, contributed largely to such a possibility. Yet his love of beauty and all living things, especially his own kind, along with its seeming antagonism to the dogma of the Shorter Catechism, kept him in sore doubts; and he had not yet cast off its chains, even though his sinews were fast hardening for the task. To some—not his father, I think—this indecision may have seemed temperamental rather than due to his honesty. But the Celtic tendency to drift was never his: no man was ever less given to procrastination. Instinctively he always saw at once the right and wrong of any question; even if in the present matter he had not the data before him that alone could justify a decision.

Hence it is not surprising that, having that rare gift of teaching which makes learning a delight, he sought a tutorship, if only to get time and opportunity for feeling sure of himself.

The Rev. John Morison, D.D., was then one of the most fashionable preachers in London. The Trevor Chapel in Brompton was built for him. He preached there from 1816 to 1856, and his influence was orthodox and far reaching. Yet another of the strong men that Aberdeenshire was producing, he had been in early life apprenticed to a watchmaker in Banff. He was the same age as George MacDonald senior, and I do not doubt that my grandfather, attracted to the young man by his religious ardour, would meet him frequently on his visits to his future brother-in-law, Lieut. George MacKay, possibly while courting the lady who became my grandmother. It may even be that my great-grandmother, Mrs. Charles Edward MacDonald, the enthusiast for missions, had something to do with the lad Morison's giving up his craft for the ministry. Anyhow, a friendship was struck between the two young men that lasted throughout their lives, though supported chiefly by correspondence. So when young George MacDonald sought a tutorship, it was Dr. Morison who found it for him in the home of his Church-member, Mr. R—, living in Fulham. This gentleman and his wife were kind so far as their conception of a University man's dues instructed them; but the young Scot's fine physique led the lady of the house to deny him the care necessitated by his frequent ill-health. He had three pupils. There were two little girls besides, whose unruly screaming he found hard to bear. Once when he was reading to the boys, one asked if Jesus Christ wasn't crucified four times, though the elder brother indignantly insisted it was only twice. He was expected to take them twice on Sunday to the Trevor Chapel. Although he found this irksome enough, he sought the minister's advice in the matter of his own Church-membership. His great hope, now he was earning money, was to be able to send some home, and pay his small Aberdeen debts.

G.M.D to his Father.

FULHAM,
[November, 1845.]

...My great difficulty always is "How do I know that my faith is of a lasting kind such as will produce fruits?"...*My error seems to be always searching for faith in place of contemplating the truths of the gospel which*

THE WOOL-WORK SLIPPERS 93

produce faith. My spirit is often very confused. My time does not come to much for reading between one thing and another, but I am improving my mind steadily, though it may be slowly. I am reading just now a recent publication, Darwin's account of a voyage round the world, which, though in many places too scientific for me as yet, I think you would enjoy very much...

The italics are mine; for I almost think we may say this discovery of his "error" was the foundation of my father's teaching.[1]

During the early part of the year 1846 he must already have been often welcomed at Mr. James Powell's house, The Limes, Upper Clapton, to which, as has already been told, he was introduced by his Cousin Helen, now the wife of Alexander Powell. For in June I find his first extant letter to Miss Louisa Powell, already addressing her by her Christian name and signing himself "Your affectionate cousin." From this time onwards the increasing freedom of his pen, the lessening tendency to introspection, and a surer hope are very evident. No one but himself ever knew in what way his prayers were answered, or whose the hand that unconsciously upheld him. This letter was written two years and four months before they were formally engaged.

As an indication of his dawning happiness and of his invariable industry, whether of hand, mind or spirit—a man of action I repeat, quite as definitely as he was one who could wait patiently—I may here tell of a pair of slippers he made at this time for his mother.[2] My Aunt Jeanie, Mrs. Crawford Noble, tells me that she remembers them perfectly: "they were in cross-stitch, representing acorns and leaves in shades of green with a scarlet grounding. His mother had them made up, but never wore them: they were too precious." Berlin wool-work was then coming into fashion with

---

1 Indeed, I have throughout ventured to italicise certain notable passages in the letters.
2 He never spoke or thought of that loving and wise woman as *step*-mother.

young ladies, and we can easily surmise whose fingers taught that young man his use of the needle. My mother had most beautiful hands and the finest eyes I ever saw.

G.M.D to his Step-mother.
LONDON,
June 15, 1846.

MY DEAREST MOTHER,

Will you accept of some of my *work*? You will excuse faults, seeing it is my first attempt. I should have got them made up, but both my time and purse were very limited, and I was not sure that they would fit you. I can sew very well now—always mend my own clothes—use my thimble—a nice silver one [1]—like a lady. I have patched my trousers two or three times—an accomplishment I have attained since I came to England, and a most useful one I find it to be! I don't know when I heard a word of little Jeanie. Tell me about her when you write...God is very good to me. Oh! I was so far from him two or three years ago, and I trust I am always coming nearer to him now.

I would like to quote many of my mother's letters written in these early days. But they are very ordinary—like primroses and hedge-roses and shy violets and quiet pools of blue-bells—just ordinary. We have all memories, besides some gift of imagination. So I will, for the most part, leave them where they lie. But here is one of the many preserved by my father, dated July 20, 1846, showing in what manner he would write to his "Cousin Louisa," and how her doings and well-being had become so important to him. Moreover, it bears upon future events in a way that will become obvious. He is urging her not to lose interest in her scrap-book and sends her a poem which he had already written; "I am not sure if I have given it to Helen, but I intended doing so." They are, by the way, better than anything he ever did for that cousin so far as records go; they are not to be found in her book:

---

1 An earlier letter to Miss Louisa Powell apologizes for having inadvertently carried off her thimble. I do not doubt that a reply-note instructed him to keep it if it would be of any service.

THE WOOL-WORK SLIPPERS

> The mysterious night,
> When but a tip of the low hornéd moon
> Looks o'er the crest of a peaked cloudy height,
> Edging it with glory—fading soon:
> A few pale stars are through the cloud-rifts strewn,
> And the low wind is running to and fro,
> Like a forsaken child, that knows not where to go.
>
> O to have the silence of such a night round me once more!
>
> I am, my dear Louisa,
> Your affectionate cousin,
> GEORGE.

A comment written by Louisa Powell at the foot of this letter brings her close to any reader's heart, and not a whit further from his reverence. *"My Dear, my Dearest!"* she writes, while her penmanship breaks out into little spasmodic sprays and stars of a decorative anguish, *"I am an overgrown baby with manners like a bear vexed!"*

Among the many scraps of verse, published or not, scattered through my father's promiscuous manuscripts, I find these lines without emendation and with their date subscribed:

> Time dieth ever,
> Is ever born;
> On the footsteps of night
> So treadeth the morn—
>
> Shadow and brightness,
> Death and birth,
> Chasing each other
> O'er the round earth.
>
> But the Spirit of Time
> From his tomb is springing.
> The dust of the world
> From his pinions flinging.
>
> Ever renewing
> His glorious youth,
> Scattering around him
> The dew of truth.
>
> *January* 1847.

CHAPTER II

THE FAMILY OF JAMES POWELL

SOMETHING must be told of the English household into which George MacDonald was welcomed by James Powell and his wife, their sons and daughters. Thanks to many letters of my parents to one another as well as to and from other members of the family, together with reminiscences[1] set down for me by my Aunt Angela, Mrs. Francis, I can give some impression of the enlightening influence George MacDonald brought to this large family, as well as of what their lavish hospitality did for him during the period 1847-51, before he married Miss Louisa Powell.

Concerning my grandfather's family no very exact particulars are forthcoming. His eldest grandson, Sir Leonard Powell, advises me that our ancestors were *Knights of the Shire* in Wales, and until four or five generations ago were buried in Abergavenny Churchyard. When the standing army was first inaugurated in England in 1645 these knights, who had been endowed with land for the support of the soldiers required of them, were divested

---

1 She prefaces her reminiscences with the "Spring Song" of her subject:

"Days of old,
Ye are not dead, though gone from me;
Ye are not cold,
But like the summer-birds fled o'er some sea.

"The sun brings back the swallows fast
O'er the sea;
When he cometh at the last,
The days of old come back to me."

(*Poetical Works*, vol. i, p. 339.)

CHARLOTTE POWELL

ANGELA AND CAROLINE POWELL

JAMES POWELL, age 86

MRS. ALEXANDER POWELL (*NÉE* HELEN MACKAY), age about 23

of all such real estate; and it went back either to the Crown or to the superior landlord. A certain Thomas Powell, one of these impoverished individuals, came to London with, my mother used to say, the half-crown so essential to mercantile success in his pouch, and started a leather business in Whitecross Street, E.C. This expanded so greatly that his successors, Messrs. T. J. & T. Powell, would transact every sort of business connected with the leather trade, importing tanning materials and hides from all parts of the world, exporting again to the Continent and selling to manufacturers or advancing money to tanners. Originally, my grandfather lived upon the business premises, my mother being born in Whitecross Street, "within sound of Bow-Bells," she would say. The firm took first rank in the leather trade, removing to 36 Lime Street and latterly to London Bridge. The whole family were profoundly religious and all, at any rate of the later generations, Nonconformist. [1]

The young tutor just graduated from Aberdeen paid frequent visits to his Cousin Helen, by this time married to Alexander Powell, at Stamford Grave, Upper Clapton. Unquestionably not robust in health and much in need, I take it, of ordinary sympathy and kindness, he was always welcomed by them. Mrs. Alexander, it will be remembered, upon her introduction to the family in 1844, had taken by storm the very hearts of this conventional and chapel-disciplined family; and some of the girls at least must have been, to judge from their characters, restless for fresh influences. Helen MacKay was a great beauty. Her charm of manner, sweetness of smile, the tenderness of her voice in speech and song, her captivating eyes, bewitched these six

---

1 The original Thomas Powell was well known as a lay preacher of terrible long sermons, and was sometimes inaudible. Once a sailor at the back of the chapel, it is recorded, unable to hear him, called out in a voice that might have shamed the stormy waves themselves, "I say, if this is a secret, keep it to yourself," and upset the congregation, if not the preacher.

sedate, if handsome and accomplished, young ladies: Louisa almost worshipped her, and her brother Alexander went crazy about her beauty. Nor was she slow to hint a delightful and proprietary right in her Cousin George of whom she expected great things for the world's uplifting. To-day we hardly realize how large a factor in daily life were matters of religion at that time, and how important was correctitude upon doctrinal points. Thus one of the Misses Powell deferred for many months accepting her lover until he could formulate satisfactorily his views on the Atonement: which at last, and most fortunately for the world, he contrived to do. But now Helen MacKay, with facile suggestions of having a wider outlook than the Misses Powell's eyes had ever dared—suggestions that set at least one of them wondering how much this cousin from Aberdeen had contributed to such eye-opening—and yet altogether orthodox and devout in her observances, had prepared the way for George MacDonald's welcome. She had been married already a year when she took him to her father-in-law's house, The Limes, an old Georgian house, with good stabling and a three-acre garden, whose tea-roses I still remember with rapture as one morning my grandfather held a dew-laden bunch of them to my four-year-old nose as I sat hungry for my breakfast.

Louisa was away from home when George first came; but her sister Angela—Annie, she was named—wrote that Helen's cousin would "explain everything that puzzled her and make her life happy!" She adds in her reminiscences:

> He showed me new life in everything, understood me as an equal. This was very wonderful to me, as all my life I had been the fool of the family for my inability to spell and commit to memory. Great was my astonishment when he wished me to learn mathematics and began himself to teach me.

Although my Aunt Angela could never spell better than an average ten-year-old child, she and my mother excelled perhaps their more brilliant sisters in originality. And now George MacDonald discovered to them the great writers in place of "hymns for Sundays and pretty bits for weekdays." He read first to them Scott's *Marmion*, and then Wordsworth, opening their eyes to the world that had been always about them. Then came Tennyson's early poems and *In Memoriam*. In 1845 Browning's *Saul* appeared, and this also he read to them. The smallest of their doings interested him; and my aunt says:

> Once when I was ill he came to see me in the old schoolroom, because I was naughty and would not take my castor oil. He had not talked to me for many minutes before I gulped it down without a murmur, and was rewarded next day with a box of sugar-candy—a rare luxury at that time.

The rebellious child could not have been less than seventeen!

But some account must be given of these six girls, to three of whom he was so noble a being that they swallowed Browning and physic with equal obedience—if differing appreciation. They were congregational, quite orthodox, and not more narrow-minded than a respectable and well-to-do city merchant's family would be. Their mother was a tender-hearted lady, the refuge and help of all her children; for they had individualities of character too strong to be always comfortable with one another in spite of an enthusiastic admiration for each other's special merits. Louisa and Angela paid the penalty of their gifts in often resenting and even ridiculing the correct deportment of their two elder sisters. The eldest, Charlotte, who afterwards married Professor Godwin, George MacDonald's teacher at Highbury College, certainly was a highly gifted woman. The others looked up to her so much that there was no jealousy of their father's favouring of her beyond her sisters. The mother's frail health—she had lost five children, having had thirteen in all—gave this daughter much responsibility.

She even had more expensive masters than the others. Her pure soprano voice was the joy of the home and all its guests. In her rendering of "Rejoice greatly" and "He was despised" in the *Messiah*, it was said that only Clara Novello could surpass her. Then her power of describing anything she had seen, her facile mimicry and portrayal of character made a great favourite of her. Yet she was a very active member of the Society for converting Roman Catholics, and belonged to several other missions. Her exactions in matters of propriety invited the ridicule of Louisa and Angela, in which the youngest sister Carrie, who was at this time but fourteen, would ardently sympathise.

The next in the family was Alexander, who, like his father, was an excellent hand at his carpenter's bench. He had much of his sisters' eccentricity of character, and, I believe, his practical jokes of a rather alarming nature, and a tendency to roughness in fun hard to bear by a hyper-sensitive, hysterical wife, made her married life difficult at times. They had no children. But he had been an ardent lover. It was in 1840 that alarm was first felt concerning the Chartist movement, and in London an increase of crime, especially burglary, was attributed to political sources. Alexander Powell and his cousin, Edward Sharman, were enrolled as special constables, and secured the right to patrol that region of St. John's Wood where the Abbey Road lies, in which was the school where Helen MacKay was being *finished*. The two young officials called at the house in the exercise of their duties and asked for the Head Mistress. Informing her that they had been instructed to pay her school very particular attention, they desired, for reasons they would not particularize for fear of unduly alarming the ladies, to search the school premises for suspected burglars. Permission was eagerly accorded; but whether their effrontery was rewarded either by the capture of any miscreant, or by a glance from a pair of irresistibly fascinating eyes, history has no record. Anyhow, we see in

Alexander Powell the spirit of his sister Louisa who used to delight her children with wonderful stories of her innocent escapades at school, which generally ended in her admiring schoolfellows being reprimanded, but only herself punished. At the same time she would make us realize what a wonderful woman her mistress, Mrs. Laurie of Reading, had been, and how much she owed to her loving discipline.

Phœbe followed. Her characteristic was a genius for philanthropy so dominant that she could ignore all the pungent criticisms of her family. She was even negligent about her dress, if to make herself tidy before going to chapel would interfere with her preparatory prayers: "so that at the last moment she would rush on her bonnet over her beautiful, untidy hair and her shawl all askew, caring nothing for what people said."

She was scientific in her tastes and particularly interested in Natural History, besides being the best water-colour painter of them all. Her fine character was shown in the work she did for the Irish Famine. "Long before Gladstone took up Ireland," says my Aunt Angela, "Phœbe's heart was indignant at England's treatment of that sore, ill-used country." When the famine broke out in 1845, her personal self-denial did much to convince visitors to The Limes of the urgency; and she collected a great deal of money for the cause. Her intimacy with destitution at home was quite as keen, and she would take her sisters and young-men friends as far as Bethnal Green, right into the haunts of thieves and worse, to compel their interest: and that in days before "slumming" had become respectable, or even fashionable.

These two elder sisters, much, it may be safely presumed, as they admired George MacDonald, had no need of the help he gave Louisa, Angela and Carrie. Louisa, born November 5, 1882, was to my own eyes—and I scorn to have prejudices in treating of so delicate a matter—unquestionably the pick of that remarkable bunch of sisters; and my Aunt

Angela agreed with me: "The home was always dull when Louisa was away: she was the gay influence. Like the twinkle of her wonderful eyes, she brightened all around her; they could always and at once see the ridiculous in everyone and every situation." Humbug was to her all through her life so absurd and funny that one wonders why it ever made her angry. Either her sense of the ridiculous or her honesty prevented her joining their Church till much older than was customary. When at last she consented to it, along with her young sister Flora, my aunt tells how two grave old deacons came to ask them questions and to pray with them. One was an undertaker, very old and fat. He asked Flora whether she "wrestled in prayer." Whereat Louisa could but half conceal her naughty delight; for she pictured this sister, who shared her bedroom, so often fast asleep already when kneeling at her bedside.

Louisa was the smallest of the family, slim and perfectly proportioned. Indeed, I think she was well aware of her pretty figure. My sisters assure me she never wore stays; yet I find an envelope containing five specimens of doggerel verse, written by her brothers and sisters in gentle ridicule of her small waist. Here is her eldest sister's:

> List ye who would a marvel hear,
>   Whilst I a story tell;
> Come look upon this waist so dear,
>   And mark this wonder well.
>
> A little waist it always was,
>   A man might well it span;
> But now 'tis smaller than it was:
>   A child I'm sure now can!
>
> Yet more this flesh and skin surround
>   Than ere they did before:
> Of old one heart alone was found
>   Now two are there—Oh, Lor!

THE FAMILY OF JAMES POWELL

Another seems to match the handwriting of Miss Phœbe:

You know that our Lou has grown graceful and slender;
Like the breeze on the aspen, a zephyr may bend her!
Is it squeezing and pulling, and tugging and pressing
With steel and with whalebone, with jaen and with lacing?
Oh, no! but give ear and the reason I'll tell
Why a finger and thumb her waist may span well:
She has lost her large heart, and there's nothing within
But back-bone and ribs, nerves, muscle, and skin.

The other specimens hardly reach the same literary excellence, though two seem to be Angela's and Carrie's. They are dated May 27, 1850, a month before Mrs. James Powell's death and ten months before my father and mother were married.

George was the next—May 12, 1824. He was the pet of his mother, and always held up to Louisa as a model for her to copy. Not only was he a very pretty child—and here again in contrast with Louisa, who was perhaps in her young days the least good looking of the family—but he would incite her to commit naughty acts, such as pulling an old gentleman's hair in the pew in front of their own—but only to settle the question as to whether he wore a wig. He didn't; and the little girl had to pay the price for her admirable fortitude. If George Powell was suspicious of the adopted cousin George MacDonald's orthodoxy, he was the very best of brothers when anyone was in trouble; and he adored his sister Angela in particular. Indeed, he was also the best of uncles to several nephews, one at least of whom could hardly have completed his medical studies without a hospitality generously bestowed.

Angela was born on December 15, 1826. She became her mother's "little needle-woman." Because she spelled so badly, her parents had some doubt of her intelligence. But after George MacDonald found her surprisingly receptive of any imaginative appeal to her understanding, no one any more questioned her abilities.

Florentia (born August 13, 1830) was the quietest of all, the most submissive perhaps. Chief among her gifts was her piano-playing. She loved warmly and got much petting in return.

Caroline (December 11, 1832) the youngest, was always delicate in health, but became perhaps the dearest of all these sisters in her sympathy with my parents and ministrations to their family. Of all our aunts we loved her best in our young days.[1]

The family life is interesting to look back upon. All well-educated, even judged by the standards of to-day, no excessive brain-work spoiled them of their normal duties in life. Excluding the youngest, they all married, and very happily. Excepting Mrs. Godwin, they had families; Louisa, George, and Flora very large ones. Besides being unusually musical, all the girls as well as Alexander showed pronounced histrionic gifts, which they bequeathed to many of their children. They would necessarily have felt that all play-acting was wrong; but I think my father, who even then went occasionally to the theatre, must have changed their views. Anyhow, they contented themselves with charades, then a fashionable amusement which gave wide scope to their talents.

Even more important, however, in the domestic happiness was my grandfather's excellent taste in music. Himself an accomplished violinist, he had regular quartette parties at The Limes, where none but classical music was ever played. Erard, the piano manufacturer, the Novellos, Clara Macirone—a favourite pupil of Mendelssohn, and the Misses Powell's teacher of the piano—numbered among their guests. Mr. Powell, a severe disciplinarian, did not allow dance-music on

---

[1] These dates are got from the books of the Old Gravel Pits Meeting House, where on January 26, 1836, Louisa, George Holt, Florentia, and Caroline Chase were baptized. The delay suggests that my grandparents did not favour infant baptism.

THE FAMILY OF JAMES POWELL

his pianos, so that dancing formed no part of their pleasures.[1]

He himself was a good handicraftsman, whether at his carpenter's bench or bookbinder's press, and would be terribly severe with all idleness. Industry and a generous economy ruled the house.

Less entertaining, I presume, were the dinner parties, which sometimes included renowned ministers of the day. My Aunt Angela remembered one such guest declaring, *à propros* of the Atonement, that if Jesus Christ had been born one day and crucified the next, His work for the world had been accomplished.[2]

It is small wonder if young George MacDonald seemed to these young ladies the very model of a poet.

He came (wrote my Aunt Angela, in her enthusiastic way) not a conventional youth, with polite smooth talk, but like a prophet of old. Long

---

[1] Often to the astonishment of his guests, my grandfather, after a formal dinner, would lightly tap the table, and give the keynote, when the family would sing a thanksgiving in exquisite harmony. In later years it must have charmed his old heart, when he gathered his grand-chicks around his table at Christmas, to hear their little voices piping the sweet air and harmony he had made that their fathers and mothers might sing Milton's words:

> "Let us with a gladsome mind
> Praise the Lord, for he is kind:
> For his mercies aye endure
> Ever faithful, ever sure.
>
> "All things living he doth feed,
> His full hand supplies our need:
> For his mercies aye endure
> Ever faithful, ever sure.   Etc.

One of those grandsons will never forget, though he himself is now old and deaf, how, after trying to give the little boy a preliminary lesson on the violin, the old man, with a deep sigh, replaced it in the case saying he was too old and deaf even for that.

[2] In further illustration of that day's orthodoxy, I may tell how an aunt of my mother, Miss Eliza Sharman, used to vow she could never lie comfortable in bed if she might not believe in hellfire and everlasting pains! On the other hand, a racy story used to be current in the family of a brother of my grandmother's, Mark Sharman, who lived at Wellingborough. One day he was telling at his table of an infant who had died in the night. "Mr. Sharman," asked a guest, "I hope the poor thing was christened?" "Well, ma'am, *no*," he replied; "the parson couldn't get his breeches on fast enough, and the puling little sinner went to hell."

before we thought of him as having any religious message to us, gradually we found he knew about everything and could put any difficulty right, be it to answer "Is there a God?" or "What is poetry?" or "What about ghosts or fairies?"

Nor must we forget the swallowing of physic.[1]

Yet while my aunt relates how they came to realize the poverty of their rigid dogmas, we must not lose sight of the sweetness and tenderness of this unusual family in their daily life. What with the father's music and the gentleness of the mother's spirit throughout her long suffering, no unintelligible dogmas could harm the innate simplicity of their religious thoughts. In the case of my mother, this shines in all her letters to my father; and I do not see that the spiritual tone of them is in any way altered or improved when her freedom of thought became assimilated to his own. Her modes of expression became more modern no doubt; but this was due to mental changes rather than to any modification of the great truths that lie behind the most repellent of ecclesiastic dogmas: the illumination of which truths, not their abolition, was the life-work of George MacDonald.

---

1 A tragi-comic thing happened to this ardent girl Angela when she was nineteen: her aunt took her into her bedroom one day and catechized her, the result being that the next day she made a new will, omitting the name of Angela Powell. She had originally left to this favourite niece all her books of prayer and meditation and her guides to Heaven, but now bequeathed them, along with her wardrobe, her poke-bonnets and crinolines, to the heathen.

It was for Angela—perhaps as a consolation for some such disapproval—that George MacDonald wrote the poem beginning:

> "Were I a skilful painter,
> My pencil, not my pen,
> Should try to teach thee hope and fear,
> And who would blame me then?
>
>   (*Poetical Works*, vol. ii, p. 10.)

CHAPTER III

THE NEW OUTLOOK

THE days of George MacDonald's tutorship brought him much mental conflict and discipline. Teaching dull, spoiled children, and propitiating a resentful mother none too hospitably inclined, were spiritual sackcloth to the poor and sensitive young Scot. His letters to his father reveal this to the full, even though he never indulges in incrimination or self-pity, rather blaming his own irritability of temper. He prefers to discuss with his father the principles of Church government, and wishes "our churches were like the primitive ones in more than the mere theory." He would "rather be of no sect than a sectarian." He describes Dr. Morrison's sermons, even questioning his policy and taste in singling out individuals of his congregation for public reproof. Then he has destitute friends in London who get every penny he can spare from his narrow earnings, and asks from his father oatmeal for them; or, on the other hand, ten shillings from his employer for the famine-stricken Highlanders. He sends accounts home of every penny spent, and fears his father will hardly understand how the money flies in London, if only in shoe-leather.

In reading of George's satisfaction over his brother Alec joining the Church at home, it is interesting to compare his conventual phraseology with his later imaginative freedom of expression.

In several letters he discusses his increasing hope of being a minister, though constantly feeling and stating his unfitness. His candour with his father is entirely consistent with his open-mindedness to his own sons in later days, and indeed to all who sought his help. But as to a proposal to study at a theological college, he will decide nothing before seeing his father.

G.M.D to his Father.

FULHAM,
[*undated.*]

...I did not wish you to understand me as having finally made up my mind as to the ministry. 'Tis true this feeling has been gradually gaining ground on me. What a mercy I was not allowed to follow out Chemistry! But, on the other hand, I fear myself—I have so much vanity, so much pride...I have not prayed much about it, for it has seemed so far in the distance, as if it was scarcely time to think of it yet....I love my Bible more—I am always finding out something new in it. All my teaching in youth seems useless to me. I must get it all from the Bible again....If the gospel of Jesus be not true, I can only pray my maker to annihilate me, for nothing else is worth living for; and if that be true, everything in the universe is glorious, except sin....One of my greatest difficulties in consenting to think of religion was that I thought I should have to give up my beautiful thoughts and my love for the things God had made. But I find that the happiness springing from all things not in themselves sinful is much increased by religion. God is the God of the beautiful, Religion the love of the Beautiful, and heaven the home of the Beautiful. Nature is tenfold brighter in the sun of Righteousness, and my love of Nature is more intense since I became a Christian—if indeed I am one. God has not given me such thoughts and forbidden me to enjoy them....

To answer another question. I have smoked a good deal since I came to London, though not much lately. When I am well it is a great enjoyment to me. Mr. R—is a smoker. He gave me a beautiful pipe. But I should not have much right to claim much love for you, if I would not give it up at your request. I was almost sorry it was not a greater sacrifice. And yet I would not have you think it no sacrifice. So I promise you never in this world to smoke again. That is settled now.[1]

I should have much to say to you if I were with you, and many a long conversation I trust we may have before *very* long. May I never cause you a thought of pain, as I have so often done in years that are past....Give my love to Johnny; to grandmamma too....

---

1   He did not smoke again till his visit to Huntly in 1855, when his father gave him a cigar, the consequence being confessed in a letter to my mother.

THE NEW OUTLOOK

Another letter belonging to this year is even more interesting. Though it reads strangely to modern minds, the views expressed did not ever, I think, undergo much change throughout my father's life. It is written to his uncle, a man of astute ability and with considerable literary gifts:

G.M.D to James MacDonald, Huntly.
LONDON,
May 22, 1847.

MY VERY DEAR UNCLE,

I called on Dr. Adams, but had again the misfortune to find that he was out. I do not think I am right to use the word *misfortune*, for the conviction is, I think, growing upon me that the smallest events are ordered for us, while yet in perfect consistency with the ordinary course of cause and effect in the world. I am strongly inclined to think that whatever has a moral effect of any kind on our minds, God manages for us—and even much more than this. How far the events of those who do not at all seek to serve Him are controlled by him, in regard to these individuals personally, is a question about which I have no opinion at all—at least not a settled one. Perhaps it would be presumption to form one on such a subject....

Your very affectionate nephew,
GEORGE.

CHAPTER IV
BETROTHAL

LATE in the Spring of 1848 George MacDonald relinquished happily his tutorship. The following letter was written after his resignation was determined upon:

G.M.D to Miss Louisa Powell.

FULHAM,

[undated].

...The difficulties with which I told you I was surrounded are not the results of my situation. However ill I may bear them at times, I regard my trials here as helps, not hindrances. But my difficulties are those which a heart far from God must feel, even when the hand of the Heavenly Father is leading it back to himself. It seems a wonder that he can bear with me.

What is it that is the principal cause of everyone's unhappiness who is not a Christian? It is the want of enough to love. We are made for love—and in vain we strive to pour forth the streams of our affection by the narrow channels which the world can give[1] —and well it is if, stagnated in our hearts, they turn not to bitterness. The religion of Jesus Christ is intended to bring us back to our real *natural* condition: for all the world is in an unnatural state. This will give us that to love which alone can satisfy our loving—which alone , as we climb each successive height, can show us another yet higher and farther off—so that, as our powers of

---

1   These words call to mind some of later years:

"I love thee, Lord, for very greed of love—
Not of the precious streams that towards me move,
But of the indwelling, outgoing, fountain store:
Than mine, oh, many an ignorant heart loves more:
Therefore the more, with Mary at thy feet,
I must sit worshipping—that, in my core,
Thy words may fan to a flame the low primeval heat."
(*The Diary of an Old Soul*, March 13th.)

loving expand the object of loving grows in all those glories which excite our love and yet make it long for more.

He had been for the last year supported in his difficulties by the hope of visiting his home that summer. And now the step became imperative because of the need to talk to his father of these two things: he must ask advice and help for the proposed theological studies in London; he must get approval for his hope of securing a certain adorable young lady for his wife. My father once told me that he had never asked his father for anything, as boy or man, but it was given. The fact revealed to me the perfection of their unity. Hence it was now quite imperative that George MacDonald should go North and ask these things of his father.

Moreover, he was pining for his home, the winds of its hills, the rush of its rivers, the touch of its many dear belongings; but, far more than these, for his mother and the baby-sister he had not yet seen. So he spent the summer of 1848 at home. Consequently we have no letters between him and his father concerning his outlook and duties, and no words as to how the fresh expenses for classes and sustenance were to be met—expenses that, modest as they were, must have looked heavy in comparison with Aberdeen. Certain it is that this holiday was one of extraordinary joy—not only to himself but to those he loved. For that faculty of subconscious personal appeal, to which I have referred, and which inevitably met always with its corresponding response, made the family life a close bondage of interplaying joy, worship and service. Even when the sons had reached independence, they would ask their father's sanction for their doings.

> With simple gladness met him on the road
> His gray-haired father—elder brother now.
> Few words were spoken, little welcome said,
> But, as they walked, the more was understood.
> If with a less delight he brought him home
> Than he who met the prodigal returned,

> It was with more reliance, with more peace;
> For with the leaning pride that old men feel
> In young strong arms that draw their might from them,
> He led him to the house,...
> Set him beside the fire in the old place,
> And heaped the table with the best country-fare.[1]

Speaking of this visit my grandmother used to give an instance of her son George's athleticism. His two youngest sisters were then four and two years old. She saw him upon one occasion whip them up, one under each arm, run round the house with them, and then leap over a hedge which was probably four feet high. Another feat was taking a twenty-eight pound weight in each hand and lifting the two together up to the level of his head. The former story seems almost incredible, though remembering his statement to myself that when he was a young man he would put two chairs back to back and from standing would leap over them, I can accept it.

It is curious that no letters seem to have passed between the lovers—not yet engaged—during this holiday. Perhaps they had agreed to suspend their letter-writing. Yet it is clear enough that my mother was happier than she had been; for, writing to her betrothed a year later in Cork, she encloses a note that had been written during his holiday in Huntly, but not—whatever the reason—for his immediate perusal.

> ...I have just found in my paper-case what I wrote last year in the Forest on the picnic day, when you were in Scotland. If you like, dearest George, you can try and read it, though it is not worth sending. I think I told you I would give it you, and I came upon it just now unexpectedly.
>
> High Beech, Epping Forest
Under the trees alone.
>
> Oh, the air is so sweet, the trees so beautiful, the sky so bright! All nature looks so glorious, and the silvery clouds soften the heat; and my heart feels so much quieter having so much more hope now to rest

---

[1] A custom absolutely characteristic of Scotland, and not least in the poorest Highland home. ("A Hidden Life," *Poetical Works*, vol.i, p. 146.)

upon—and, I think, more love than when I was here last year. I cannot (now all is quiet and still, and all our party are somewhere else) help thanking God for this, and you his instrument. Oh, here I do pray God, your Help and Shelter, to give you health, strength and much of his love, that you may glorify him now on earth and for ever in his Heaven.

Robert Troup was also in Huntly after his first year's course at the Highbury College, where he had again met George MacDonald as a visitor. Unfortunately Mr Troup tells us little of that holiday. One incident, however, he relates. My father at the request of some friends held a little meeting in the cottage of one Tibbie Christie, a blind woman of ninety,[1] confined to bed and unable to go to church. Ten or a dozen friends were present.

> He prayed with simplicity and spoke on the words of Mark vi. 48, "He saw them toiling and rowing." He pictured Jesus looking down from the hillside on the raging sea, the tempest-tossed boat and the anxious disciples, thinking of them when they thought he had forgotten them, and then coming to their rescue. This he then applied to Christ's unseen care of the toilers, the oppressed and afflicted, and of those who sit in solitude and sadness.

In September George MacDonald once again left home, now not launching into the unknown, but making sail for a harbour where hard work and romantic joy were awaiting him.

At that time there were no less than five Congregational Theological Halls in London. George MacDonald in September, having several friends there, entered his name at the Highbury College.

The professors there were three in number: Dr. Ebenezer Henderson, a great linguist and Hebrew Scholar; Dr. William Smith, of dictionary fame, but a somewhat dry pedagogue; and Professor John Godwin, a man of acute intellect, and said to have great influence with the students, though suspected of heretical latitude by some of the Council. His Chair

---

[1] We meet this old blind woman again in *Alec Forbes*.

was that of Systematic Theology and New Testament Exegesis. His mode of thought appears to have been independent, with leanings towards Arminianism. It was for his exposition of the New Testament that my father was most indebted to him; but though he was inclined to more generous interpretations than were usual, he would not—to judge from his dealings with my father—advocate the free expression of opinion if it was to interfere with a successful career.[1] Being the only resident authority of the College, he was regarded as its Principal. The students lived together under one roof, each with his own study and bedroom, the senior students on one side of the quadrangle, the juniors on the other. All meals were taken in common, and the dietary was excellent, arrangements in striking contrast with the Aberdonian student's life. The men met together also every morning and evening for scripture-reading and prayer.

My friend, the Rev. Charles Green, a fellow student of my father, and now in his ninety-fourth year, tells me of their debating society and how upon one occasion he himself read a paper on the "Æsthetics of Public Worship," and how George MacDonald joined in the discussion and supported the opener in his condemnation of the general lack of any appeal to taste and natural sentiment in dissenting chapels.[2]

It is on record also that once George MacDonald

---

[1] Much later, however, in 1859, he expressed himself so freely and publicly, that the Committee of the New College could not overlook it: he resigned the Greek Testament Chair, but retained that of Theology.

[2] Mr. Green points out that of that meeting the two chief speakers ultimately separated from the Nonconformists, he himself taking Holy Orders, and my father becoming a lay member of the Church of England. The year my father left Highbury, the College was transferred to its new home and became the New College at Belsize Park. But it was no longer residential, being more on the plan of the Divinity Halls in Scotland. Mr. Green spent his second two years in the new building. He tells me that during his time some students were expelled, because they could not accept "verbal inspiration". One student, Arthur M. Francis, who subsequently married my Aunt Angela, was urged by Mr. Godwin to relinquish all idea of the ministry because of his free and fearless views, and his advice was adopted. One of those expelled was Hale White, better known as Mark Rutherford, the father of my friend Sir W. Hale-White, the distinguished physician.

introduced a discussion on Ghosts.[1] Occasionally, braving Professor Godwin's openly expressed disapproval, he would persuade one or another student to accompany him to lectures at the Marylebone Institute by A. J. Scott, later the Principal of Owens College, and my father's most steadfast friend. But few were well enough educated to appreciate that mighty intellect, most having been engaged in some secular work before entering the College. So my father's friends were few. Among them James Matheson[2] stands out conspicuously, excepting whom, together with Charles Green, Hardwicke Smith, the writer, and Robert Troup, not many were of any intellectual distinction. George MacDonald was senior to most of them. With a University degree and his three years' experience of teaching, he was so much above his fellow students that his volunteered help—to dull students, or in the Chemistry class he instituted—was much appreciated.

But (writes Mr. Green to me) conscious as he must have been of such manifest superiority, it never generated any resemblance to those grand airs attributed to Matthew Arnold...He had no eccentricities of manner or dress...He was at all times perfectly natural and easy to approach, though so innate was the poetic and mystic element that he might well have appropriated to himself the memorable words of Coleridge:

> "A sense o'er all my soul impressed
> That I am weak yet not unblessed,
> Since in me, round me, everywhere,
> Eternal strength and wisdom are."

---

1   On which subject perhaps his views did not much change in later years. Reading such a fearsome story as that in chapter xiii (vol. i), of *Castle Warlock* (1882), one cannot restrain the conviction that at least in some one chamber—perhaps an oubliette—of his Castle of Imagination, he did firmly believe in ghosts and ghostly re-visitations of the earth. But in chapter x of the same volume the subject is rationally discussed, and we are reminded that "the roots of the seen remain unseen."
2   James Matheson was noted for his keen and vigorous intellect. After finishing his theological course, he settled at Nottingham, remaining there all his life, greatly beloved. He had a large family, among them my intimate friends, Leonard Matheson, who has done so much to raise the tone and status of the dental profession, and Annie Matheson, the poetess who wrote the article on *George MacDonald* in the *Dictionary of National Biography*. Another son is Percy Matheson, Fellow of New College, Oxford.

As soon as George MacDonald settled at the College, he wrote, on October 19, 1848, a formal letter to Mr. Powell, begging to be allowed to visit his daughter in hope of one day making her his wife. The reply, I cannot but think, must have surprised almost as much as it rejoiced him. He was accepted. Though but a needy theological student, with indifferent health, and no *personal* ambition, whose father, a tenant-farmer in the impoverished North, could give him no pecuniary help, he was yet welcomed as son-in-law by this prosperous, stern disciplinarian, whose smile was not a ready one, who seldom petted his daughters, and who was yet curiously jealous when any lover came about them. True, Louisa's mother loved the young Scot dearly, and what the wise little invalid lady felt to be right, could not be questioned by her devoted husband. But here again the personality of the young man was unconsciously persuasive. To the heads of the house no less than to the daughters, it was something different from any that had hitherto come into their home. The austere merchant who could put his soul into his violin-playing, recognized with sure instinct that a daughter given to this lover of God, this poet who opened the eyes of all who were not slaves to pharisaic convention, was in good keeping indeed. There was always a mystical quality in my father's influence: to come within it was to be convinced.

Four betrothal letters lie before me, each so simple and direct that the writers' characters seem still to radiate from them in their loving and wise if formal words. The young man's humbleness and fortitude; the old man's acquiescence because he and his wife had long agreed not to interfere with their children's choice, save in the matter of advice; the mother's tender and profoundly religious welcoming of him as a son—are just what they should be, and would be quoted did space allow. My father's, however, must be set down because the first of a long series from him to my mother—to me almost holy as scripture. It is only because I am sure that any reader, who has got thus far in this life of my parents, will feel at once uplifted and chastened when he reads such words, penned in secret with closed door, that I dare present even one of them.

G.M.D to Louisa Powell.
HIGHBURY COLLEGE
My Study, Oct. 23rd, 1848.

...I meant to write a much longer letter to my Louisa and many beautiful and wise things (to me) I wanted to say, but now the impulse has left me. May our Father in Heaven be with you and bless you, and make you better of your present suffering.

Is love a beautiful thing, dearest? You and I love: but who *created* love? Let us ask him to purify our love to make it stronger and more real and more self-denying. I want to love you forever—so that, though there is not marrying or giving in marriage in heaven, we may see each other there as the best beloved. Oh Louisa, is it not true that our life here is a growing unto life, and our death a being born—our true birth? If there is anything beautiful in this our dreamy life, shall it not shine forth in glory in the bright waking consciousness of heaven? And in our life together, my dear Louisa, if it please God that we should pass any part of our life together here, shall it not still shine when the cloud is over my head? I may see the light shining from your face, and when darkness is around you, you may see the light on mine, and thus we shall take courage. But we can only expect to have this light within us and on our faces—we can only expect to be a blessing to each other by *doing* that which is right....

CHAPTER V
NEW FRIENDS AND DUTIES

GEORGE MACDONALD being a Master of Arts, spent only two years at Highbury instead of the full course of four; and during that period he was allowed many interruptions to gain experience and confidence in preaching. For it must be remembered that in Nonconformist communities preaching was always, and still is, held to be the minister's chief duty. If he also seems to act as mediator between God and man in devising suitable prayers for the lay-worshipper to acquiesce in, these were usually but another form of sermonizing. Indeed, worship and praise were technically distinguished from the sermon as the "Preliminary Exercises." Consequently the theological students, to become expert in pulpit fervour and exposition, must have experience; to gain which they accepted invitations from any Church temporarily in need of a pastor. For such duties an honorarium was given. Thus in June 1849 my father took temporary charge of a pastorate in Cork, where he remained for three months.

How much he gained from his theological course we do not know. But likely enough, his studies were of other importance than the professors presumed: they were strengthening his suspicions already germinating, that mere scholarship in the interpretation of Christ's words was of small worth, if not often dangerous; though almost up to his last days he was searching his Greek Testament for its innermost meanings. At any rate Mr. Godwin must take him to task for his informality in speaking, for his tendency to be intellectual and poetical in his expositions, and for his doctrinal insecurity. None the less his affection for this pupil was genuine. He secured many engagements for him, and at last confessed to him that wherever he went he "gave satisfaction." Mr. Godwin later became his brother-in-law and lifelong friend.

A more important gain through Highbury College was the friendship with a man of his own mental and spiritual degree, one who was destined to do more for him, with wise admiration and keen criticism, than perhaps any man-friend of later years. For both these services were the outcome of that deep unuttered affection between man and man, potent as it is rare, of which common minds know but little. I refer to Greville Ewing Matheson, James Matheson's elder brother. Their widowed mother, with a minute income, had achieved wonders in educating her family of seven boys and one girl, all of unusual aptitude. They lived in Barnsbury Street, Islington, not many minutes' walk from Highbury Park, where the College was situated. So that her home and her gentle wisdom, freely open to any friend of her sons, played a vital part in my father's Highbury days.[1]

It was not long before the Matheson young men were introduced to The Limes. My mother, always shy and diffident in making advances, called upon Mrs. Matheson at her lover's request and then sent formal invitations to a charade-party. To him in Cork she describes the event, and gives us some sense of how a little genius united to a generous gaiety can use the simplest resources triumphantly. For so it always is with Art: any clay will serve to give her some means for expression.

Louisa Powell to G.M.D.

...I do not think I sat down for more than ten minutes altogether last night, and I was galloping about into all the corners of the house for

---

[1] Mrs. Matheson's father had been the Rev. Greville Ewing, one of the leading ministers of the early Independents in Scotland.

dresses, etc., to dress up the actors. We had two excellent charades—*Countryman and Bradshaw*. David Matheson acted to immense admiration as a most absurd little French valet—he perfectly convulsed the whole room...I never saw Papa laugh more.

The hard work and close study of these two years at Highbury had frequent interludes of minor ailments, such as headaches, great fatigue, and more than one sharp attack of bronchitis. But pleasures came too. There were concerts and oratorios, May Meetings at Exeter Hall, Royal Academy Exhibitions, then held at the National Gallery, and occasional outings to the Forest or expeditions with Powells and Mathesons to Greenwich or Richmond or even Rosherville; more rarely, I think, and in Matheson company, an evening with Phelps at *Sadler's Wells* or Robson at *The Grecian*. I am told by a correspondent how after once such occasion my father received an anonymous letter the following morning, advising him that he had been closely observed by a well-wisher, who, if such promptings of Satan were ever yielded to again, would secure his expulsion from Highbury. But some trick in the penmanship revealed the perpetrator of the joke to be one of his companions in the iniquity: I presume it was either Greville or William Matheson. Then my father would often be given a mount by Mr. Powell and would accompany one or more of the young ladies on a round of calls, they also being on horseback. One of the many points in the young man's favour with his prospective father-in-law was his excellent seat in the saddle, a gift that matched his quick adaptation to the niceties of London ways. Indeed, Mr. Powell was openly proud of his young friend's breeding; at any rate, until the day when George returned from Cork with that on his face which recalled man's unregenerate days and savage origin—to wit, a beard. The delinquent had been three months away, yet when Mr. Powell returned from the city and found him in the drawing-room with his daughters, he hesitated for one moment, gave him a second look, then, without greeting, turned and left the room. My father, so my mother would tell us, immediately went to his own room and, with soap and razor, obliterated his offence.

In the spring of 1849 Miss Louisa Powell accompanied her dearest friend, Miss Josephine Rutter—a lady of great sweetness and strength of character—together with a younger sister of the latter, Hannah, to Hastings. The doctor had ordered sea-air for Louisa, who was not then very robust. A long series of letters was exchanged between the lovers, of which, though I have a great number of my mother's, only two of my father's have been preserved. In the first of these I find the earliest mention of A. J. Scott, of whom in later years he wrote as "The man who stands highest in the oratory of my memory." [1]

The letter is full of the domestic details so dear when related by the man she loved: how Phœbe wrapt him up in her boa; how her mother is to take Annie's reading more seriously in hand, and how he is determined to help by giving her lessons in mathematics, if only she will consent; how Flora can be helped; how a whole day of his own is used up in little services, such as getting Louisa's concertina mended, looking after a place in the city, though not very hopefully, that might suit his brother Alec. But the end of it must not be epitomized. For this and the following letter have lovely words about Nature. We see in them how his expressions about beauty are strengthening, his vision is growing clearer, and all, we may conjecture, because of that new love which had come to illuminate his world.

G.M.D. to Louisa Powell.

May 12, 1849.

You tell me about the sea and the sky and the shore so beautifully, so lovingly, so truthfully, that I love you more for it....Tell me again about everything round about you; every expression the beautiful face of Nature

---

[1] Dedication of *Robert Falconer*.

puts on. Tell me, too, about the world within your own soul—that living world—without which the world without would be but a lifelessness. The beautiful things round about you are the expression of God's face, or, as in Faust, the garment whereby we see the deity. Is God's sun more beautiful than God himself? Has he not left it to us as a symbol of his own life-giving light? But I cannot now explain all that I mean....

G.M.D. to Louisa Powell.

Highbury,

May 15, 1849.

I have just read your letter, dearest. My hands were cold, and when I opened the bit with the flowers they felt warm....I have had a letter from you every day as yet. Only a week to-day since you went! Well, I would not have you back one hour sooner, if my heart were like to break with its longing. You have beautiful things around you, and beautiful things are creeping into your soul, and making a home for themselves there—and my wife is growing more beautiful for me. Does not He deserve thanksgiving who made man male and female? ...Write to me about the sea and sky, and all those never-ceasing beauties, ever changing yet still the same, which are common to all men—like those great truths the *sense* of which makes a man feel great too—those truths ever the same yet ever presenting new aspects of beauty, different to different minds, different to the same mind at different times—yet ever in essence one and the same. I am indeed glad to hear you are so wild!

I have been trying to translate a little poem of Goethe's, entitled

Nähe der Geliebten

I think of thee when of the sun the shimmer
   From the sea streams;
I think of thee when of the Moon the glimmer
   From deep wells beams.

I see thee, when upon the far Way's Ridge
   The Dust-cloud wakes;
In the deep night, when on the narrow Bridge
   The Wanderer quakes.

I hear thee there, when with a rushing low
   Falleth the Wave,
In the still Thicket loitering oft I go
   Quiet as the grave.

NEW FRIENDS AND DUTIES

> I am with thee, and tho' thou art so far,
>   Yet thou art near!
> The Sun doth sink, soon lighteth me each Star—
>   Oh! wert thou here!

> What a strange picture of Turner's I saw yesterday at the Exhibition. A Rainbow over a stormy sea, ships far and near, boats and a buoy. I could make nothing of it at first. Only by degrees I awoke to the Truth and wonder of it. I lost much enjoyment, however, by going without any optical assistance.[1]

If there be such things as milestones on a man's spiritual pilgrimage, then I think these two letters must stand as such. They indicate the long road already travelled and recall something won; but they also suggest the many miles yet to come. My father's words are the poet's who knows what eyes and ears are given for; they are the philosopher's who amplifies and explains every sentiment the senses awaken; they are the prophet's who bids the weary and travel-stained lift their eyes to the hills whence help always comes: and then, on for another milestone. But some of us who have been led by his later imaginative writings to get sense of the fairy realms which not even his poesy can wholly reveal to us, will, in looking back upon their master's earlier journey, see that himself at twenty-five had but reached the little wicket-gate, to which, later, he led ourselves—children, lovers, parents—bidding us enter and take each our own way.

In his most imaginative stories he is constantly offering help to the divine questionings. In *The Princess and the Goblin* it is a little invisible clue, which when at last we have hold on it, we dare never lose again. And in his novels he teaches the same truth more directly, if to some less arrestingly. Compare this passage about Nature, from the novel *What's Mine's Mine*, written almost forty years later than these letters:

> If you would hear her wonderful tales, or see her marvellous treasures, you must not trifle with her; you must not talk as if you could rummage her drawers and cabinets as you pleased. You must believe in her; you

---

1 My father was short-sighted.

must reverence her; else, although she is everywhere about the house, you may not meet her from the beginning of one year to the end of another....I have all the time been leading you toward the door at which you want to go in. It is not likely, however, that it will open to you at once. I doubt if it will open to you except through sorrow....When you have got quite alone, sit down and be lonely...fold your hands in your lap, and be still. Do not try to think anything...by and by, it may be, you will begin to know something of nature. Nature will soon speak to you, or not until, as Henry Vaughan says, some veil be broken in you.[1]

The next letter is to his father. In it he refers to the possibility of going to Cork for three months' temporary work. Second only to his longing to do God's work, I think, was the craving to be no more a burden upon his father and to pay his inevitable but modest debts. If, judging from the frequency with which details of payment for his pastoral services are discussed with his father in the correspondence of this period, one be inclined to honour him for being so practical, I would beg the reader wait till he learns how, many years later, when far more heavily weighted with money responsibilities, he refused a pastorate with stipend equalling that of an Anglican bishop.[2]

He left for Ireland on June 19th. It is particularly during the ensuing months that Louisa Powell began to realize the suffering that such consecrated companionship as was theirs must necessarily invite. Her letters written during this period are full of strange variations in mood, though every aspect, sometimes sad enough, is accounted for by her overwhelming love for this rare lover. Now and again it seems as if she could not bear to read his exalted thoughts. She is oppressed by her inability to share in his joy over God's glories. Then she responds in most touching words claiming her unfitness, almost begging him to let her go, saying she could bear anything that was for his good. Again

---

1   *What's Mine's Mine*, vol. ii, pp. 182 and 213. The reference is in Vaughan's *Cock-crowing*. Compare also *David Elginbrod*, vol. iii, p. 372.
2   *Vide* p. 459.

she breaks out into simple yet anguished solicitude for his health; his cough is constantly mentioned. She responds to all his interests, tells of her gladness that he has found in Mr. A. J. Scott at last a man who could preach and give the message from God direct, and hopes he will miss no opportunity of hearing him when he comes home.

Charles MacDonald came to London during his brother's absence in Cork, and Miss Louisa Powell was invited to meet him at the house of her sister-in-law, Mrs. Alec Powell. He expressed himself very freely as to George's mistake in undertaking the work in Cork, when his prospects would have been so much better in Manchester. She wrote of the interview to her lover, was afraid Charles might think her lacking in modesty for the way she talked of him, and expressed herself very indignantly at the way Helen spoke, "as if she was so much George's superior!" The maternal sense in loverhood was already strong in this brave young lady.

Louisa Powell to G.M.D. at Cork.

August 6th, 1849.

...I had such a very beautiful dream last night, dear. I dreamt I had a vision, it was so beautiful! I think it was at sunset. I was looking earnestly at the clouds when one thick volume of pink and white cloud had two faces; the cloud was all the shape and colour to show them. I looked at them for a long time not knowing who it was, but soon discovered your face, only grown into a beautiful old man with the most glorified and perfectly beautiful expression upon it. The other for some time I thought was Mama, but upon looking and thinking, hoped it was I, with long white hair. I held a book out of which you were reading. You had your arm round my neck. Was it very conceited of me to imagine that I should ever grow into anything like Mama? Of course my features never can. I dreamt that, after looking for some time, the cloud melted away: then someone told me it was a vision sent to me that I might not fear present evil to either of us. Perhaps this is hardly worth telling you about; but I do not know when I have had any so beautiful a dream, or any that has made so strong an impression on my waking thoughts...

How much my mother in later life came to resemble her own mother, how she became in old age the most beautiful among sisters much handsomer in youth, her portraits only partly declare. But her vision was surely prophetic.[1]

When he was ill at Cork she says he ought to have some angel to take care of him; "but oh, how I should like to be that angel!" Once there is some real distress at his having reproved her for writing unkindly about Unitarians, a certain member of which community a friend was about to marry. She is heart-broken at his reproof, and yet breaks out eloquently into saying what the Divine Man means to her—to qualify which understanding of the Trinity would take from her all faith and hope. She would rather see her friend married to a Roman Catholic than a Unitarian! It is a good instance of the way this worshipping young woman could, when she felt she must, stand up even against the man she worshipped. Yet here the difference, as in every other instance occurring in their letters, arose from a misinterpretation, and not from any disagreement in principle or faith. Another time she assures him that in his soul he is truly musical, even if he knows no music and cannot sing the simplest hymn tunes. Thus most deeply did she already understand him.[2]

---

[1] Here I recall certain words of my father on plain and handsome faces: "I would advise any young man of aspiration in the matter of beauty to choose a plain woman for wife—*if through her plainness she is yet lovely in his eyes*; for the loveliness is herself, victorious over the plainness, and her face, so far from complete and yet serving her loveliness, has in it room for completion on a grander scale than possibly most handsome faces..." (*What's Mine's Mine*, vol. i, p 9.)

[2] "It seems to me at least, in my great ignorance, that one cannot understand music unless he is humble towards it, and consents, if need be, not to understand. When one is quiescent, submissive, opens the ears of the mind, and demands of them nothing more than the hearing—when the waters of question retire to their bed, and individuality is still, then the dews and rain of music, finding the way clear for them, soak and sink through the sands of the mind, down, far down, below the thinking-place, down to the region of music, which is the hidden workshop of the soul, the place where lies ready the divine material for man to go making withal." (*Mary Marston*, vol. ii, p. 280.)

It strikes me in passing how much more imaginative and convincing is such a conception of the subconscious mind than that of the modern psycho-analyst. It gives one hope in infinite possibilities in place of disgust at the remnants of a bygone barbarism.

She would always vanish, if possible, to read and write these letters which were so inseparable from her religious thoughts. There was a great oak-tree in the old garden of The Limes. Up its huge bole her father had constructed a perilous stairway and a platformed seat in the fork. From this eyrie her dovelike heart would unfold its wings and roam afar, while her pencil would be setting down self-obvious facts for her lover's perusal, such as there being just room for him beside her on that uplifted seat!

She could be comical, satirical, sometimes cruelly so, and witty, besides being easily moved to tears by others' suffering of mind or body. Like all great souls, she could give much because she could suffer much; and so ardently did she love Truth that hypocrisy must be met with its penalty in satire or scorn.

I cannot conjecture how far the habit of elaborate introspection, fostered, no doubt, by that day's constant chapel-sermonizing, tended to alienate from the lives of young people their natural joy of life; but I am sure my beloved mother, in the hope of becoming a fitter wife, tortured herself because she could not love God as she ought! Towards the end of their three-months' separation there is much said between them about her own temper—"a gnawing plague that has fastened itself to me"; and her friend's sister, "the adhesive Hannah," is source of much irritation. But Louisa Powell is determined to overcome this temper of hers, and begs for her lover's help and prayers. One letter to him is quite heart-rending and elicits from him the question whether she is "taking a rest from loving him." But to this terrible suggestion she replies that if it appears so, it is,

I think, rather that my not expressing it would arise from the calmness and repose which the confidence of loving you and of possessing your love gives me. Now I am sure I have been improper enough even for you! But I could not bear you to think I *rested* from that same. How often when I am writing to you I wish I could just look into your face to see what you think about it, to see if I have said anything that would at all displease you.

The letters written by George MacDonald from Cork to his father suggest some conditions of his work there. Certainly he gained knowledge of the world, while the Irish hospitality took him into the people's hearts and made him happy. One of the deacons lent him a horse, and he rode often. Yet he was again laid up with bronchitis and suffered from low spirits—"no new thing with me," he says.

G.M.D. to his Father.

CORK,
July 25, 1849.

My conscience has never been more at ease with regard to my studies. I am very glad I came here, to let me try myself a little; and though I have not so much confidence in my capabilities as perhaps you have, yet I get on pretty well, tho' I am very doubtful how I shall ever be able to write more than one sermon a week....Yesterday morning I went some six miles east from Youghal to see the devotions of the poor Catholics at one of the round towers of Ireland and by two holy wells, and a holy stone, said to be floated from Rome, under which they creep for rheumatism, etc. They were kneeling on the graves and by the wells and by the stone, counting their beads and washing themselves. They want me to go to Killarney before I leave, and indeed I should be sorry to leave without seeing those lakes; but, though I think this more valuable than many a book that you would quite approve of my laying out the money for, I don't know what you will say to it. You are a lover of nature, too—and yet I think perhaps it is more to me than to you—I don't know, though.

By the way, the Queen was here last Friday. I didn't see her—for I am no worshipper of royalty....I believe there was no great enthusiasm amongst the lower classes—how could there be!—but she was received with every possible demonstration of loyalty—a great deal more show than I was pleased with, considering the state of the country....

In the reply to this letter his father urges him to return by Manchester and see his brothers, but adds that if he preaches there, it will not be the first time they have listened to him. Then he related the story already told of a basin-stand serving for a pulpit.[1]

---

1   *Vide* p. 59.

CHAPTER VI
FATHER AND SON

ON his return from Cork, George MacDonald settled down to his studies again at Highbury, perhaps with less interruption that Louisa Powell was gone to Lynmouth with her sisters and her mother, who was recovering from a grave attack of hæmorrhage. His letters to his father are full of interest. They tell of the Chemistry lectures he is giving gratuitously to the other students, his closer reading and his better health. In sending his love to his step-mother, he writes: "By the way, Father, I've hardly seen her match for a lady of God's making yet."

My Uncle Charles, now a partner in business with a friend, and a deacon in a fashionable Manchester church, was just married and wrote that with his influence George ought to get the post of assistant to Dr. Halley, its minister: he even promises a salary of not less than £200 a year. But Manchester failed to tempt the young minister, and Louisa was not attracted to the great Cottonopolis. Moreover, I gather, my Uncle Charles's optimism and love for playing the patron were already understood and the offer was hardly even weighed.

There were inevitably disappointments to face.

G.M.D. to his Father.
HIGHBURY,
Feb. 23, 1850.

...Yesterday, however, a note came from one of the deacons at Stebbing, telling me that I had better not go, as I was not acceptable to many of the people....The more intellectual part, I believe, would have liked me to go—indeed, I think this is the feeling about me generally in other places; [but] many say they can't understand me. I tried to be as simple as possible at Stebbing. They are a nice, kind-hearted country people, but I cannot say I am disappointed at not going—rather the contrary....But God takes care of me—though I don't deserve it. Perhaps my manner is too quiet to please dissenters commonly. However, I must not do violence to the nature God has given me, and put anything on. I think, if people will try, I can make them understand me—if they won't, I have no desire to be understood. I can't do their part of the work....

But his father's sense of humour must combat the remark, "I must not do violence to the nature God has given me." Among other and racier illustrations, he points out that his maternal grandmother was born duck-footed. "Was the doctor," he asks, "doing violence to the nature God had given her when he set free the little toes from their bondage?"

Once again Mr. Godwin found work for his favourite pupil, and on April 4th the latter began a month's duty at Whitehaven, Cumberland, where his father hoped "he would find mountains ready made to please his poetical mind without putting it to the labour of portraying imaginary ones."

But few of his letters, either to his father or his betrothed during this year, remain. On the other hand, the number of letters received by him from both of these is very great. So important are his father's as indicating the spirit of the son, though they still continue their old-fashioned tone of parental advice, criticism and admonishment, that some must be given. For it is impossible, let me repeat, to give any whole idea of the son without picturing the father and brothers, the mother and little sisters, who were so literally, though miles might keep their bodies far separate, part and parcel of his welfare. So when one by one they were taken by death, just as, years afterwards, one by one his own children were taken, each occasion was a shattered hope—and this in spite of his enduring and always increasing faith.

In the first he answers his son's question as to what sort of stipend ought to content him; and in the second he gives a lovely picture of life at The Farm:

George MacDonald Senr. to his Son George.

HUNTLY
29th April, 1850.

...As to ministers' stipends in general, they are in most cases but too small. I have always preached up this doctrine, and I am safe to say that my *practice* in support of a better paid ministry has been quite consistent with my profession...Should you prove acceptable and receive a *call* [to Whitehaven], I trust you will, as in the sight of God, seek to discharge the duties of the *Office* with the main design of glorifying God by doing good to souls...You may find yourself more comfortable than in a place of greater *genteelity*, where much of the conceit of this world and the pride of life frequently prevail, making a minister's position anything but comfortable.

I consider the salary could not well be less than what you mention....It requires *much prudence* on the part of *any* minister, whether old or young, when necessity compels him to bring his own necessities before the church. Not a few who would hug to their bosom the *poor starveling*, would dash him from them to be trampled under foot when the necessity of an increased stipend was needed!...I hope you will by and by be in circumstance to pay off your small debts, and make conscience of never venturing on taking a wife before then. If you begin thinking lightly of such a case, depend upon it the carelessness will increase until none but yourself and such as are in similar circumstances can paint the agony it will entail...

HUNTLY,
24th May, 1850.

MY DEAR GEORGE,

Almost all the family have gone to meeting save myself, and I am just away from having worship with the farm servants. The children are off to help each other to bed, the voice of the mill has ceased—the falling water alone with its continual buzz is the only thing that falls upon the ear, where I am sitting. The evening is calm, warm and beautiful. The midges sport in thousands above the water, and nature, long detained from its summer garb, is now getting into lovely verdure. What a change in the course of one short week!—plenty of grass now for the starving cattle, and the corn crops are advancing as if within the tropics. But our seasons are changeable, as you may well remember, and how long such a state of things may remain, it is impossible to say....We have ground for confidence in our God, the author of all blessings, that He who spared not His only son, but delivered him up to the death for us all, will with Him also *freely give us all things*....Charles wishes you to go to Manchester, and says that Dr. Halley seemed anxious to see you. But perhaps Charles only *thought* so, because he might so wish it...

The final letter of this series indicates even more clearly what a close observer and what a thoughtful believer was George MacDonald's father.

George MacDonald Senr. to his Son George.

HUNTLY,

31st May, 1850.

...Your long letter yesterday gave me something of variety to think about which pleased me, notwithstanding that part of it was rather too philosophical for the cast of my mind; but in so far as I am able [to] see, the views of both of us are very much alike...Like you, I cannot by any means give in to the extreme points either of *Calvinism* or *Arminianism*, nor can I bear to see that which is evidently *gospel mystery* torn to pieces by those who believe there is no mystery in the scriptures and therefore attempt to explain away what it is evidently for the honour of God to conceal. I see so much of mystery in nature, and so much of it in myself, that it would be a proof to my mind that the scriptures were not from God were there nothing in them beyond the grasp of my own mind. As to the responsibility of man and his power of choice, I think there can be no doubt.

As to the *"new faith"* folks, I believe they hold many important things in common with ourselves...They have without the least compunction split in pieces many churches and in various places kept possession of the places of worship. ...Is it to be endured that for the sake of a few speculative minds a whole community of commonsense but pious Christians shall become agitated as the billowy ocean, and the pulpit and the house of God made the place and the season for a sort of *debating society*? I consider the peace of a Christian Church too important a matter to run the risk of the disunions and hatred which have been created in too many quarters around us.

Let me hear from you before leaving the College, and I shall do my best if need be....

BOOK III
CALLED AND REJECTED

CHAPTER I

THE CALL TO ARUNDEL

THE years 1850-51 are full of news as regards the story of George MacDonald's life. They include his invitation to the pulpit at Arundel; the threatened wreck of this hope by alarming illness; the story of Louisa Powell's brave support; and his marriage. On his return to Highbury from Whitehaven, his life became more and more interwoven with the family at The Limes, although anxiety concerning Mrs. Powell clouded their whole horizon: she died in the second week of June 1850.

During August and September Mr. Powell took a furnished house at Brighton for his family, he himself travelling up and down every day from London. The journey even then was accomplished in an hour, and it did not appear to overtax his strength, though he was now seventy. Small and abstemious, he had kept his youth remarkably.

While his friends were at Brighton, George MacDonald had an invitation to take temporary duties at the Trinity Congregational Church, Arundel, and it soon appeared highly probable that he would be asked to remain. Arundel being only twenty-five miles from Brighton, occasional trips between the places were not difficult. On August 27th, Charlotte, with Louisa and Mrs. Helen Powell, visited Arundel at its "supply" minister's invitation, and the next day Louisa writes thus of it:

Miss Louisa Powell to G.M.D.

[BRIGHTON.]

...I did not go to bed before we had unpacked our treasures, looked at the figs and butter, put the sweet flowers into water, and gave the bits of wild roots and flowers a little too; I felt so happy...I cannot imagine my ever living in so lovely a place; so near to such beauties. There would be one disadvantage which I felt when we were left quietly in the carriage, that in such a secluded place I should not be enough for you, dearest. My heart sinks sometimes, oftentimes, when I think of my unsuitableness in so many ways. And oh, if you found it out too late! And Helen gave me such a long lecture upon matrimony after we were in bed, as has made me afraid even more than before *for you*, not for myself. I wish she would in some things take the advice she gave me...But I was pleased to hear her say what she did, as it shows she must try sometimes...How kind Mrs. New[1] was to think of taking us to see your rooms...We are quite sorry to lose Helen. How I wish I were as *bewitching*! but I must learn to be content.

Believe, my dearest George, in the love of your most unworthy child,
LOUISA.

P.S.—I have read three or four pages of Uhland's poems. I was so delighted: I quite thanked him for writing such lovely verses—and a dearer than he for leaving me the book.

To me at least it is touching to read how often my mother signs herself as her lover's "loving child," especially when she is troubled with the sense of unworthiness Helen Powell could so readily excite. Another letter, to be quoted presently, throws more light upon the writer's trials at the hand of this sister-in-law whom she had almost worshipped. Nevertheless, my mother after her marriage banished all her resentment and wholeheartedly identified herself with the two cousins' friendship.

Here I may give the new minister's own description of Arundel's surroundings, extracted from a letter he wrote in January 1853 to his twelve-year-old half-sister Bella. A portion of it is already quoted in the description of The Farm at Huntly.[2]

---

1 This landlady proved a true friend in the distresses that fell so soon upon the minister.
2 *Vide* p. 56.

THE CALL TO ARUNDEL

G.M.D. to his Sister Bella.

...Behind the town there are very low hills, with sweet short grass, on which numbers of fallow deer are feeding. Here and there are plantations of very fine trees, and down in one of the hollows rises and runs a stream of water, clearer than the Bogie, and so nice to drink in the hot days...We have a river that runs through the town, up which vessels come of a good size, bringing things and taking away things; but it is a very quiet little town—not so much bustle as Huntly....The fields grow much richer crops than with you, and there are many more trees growing about the fields; but it is not such a beautiful country to my mind, nearly, as the one I left...

The following Sunday Mr. Powell took his daughter to Arundel to hear George MacDonald preach. Before breakfast on the Monday he wrote a long letter to the minister concerning his methods. For itself alone the letter is worth quoting, so openly grateful is it to this young man who had not yet received any *call*, so modest and respectful is it in tone, and yet so definite in the advice he has to give. It is interesting, too, for its quotation of remarks, once made to him, *à propros* of rival systems in education then much discussed, by his "late illustrious friend," Samuel Taylor Coleridge.[1]

Mr. James Powell to G.M.D.

BRIGHTON,
30th Aug., 1850.

MY DEAR SIR,

...Perhaps I ought to apologize for assuming the critic. I only, however, do it on the plea of age, and I then only make these remarks to be received by you if you on consideration think they have any reason in them. I ought perhaps to have commenced with saying how very much I was pleased with your professional services...If in my earlier life I had been asked what I thought of your reading the Scriptures, I should have given an answer of approval, because you avoided monotony by giving the emphasis natural to the various speakers in the narrative parts. But the

---

[1] Coleridge died in 1832. He had been professionally intimate with my grandfather's eldest son, James, by his first wife, a surgeon practising in Hackney, who was often compelled, my mother has told me, to incur his patient's displeasure, and sometimes anger, by refusing to supply him with laudanum or crude opium. Coleridge was then living at Highgate.

remarks of my illustrious friend, S. T. Coleridge, modified my opinion...I wish I could give you a tithe of his eloquent words, but his meaning was that in reading the Scriptures, while monotony is avoided, the divine source should never be forgotten, and they should be delivered more as the Oracles of God than the opinions of man...

For the remainder of September my father was at Arundel, while my mother at Brighton found herself, I presume, now busier than ever with the shirts and the stock-cravat she was making up for him. In October he received his *Call*.

G.M.D. to his Father.

Arundel,

[Oct. 4., 1850].

In great haste and half-dressed I am writing, my dear father, to tell you that the Church at the meeting last night [determined] that I should be their minister...They give me £150...I expect to find the work of preaching grow easier and easier, but will be oppressed at first, I fear. That will teach me more faith. Mr. Godwin told me that the accounts he had heard lately of my acceptableness were very gratifying to him. This is something from him, as my sermons have seldom been other than censured by him as unsuitable for the people. I will send you some of my poetry and a sermon or two soon; for I have not time to spend on the composition of sermons, which I preach in a very different style from that in which I write them...

October 16th, 1850.

...The invitation was signed by all the Church except five, who had not heard me. I preach for the first time as their Pastor next Sunday...In all things I hope God will teach me. To be without him is to be like a little child, just learning to walk, left alone by its mother in Cheapside—and far worse than that faint emblem.

We hope to be married in the spring—to which Mr. Powell is quite favourable—and if you would receive us, we should like, if we could, to visit you then—perhaps in April. I should, of course, have much pleasure in letting you and Louisa know and speak to each other, and should like her to see the sky and the hills which first began to mould my spirit.

You ask whether the Church is of long standing. I cannot say how long—but there is a very old lady still alive, though in her dotage, who was principally the means of forming the Church. There are fifty-seven signatures to the *Call*...They seem a people that would make much of their minister...The congregation increased while I was there...The people are a simple people—not particularly well informed—mostly tradespeople—and in middling circumstances. They chiefly reside in the town, which has between two and three thousand inhabitants. There are none I could call society for me—but with my books now and the beautiful earth, and added to these soon, I hope, my wife—and above all that, God to care for me—in whom I and all things are—I do not much fear the want of congenial society...

While expecting this call, George MacDonald had been approached by a Church in Brighton to ascertain if he would accept an invitation from themselves. But, attracted by the simpler ways and affection of the Arundel folk, he felt under some obligation to them, and therefore believed he was definitely led to their pulpit rather than to Brighton with its well-to-do and better-educated society. Towards the end of October he settled down into his lodgings at Arundel.

A curious incident now occurred which I tell because of the light it throws upon the chief characters of these memoirs. It largely explains Louisa Powell's freaks of misery about her imagined lack of "fascination." The word crops up again and again in half-playful or wholly serious reproach. There can be no doubt that this feeling was kept alive by her sister-in-law's gifts and graces: had not Miss Louisa herself been fascinated by them when the beautiful schoolgirl first came to The Limes? I am reminded by another of her nephews that our Aunt Helen had an irresistibly sweet smile, which, of course, was the outward sign of inward grace, although it might well be used in exercise of her power.[1] Yet, judging from my father's estimate in

---

1   Little reason had my mother for fearing the personal attractions of any woman, if only because of her eyes' beauty. One of her sons was her worshipper always; well he knew that to look deep into those tender eyes brought instant repentance for his sins and then a perfect forgiveness. He remembers an occasion when, as a very young man, he called upon a physician of high distinction in reference to an appointment he sought. He was recounting his own record and qualifications, when the great man, who had been absent-mindedly gazing into the fire, suddenly wheeled round and irrelevantly exclaimed, "Your mother has the most wonderful eyes I ever saw in the face of a woman!" The applicant did not know he had ever met his parents. He did not get the appointment.

later years of his cousin's character, it is probable that her love of power, rather than intentional unkindness to my mother, accounted for her unwillingness to relinquish the influence she once had with him.

Certain pocket-books, full of his boyhood's scribblings, my father was now preferring should be in my mother's hands rather than any longer in Cousin Helen's. So he writes asking Louisa to get the little books from her sister-in-law. The fact that he did thus commission her proves—if proof could be needed—that he had nothing to keep from my mother, and that he preferred that his cousin should know this. Mrs. Alex was on the eve of leaving town for Banff, where her husband was to join her for Christmas, so that my mother had to pay her visit immediately. The result she tells in the following letter:

Miss Louisa Powell to G.M.D.
THE LIMES,
Oct. 24, 1850.

...I went to Helen's last night...I felt very much inclined to beg you to write to her, instead of my asking about the books; but when I thought how seldom I can show my love to you by doing anything I do not quite like, I determined not to miss this opportunity, and found it indeed much easier than I expected. She pretended not to know what I meant at first. She thought I meant some of her note-books that you had of hers and which, as I understood her, you had returned to her. However, she soon understood me, and when I asked for them, saying Papa would perhaps take them, she said, "Very well, Louisa, I will make up a little packet for him." We are all going to tea there to-night—for the last time. She was very pleasant and more natural than sometimes, I think, and so we were more cordial friends. I should not like her to go away with all the uncomfortable feeling that I am sure has existed on both sides...I hope your pocket-books have not shared the fate of the poetry she told me was for no eyes but her own and was therefore put on the fire... [1]

---

[1] The inclusion of these letters has been much criticized by some members of the family; yet I adhere to my decision, seeing that they are so entirely creditable to the two persons chiefly concerned. That my father should have written verses to Helen MacKay

The final letter relative to this incident I also give, because I would have every reader know how perfect was the love that held my father in all the many and severe trials that beset him; how humble and strong was my mother in its offerings; and just why it was so vigilant and sustaining.

Miss Louisa Powell to G.M.D.

Nov. 2 [1850].

...You were not obliged to say a word about these pocket-books, and, had you loved me less, I am sure you would not. You know how much and often I regret my want of the *enchanting* for your sake...but indeed, dearest, believe me, in truth I say the better part of me would choose rather to be loved, as I believe you love *me*, than with the more *intoxicated admiration-love* that at first sight seems so enviable. What could I ask for more than the enduring affection I believe you have for me which you know is appreciated and treasured by me?...It is dear of you to say *we will love each other for ever*—it makes my heart happy every time you say so; for it is a strange one for fancying miseries and dreading the time when you will have got tired of me, and I shall have no genius, no talent, no poetry, no beauty to win back the dear, cherished love. My real hope is in growing better and in trusting that goodness may do what the others could not.

But enough of this. Your dear, dear letter requires no other answer than that I too love you more than ever—and that is saying a great deal. I feel so frightened sometimes putting such thoughts on paper, but no one knows but you—and you will not be shocked. The thought of our Heavenly Father knowing every word and seeing my thoughts does not distress me, but the opposite...

* * * * *

It was proposed that the ordination should take place at the end of November, and my father was anxious that a valued

---

in his boyhood is as normal and inevitable as that my mother should be jealous of any one thus honoured. Both would be less lovable, less than human, had such things been impossible to them. My mother's alert sense of humour would certainly repudiate any presentment of herself as a plaster saint, and to my father it would be no less intolerable. The letters reveal their sure confidence in one another: there was nothing to hide and nothing was hidden. And if, now and again, the cousin could not withhold her pin-pricks, nor my mother her momentary wincing, the affectionate understanding and intimacy ultimately arrived at between the two ladies was patent to all their friends.

friend, the Rev. Caleb Morris—a man whose wide outlook and simple eloquence, as well as his spiritual courage, made him a real power in non-conformity at that time—should be asked to officiate. But the ceremony had to be postponed for the present.

George MacDonald himself, it appears, had no strong feeling as to the necessity of ordination, adopting the view generally held to-day that the *call* itself implies and constitutes ordination. It appears from one of my mother's letters that some of the Arundel congregation were questioning the efficacy of a minister's administration of the Sacrament until some rite of ordination had been performed. My grandfather was strongly in its favour on the score that "a suspicion might arise of something wrong in doctrine or character."

G.M.D. to his Father.
Arundel,
October 29th, 1850.

...My congregation I think increases, and the week meetings on the whole are better. We have a prayer-meeting every Monday, and a lecture on Thursday, for which I do not make much preparation—but gather up the gleanings of the Sunday. I mean on those same evenings to have Bible classes, one for young men and the other for young women. I shall have plenty to do....I hope to be able to visit a good deal amongst the poor and unwell.

I expect the ordination will take place towards the end of November. I don't like it....

It will depend on Mr. Powell whether I take a house at once—there happening to be a desirable one vacant now, and houses being very scarce in Arundel. He is coming down to me Saturday to stay till Monday....

CHAPTER II
MARRIAGE

BUT a catastrophe was awaiting all these plannings. Miss Louisa was hoping she would be allowed to attend the ordination. But a long-promised visit to her aunts at Leamington stood in the way. She had a warm affection for them and visiting would be more difficult after her marriage. She feared her father, owing to the expense, would bid her choose one or the other. Already he was doing much for the young couple and would soon be going to Arundel to inspect a house, and, if approved, to furnish it for them. Incidentally, in relating these points, she tells of her birthday on November 5th and her many presents— as, for instance, the tea-caddy given by her father:

the loveliest I ever saw. I know it will just suit you—it is so neat and elegant-shaped, with a likeness of York Minster at the top done in that coloured mother of pearl. All the others were housekeepingish except the preciousest which Annie has given me [a chain knitted of her betrothed's hair]. You are in part round my neck now, my dearest...Helen has behaved very strangely about a present she bought me. I am so sorry, for it has spilt our comfortableness.

My father's birthday present had been Tennyson's *In Memoriam*, copied out in his exquisite penmanship.

Her father wished her to visit the aunts, though herself would have chosen the ordination at Arundel if only because she was anxious about her lover. The young minister had been much troubled by a cough. She implores him to rest. She tells how Angela had been cured in a night of a very bad cough by taking homœopathic *bryonia* and *mercurius*, and begs him to take them. She encloses two minute packets of globules, with full directions for their use. The innocent things lie beside me as I write, treasured but untouched for seventy-two years.

On November 7th she left home for Leamington, where she should arrive at 5.26 p.m. She took to read in the train a volume of Ruskin which George MacDonald had sent her, as well as, nearer her heart, a pencil-addressed letter from him that had arrived just as she left home, but which she did not then open in the hurry of departure. Comfortably settled, and the November fog soon left behind, she opened it. It was only six lines telling of a broken bloodvessel and furious hæmorrhage from the lungs. Out she came at Bletchley, the first station where they stopped, and took the next train back to London. She would, in spite of the impropriety, have driven across to London Bridge station and so to Arundel; but there being insufficient money in her purse, she arrived home again in the late afternoon. Her father was quickly told. In his distress he took her in his arms, and said he feared it might be a sign that she was never to marry George MacDonald. But, "No, Papa!" she exclaimed in finality; "it is a sign that I must marry him at once and nurse him!" Though, I do think, thanking God for his courageous child, he turned away and left her, but very soon came to uphold her decision. A second letter quickly followed with reassuring news.

But Louisa hardly dared think again of going to nurse her lover: it would be hardly proper, they said. Besides, having met Mrs. New, she felt content in her goodness; and though he was condemned to lie motionless on his back, with leeches on the chest, he was not too ill to pencil her little notes.

Alex Powell, kind brother that he always was, took pity on his sister and went to Arundel for the week-end and

MARRIAGE

brought back better news. Here is her first letter after the attack:

Miss Louisa Powell to G.M.D.

The Limes,
Nov. 7th.

...How dear of you to write; but you must not do it if it is at all likely to hurt you one bit. Mrs. New or somebody would send me a report. God keep you and both of us in willingness for His goodwill...Papa has been so very kind to me. I know he loves you. He says he will find a corner somewhere when you are quite better enough to come. [The house was then very full of guests.] Good night, my best and dearest...I should like to be an angel or fairy just to see how you are sleeping. But He is keeping you and I will praise Him...

Nov. 8th, 1850.

...I suppose you feel weak after the leeches, but I hope they will have had the desired effect by this time. Do not think that you must write to me; I should not be frightened if you think it better to let someone else. Alex will write for you while he is with you...I hope, dearest, you will try and keep your thoughts and mind very peaceful. You have all the love you could wish, but till you are a little stronger, only think of it as a very commonplace sort of thing, and only just exactly what you have a right to. Think no more of me than as a good little girl that will be quite pleased when God makes you better enough to come...I must tell you that I feel quite well today. I walked down to Hackney before breakfast with your letter...Dear Papa sent me his love last night and said that he loved me very much, and that he loved you very much. This was precious to me.

Mr. Powell urged his coming, as soon as the doctor would permit, to consult the great Dr. C. J. B. Williams,[1] who, on November 14th, pronounced the lungs to be affected. George MacDonald wrote of this to his father, but does not appear to realize its gravity.

G.M.D. to his Father.

The Limes,
Nov. 15, 1850.

Louisa has told you of my visit to Dr. Williams and of his orders not to preach for six weeks or two months. He has ordered me cod-liver oil. I have

---

1 Father of the late Dr. Theodore Williams, the earliest advocate in this country of outdoor life and mountain-air for the tuberculosis.

very little fear that my complaint is slight and will soon leave me with proper care. But I believe the lungs are in some measure affected. It is somewhat discouraging to be thus laid aside at the beginning—but the design of God in doing so will perhaps appear soon—or if not now we shall know afterwards; and if never, it is well notwithstanding. There is a reason, and I at least shall be the better for it.[1]

Now the question is, what am I to do with myself. I must not stop here much longer. And then I have no money. All my spare money I laid out on books—very necessary to do when going to a country place like Arundel where I can have no *society*, and no books of any kind except what I have of my own...I expect the people will wait for me, though £2 a week [to pay substitutes] out of £150 a year won't leave much...

At this period my grandfather wrote frequently from Huntly full of encouragement though deeply anxious. He relates many instances where a serious hæmoptysis was followed by no lung-disease. And I confess I am astonished to learn how many of my relatives were thus attacked and yet recovered. When, however, a little later, my Uncles Alec and John suffered from this bleeding, rapid destruction of the lungs ensued.

So the young minister, at the very beginning of his career, was struck down. He spent his days of convalescence with his paternal aunt, Mary Spence, at Newport, Isle of Wight, and then at Niton, doing no work beyond writing, trying to digest his food in spite of the cod-liver oil, and taking gentle exercise.

On December 9th his father writes cheerily to brighten these anxious days.

G.M.D. Senr. to his Son George.

THE FARM.

...Janie is getting on with her little words remarkably well. She is a strong, healthy little thing and a great pet with all and sundry. She is very fond of her *piece* and her pottage [porridge] and almost anything of an eating-kind. Her sisters the other night were somewhat amused with her: the last part of her *grace-before-meat* was—"May we eat and drink to Thy glory for ever and ever. Amen!"

---

1 "I do not myself believe in misfortune; anything to which men give the name is merely the shadow-side of a good." (*Castle Warlock*, vol. ii, p. 127.)

MARRIAGE

G.M.D. to his Father.

Newport,

Dec. 17, 1850.

It is very kind of you to write to me so often....I feel very doubtful whether I shall preach much longer. I feel if I were to begin again now, it would bring back the attack....I know you have often thought I fancied I could not work: often it may have been so, but not always; but lately I was sure something was wrong. It was in the very midst of forcing myself to do what I did not *feel* as if I were able for, that my attack came. However, it may partly be fancy. All that I know is that when I have work to do, I will try to do it with God's help, and then if I fail, it is not my fault. But I am not unhappy about it....Perhaps such attacks might come and go, and one yet *wrastle on* for some years. But I have no *idol of chance*,[1] as many called Christians seem to have. All will be well with me. I know you would give me my heart's desire if you could. And I know God is better than you—and it was Christ himself that taught us to call him *Father*. If I were to die to-morrow, I would thank God for what I have had, for he has blessed me very abundantly: I could say "I have lived."

I would here record a fact that should not be forgotten throughout this story of my father's life, that he had scarcely ever any fear of death, and none when it faced him.

In the above letter his reference to his work implies only his pastoral duties. But now when writing to my mother he often mentions his poetry as his work; and we know that *Within and Without*, his dramatic poem which brought him immediate recognition when it was published in 1855, was entirely written at Niton and Newport.

Greatly encouraged he must have felt at receiving on December 23rd the following letter from Mr. Powell. I quote it in full for its unqualified testimony to the high esteem and affection in which he held my father, not only then, when his responsibility in allowing his daughter to marry this invalided

---

1 This recalls a word of Sir Philip Sidney that my father would quote in later years: "Since a man is bound no farther to himself than to do wisely, chance is only to trouble them that stand upon chance." The axiom of my father's, already quoted, is even more notable: "*The roots of the seen remain unseen.*" (*Castle Warlock*, vol. i, p.124.)

man was heavy upon him, but far more in later years when he knew he had not decided amiss.

Mr. James Powell to G.M.D.

THE LIMES,
22nd Decr., 1850.
Sunday Afternoon.

MY DEAR SIR,

After dinner to-day I turned to the fire with a rather heavy heart—the recollection of the many, many Sabbath afternoons when I had playfully asked leave of my dear companion to quit the table and go to the fire, forced a tear from my eye and a pang into my heart. But I did not, when I took up my pen, intend to name this, but to tell you that after a glass of wine, we took up your 116 Psalm and sung it in the four parts.

I want a bar or two of suitable interlude between each verse, and if you could write music as well as you can poetry I should send it to you to compose it; but we have talked of sending it to Rome—to ask Novello to do it. He is there to spend the remainder of his days. I have not yet seen Alfred N., his son, but I do intend to take it to him that it may be published...[1]

When you return home—for so I suppose I may call Arundel—I shall be happy to run down any Saturday with Louisa—returning on Monday—if you will get us a couple of beds and a sitting-room for two nights...

The following letters are closely associated with the writing of *Within and Without*:

G.M.D. to Miss Louisa Powell.

NITON,
Dec. 27th, 1850.

I had your sweet letter to-day, when I posted my one to you....Caleb Morris is one of the few who stand so high that they can see a good many things at once. Most people are always peeping through pin-holes in bits of paper; and often very ready to tell the man on the hill top with his eyes wide open what wonderful things they see....I think I should like Caleb Morris to marry us better than anyone except Mr. Scott....I am surprised

---

1   Psalm 116: "I love the Lord, because he hath heard my voice and my supplications.
    "Because he hath inclined his ear unto me, therefore will I call upon him as long as I live," etc.
    I cannot find the *version* of this psalm by my father. Messrs. Novello advise me that they did not publish it.

MARRIAGE 149

to find so many of my notions in Dr. Arnold's letters—only much enlarged and verified beyond my shelled-chicken-peepings....I wish the Church were better. I think I should almost go into it. Don't fancy I am changing. Indeed I am not saying more than I have always said, that my great objection to it was the kind of ministers the system admitted. If Dr. Arnold's plan could be carried out—which it never could till all men, or nearly all, are not *merely Christians* (that sounds very dreadful, does it not?) but thoroughly earnest men—I should have very little objection left.

Saturday night. I had your letter to-day and the poor flattened rose—crossing your violets on the way. I was out nearly an hour and a half and enjoyed it, this bright beautiful day. I walked down nearer the sea, but yet a long way above it. I could see the blowing of the irregular tiny waves over the level sand, of which a little was bare, and a man or boy, I don't know which, was walking on it, with such a clear black shadow. The sun flashed on the sea, and a sloop-rigged boat left a snail track behind it. The horizon was a luminous mist, I enjoyed it more than yesterday.

Sunday morning. I lay simmering in bed, till half-past ten this morning, without mental energy enough to look at my watch. I have been out before the door and it is very mild, and the sea sounds on—the first time I have noticed its low monotonous tune. I have had your dear little letter this morning. Thank you for all your dear love...I shall write a little of my poem this evening. I fear it will disappoint me as usual....It is little more than a week now till I see you once more. I am sure I shall never be well until I have you with me always....

G.M.D. to his Father.

UPPER CLAPTON,

Jan. 9th, 1851.

I have just come from consulting Dr. Williams. He seems so far satisfied with me—but not pleased that I did not take the oil constantly—which now I will do, sick or not—but he says that will go off.[1] He allows me to preach if I begin gently....Many thanks to you, my very dear father, for writing

---

1 The oil was a constant trouble. The following from his father is amusing enough: "...When you told me of having bought two gallons of Oil I thought I saw you scouring the country with an oil pig carried by a string tied round the neck—a strange piece of clerical luggage. It brought also to my recollection the *true* story of the late F—E—, minister of C—. He went drunk to the pulpit one Sabbath, and after the people had finished the first psalm-singing, he got up out of *a sleep* he was indulging in and bawled out to the congregation 'Roar on boys, there's *mair* in the *black pig* in the foot of the press.' I hope then that the oil pig will do you more good than the *black* one did to F—!"

so often and so kindly. I hope to be married in March. Mr. Powell quite intends it. I fear we shall not be able to come to Scotland. Dr. Williams does not approve of it. But we will hope to see you in the South.

When George MacDonald resumed his duties on January 16th at Arundel they received him with a quiet joy that was very gratifying. But he is clearly not very fit for work and has to spare himself all he can. He grows more emphatic when writing to his father as to what sermons ought to be, arguing strongly in favour of extempore speaking:

> Most preaching seems to me greatly beside the mark. That only can I prize which tends to make men better—and most of it "does na play bouf upo' me" [*does not even bark at me*]....I finished my poem at the Island, but it must wait your perusal when you come to see us, for I cannot copy out more than 2,000 lines. Will you come and see us in the summer?...Mr. Powell is to bring Louisa down to see me some Saturday soon and stay till Monday.

Speaking of his library, he says it will always be a small one, "but I expect rather unlike most dissenting ministers,... You may be sure I never buy a book except I have just reason for believing it a pearl and no paste."

On February 26th he writes about the arrangements for the wedding. After the first Sunday in March he is to go to London, it being fixed for the 8th. He hopes his brother Alec will be with him. John cannot, but will visit them in May when he comes to London for the Great Exhibition. He himself is to stay at the Mathesons, till the 8th.

> By the way, some of them are the only young men I know fit to be companions—intellectually, of course, I mean—to John. I am so astonished at his *growth* as shown in his letters. Very few men could write as he does. One of the Mathesons, even younger than he, is extraordinary.[1]

---

[1] This, apparently, was David Matheson, father of Greville Ewing Matheson Junior, my lifelong friend and author of some very brilliant light verse.

MARRIAGE

The last extant letter of my father as a bachelor to Miss Louisa is delightfully commonplace; the kitchen-range, the book-recess, the blinds of the little house in Tarrant Street he had taken, the need of cards and calling, the wedding presents, fill four pages. Crossing it he says he has been reading Mrs. Matheson's memoirs of her father, making him "resolve as soon as I am able to do what I can in preaching in the country round about...You shall have only two more letters from me—don't cry!"

George MacDonald and Louisa Powell were married on March 8, 1851, at the chapel known as The Old Gravel Pits.[1]

Among the facts on record concerning the ceremony are two of interest. The bridegroom wore a white satin waistcoat beautifully embroidered with sprigs of gay flowers, lent him by a friend. According to my Aunt Angela, Mr. Powell discovered that he had most important business at Bristol which would make it impossible for him to be present at the ceremony.[2] At the last, however, matters were adjusted, and he reached home in time with a beautiful white scarf for the bride, which she wore. But, at the most solemn moment—so my Aunt Angela told me—she espied the grin of a shop-ticket on one corner of the scarf, and her ineradicable sense of the comic took her unawares. I suspect it was rather that my aunt

---
1 The Old Gravel Pits was a meeting house in Hackney. Its original congregation had become Unitarian but later scattered. Then the Rev. John Pye-Smith, D.D., gathered about him a Congregational Church which met first at Homerton College, but moved in 1810 to The Old Gravel Pits Meeting House, where they worshipped till 1871, when Clapton Park Chapel was built. It was the old Meeting House that my grandfather's family originally attended when they lived at Grove Place, Hackney, before removing to The Limes. Dr. Pye-Smith was succeeded in 1850 by the Rev. John Davies, who married my father and mother.
2 Probably this was but an excuse to cover a fear lest he should not be able to control his emotion, without his beloved wife's support. We have seen how readily moved he was to tears. I cannot believe, judging from his undertaking to pay the rent at Arundel, his furnishing the little house to its minutest detail as his wedding present, and his letter given a few pages back, that my grandfather had opposed the marriage, though in certain quarters this has been asserted.

attributed her own quizzical acumen to the bride—with whom the wonder and sweet solemnity of the occasion must have overruled all other feelings.

The wedding took place on a Saturday, and on the following morning the bridegroom was to preach at Rugby, *en route* for Leamington, where the bride's two maiden aunts had lent their house for the honeymoon. But if George MacDonald looked to no "idol of chance" to set things right, some demon of mischance awaited the happy pair on unpacking their luggage at Rugby: the bottle of cod-liver oil was broken, its contents reaching even the Sunday trousers of the morrow's preacher!

My father's wedding present to my mother was the following poem—so strange and tender and prophetic that, though it was subsequently published in *Within and Without*,[1] its six concluding stanzas must be given here:

> Love me beloved; for thou mayest lie
> Dead in my sight, 'neath the same blue sky;
> Love me, O love me, and let me know
> The love that within thee moves to and fro;
> That many a form of thy love may be
> Gathered around thy memory.
>
> Love me beloved; for I may lie
> Dead in thy sight, 'neath the same blue sky;
> The more thou hast loved me, the less thy pain,
> The stronger thy hope till we meet again;
> And forth on the pathway we do not know,
> With a load of love, my soul would go.
>
> Love me beloved; for one must lie
> Motionless, lifeless, beneath the sky;
> The pale stiff lips return no kiss
> To the lips that never brought love amiss;
> And the dark brown earth be heaped above
> The head that lay on the bosom of love.

---

[1] *Poetical Works*, vol. i, p. 79

MARRIAGE

Love me beloved; for both must lie
Under the earth and beneath the sky;
The world be the same when we are gone;
The leaves and the waters all sound on;
The spring come forth, and the wild flowers live,
Gifts for the poor man's love to give;
The sea, the lordly, the gentle sea,
Tell the same tales to others than thee;
And joys, that flush with an inward morn,
Irradiate hearts that are yet unborn;
A youthful race call our earth their own,
And gaze on its wonders from thought's high throne;
Embraced by fair Nature, the youth will embrace
The maid beside him, his queen of the race;
When thou and I shall have passed away
Like the foam-flake thou lookedst on yesterday.

Love me beloved; for both must tread
On the threshold of Hades, the house of the dead;
Where now but in thinkings strange we roam,
We shall live and think, and shall be at home;
The sights and the sounds of the spirit land
No stranger to us than the white sea-sand,
Than the voice of the waves, and the eye of the moon,
Than the crowded street in the sunlit noon.
I pray thee to love me, belov'd of my heart;
If we love not truly, at death we part;
And how would it be with our souls to find
That love, like a body, was left behind!

Love me beloved; Hades and Death
Shall vanish away like a frosty breath;
These hands, that now are at home in thine,
Shall clasp thee again, if thou art still mine;
And thou shalt be mine, my spirit's bride,
In the ceaseless flow of eternity's tide,
If the truest love that thy heart can know
Meet the truest love that from mine can flow.
Pray God, beloved, for thee and me,
That our souls may be wedded eternally.

CHAPTER III

THE PASTOR

THOSE were happy days indeed, with plenty to do among a people, simple, eager to learn, and very grateful. The majority were tradesmen, though a sprinkling of pure country-folk gave the minister easier touch with the elemental virtues, which among people belonging to the soil are less likely to be hid under a bushel of worldliness. It was at Arundel that he stored, without, I think, any definite intent, material for that best (as some think) of his English novels, *Annals of a Quiet Neighbourhood*. Its descriptions tally closely with Arundel, while one at least of the characters, Old Rogers, is the portrait and name of a member of his congregation who would come regularly to chapel in his round frock, red cotton handkerchief and tall beaver hat. His conversation in the book is based upon the old man's shrewd observations, his imaginative outlook accounted for by his having been a man of war's man. So that when he likened the pulpit to the mast-head, one is not surprised. "I love a parson, Sir...He's got a good telescope, and he gits to the mast-head, and he looks out. And he sings out, 'Land ahead!' or 'Breakers ahead!' and gives directions accordin'." It was on Arundel's beautiful bridge that my father first met Old Rogers. "All sorts of bridges have been from very infancy a delight to me. For I am one of those who never get rid of their infantile predilections, and to have once enjoyed making a mud bridge, was to enjoy all bridges for ever" [1] —a remark that holds one clue to my father's thoughts and imagery: the child was father of the man.

The serenity of the place is nowhere better suggested than in words of my mother, written in July 1853 to my father after his resignation:

> What a sweet, sunny, breezy Sunday afternoon this is! The street is so still, and our one tree is whispering most sweetly to me all about you, and Him who cares about both of us. The river is full and the lights and shadows in the meadows beyond are very beautiful.

The following letters show us the minister at his work. The first already indicates certain views upon doctrine, that were before long to be used against him.

G.M.D. to his Father.

ARUNDEL,
April 15th, 1851.

Will you excuse my writing to you on these scraps of paper, as I am not willing to call Louisa from the garden where she is sowing some flower seeds....She has been very well, I am happy to say. I am far happier, much more at peace, and I hope learning more rapidly the best knowledge....As I expect to be on very good terms with the Church people here, I hope for better congregations in the evening when there is no service in the parish church. Amongst our visitors the week before last was the vicar—I mean at our house, not the chapel....

I firmly believe that people have hitherto been a great deal too much taken up about doctrine and far too little about practice. The word *doctrine*, as used in the Bible, means teaching of duty, not theory. I preached a sermon about this. We are far too anxious to be definite and to have finished, well-polished, sharp-edged *systems*—forgetting that the more perfect a theory about the infinite, the surer it is to be wrong, the more impossible it is to be right. I am neither Arminian nor Calvinist. To no system would I subscribe....

In such manner was my father spending his renewed energy. When I recall his wonderful tenderness in any sort of trouble, so that a sufferer knew at once what it meant to have another take upon himself his or her anguish; when I recall his rejoicing with those who rejoiced, or his stories of

---
[1] *Annals of a Quiet Neighbourhood* (1867), vol.i, p. 15.

pathos and humour, of faerie and wit; then do I know how impossible it was that the folk of Arundel—barring some few who could not dissociate their religion from a belief that any increase of trade-profits and custom was proof of God's clemency—should fail to love their new minister. One of his congregation, Alpheus Smith, I knew well in later years; for he had followed my father to London. He told me how, because the minister had admired his stock-tie—of *moiré antique* it was—he made one like it, and, daring much, had it placed upon his dressing-table. It was this gentleman's wife—I had it from my mother—who, when the minister was sick, would send them all sorts of delicacies, such as were never afforded for themselves—jellies and cream-custards, even cold chicken—and without clue to the donors. In the later days particularly, when the relatively rich deacons tried to drive him away by curtailing his stipend, simple gifts, such as fruit, cauliflowers, potatoes, home-brewed beer, were offered them by poorer friends. My mother took wise and tender share in the pastoral work, her quick and sound sympathy making her loved by all. My father's flaming words against mammon-worship and cruelty and self-seeking were as thoroughgoing as the giving of himself to all who needed him. "The few young," he writes to his father in a noble letter given in full hereafter, "who are not [adversely] influenced by their parents, and the simple, honest poor are much attached to me." And again: "Some of all classes *do* understand me and I am happy not to be understood by those that do not understand. Some say I talk foolishness, others go away with their hearts burning within them."

The poor understood him—as they did his Master; but the purse-proud resented his plain speaking and turned away. "Riches indubitably favour stupidity," he wrote, "poverty mental and moral development." In later years he was once preaching at the most fashionable church in Glasgow, the

THE PASTOR

congregation mainly of the wealthiest. In the course of the sermon he remarked: "One may readily conclude how poorly God thinks of riches when we see the sort of people he sends them to!" [1]

If any should desire evidence of the young couple's happiness, it lies before me: seventeen thin quarto cards, one edge of each pasted to a separate linen strip by which they are stitched and bound between boards adorned by my mother with ferns, ivy and autumn leaves in water-colour. On each page is copied in my father's exquisite handwriting one of Greville Ewing Matheson's sonnets or poems, every one decorated with old-fashioned floral designs done by my mother. The title page has on it simply

> POEMS
> By G.E.M.
>
> Lighter and sweeter
> Let your song be;
> And for sorrow—oh cheat her
> With melody!

To me the little album [2] witnesses the great love my father bore the writer, and shows how this love was accepted as part of my mother's own happiness. She loved her husband's friends as he loved them, and would share in this homage to the chief of them. It must have been my mother's idea, and I fancy she intended it for his bride when he should find one; if so the tribute never reached its home.

In June 1851 Mr. Godwin came down for the ordination. Mrs. George MacDonald's sister Charlotte had been invited to help entertain the great man; and it was at Arundel she and the professor, a childless widower, met for the first time: they were married two years later by

---
1 It is, of course, not wholly fair to quote a single sentence, especially if ironic or epigrammatic, apart from its context.
2 Most of its poems appear, together with many of my Uncle John's, in the little volume called *A Threefold Cord*, published in 1883. They are included in the *Poetical Works*, vol. ii.

my father. My Uncles Alec and John MacDonald were also present, and my grandfather writes from Huntly on July 17th:

> John and Alec are greatly delighted with Arundel and with the *minister's wife* thereof. I am happy to think you have been so fortunate, and I pray God you may appreciate at all times the blessing...

Then my father and mother began an even more strenuous life. They had frequent visits from friends, particularly my mother's sisters, and Greville Matheson. But my father was still much of an invalid; the notoriously relaxing climate of Arundel probably helped him not at all. Nor is his father altogether happy about him, but writes urging him to

> give over the fruitless game of poetry, and apply yourself to the preaching of the Gospel and the instruction of your people. A nervous temperament and a poetical imagination are too much for a frail clay tabernacle, as witness your hypochondriac Cowper and many such like.[1]

But the young minister was happy enough in his work, and in the autumn he writes his step-mother that Louisa was expecting to become a mother at the end of the year, and begs her to write to her: "for now she misses her own mother more than ever, and cannot help having some fear."

An occasional visit to London for a day or two proved a great help to him, for he would not only see his wife's people but Greville Matheson. The latter was already giving him

---

[1] But a little later he writes jocularly to my mother on the same topic:
"6th Feb. 1852.

"...Is not *nervousness* the *tap-root* of all genuine poetry? The nervous system acts, and is reacted upon until it becomes a shaken, wasted and tattered thing. Don't get alarmed: for I say what I have done jocularly. You may please tell George that Alec and John sent their little sisters Sir Walter Scott's poems, which I have read out and out, and which so set in motion within me the *deep springs of latent poetry* that when I went to bed my nightly visions were often such as I am sure Sir Walter himself would many times have been *proud of*—my *rhyming* too was *beautifully correct*; and as to the *real poetry* I shall say little of that—sooth to say it would not have disgraced a *Byron*!!! It is now no longer wonderful to me that the independent minister of Arundel *is a poet*..."

literary help; and at the end of 1851 he was emboldened to print in Arundel his translations of "Twelve of the Spiritual Songs of Novalis," for private circulation as a Christmas gift to his friends. The mystic pietism of these songs, outcome of Novalis's anguish over the death of his betrothed, had gripped my father's imagination in, I think, his student days; and now at last he must, with true poetic instinct, give of their riches to his friends. It is quite clear that these songs found in their translator something more than a "mere lamp lit behind them" as, in the introductory note to the collection, he claims his own work to be; for the songs are made to shine anew by a light that is brotherly-kin to that of the mourning lover. Thomas T. Lynch, the well-known hymn-writer, who was very intimate with my father, thus acknowledges the gift of these songs:

...Any one who will give not perusal only but re-perusals to your Songs of Novalis will understand how every line may to author and translator have gleamed with that peculiar magnetic light of which Literature as well as Science knows something, which is not for all eyes, nor for the eyes sensitive to it at all times, or without darkened privacy and discipline of patience....

On January 4, 1852, the first child was born, Lilia Scott, the former name after the child in *Within and Without*, the latter after A. J. Scott. To the little one's parents not one of their Master's miracles could exceed this everyday creation of a little child; and none felt its happiness more than the two grandfathers. The one at Huntly, as so often happened when he was very happy, let fun creep into his letters:

So little Lilia grows greatly. If she holds on as you would lead me to think, I may expect to see you, if I live so long, travelling north with her in a *caravan* as one of the "wonders of the world"!

As for the grandfather in London, though I find no written word of his on the subject, one needs only recall the letter written to George MacDonald on December 22nd to understand his feelings.

CHAPTER IV
THE THREE BROTHERS

I MUST now give some account of my father's two dearest brothers. However great were George MacDonald's friendships, they could not compare with his attachment to father and brothers. The love which is mutually instinctive, which is centred in parents and children, brothers and sisters, to radiate from the home in diminishing intensity over clan and nation, is purely religious. It is firmer-rooted than the love of lovers; though if these become husband and wife it thrusts roots into the heavenly ground, and remains, among simple and virtuous folk, as ineradicable as the love of mother and child. And when the natural bonds of family and home are strengthened by sympathy in spiritual outlook and intellectual culture, then we have love of the very highest order. Thus my father and mother had found this greatest love. George, Alec and John MacDonald, bound together in the first instance by the most tender family-love [1]—with a father of exceptional wisdom always thinking of them, the memory of a beautiful and idolized mother, and a mother of adoption than whom no actual mother could have more wholly endeared herself—discovered a common spiritual taste in literature and philosophy. George and John, fearless in poetic imagination, and Alec, with less genius, simpler in mind, though not less honest, were equally

---
1 *Vide antea*, BOOK II, Chap. III.

GEORGE MACDONALD, 1855

MRS. GEORGE MACDONALD

ALEXANDER MACDONALD 1852

JOHN HILL MACDONALD, 1853

beloved by one another. My mother took them both into her heart and keeping.

My Uncle Alec evinced early the business instincts of his father's family—instincts which were altogether submerged in John, while in George, though sufficient for practical needs, they never assumed any importance of their own. The inherited instinct for enterprise and adventure showed itself in all four brothers. In Charles the ambition to get rich without labour seemed most easily indulged by exploiting patents and gold-mines or other men's money. In George it inspired the need of a wider spiritual knowledge than could be found in the mother-country of Calvinistic doctrine and literary convention. Alec's enterprise took form in an eager throwing of himself into reform movements, his quick sympathy with his more gifted brothers' different lives, his keen poetic intelligence rather than creative gift. But in John the inherited strain produced a restlessness that made of him a wanderer, and accounted for his lack of persistency in everything he undertook. Every bit of work he set hand to, or others set him to do, he carried out with fiery enthusiasm; but the inevitable restraints of system and time-orderliness—which often invite the imaginative temperament to slovenliness in uncongenial work—drove him away from it altogether. As schoolmaster he won highest praise from his chiefs and was adored by his boys; yet he must always break away from every such work after a while lest the necessary methodical routine—which he could accept with rational dutifulness for a period—should overwhelm his free spirit.

The poet is necessarily a nomad, and the purpose behind his *Wanderlust* may be no more obvious to himself than to his friends. In the dreaminess of my father's boyhood and student days, in his "longings after visions and revelations"—to quote his father's words—"awakened by Louisa's beautiful voice and her rendering of Handel and Mozart on the piano," we see this traditional nomadic instinct rising out from its shallow submergence in the subconscious. But the inherited sense of stern duty and of loyalty to father and wife and child—attributable neither to clan system nor Calvin doctrine, but to his vitality of instinct—gave to all his travels in the fairyland of children and lovers—in the heavenly kingdom of men's hearts—a pole-star in the heavens.

In the comparison of the two brothers' temperaments it is interesting that in their student days the elder won distinction in Chemistry and Natural Philosophy, the younger more particularly in Logic and Moral Philosophy. John was certainly the profounder in metaphysical thought, George the happier in poetic vision. If John was more nomadic, George was more pastoral. Any close critic of the two brothers' poetry would see very clearly this difference in them, though it would be unfair to force the point by special quotations. If the elder's appears sometimes checked in its freedom by the restraint of high finish—and such polishing of rough strength seems more evident in some late emendations—the younger's poetry, submitting less skilfully to technical requirement, often seems to forget its initial aim, and so fails in efficiency. The contest between the old rivalry of free imagination—or "intuitive sensibility," as my Uncle John defined it—and stern discipline—or "categorical logic"—was in the coming Manchester days often discussed by the two brothers, Charles joining in with his quick admiration for his brothers' intrepidity, and Alec eager to learn, taking small part in words, and sympathizing more intelligently than perhaps he understood. And yet in 1888, my father, in a letter home, speaks of meeting a Rev. Mr. Hutchinson who had been intimate with my Uncle Alec and now was master of a co-education school at Ashton-under-Lyne. This gentleman related how finely my uncle had, to quote the letter, "stood up for Wordsworth against himself, who was fresh from college-logic and on the philistine side."

THE THREE BROTHERS

All the brothers were well above the average height, and Alec, with his winning smile, was, so his father said, more like George than the others in features. My father at five feet, ten and a half inches, was the shortest of the three. Writing to my father at Whitehaven, my grandfather contrasts the characters of Alec and John.

> ...Alec is a great favourite here with great and small, and John would be equally so; but he is more reserved in his manners and apparently few are intimately acquainted with him. He has talents of a very high order, tho' sometimes for his own amusement he clothes them in the strangest *tag-rag* of drollery. If you saw him, for instance, walking up to you after the manner of a lame begging impostor, you would run the risk of splitting your sides with laughter.

Two months later he refers again to John's humour:

> I heard to-day from John and am glad to think he is comfortable. He says a lady wished him to say something in Scotch that she might hear it. He immediately replied in emphasis, "Fat are ye efter noo, ye shochlin vratch!"[1] The lady was quite delighted, and said it was *beautiful!*...

John had just obtained a good post in a boys' school near Sheffield. He "was a born teacher" wrote my father of this brother's counterpart, Ian, in *What's Mine's Mine*,[2] "and found intensest delight, not in imparting knowledge—that is a comparatively poor thing—but in leading a mind up to see what it was before incapable of seeing." He had graduated in Aberdeen with greater distinction than my father, and in October of this year (1851) came of age. On April 15th the minister at Arundel had thus written to his father:

> I have a most interesting letter from John, and am delighted at the thought of seeing him here next month as he promises. It will then be almost six years since I have seen him. It will be deep pleasure to me to exchange thoughts with one who is now passing through an earlier stage

---

1 "What are you after now, you wriggling (or paltry) wretch?"
2 Vol. ii, p. 64.

of the same spiritual transformation which I trust has begun in myself, though I think his mind is on a bolder scale than mine. However, growth for him as for me is infinite—for it is in God we have our life...

The following poem, written to his brother George on his twenty-first birthday, must be partly quoted for its intrinsic beauty and poetic promise as well as for the clue it gives to its writer's temperament. My father had written nothing so notable at this age. John Hill MacDonald also figures as Eric Ericson in *Robert Falconer*, where its author gives some of his brother's verses; and many more in *A Threefold Cord*.

>   TWENTY-ONE.
> Alas the day! and so I rise a man
> Who felt but yesterday milleniums old,
> Grey-hearted as the everlasting hills,
> But just a man! and life so grey and worn,
> And all my mortal records scribbled o'er
> With dateless memories—old, old as Time!
> And all the past far-stretching, crowding in
> Upon me, from passionate noon to unremember'd dawn.[1]
> But just a man!
>
>   Above me, many-voiced,
> I hear the murmurous rushing of the years;
> And before me rise dim phantoms—fears, hopes,
> Joys, sorrows, shadowy faces, vanished forms,
> Disjointed as in dreams. Dim, very dim
> As morning twilight on the distant hills,
> Now childhood beckons, and with gleaming smile,
> And light free step—herself a sunny shade—
> Leads on through realms of shadowy brightness—
> Dewy, morning-lands on which the sun
> For ever rises and the streams run sparkling,
> And the flowers bloom ever, and the glad bird sings
> In fragrant bowery woodlands and bright meads,
> Through golden cycles of immortal dawn;

---

1 This recalls four lines in my father's *A Prayer for the Past*:
>   "All the dead years garnered lie
>   In this gem-casket, my dim soul;
>   And thou wilt, once, the key apply
>   And show the shining whole."
>   (*Poetical Works*, vol. i, p. 283.)

A sunny world where never more my foot
Shall tread the fragrance of the violet out,
Or break the murmur of the streamlet more;
Or wander, spell-bound, through the hazel-copse,
Or dint the velvet verdure of the lawn;
Where never more my ear shall drink the song
At earliest morning of the piping thrush,
Or hear the hidden angel of the night
Solace her exile with all sounds of Heaven;
Where never, never more this eye shall see
The beaming faces of the loved of old.

* * * *

Peace, wailing harp!...
This life shall live for ever. Each dim hope
And frail young Joy hath immortality—
Is sown in weakness to be raised in power.
Peace, wailing harp!...
A little hence the harvest! waving fields
Of husky grain, and for each bitter want
Say thirty, sixty and a hundredfold.
...O sweet, sweet the drying
Of our tears shall be; and sweet the love
Of Him who saves us! Would that the End were even
Ready at the doors!

* * * *

October 1851.

My uncle was tall and wiry, over six feet indeed, with very slender limbs, long hands and feet. The first look of his face was that of an eagle, his nose large and fine. His forehead, if anything, was higher than my father's and with that same slight backward slope so often seen in men of poetic imaginative power. He was very absent-minded. My step-grandmother would tell how once as a small boy, when they were seated at table and a knock came at the front door, he was bidden go see who was there. He left the room and soon came back, seated himself at the table and said nothing. "Who was it, Johnnie?" asked his step-mother. "Oh, I forgot," he said; "I—I—knocked on the door—and—and I forgot!" He would not have been surprised, I imagine, if someone on the outside had opened the door to his knocking and led him away into fairyland. His hair was copper coloured, his eyes were blue, and he was much freckled. The lower part of his face was certainly too small in proportion, but though his upper lip was short, the curves of his mouth "gave an impression of sweetness and strength that robbed the disproportion of any suggestion of weakness."

I cannot help wondering whether the incident described in Robert Falconer of the lad's cutting his tethered kite adrift, and with it his boyhood, may not have occurred in my Uncle John's life rather than in my father's, as I have presumed, and that the deed gave rise to reflections responsible for the poem *Twenty-One*.[1]

I am convinced that a very true portrait of my Uncle John is given as Ian, one of the two brothers who dominate the story of *What's Mine's Mine*,[2] even if Ian more surely found himself than my uncle had time for in his short life. Certainly some of the astonishing adventures of Ian in Russia, whither John went in 1853, are based upon the latter's experiences, and certain references to him in my father's letters to their father after John's return to Manchester tally closely with some details given in the novel. One of his chief reasons for such remote travelling was the opportunity it would afford for learning Russian. He secured a post in a boys' school in Moscow kept by an Englishman. But in spite of his exceptional facility in acquiring languages, he was disappointed at the meagre opportunities for learning Russian. Everybody spoke either German or French, the former in preference. He acquired, however, a colloquial familiarity in those tongues with whose literature he was already intimate enough. He

---

1   "Away went the dragon, free, like a prodigal, to his ruin. And with the dragon, afar into the past, flew the childhood of Robert Falconer. He made one remorseful dart after the string as it swept out of the skylight, but it was gone beyond remeid. And never more, save in twilight dreams, did he lay hold on his childhood again." (*Robert Falconer*, vol. i, p. 306).

2   The noble sonnet given on page 94 of that book's second volume is, I strongly suspect, my Uncle John's. It is addressed to *Earth*.

was made much of at the British Embassy, and, through its hospitality, became more than friendly with a beautiful Russian lady of rank.

John MacDonald's letters to his father from Moscow are brilliant, particularly one describing peasant merrymaking in a village inn and a wolf-hunting expedition. It is reproduced bodily in *What's Mine's Mine*.[1]

One other incident in that novel is a fact. Certain of my uncle's friends, for some reason anxious about his safety, because, I gather, of his attachment to the lady mentioned, hastened his departure and booked his place in the *diligence*, in opposition to his wishes. There was misunderstanding at the last moment about his passport, owing to his imperfect Russian, and the police refused to let him go. That *diligence* was held up by robbers and every person on it butchered, except the driver, who feigned death. The crime may have been connected with the lady's relatives, as the novel[2] has it; or the inference may be pure fiction. But my uncle's narrow escape from death by assassins is fact. He got safely away from Moscow in June 1855, just after the assaults on the Malakoff by the French and on the Redan by ourselves had failed. One wonders if, after all, the attempt upon his life was political and not private. He remained a few weeks in Leipzig, whence he wrote home that he intended going to America; but he appeared in Manchester quite unexpectedly in the middle of August. The fame of his adventures must have got abroad, for he was invited by *Blackwood's Magazine* to contribute an article; but, what with his usual neglect of his own interests and his ingrain indolence, he would not do it. He confessed to my father that he was too much attached to the lady to give publicity to any part of the tragical adventure.

A wonderful intimacy of heart and brain certainly subsisted between these two brothers, and must have been greatly strengthened—if such were possible— when in 1858

---

1 Vol. i, p.233.   2 Vol. ii, p. 86.

my father and mother nursed my uncle at Hastings during his last illness.

Christmas of the year 1852 John spent at Arundel, and their talks must have been grand. In my father's darkest moods he never forgot the sunrise; but my uncle, to judge from the despondent note in almost everything he wrote, would be fearing lest, when at last the dawn should come, there might be no sunrise in it.

Little signs of this brother-love constantly scintillate from other faded letters. All of them poor, Alec with his £100 a year, John with his £50 and board, are rich compared with their older brother, the minister. Little sums pass between them—and indeed from them to their father—and all happily, as though money when in hand was so light a thing, though heavy enough when not to be got at. Clearly it was lack of money more than anything else that kept my grandfather from coming South to see Louisa and little Lily, as he was so constantly hopeful of doing "next summer." Such perfect understanding as these men's is perhaps found only on the rich soil of a mutual poverty. Both younger men crave for every scrap of George's verses; and John in his turn sends his own poetry—sonnets, odes and what not—to his big brother for advice and criticism. [1]

In 1852 Alec was attacked with blood-spitting. He was an extraordinarily lovable youth, three years my father's junior, with rich abilities, a curiously winning modesty and a notable facility in friendship. His verse-making was confined to humorous doggerel, though he read Wordsworth deeply. Without the intellectual power of George and John, he happily lacked the talents of his eldest brother Charles as well as his amazing facility in misusing them. He was

---

[1] In the novel are notable words about brother-love, even where there is no consanguinity. "Few men are capable of understanding the love of David and Jonathan, of Shakespeare to W. H., of Tennyson and Hallam...I am sure of this, that a man incapable of loving another man with hearty devotion, cannot be capable of loving a woman as a woman ought to be loved." (*What's Mine's Mine*, vol. ii, pp. 75 and 65.)

advancing rapidly in a mercantile house in Manchester. Unlike the other two, his religious convictions gave no anxiety to his father. Letters to my father from John and Alec illustrate those points as well as John's almost maternal tenderness over Alec's love-story; while another of the disappointed youth's to my mother, whom from the first he loved as a sister, seems to me quite beautiful. In style and directness it could not perhaps have been surpassed by either of his highly educated brothers.

John H. MacDonald to G.M.D.
MANCHESTER
Jan. 15, 1852.

MY DEAR GEORGE,
　　I should have written you ere now to congratulate you on the birth of your daughter...May every success attend the little stranger on her visit to this old crazy world. It is indeed passing wonderful...
　　And now I must say something to you about Alec. The lady to whom he is so fondly attached is a Miss R., the youngest daughter of a highly esteemed surgeon...She is a very sweet creature. It was not till the night of a soirée among the Sunday School children that he resolved to speak his mind. He walked home with her and made a manly declaration of his love, telling her plainly he had nothing to depend on but his own resources. He was received in the most gentle and ladylike manner, but was disappointed in hearing that she never had the remotest idea of his attachment...Altogether he was sympathized with in the most affectionate manner...Alec displayed a very fine spirit, expressed his thankfulness even in his sorrow for the way in which he had been treated, and, without giving way to any extravagance, sorrowed deeply and earnestly. The interview having been so short, he wrote a long letter to assure her that, so far from his thinking her behaviour harsh or unkind, he was most grateful for it, and that, although the trial was the deepest he had ever experienced, he believed it was a lesson from God and one of the most beautiful...To this letter he received a very kind reply, expressing great esteem and admiration for all she had ever known of his character, containing indeed no repetition of any refusal or discouragement, but at the same time giving no solid ground for further encouragement... Into a sensitive heart like hers such a confession as Alec made must sink deeply. But he does not seem to entertain much hope and he is very sad and looking ill, though perfectly quiet and patient.

It is sad to go into the dreary world of business again as if nothing had happened, with a young vision of the heart, which had grown up to be a life in the soul, lying cold and dead within, smitten even in its bloom and when its beauty and livingness were most refreshing.[1]

Do write him a long letter; I am sure you could give him comfort better than any one else...

In spite of his rejection, however, it would appear that the lady, beautiful, tender-hearted and deeply religious, soon accepted something of lover-like intimacy with her admirer; and he was very happy. But no engagement was entered upon. Presently we find him addressing a great temperance meeting in Manchester, his speech all carefully written beforehand and sent to his father; and we realize how much more a man of action he is than John, the contemplative, dreamy Celt, with his passionate love for beauty, his melancholy, his impersonal hopes. My father possessed beyond either the qualities of each, and both looked to him for what each most lacked himself. But Alec's happiness came only to be wiped out by his rapid disease of the lungs, for which he came to Arundel to be nursed in March of the same year. Probably it was in consequence of this that the girl's father prohibited all further intimacy: so I gather from Alec's letter to my mother written after his return to Huntly.

My uncle gained little from Arundel, perhaps because of its relaxing climate; and he was longing for home. So he went.

On August 9th he "hurt himself by rising from a bank with M. on his shoulders and walking with him some distance, 'Cockerty-huie!'" So wrote his father to George. This indiscretion was followed by more hæmorrhage, after which he rapidly lost ground. It must have been soon after this that the engagement, if such the intimacy amounted to, was

---

1 "Ah God! when Beauty passes from the door,
    Although she came not in, the house is bare:
    Shut, shut the door; there's nothing in the house!
    Why seems it always that she should be ours?
    A secret lies behind which Thou dost know."
                    ("A Hidden Life," *Poetical Works*, vol. i, p. 138.)

broken off; and he wrote this letter to my mother. The gravity of his illness he does not discuss: often in such cases, though the facts are fully realized, it seems impossible to speak of them.

Alec MacDonald to Mrs. G.M.D.
HUNTLY,
Oct. 31, 1852.

MY DEAR LOUISA,
    I think I have now received the last of a short series of her letters—the last. To me there have been connected with them many thoughts, many feelings, living anticipations of a bright future. But they are gone now. It is well. I am thankful I do not say this because I cannot help it, for I know it to be true. I did love H—R—. She was my first love. I told her so, and when she said she would love me because it made her happy, I was happy too. I did not question the reality of my feelings. I was too perfectly joyous. Nothing that has happened since has surprised me. It may have made me sad, but I was waiting for it, and now, it is well. While I sat by her and heard her say that we should be parted, for long perhaps, but that our not seeing each other should be the worst of that separation, I felt that I might hope for the future; and surely I did hope. But yesterday morning I laid it aside. I told her long ago that it was "better to have loved and lost than never to have loved at all." I can say so still. She tries to forget me now, and for her own sake I hope she will succeed. I do not blame her, she could not help it...I have no further claim. I cannot wish to forget her, but my hopes can fold their wings now, for it is winter, and for a time at least they must rest. My fears are dead....

    But it is pleasant still, dear Louisa, to think of how happy I was. It teaches me in part for what I was made...I was indeed strangely happy when I heard her speak of her love, when she said she knew she could never be more loved by anyone. I can remember those feelings and be thankful for them yet. I do not doubt the All-Goodness, my Father. He does all things well and in this too He has been kind.

    You were very very kind to me at Arundel. I have not forgotten it in the least, although I have said so little about it. Tell me about Lily—dear little creature! I think I should be able to carry her about a good deal now. I should like to hear her call me Uncle.

ALEC.

In passing I must not omit the consoling fact that on my father's visit to Manchester in that year, 1852, he had, at his brother's request, called on Miss H.R., and was able to report his happy impressions of her to Huntly. A warm letter of thanks from Alec tells of the pleasure this gave him.

In April of the following year, 1853, Alexander MacDonald died in his father's arms. His brother George had not seen him again; but my Uncle Charles saw him just before the end, and could not suppress his emotion. So the dying man must comfort the living, and with his old smile he said, "Never mind, Charles, man! This is nae the end o' it!"

Some may turn to the next letter again and again. Every time they read it, they will know better why George MacDonald's love for God made of him a mystic and poet and revealed Love at the heart of every living thing. Once one of us said to him: "It all seems too good to be true!" But he answered: "Nay, it is just so good it *must* be true!"

G.M.D. to his Father.

Arundel,
April 5, 1853.

My very dear Father,

I thank you gratefully for your last precious letter, which I shall not lose sight of as long as I live. It was very kind of you to write so much and so freely about my beloved brother, who is dearer to us all now than ever before. Of him we need never say he *was*; for what he was he is now—only expanded, enlarged and glorified. He needed no change, only development. Memory and anticipation are very closely allied. Around him they will both gather without very clear separation perhaps. He died in his earthly home and went to his heavenly.

Louisa will write to my mother herself. She is very grateful to her for sending the beautiful hair to her. He is more to be envied maybe than if it had been his wedding-cards. But for them that love God, no one is to be envied more than another; for all are clasped to the bosom of love and fed daily from the heart of the Father, whether here or in the other world—all one.

I too am thankful to dearest mother, not for the love and care she showed him, for of that it would be irreverent almost to speak—but that she would not let them hide his beautiful face with the hideous dress of that death which the vulgar mind delights in making as frightful as the power of ugliness can.¹ Let the body go beautiful to the grave—entire as the seed of a new body, which keeps the beauty of the old, and only parts with the weakness and imperfection. Surely God that clothes the fields now with the wild flowers risen fresh from their winter-graves, will keep Alec's beauty in His remembrance and not let a manifestation of Himself, as every human form is, so full of the true, simple, noble and pure, be forgotten.

Turning back to the other two brothers, the following letter tells of their great love and faith in each other:

John H. MacDonald to G.M.D.

[STONEGROVE], SHEFFIELD,
March 23, 1852.

MY DEAR BROTHER,

...We had all a holiday this afternoon, and the day being beautiful, Mr. Cecil² and I sat in an arbour looking down from an eminence upon the budding trees and read over all your poems with unutterable feelings. But, my dear brother, I do wish many more could be refreshed and strengthened in like manner. When do you think you can publish? ...As regards myself, I am seriously tempted now to give up writing and assume my legitimate attitude of listener and learner from others more gifted. You will make music to me whilst I fill the little humble sphere which God has appointed me. *I feel like one who is perpetually on the edge of vision but who is destined to be as perpetually snatched backwards by invisible hands.* I must wait awhile for wings and be content in the meantime with the glorious reports of the good land brought by souls stronger and more adventurous than mine. And I hope, too, to have courage to bear the fearful trial of groaning under a burden of unuttered thought...

This letter suggests the prevailing difference between the two brothers' poetry. George, if we may compare his blank verse with his songs and ballads, excelled, most critics agree, chiefly in the latter; John realizes the merits of rime only in the sedate sonnet, and appears never to have felt the urgency of joy to break and blossom into lyric. In him that

---

1   *Vide* sonnet "A.M.D.," *Works of Fancy and Imagination,* vol. ii, p. 188
2   Henry Cecil, a fellow-master with John MacDonald at the Sheffield Academy, became the latter's best friend. Each called the other "brother," and were united in work of some difficulty. Cecil held his friend to be a man of immense power and likely to prove of great influence in the world, sharing with him an unbounded admiration for my father's poetry. The latter, in his middle life, counted Henry Cecil among his warmest friends.

melancholy of youth, from which his elder brother suffered so much before he met Louisa Powell, grew upon him.

I shall close this account of the three brothers with a letter from my Uncle John, written after his return from Russia, to my father, then wintering in Algiers. He had secured the post of tutor in an old moated grange near Warrington and had leisure for much reading. The letter surely gives insight into a rarely philosophical imagination in this twenty-six-year-old man.

BARROW HALL, PENKETH,
WARRINGTON,
28 Feb., 1857.

MY DEAR BROTHER,

...I seem to myself at times like a curiously contrived machine exquisitely adjusted up to a certain point—where the Maker seems suddenly to have relaxed his efforts and given so hurried a finishing touch as to spoil it for going to all coming time. But I know this figure will not please you, who prefer to consider the mind itself as the creator and upholder of the organism.[1] This much, however, is now plain to me, that life can only be measured by a series of activities, and that for those who cannot realize existence at all except under some form of beauty and loftiness, life ceases when these activities do not tend to the production of these conceptions. And here I think is the true province of faith which assures us that these things do in fact exist, although we can only come temporarily in contact with them—yea, that nothing else can be truly said to BE at all, however it may possess a temporary and transitory existence, except what is great and worth living for. This assured conviction must be the faith of which Christ speaks when he will be in a man as a well of water springing up into everlasting life. As Goethe says:

> "Wer nie sein Brod mit Thränen ass
> Wer nie der kummervollen Nächte
> Auf seinem Bette weinend sass
> Er kennt euch nicht Ihr himmlischen Mächte."[2]

---

1 This recalls Spencer's *Ode to Beauty*, and the lines:
  "For of the soul the body form doth take
  For soul is form and doth the body make."

2 Some readers may like a translation:
  "Who never ate his bread with tears,
  Who never spent sorrowful nights
  Weeping on his bed,
  He knows you not, ye heavenly Powers!"

> I like Goethe because he rebukes my laziness and absurdities without ever losing hold of my sympathies...He is honest, and that is everything, wholehearted, *heroic*; and in most modern writers, except Carlyle, I think the deficiency lies there. There is an obvious effort to smother, harmonise and reconcile whatever is discrepant or calculated to arouse a difference of opinion—instead of wresting great thoughts out of unorganised heaps—and doing battle with the Devils and Phantoms and all the brood of Hell which consistently hinder our path into the light regions. I like what you say of Christ. I rejoice to think he was a man and fought *his* battle with the long-eared stupidity, subtle casuistry, and arrogant presumption—yes, and with brute force itself, the last of his antagonists, which nailed him finally to the cross...

A year later, viz. in 1858, my Uncle John also was attacked with hæmorrhage followed by rapidly advancing destruction of the lungs, and he died in July of that year.

One more word must be added, if only because George MacDonald's story, in spite of his many and desolating losses, is one of jubilant faith. In the three brothers we have instances of as many orders of belief. While George and John openly admitted the fact that their faith was *unprovable*, Alec, perhaps more simply romantic in his child-like acceptance of the Gospel-story, would not have allowed any intellectual conditioning of its credibility. John, the philosopher and dreamer, found his theorizing and his visioning as constantly in conflict as were the terror and beauty of the universe, or the sadness and aspirations of his own inner self. His honesty of mind so often overwhelmed his imagination that his faith never got beyond that of a great and uplifting hope. George, with stronger flame in his inner sanctuary, and so with less fear of mind, braggart of its integrity, overawing the spiritual instincts, honouring honest doubt in his brother and in all men, knew of truths outstripping ratiocination and evidence, and fought the fight that is won only by losing the life. Yet the anguish of John MacDonald's doubts were testimony to the faith he could not subscribe to: at times he might cry out that God had forsaken him, but he was always, if silently, commending his spirit into his Maker's hands. If Alec's unquestioning faith gave him sooner the freedom of the Kingdom; if John's was little more than a passionate hope; their brother's was at once childlike and critical, prophetic and triumphant.

CHAPTER V
THE HERESY HUNT

THE year of 1852 was already bringing criticisms of the minister's orthodoxy, and these were curiously coincident with the discovery that his residence, rented from the most influential of the deacons,[1] was not large enough for his needs. The fact may have had no bearing whatever upon subsequent events; but my mother strongly suspected it, as well as some members of the congregation. Anyhow, erroneous doctrine would be highly objectionable to a mind like this man's; and a mere suspicion of heresy with such respectable support as his would be very grave. There were, however, easier points than those of the Westminster Confession for the simple-hearted to discuss. The new minister's teaching with regard to Sabbath-keeping, although it involved nothing heretical, was suspect. For between the Scotch Sabbath and the Dissenters' Sunday in England there was little to choose. Another point of even less importance, one would think, made certain elderly ladies, as I heard from one of that very congregation, furiously indignant; for gossip had it that their pastor had expressed a hope that the lower animals too would be sharers in the better

---

1 In *David Elginbrod* (vol. iii, p. 106) my father introduces him in the person of a rich grocer, together with his wife and her absurd drawing-room. The hero, almost starving, is engaged to teach, at eighteen pence a lesson, their little son, who, on his first introduction to his tutor, boasts that he has five bags of gold in the Bank of England. My Aunt Angela, who shared so much in these Arundel experiences, told me this remark was actually made to the minister by the deacon's son.

life to come, and this although there was no Scripture warrant for such a hope.[1]

These early experiences of George MacDonald may seem to many strong argument against the Congregational system of Church government. But they must remember how an Anglican congregation sometimes dwindles almost to vanishing point because it is impossible to get rid of an undesirable incumbent. With the tendency of every half-educated authority to tyrannize over any scholarly person in its employ, such deacons are in danger of treating their minister as if he were "their servant instead of Christ's," as my father subsequently expressed it.

One day at the end of June 1852 the deacons formally waited upon the minister. Pretending, since he was contemplating a larger house, that his stipend was unnecessarily generous, they found herein apology for the subterfuge they had agreed to adopt. They came, he was assured, with the unpleasant duty of informing him it was no longer possible to pay him as much as £150 a year. It was hard enough to make both ends meet, but for him such a matter was in the hands of God.

"I am sorry enough to hear it," he replied; "but if it must be, why, I suppose we must contrive to live on less."

The answer surprised them: "O, but—er—we thought—" stammered out the minister's landlord, "—er—we thought you would take it—er—as a kindly hint, so to speak—"

"Of what?" asked George MacDonald.

"That your preaching is not acceptable, and that you should resign," was the reply.

Then it appeared that there were two charges against him. The first was a sermon he had preached from the text, "He that doeth my will shall know of the doctrine," in the course of which he had expressed his belief that some provision was made for the heathen after death.

---
[1] *Vide Paul Faber*, vol. ii, p. 90.

THE HERESY HUNT

The second was even more shocking, and probably originated in his *Songs of Novalis*: he was tainted with German Theology.

Though he accepted without demur the deacons' reduction of his stipend, which was within their rights,[1] he determined to submit the question of resignation to a meeting of the whole congregation by whom he had been called. Of the number that responded there is no record, unless the resolution, of which the official copy is before me, was passed at this meeting after the pastor had retired; in which case there were but twenty present. Such a small number suggests either that the active objectors were few, or that the majority had not the pluck to stand up to the deacons.

My father read a concise address, of which I have the draft copy in his own hand:

> It having been represented to me that a small party in the church has for some time been exceedingly dissatisfied with my preaching, it has become my duty to bring the matter before the assembled church. My first impulse was at once to resign, as the most agreeable mode for me to be delivered from the annoyance. On mentioning this to some of my friends in the church, the proposal was met with no opposition, although it drew forth expressions of sorrow, and the declaration of benefit derived from my labours. But from the advice of two of my friends engaged in the same work, and from the awakened perception in my own mind that, *as I came at the invitation of the whole church, it would be unfair to the other members of the church to resign unconditionally on account of the dissatisfaction of a few*, I resolved to put it in the following form: Will you, the Church, let me know whether you sympathize or not with the dissatisfaction of the few? Such a communication from you will let me know how to act: I put it thus from the feeling that this is my duty. With my own personal feelings I have nothing to do in this assembly. I retire and await your decision.

The official record of the ensuing proceedings runs as follows:

> At a Meeting of the Church of Christ assembling in Trinity Chapel, Arundel, held July 5th 1852 to consider a request from the Revd. G. MacDonald.

---

1 According to the chapel books, the stipend paid him for his final half-year was £56 16s.

Mr. New in the Chair.

1st. It was proposed and resolved unanimously to express their respect and esteem towards him as their Pastor.

2nd. In reference to the dissatisfaction expressed by some members of the Church,

We do not by any means sympathize with the statement which has been made that "there is nothing in his preaching." But we do sympathize with those who were dissatisfied with the statement from the pulpit "that with the Heathen the time of trial does not (in his, the Revd. G. MacDonald's opinion) cease at their death," which certainly implies a future state of probation. And this Church considers such a view is not in accordance with the Scriptures and quite differs with the sentiments held by the Ministers of the Independent Denomination.

It is by no means our wish that the Revd. G. MacDonald should relinquish the office of Pastor of this Church; such a course would cause much regret. But if on reflection he continues to hold and express such an opinion it is evident that it will cause serious difficulties in the Church.

These propositions were agreed to by about 20 members.

I do not doubt that my father refused to accept this resolution. His *call* had been signed by almost every member of the Church, and he could not take his dismissal from so small a minority. What his actual reply to the twenty was, I do not know. But it goes without saying that, so far from trimming, he strengthened the points that gave dissatisfaction; and he did not resign till a year later.

G.M.D. to his Father.

ARUNDEL,
July 27th, 1852.

...I have been very much occupied with some annoyance given me by some members of the church who are very unteachable. I thought it not unlikely at the time that I should have to leave...If God put the means at any time in my power, I mean to take another mode of helping men; and no longer stand in this position towards them, in which they regard you more as *their* servant than as Christ's...

Little Lily grows nicely—is a little fretful with her teeth. *Fat* you cannot call her—her largeness seems all of firm muscle—and a great child she is. I was absent more than last week, but when I returned, she had not forgotten me....

I suppose you are enjoying John's society very much. He is a most superior youth. I think he is decidedly the first of the family in talent and a great one amongst his generation, as time will show. I hope he will take no steps *whatever* about going to a dissenting college without letting me know. I hope he and his colleague Henry Cecil will come and see me at Christmas.[1]

I half expect a visit from Caleb Morris by and by. I have a great affection for that man. He is almost the only minister of standing whom I respect intellectually, morally and spiritually....

Naturally during these early years of married life there were not many occasions for correspondence between my parents, though it is fortunate, from such point of view, that the minister needed, for his health's sake, an occasional change. Thus we find him exchanging pulpits with ministers in Worthing, Chichester, or Brighton, more particularly with his great friend Mr. Ross of Brighton, who was going through similar troubles with his congregation and enduring worse libels. In the summer of 1852 he visited The Limes and in the autumn went to see his brother in Manchester. So I find letters of my mother covering these periods. Her humour was fine support for this troubled man, and his words in meeting her occasional self-reproaches are lavish in tenderness. She is critical of the "supplies" who take his place in the pulpit. Some were amazingly illiterate, and generally she would have to entertain them. Once, Baby Lily being just six months old, a Mr. Champion said grace at their dinner, beginning with: "O indulgent Parient!" and beseeching Him "that our *habsent* Pastor may be given *henergy* from on 'igh to preach the gospel, and all of us grace to perceive our sinful *herrors*!" My mother had spared herself his sermon, which, she was later informed, had twenty-five headings. But, it is only fair to add, all my mother's aversion vanished when the simple man told her of his troubles, his children's ill-health, his wife's coming confinement.

---

1 This intention was carried out. Mr. Cecil writes to my mother in the following March of "the agonizing regret" with which he thinks of Arundel, "yet with a warmth that would thaw me were I in Nova Zembla!"

She was particularly indignant against another substitute because in the course of his sermon he declared that no real benefit was to be looked for from religion until we got to heaven.

Again she writes a chatting letter about the maid's iniquitous flirtations, saying: "I cannot write better with Baby in my lap trying to choke herself with the sealing-wax..." It was a wonderful baby, though "her little white-speckled gum troubles her sorely, if I may judge from her little squeaks and most queer grimaces." In my mother's descriptions, here and elsewhere, of the child's emotions and tricks in expressing them, I see so plainly my eldest sister, as I remember her long after, full of pity for my boyish griefs and delinquencies, or sometimes indignant with me for some littleness in thought or conduct.

All the pastoral gossip must be told in the letters. Old Rogers comes in his smock with a gift of golden gooseberries from his garden, and has given to him the remains of the cold mutton, which, having cleaned it to the bone, he pockets, saying that "the missus will get summat out of he yet."

Little Mary Ann, whoever she may be, brings a present of home-brewed beer,

> "very strong and good for nursing." She was looking out of my bedroom window and exclaimed, "O what a beautiful garden!" Whereupon I gave her plenty of carnations and went into the garden to get her some jasmine, roses, &c., which delighted her immensely. She kept saying, "I shan't know what to do with myself if I have such a lot of flowers! Oh what will my mother say to such a beautiful nosegay!"

Then comes Mr. Bull. He called to tell her how sorry he was not to get his way at the meeting.

> He proposed a "resolution of attachment and affection" which was most warmly responded to, until someone referred to your sermon. I told him if such words (from the chapel) had come before, you would be feeling quite differently about your position.

THE HERESY HUNT

These letters show also how my mother determined to add to their curtailed income by taking into the family three or four little girls to educate, offering "a good English education, with music and the rudiments of French, Italian and German," for £60 a year. A prospectus was printed and an advertisement inserted in *The Patriot*. But I do not think any pupils came.

By what steps, by what annoyances, by what spiritual wickedness in high places, the resignation became at last inevitable, is not on record. But, although the love of many was unwavering, it was no longer possible for my father to remain, because of the dissension now at work. Chiefest of all the Christian blessings was peace, chiefest of all terrors was schism. He resigned in May 1853.

But the house was not left immediately, as my mother had to remain in Arundel with one or other of her sisters, Carrie or Angela—"George's secondary wife," my mother named her—till after the second addition to the family, which was expected during the summer. In July my father was to marry the Rev. J. H. Godwin to my Aunt Charlotte. But he dreaded the meeting with his future brother-in-law, disliking the inevitable clash of opinion with this friend. Just after he left Arundel for London and the happy event, a letter arrives which my mother forwards with the words, "Here is a stiff letter from Brother His Holiness!" It shows very clearly why my father found intercourse disconcerting with this affectionate, devout, yet at that time worldly-wise man.

Rev. J. H. Godwin to G.M.D.

...I may be wrong, but I do not think you have done that to ensure your success in the ministry which you would have seen to be requisite in another occupation. Sympathy with those you would influence, and the study of the works of those who have succeeded, appear to me the obvious conditions of success. He who will not, in things of chief moment, sympathize with the multitude, cannot reasonably expect to influence them. And he who cannot profit by the labours of those who have gone before him, must work at very great disadvantage. In looking over your books[1] I could see very few that appeared to me likely to be of much service to you, in respect of your chief work, etc.

Yet Mr. Godwin must have greatly respected this pupil of his before he could consent to be married by him. His eyes would perhaps have been opened wider by some letters of George MacDonald to his father in these days.

G.M.D. to his Father.

ARUNDEL,
April 29, 1853.

...But indeed my way of thinking and feeling would not help to make you more sad. I grow younger and happier...O I know a little now, and only a little, what Christ's deep sayings mean, about becoming like a child, about leaving all for him, about service, and truth and love. God is our loving, true, self-forgetting friend. All delight, all hope and beauty are in God. My dear and honoured father—if I might say so to you—will you think me presumptuous if I say?—leave the Epistles and ponder *The Gospel*—the story about Christ. Infinitely are the Epistles mistaken because the gospels are not understood and felt in the heart: because the readers of the Epistles too often possess nothing of that sympathy with Christ's thoughts and feelings and desires which moved and glorified the writers of the Epistles. The Epistles are very different from the Apostles' preaching; they are mostly written for a peculiar end and aim, and are not intended as expositions of the central truth...

God has provided for us very lovingly. Our salary is reduced—but not so much as we feared, and our sister's boarding with us has helped much to take us through...

ARUNDEL,
May 20, 1853.

...I am always finding out meaning which I did not see before, and which I now cannot see perfectly—for, of course, till my heart is like Christ's great heart, I cannot fully know what he meant. The great thing for understanding what he said is to have a living sense of the reality that a young man of poor birth appeared unexpectedly in the country of Judaea and uttered most unwelcome truths, setting at nought all the *respectabilities* of the time, and calling bad, bad, and good, good, in the face of all religious perversions and false honourings. The first thing

---

1   Eight pounds' worth of which had been bought of my father by his sister-in-law, Charlotte, when the break-up of the Arundel home was determined upon.

is to know Jesus as a man, and any theory about him that makes less of him as a man—with the foolish notion of exalting his divinity—I refuse at once. *Far rather would I be such a Unitarian as Dr. Channing than such a Christian as by far the greater number of those, that talk about his Divinity, are.* The former truly believes in Christ—believes in him far more than the so-called orthodox. You will find some thoughts of mine on this matter (though the Editor begged leave to omit the most important portion) in the *Christian Spectator* for May. They are in an article headed "Browning's Christmas Eve."[1] The life, thoughts, deeds, aims, beliefs of Jesus have to be fresh expounded every age, for all the depth of Eternity lies in them, and they have to be seen into more profoundly every new era of the world's spiritual history...

You must not be surprised if you hear that I am not what is called *getting on*. Time will show what use the Father will make of me. I desire to be His—entirely—so sure am I that therein lies all things. If less than this were my hope, I should die.

I expect to find a few whom I can help in Manchester. The few young who are here and not [adversely] influenced by their parents, the simple, honest and poor, are much attached to me—at least most of them—and that means but a very few. If I were in a large town I do not think I should yield to them and leave—but it is better for me to be driven away than to break up such ties as may be supposed to exist between a true pastor and true people for the sake of getting a larger salary...

WORTHING,
June 3, 1853.

...Mr. Godwin says I want a place with a number of young men. He says they can't understand me in Arundel; but I know that *some* of all

---

[1] There are many notable passages in this article, for instance: "As a mathematical theorem is to be proved only by the demonstration of that theorem itself, not by talking *about* it; so Christ must prove himself to the human soul through being beheld. The only proof of Christ's divinity is his humanity. Because his humanity is not comprehended, his divinity is doubted...There are thoughts and feelings that cannot be called up in the mind by any power of will or force of imagination; which, being spiritual, must arise in the soul when in its highest spiritual condition; when the mind, indeed, like a smooth lake, reflects only heavenly images..." "The life of a man here, if life it be, and not the vain image of what might be a life, is a continual attempt to find his place...to know where he is, and where he ought to be, and can be...The quest for this home-centre in the man who has faith, is calm and ceaseless; in the man whose faith is weak, it is stormy and intermittent. Unhappy is that man, of necessity, whose perceptions are keener than his faith is strong..." *Christian Spectator*, May 1853, p. 261. The article is signed "G.M.D." Reprinted in *Orts*, 1882.

classes *do* understand me, and I am happy not to be understood by those that do not understand...Some say I talk foolishness, others go away with their hearts burning within them. May God fashion me after *His* liking...

Whether I shall go at once to Manchester and preach wherever I have an opportunity, remains not yet decided. I should be glad to rest, and preach nowhere for a month...

I can hardly say I have any fear, and but very little anxiety about the future.[1] Does not Jesus say, Consider the lilies? We have only to do our work. If we could be forgotten, all Nature would go to wrack...Jesus lived a grand, simple life in poverty and love...His spirit is working in the earth—and in my heart too, I trust. But no man can speak the truth in a time of insincerity—like this and like most times—and tell people to their face that they cannot serve God and Mammon, without making foes...

How strange the dear old fields will look to me with the iron nerves run through it, which makes the dear, rugged North one body with the warm, rich, more indolent South![2] When I think of that noble brother of mine for whom the evening and the rest came so early in the day, it is oftenest as running with him through the long grass of that same field on a warm summer night, trying to catch the corn-scraich, till recalled by you and reprimanded for trampling down the grass. And the well, too! from which on hot noon-days I so often fetched you a jug of cold water when you came into the house hot and thirsty...On the next page to fill up I write a little hymn which I made for a dear friend of Louisa's and mine [Josephine Rutter] after her recovery from a very severe illness...[3]

Two more short letters belong here, and indeed are necessary to point the tender ministry to small as well as great needs, and the abundant gift of gaiety possessed by this lover of God, of father and brother, of friend in sickness, of insignificant bird in its burial; and how this all made for recreation of mind and heart when most needed. The letters refer to the marriage of Mr. Godwin with Miss Charlotte Powell.

---

1   "There are those who say that care for the morrow is what distinguishes the man from the beast; certainly it is one of the many things that distinguish the slave of Nature from the Child of God." (*Castle Warlock*, vol. ii, p. 132.)
2   The railway just opened cut through The Farm.
3   I do not give the verses, because a much improved version appears in the *Poetical Works* (vol. i, p. 296) under the name of "Hymn for a Sick Girl."

THE HERESY HUNT

G.M.D. to his Wife

[THE LIMES,
July 1853.]

...It is all over now and they are gone. Everything has gone very well—No drawback. We are going to the Forest where we went last time to tea. Lily has been *very good*...She looked so sweet in her pretty white dress and bonnet they got for her...She had a little champagne, a little raspberry ice and some grapes...

...I have been very idle with the girls all the morning; but we have been very happy for the day after the wedding. We romped a good deal at the Forest. I laughed very much, and was merry, and seemed to have clearer brains for it. I am sure it is good. I understand the Bible better for it, I think. It seemed to me there was one, more lady-like than anyone there, wanting. Is it my imagination that makes you seem so? ...Or is it a fact? I think perhaps you would be even more pleased with the former supposition than the latter. Carrie and I found a dead bird yesterday and we went out this morning and got a spade and went and buried it under a tree, and Carrie put roses over it before the earth. And when we had buried it, we found another lying close to the grave, which we buried too...Mr Godwin and I were very good friends. I wish he would say nothing more—we should get on so nicely—for I cannot help and do not wish to help loving him...

The second daughter was born on July 23, 1853, and named Mary Josephine.

BOOK IV
MANCHESTER

CHAPTER I
ALEXANDER JOHN SCOTT

NO greater change in environment, physical or social, intellectual or spiritual, can well be imagined than that from Arundel to Manchester. The beautiful, sleepy town of the South Downs, with its ill-educated society, its mental torpidity and a theology as comfortable to the vulgarly prosperous as it was cruel to a fearless thinker, was now done with, and in a city of ugliness, fierce competition and atmosphere black with its factory-scourings,[1] George MacDonald was to find sympathy and uplifting from the man he revered beyond any met since leaving home—Alexander John Scott, the first Principal of Owens College.[2]

Though my father upheld the Liberalism of Cobden and Bright, he was little of a politician. Nevertheless, the integrity of these Radicals induced a feeling that Manchester

---

1 "The cloud has fallen and filled with fold on fold
    The chimneyed city; and the smoke is caught,
    And spreads diluted in the cloud, and sinks,
    A black precipitate, on miry streets,
    And faces gray glide through the darkened fog.
    Slave engines utter again their ugly growl,
    And soon the iron bands and blocks of stone
    That prison them to their task, will strain and quiver
    Until the city tremble. The clamour of bells,
    Importunate, keeps calling pale-faced forms
    To gather and feed those Samsons' groaning strength
    With labour.
        ("A Manchester Poem," *Poetical Works*, vol. i, p. 422.)
2 Which my paternal grandfather, delighting to make fun of as typifying the new *progress* that brought ruin to the land, once wrote of as "the embryo university of the Cotton Lords," offering, however, to send "a cold shoulder of mutton for their opening soirée!"

stood for liberty, even if the freedom they fought for had scarcely higher aim than more money for the few, less slavery for the many. But Owens College was inspired by nobler ideals. The new principal was a chief among leaders; and it was he who, although offering no immediate encouragement or advice, attracted the penniless, discarded minister to the city of Fog and Freedom.

But before proceeding, I must tell something of A. J. Scott, who takes rank with Greville Matheson, John Ruskin and Frederick Denison Maurice as the choicest friends of my father. His name is now forgotten, mainly because he had little gift for writing. His spoken word was an uprush from living springs. My father always thought him the greatest intellect he had known. Men like Frederick Denison Maurice, Thomas Erskine of Linlathen, Dr. W. B. Carpenter, Archdeacon Hare, Thomas Carlyle, fully realized his phenomenal abilities. The last spoke of him as "a man whose rare merits the whole world might come to realize"; and the first wrote of him as one who was "unrivalled as a lecturer for the highest kind of eloquence, and for self-restraint in avoiding all useless and idle displays of it." Archdeacon Hare maintained there were "scarcely three men in England who have meditated so deeply on the great moral and political problems of his day; and assuredly there is none who would possess the same power of uttering his thoughts in clear, strong, convincing words."

On Scott's death in 1866, Ruskin, writing to my father, claimed to rank himself "among his lovers," and spoke of "the tranquillity of his faith." Maurice dedicated his *Mediaeval Philosophy* to him, and my father his *Robert Falconer*.

Prior to Professor Scott's election to his Chair at University College in 1848 he had been minister to the Presbyterian Church at Woolwich, where, till he went to Manchester, he remained, although found guilty of heresy by the Presbytery of Paisley and deprived of his licence to preach. This decree had been consequent upon his preaching for the Rev. J. MacLeod Campbell, who fell under like penalty for refusing assent to the doctrine that only the Elect are redeemed by Christ.[1]

In 1851, the year my father went to Arundel, Scott was appointed Principal of Owens College, holding there also the Chairs of Logic and Mental Philosophy and of English Literature. Whatever his subject, Vernacular Literature, the Middle Ages, Socialism, Church History, or Chartism and the Ballot-box (which he condemned as repulsive to every class of voter), he spoke always without notes, pouring out his immense learning in appeal to mind and heart such as few can ever have rivalled.

So it is small wonder that George MacDonald gravitated to Manchester in response to this compelling force. Both Scott—nearly twenty years my father's senior—and his wife proved the staunchest of friends in all my parents' troubles. Yet the rejected minister's going to Manchester, with no certainty of employment, must have looked to many like foolhardiness matched only by his failure at Arundel. Naturally he had but few offers from other Churches, for in the eyes of the orthodox his career had been short of creditable.

My mother's bright letters indicate her perfect agreement in his adventure, even though my father realized that, even should he get a pulpit, it would only be to find himself once more in an impossible position. The letters to my mother,

---

[1] An old disciple of Scott once wrote thus of him: "I attended all his lectures, and well do I remember those frequent times when he would suddenly turn half round in his chair, and drawing his gown over his knees and closing his eyes, would rhapsodize, so that one felt one's heart beating and brain whirring. Even now as I write I can hear that vibrating voice and see again the sunlit room, which was to me a very grove of Academe, though it only looked out upon St. John's Churchyard." (*Manchester Old and New*, by Wm. A. Shaw, M.A., Fellow of Owens College, p.98.)

In his earlier days, when the advisability of lowering the standard of Owens College to the level of a training school, in order to increase its popularity, was hotly debated, Scott stood so strongly for an even higher standard that Owens rather raised other teaching institutions to its own level than modified its own ideals.

she having to remain at Arundel through July, for family reasons already given, explain the situation. Already he had hopes of "raising a Church" of his own; for in that city—the economist's apology for wealth as over against Gospel-teaching—few ministers dared speak openly. Yet, money and luxury notwithstanding, Manchester people were generous and hospitable; while Owens College, with Scott as its Principal, evidenced the Cotton Lords' respect for learning and culture.

Of these letters space allows only one or two quotations. He calls on Professor Scott, tells him that his heterodoxy has driven him out of the Church, that he has no work, and would employ himself in tuition until the right work is found. "Mr. Scott came close to me," he writes, "to help and encourage me." These words throw a warm light upon this first meeting of the great thinker and the broken, keenly listening minister, frail in health, poor in purse and strong in spiritual freedom; and they suggest the immediate understanding of the two men, each so different in power of work and mode of expression, and yet one in the colour and courage of their faith. Of the religious (orthodox) society of Manchester my father writes that "they talk there of nothing but getting on," and then rejoices in being at last among such "great-hearted loving friends" as the Scotts and their far-reaching circle.

The story of the two and a half years' life in Manchester is one of unfailing hope and recurrent disappointment. But they held, too, some happy consolations—intimacy with men and women of rare excellence, a home once more, his own place of preaching, and, most notably, the instant success of his first book. *Within and Without* (1855) brought a succession of new friends, amongst them Lady Byron (the poet's widow), Thomas Erskine of Linlathen, that loving support to all who dared preach universal redemption, the Russell Gurneys, Frederick Denison Maurice, John Ruskin, and so, indirectly, a host of others.

But before this, many minor troubles and ominous disappointments were his. Thus Mr. Powell seems for a while to have been "a little less cordial." Possibly he was unconsciously influenced by the professionally successful Professor Godwin; possibly it was not more than regret in finding his brave Louisa and her two babies without a home; and certainly George MacDonald was not "getting on." Mr. and Mrs. Godwin had just returned from their honeymoon and were to visit The Limes. My father writes to my mother, when she went there after leaving Arundel, a little anxious as to what "our brother His Holiness"—my mother's nickname—might be chattering, though "my wife will not be afraid," he says; "and if she cannot avoid the subject, will speak as plainly as necessary to let him know that neither of us is to be blown about in any direction."

Again, his own father seems to have doubts and fears. With the debts of his long deceased brother Charles still weighing upon him, it is small wonder if at times he wished his sons were more like other men. Alec, so full of promise, was dead; John, the youngest, only just three-and-twenty, and the most brilliant, was constantly flying off at unreasonable tangents, and now proposed going to Moscow. Charles had made a humble marriage, and before long was to plunge his father in new money troubles. Finally, George, his favourite, whom he had not seen for four years, was utterly unsuccessful, beyond getting an incomparable wife and two bairns; and yet he was refusing the manna offered from above! But George MacDonald knew his father's heart too well to have any fear of lasting mistrust; his letters all reveal this. On the other hand his wife's close touch with her home would assuredly keep her father patient with the husband to whom she had entrusted her heart and soul, giving him in exchange so much of her own fortitude throughout his life.

CHAPTER II
THE WILDERNESS

GEORGE MACDONALD'S gift of imaginative eloquence, his power in appeal and passion of faith could have quickly made him the most popular preacher in Manchester, if, following Professor Godwin's counsels, he had given just such attention to success in the pulpit as other walks of life demand of ambitious men. Less worldly Christians than the kindly professor of Greek Exegesis have argued, in good conscience, the futility of giving people what they could not accept; and have urged that, by offering only what is within their present understanding, they may gradually be brought to higher and wider vision of truth. But George MacDonald knew it was never the prophets' way to entice change of heart by temporizing with eternity or qualifying the truth.

It is curious to note the position in which he stood towards the two greatest men he had ever known, namely his father and A. J. Scott: the one he loved best thought he might be presumptuous in the stand he was taking; and the other, whom he honoured intellectually beyond all, supported him by every means in his power. His defence to his father in the following letter is so direct and logical that we may be sure it brought content. A little earlier he had written to my mother concerning the entire distastefulness of all he heard in the chapels, and that he "almost hated" going to them, dreadful though it was to confess it; and no doubt he had been writing similarly to his father.

THE WILDERNESS

G.M.D. to his Father.

[*Undated.*]

I am sorry that you should feel any uneasiness about me and my position. It is unavoidable that the friends of any public man who cannot go with the tide, should be more or less anxious about him...But your faith in God, and the faith of individual good men in me, should quiet your fears. As to the congregational meetings and my absence from them, perhaps if you saw a little behind the scenes, you would care less for both. I will not go where I have not the slightest interest in going, and where my contempt would be excited to a degree very injurious to myself. Of course, when I disclaim all favour for their public assemblies, I do not deny individual goodness. I have no love for *any* sect of Christians as such—as little for independents as any. One thing is good about them—which is continually being violated—that is the Independency. And independent I mean to be, in the real sense of the word...There is a numerous, daily increasing party to whom the charge of heterodoxy is as great a recommendation, in the hope of finding something genuine, as orthodoxy is to the other, in the hope of finding the traditions of the elders sustained and enforced. For popular rumour surely you need not care—as if it *could* be true, and were not the greatest liar under the sun! And from all its lies God can keep his own. For my part I do not at all expect to become minister of any existing Church, but I hope to gather a few around me soon—and the love I have from the few richly repays me for the abuse of some and the neglect of the many.

But does not all history teach us that the forms in which truth has been taught, after being held heartily for a time, have by degrees come to be held merely traditionally and have died out and other forms arisen? which new forms have always been abused at first. *There never was Reformation but it came in a way people did not expect and was cried down and refused by the greater part of the generation amongst whom it began.* There are some in every age who can see the essential truth through the form, and hold by that, and who are not alarmed at a change; but others, and they the most by far, cannot see this, and think all is rejected by one who rejects the *form* of a truth which they count essential, while he sees that it teaches error as well as truth, and is less fitted for men now than it was at another period of history and stage of mental development.

But why be troubled because your son is not like other people? Perhaps it is *impossible* for him to be. Does not the spirit of God lead men and generations continually on to new truths? *And to be even actually more correct in creed with less love to God and less desire for truth, surely is* INFINITELY *less worthy! But if you believe in the spirit of God—why fear?* Paul, I think, could trust in God in these things and cared very little about orthodoxy, as it is now understood. "If in anything ye be otherwise minded, God shall reveal even this unto you" are words of his about the highest Christian condition. And Jesus said "If any man is willing to do the will of the Father he shall know of the doctrine." *Now real earnestness is scarcely to be attained in a high degree without doubts and inward questionings and certainly divine teachings*; and if you add to this the presumption that God must have more to reveal to every age, you will not be sorry that your son cannot go with the many...If there is to be advance, it must begin with a few, and it is *possible* (I cannot say more, nor does modesty forbid my saying this) I may be one of the few.

Increase of Truth will always in greater or less degree look like error at first. But to suffer in this cause is only to be like the Master; and even to be a martyr to a newer development of truth (which certainly I do not expect to be required of me) is infinitely nobler than *success* in the common use of the word...I believe there is much more religion in the world than ever, but it is not so much in the churches, or religious communities in proportion, as it was at one time. Your Huntly young men would not refuse me, however the be-titled and pompous doctors of the law would set me down—and better men than I—with the terms of "*German*" and "*new view*." If this seems like glorying, I will venture to take Paul's defence, of being compelled thereto! For if it be alleged against me that some condemn me, what have I to say but that others, and they to my mind far more estimable, justify and receive me? Your own Troup would be cast out by many. But I will not write more about it, sure that one day, either in this world or the next, my father and I will hold sweet sympathetic communion with each other about God and Jesus and the Truth.

A few young men in Manchester are wishing to meet together in some room, and have me for their minister. That is what I have wished from the first; and if they give what they can to support me, I will be content and try to make it up in other ways. But it does not seem very improbable that if I had a beginning once, I should by and by have a tolerable congregation. But may God keep me from trying to attract people...

Along with this I give one to my mother written soon after a little bronchitic attack he had had on arrival at Radnor Street where his brother Charles lived. He speaks of the general awakening among ministers to the larger faith and the consequent pastorless condition of many chapels. The leaven was at work.

THE WILDERNESS

G.M.D. to his Wife.

RADNOR STREET, MANCHESTER,
Sept. 7th, 1853.

...Here is a little hymn I made for you last night, to keep away other thoughts, and because I could not sleep....

Is it not nice that I have had so much employment lately?...There will be many vacant chapels in Manchester soon, but I have no chance of any of them. But if I could get begun, I should probably have a large congregation soon....

Thank you for your much precious love—the most precious thing I have; for I will not divide between the love of God directly to me and that which flows through you. Your love makes me strong....

A MOTHER'S HYMN.

My child is lying on my knees;
    The signs of Heaven she reads:
My face is all the Heaven she sees,
    Is all the Heaven she needs.

And she is well, yea bathed in bliss,
    If Heaven lies in my face;
Behind it all is tenderness
    And truthfulness and grace.

I mean her well so earnestly;
    Without a questioning,
'Twere little to let life go by
    To her a truth to bring.

I also am a child, and I
    Am ignorant and weak;
I gaze upon the starry sky
    And then I must not speak.

For all behind the starry sky,
    Behind the world so broad,
Behind men's hearts and souls doth lie
    The Infinite of God.

If I, so often full of doubt,
    So true to her can be,
Thou who dost see all round about,
    Art very true to me.

If I am low and sinful, bring
  More love where need is rife;
Thou knowest what an awful thing
  It is to be a Life.

Hast thou not wisdom to enwrap
  My waywardness around,
And hold me quietly on the lap
  Of love without a bound?

And so I sit in thy wide space
  My child upon my knee:
She looketh up into my face
  As I look up to Thee.

L. P. McD.,   G. McD.[1]
  September 7, 1853.

One point in my father's character is very clear: he had no intimacy with Fear. The foregoing letter to my grandfather shows this in its spiritual aspect; but his faith no less took the sting out of all physical terrors. We shall see at the close of these Manchester days with what equanimity he looked death in the face; and I remember how some twelve years later he visited a friend struck down with smallpox and so maniacal that no one else could control him. It was his personal embodiment of the sixth beatitude that made him not only fearless of spiritual and physical danger but regardless of any accusation of improvidence which Society, that "all-pervading, ill-odoured phantom," that "rag-stuffed idol," [2] could bring against him. To keep the mind serene in expectancy of death, to risk contagion of a horrible disease for Love's sake, to wait upon God for bread, is to leave all for the Truth: to consider first a piece of ground, or a five-yoke of oxen, or a wife as apologies for fear, was never his way. He knew he could fill at once any one of these pastorless chapels if it had been right to accept them.

---

1   This is reproduced in *Within and Without*, Part IV, Scene 4, with some improvements, one verse perhaps being less pleasing.
2   *Castle Warlock*, vol. iii, p. 314

THE WILDERNESS

But it was not. Though he could not see where food and clothing for wife and children were to come from, he would not even for them accept the stones in the wilderness as bread.

In the early days of September he applied for the advertised post of librarian to Owens College, at a salary of £100 a year.[1] He hoped it would prove a nucleus, to which he would be able to add, in one way or another; for the work would leave him free for what he most desired, viz. calling together a little Church.

G.M.D. to his Wife.

MANCHESTER,
Sept. 26, 1853.

...I have spent rather a sad morning in my own company. Purely physical sadness—if such a thing could be: as if all our ailments were not mental! But I mean it was the sadness, which, if I had been a woman, would have been relieved by tears, and, as I am a man, was bettered by a long walk through wind and sunshine, and green fields and cows. I came home better. I could know that all around me was peace, that it was well with all the world and with me; that God was at the heart of things; and yet I was one Unrest in the midst of the Rest. Well, it is God's business, and he will mend it. Oh, the great Fact of God shooting up into great heights of space, grand indisputable Reality! *God and I—I a creek into which ebbs and flows the infinite Sea!*...It is worth all suffering to be at length one with God; when my being shall be completed by having all the veils between it and the full consciousness of the Divine rent asunder—when it *will be flooded* with the central brightness. Here is a little sermon for you, dearest. Not untrue because a sermon—nor even untrue, because I feel I might feel it much more than I do: for surely it is my hope and the deep ground of all my looks into the future which shall become the present....

I am very pleased with your account of how Lily received Mary

---

[1] He sent in testimonials from various notabilities. I quote a few words from that of Thomas T. Lynch, who the year before had been delivering a course of lectures at the Royal Institute in Manchester, and who was one of my father's greatest admirers, though I do not think they often met: "...Your love of literature and familiarity with books, and not less your native courtesy and sympathy with all who are wishing at the same time to be free and wise, make the position one which you would find as congenial as you would be able, I feel convinced, to fill efficiently."

Anne [the nurse]. I love that deep, quiet way—I would rather have the blood eloquent on her face than the words on her tongue....It is a very good thing for us to be parted sometimes. It makes us think, both more truly about each other, and, [because] less interrupted, about our God....We must seek Him. We may, however, say to ourselves— "One day these souls of ours will blossom into the full sunshine;" when all that is desirable in the commonness of daily love, and all we long for of wonder and mystery and the look of Christmas-time will be joined in one, and we shall walk as in a wondrous dream yet with more sense of reality than our most waking joy now gives us. How is my Lily? And my sweet Blackbird? She laughs as the Blackbird sings.[1]

But the librarianship was given to another, and some friends were not altogether sorry. Then he caught a bad chill. Although tenderly nursed by Charles and Jane, his wife, he was sad enough: men of strongest mind become so quickly dependent upon the wives who love them for such weakness. "Dear, how sad that you should be so poorly and no wife to nurse you," writes my mother on September 29th. "I do not think I can bear it much longer for you to be living without me to help you when you are not well...."

The hope of hiring a room in the most densely populated part of Manchester in which to begin his preaching was foremost of all hopes, I think. What with his brother Charles, who *hoped* to contribute £20 a year, and his ardent friend, Arthur Morley Francis, an increasing number of earnest students from the College, and the strength of his message, which he knows will find the ears to hear, he is confident of success.

And now the furniture at Arundel was all packed by my Aunt Angela and sent by barge to London for storage in the Powell firm's warehouses. But there is a most terrible incident! Angela had to write of there being still £6 to pay for rent, though both my parents thought it was settled. The error is curious, as my father's money accounts were throughout his life conscientiously kept. However, the receipt of the landlady's solicitor for the sum in question,

---

[1] Mary Josephine had as child and woman the most beautiful bird like voice.

THE WILDERNESS

the final quarter's rent, dated November 28th, lies before me. Concerning this blow my father writes:

> I hope it will not trouble my sweet wife. It has done me a real good, I think; for even in poverty like ours, one is so much more ready to trust in what oneself has, than in what God had ready to give when needed.

The little family, on October 10th, left London on a visit to Mr. and Mrs. Alex Powell in Liverpool, settling down as best it might to conditions which, however generous the hospitality, were to my mother always irksome. In a letter she opens her heart on this point and upon matters of profounder interest, such as Lily's terrible cold, and Elfie's vaccination; and then she announces the Rev. F. W. Robertson's death at Brighton.

> He died, Mr. Griffith says, of a broken heart from what he has endured from persecution. He has been hunted to death for his liberality and goodness.[1] Is it not fearful to think of the *piety* of the churches? I am, my very dear Husband, heart and soul and life yours.
> P.S.—I would rather be with you on starvation diet than anywhere without you but with all the luxuries of creation.

George MacDonald joined his family at the Alex Powell's in December. He had then eight preachings at Newington. A few letters of this period give us fresh insight into his determination to take no pastoral work that would demand any temporizing with his convictions, and we learn of his first disappointment in publishing.

G.M.D. to his Wife.

Nov. 29, 1853.

...The change of feeling on many points of common belief spreads much among the ministers, although of course most can only follow in

---

[1] There appears to be good reason for the surmise that the virulence of religious cliques and the animus of absurd individuals found in this fearless champion an all too sensitive fighter. His very vehemence and passion against his detractors worked for his undoing. He died August 15, 1853.

the wake of the few. Cant is giving way to real thought and action—a true revival springing up in other quarters besides Arundel. But our great danger lies in acting or feeling as *a party*. I wish to be in a condition in which I can do my work for the Truth's sake, without any reference to others who oppose my teaching. *We ought never to wish to overcome because WE are the fighters, never feel* THAT IS MY TRUTH. *Every higher stage of Truth brings with it its own temptation like that in the Wilderness, and if one overcomes not in that, he overcomes not at all.* The struggle may be hard. I would I could be sure of the struggle, and then I should of the victory....Oh, dearest, whatever you may feel about our homeless condition at present, I hope it has helped to teach your husband some things....We may wait a little for a home here, for all the Universe is ours—and all time and the very thoughts of God himself....

G.M.D. to his Father.

ASHLEIGH, ANFIELD, LIVERPOOL,
Dec. 21, 1853.

...I am sorry to say—sorry because it will disappoint you—that my publisher [his name was Freeman] having accepted my poems on the testimony of others, now, on reading them himself, wishes to be clear of the engagement; which he certainly shall be. I am thankful to God for the pleasure the expected publication gave me, and so helped to keep my spirits up. Now I am able to let it go.

We are with Alex and Helen [Powell] now, but we long much for a home of our own. Much rather will we live in poverty than be longer dependent...It is a blessed thing for me that my wife does not pull one way and I another. Our children are well and consequently happy. We are going through the hard time now, without which never man was worth much in the world—I mean for its salvation. May He keep me from being a time-server....

But now, because the chapels on every hand were throwing out their free-thinking pastors, substituting time-servers and dullards, and losing their congregations, there came a big movement to counteract the danger, and several important people were interested in it. It was hoped by my Uncle Charles that his brother would be offered the leadership of this movement, though its more influential supporters maintained that some distinguished minister from London should be invited. But the scheme fell through—at any rate so far as George MacDonald was concerned— "wrecked by the rich man getting control," he says very positively. Nevertheless, the arrangements for securing a room for his preaching in the very heart of Manchester matured; and it was the poor men, who could scarce contribute to the minister's maintenance, who brought them to fruition.

CHAPTER III
A HOME AGAIN

THE visit of my mother and her two children in October 1853 to the Alex Powells, who, having a large house and no family, could easily accommodate them, lasted until after Christmas. But they then determined to make a home again, and my father, returning to Manchester before them, set about finding lodgings.

G.M.D. to his Wife.
MANCHESTER,
[*December.* 30, 1853.]

...It is rather a sad time for us to begin housekeeping (he wrote), for everything is very dear—coals themselves 20s. a ton, and war threatening. But it is all the same to God whether we begin with £10 or a thousand...I am very rich in my wife and children, but wish I could support them...

G.M.D. to his Wife.
Jan. 4, 1854.

...Thomas Pass has called to see me....I am delighted with the man. He is a carpenter by trade, a young handsome man. I made him tell me something of his history. He was so fond of Alec. He is a reader of Carlyle, and all good books, with a most open noble human heart. You will be very pleased with him. He says it is not true that the workmen are such infidels, but they have no confidence in the ministers.

...I am waiting for some account of my darling Lily's stormy birthday. Not for many years has there been such a day here....Surely, dearest, she comes up to all we could desire. I wonder whether you were allowed to give her the Clapton presents. I think it is not very

A HOME AGAIN

delicate not to give them to you at once; but never mind. Some are very fond of power in the most paltry shapes. But perhaps there may have been some good reason for it...Tell me the things that were given to Lily....

My grandfather MacDonald—in vague agreement, I think, with the notion that success in the world may be taken as indication of divine approbation—fears that his son, in refusing those means of respectable livelihood that ordinarily seem right, may be "presumptuous." He still fails to see that to his son's impassioned faith the doctrines and conventions of the comfortable pulpit are intolerable. Intellectually at least the position of father and son was becoming reversed. But I think the elder's admonishing is impelled rather by a sense of duty than real anxiety. Sometimes his lectures break down in a little laugh at himself or in a ridiculously funny illustration of his wordy advice, or in a reminder that he is "never given to *laudation* of his sons." His deep piety, his sense of accountableness to God for his sons and his occasional austere attitude towards them lest, rejoicing too much in the world, they forget God, remind one of his own mother. Now and again his tenderness breaks out in a word: in thanks for a poem, he says, "I like your little poem very much and so does your mother. I thank you, *laddie!*"

The following letter tackles the accusation of presumptuousness. The little family were once more united in lodgings, after spending a few days with the Scotts. Whatever the inconveniences, they were happy in one another, in their independence, and in their new, yet already dearest, friends as neighbours. Increasing engagements for preaching were at first the sole means of livelihood. That my father left no stone unturned—as if any stone might be covering sealed orders from his Chief—is proved by his now applying for the post of sub-librarian at the College, though in this also he was unsuccessful.

G.M.D. to his Father.

Manchester,
Feb. 6, 1854.

...I think if you saw everything in us you would not judge, even if you should think us mistaken, that we had acted presumptuously....All I meant to say was, that though you have good and just cause to be anxious about our proceedings, I *think* that you would be relieved, if you could see simply how we thought and acted. And all that has happened since has been of a kind to make us never think of regretting the step we took in coming here to lodgings....Pray to God to make me more humble and wise and earnest, and not self-seeking. Would you be so kind as to send us some meal now?

But having to preach in Birkenhead, he visited a Mr. Rawlins, in whose house he was laid up for three weeks by a severe attack of "congestion of the lungs" and a warning of hæmorrhage. The hospitality was unbounded, and my mother and little sisters were guests also. The patient was forbidden to preach for some weeks, and the blow was serious. Then Miss Ker, a sister of Mrs. A. J. Scott, lent them for his convalescence a farmhouse at Alderly, which she rented and had made very comfortable; and they proposed a visit to Huntly after that.

My mother's longing to meet her husband's parents grew stronger every year. At the same time a permanent home was becoming increasingly necessary, and certain plans in hand depended upon getting a secure foothold.

G.M.D. to his Father.

Alderly Cross, Alderly,
Cheshire,
March 17, 1854.

If you could have a panoramic vision of our changes of abode for the last six months, you would see that the last two residences, although both by far the most comfortable we have occupied, are very interestingly contrasted. We have left the town-residence of a rich manufacturer, with a carriage at our command almost, and are now since yesterday morning, resident in a large, low, stone-floored, four-doored room in a farmhouse

A HOME AGAIN

in the rich dairy country of Cheshire. We have this large room, called the *house-place*, and two large bedrooms over it. The room is not much more than seven feet in height with two large beams crossing the ceiling; and the old bookshelves and cupboards are fitted with excellent books in English, German and Italian. Over the fire is the only specimen of the kitchen crane I have seen since I left Scotland—only more complicated and perhaps more convenient than those at home. The country round is *very* beautiful….

Do not give yourselves any annoyance about accommodating us, else we shall hesitate about going….I assure you my wife is a better one to do without than I am; and I think I am very fair….But I know well what real comforts there are in my [old] home….One thing however, we must have—that is, a promise that you and mother will not leave your room. And for fare, Lou is more Scotch than I am, and devours pottage [porridge] and cakes like any native—so does Lily. So you see we are not dainty.

My book, *Within and Without*, is in the hands of an Edinburgh publisher, and I think he will publish it. He is strongly urged to do so by a sister of Sydney Smith into whose hands he put it for her opinion….

But the book was refused, and the doctor forbade the journey to Huntly so early in the year. Cold weather had always done my father noticeable harm, even when he was fairly well.

It looks as though disappointment met every plan and hope; but "we must not judge from one consequence where there are a thousand yet to follow," [1] he wrote in later years, when he could look back upon his life and find every incident providential—not one "almost a providence" as the saying has it.[2] And this disappointment was almost as grievous to my grandfather, who yet, once again for encouragement, could write jocularly about the cod-liver oil.[3] He had strong

---

1 *St. George and St. Michael* (1876), vol. ii, p. 256.
2 "I min' ance hearin' a man say, 'It's maist a providence!' I doobt wi' maist fowk, it's only at best, 'There's nearhan' bein' a God.'" (*Castle Warlock*, vol. iii, p. 320.)
3 "I have much faith in it," he writes, "far more than in some points of Homœopathy: for instance, that by swallowing *half a hailstone* a man dying of cold will be thrown into a profuse and healthy perspiration! This, however, I should say is a prescription of my own—not the less valuable, I hope, on that account, though I must say looking a little quackish!…"

hope, however, of coming South in the summer when they were settled in a home. But he never did so.

Such courage of man and wife—further exemplified in the next letter—was, I think, rare even then, but is certainly rarer in this day, when young people expect everything to be provided and done for them, whether by parents or society, by the world or the devil. I feel sure the venture upon house-keeping upon an assured income, for an uncertain period, of 10s. a week, was due to my mother's pluck. Her quick perception in affairs, no less than in matters of character and art, was seldom at fault, and she knew that, with their influential friends, she could add to the income by taking pupils to live with them. She was gifted and skilful in a social sense. She either instantly made friends, or set people aside for later decision; but, unlike my father, she did not scruple to make antagonists of any she knew to be insincere. Quickly enough she had found her place in Manchester's social doings: and wonderful doings they were in days when the second generation of mushroom cotton-lords were asserting their right to a sunny place in *Society*. My mother would tell us of bizarre entertainments, mostly of an afternoon. The display of expensive costumes with wide swooping crinolines and waspish waists was astonishing, not to mention the bare arms and bosoms, exhibiting as much ruddy area as the comparative modesty of that day would allow, and adorned with outrageous costly jewellery—and this by daylight! But the kindness shown was never patronizing like that so often of the better-born, whose condescension to herself my mother could ill bear, nor forgive it when offered to her husband.

In the late spring they took No. 3 Camp Terrace, Lower Broughton—"a nice house, large and in some respects handsome"—for £35 a year. Originally it had been £55, but its locality was not so fashionable as it had been. Arthur Morley Francis was to lodge with them, paying 10s. a week. Here my father intended to give lectures on English Literature, and sufficient encouragement was offered on all sides.

But (he wrote from the new home to his father on May 4, 1854) congratulations sound strange while we have no money. Mr. Powell has been very kind, but we have nothing to go upon....I was possessed by an angry evil thought yesterday and went out of the room to get rid of it. Coming upstairs to my study, the moon shone bright in the high heaven, and the conviction arose within me that God cared for his children. Did he really, I thought, put that shining thing up there to light up this round earth, and will he not minister to my wants?

Then follow words which to some will read as very significant:

....Everyone mostly who speaks to me, so Louisa and I remark, talks kindly—with a marked softness of manner, for which, if it means what I hope it does, I have reason to thank God.

My Aunt Angela now joined them once more for the furnishing of the home. She was never so happy as with them, for they understood her eccentricities better than most, as well as her hearty imaginative wit. We now find her on the floor stitching at carpets and curtains, with Arthur Morley Francis—once student with George MacDonald at Highbury—in attendance upon her. "Bees-wax and whitey-brown thread was my first love-present," she writes. And from that time onwards, until her sister's first son was born in January 1856, she remained on and off, "sister-help to Louisa, nurse and playmate to the children."

CHAPTER IV
THE PREACHING ROOM IN RENSHAW STREET

THE room of his own in which George MacDonald could preach freely was at last taken in Renshaw Street, in the heart of Manchester, and a few earnest disciples gathered round him. He had now fairly regular literary work for *The Christian Spectator*, and was feeling more secure, if only his health remained good. Following his brother Charles's example, he grew his beard, encouraged to such defiance of fashion by his doctor's opinion that it would be protective. His defence of it to his father involves greater matters however:

G.M.D. to his Father.

3 Camp Terrace,
Lower Broughton.

...My best thanks for your letters and for the cask of provisions...Give our love to dear Mother and thanks for the beef, which if it be only nearly as good as the last she sent us, we shall excessively devour. It is very kind of her to send it.

You send us good news, too, of John.[1] I wish he were near us now. Alec and he would be such a comfort to us. Charles is a true friend—but how strong we should be if we were all together! But we are all together in God; and that is enough....

You seem amused and somewhat indignant at my wearing my beard. Don't fancy it a foot long though, in place of an inch; and believe that I feel nearer to nature by doing so. Having been an advocate for it from my boyhood, I hope ere I die, when my hair is as grey or white as this

---
1 They were all anxious about my Uncle John. He was still in Russia, and on account of the war would have considerable difficulty in returning.

paper, and when no one for whose opinion I care a rush will dare to call me affected, to wear it all just as God meant it to be, and as men wore it before some fops began to imitate women...

In the next letter we find him almost exultant in happiness over the new opportunity for preaching.

G.M.D. to his Father.

3 Camp Terrace,
June 26, 1854.

...Louisa and I send our best thanks for your very kind gift. Indeed it goes into my heart to think you should be sending us this when I fear you are ill able to do without it. It is a precious gift to me, as coming from you especially, whom, but that I think God has chosen me for other work, I ought to be helping now. The only reward I wish you to have for it, is to know certainly at some time that in thus helping your son and his family, you have been helping one whom the Father has been teaching through suffering to help the rest of his children. [1]

Meantime I was never so happy all my life....Next Sunday evening I begin the realization of a long cherished wish—to have a place of my own to preach in where I should be unshackled in my teaching. This I now possess. May God be with me. No one can turn me out of this. It will be taken and the agreement signed in my name. If anyone does not like what I say, he can go away and welcome; but not all can turn me away. I call them together—not they me. A few friends contribute the rent of the place, and a box will be at the door for contributions of free will for me. We will have no odious ungodly seat-rents and distinctions between poor and rich. But you know comparatively little of this in your place....

3 Camp Terrace,
July 19, 1854.

Thank you for your kind letter containing the good news about John's safety. I suppose he could not now leave Russia if he would except by

---

1 In the all too short but delightful and tender essay, "George MacDonald: A Personal Note" (*From a Northern Window*, 1911), my brother Ronald asserts that our father, "in speaking of himself and his work, said nothing of mission nor of message." Yet the above letter comes near, I think, to the claim of such. "So simple and modest a character" would shrink from making it to any ears but those that could not accuse him of hypocrisy or egoism. "But"—I still quote my brother—"to carry once more the news which grows greater with age, to carry it with the freshness and new brilliance that come from the mouth of a new poet to his own and succeeding generations, was none the less the moving principle of his life."

stealth...I have preached three Sundays now, and am quite satisfied as far as I have gone. I want no hasty success. I want to do God's work and be God's servant. Who ever did this fully without more or less failing?—according to the world's idea of failure and success. The world's judgements are simply those of Peter when he opposed Jesus, and said "This be far from thee, Lord." No man ever failed, according to this judgement, as Jesus himself failed.

My principal temptation to desire success is that you should one day have the pleasure of seeing your son honoured before you die. In a small (and I may without ostentation, and quietly to you, say) select circle, you would find this the case already. Popularity I can hardly expect, for reasons which my friends could tell you better than I.

I am so pleased you like my writings [in *The Christian Spectator*]. Much of my taste for literature has come from you. It is not therefore wonderful that you should like my little sketches. You will find one in next month's, I believe—"The Broken Swords."

I don't know if I told you I am making 9.s. a week—that is by three lessons a week—during the College vacation....

Now, could you not come and see us this summer or autumn?—for I do not see how I can go Northwards—for lack of money and time too. We could receive you very well now—for we are quite settled. We expect another little child in September. Do not let this make you uneasy about us. In the story about the Schoolmaster you have just what I think about it.[1] God cannot forget his children.

The numbers attending the Sunday services in Renshaw Street were small and did not materially increase. They were mostly personal friends and intellectual. The working people do not seem to have been attracted, and some of the preacher's truest friends dared attend only occasionally. Among these the Miss Colemans, who kept a fashionable school, were nervous as to the propriety of going often. "How it would help us through the week!" one of them exclaims. But "though they are of the Maurice and Kingsley school," my mother writes to her sister Carrie, "their school is too dependent upon the Bishop's patronage!"

My father's time was now fully occupied. He was busy preparing his lectures for the winter. His contributions

---

1 The story had just appeared in *The Christian Spectator*, and was reprinted in *Adela Cathcart*; but as this is now out of print, it is not available. Nor is it of first importance.

to *The Christian Spectator* were becoming important to that magazine, whose increasing excellence he must have been in some measure responsible for. "The Broken Swords" is a model of how much the short story can do.[1] Concerning it he writes thus to Huntly:

> ...My object was principally to show that the most external manifestations of manhood are dependent on a right condition of heart; at least, it was only after, and by means of the most painful self-denial in the case of the girl, that the youth regained his moral and physical equilibrium. I quite agree with you that there are far worse things than any amount of war and bloodshed; but I am not politician enough to be able to apply my principles to the settling of the question of *this* war. It seems base to help the Turks instead of the Poles or Hungarians—one of whom is worth 100,000,000 of the other. But I am ignorant in these things....

My father corresponded with Dr. MacIntosh MacKay, now in Australia—whither he had followed those famished Highland emigrants for whom he had organized Lord MacDonald's bounty. However distressing his nephew's heresies, the old man must have honoured his refusal of success to follow his Master: he himself had done no less when a prime mover in the disruption of the Scottish Church. Anyhow, my father began to think seriously that the colonies might be more receptive of the simple Gospel than the old country; and this feeling, with the possibility of relief from the bronchial attacks and headaches that constantly nagged at his energies, might have changed the whole story of his life but for my mother's sea-sickness. Nevertheless, she bravely faced the Atlantic with him seventeen years later.

On September 16th a baby-girl arrived, "Somewhat to the disappointment of her mamma, who wished for a boy," the father writes to Huntly. "Not I, I like girls best....What a wonder it is—this miracle that happens every day and every hour! Only, the unusual strikes us more. God is *always* doing wonders."

---

1 The story was republished in *Works of Fancy and Imagination*, 10 vols., 1871; also in *The Portent and Other Stories*.

She was named Caroline Grace. Three days later he writes again to his father asking for the books his brother John had offered him, particularly the Goethe which the Stonegrove schoolboys had given their master. Also he would like his brother's prize book—*Compendium of Natural Science*—a request suggesting that he was already contemplating lectures on Physics. Then he speaks of going to London shortly to try and get more remunerative literary work—"and could mother spare me half a pound of fresh butter? I should like to taste it again—there is nothing like it here. Please don't think me greedy...."

The lectures in the new drawing-room were well attended, and had much to do with the founding of the Ladies' College in Manchester. He was one of its original lecturers, and, along with a course on English Literature, he presently undertook one on Physical Science.

I would give much to have some record of my father's lectures on Natural Philosophy and Chemistry. His delight in turning yet again into the paths of his Aberdeen days must have been great, for we remember the assurance to his father, amid theological doubts, that he could at least make a good chemist. His talks about the rigid Law of the atoms, their unascertainable minuteness yet indivisibility and unalterable ratios; the contrast of their fixed dimensions with the plastic dimensions of Life, which are always making for increase and freedom, and yet penalize any aberration from type; such thoughts coursing through his brain would have found choice words for their utterance. He knew enough of Swedenborg's teaching to feel the truth of *correspondences*, and would find innumerable instances of physical law tallying with metaphysical, of chemical affinities with spiritual affections; of crystallization with the formulation of purpose; of solution with patient waiting till the time for action was come; and so forth. "All deities reside in the human breast," said William Blake; and my father's master-mind had its integral subordinates: the philosopher sitting in the observatory of the brain, the priest in its oratory, the musician at its organ, the poet before its open window, the student in its library, the experimenter in its museum and laboratory, would all join mind to mind so that their learning would find single-souled utterance to claim God as the life, and Christ the type, of all incarnation, of all obedience, of all salvation from the Law's rigidity. My father's sense and understanding of ethical Evolution is implied throughout his writings, and must have discovered itself in quite early days long before he knew anything of the *Descent of Man* or the *Origin of Species*.

Of the many new friends he made, some won the right to a permanent place in his heart. To Dr. Harrison I give thanks for his ceaseless unpaid services, and am made happy in finding him among my father's disciples in Renshaw Street. Only a year later this good and wise doctor saved his life. Another lifelong friend, only a year my father's junior, was Henry Septimus Sutton, who early in these Manchester days came to sit at his feet. He published in Manchester his best known poem, *Rose's Diary*, in which his religious feeling radiates from simple-phrased yet imaginative lines: a book highly rated by his friend, F. T. Palgrave, and Dr. Martineau. Judging by the date of this volume's appearance and from a letter Sutton wrote my father when in Algiers in 1856, one sees that George MacDonald's teaching had something to do with the book's inspiration.[1]

Indeed, my father made many friends in Manchester, young men and women whose virility of mind and fearless

---

[1] *Quinquenergia: Proposals for a New Practial Theology*, 1854. Much of Sutton's verse reminds me of my father's, particularly of his *Diary of an Old Soul*; much of George Herbert's; for instance:

> "If my shut eyes should dare their lids to part,
> I know how they must quail beneath the blaze
> Of thy love's greatness. No: I dare not raise
> One prayer to look aloft, lest I should gaze
> On such forgiveness as would break my heart."

Sutton died in 1901.

outlook gave strength to his own hope and courage. Besides these he got intimacy through his lectures and the new College with many good friends whom he would not at first have chosen. An occasional visit to London gave him touch with old friends. We find him going with Miss Phœbe Powell on horseback for a sixteen-mile round of visits, calling upon Thomas Lynch, Garth Wilkinson, the Godwins, etc. He takes Carrie to the Crystal Palace, now removed from Hyde Park to Sydenham, and finds Mr. Powell in every way faithful and kind. At home the baby Caroline Grace and her mother are thriving, and in London the father reads his manuscript of *Within and Without* to audiences of Powells or Mathesons. On October 1st he goes with Greville Matheson to the Working Men's College for the inaugural address by Frederick Denison Maurice, who before long became one of his closest friends.

My parents were amply justified in their enterprise. It saw the Ladies' College fairly established, and George MacDonald, besides lecturing there on English Literature and Natural Philosophy, a little later held classes in mathematics. His lectures for the twelvemonth were calculated to bring him in £30, an amount that was gratifying. Still he was preaching in one place or another almost every Sunday, each occasion bringing him as honorarium at least a guinea. He was writing, too, in all his spare moments. For a man with the faculties of dreaming, as well as, he freely admitted, the Celtic liking for indolence, his industry was amazing; and it found outlet, when brain and pen were weary, in all manner of domestic services. In the early part of this year he had put the last touches to *Within and Without*. The labour he always gave to making his manuscripts as truth-transparent as might be, was a matter almost of religion.[1]

---

[1] A reminiscence of my own illustrates this feeling of his for finest craftsmanship. "Be sure," he said to me as a boy, when, tired over a little carpentering job, I had exclaimed, "O, that will have to do!" "be sure if you say that, it will not do; it mustn't be allowed to do!" And I hope I have never forgotten the reproof.

If sometimes his polishing seemed to hide the inherent strength, that is but the danger always waiting upon the conscientious craftsman. So much of the beauty and convincingness of my father's letters come out of the fact that in them he just lets his light shine before the one beloved man or woman without any subsequent trimming of wick or furbishing of the lanthorn's windows. They are just simple and direct as the heart would have them.

CHAPTER V
WITHIN AND WITHOUT

CHRISTMAS, 1854, was spent by the little family at The Limes, and my father left them there a few weeks for their own and the grandfather's pleasure while he resumed his teaching. The letters are now good reading indeed. They let us feel how inevitable it is that husband and wife united like these would, if they tried to spare one another the suffering of reading about their personal troubles, be in danger of weakening their mutually invigorating dependence. Yet they are heartrending too, especially if we, for whose ears they were not meant, forget how strong was their fortress. While my mother was still staying at The Limes, certain devoted women friends of hers and her husband's did what they could in looking after him: helping him in research-work at the public library and copying passages for his literature lectures,[1] especially from Sir Philip Sidney's *The Countess of Pembroke's Arcadia*; giving him dinner or tea at the College; and even invading No. 3 Camp Terrace and carrying off socks in need of darning. Now, although in her heart my mother was thankful to these ladies—really loved friends of her own—and tells him so in true simple words, she finds it hard to forgive them, and is even a little naughtily satirical about their worship! So loyal, moreover, is he—not from sense of duty, but just because he adores his wife always—that all such little services have to be told, just as

---
[1] Many of which he published in 1891 under the title of *A Cabinet of Gems*.

he refers to his headaches, his better or worse success with this or that lecture, his undertaking a class of arithmetic and mathematics at the College, the terrible coal-bill that must be paid, or the dirty, asthma-breeding fogs; and he makes a surprise visit to her—a seventeen-shilling excursion to London allowing this—though she knows of it only a few hours before. On the other hand, we hear of the children's sweetness and ailings, of her talks to them about Papa and his love for them and his trust in their good behaviour; of how Mr. Powell is reading *Within and Without*—doubtless the exquisitely penned MSS. that its author had copied for my mother—and how she found him with the volume in his hand and the tears streaming down his stern old face.

But the last word of this series of letters, thus reluctantly dismissed, must be given:

G.M.D. to his Wife.

...I was preaching last Sunday about forgiveness, and I felt that not to forgive was just to send one to the hell of our little universe. Not to be forgiven and taken in by any human heart is the worst mishap that can befall. May I be taught a lesson hard to learn. You do not need it so deeply as I do—you only break out in thunder and lightning! I have a cold smile deep in my heart like a moth-eaten hole, when I feel really wronged....[1]

Macmillan had refused to publish *Within and Without*, but in the next two letters we learn of a generous offer from Longmans, then the foremost of all publishing houses; and the author's spirits are running high. My mother had been compelled to prolong her absence and help nurse her sister Carrie who was very ill at Hastings.

G.M.D. to his Wife.

[Feb. 5, 1855.]

My poor dear child, what is to be done with you and all your sad household? I wish I were there to be nurse in general, and to you in particular, and Carrie too when I might....

Well, you will be glad to hear that at last I have found a publisher—the

---

[1] I profoundly question the introspective diagnosis!

great house of Longmans. But we *may* quarrel yet, so say nothing about it, except to Carrie, with my dear dear love, if she is able to hear it, and say she must get well and read her brother's first book....Mr. Scott thinks me very fortunate. Carlyle's first offer for the *French Revolution* was that he should pay £20 or something and have none of the profits. He finally agreed as I have done or rather will do...

On February 7th of the year 1855 Longmans signed the agreement.

In explanation of the next letter it must be stated that my father's sister Bella, then fourteen, had been stricken with lung disease, and he was therefore the more anxious to go home. My mother had hoped to persuade them to let the child come to Camp Terrace and attend the Ladies' College, but Manchester was now out of the question.

G.M.D. to his Father.

MANCHESTER,

Feb. 8th, 1855.

...I send back by this post to Messrs. Longmans of London the signed agreement between them and me for the publication of one of my poems. I have now got the right publishers and it is a very advantageous agreement for an unknown author....Next week I commence two courses of lectures—one for ladies in the morning, the others for anybody in the evening—both at my house. I hope they will bring me in enough to leave a possibility of visiting you in the summer. I can hardly go another year without seeing you....

Will you allow me to tell you one thing founded on the deepest conviction—that in Scotland especially, and indeed in all dissenting modes of teaching in England, a thousand times too much is said about faith....I *would never speak about faith, but speak about the Lord himself—* not theologically, as to the why and wherefore of his death—*but as he showed himself in his life on earth, full of grace, love, beauty, tenderness and truth. Then the needy heart cannot help hoping and trusting in him, and having faith, without ever thinking about faith. How a human heart with human feelings and necessities is ever to put confidence in the theological phantom which is commonly called Christ in our pulpits, I do not know. It is commonly a miserable representation of him who spent thirty-three years on our Earth, living himself into the hearts and souls of men, and thus manifesting God to them. Can anyone fear the wrath of God, who really believes that he is one with that only Saviour?*[1] If your suffering friend could but see in her fear how full of love God's heart is to her, by seeing his real nature expressed in the most tender-hearted helpful man that ever lived, while he would not yield one hair's breadth from the will of God, surely fear would go, and love would come.

I am pleased to hear the news about Margaret and Mr. Troup. They will make a very suitable couple, I think. Maggy has always been a favourite of mine; and for Troup I have a real esteem as you know....

I hope we shall have peace now—but who can tell? Any more word from John?...

On May 18, 1855, *Within and Without* appeared, and the publishers did all in their power to give it the chance it deserved. The reception of the new writer was remarkable. Before long the reviews were so enthusiastic that it was determined to advertise it largely with extracts from the Press; though, seeing that some inevitably were foolish, some cynical, and some even spiteful, the author thought the unfavourable ones should be given the same publicity as the eulogistic—an opinion that did not tally with the publishers'. *The Scotsman*, then perhaps the most literary of the newspapers, thus spoke of it:

> This strange and original drama is full of the most exquisite poetry sustained at the pitch of sublimity with immense yet apparently effortless power....A very remarkable production of intellect and heart united as perhaps they seldom have been before....

But *Within and Without*, with so much of its author's life-story before us, assumes new importance. We have seen some of the inner strife of his soul; have been given hints of the way in which his love for God and his love for the woman he adored were brought into harmony. We have felt something of the suffering both must endure until the revelation came that the perfect love of man and woman is but offshoot of that love for God which bids them leave all lower ties to follow Him; that in thus following Him their own love becomes perfect.

---

[1] The italics are again my own.

With such reminders before us, remembering too that pearl among all the lyrical gems of this book, *Love me, Beloved*, his wedding-gift to his bride,[1] we may know that the drama touches the deeps of its writer's faith.

Hence it will be apparent to some who see human love as offshoot of the Divine, that *Within and Without* just *had* to be written. For it brought direct from God to my father a message which he must give to my mother also—hardly less direct from God for that. For my mother's earlier trouble was simply this: seeing this man of her own heart so much absorbed in adoration of Him—and those letters of his which she has denied us sight of must have constantly revealed this to her—she felt that his love for her fell short of what it might have been, had she been gifted as some other women were. The divine Fatherhood had been revealed to her when her whole soul was swept into her love of this man; was it not greater than his who gave the first-fruits of his love to God? He was all Heaven and Earth to her; she, she feared, but a possible earthly-paradise to him. If the poem is actually pertinent to my parents' rarely troubled courtship, it suggests very plainly that my father had long since discovered this truth—that in bringing the firstfruits to his wife he was still rendering to God the things that were God's.

Thanks to the courtesy of Mr. C. J. Longman, of Messrs. Longmans, Green & Co., I am able to give an abridged analysis of *Within and Without* made by its author for use in that firm's "Notes on Books" which they issued quarterly.

Within and Without: A Dramatic Poem. By George MacDonald. Crown 8vo, pp. 188, price 7s. 6d. Cloth. May 18, 1855.

This poem is an attempt to represent the history of a man who, *apparently* disappointed in all his secondary aims and hopes, attains, partly through means of these disappointments, to the freedom of faith;

---

[1] It was with some real touch of heart-break that my mother, so she has told me, consented to its publication: yet she has thereby given to the world a privilege that a few, if not a many, will always bless her for.

and finds that in gaining this he has gained everything, in a higher form, too, than he had ever anticipated....But the real cause for his disappointment is, that he has been seeking the knowledge of God by aspiration and abstraction alone, instead of seeking it in active life. He escapes from the monastery, finds a long-lost lady still true to him, rescues her from danger, and escapes with her to England. Here the greatest trial commences. From the different mental conditions of his wife and himself a gulf gradually opens between them. She cannot sympathise with his absorbing hunger for individual communication with the source of life; and he is too engrossed to minister his share of the beautiful to a nature that can only exist on the favour of the world. But each loves the other, and both love their child, who is more of a companion to them individually than they are to each other. At length an Englishman makes his appearance. The husband thinks his wife unfaithful; and in his conduct to her appears the result which the increasing knowledge of the divine humanity of Jesus exercises upon him. Then comes the final deliverance. He who had been seeking good for the sake of personal perfection to a degree that interfered entirely with what he owed to her who was nearest to him, comes to feel the baseness of even such lofty selfishness as this, and abjures it and himself with it; confesses that less than all was too little to cast at the feet of his wife, in whom God was present in his eyes. Then he has leave to die, and...finds the realisation of all the hopes which he had cherished in his former state. To the wife her temptation is such a spiritual awakening that ere long she joins her husband and child, having learned to love not the Beautiful alone, but the True in the Beautiful.

The abstract gives but a poor idea of the work's originality. If some do not care for its poetical metaphysics, they will admit its lyrical beauty and power. In the latter its author had discovered his higher art.

The appearance of the book put husband and wife in good heart. The vacation was at hand, and the author was greatly in need of a holiday. My father again made plans for taking my mother to Huntly. But money was very scarce, and no arrangement could be made by which the children could be left. Arthur Francis was still living with them, and even if relations between that gentleman and Mr. Powell had not been a little strained, my Aunt Angela could not have taken charge. In June worse news of Bella came from The Farm, and my mother insisted that my father must go without her. Moreover, Robert Troup and Margaret MacDonald were anxious for him to marry them.

My mother's constant vigilance over my father in his sickness and pleasure, his bodily and spiritual needs, is a very notable point in my parents' life. Always as keen and instant, whatever her own ailing or weariness of heart, it becomes more and more needed. Particularly in the American experiences in 1873, and in the means she devised later to secure his wintering always in Italy, may we realize its indefatigable zeal. If such devotion be quite ordinary, it is not therefore less sublime.

G.M.D. to his Father.
MANCHESTER,
June 3rd, 1855.

Thank you for letting me know about dear Bella....How does dear mother bear it? It must be a dreadful trial to her, but no trial is too sad which makes us look more to the eternal love—the great sea on which all other loves are but the surface waves. None of us will live very long here, and then we shall go into the great unknown wondrous world, which so many of our dear friends know already, and where they are quietly waiting our arrival....

On July 1st my father left Manchester for Huntly. On the following day my mother writes him all the news and much else of more import.

Mrs. G.M.D. to her Husband.
CAMP TERRACE,
July 2nd, 1855.

...Here I am in the denuded drawing-room, and here you are not. And I delight in the thought that you are so far on your road to home and your father. If it is such an evening as this in Edinburgh you will enjoy a night's sojourn in that princely city, though you be ever so tired—which you certainly will be by this time, half-past seven. I wonder how the hard-boiled eggs fared? Were you very weary? Such lots of little questions I should ask were I at your side—where I enjoyed being so much this tearful morning. Oh, how the whole world cried as I walked home! So I thought I would try and look for the bright pieces of this "mysterious dispensation." I could not find any bright, but I saw the calm and felt content, only anxious for fear I should not do all and become all that seemed pointed out to me.

We have all been very busy clearing out, folding up, locking up, shaking carpets and curtains, putting away and effecting clearances by wholesale....What nonsense I am writing! When I have paid Woodhouse, Butcher and Milk I shall have £1 something left.

What would I not have given to have seen the beautiful Father meet the lovely Son! How happy and how sad you are by this time....Mrs. Andrew says that, as everyone has to eat a peck of dirt, so she believes everyone has got to get through a peck of disagreeables in life; and she thinks our peck must be nearly out....I am so anxiously waiting for your first letter, and still more for the first from Huntly. I wonder what your impression is of the dear invalid? I suppose you would scarcely have known her. But you will, I know, love, tell me all you can. Oh, this is my happiness—to know that you love me so truly in spite of my plainness and *ignorance* and temper. God help me! May I send my love to your loves?...

CHAPTER VI
THE PAINTED TABLE

THIS visit to Huntly, the first since George MacDonald married, was full of sadness because his sister was dying; but it was no less full of a joy that sorrow could hardly darken. The letters thence to my mother are clear in descriptive touch, shining in portraiture, tender in solicitude for her joining him. Many are pencilled on odd scraps of paper, here and there torn or illegible, and but few have their dates. Yet their interest is hardly dependent upon the narrative of my mother's corresponding letters.

Sensible of his wife's suffering on parting from him, the traveller homewards from his home, pencils her a letter at the first opportunity. It was his first visit to Edinburgh.

G.M.D. to his Wife.

EDINBURGH,
Monday night 11 *o'clock,*
[*July 2nd,* 1855].

It has been a long day since I saw the last of your eyes at the station. The rain cleared off when half our journey was over. I lay down and slept. I hardly remember anything, but I wish you had seen a sweet-looking Scotch woman with whom I fell in love—a country woman between 40 and 50—oh, so sweet and simple! G.—S.—is with me still; and we have been wandering about till 11 almost—chiefly through the old town— which has *all* the attraction for me. We went on to Calton Hill and from there into the old Canongate, at the end of which stands Holyrood House, the outside of which I contemplated for some time, especially the *storm- windows*, as in Scotland we call the projecting windows on the roof....I don't care about Queen Mary though. She was too naughty to love—and Holyrood House is hardly as interesting to me as it is to most Scotchmen for *her* sake. But the Canongate and the Cowgate! oh such houses! oh filth! and misery! and smells! and winding common stairs! and *grated* unglazed windows on all the landings! And squalid figures looking down from two, three, four, five, six, seven stories! (Some houses we counted ten stories at the back, and there are others of two, or three, or four more!) Such curious houses they are, with crowded gables to the streets, and every few paces a narrow court running between to more and more mysteries of stairs and lofts—crowded, abominable dwellings. Some of the dark *closes* and entries look most infernal, and in the dim light you could see something swarming, children or grown people perhaps, almost falling away from the outlined definiteness of the human. It was more like some of the older parts of Aberdeen than anything else I had seen, but worse, much worse. Dearest, you must come here with me, you would be so interested. It is like no other place. To think of it after our orderly *clean* commonplace well-behaved Manchester, it is hardly credible! And yet I saw nothing wrong—though much that would be wrong when I could not see it. You know Edinburgh is built very much up and down hill; and so in some parts narrow closes, some so narrow that your little arms could touch both sides, run from top to bottom of the hill through these great, tall houses. Glancing down one of these I was arrested. It was very narrow, and went down, as if to Erebus, and suggested bad and dangerous places, down into the unseen and unknown depths. But across the upper part was barred the liquid hues of the sunset, against which stood the far off hill with some church tower or something of the sort in relief against the infinite clearness. It is twelve—and I am going to bed. Dearest, I hope you will not be frightened to-night. God, the Sky God— the Green Earth God be with you; *our own God*, as David says. I don't go till 10 ½ to-morrow morning. Kisses to my brood....

He arrived too late at Aberdeen and missed the connection for Huntly, so he spent the evening visiting old friends. But in the train from Aberdeen to Huntly—instead of by coach as hitherto—he writes on odd scraps of paper:

G.M.D. to his Wife.
[July 4th, 1855.]

I am seated alone, a few miles on my way to Huntly. I have passed in the distance the stone crown which tops the square tower of my old college, and the pagoda-looking towers of the old cathedral—and beyond lies the sea. ...When I get nearer home I shall want to be looking out, and not to write. It would be pleasant to point out to you the old places where your husband wandered and grew, and partly became the man you love now, notwithstanding his faults—which I hope will always be growing less....

I shall feel something like the Ancient Mariner. "Is this the kirk? Is this the mill? Is this my own countree?" A girls' school is crowding into the carriages—not mine; and a country girl has flashed a look of you on me, darling, and it makes my two weary eyes rather dim when I write about it to you. We are passing through a bleak country now. Now we are at the town of Inverury, 20 miles from home by the old road—how far by this I don't know. The country folks stare rather at me, and the louts laugh—my red cap[1] and hairy face afford them amusement. It is a beautiful bright morning with a pale blue sky, and white clouds sleeping in light, and a triumphant God-like sun....I seem to see better in this clear air and plentifulness of light than I have seen for a long time. I hardly wish to put my spectacles on...

                            The Farm, Huntly.
                                       [*July 4th*].

Dearest, I am sitting on grass with water bubbling on both sides of me. We have all met and I am loved to my heart's content. My father is not much changed, only stouter, and fuller in the face. My mother is very dear....My sisters met me at the station, and now as I sit here they are ministering to me with wild roses and wild peppermint beloved, like two fairies. They are sweet dear things. Bella and I both cried. She is so thin, I should not have known her. Mother was very pleased about the cakes, but Bella has not tasted them yet. When I put your letter in my pocket my father quoted that line about not reading dear words with others near. [2] Uncle and Aunt and cousins are all so loving....

There are two letters awaiting him, one from his wife, already quoted. The second says: "We are, during the holidays, like gardeners *frozed out* till the thaw comes." But it enshrines tenderest words of her love, and tells my father of an appreciative review of *Within and Without* in the

---

1 A tasselled red smoking-cap he travelled in.
2 "Julian (feebly), 'A letter from my Lilia! Bury it with me—I'll read it in my chamber, by and by; dear words should not be read with others nigh.'" *Within and Without*, Part IV, close of Scene XXV.

That a line of so little note could be quoted by my grandfather is evidence of his intimate acquaintance with his son's writing and of his own fine memory. The trifling words must have given my father much happiness.

Globe and an "insulting one" in the *Leader*, which yet Dr. Harrison had brought her for her pleasure! The least adverse criticism of her husband's work would always blind my mother's indignant heart for the moment to any praises, however apt and generous. So, sometimes, would she misunderstand her friends, though always wanting to be fair, always ready to admit her own errors.

My father's letters must have been milk and honey coming to that dull street with its heart-rending cares. *À propos* of which, a certain Painted Table, to which ensuing letters refer, must be here mentioned because it gives picturesque and poignant glimpses into the poverty of 3 Camp Terrace. It was a circular slab of slate ruled for chess, which my mother was painting to imitate inlaid squares of marble of great variety in colour and markings. She was doing it for her brother Alexander, who was to pay her £5 for it. The possibility of joining my father in Scotland depended mainly upon its completion. She was too proud to ask payment before it was done. But soon, what with the unlikelihood of getting it finished amidst all the household difficulties, the table became a great disappointment. Indeed, it was not completed until after my father's return.[1]

G.M.D. to his Wife.

Huntly,
July 5th, 1855.

....I have brought out a table and chair from the house and am sitting under the overhanging boughs of a small tree which was just planted when I visited home last. It is evening, and the birds are singing, and this afternoon I have been walking through one of the fields with my father, so full of the flowers of which I send you some; and down in the nursery lies my poor thin sister, very quiet—or rather sits, for she sits in bed with her knees up and

---

1 As a matter of fact, though duly sent to my uncle, Alexander Powell, it was first unpacked by myself just fifty years later. It was a wonderful work of ingenuity and beauty. But on exposure the paint crumbled off in a very few days. Only the bare slate remains, and it serves now for a garden table.

her head leaning upon them—so thin is she!...She lies like a seed waiting for the Summer to which this Summer is but a Winter. My father is so kind and liberal—more so even than I had expected: he has no objection at all to my moustache, though he would like it off to make me more acceptable; but he does not seem to care much....He enjoys Browning so. I have been reading several, amongst them—*The Spanish Monk*. He seems so to enter into the dramatic, and sees no reason why I should not read it to anybody.

Dear love, I can hardly bear your not being here....It comes so often when I see beautiful things. There is not *much beauty* here, but much to my heart: and there would be to yours, and you would love my home, with its rough stones nearly covered with ivy. Here comes Louie hauling a great mat from the lobby, which she has now put under my feet, lest the grass should be damp.

How do you sleep, dearest? Have you been frightened at night? Why have I not a letter from you? Here are some flowers we picked from the field. The forget-me-nots are from Louie and Jeannie to you, and the roses are from the same for Lily, with love to you both.[1] ....I must write a story here. I am looking for one somewhere in my brain. I will pray to God to let you come if it pleases Him; and then perhaps you will....How you and my mother would love each other! Get as much of the table done as you can without hurting yourself—and then perhaps we can somehow get you here.

I think Bella is a trifle better to-day, but she has not been up since I came. She does not suffer much. It is touching the interest with which she shows me little trifles of gifts and thinks so much of them, the darling!—do send the handkerchief.

Mrs. G.M.D. to her Husband.

CAMP TERRACE,
July 8, 1855.

I was very sorry not to write to you yesterday, dearest George, because I was reckoning of[2] doing so all day and it seemed the only very pleasant duty I have to live for. I had a great deal to tell you too....

I hope the showers of rain that your letters bring daily will do me good and humble me. I hardly know how to read them for sorrow that I was not worthy to be allowed, i.e. by Divine Providence, to share such sweet joys with you. Then I felt Mr. F....'s unkind letter very much, but I should not put that

---

1 The wild roses and harebells particularly are there finer than any we get in the South.
2 It is pleasant to find my mother unconsciously adopting my father's Scotticisms.

beside my weeping for my want of worthiness to be your wife....Mrs. Andrew is very sweet and quite tender. I breakfasted there this morning. I am up at 7 every morning now and dress the children myself....

Then my father had to learn that the children were ailing sadly. The intolerably insolent little nursemaid had broken their carriage so entirely beyond repair that a new one must be bought, otherwise the two youngest would get no fresh air. But it cost 24s. and proved very heavy for the mother to push, especially when the little ones were so troublesome at night that she got but little sleep herself. She tells of an invitation for herself and the children to spend a week or two with her sister Flora, Mrs. Joshua Sing, in Liverpool; "but," she adds, "the expense will be greater than to stay here. Besides I cannot begin painting The Table till I come back...."

With this she encloses a letter from Charles Kingsley in appreciation of *Within and Without*. Indeed, one of my mother's solaces was the fairly constant receipt of highly gratifying reviews.

To understand my mother's determination that my father should have perfect rest and recreation now that it was vacation, one must remember how his irrepressible intellectual energy was always in conflict with his frail health. She knew how much to him was opportunity for dreaming, and that it could seldom come to him through the rain and fog of a great city, however dear its fireside and friendships. Huntly, his home and cradle, must ever be to him the land of dreams; and she was Celt enough to realize that his genius must hunger and thirst for its inspirations. One who remembered him on that visit to his home spoke of "the tall, delicate, kindly-eyed, Glengarry-bonneted man taking his walks by the castle, or his rides among the heather and dark topaz streams of his native hills." The man was offspring of that boy who would lie on the sofa or on the horse's back for hours reading when others were at play, or who none the less would be first and most furious in their "ploys" or protagonist in a Juvenile Temperance Society.

G.M.D. to his Wife.

Friday afternoon, HUNTLY,
[*July 8th*, 1855].

I wish you were here. My father and mother are so kind....My beard is safe, I think! I talk Scotch to all the people, and one old school-fellow tells me that will get me over the effect of my beard and moustache!...O, I want you so much. It is so often on my lips, dear wife....What money have you? I am going to write something for *The Spectator*, and ask him to advance something on it. Charles owes you about 25s. Shall I write to him to take it to you? Oh that fine old man, my father! He *is* the man to tell anything to. So open and wise and humble and kind—God bless him! [1]...My father will be 63 on the 3rd of Dec. I asked him to-day. It has been so hot to-day, and Bella has been sitting out in the shade, but there is very little hope of her. She is very patient, the dear child. O how you would luxuriate in the sun! I am sitting now with a jug of milk by me, drinking away....

Saturday night.

"Thou mightest have left us in darkness, but that would have been unworthy of God." This is a sentence in my father's prayer this evening, which will just be a little window into his thoughts.[2] ...Could you go to Cornish's opposite the infirmary and get a fairy tale book of Grimm's—3s. 6d. I think. It is in red boards with woodcuts—I think it would amuse Bella. My uncle offered me a guinea for my moustache[3] to-night, seriously though funnily. If he knew how bitterly hurt his own son was at his compelling him to shave, he would not have risked it. If fathers knew how liberality

---

1   "Whole-hearted is my worship of the man
    From whom my earthly history began."
    (*Diary of an Old Soul*, January 4th.)

2   The character of David Elginbrod, it will be remembered, was drawn from my grandfather. The above calls to mind the prayer in the novel (vol. i, p. 44): "O Thou who keeps the stars alicht, an' our souls burning wi' a licht aboon that o' the stars, etc."—surely one of the noblest utterances in all my father's writings. When the late Dr. Clifford preached his sermon on my father's life and work on the first Sunday after his death in 1905, he quoted the whole of this prayer and said: "I know nothing finer than that in the English language."

3   If in Scotland it was *heathenish* to grow a beard, it was, then, in England, *fast* to cultivate a moustache—at least for a civilian.

makes their sons love them, they would exercise it oftener. But my noble old father told me that for his part *I might let it grow till I stuffed it in my trousers!*

[HUNTLY, *July* 10.]

My days pass so quietly—I hardly go anywhere but saunter about the house with Shakespeare in my hand or pocket. If you had been here after I wrote to you last night, you might have seen me in less than an hour on the far horizon—the top of a hill¹ nearly 1,000 feet high 2 ½ miles off. You would have seen my white mare and myself clear against the sky.... She is a dear old mare. I love her, and cannot believe that she returns to the elements when she dies. She will perhaps be *our* mare in a new world—though this thought is too covetous to enter the new heavens and the new earth perhaps. However, if only she lives I don't care so much about having her.²

[*July* 10.]

Dearest, my mother has got such a nice servant that she longs for us to have to take care of the children. She was three years with her and she was so kind to them and good-tempered, and cares for her master's interest—a good-principled girl—and she would come with me.

We have had a letter from John to-day from Moscow, but by this time he is at Leipsic, where he expects to find a situation, and if he fails he will sail with a friend for America. There is no word of his coming home....

I have been in my old room for the first time now, this minute—and have seen dear Alec's hat which my sisters take care of. You would like my little sisters. Louie sends her love to you and Lily and all of them.

...I hope poor baby is better by this time, and that you have been sleeping better. I wish I could get you here. Perhaps still. I will stay over the wedding, which is to be in a fortnight—perhaps I will not stay longer except you come....You are a dear, good, sweet wife, soul and body. Now I must stop. I have just been out to drive away a cat—for they kill the little birds....

[HUNTLY,]

11 *July*, 1855.

...I had such a nice ride last night, and met a countryman who had heard me preach (and who had been at school with me, I am since

---

1 Clashmach.
2 She must have been a great age when she died. Her hide was dressed, dyed green and sent to my father. To myself was later deputed the honour of covering with it the study-sofa, upon which her old lover would spend an hour or more every day, resting or sleeping...

reminded). His face was radiant through a profusion of dirt caused by a hot day's work in the *peatmoss*. He went back with me and accompanied me through a great part of my ride, talked about the different birds and flowers, and showed me a nest of the rose-linnet....Do put things in train so that you could come as you say for the last week of my stay, if I can manage it. I have not quite lost hope yet, but it is very indefinite.

Thank you, my wife, for being so kind to my sister. My little sisters have come in. The youngest has a half-grown yellow-hammer perched on her shoulder, which she found a fortnight ago, and which is now very tame. It is now biting her tongue and now being fed with meal and water. I eat cakes made with cream every day. I have not tasted water since I came, but milk and bitter beer—not so strong as ours.

O dearest, I *must* have you here for a week, *but, but*—I don't know. You would be very pleased with my cousin Margaret who is going to be married. She is so sweet and loving and quiet....

A letter of my mother's, written on the 12th, just before she left with the children on a visit to her sister Flora, in Liverpool, concerning which promised visit she had changed her mind, speaks of her success in getting the Grimm Fairy Book and sending it off, together with a handkerchief she embroidered with a flowery wreath for Bella. One wonders how many shillings were left in her purse to take the children and their nurse, the impertinent Charlotte, to Liverpool. Anyhow, she writes happily:

"One of the Miss Kers has made a beautiful frock for Lily. New friends are best," adds my mother with a touch of despair. In this frock the child went to spend the day with Mrs. Henry Sutton. When her mother went to fetch Lily, Mr. Sutton, she says, "came rushing downstairs to open the door for me with his hair all flying back. You are the only other person—man I mean—that could forget himself to *do* such an impulsive and warm-hearted *fly!*..."

At last they left for Liverpool and locked up the house, my mother being greatly distressed that "the cat—*your* cat"—cannot be found anywhere; but more than one good neighbour had promised to look after the creature.

THE PAINTED TABLE

For the rest of the month my mother and her little family were at Mrs. Sing's, where, although she is constantly referring to the kindness of everyone, she is clearly oversensitive about her position. Contrasting her younger sister's luxurious home with the poorer furniture her husband had to put up with—he who worked so much harder and had so few comforts, who was always fragile and was now acknowledged to be a great poet—she finds it a little hard to bear. But surely her feeling of being patronized was more imaginary than just. She says: "I must learn to take people as I find them and not to be out of patience with them for not being what I want them to be...." Little Mary, too, is teased by her cousin James and bites him; and my father's defence of her fierceness is perhaps more consistent with his affection than his ethical principles: "Poor little Elfie," he writes, "what could she do but bite? It is the only gift she has in self-defence!" Anyhow, little Mary is whipped by her mother, and James, though goading her to the crime, escapes Scot-free.

...Do not come back for me a day sooner than you need, if you are well and enjoying yourself, which I know you are intensely. I shall have had a nice change here and shall be better when I go back, although I do not think I can do any *table-painting* unless I have another servant...

The letters are full of details about the children, mostly lovely for the father to get, and worth quoting if space allowed. But she is hard at work on their under-clothes, which seem to be in a sad condition, and soon begins wondering how they are to get back to Manchester, as all the money she has in the world is 15s.

G.M.D. to his Wife.

Huntly,
July 13, 1855.

...I have just had your letter and the book....How much you have been doing and how tired you must be! You will have some rest, will you not now, in Liverpool?...I shall not stay very long after the wedding, except I find I can propose your coming once more...

New true friends are better than *old false* ones, but it needs time to test them. Only I think the friendship of the Scotch has more foundation than much of the other countries...I don't speak of individuals, you know. How could I, with your great big heart, which is big enough for me to lie down in and go to sleep, so warm and safe....

In truth the mother is having a very hard time, what with herself and the ailing children, the fear of outstaying her welcome, the provokingly comfortable and roomy wardrobe, the drawers of which absolutely refuse to stick and squeak and run askew like the cheap things at Camp Terrace! She is determined to find a place for the impudent Charlotte and not to take her back to Manchester; but she looks forward to having the Huntly maid, Elsie—who, by the way, proved almost perfection. Yet Charlotte's wages had to be paid. Then a probably imaginary coldness in her hostess made it impossible for the pathetically sensitive mother of three to stay. On July 19th she writes:

I have been reading the life of Mary Powell—Mistress Milton—and as I started determined to be cross with it, I enjoyed it very much. It ought to do me good. Some of it reminds me very much of you and me. I sometimes think I should like to keep a journal for the sake of the children. I think it would be very interesting if written for them; there would not be so much difficulty in keeping it simple and honest.... [1]

Mr. Powell, her father, had come on a visit to Flora, and it makes my mother very happy. She speaks of everyone being so intensely kind to her—even Alex and Helen.

But I find it difficult to bear the much greater love Papa has for Flo than me. But he is very kind and loving to me. I miss nothing but my companion. It is the old story: if you were with me I should hardly see the darkness. However, dear, I do not want you to come back so soon as you say....

---

[1] Little did she realize how priceless her "simple and honest" narrative would prove to her children.

Then the next day's letter is important to anyone interested in old Mr. Powell. His bearing on his visit may seem unintelligible, though only that of the average healthy man in face of sickness and ill-success.

Mrs. G.M.D. to her Husband.

[LIVERPOOL,]
Friday, July 20.

...I have been out a little with Papa. I do not think he will say anything about our pockets. Everything is too bright and glowing and rich and plentiful here to think of such words as "no money" or *getting on*. Indeed Manchester is altogether too disagreeable a place to mention. He is very kind to me, quite tender and sweet, and most in speaking about you and very loving to the children. So I must not mind if he shrinks from talking about our circumstances—as children do from the uncongenial subject of death. I have been in with Baby and Lily to Helen, and your Lily was so naughty. I intend to go back to Manchester next Wednesday or Thursday....I am as pleased as you can be at the prospect of Elsie. What a pretty name! Do not take your father's money, dear. I have 12s., which must take me home. And then we must go upon tick till I get the table done. You good husband to write so much to me....

G.M.D. to his Wife.

[HUNTLY, *July* 14.]

...Surely our hard time will wear over by degrees. It will, if it please God: that is, if we are ready to stand the harder trial of comfort—not to say prosperity. I wish I could get a situation in Somerset House that would leave me time. I would gladly go to London, and write and preach. Would you not like it? To leave Mr. Scott would be the chief difficulty to me. I shall feel it rather painful to leave my father and mother again, but it will be with the hope of seeing them again with you next year.[1] I am glad you have enjoyed your papa's visit. Never mind, that he makes more of Flora. *I* know something of what my wife is worth. You have a harder trial than the others, dear, both from your husband being what he is, and poor besides—but perhaps that may be made up to you some day.... May the wonderful Father draw out the end as He pleases. Oh, God is so true and good and strong and beautiful! The God of mountain lands,

---

1 When an utter breakdown in health caused the whole family to be entertained for three months at The Farm.

and snowdrops, of woman's beauty and man's strength—the God and Father of our Lord Jesus Christ. I wish you saw the sky away to the North. It is so lovely—orange on the horizon, fading up through yellow and pale green into blue. This is at 11 o'clock at night. There is a slight frost....

In my mother's over-wrought condition and the financial uncertainties, the success of *Within and Without* must have uplifted them both into real happiness. Mr. Longman, the publisher, writes very happily to the author concerning its sales and its recognition, and the need to advertise it more. His kindness must have been very sincere, for there could at best be but little profit to him in the matter.

CHAPTER VII
LOOKING AT DEATH

THOSE who remember that in *David Elginbrod* George MacDonald gives a portrait of his own father, will not miss the significance of this visit to the old home. The letters make even more obvious the old man's character; and they are the last to give us touch with him. In the care—like woman's rather than man's—with which he tended every human and humbler creature committed to him we behold the strong man. My father knew no fault in him: even as those who are entitled to say it, found no fault in his son.

G.M.D. to his Wife.

HUNTLY,
[*July* 14, 1855].

How careful my dear father is of everyone. I have just heard him calling in at the kitchen window to the servant to go and open the children's window, for it had been shut for the rain (which poured so richly this morning) and it would be very hot. He shuts my windows himself lest I should hurt myself....

My father was disappointed that he was not asked to preach. He tells my mother that many were afraid of him: his unorthodoxy was so notorious that some were annoyed at their minister marrying his cousin.

...I think there is scarcely one other manly, straightforward man to equal my father. But he takes very little hand in outside things. I have more and more cause to rejoice that I am not connected with any so-called church under the sun....

My grandfather, though a deacon, took little part in church or public affairs. But his more orthodox brother James had great influence among the Congregationalists. He was energetic in the Sunday-schools, and so strong an advocate for prudence and self-denial that he instituted the savings-bank. His literary gifts were undeniable, if the only evidence were his authorship of *The Huntly News for* 1937 (*sic*), which, full of the changes to be realized in another hundred years, had been printed in 1836 as a preliminary canter for the printing press then first set up in Huntly. But he looked askance at his nephew's emancipation, and now opposed the wish of many that Huntly should hear my father preach, his avowed objection being his beard. But he gave way at last. Twelve years later, when *Robert Falconer* began to appear serially in *The Argosy*, he wrote sternly to its author on the ground that so many of its characters were portraits and would give offence. He even drove his gig post-haste to Banff to warn the editor of the admirable *Banffshire Journal* against reviewing it.[1]

G.M.D. to his Wife.

HUNTLY,
[*July* 17, 1855].

...The servant Elsie Gordon is engaged for £7, and she will be ready in a fortnight. My mother says she will do anything she is wished to do. She can wash well and make the children's clothes, do a room very well, cook plain Scotch dishes, bake cakes, etc., gets up very well in the morning, is exceedingly good-tempered and very kind to children....

...The chief difficulty in getting you here is the money. I shall have to get some from my father to bring me back, for I have just 2s. 6d., and I should hardly have the face to propose your coming except we could pay for that. But if Mr. Troup asks me to preach in his absence, then perhaps I could manage it. Perhaps I may be able for a story in a day or two. Once begun I could soon finish it....Cannot you send me an idea to work into a tale?...

---

1   As far as I can ascertain he succeeded.

LOOKING AT DEATH

G.M.D. to his Wife.

[HUNTLY,
July 17, 1855].

...Do not think, dearest wife, that it is for your fault that you are not permitted to come. Perhaps it is only to make you love me more by being away from you, for you know what I think about that....But it will not do in the present state of our pockets....My father is so often talking about the book and me. He at least receives his son with honour. I am afraid I have troubled him very much to-night by telling him how ill-off we are....

[July 20, 1855].

I have been out since twelve o'clock, have had 18 miles on horseback, and some delightful feelings floating into me from the face of the blue hills, and the profusion of wild roses on some parts of the road. The heather is just beginning to break out in purple on the hillsides. Another week of warm sunshine will empurple some from base to summit. How much more I understand nature than I did!...

On the 23rd my mother writes reminding him it is Mary's birthday. She is two. "Do you remember this day two years finding the lark's nest with the six little ones?"
So he wrote these verses about the little Elfie:

> I have an elfish maiden child;
>   She is not two years old;
> Through windy locks her eyes gleam wild,
>   With glances shy and bold.
>
> Like little imps, her tiny hands,
>   Dart out and push and take;
> Chide her—a trembling thing she stands
>   And like two leaves they shake.
>
> But to her mind, a minute gone
>   Is like a year ago;
> So when you lift your eyes anon,
>   They're at it, to and fro.[1]

---

1   *Poems*, 1857, "Little Elfie."

G.M.D. to his Wife.

[*July 25, 1855, the day after the marriage of Robert Troup and Margaret MacDonald.*]

...I *cannot* bear to force my departure. They are very sad sometimes, and I am sure I am a comfort to them....That dear child Bella has been saving up her money for some time, as she always does to give presents—she had nearly a pound—and to-day she gave me two sets of flannels for the winter, which I should think took all she had. Her little body will be cold before I wear them. I *am* going to preach next Sunday evening. I cannot *write* more just now....

On the 28th my mother and the children returned to Manchester, Mrs. Sing sending them 1st Class, and everything was happy between the two sisters.

G.M.D. to his Wife.

[HUNTLY, *July* 28,]
6 o'clock Monday morning.

I preached yesterday about the little child. After, one old woman said she thought I went rather too far *on that side* of God's character. Another said to my father: "When I saw him wi' the moustaches I thoucht he looked gey and rouch-like; but, or he had been speakin' lang, I jist thoucht it was like Christ himsel' speakin' to me."

Since writing the above my Uncle has called me aside and given me from Mr. Troup £1 1s. to get something in remembrance of the marriage, and £1 1s. besides from himself in acknowledgement of last night's sermon. My father has some money ready to send us home. Thank you...for the *Scotsman*. It is very gratifying. It is thought a good deal of here, but because of its *latitudinarian* opinions, has ceased to be read in this neighbourhood. I hear some unfavourable notice had reached Huntly before, in what paper I don't know, and probably made the first impression....

Then comes a letter from my mother with a distressing revelation: Harrop, the grocer, asks for his money, £4 13s. by the end of the week!

So dear, after thinking over everyone, right and left, and all the pros and cons and some tears—not naughty ones, though, I think—only rather hot ones—I have determined to write to Mr. Bateman to-night. I shall ask him to lend me £5. I am sure it is the best way. Then I will work very hard at the Table....[1]

When, by the way, she had gone to see Mr. and Mrs. Alex Powell to bid them good-bye, Helen had given her a sovereign, and her brother had scolded her for not having yet finished the Painted Table. They could hardly be ignorant of her poverty and the brave fight she was making. Since it is unbelievable that the kind-hearted Flora did not sometimes gossip with Helen about the little socks darned and darned again, the neatly mended embroidery-edgings of the little trousers, the much-wrinkled shoulder-ribbons that would not be smoothed back into youthful smiles, one can only surmise that Mr. and Mrs. A. Powell felt it wrong to interfere too much with the dealings of Providence, lest Louisa never learn prudence and economy.

G.M.D. to his Wife.

[HUNTLY, *July* 31],
Sunday afternoon.

...I have a little cold, but I don't think it will interfere much with my preaching this evening. I am regarded with some jealousy here I think, but I don't care much for that, as my nearest friends have faith in me. I think my father and mother will both go to-night, though it pours with rain....They are very sad about Bella. My father says that she suffers very much after they have gone to bed, and all is still and dark; and that seemed to distress him so much. It will be our turn sometime most likely to go through this.[2] I will be more gentle with Lily and Mary, I think, when I return. We must try all we can for their sakes as well as our own to be good, for it will never do to *look* better than we are. My love to my bairnies. And my love to their dear...mother from her own Husband.

---

1 Mr. Bateman was an old family friend of the Powells. His reply is worth quoting, not only because he sent as a gift more than was asked: "Give your nestlings each a kiss and say 'An old true friend of mother sends you this kiss and something else, dear child, as loving *gift* to help and comfort her and you.'"
2 Little could he guess that each of his three eldest girls would die, though later in life, just as their Aunt Bella died.

Aug 1st.

Thank you...for your letter to-day, such a nice long one. Thank you for your precious love....I never wanted you like this before. But I have been planning how and where to take you for a night—now and then perhaps—after I return, before the work begins again. It will be delightful to be able to leave the children [with Elsie] without fear. My father will send me home, though it is very little he can do. I have just 2s. 6d. I spend nothing here. I had 4s. when I arrived and I have spent 1s. for stamps, which I need not do except I liked. But one doesn't like to be going to the office for stamps always....

My father has just come in (I am writing in my bedroom) and offered me £3 to send to you. I have not taken it yet, for I daresay you will not want any before you can answer this and tell me how much you will need till I see you again....

If I am asked to preach again next Sunday I will preach about the young man who was told to leave all he had—for the people are getting much more up in their way of living than when I left, and will need to be reminded; not that there is any harm in the thing itself. I think you could follow Him up and down, dear sweet-eyed wife.

This crossed my mother's of the same date telling of a respectful and admiring review of the book in *The Christian Spectator*. But it hurt once more—just a little—to see her own poem, *Love me, Beloved*, reproduced in its pages.

In the very next letter, however, we find her greatly overwrought again.

Mrs. G.M.D. to her Husband.

[MANCHESTER],
August 3rd.

...I am so glad you are not coming home to-night, for I got no sleep till 4 o'clock this morning, the children screaming in turns, and sometimes all together, and alternatively playing till then. I *am* so tired. The new carriage is very heavy, and I have been pushing them out to-day. It has done them good. I do think they will sleep to-night.

I was almost mad with weariness, children and jam-making all day long, when Charles and Ellen Coleman began talking about honesty and truth in friendship and real friends and true people, and I talked such stuff about not believing in anyone, and the last six months' experience having taught me a great deal! I said a great deal I didn't mean but thought

I did then—but she and I were in very different physical conditions. She looks so very well and plump and pretty and cheerful and full of hope such as I felt (*not* pretty though) a few days ago. And now it is all drained out of me, everything looks so impossible—so unlike the beauty and life there is in flowers. Ellen looks like a flower, I like a potato rind. I am so very sorry I talked so to Ellen.

I suppose you have seen *Maud* [Tennyson's latest poem]? Everyone I have heard speak of it is disappointed. There is so much about war....

Everyone wants you back....

In quoting sad words like these, one has to remember that my mother was in distressful need of rest. "What we need for rest as well as for labour," wrote my father in *Castle Warlock* many years later, "is Life"; [1] and my mother was giving hers to a new life on its way.

G.M.D. to his Wife.

[HUNTLY,
Aug. 6, 1855].

...Since dinner I have had a saunter up towards the hilly regions, and have looked down on all the Huntly valley beneath me. What a multitude of harebells there are this season! I brought home two or three white ones this afternoon to Bella. I never saw any before. But poor Bella had a bad night again, and seems to me looking worse than I have seen her before....I think I shall leave in the beginning of next week—and I hope to be a better husband to you and father to my children....I shall be altogether yours some day. You know what I mean. I am not all Christ's yet.

Monday night.

Just a few words, dearest, for the last time from here. I have been with my father to see Alec's grave, five miles away. He lies beside my mother and my two brothers. I thought—oh, there is room for me between him and the wall. But I must be where you are, my own—only I should like if we could both be in that quiet country churchyard. My father was a good deal overcome, for it is not only the dead but the dying he has to think of. Mrs. Wilson gave me £4 to-day "for the children." My father gave me

---

1 "Thank God for the night and darkness and sleep, in which good things draw nigh like God's thieves, and steal themselves in—water into wells, and peace and hope and courage into the minds of men." (*St. George and St. Michael*, vol. ii, p.17.)

£4 too to bring us [himself and Elsie] home. I shall not want quite £3 and have £2 besides; so I shall come home with more by far than I could have made by staying. My father is so dear and kind. My mother is working away ironing my shirts now. You will love her...next year, I hope. I think more of home, a great deal more, then ever I did. Thank you for your two letters received yesterday. I have been troubled about your talking so before those who cannot understand you as I can. Do not let your horns out of your shell, darling, except to your own friends—for you have two or three yet, though you may not believe it! You are true except in trust. But....I know the darkness and trouble you are in, and you are safe with me.

And so the visit ended, and my father brought back with him armfuls of imaginative grain waiting for future germination and life—to be increased, there can be little doubt, when, less than a year later, the whole family went to Huntly on a three months' visit. The stimulus he got from the literary praise of his dramatic poem coincides well with this return to the land whence was to come the rich milk and wild honey, the sturdy oats and roses and wild peppermint of his finest novels. Those long and loving talks with his father had been full of family lore and racial traditions—full also of the wisdom, austerity and deep, if hidden, tenderness of his grandmother.

But the parting was full to overflowing in its sadness; for little Bella was waiting for her call, and, child though she was, longing to go. In a letter dated from Edinburgh, on his way back to Manchester, my father thus refers to her:

G.M.D. to his Father.

...Give my love to them all—especially Bella. I fear I shall have no better news of her. But, dear father and mother, death is only the outward form of birth. Surely it is no terrible thing that she should go to Alec. And we can't be very long behind her. There is room for us all between Alec and the wall in the churchyard. I hope it will not hurt you more to write thus. Surely if we are sure of God, we are sure of everything: He never gave a good gift like a child to take it back again....

LOOKING AT DEATH

Almost immediately on his return home work began to pour in, so much so indeed that there can be no doubt that my father gravely overtaxed his strength. Nor was my mother at all in fit condition for the increasing demands upon her. But Elsie proved a most capable and affectionate servant; and the children loved her.

My Uncle John arrived in Manchester unexpectedly in his erratic way, and notwithstanding his intention to remain in Germany or go to America.

G.M.D. to his Father.

[Aug. 1855.]

MY VERY DEAR FATHER,
I have long meant to write you some notices of my book....

I will send you the *Brighton Herald* and the *Morning Post*'s opinion—also a letter most gratifying from Mr. Maurice....John is with us—very tired. He is waiting to see if he can get a situation. ..you will be glad to hear that I have as much teaching already as I think will bring me in £3 a week. We hope for an Owens College student to board with us—may be, more than one. My lectures will bring me something—altogether we have good hopes for the winter. I am better, though I still cough. How is dear little Bella? Give her my love.

I have heard several things about my book since I returned—the principal of which is the interest Lady Byron, the widow of the poet, has taken in it. It seems to have taken a powerful hold on her.

I hope you will be happy in John's visit soon. It seems a really painful effort to him to write....

The next, undated, tells of Mr. Scott's great care for him, and quotes a translation of the German song in *Within and Without* by Henry Cecil—my Uncle John's great friend—which some others may be glad to have.

G.M.D. to his Father.

[Aug.? 1855.]

...Mr. Scott called on Friday, and before he left, told Louisa that, not thinking either of us very worldly wise, he must enquire into our circumstances, etc., for though he was not rich himself he knew many who were, and who at a word from him, would be glad to render us assistance. He is indeed a true friend. Is it not a great thing to me to have the man whose intellect and wisdom I most respect in the world for my friend, he not being ashamed to acknowledge the relation? He said he heard of my book from many quarters while in London, and that it has got into the best literary circle....

I think you would like to know this translation by young Cecil of the three German verses in *Within and Without*:

> "When thy present voice I hear
> In the leafy murmurs near,
> When I feel Thee far and wide,
> Father, who hath bliss beside?
>
> "Now the loving sun outshines—
> Me with Thee and all entwines;
> To the flowers hastes the bee—
> To Thy love my soul doth flee.
>
> "Till Thy love to me be less,
> Life is no more weariness;
> So I see and hear but Thee—
> That alone sufficeth me."

George MacDonald at last had a pulpit offered him where he could preach freely. The particulars appear in the next three letters. The first begins with an answer to his father's request that he should define his objections to public prayer:

G.M.D. to his Father.

[Aug.? 1855.]

...My objection is simply that I do not think one-third—perhaps one-tenth of it is prayer at all. If your experience leads you to *believe* that there is more praise or *speaking* to God in these prayers than a dreary recurrence of vain repetitions in the form and in the name of prayer, my experience does not. There may be times when such assemblies are very suitable; but my impression is that there would be perhaps more real prayer if there were less public praying. But more knowledge *may* lead to a modification of my opinion.

I am glad to tell you that I was unanimously invited last Sunday by a company of 70 seat-holders to preach to them. I agreed to do so for a year to see how it will do. I was never treated with so much respect. They say: "Speak out; tell us what you think; no one will interfere with you; that desk is yours." And all that the chapel raises, which will not probably

LOOKING AT DEATH

exceed £100 and may be less, will be mine....Indeed they give me all the liberty I could wish; nor have I ever seen such promise of generous faith in a spiritual teacher before....I mean to have a week-evening for religious help to my friends here, either at the Schoolroom or in this house. I am gradually becoming known in Manchester, but I have not much to do that brings in money. Only when one thing is taken away, another comes—from God I think and hope....

On August 24th Bella died.

G.M.D. to his Stepmother.

[*Aug. 26, 1855.*]

MY DEAREST MOTHER,
...Bella has only gone nearer to One who loves her more dearly and tenderly than you do. Or if you even think that she has gone to Alec, who has been waiting for her, it seems no such dreadful thing. God will let him take care of her till you go. I feel that if I had been in the spirit world before she came, I should have taken her to my heart so warmly that my little sister would soon have felt at home in the new place. We must weep often in this world, but there are very different kind of tears. Bella will be kept quite safe for you there, and you will never be separated from her in heart. Schiller says—"Death cannot be an evil because it is universal." God would not let it be the law of His Universe if it were what it looks to us. And dear Mother, who could wish an easier, quieter, simpler death than my dear sister's? I should like to wither away out of the world like the flowers that they may come again....

This letter reminds one of David Elginbrod's prayer when the young man Hugh Sutherland lost his father:

O Thou in whase sicht oor deith is precious, an' no licht maitter; wha through darkness leads to licht, an' through deith to the greater life!—we canna believe that thou wouldst gie us ony guid thing, to tak' the same again; for that would be but bairns' play....[1]

A letter from my grandfather at Huntly tells of their return from a visit to the Cabrach,[2] the Banffshire Hills, after Bella's death, how the mother since her return home "feels

---
1   *David Elginbrod*, vol. i, p. 142.
2   I can hardly refrain from quoting, as a notable instance of my father's pictorial writing, his description of the Cabrach. Readers of *Castle Warlock* will scarcely have forgotten it. (Chap. i, pp. 1, 2, 3.)

better for the 'caller' air, but misses her lassie greatly. I trust time will heal the wound which is liable on many occasions to be torn open again."

Then he quotes his brother-in-law, Mr. A. S. McColl, a great Shakesperian student to whom my father later dedicated his *Hamlet*, as pronouncing *Within and Without* "the finest poem that has appeared for twenty years." But here the loving father proceeds to warn his son against the dangers of so much praise, and tells him how the only protection against conceit is to stretch forwards to higher and ever higher attainment. The reply must have relieved my grandfather's mind of all anxiety, if he ever really had any:

G.M.D. to his Father.

Sept. 27, 1855.

...I thank you for your anxiety about the so far success of my book. True love must be uneasy. I hope I know enough of my own failings and ignorance to keep me from becoming conceited, and perhaps I don't think the success so great as you do. Certainly there is always danger, and perhaps a usually modest man may at moments be over favourable in his judgments of himself. I think I have more consciousness of weakness than of strength. But our safety is in God's keeping, not in our own. May He take care of me, and do what He will with me.

It is a great pleasure both to Louisa and me to have John near us—we see him often. I go and see him and he comes and sees us....He has very keen feelings, and if he came to see you now, he could not have borne the thought of leaving again; and he could have stayed but a very little while. He is subject to melancholy, but I hope I may be of some use to him. I love him very dearly....

Agreement was made with the Bolton people. His only duty would be Sunday ministrations to a congregation largely composed of spinners, weavers and mechanics, all with terribly long hours and insufficient wages, with Chartist passions still surging in their bosoms and the Peterloo massacre keeping alive their indignation against mill-owners grown suddenly rich and powerful.

But barely had two months elapsed when my father was struck down with the worst hæmorrhage from the lungs he had had. For many days he lay at death's door, the doctors unable to stanch the incessant flow of blood. Nothing but absolute rest from movement, from cough, from speech, with ice-bags on his chest, would give him a chance. My mother was quite unfitted for much nursing; so her sister Angela came from Liverpool to help. The two Miss Kers, Mrs. A. J. Scott's sisters, came one or other of them to his bedside to read or sing to him for hours together. Dr. Harrison declared that never had he known any patient who, fully aware that he might be dying, looked death in the face with such perfect equanimity. It was then, surely, that these thoughts came to him:

> I was like Peter when he began to sink,
> To Thee a new prayer therefore have I got—
> That, when death comes in earnest to my door,
> Thou wouldst thyself go, when the latch doth clink,
> And lead him to my room, up to my cot;
> Then hold thy child's hand, hold and leave him not,
> Till death has done with him for evermore....[1]

Nevertheless the blood-flow did not lessen; and at last the doctor, urged by a possibility that it might be diverted and give the breach in the vein opportunity to close, bled him at the arm. The blood-spitting at once ceased and did not return. As Dr. Harrison was a homœopath, his treatment was the more remarkable.

On December 30th he was able to write his father a long letter:

G.M.D. to his Father.

Sunday evening,
December 30, 1855.

MY VERY DEAR FATHER,

....I am much, much better....Louisa is wonderfully well now....Phœbe, her sister, is to be married to a Liverpool gentleman [Joseph King, M.R.C.S.] on the 18th of February, when we shall all, I hope, be at Clapton....After the wedding we talk of going to Devonshire for two or three months. Mr. Powell has expressed himself very ready to help us, and had already paid the

---

[1] *Diary of an Old Soul*, January 28th.

last quarter's rent for us. We seemed likely to be better off than we had ever been before—and now I think, in some way or other, we are meant to be much better off yet. I think we shall be able to clear off all our debts—£25, I think—however, without troubling my father-in-law....

The interesting fact I wanted to tell you about my poem [*Within and Without*] is this. I had doubted whether I had not offended against probability in making an Italian the subject of such emotions as I have represented in Julian. I had therefore given him a German mother. But just before my illness, I made the acquaintance of an Italian nobleman, Count [Aurelio] Saffi, who having been one of the Triumvirs in Rome, along with Mazzini, is now a refugee in this country, supporting himself by giving lessons in Oxford. He is a literary man and was giving some lectures at the Royal Institution here, residing for the time at Mr. Scott's house. He was much struck with the book, he told me, considering it the best expression of the religious feelings of the age. This, though himself a Roman Catholic. Indeed we soon formed a warm friendship for each other. He came to see me before he left, while I was yet unable to sit up in bed. Mr. Scott says to hear Saffi speak of anything mean or base would be almost a new sensation. He seems to speak from such a height above it.

Once again we find friends flocking round the broken man, almost vying with one another in heaping benefits upon him.

G.M.D. to his Father.

MANCHESTER,
2nd January, 1856.

...On New Year's Day two gentlemen called on me, who along with a third—none of them much known to me—had made up a purse of £30 for me, which they offered in the most delicate and kind way. One of the three is an Independent, another a Churchman, and the third a Unitarian.

This morning's post brought me a bank-order for £5 from Miss Ross, as unexpected as welcome, and I have written to thank her for her great kindness.

Then this afternoon some of my Bolton people called on me, bringing me my quarter's salary in advance. They had paid me up to Christmas, just before I was taken ill. This will leave something considerable over after paying all our present debts....

Miss Ross, her mother being sister of Isobel Robertson, had kept a young ladies' seminary in Huntly, but had recently retired.

LOOKING AT DEATH

G.M.D. to Miss Ross.

Manchester,
Jan. 2, 1856.

....Please to receive my warm thanks....And if we have not learned by this time "to cast all on Him who careth for us," I think we are getting to learn it. Indeed, I have so much hope along with a little faith, that I have not been troubled—scarcely at all. I can see more and more that nothing will do for anybody but an absolute enthusiastic confidence in God....You once told me of some of your early experiences; and now that you have plenty, you have not forgotten your former needs. May God bless you for your kindness....

Then comes a bit of news gratifying and astonishing to the one who now made a fourth in the little family: the first son is born.

G.M.D. to his Father.

Monday evening,
Jan. 21st, 1856.

My dearest Father,

I am too tired with writing notes to do more than tell you that I have a son at last. Before ten last night he arrived. Louisa behaved so courageously. He is a great boy—might be three months old, they say! He has a baby's accomplishments of feeding and sleeping perfectly....

Less than a month later my mother was hard at work dismantling the house.

BOOK V
MIGRATIONS

CHAPTER I
KINGSWEAR AND HUNTLY

IN spite of George MacDonald's protestations of recovery, it is not difficult to read between the lines that he was weak and ailing. As soon as my mother was through her trouble, Mrs. Scott fetched him away to their home at Cheetham Hill, no great distance from Camp Terrace. There he was nursed into greater security, leaving the mother and baby to her great friend, Mrs. Andrew and her sister Angela. The former was a lady of rare cheeriness and wisdom, as well as of foresight, if I may judge from the fact that, after leaving the little son snug in his mother's arms for the first time, she instantly returned and, putting her face round the door, whispered anxiously, "Has he asked for the latch-key yet?"

G.M.D. to his Wife.

[CHEETHAM HILL],
Jan 24, 1856.

DEAREST, SWEET WIFE,
   I think I am a little better to-day. I need hardly tell you I enjoy myself. They are all so kind. I was left quite alone, and spent the time meditating in spite of stupidity—and in reading Hoffmann's *Golden Pot* again. It is delightful.[1] ...I never saw Mr. Scott so happy, so merry or so loving as last night. He talked a great deal yesterday about Art, and I have some new thoughts about it from him....It was a divine day and I saw things as I had not seen them before. May our Father teach us—for no one, not even Mr. Scott, can teach us but Him. Indeed we have secrets of our

---

1   In a later letter he writes again about *The Golden Pot* in even higher terms of praise. Reference is made to the point later (p.297).

own with Him and no one else.[1] Think of and to Him while you lie there. Tell me about little Greville. Is his hoarseness gone?...My love to Annie please. To-morrow we will come.

With his hopes of providing for his family and of holding together his two sets of disciples—at Renshaw Street, the intellectual, and at Bolton, the working folk—fallen into chaos, it is small wonder if now some lowness of spirits should assail him. But nothing ever quenches his optimism:

> My harvest withers. Health, my means to live—
> All things seem rushing straight into the dark.
> But the dark still is God....
>   ...Am I not a spark
> Of him who is the light?[2]

G.M.D. to his Father.

MR. SCOTT'S HOUSE,
Feb 18th, Monday.

We have been in great confusion and haste for some days getting our house in order to be left for an indefinite time. Now it is abandoned to the care of a man and his wife who are glad to live there rent free, and we are with our friends, the Scotts. To-morrow we leave for London. Phœbe is to be married on Wednesday. We shall rest in London a while before we proceed further....Louisa is surprisingly well, and little Greville is a great thriving boy....It is only a month to-day since he was born, and Louisa has done a good deal of work....The same friends whom I mentioned to you before sent me £20 (additional to the other £30) the other day. Mr. Scott tells me a friend in Wales has sent me £20 through him besides; and he says whenever I want money he can get it for me. Mr. Powell has been very kind too, and promises to help us....

UPPER CLAPTON,
Feb 27th, 1856.

We bore the journey here very well indeed, but after the wedding was over, we got very tired. I have not much strength, and Louisa too is far from strong. I have been to see Dr. Wilkinson,[3] who is a personal friend and a

---

1 This recalls two verses in "The Disciple," *Poetical Works*, vol. i, p.208
2 *Diary of an Old Soul*, January 15th.
3 Garth Wilkinson, M.R.C.S., a homœopath, was the well-known Swedenborgian who first re-introduced William Blake's poetry to the world—often spoiled by his own emendations. He proved very kind and most useful, introducing my parents to many who became life-long friends; more particularly to Miss Anna Leigh-Smith.

KINGSWEAR AND HUNTLY

homœopath. He agrees with Dr. Harrison that there is no mischief in my lungs, and says that after this I may be better than ever—but that I must have entire rest for six months at least. We expect to go to Devonshire for a couple of months at least. After that perhaps we may think of coming to see you if you will have us. [A hope that at last was realized.]...

We are in no anxiety for a few months at least. I am ashamed to have written that last sentence—as if we should feel safe only as long as we had means laid up in store!...

Angela was now mistress of her father's house, and found it very pleasant to be hostess to those whom her love had delighted to serve so often and so long as "nurse-friend and playmate." One day she took her guests for a drive in Victoria Park, only recently opened, and a little incident cheered my mother so much that she wrote it as a small story, which my father published—a little retouched perhaps by his own pen—along with other short stories gathered together in the novel—not very notable except for them—which he called *Adela Cathcart*.[1] The final point, that of my mother giving her last sixpence to the imbecile boy to buy a kite with, is literally true: it was, like so many of her larger deeds, little short of divine in its improvidence. Her account of her weariness is worth quoting:

> I had been ill, and my husband was ill, and we had nothing to do, and we did not know what would become of us....I knew that all was for the best, as my good husband was always telling me; but my eyes were dim and my heart was troubled, and I could not feel sure that God cared quite so much for us as he did for the lilies.....The very colours of the flowers, the blue of the sky, the sleep of the water, seemed to push us out of the happy world that God had made. And yet the children, two of them [they were now out of the carriage and feeding the swans], seemed as happy as if God were busy making the things before their eyes, and holding out each thing as he made it, for them to look at....

But it was imperative to get my father into the sun, and his father-in-law made it possible. He had grown mightily fond and proud of the little grandchildren, the little white Lily with

---

1   1864, vol. i, p. 73

her wondering grey eyes, her sensitive nostrils, her rare sweet smile and that captivating, quick-blossoming of her roses; the little dark-haired elfish Mary with her blackbird's voice and a sweetness more instant than Lily's; the solemn, less pretty Gracie, but with her mother's wonderful eyes; and the great greedy baby, his brown eyes all for his mother. They were so much the old man's own that their father became once again something more than a duty for his stern solicitude.

And so my parents with Lily and the baby went to Kingswear early in March. But hardly were they settled in lodgings upon the hillside when my father was again seized with hæmorrhage, though far less severe than that of two months before. My mother "nearly killed herself racing in the dark down some thirty odd steps" to the Vicar's house for help. He was the Rev. John Smart. His immediate response, his wife's solicitude and his daughter[1] flying for the doctor, endeared them to her at once. Again my parents' need brought them life-long friends. Mr. and Mrs. Smart gave of their best to that brave man and wife, and their grandchildren will not forget what came of it.

G.M.D. to his Father.

[*First week in March* 1856.]

...To-day I feel somewhat alive again, especially as a stiff breeze has been giving a rapid motion to the surface of the river, and the white sea birds have been darting about, in and out of the water....Louisa will write soon when she gets [from her brush] a picture of the place to send you....We have a strong, cold east wind, so that at Dartmouth on the opposite side they are glad to shut their shop shutters—while we under the eastward hill scarcely feel it....My spirits are not very bad now. Nor can I pity myself very much when they are, for I have hope that no dejection can touch. At the same time I shall never be in good spirits till I can employ myself in something that seems worth doing. I cannot even write verses for any length of time—at least I have done nothing to speak of in that way for a long time, but I hope soon to be able again though the doctors do forbid it...

---

1   Viz. the eldest, Annie. She died the same day as her youngest sister, Mrs. Ewing Matheson, at Dartmouth only last year.

The east wind, however, was as rough with the patient's bronchial tubes as with the Dartmouth shops, and his recovery was slow. But in a very few days he was lying on the sofa "looking out from the window," he writes, "through the mouth of the river Dart (as Jonah might through the jaws of the whale) into the great Atlantic."

A week later they removed from their lodgings to Little Ravenswell, a wonderfully pretty cottage, where later a wealth of apple-blossom would be looking in at the drawing-room window, with its garden running down to a low sea-wall that kept out the waves of the great estuary, and over which they might watch "the broad low moon throwing great splashes of light on the tops of the water-mounds, heaving too slowly to be called waves." My father spent much time on the water, and the air got thus was especially helpful. "The clergyman and all his family are such simple good people. I went to church last Sunday and enjoyed it."

During the spring he copied his collection of poems in his perfect handwriting into a pretty volume, dating it "Kingswear, Lynmouth, Lynton," and gave it to my mother at Huntly in the summer. In a letter of this month to his father, he says:

>...Will you please give up *the Rev.* to me, I never liked it. I only say *please*—if you have no particular reason for doing so.

In spite of the sunny and sheltered spot and the primroses peeping and leaping up in the quiet woods that here run almost into the sea, the patient made but slow progress; so that my mother, remembering the delicious days she had spent at Lynmouth and Lynton with her mother eight years before, determined upon a move thither. There the following two months were spent while the visit to Huntly was arranging itself.

G.M.D. to his Father.

Lynmouth, Devonshire.

We came here yesterday by steamer from Kingswear....This is a most romantic country; crowded hills, with wood climbing up to the tops of some from the bottom of the valleys—while others are as bare as any in Scotland; brawling, rocky streams—of which one, the Lynn, at the mouth of which we are situated, runs into the sea direct....We have left warm friends behind us in the clergyman of Kingswear and his family. You should have seen him pulling us and all our luggage in his boat to the steamer, like a ferryman!...We shall be here a week at least—after which Louisa will go to Manchester and I by sea to Aberdeen on our way to you....

Three months were spent at Huntly. For once the imagination must tell of my mother's delight in at last meeting that father whom she already loved hardly less that she had never seen him face to face; of her pride in showing her four children; and of my father's joy in being at home again—little less in his heart a boy that he now had the "wifie," whom when six years old he had boasted he could do so well with, although the watch he had protested he could do without was, in fact, but a sorry affair. Also we can well picture the old father's and somewhat younger stepmother's quiet joy in realizing at last how tender a wife God had given their son—a joy that could hardly have been greater had they known that a few years thence it would be said, "George MacDonald had done for Scotland what St. Paul did for Asia Minor: he opened the windows."

But no word to or from any correspondents touch upon this period. It is more than likely that my Uncle John joined us there; for his pupils in Manchester would have their holidays, and the opportunity of seeing his brother and sister must have been irresistible. On the other hand, my Uncle Charles at this time may have been too deeply involved in his already hazardous business affairs to spare much time for a visit home. Anyhow, my mother could rest, my sisters could grow fat upon porridge, white scones, eggs and cream without stint, the baby having no need of better food than he had always got, though soon to realize the merits of dairy milk. But my father, we must infer, did not gain much strength; and the need of his wintering in the South was urged by all his friends. Not least in such promptings, I take it, was Lady Noel Byron, who must already, if for the present only by correspondence, have begun their fast-ripening intimacy.

CHAPTER II
ALGIERS

LADY BYRON in advocating Algiers for the winter seems to have realized that for the new poet a change of scene and society might be as beneficial to his genius as dry air and sun to his lungs. At any rate, she provided travelling expenses[1] and gave him introductions to some who proved lifelong friends. She had not yet met him, nor, though their correspondence had made them well acquainted, had he yet realized how deep was her sense of debt to *Within and Without*. Possibly it was through A. J. Scott, with whom, I believe, she was intimate, that she heard of my father's empty purse. They were to leave about the middle of October; and my father was again prevented from seeing Lady Byron owing to her own illness. Lily was to be left with Mrs. Godwin, Grace and the baby at The Limes. Mary had gained less than the others from the bracing of Huntly, and was so easily upset by changes in the weather that she was

---

[1] At what date he sent her this poem I do not know. It was first printed in the *Disciple*, 1868, p. 331, and again—altered, not for the better, some think—in the *Poetical Works*, vol. i, p. 441.

"To A. I. N. B.

"They followed hard, for riches' sake,
 The searching men of old,
After the secret that would make
 The meaner metals gold.

"A nobler alchymy is thine,
 O lady born to bless;
Gold in thy hand becomes divine—
 Grows truth and tenderness."

to accompany them. Perhaps the sweetest, least exacting of all the children that trooped along in after years, she gave no trouble. When her parents went out sight-seeing of a morning she would be put to bed for an hour or two, and on their return would be sleeping or quite happy with her doll and toys.

The journey was at last accomplished in spite of delays due to bitter weather and mistakes, besides an attack of bronchitis which kept them a week at Valence. It was full of interest, although as specimens of George MacDonald's descriptive powers we shall prefer his letters from Algiers:

G.M.D. to his Father.

ALGIERS,
Friday, Nov. 28, 1856.

...Under the windows of the hotel there are trees with many yellow oranges. Before us lies the bay of Algiers, filled with the blue Mediterranean—for it is bluer than other seas, or rather more habitually blue....Oh, the multitude of costumes! I have been able to classify them only partially as yet. I will not try to describe them, but my delight in colour is gratified here. I have, however, with my Rob Roy plaid and Glengarry bonnet, added one to the multitude of costumes, and seem to amuse some of the people as much as they amuse me. The town is full of French soldiers in all variety of uniforms; and what with their infernal drums and trumpets, and the noise of French and Arabic and the waggons and horses with bells—and, beautiful in themselves, the fountains before the door, we long for quiet....We cannot lead a hotel-life long, for our money would soon be gone....The town is built on the hillside, covering no great extent, but very closely built—so closely that a peep of the blue sky is something. The lower part of the town is French, though tinctured with Arabesque; but above, you might fancy—what with narrow passages, the only streets, what with arched ways, and houses projecting till the walls touch, and a constant succession on either hand of courts with Moorish arches, and stairs up and down—that you were in the time of the pirates! Even now the succession of strange countenances is startling—Arabs, Jews, French-Moorish women, all in white, of whom nothing is visible but the eyes, and perhaps the bare feet—Negroes as black as soot nearly, with features of whose breadth and thickness there could hardly be an exaggeration—children with purple hair! Some that we suppose Turks, and Armenians or Persians—multitudes of donkeys and mules; oxen yoked by the horns; beautiful Arab horses, very small and elegant, mostly white; and yesterday we saw one camel walking along with an Arab or somebody on his hump....There does not seem nearly the misery that we see in London or any of our large towns.

The countenance and forms of the Aborigines seem much more noble than those of their conquerors. Prominent regular features, dark eyes, slender limbs (the bare legs, bronzed and smooth, would need two to make an English footman's), long, swinging gait—are contrasted with the more common features and most insignificant persons of by far the greater part of the French soldiery. The French are, however, very pleasant people to have to do with....

Before the year was out they had found apartments in an old Moorish house on a hillside, surrounded by olive groves, and a little way inland from the western suburb of St. Eugène. They had the ground floor, which was chilly from lack of sun, and damp like all the houses. The floor above was rented by an Archdeacon and family, who proved kind neighbours.

The description of the rooms written to Miss Annie Smart comes appropriately here, though the date anticipates:

G.M.D. to Miss Smart.

January 12, 1857.

MY DEAR ANNIE,

(How would you like to buy oranges at 3 half-pence a dozen?)...What shall I begin by telling you? First that if you were suddenly transported into the little room in which I am writing, my wife working, and little Mary chattering like a Kalmuck praying-machine, you would stare a little....In the first place, the room is long rather, and would be narrow, but for two deep vaulted recesses, in one of which stands a piano, in the other a cupboard of ugly painted wood. On the other side are three small windows of different sizes and elevations. The walls are 2 ½ feet thick, for the roof is vaulted with crossing arches. The floors, and two feet up the walls are covered with coloured tiles, yellow and green and blue and black, of somewhat varied but not very interesting patterns; and the absence of red either pure or in combination gives to my eye a dingy appearance....We have only two or three little bits of carpet. Out of this room lead two others, paved with red tiles—one of which is our bedroom, and the least comfortable part of our interesting abode. A few steep steps lead up to the kitchen, at which, from the paucity of utensils and the oddity of the charcoal fireplaces, an English cook would be considerably puzzled. We have a very stupid French girl from the Hautes-Pyrénées....From our windows we look out on the Mediterranean with its infinite varieties of colour and shade, and for the last few weeks with plenty of ragged waves. From our door we see eastward across the bay the distant snow-capped peaks and the Lesser Atlas, towering over nearer ranges of lower hills. This is, of course, the grandest part of our landscape....You should have seen how I made a conquest of the affections of an Arab horse to-day. They are such beauties, but they do not use them well....

Other friends near at hand were Mr. Leigh-Smith, lately Member for Norwich, and his three daughters. One of these became Madame Bodichon, who founded Girton College and was the intimate friend of George Eliot; and another Miss Anna Leigh-Smith, for whose health the family were wintering in Algiers. The latter became our life-long friend, a woman of stern intellectual vigour and an unwavering kindness, characteristics she still made clear to one of us on her death-bed in 1918. They all sketched very cleverly. I think their brother, Captain Leigh-Smith, R.N., of Arctic renown, was with them also for a part of the season.

So here, as usual, friends were ready waiting, as it were, for George and Louisa MacDonald; and it is interesting to note how some of these impressed them when first introduced:

G.M.D. to Miss Caroline C. Powell.

ALGERIA,
Christmas Eve of 1856.

MY DEAR SISTER,

Our days move on without much variety, for I am not able for long walks or much exertion....If I were able I should go to high mass at midnight to-night, which I do not think would shock Archdeacon Wix[1] and his lady so much as they will be shocked when they find out, if ever they do, that I count *The Church* as much a sect as the Independents or the Mormonites! They are very kind to us and we like them....I was interested to find when

---

1   The Rev. Edward Wix, sometime Archdeacon of New Zealand, then vicar of St. Michael's, Swanmore, Ryde, and a frequent contributor to the *Gentleman's Magazine*.

we saw the Miss Leigh-Smiths last that they expect a Miss Bessie Parkes, somewhat known as a poetess and a friend of our Mr. Sutton, to visit them this week. They are rather fast, devil-may-care sort of girls [!] not altogether to our taste, but very pleasant; and they seem to draw and paint well. One of them [Anna] who is in poor health, is more sweet and womanly. But what is all this for? I had better have told you of the silvery-grey sea of this day, bounded by a narrow horizon-belt of intense and dazzling blue; over which silver-grey, immense lateen sails, with an enormously deep-reaching reflection, went crawling, moved not by the wind, for there was none, but the oars of the boat below. Meantime I have learned something of the face of Nature and the face of man—very little of the face of woman though! I look keenly through the thin Manchester stuff over the Moorish faces, but I see almost invariably a sickly, thin countenance—at least in appearance through the veil, with soft black eyes over it, and often made hideous by stained eyebrows, meeting in Moorish arches over the nose. The Jewish women, who expose all the face but the chin, are gorgeously dressed as to colour, but odiously as to form, and are invariably unpleasant looking—I would say *ugly* if I were not writing about women. But the men are often superb—the Arabs especially. I think the most beautiful arm for texture and form I have ever seen is the property of a negro, a right black one too; and he seemed to prize it, for he had on it, more than half way above the elbow, a pale-red flat tight bracelet, which set the black off well. This is certainly the place for the study of the human form....

A small party of English people so far from home, the nearest shopping centre, so to speak, being Marseilles, were necessarily thrown much together. They met frequently at one another's apartments in the evenings for tea and talk, with an occasional picnic expedition into the desert. At such gatherings, none being blessed with superfluity of china and so forth, each would bring what they could. Mr. and Mrs. Oliphant,[1] with their son and daughter, now Lawrence Oliphant, M.D., and Mrs. Ormond of Southbourne, possessed the only large china teapot, as I am advised by the latter, as well as six silver teaspoons. These were in great request. Mrs. Ormond sends me a

---

[1] This gentleman's father was William Oliphant the publisher in Edinburgh. The family were wintering in Algiers for Mr. Oliphant's health. I am grateful to Mrs. Ormond for many particulars of this winter's incidents.

few extracts from her mother's diary, and among them this scrap:

> The George MacDonalds we see almost daily. His conversation is clever, and when for the time his writing is cast aside, he is like a merry schoolboy enjoying his recreation hour, unsophisticated, genial and good hearted.

It is delightful to be reminded yet again of my father's gaiety of spirits. The intimacy with women so well read and cosmopolitan as the Leigh-Smiths, and belonging to an order of free-thinking intelligence different from any he had yet had intimacies with, offered, I conceive, a new outlook. My parents had brought an introduction to them from Garth Wilkinson, and the two young ladies had been asked by Lady Byron to call upon the young poet's wife. It must have been their intellectually emancipated conversation—a little aggressive, to judge from my own intimacy with one of them—their wealth and their disregard for convention, that gave him the impression on first meeting that they were a little "fast and devil-may-care." They were, by the way, cousins of Florence Nightingale, and were not unlike that lady in their decisiveness of utterance and their tendency, with all their liberality of mind, to intolerance of weaker understandings and less wise dogmatics. The impression of *fastness* may have been strengthened when at a picnic to Pointe Pescade, four or five miles north-west of Algiers, lunch being laid in the shade of an old Moorish Café, with olive woods all around, Miss Bessie Rayner Parkes, a cousin who had recently joined their party, asked Mr. Oliphant for a cigar, which she lit and smoked as if, Mrs. Oliphant wrote, the experience was not new to her.[1]

---

[1] Miss Parkes was a daughter of Joseph Parkes the politician, her mother being the youngest daughter of Joseph Priestly, who discovered oxygen and supported the Unitarian Creed with such fine animus. In 1868 she married M. Belloc, and became the mother of Hilaire Belloc. She wrote on literary and social subjects, and had published a volume of poetry.

The climate did not suit my mother, and she suffered—like so many others, my father told me—from the sirocco and the melancholy it induced. Though the news of the children was good, she pined for them, in spite of the small Mary's bright chatter and singing. The child, moreover, contracted the endemic ophthalmia. Yet my mother joined in all the simple pleasures.

Mrs. G.M.D. to Miss Caroline C. Powell.

[1857, undated.]

...We gave a soirée the other night, and with flowers made the room look quite pretty—great boughs of lovely scented acacia and lots of hawthorn and dear dark rich roses and wild pimpernels, large dark blue ones, and though they were all people with lots of money, I think they enjoyed themselves without wine or delicacies.

But even in this climate George MacDonald could not outwit the bronchitis, and he had more than one severe attack in the spring. So they remained till the end of April, and then, as he said, he would give up invalidism altogether. "Indeed, I would rather die trying it than live as we are doing now," he wrote to his father. And yet he was writing, writing always, one result being that his first volume of poetry was published the following year.

G.M.D. to his Father.

ALGIERS [1857, *undated*].

...I feel with you in the fact that your sons have needed so much to be done for them.[1] *For me, if it please God, I shall do better by and by. If not, I hope He will let me go very soon—for if I cannot provide for my family, I would rather not add to the burden. At the same time, some of what is given to me must be regarded in a very different light from charity in the ordinary sense of the word. True, it would not be offered to me if I did not require it; but if I contribute to make life endurable or pleasurable or profitable, I do not see why I should be ashamed of having that acknowledged in the way I need, any more than if I were paid for keeping a merchant's books....*You may hope that I shall not

---

1 My Uncle Charles was leaving for Sydney after his father had settled his heavy debts.

refuse to do anything that I can honestly undertake to provide for my family as soon as I return. I would far rather take a situation in a shop than be idle.

A new edition of *Within and Without* will be published in the spring; and I expect it will be accompanied by a new volume....

I have italicized the above passages because they express very simply how my father's work had to be apprized rather by some law of spiritual economics than condemned by the world on the score of his not "getting on." His work was the scattering of seed wide flung and free for whomsoever, even fowls of the air, might need them. Having thus no market value, in spite of increase a hundredfold, they could not expect just wage. A few, like Lady Byron, understood this. His services to the world being poetic—miraculous, not to be appraised—stood above economic law and custom, and might find their dues only through channels of love—which also are miraculous always.

BOOK VI
HASTINGS

CHAPTER I
THE TACKLEWAY

AT the end of April 1857 George MacDonald with his wife and little girl returned from Algiers. They had a bad crossing to Marseilles, and my mother suffered severely, though the hope of again holding her children sustained her. She used to tell how the youngest, now fifteen months, all through the first night after their return howled afresh every time he was put into his cot until taken back into his long lost place of rest, and how happy his naughtiness made her, notwithstanding her fatigue.

The first thing to be done was to put the volume of poems through the press, as Longmans must have it published by the end of June; and the second to find a home that should offer some hope of permanency. Medical advice was against a return to Manchester, and my father's best friends favoured his living in or near London, as the centre of literary and educational activity. But as he was almost immediately ill again with a bronchial attack, it seemed that their home should be sought on the South Coast if possible, at any rate for the following winter. Meantime the summer was spent at The Limes. My father paid a visit to Manchester at the end of May to settle his affairs there, to bid farewell to his little following at Bolton, and to see the Scotts, the Suttons, the Andrews, the Colemans, but more particularly his brother John, now teaching at Barrow Hall, near Warrington, the moated grange four hundred years old, where he had much leisure for reading.

On his return to London my father at last met Lady Byron; and one may presume she had been hardly less desirous of meeting the writer whose health she had done so much to restore. Something of his first impressions of her he tells his father:

> G.M.D. to his Father.
>
> THE LIMES,
>
> [*June* 1857].
>
> ...I have been to see Lady Byron. She is the most extraordinary person, of remarkable intellect, and a great, pure, unselfish soul. She has made a proposal to me to edit a number of letters which she has at different times received from distinguished persons. But this must not be mentioned to anyone. Even if it is published, I presume her name will be quite concealed. If all goes well, and she commits the papers into my hands, I presume she will advance me a little money to work upon, which will deliver me from immediate difficulties.[1] By the post preceding this, I have at length sent you a copy of my new book, which I hope you will accept—both in itself, and in its dedication to yourself....I wish I could come and see you, but I have no money, and I cannot very well leave Louisa just now.

The closing lines of the dedication must be quoted here:

> Thou hast been faithful to my highest need;
> And I, thy debtor, ever, evermore,
> Shall never feel the grateful burden sore.
> Yet most I thank thee, not for any deed,
> But for the sense thy living self did breed
> That fatherhood is at the great world's core.

If in *Within and Without* we have some reminders of his youth's passionate immaturity, of a spiritual gloom contrasting strangely with the songs and sonnets that flash out like stars for an enduring glory, perfect in form and clarity of utterance, this new volume was of the day-spring purely.

Take *Lessons for a Child* as expressing his *pantheism*: a word I use in Wordsworthian sense, and antithetic to any crude theory that, admitting God's manifestation in natural

---

[1] The proposition went no further. It may be noted that Lady Byron's age was then sixty-five—that of George MacDonald's father.

phenomena, denies His personality and transcendent, creating presence—and there an end of it. George MacDonald's *pantheism was faith in the Father of all life, whose living word perpetually creates, inspires and redeems the whole world*:

> There breathes not a breath of the morning air
> But the spirit of Love is moving there;
> Not a trembling leaf on the shadowy tree
> Mingles with thousands in harmony,
> But the spirit of God doth make the sound
> And the thoughts of the insect that creepeth around.

Or again, as expression of the inevitable mutual dependence and co-operation of all things—their *commensalism*, to use a suggestive word from Science's vocabulary—implied in this sense of God's universal immanence, take *The Tree's Prayer*:

> Oh for the joyous birds,
> Which are the tongues of us mute longing trees!
> Oh for the billowy odours, and the bees
> Abroad in scattered herds.

The collection brings assurance of the writer's lyric power in expressing the deep truth in common things. Nothing more simple has he ever written than *Better Things*, of which I quote but three verses:

> Better to love than be beloved,
>   Though lonely all the day;
> Better the fountain in the heart,
>   Than the fountain by the way.
>
> Better than thrill a listening crowd,
>   Sit at a wise man's feet;
> But better teach a child, than toil
>   To make thyself complete.
>
> Better a death when work is done,
>   Than earth's most favoured birth;
> Better a child in God's great house,
>   Than the King of all the earth.[1]

---

1   It is interesting to compare two of these selected verses with their changes in the *Poetical Works* (vol. i, p. 403).

Alongside with such examples, I am constrained to quote a passage illustrating the power of my father's prose in poetic diction as well as defining, as poetry is not called upon to do, one aspect of his faith:

> All about us, in earth and air, wherever the eye or ear can reach, there is a power ever breathing itself forth in signs, now in daisy, now in a windwaft, a cloud, a sunset; a power that holds constant and sweetest relation with the dark and silent world within us. The same God who is in us, and upon whose tree we are the buds, if not yet the flowers, also is all about us—inside, the Spirit; outside, the Word. And the two are ever trying to meet in us; and when they meet, then the sign without, and the longing within, become one in light, and the man no more walketh in darkness, but knoweth whither he goeth. [1]

If his fairy stories are the best of George MacDonald's imaginative prose, then his lyrics are the best of his poetry. The secret even of the didactic in *Better Things* is its magic. Even the homeliest of ballads, be it of tears or laughter, appeals to that instinctive apprehension which schoolteaching tends to discredit. In the ballad, however, my father had hardly yet shown his vigour and raciness, for *Phantastes* was not published. But apart from its riming stanzas, this volume of *Poems* manifests an increasing freedom in blank verse, particularly in *A Hidden Life*. Its poetical vision into the life of sweet common things makes it ring truer and simpler than *Within and Without*, even though it has none of the matchless songs of the dramatic poem. In *The Lost Soul* there is such obvious tragic power that, once read, it can never be forgot, even if some reviewers stigmatized it as belonging to the "spasmodic school." [2]

Some points of the *Scotsman's* critique (August 12, 1857) are interesting:

> This second volume from the pen of Mr. MacDonald is marked with the striking characteristics which distinguished his former work; the earnestness of thought, the deep religiousness, and the mingled simplicity

---

1 *Thomas Wingfold*, vol. iii, p. 135
2 That brilliant critic, Prof. W. E. Aytoun's term for a group of poets like Philip James Bailey, Alexander Smith and Sydney Dobell.

and power of utterance are the same....His poetry is not for the few who have erected a particular standard of taste, but for the many who are scattered, for the sheep having no shepherd. The dogmatist, if he lingers there, will find the tightly-wound coil of his prejudices unwinding he knows not how, and the child-heart, somewhere hidden in the breast of every living man, awaken and yearn towards the truth....

But to return. In spite of all the difficulties, my father went to Huntly on a short visit; and most happily, for never on earth was he to meet his father again. How long he remained I do not know, as only one letter thence remains—and that undated.

On his return to The Limes, where he found my mother in very poor spirits, he writes his father of their need to make a home again:

G.M.D. to his Father.

THE LIMES
August 27, 1857.

We find it is useless to try anything till we have a house. We had a prospect last week of getting a young man to live with us for twelve months for which we hoped to have £100, as I would have given him three hours a day of instruction. But the fact that we had not a house was made the ground of postponement, though perhaps the real reason was that we were not Church people....Thank you very much for both your letters and for the *Scotsman*. It is a very gratifying review. We are anxious to get by ourselves again and have our children with us. If we could but get *bread literally* we should be content, and might perhaps thrive better on it than on dainties unearned....

On August 31st another baby-girl came, and she was named Irene. A day or two before my father dined alone with Lady Byron in Dover Street. She asked him to tell her absolutely of his affairs, saying: "I hope it is no disgrace to me to be rich as it is none to you to be poor," adding in her simple, most matter-of-fact manner: "If I can do anything for you, you must understand, Mr. MacDonald, it is rather for the public than yourself." A few days later she wrote, and enclosed a cheque for £25, and promised him £50 at Christmas. At that time she kept no horses so that she might have more to give away, says my father.

But Lady Byron was not in favour of Hastings—a place she knew well. She writes: "there is no life of mind in the place, except under clerical influence; and in the matter of pupils Brighton is too fashionable a competitor."

Nevertheless, Hastings was chosen and a house on the already decaying Tackleway[1] was found to be suitable for economy and shelter. Lady Byron herself, I learn from other sources, had spent some months at East Hill House, immediately below the Tackleway at the south end of All Saints Street, and may possibly have suggested this part of the old town.

The house chosen was and is still named Providence House; but however truly it was divinely provided, its simplicity hardly tallied with its pretentious name, and my parents during their tenancy re-styled it Huntly Cottage, though it had thirteen good-sized rooms. Its low rent of £35 was accounted for by its unfashionable situation. It is now divided into shabby tenements and has reverted to its earlier name. But it was in fair condition then, and would have been roomy enough to accommodate one or two pupils, should such be forthcoming; while its first-floor drawing-room was large enough for lectures.

G.M.D. to his Father.

East Hill, Hastings,
October 15, 1857.

We are in our own house at last, and our landlady has let us have the use of her furniture till our own arrives, so that we can manage pretty well, having only two of the children and a nurse with us....We have got a very pretty house, though not in a fashionable part of the town, which may interfere with our success. However, we could not do better....I hope to keep well enough to be very busy, and deliver lectures as I did in Manchester....

---

1 The Tackleway in older maps is named East Hill Walk, and had a row of grand old trees. But when the fashion left it they were cut down. Thereafter it was used as a ropewalk—hence its name of Tackleway.

Before they were really settled he was again laid up, but in early December he is able to write thus:

> *G.M.D. to his Father.*
>
> Hastings,
> Dec. 2, 1857.
>
> ...I had hoped to have a fairy tale or something of the sort ready by Christmas, but that has been quite prevented by my illness. I send you one of Lady Byron's letters in which she mentions my books. Poor lady, she is very ill. She sent me the other day the £50 she promised for Christmas, with just a note on the envelope that she was too ill to delay sending it.... You must not lose heart, my dear Father, for your family. You have got through so far with great difficulty, and so shall we, but as long as God thinks it worth while to let us suffer, it is worth while. If success in this life were an end, we might say all our family has failed, on all sides; but this life is but a portion and will blend very beautifully into the whole story.[1] May the one Father make us all clean at last, and when the right time comes, wake us out of this sleep into the new world, which is the old one, when we shall say as one that wakes from a dream, *Is it then over, and I live?* I for my part would not go without one of my troubles. The only one I fret at is being dependent....

The new house, to judge from its rather inaccessible roadway, its quaint old surroundings of irregular gables and red roofs, its timber-and-slate construction, was unpretentious enough for any poor poet to work in and shelter his family. But it was larger than its frontage suggests, being built on a hillside; so that what was basement as to the front of the house looked at the back over the roofs of the houses below it. The drawing-room on the first floor had a great bay extending the whole width of the house, affording a splendid view of the old town spread up and down in the valley below. The churches of St. Clements and All Saints stood above the red roofs to left and right; while above them to the west rose sharply the Castle Hill, which, surmounted by its hoary ruin looking out to sea, ran with grassy sheep-

---

[1] "Poor indeed is any worldly success compared to a moment's breathing in divine air, above the region where the miserable word *success* yet carries a meaning." (*St. George and St. Michael*, vol. iii, p. 284.)

cropped braes and spinneys of fir and oak northwards till joined by the rising vale at the village of Ore. To the south, over the low-lying town, was the sea. Rising sharply in front was the East Hill, giving protection from all wind in that quarter, yet offering fierce bracing at the cost of a sharp climb. The Tackleway ends in All Saints Churchyard up-climbing steeply, and at its south in a flight of steps leading down into the midst of those tarred-wood, two- three-, or four-tier huts where the fishermen store their nets and tackle. Vehicles get to the Tackleway by two narrow roads of steep ascent and by many alleys, into one of which the kitchen of Huntly Cottage opened immediately opposite the back door of the next house.[1]

The furniture arrived at last, a good deal spoiled by its storage and travels. Its unpacking, thanks to the cayenne pepper used to keep moth away, gave the master a severe attack of asthma and bronchitis; so that, till the sorting and cleansing was over, he fled to friends in Brighton for a week.

The children were gathered together again, and my mother, as usual, wrought miracles. The only servant at first was, in her master's words, "a girl of fourteen or fifteen with joints like a Dutch doll and a brain like a Dutch cheese." They were hardly settled when Christmas was upon them; and my mother, though almost worn out, would not let such a trifle as a half-settled house interfere with the children's happiness on the Day of Days, or their sharing it with others less fortunate.

---

[1] It belonged to a Mr. Inskip, the Town Clerk. I take this opportunity of recording my personal indebtedness to his two charming daughters—one or other of whom I am proud to regard as being the first to tempt my heart out of my mother's safe keeping. Was it not she who awakened in my three-year-old bosom its quite passionate and not yet defunct love for a cold potato in curling brown jacket, to be eaten from the fingers only? Across the steep alley I would step into the opposite door emboldened rather by a seductive larder than the ladies' lavish embraces.

CHAPTER II
ADESTE FIDELES

IN a collection of manuscripts written by the Powell family for their father on his seventy-seventh birthday, I find my mother's description of the first Christmas, 1857, at Hastings. Whose ever the project had been, it was the mistress of Huntly Cottage who took upon herself the copying into fair hand and the decoration with her brush and colours of these literary items, each separately removable by two little silk tassels of various colours from the leather portfolio daintily embossed on one side with a basket of coloured flowers and on the other bearing the legend in painted lettering, "Dear Papa from Your Children's Thoughts." The contributions were not signed, so that, being all copied out by the same hand, the authorship cannot in every case be determined. One contains the germinal idea of *The Shadows*—a story subsequently to appear in *Adela Cathcart* (1864), and *Dealings with the Fairies* (1867).[1] It was probably written down by my mother after oral telling by my father, for the diction is not his. Other items were a translation of a German fairy story; little essays on "Happiness" and "The New Year"; a school-boy incident written probably by my Uncle Alec Powell, with youthful vigour and exaggeration; some indifferent verse and the love story of a friend who died in his youth. But the chief contribution is my mother's picture of their simple Christmas hospitality.

---

[1] And now in *Fairy Stories*, by George MacDonald, Centenary Edition, 1924. Allen and Unwin.

On Christmas Eve had arrived two parcels from The Limes and a "bran-cake."

Everyone was busy, parents, children and servants [there were now two, Sarah, the Devonshire nurse, and Elizabeth, "the Dutch cheese"], adorning the Christmas-tree, making dresses, puddings, caps, and the father sticking up Christmas pictures on the nursery walls to delight the little ones in the morning.[1]

The only sadness was little Mary Josephine's eyes, which had never quite recovered from the Algiers ophthalmia.

Christmas Day, 1857. Poor little Elfie's eyes are quite shut. She is very patient, and listens quite quietly to all the talk about the presents and the company expected. Husband and I walked to St. Leonards-on-Sea to see the doctor. A beautiful Christ's Day it was. On our return we found our first guest, little Annie—she owns no other name, her very existence being ignored by her parents—joining our little ones in games of scampering and taking in turns to lead about the poor little blind girl, who looked most pathetic with her outstretched hands feeling everything. Her little new black frock and scarlet jacket with its little gold buttons could only be felt, stroking its soft texture and feeling the buttons. After a short early dinner the thirteen poor children came in, with clean frocks and bright faces, to see the Christmas tree. Husband told them the story of the Ugly Duckling.[2] The big ones enjoyed the history, the little ones wondering at everything they saw from the big tree and the big gentleman and his books down to the little baby—though all of them had "got one at home too."...

They all had some 1d. toy or 1d. book, or pair of warm mits from the tree, which, however, was not lighted yet. Then they all went into another room, where they ate a cake or a bun, and husband talked to them again and told them the true story of the day—about the good Christ-child. They were all so modest and happy—even the aristocracy of our company, the carpenter's children.

Then they went away glad enough with half a Clapton orange each. At five o'clock we lighted the tree in the middle of the tea-table, at the top of which was the day's luxury, the Plum Pudding....How happy everyone looked! The big ones, none of them thinking of themselves, but all pleasing

---

1 I well remember among these the big Robin in the snow.
2 *À propos* of my father's gift in story-telling the late Mr. Oliphant Smeaton wrote thus in 1905: "To hear him telling a fairy or a brownie or a goblin romance was to listen to a master in the art. I remember him long ago [1865, probably], when I was very ill, sitting by my bedside for hours telling me tale after tale from his inexhaustible fairy wallet." (*The Scottish Review*, September 28, 1905.)

the little ones; and thus came in their own pleasure. A teetotum, Sarah's present for Greville, which had been hanging and twirling on the tree all tea-time,[1] was now brought down, and reels of cotton, 1d. candlesticks, nuts, figs, oranges were numbered and gambled for. The little brooches on the tree for Aunties were to be sent on New Year's Eve.

Then followed the mysterious bran-cake which had been the cause of much wondering anticipation all day. The poor Elf had been all the while feeling everything and getting the little gifts described to her, but never able to open her eyes. Once she said, "I suppose God doesn't wish me to see to-night." The delight of diving the hand into the "soft bran" as Elfie called it, and pulling out a treasure for somebody was something delicious. I wish the senders of the bran-cake could have seen the faces, and heard the exclamations! A history of Punch and Judy was one of the presents the tree afforded Papa, and great glee was there over the display of his elocutionary talents in giving it to our party. I like just to note our pleasure that Sarah and Elizabeth were kindly recognized from Clapton as part of our household, just as we like to do here.

Sunday, December 27th. A beautiful holyday! Husband and I and all the children down on the beach. All at once a little whisper from Elfie—"Mama, I can see a little!" Then, in a few minutes she bounded away from me, jumping over the breakers—it being low-water. Then the exclamations, "Oh, there is my darling baby, how sweet she looks! Papa! Mama!" scampering to our sides. We were as glad and light-hearted as she: the lost sight was found again!

In the evening talking to them both delighted me, Mary with her loving assurance about God being so kind. "I should like to see God so much and tell him how glad I am he lets me see again!" and Lily with her puzzled anxious looks about almost all I told her. Her tears came fast in her distress at Jesus lying asleep when they were all so frightened in the boat in the storm, but Mary was sure he had not forgotten them, though he was asleep.

December 30th. To-day comes news of the little new cousin's birth. [2]Mary jumped about the room and danced with delight. Her face got so red. "I'm so glad, for we often wanted a baby and a nurse when I was at Auntie's. Mama, I daresay God knewed Auntie wanted a baby—p'raps she asked God to give her one, so he made her a little girl. I wonder where he gets our bones from. I wonder how he puts our feet on. Mine are so nicely put on."

---

1 Ivory it was, and remained my greatest treasure for many years, its companion a Black-Forest, unpainted horse of matchless merits, and a china medicine-spoon no less cherished. They all keep company in my old heart with Sarah, my Devonshire nurse.
2 Mrs. Joseph King's first child. Mary had been staying with her while Huntly Cottage was furnishing.

That the inspiring spirit of these festivities was my mother is obvious enough, a spirit we shall often see in like transformations of forbidding circumstances. If "more are the children of the desolate than the children of the married wife," then my mother usurped the privilege of the former in addition to her own. I can conceive of no more perfect counterpart to my father's faith than these practical works of my mother, so literally creative, "as the clay is in the potter's hand."

The following letter comes well in sequence to the manuscript just quoted and adds some details to its picture:

G.M.D. to his Father.

Huntly Cottage,
January 2, 1858.

...I am wonderfully better. The weather is very fine. Christmas Day and New Year's Day were both fit for Algiers...The house is pretty comfortable now, but the floors are very open between the boards. Through these the wind blows like knives. But I shall put the demon out by degrees. I have pasted brown paper over the cracks in the floor in two rooms, and we have two more that want it very much....I am writing a kind of fairy tale [*Phantastes*] in the hope it will pay me better than the more evidently serious work. This is in prose. I had hoped that I should have it ready by Christmas, but I was too ill to do it....Louisa is very well, and the children—except Mary, who constantly suffers from her eyes. She has wonderful spirits, though almost too good sometimes. She is a strange child. We think sometimes that she will not live long.[1] She is very thin and delicate—a most elfish creature. We call her *Elfie* when she is good and *Kelpie* when she is naughty.

Could you send us some more meal soon. This is not finished, but I have taken to eating a good quantity every morning myself. Indeed, I take nothing else but a cup of tea....

The household now settled down into regular ways, its master with a study that he could once more call his own. The children with the strong feelings of their parents reproduced in them, their vigorous individuality and constant need of caressing, besides their frequent illness, would have been

---

1 Her death in 1878 from lung disease was the first break in the family.

difficult but for discipline that secured an obedience less passive than co-operative. An illustration of this is given by a friend presently introduced by Miss Anna Leigh-Smith, for hospitable entertainment—a Miss Blythe, who later married Mr. Charles Matthews of Birmingham. The visitor thus describes the home's old-fashioned orderliness:

> I was delightfully received by a strikingly handsome young man and a most kind lady, who made me feel at once at home. There were five children at that time, all beautifully behaved and going about the house without troubling anyone. On getting better acquainted with the family, I was much struck by the way in which they carried on their lives with one another. At a certain time in the afternoon you would, on going upstairs to the drawing-room, see on the floor several bundles—each one containing a child! On being spoken to, they said, so happily and peacefully, "We are resting," that the intruder felt she must immediately disappear. No nurse was with them. One word from the father or mother was sufficient to bring instant attention....In the evenings, when the children were all in bed, Mr. MacDonald would still be writing in his study—*Phantastes*, it was—and Mrs. MacDonald would go down and sit with her husband, when he would read to her what he had been writing; and I would hear them discussing it on their return to the drawing-room. To hear him read Browning's *Saul* with his gracious and wonderful power was a thing I shall never forget. Mrs. MacDonald's energy and courage were untiring and her capabilities very unusual.[1]

---

1 I am indebted to Mrs. Matthews' daughter, Mrs. George Rathbone of Liverpool, for this reminiscence.

CHAPTER III
FATHER AND BROTHER FALL ASLEEP

FEBRUARY 1858 brought news that John MacDonald was ill, his lungs gravely affected. Early in April he came to Huntly Cottage, to be nursed; but neither the sheltered bracing nor my father's and mother's devotion did much for him. Dr. Hale, their generous adviser, gave but little hope.

The following letter mentions for the first time a visit to F.D. Maurice, who introduced my father to Smith, Elder & Co., as possible publishers of *Phantastes*. Their immediate acceptance of it and payment, as well as the statement that it had taken but two months to write, are interesting. My father's industry was amazing.

G.M.D. to his Father.

[*Undated.*]

I had a most successful visit [to London]—got some books I much wanted at moderate cost—visited Mr. Maurice and Lady Byron—put a little MSS. that took me two months to write without any close work—a sort of fairy tale for grown people, into a new publisher's hands and two days after had £50 in my hands for it.[1] I likewise have plenty of work on my hands for printing in one way and another. Indeed I shall now be *fully* occupied for some time. I am going to give some lectures, too, here, as I did in Manchester....

G.M.D. to his Father.

HASTINGS,
April 18*th*, 1858.

...Our Doctor says it is out of the question for John to go to Scotland in May. He must not think of doing anything for eight or ten months....We are most happy to have this charge given to us. Louisa is only most pleased that *we* should have it to do. Though I say it that shouldn't, she is a first-

---

1 This sum was paid for the copyright.

FATHER AND BROTHER FALL ASLEEP

rate nurse—and we both know something of the sick room. So you may be comfortable about him. The Doctor attends him as my friend, and charges nothing. I think he will be interested in him for his own sake. I am very glad to have him with us; for we understand each other so well. And as to expense—never think of that. Thank God He takes all anxiety off us. The more we want the more we have and shall have. Things are looking well for us—but God is the giver—and He has plenty. It is very sad for those who cannot trust in him: it is miserable slavery.

About this time my Uncle Charles returned from Sydney, apparently with schemes for making his fortune and that of his many friends. He assured my mother that in a few months he would be able to write her a cheque for a thousand pounds and never miss it. Though his intentions were honest and generous, his brother throughout his long life had constantly to supplement his precarious supplies.

My father was now giving lectures on English Literature in the drawing-room of Huntly Cottage, and although they did not yet attract many hearers, they were bringing in something.

G.M.D. to his Father.

HASTINGS,
May 20, 1858.

I returned last Saturday, having seen a number of different people in London. I spent some time with Lady Byron, dined with the Recorder [Russell Gurney], spent a day with Caleb Morris, etc., etc., and came home tired rather. Perhaps I may bring John home to you in a little while....His cough seems to us less, and certainly the pain is *very* much less. He is decidedly more cheerful, and eats better, though doubtless he is in a precarious condition still. God's will be done. If He make your sons—after (it may be) a long time—good men, you will be satisfied that none of them had the success which on many accounts would be desirable. I have just had a note from Lady Byron announcing the sending of a mantle for my wear....I am very well.

But my Uncle John's condition soon became hopeless. His one desire was to go home and my father was planning to take him.

Sunday evening,
[June (?) 1858.]

MY VERY DEAR FATHER,

John has had a bad turn again since you wrote, but he is now almost over it again. He cannot travel yet, though....Meantime I believe he feels quite at home with us, and all we can do for him we will. We both read to him when we can, but he is only able for a bit of a story at a time and is soon tired even of that. He is certainly in a very doubtful condition—but God's will is best. As to what you say in your last letter about giving up to the will of God, and then taking it again—I would just say that it is only by having wishes of our own that we are able to give up to the will of God. It is live things, not dead carcases that must be brought to his altar. And then we do not know what his will is—it may be the same as our wish, for all that we know.

God is good to me. I have prospects of lectures in London that will bring me in the necessary money for another few weeks. If the plan succeeds I shall be the guest part of the time of the Recorder—whose lady is managing the affair for me.[1] I expect to go to London next week, and John bids me say that if he is able he will accompany me to London, and sail from there for Aberdeen. But *I* doubt it....

And out of all the letters written to his father by George MacDonald from his tenth to his thirty-fifth year, this is the last extant.

Either my father or my Uncle Charles must have gone with my Uncle John to Huntly, where he arrived safely, and died on July 7th, aged twenty-eight.

> In the hush of noon he died,
> The sun shone on—why should he not shine on?
> Glad summer noises rose from all the land;
> The love of God lay warm on hill and plain;
> 'Tis well to die in summer.
>   When the breath,
> After a hopeless pause, returned no more,
> The father fell upon his knees, and said:
> "O God, I thank thee; it is over now!
> Through the sore time thy hand has led him well,
> Lord, let me follow soon, and be at rest."[2]

---

1 Thomas Erskine of Linlathen had written in July 1855 to Mrs. Russell Gurney thus of *Within and Without*: "I like it better than any poetry and most prose that I have read for many years."
2 *A Hidden Life*, p. 167.

FATHER AND BROTHER FALL ASLEEP

A few days after the burial, my grandfather was at dusk going out at a little gate that opened from the farm precincts to a back road running up on to the moor, and saw a figure coming towards this gate. He stepped back within the gate. The figure passed on, but then turned, and my grandfather saw it was John, with plaid over his shoulder in his customary manner. The old man hastened after, but, because of his lameness, failed to overtake the wayfarer before he disappeared at a bend of the ascending road. When my grandfather reached the turn, the figure could not be seen anywhere, though the road and country were so open that no one could have found covert. A man not readily conceding supernatural manifestations, my grandfather hurried home, quite awed and disturbed—so my grandmother told me; for he did not doubt that his beloved son had come back to him and was for conducting him somewhither.[1]

It was but a few weeks later, August 24th, that himself, apparently in perfect health, was seized by a fatal heart-attack. The previous night he had as usual walked round the farm to see that everything was in order. On his return he was stricken with violent pain in the left side of his chest. His brother was summoned and the doctor sent for. They poulticed him all night, and with some apparent relief. At eleven o'clock in the morning little Jeanie, then twelve years old, came to the room to ask her mother something. He was then lying in bed, the child's mother sitting by his side. He turned his head to see who was at the door, looked straight at his little daughter and smiled to her. But her mother then saw a death-like change pass over his face and called out to the child to run for the doctor; but he died immediately.

My Uncle Charles was at home. My father, who hurried northwards instant upon the telegram, did not see him alive.

My grandfather left his property, amounting in all to £1,100, to his wife, who at the end of the year left the old home.

---
1 This is the sole recorded instance of Celtic second-sight in my father's family.

CHAPTER IV
PHANTASTES

NO such sorrow as this loss of father and brother had yet ever touched George MacDonald. My mother has told me that, though tears would readily come over any tale of suffering, or when sharing another's joy or hearing fine music, he seldom wept even when his children were taken. Yet those who have found touch with him in his writings, particularly the *Diary of an Old Soul*, need not be told how the death, almost as if together, of these two men—the one his tower of strength, the other so much leaning upon him—wrung his very soul. The two dearest brothers and the strong father from whom their "earthly history began" were now gone, and himself stood in the front rank of those who wait.

How long my father remained at Huntly after they laid the beloved body in the family grave in Drumblade churchyard I do not know—enough to be assured that his mother would win through her suffering. For days she would pace the meadows, with bowed head, clenching and unclenching her hands held to her bosom in mute appeal against the inexorable; for few wives have such husbands as hers, few husbands such a wife as this, now left alone. But she could not live on at The Farm without him: she must take her two bairns away. My father knew he was uttering my mother's thoughts when he offered them his home and showed her how well they could now afford it.

G.M.D. to his Wife.[1]

[HUNTLY, *August* 26, 1858,]
Sunday night.

...My mother seems a little more cheerful to-day. Charles and I went to see some poor people this afternoon. It is very pleasant to hear how they all talk about my father. You would almost fancy he had been a kind of chief of the clan...

Now I have had your sad, sad letter. I do love you, and am so grateful for the love you give me. I think God will show himself very kind somehow or other to us both—not that I deserve it, but you do.... Do not think I am unhappy. I am glad my father has got through. I love him more than ever. I am cheerful and hopeful. My love to Lily. Tell her I will pull her tooth out for her if she likes. My love to them all and to you, good, kind, beautiful wife....

From this time onwards my father wrote as regularly to his stepmother as hitherto to his father, though the letters, being more concerned with family matters, invite only occasional quotation.

G.M.D. to his Stepmother.

[HASTINGS,
October 15, 1858.]

...My new book is just out, and I am asking my publisher to send you a copy. I am very well, and have the prospect of a tolerable amount of employment. I dreamed last night I saw my father. I felt I loved him so much and was clinging to him, when to my surprise I found he was so much taller than I, that I did not reach his shoulder. There is a meaning in that, is there not? His great soul has already learned so much more than we know. But we shall all find him again, and that will be a blessed day....Louisa joins me in warmest love to you....

My chair and all my things arrived quite safe.[2] I will write you a few words every week....

May God help you, dearest Mother, to go nearer to Him—that is the only thing that can comfort you for the loss of my father. There is no gift

---

1 Already quoted in part, p. 37.
2 Things of his father's. His special chair, in which I now sit, was my father's study-chair for longer than I remember. The only other thing remaining to me is a deep-mauve whisky decanter with silver-mounted cork. It always stood well filled on the sideboard at The Farm; yet, until the last few years, my grandfather never took any spirit, and then only one tablespoonful, always measured out by my grandmother, as a night-cap.

so good, but its chief goodness is that God gives it, and what he gives is not to be taken away again. Whatever good things we can fancy for ourselves, God has better than that in store for us. Even your sorrow is turned into joy, if you can say to God, "I am willing to be sorrowful, since it is thy will."...I am much obliged to Jeanie for her little letter and the feathers, which are already planted in Greville's cap....

During the next few months courses of lectures were given at Huntly Cottage and at Brighton. But they were not financially successful, and those at Brighton were abandoned. In later years my father refused absolutely to preach or lecture in any South Coast watering place, so little desirous of his help did he find their people. But his consolations were many. On October 28th *Phantastes* was published; and on November 6th, the fifth daughter, Winifred Louisa, was born, to be generally acknowledged as unusually pretty and well-behaved. The book, too, was well received—so well indeed that the hack reviewers were driven to vituperation.

Phantastes: A Faerie Romance for Men and Women, to give its full title, was a new adventure, and one into the highest realm of imaginative literature, that of symbolic presentation. That such mode of teaching is more instant in appeal and leaves more permanent impression than others of exact formulation, my father well understood. It was indeed the mode of his Master. Yet, because of commonplace, didactic mishandling, symbol, allegory, parable are nowadays often resented as puerile or pedagogical. We may be sure the scribes and pharisees would, in the cant of to-day, say Christ's parables and poetic symbols were unliterary and suitable only for the ignorant. Yet the finest art consists in allusive presentation of truth in outward form of beauty.

But *Phantastes* is more than symbolic, even though the *Athenæum* stigmatized it as no more than "a confusedly furnished, second-hand symbol-shop." Through its beauty it does something more than appeal to our feelings: it rouses them from sleepy contentment, sets us first wondering, then thinking, and at last awakens the resolve to set about some husbandry of life, or some defying of death.

All poets are preachers; a few are prophets. George MacDonald's fairy stories, as dear to children as to right-minded parents, are as full of hope as rainbows. The prophetic, like the poetic, depends upon its appeal: while the latter claims the illumination of feeling as its mission, the former compels thought and action, conversion and heroism. *Phantastes*, with its grace, its wit, its irony, makes us conscious of real magic in the air we breathe: it is a "candle of the Lord, searching all the inward parts." More, its symbolism appeals not only to the light within a man's own soul, but shows him his own shadow spreading over the world if ever he looks upon poesy as a mere anodyne to the chatter of facts that will not let him sleep.

In a letter to Mrs. A. J. Scott, my father thus refers to the book which he is sending her husband:

> I hope Mr. Scott will like my fairy-tale. I don't see what right the *Athenæum* has to call it an allegory and judge or misjudge it accordingly—as if nothing but an allegory could have two meanings!

Yet I do not quite see why my father should object to the definition; though, if we accept, say, the *Pilgrim's Progress* as the typical allegory, then should *Phantastes* be likened perhaps rather to the *Faerie Queen*. It is a story of chivalric romance; and if its hero never reaches the country he sets out to discover, he gets sufficient touch with it to believe thereafter more in ideal Truth than the passing beauty of a ponderable world. It is full of priceless gems, with barely a hint of preaching.

It may be remembered that immediately after my father's break-down in Manchester, he wrote to my mother in high praise of Hoffman's *Golden Pot*. I think it must have been Carlyle's translation, for I have that from among his books; but probably it led him to the original also. On reading this translation myself, in study of my father's intellectual position in 1856, I cannot but think it made an arresting impression upon him. It is splendid, dazzling in colour, very mad in a sort of riotous detail, but with a *meaning* which is stated at last when there can no longer be any need for it. Its moral is far more philosophical and definite than, as a work of art, it should bother itself to be; indeed, the story is greater than its writer knows: it transcends its apology. Its very madness, its rampant magic, its wit and tragic humour, its gentle touches of pathos, its faculty of *bi-local existing*—though this is suggested better by George MacDonald in *Phantastes, The Princess and the Goblin, The Back of the North Wind*, and, at the last, *Lilith*—must fascinate the imaginative reader.[1]

We have but to compare the opening of Hoffman's tale with the manner in which, in *Phantastes*, Anodos steps from his own bed into the daisied grass to see how both Celtic and German poet would have us understand that quite easily and unexpectedly we also may step—not *if we will*, but rather *if we are led*—out of the common tangible world into that truer land of faerie and imagery; and that having once set foot in it, we can never quite leave it, even though shadows of the tangible overwhelm the gentler beings of impalpable beauty. We may perhaps lose our soul, yet never more can we be unbelieving.

Should any who love my father's fairy-tales for their beauty alone—and they can never love amiss if they see their beauty—feel annoyance at my hampering them with a specific message—the *spiritual* quality they will not deny—he must turn to the penultimate page of *Phantastes*:

---

[1] To help the realization of *Phantastes*' place in imaginative literature, let me give one passage from *The Golden Pot*:

"'But,' said the student, 'don't you see that you are, everyone of you, corked up in glass bottles, and cannot for your life walk a hairs-breadth?'

"Here the Church scholars and Law Clerks set up a loud laugh, and cried: 'The student is mad; he fancies he himself is sitting in a glass bottle, though all the time he is standing on the Elbe-bridge and looking down into the water! Let's be off!'

"'Ah!' sighed the Student, 'by reason of their folly they don't feel the imprisonment which the salamander has cast them into.'"

I have come through the door of Dismay; and the way back from the world into which that has led me, is through my tomb. Upon that the red sign lies, and I shall find it one day and be glad.

Phantastes, in a word, is a spiritual pilgrimage out of this world of impoverishing possessions into the fairy Kingdom of Heaven:

> Surely Thy ships will bring to my poor shore
> Of gold and peacocks such a shining store
> As will laugh all the dreams to holy scorn
> Of love and sorrow that were ever born.[1]

As in such sublime utterances George MacDonald compels us to fresh adventure beyond the common arid concepts of a wholly undesirable future life, so does *Phantastes* bring home to us in allusive burgeoning the celestial purpose of our daily existence. Its very religion is fairyland—and how much more George MacDonald would have ourselves set out and discover.

Yet one other point is noteworthy in this book. Its author has discovered his lyrical felicity in ballad-writing. It was then still customary, in spite of Wordsworth, for the common critic to despise the ballad, though elemental and immortal in all folk-literature; but George MacDonald now realized to the full its possibilities. *Phantastes* has many snatches of ballad-verse, and in *"Sir Aglovaile through the churchyard rode"* we get it in complete and masterly style. As the inspiration of his fairy-tale was the spirit of the *volk-mährchen*, so the soul of folk-music took possession of his muse. Without the thatched cottage no cathedral had ever soared; without folk-song no oratorio; without ballad no ode or sonnet. The child is father of the man; and from now onwards we find the child's simple faith dominating all his writings as surely as in his youth it first took control of his theology.[2]

---

1 *Diary of an Old Soul*, August 28th.
2 In the Foreword to the edition of *Phantastes* in Everyman's Library I have explained the origin of its title. Unfortunately, the publishers (Dent) have listed it among "Books for Young People"; whereas the title-page of the first edition specifies it as *"A Faerie Romance for Men and Women."*

CHAPTER V
LADY BYRON

THE year 1859 brought further changes consequent upon George MacDonald's need of more money than his pen could earn. His reputation as a lecturer was rising steadily among intellectual circles in London. Lady Byron had introduced him to the Recorder of London, Russell Gurney, and his wife, they to Frederick Denison Maurice, and hence to a wider literary society. Through the Gurneys again a warm friendship was struck between Mrs. La Touche and my parents, but particularly my mother. A little later Mrs. La Touche introduced George MacDonald and John Ruskin. My father and mother, what with his ill-health and the demands of the young family upon herself, together with their poverty, could not move much in the social world. Yet Miss Mulock, Mrs. Oliphant, Charles Kingsley, Matthew Arnold and Henry Crabb Robinson ranked among their intimates, even if they did not meet very often; while Madame Bodichon gave them touch or intimacy with Mrs. Reid, the founder of Bedford College, Dr. Elizabeth Garrett, Mrs. Josephine Butler, whom they loved and deeply honoured, and other advanced thinkers.[1] North of the Tweed were such stalwart friends as John Stuart Blackie,

---

[1] Indeed, for a time, thanks to the frequent talk of women's rights, adopted even by my three elder little sisters in their white stockings, crinolines and Sunday, straw-poke-bonnets with pink bows and curtains, I am still crushed at times by the conviction—originating, I believe, when I was five or six, in the obligation to be polite to *ladies* (whom I heartily hated as an objectionable tribe)—that I, as a male, am still a worm. I even remember wondering how my mother could ever have married my father, he, with all his merits, being after all only a man!

Alexander Smith and Norman McLeod. One especially intimate in our home, as in our hearts, was the Rev. C. L. Dodgson, better known as Lewis Carroll, his friendship dating from the days of the Tackleway. I believe his troublesome stammer kept this most devout, learned and humorous lover of children from undertaking any clerical charge; but it was this misfortune that brought him into touch with my father. Our best friend at Hastings was the wise homœopath, Dr. Hale. His heretical sect in the profession were curiously addicted to philosophic studies and speculations, and probably had more sympathy with questions that bordered upon yet transcended medical science than most of the orthodox. Dr. Hale at any rate had a friend of some distinction as a philologist, but more as a curer of stammering, in James Hunt, Ph.D. Among the latter's patients at Ore was the author of *Alice in Wonderland*, and it was through Dr. Hunt that he and my father first met.

Another great friend was Alexander Munro, the sculptor. It was later, however, in his London studio, when I was sitting to him, or rather standing and shivering, as model for his fountain in Hyde Park, the boy and dolphin, that I remember some talk with the creator of *Alice in Wonderland* concerning the advantages of a marble head.[1] Once when Munro visited Hastings my father, coming indoors upon a windy day with his thick curling hair blowing all about him, arrested the sculptor's eye. Then and there he modelled the medallion of him, two replicas of which were later cast in bronze, one being now in the Scottish National Portrait Gallery in Edinburgh, and the other in King's College, Aberdeen. Like much of Munro's work, it lacks something in character.[2] A little later he introduced

---

1 Related in Lewis Carroll's own words in his *Life* by Collingwood (p.83.) I was probably five years old, and the year 1861. I doubt if any other member of my profession has his statue in Hyde Park!
2 Among Munro's public works may be mentioned the colossal statues of James Watt, outside the Town Hall, Birmingham, and that of Sir Robert Peel at Oldham.

Arthur Hughes, the Rosettis, and Maddox Browne to my parents.

A point of some interest is my father's attending at Hastings the lectures of a mesmerist, a Pole named Zamoiski, who was then exciting a good deal of talk among the clergy and fashionable intellectuals. On one occasion, I have heard, he challenged any member of the audience to mount the platform and tell his name. Greville Matheson boldly accepted; but when assured by the lecturer that he had entirely forgotten both Christian and surname, he failed in the test. It was this man that suggested to my father the character of *von Funkelstein* in *David Elginbrod*.[1]

Besides giving four lectures at the London Institution, an engagement that led to many others, my father was invited by the Philosophical Institution of Edinburgh to lecture in the summer of 1859—an apt tribute to his increasing renown as a speaker; and the Royal Institution of Manchester, realizing perhaps the crusts their city had formerly thrown to its guest, also secured him as a lecturer. So in May and August of 1859 we find him lecturing to large audiences, honestly enthusiastic in Manchester, critically approving in Edinburgh.

But earlier in the year—in February—the whole family went to London on various visits.

Now at last my father saw much of Lady Byron, and my mother, to her delight, shared the increasing intimacy. We find Lady Byron sending her carriage for them to luncheon or "tea-dinner"—in her wise and simple way. Indeed, so definitely did she make my mother one with my father in her heart, that she told both—a privilege accorded to very few—the

---

[1] An abstract of one lecture taken from the *Hastings and St. Leonards' News* gives an idea of the sort of stuff, that, under the name *Electro-biology*, passed for science then: "The lecturer explains all mesmeric phenomena by attributing them to the universal law of equilibrium. Like the passage of electricity from one overcharged cloud to another, so the animal magnetic fluid passes from one to another, seeking to produce an equilibrium. The first effect in the recipient are a coldness of the head and a state of insensibility, etc., etc...."

story of her separation from Lord Byron. Her reticence to the world set her even higher in their estimation. Neither of my parents, even in late life, would speak of it to anyone.

G.M.D. to his Stepmother.
Huntly Cottage,
Jan 19, 1859.

...I hope you will gradually be able to sleep better, dearest mother. May you know, when you are lying awake, that God is with you—our perfect good. My father is nearer Him now, and you will get nearer Him by losing my father. Even the bodily presence of Jesus in some degree prevented the disciples from finding God for themselves—the spiritual God, present to their hearts; and therefore it was expedient for them, as He said, that he should go away from them....Louisa longs to have you with us. We should make you as happy as you can be now in this world, we think. And you would help us so much....I am glad to hear Uncle and all of them are so kind. I should not wonder if they too learn more what my father was worth by his being taken away....

In April, lectures in London and the need to give Huntly Cottage renewals of paint and paper made it convenient to accept an invitation from Lady Byron.

Lady Noel Byron to G.M.D.
March 29th, 1859.

You shall be treated most inhospitably, dear Mr. MacDonald—put into a room apart where you can have as much solitude as you desire—with a private entrance-key that you may feel quite independent. No note will be taken of your goings out and comings in—when socially disposed you will *invite yourself*. A casual conv^n with you on one or two points might at that time help me.

Yours,
A.I.N.B.

He enjoyed her hospitality at 11 St. George's Terrace, Regent's Park, for a fortnight; and probably more than one "casual conversation" with his hostess pointed the advisability of living in London where the opportunities for work were increasing. Moreover it was quite clear by this time, that, so far as his bronchial and asthmatic tendencies were concerned, London suited him better than anywhere. About this time also the possibility of securing the Chair of English Literature at Bedford College came to the fore. Though the remuneration would be small, it would serve as a nucleus for other work; and his sister, Louie, who would have to earn her living before long, could attend the College and live with them. Lady Byron was at this time looking for a middle-class house that would be suitable as a home for young women thrown out of employment;[1] but at present her health would not allow her to begin this long-cherished project. Now, however, if she took the house she had in view, she could let my parents use it until they felt secure enough for other venture: herself as landlord would be easier for them than any other! The correspondence makes it clear—seeing that she discusses the expense to herself of furnishing—that she had in mind some ulterior scheme.

Professor de Morgan and his wife were, as everyone knows, intimate friends of Lady Byron. They lived at 7 Camden Street, N.W., a house that was afterwards Miss Buss's celebrated school. They left it in 1859.[2] The correspondence with William de Morgan, then seventeen, is amusing; and the two following letters explain matters:

Lady Noel Byron to Mrs. G.M.D.

August 4th, '59.

Dear Mrs. MacDonald,
   Illness prevented my being explicit enough. It had been a question between the de Morgans and myself about my purchasing the remainder, 6 years', of the lease, which might enable me to let you have it for somewhat

---

1   At least so I gather from the references to her generosities in my father's novel, *The Vicar's Daughter*, vol. ii, p.75.
2   According to Wm. De Morgan, the date was 1858, though Lady Byron's letter is dated 1859. In 1858, moreover, my parents had not thought of leaving Hastings. Vide *Wm. De Morgan and His Wife*, 1922, p.51.

Bronze Medallion by] GEORGE MACDONALD, 1855 [A. Munro

less than the £65 rent, without loss to myself....The garden has been invaluable to Mrs. de M. for her family.

My eldest grandson has returned. He has been working at his trade in the U.S.—and earned his passage on shipboard as a common sailor—a *man* in one sense at least.

Yours most truly,
A.I.N. BYRON.

[I enclose] this calculation from young de Morgan, for consideration on your journey. It is in favour of the purchase of the remaining terms. Hope to see you to-morrow.

The fragmentary enclosure dated July 29th gives his and his mother's calculations for a proposed expenditure of £800:

Purchase money of this house for 5 years at £60 a year and 6 per cent.—£335;

To furnishing said house—Imperially, £350; regally, £300; aristocratically, £250; respectably, £200; genteelly, £150; decently, £50. Taxes for 7 years, £100.

Choosing respectability we get a total of £635.

...with children a garden attached to the house is preferable to a *detached* garden (like Gordon Square), as in Gordon Square children have to be dressed and nursemaided regally, aristocratically, etc., according to means, while in Camden St. they...

The negotiations, however, failed. Lady Byron wrote that she had been unfairly treated by the superior landlord, her offer being superseded by a better. "I hope as usual for better in compensation," she adds.

But my parents, acting upon Lady Byron's belief that the house was secured, had disposed of the Hastings home, and so found themselves in an awkward position. They therefore rented 18 Queen Square, which seems to have been available for six months only. It would have been too large and expensive for a permanency, but would give opportunity for house-hunting at their leisure. Lady Byron was once again taken ill and had to leave London.

Since it is but due to my parents that their love for this great-hearted woman should be fully understood, something more must be said about her. Her peaceful outlook from the ruins of her own hopes, her serene waiting upon those who were troubled, must have left indelible impress upon both my father and my mother. Besides which her material help, rendered with quite lovely tact, could never be forgotten.

I may assert that whenever my father painted portraits from the life everyone instinctively feels they *are* drawn from life, with none of the commoner artist's temptation to enhance effect. This is true of old Mrs. Falconer, of Thomas Crann, of David Elginbrod, of Ian Macruadh, of the clergyman in *David Elginbrod* (F.D. Maurice); and it is correspondingly obvious that Lady Byron is given us under the name of Lady Bernard in *The Vicar's Daughter*. Moreover, in the last, apart from its intrinsic convincingness, every point tallies with the descriptions given by others who knew her intimately—William de Morgan, Mrs. Beecher-Stowe, and even Lord Byron in his word of her before he neglected and slandered her; besides my father's letters to my grandfather. In Lord Byron's words she had "small and feminine though not regular features; the fairest skin imaginable, perfect figure and temper and modest manners." From this as starting-point, I quote my father's delineation in *The Vicar's Daughter*:

> She was like a fountain of living water that could find no vent but into the lives of her fellows. She had suffered more than falls to the ordinary lot of women, in those who were related to her most nearly, and for many years she had looked for no personal blessing from without. She said to me once that she could not think of anything that could happen to herself to make her very happy now—except a loved grandson, who was leading a strange wild life, were to turn out a Harry the Fifth—a consummation which, however devoutly wished, was not granted her, for the young man died shortly after....She was slight, and appeared taller than she was, being rather stately than graceful, with a commanding forehead and still blue eyes. She gave at first the impression of coldness with a touch of

haughtiness. But the moment her being came into contact with that of another, all this impression vanished in the light that flashed into her eyes, and the smile that illumined her face. Never did woman of rank step more triumphantly over the barriers which the cumulated custom of ages has built between the classes of society. She laid great stress on good manners, little on what is called good birth; although to the latter, in its deep and true sense, she attributed the greatest *à priori* value, as the ground of obligation in the possessor, and of expectation on the part of others.[1]

So my parents in October removed to Queen Square, Bloomsbury. My father secured the Professorship at Bedford College. For some years now his sole income was derived from teaching and lecturing. Yet whatever else he might be doing, helping the little family over their lessons, or fighting asthma, or upholding the wife in her domestic difficulties, or very occasionally preaching (for which henceforth he never took any payment), or studying life in Ratcliffe Highway, he was always, always writing. His first venture after *Phantastes* was a play—the one, I believe, which, after many re-writings to please this or that manager, he published at last in 1882 in a volume of short stories, naming it *If I had a Father*.[2] Upon the advice of Mr. George Murray Smith, the publisher, he incorporated its idea—that of a father returning after many years' absence in India, and then serving as a valet his almost forgotten son, a young sculptor—in a novel named *Seekers and Finders*. But it was too metaphysical and argumentative to attract any publisher, in spite of much terse, epigrammatic writing and the introduction of the most typical character in all his fiction, Robert Falconer.

But before leaving Hastings, he went North to lecture in Edinburgh, and to visit Huntly, where he stayed a fortnight and rested.

The following letter, answering certain questions of my father, who was then seeing through the press his article on

---
1 *The Vicar's Daughter*, vol. ii, pp. 90 *et seq.*
2 "The Gifts of the Child Christ and other stories."

Shelley for the *Encyclopædia Britannica*,[1] shows that Lady Byron was no prude, as her detractors claimed her to be:

> *Lady Noel Byron to G.M.D.*
> St. George's Terrace,
> Augt. 6th, '59.
>
> As far as I have read of the "Memorials of Shelley," I find much to put the reader on his guard. There is, I think, an intentional omission of dates.
>
> Separation from his first wife "towards the close of 1813" *is* stated—her death followed—and *before* "*the peace of 1814*," but how soon after *not* stated, his proposal of [marriage] to Mary Godwin, who "unhesitatingly placed her hand in his and linked her fortunes with his own." This seemed to me rather hasty as a marriage; but I was a dupe of the equivocal mode of expression, till I read that "on the 30th Decr. 1816 Shelley's second marriage took place." It is added—"she who was thenceforward the companion of his existence" as if she had not been as much *the companion* for nearly 3 years before! As far as my own feelings are concerned, I should very much have preferred an open vindication of Shelley's defiance of social law, to this attempt to gloss it over (p.68)—"that Marriage was one of the many Institutions which a new Era in the history of mankind was about to sweep away." Mrs. Shelley, notwithstanding her antecedents, is from that time made a heroine—I ask you as a judge of human nature whether her journals, after her husband's death, are natural—whether *self-representation* is not their prevailing character, and his memory made subservient to that object. Cold is the heart that could so write—"How lonely I am"..."But I am a lonely, unloved thing," etc. This last sentence is believed by eyewitnesses not to have been true *in fact*.
>
> I like Shelley's Essay on Christianity as of a fair and impartial character, and showing how much of the Christian there was in him.
>
> A.I.N.B.

While at Huntly he hoped to get time for solid work upon the play, but it was a sad holiday. He writes to my mother that:

> The beauty of this place—the central beauty is gone. I see his spectacles lying. My mother wears them now. It makes one feel that it is all passing. But God is rich who has all persons as well as thoughts and things in him....

---

1 Eighth edition, 1860, vol. xx, p. 100, signed "G.M.D.", reprinted and enlarged in *A Dish of Orts*, 1893.

The following letter, in a portion not quoted as too lengthy, suggests to me the possibility that Lady Byron had been afraid lest my father in his devotion to my mother was in some danger of deferring too absolutely to her in matters of criticism. But other parts are worth quoting for the remarks on Mrs. H. Beecher-Stowe, who later abused her confidence so signally.

Lady Noel Byron to G.M.D.

RICHMOND,
Augt. 23rd, 1859.

Mrs. H. B. Stowe has been with me—she only came to this country for 3 or 4 days on her way to Paris—looking so well, younger far than in 1853, when I first saw [her] in the midst of evanescent homage—and why? I feel as if the expansion of her countenance, the obliteration of its hard lines, were from a theological change—she has emerged from the "Silva oscura" of Calvinism. Seven years ago she held with a terrible tenacity the tenet of eternal perdition. It is difficult to account for the kind of fondness with which some minds cling to the monstrous, whilst it grieves and appals them. She has made no statement to me of the change, but it is infused into her religious sentiments....She seems to have carried her husband along with her: he said to me, "Calvinism is the only Theology that makes out a *perfect system*, but that does not establish it as truth."

These scraps of other scenes will not, I hope, interrupt those of the Drama. I only fear in your compositions that your love of the good and beautiful may exclude too much that which is essential to bring it out *by contrast*. A course of "Newgate Calendar" might be of service, though I do not desire to see you an Eugene Sue.

To which this reply:

G.M.D. to Lady Byron.

HUNTLY,
August 25, 1859.

I am both too busy and too tired to do more than thank you for your delightful letter which I had to-day....I have almost finished the third act of my play—I hope it will be wicked enough to please you—if not, I shall try one in the style of Titus Andronicus, or the Jew of Malta....

While at Huntly my father received a letter from Henry Crabb Robinson, then in his eighty-fifth year, another friend of Lady Byron and A. de Morgan. To this I refer only for noting the friendship between George MacDonald and this generous friend of literary genius, whose *Diary* has become a classic if only for the fact that as a young man he had sat at the feet of William Blake, and has in it given us one of the best descriptions of that poet, his person, his philosophy, his simple faith. In it too he refers in his old age to meeting my father.[1] When he died in 1867 he left him a legacy of £300. The letter gives us sense of the political atmosphere and literary gossip in that year, but is too long for quotation.

No. 18 Queen Square, long since pulled down, and its site on the west side now occupied by the Hospital, served for six months only.[2]

Then comes the last letter that I have from Lady Byron to my father, and his reply:

Lady Noel Byron to G.M.D.

October 26, '59.

DEAR MR. MACDONALD,

Tho' I have begun my Hybernation I hope you will penetrate into the Molehill before long....I could not see the possibility of your doing without help after you had so strenuously fulfilled the first part of the saying "*Aide-toi*." In such cases, it is an honour to be instrumental in fulfilling the second part—"*et Dieu t'aidera*"—which would remain a consolation should you at this "Sink or swim" crisis, be unable after all to battle with the waves.

You will allow me to be quite open. Between you and me the ease is totally different; but in regard to other (may I say?) more worldly connections, beware of *borrowing*, as I know nothing which has been more injurious to the rise of a half-known author than that reputation. I could not say this unless I had desired to be your creditor rather than let you be indebted elsewhere. In the meantime £50.

Your faithful,

A.N. BYRON.

---

[1] Among his intimates also were Lamb, Coleridge and Wordsworth. In 1801 he had met Goethe and Schiller in Weimar, where he studied. He had been Special Correspondent of *The Times* in the Peninsular War, and was with the army of Sir John Moore at Corunna.

[2] I remember dancing with my little sisters before the statue of Queen Anne in the garden, and then, after making curtsies and bows, retiring backwards, not always without disaster; and I recall the more enjoyable duty of helping the gardener gather up the dead leaves for his bonfire.

Then he sends her his poem: *The Sangreal*.

G.M.D. to Lady Noel Byron.
[Nov. 2, 1859.]
18 Queen Square, W.C.
Tuesday.

Dear Lady Byron,

All that I know of the legend of the Sangreal is that Sir Galahad sought it and found it: at least that is all that is *non-original* in the poem.[1] Both the story, the mode, and the deeper meaning are original. The meaning of the 3rd part is that, ceasing to seek the central good in its highest manifestation, he failed to find the central good in the individual good thing. *But finding God in Christ, he found God in all things—as certainly, though not so fully manifest.*

I sent the poem to *Once-a-week*. It was refused on the ground that one of Tennyson's best poems is *Sir Galahad!*

You kindly ask me to tell you about my debts. I meant to do so, had I an opportunity. I am not in debt at all from having borrowed money—it is only some tradesman's bills at Hastings—amounting perhaps to £20. So far for confession!

Now about my drama. You will be amused to hear, as showing how differently different minds are impressed with the same thing, that where you apply the epithet *flat*, Mr. Scott applied the epithet of *effervescent*—saying, that there was a fine effervescence about the conversation: that as conversation it was much superior to some successful plays which he knew; that in fact it had rather surprised him; but that the wit was too refined, and the intellect too much occupied with the edges of things for a play.

My best thanks for giving me your ideas about it. You will not mind my meeting them with an opposite impression. I hope to benefit by both.

Glad enough were my parents when they found a little house—built by Charles Lucy, the historical painter, for himself—in Albert Street, Regent's Park. In it lived Thomas Lynch, the hymn-writer, and Arthur Phillott, whose daughter, an inseparable friend in those days of my eldest sister, married Professor J.R. Seely, the historian and author of *Ecce Homo*. The house was of red brick with stone-mullioned windows, and had a little front garden with a weeping ash, and a

---

1 *The Sangreal: a part of the Story omitted in the old Romances.* Published in *Good Words*, 1863, and in *Poetical Works*, vol. ii, p. 65.

larger garden beyond, packed with riotous marigolds and wallflowers and weeds. In the wall of the little hall still may be seen the cast of an unfinished Madonna of Michael Angelo's let into the wall.

Tudor Lodge was a pretty little house, but with its bedroom accommodation all too small. Its chief feature was the big studio that served admirably for study and lecture-room. It was built out beyond the house, and with a small steep stairway leading down into it through a door at the end of the hall. Once I stood at the top of that stair, hesitating because I was sent to tell my father that I had been guilty of pulling Irene's hair and making her cry, and I recall the picture of him sitting at his table in the centre of the room; on the wall, above the sheet-iron stove, a great oil painting by Lucy of King Charles bidding his last farewell to his children, which picture I held in high dread if ever I was left alone for my midday rest on the sofa; and the north skylight above. There were casts of the Elgin marbles on the other walls. My friend, Sir Johnston Forbes-Robertson—with the artist's keen observation of form, colour and character—thus reminds me of that room:

> ...You will remember, of course, how he [George MacDonald] enjoyed the children's parties your mother gave in a great studio, and how he used to cover himself with a skin rug, and pretend to be a bear to the great delight of us all! Arthur Hughes used to join in with great gusto. I recall that on the walls of the studio were some casts of the Parthenon Friezes, which at a Christmas party were all lit up with small candles artfully stuck about, a most beautiful effect.[1]

The bear performance I recall—a charade representing the *Story of the Three Bears*, my two elder sisters as the little child and the Little Bear, my father the Big Bear, and perhaps, I am not sure, Arthur Hughes the Mother Bear. Also do I remember my relief and joy, when the fur rug was discarded along with

---

[1] I well remember, on the other hand, more than one delightful party given by the Forbes-Robertsons, at one of which my friend, now the greatest of living actors, at thirteen years old, played Othello, and his sister Desdemona. It opened my young eyes to undreamed-of terrors!

the growling voice, and the actor was once again his beloved self.[1] The illumination of the friezes is also recalled to me as another instance of my mother's artistry in entertaining.

My father's sister Louie joined us at Tudor Lodge to complete her education at Bedford College, and she proved of utmost help to my mother in the house. My father held the post till 1867, and his annual remuneration varied between fifty and thirty guineas. The professors' fees were 10s. 6d. a lecture.

Lady Byron died on May 16, 1860, and on October 27th, the second son, Ronald, was born.

Now followed very anxious days, and publishers all refused his play. How many weeks or months it was after Lady Byron's death I do not know; but my mother would tell us how one day she had started out to buy certain necessaries, and in the omnibus had lost her purse with the very last sovereign in it. They did not know where to turn next for help, and there was hardly enough food in the house for the children's dinner. Only Lily, with her instinctive understanding, realized how bad things were, and found her own appetite was providentially indifferent. Then, my mother said, as the evening closed in, she and my father were standing hand in hand as if waiting for some answer to their prayers. It was in the little front drawing-room of Tudor Lodge, and the rain poured down upon the weeping ash that overspread the tiny garden. The postman walked up the steps, dropped a letter in the box, and with his double knock woke them from their quietude. The letter was from Lady Byron's executors enclosing a cheque for £300, a legacy of which they had not been advised.

---

[1] It must have been some five or six years later that he again impersonated a beast at Earles Terrace, but then in the little play written by my mother, *Beauty and the Beast*. He was terribly pathetic and brought all the children to tears. Mr. C. Edmund Maurice remembers his saying to Ruskin, who, I presume, had been praising his impersonation, "If I can act a beast I can act Hamlet," little dreaming, I imagine, that in a few more years he would play Macbeth in public.

BOOK VII
THE NOVELIST

CHAPTER I
DAVID ELGINBROD

GEORGE MACDONALD'S poetical gifts were now fully recognized by all the critics. Nevertheless, for a few years, in spite of the direct encouragement of one publisher at least, he printed nothing. He wrote with tireless, minutely painstaking energy, although often laid up by bronchitis, asthma and wretched headaches. I remember more than one grave attack of hæmoptysis in the early sixties. Once he fell in alighting from an omnibus, and cut his forehead terribly, arriving home covered with blood. The wound left a lasting scar behind it.

It is still from letters that we gather the greater events. Since all bread was paid for by casual earnings, the need of getting work, the story of failures and surprises, occupy much of the correspondence. The mother's watch and ward over her brood; their ailings, naughtinesses, puzzling sulks; their bright sayings that outshone all childhood's precedents—these needed more telling than the joys that gave heart to the sore-pressed parents. We learn too from these simple letters how the daily manna, even in that brick and stucco wilderness of wealth, always came. Other important matters are not forgotten. New figures appear, among them George Murray Smith, the distinguished head of Smith, Elder & Co., who had published *Phantastes*. He was the same age as my father and of exceptional literary acumen: had he not been the first to recognize the genius in *Jane Eyre* when he was but twenty-three, not to mention the rare qualities of

Ruskin, Thackeray, Mrs. Gaskell? He told my father that, *Undine* apart, *Phantastes* held an absolutely unique place in literature. He did perhaps more than anyone else to persuade him of his gift for fiction, though it took long for my father to realize it. "Mr. MacDonald," he said, upon the occasion of refusing his drama, *If I had a Father*, "if you would but write novels, you would find all the publishers saving up to buy them of you! Nothing but fiction pays. Yet I will publish any of your poetry."

Nevertheless, it is curious that no book was produced between *Phantastes* (1858) and *David Elginbrod* (1863). The one-volumed story, *The Portent*, appeared serially, with an absurd wood-cut, in the first year of the *Cornhill Magazine* (May, June, July, 1860), in company with Thackeray's *Lovel the Widower* and Trollope's *Framley Parsonage*; but it did not appear in book form till 1864. The story is different from almost any other of his books, but it at once convinced friends and publishers of his art in simple narrative. It deals with the Highland belief in second-sight—of which gift my father would reluctantly admit he had himself no trace. It is weird, yet strangely convincing, and has no touch of the didactic. My mother once told an admirer, that when she asked my father for the story's meaning, he said, "You may make of it what you like. If you see anything in it, take it and I am glad you have it; but I wrote it for the tale." Its author received forty pounds for its serial use, and thirty for the copyright of the book.

A review in *The Spectator* extorted from my father the following letter to the editor:

Kensington,
July 11, 1867

I do not complain that your correspondent should say what he pleases of my work, but that he should use the same freedom in representing what I say of my origin, is hardly to be ceded....Having the weakness to be proud of my Celtic birth, I do not at all relish being represented as guilty of "implicit repudiation of Celtic blood in the preface to *The Portent*." Offering the little book to a grand old Celt who knew well that I had been born in a border region whence the tide of Gaelic had ebbed away, I used these words in apology for the imperfection of my work from a purely Celtic point of view: "I can only say that my early education was not Celtic enough to enable me to do better in this respect." Is there any ground in this for your correspondent's assertion? ...To one of a race, the poorest peasant of which would be a gentleman, it is annoying to be held up as guilty of what would afford just cause to his own people for repudiating him. For surely it is one of the worst signs of a man to turn his back upon the rock whence he was hewn.

With this exception, the five years between the publication of *Phantastes* in 1858 and the first novel in 1863 were marked by what must have seemed to some like failure.

Acting no doubt upon Mr. George Smith's advice, the play, *If I had a Father*, was made the basis of a novel of some 120,000 words, named *Seekers and Finders*; but it was never published. Smith, Elder & Co.'s reader, Mr. W. Smith-Williams, gave the faithful criticism of it which I have before me. My brother Ronald and my best of friends, Ernest Rhys, have read it, and with myself endorse its author's decision that it had better remain unpublished.

With much suggestive utterance, epigrammatic diction and knowledge of human nature in certain aspects, it is often theatrical in its presentation of characters, while its conversations are more like debates of some delegates in the audience-chamber of the writer's mind than real dialogue. Yet the book is wholly consistent with its writer's life-long convictions. Its central idea is not unlike that of *Within and Without*, though characters and narrative have nothing in common with that poem. Robert Falconer first appears here, though his own story is reserved for future telling. Like Julian, he stands for the prophet who primarily has vision of the truth always supreme to its concrete expression, while his antithesis, Aurelio, a young, imaginative sculptor, finds in Beauty the manifestation of all Truth and so seeks to idealize Form without any further concept of what Truth means. Then, standing apart from each, is the idle young aristocrat with delicate and high-cultured feeling, who yet looks upon Beauty as if manifested for its own and his own sake. Naturally he is the bad influence of the story; and his father, a melodramatic yet imaginatively conceived Bluebeard, with a chamber of horrors—not for wives, but for men and women whom he has hated and loves chiefly for the sake of injuring—is horrible indeed. Yet it has many and great beauties. It reveals, too, the writer's intimacy with disreputable London—to which I think James Greenwood, the "Amateur Casual," may have introduced him. So my father's determination to leave this novel unpublished has been respected: and it is now destroyed. So the play and the novel based upon it both failed.

We now find my father in touch with literary society, although he made intimates with but a few. Thus at Mr. George Smith's business dinners he would meet Thackeray, whom he had possibly already met at A. J. Scott's house, James Greenwood, G. H. Lewes, Leslie Stephen, Leigh Hunt, James Payn, and Henry S. King. Ruskin's friendship came from another quarter, to be enlarged upon later. Smith-Williams was, I take it, more of a Bohemian. One evening at an informal supper of oysters, beefsteak pudding and bottled stout, he and James Greenwood, my father and others were consorting, when George MacDonald's attention was arrested by hearing Manby Smith, the gifted journalist, then writing regularly for the *Leisure Hour*, *Chambers' Journal*, etc., reciting a certain Scotch epitaph he had read somewhere. "What's that, what's that?" my father exclaimed, as though catching sight of some living thing that might evade him: "Say it again, Mr. Smith!" The latter repeated:

> Here lie I, Martin Elginbrodde;
> Hae mercy o' my soul, Lord God;
> As I wad do, were I Lord God,
> An' ye war Martin Elginbrodde!

Photo by] GEORGE MACDONALD, 1862 [Lewis Carroll.

My father caught and held it—the thing that grew in stature and favour till its story was written.

The proof that this event gave the germ of that novel lies in the following:

> G.M.D. to Charles Manby Smith.
>
> TUDOR LODGE, REGENT'S PARK, N.W.
> Sept 7, 1863.
>
> MY DEAR SIR,
> I meant to call and beg your acceptance of the accompanying volumes, but I cannot find time at present. I had intended one copy of the few the publishers first allowed me for you, but I found they would not go so far as I wished. Pray excuse the postponement of my offering. You gave me the Epitaph which was in a measure the germ of the whole. Please accept the result of its growth in my mind.
>
> With kind regards to Mrs. Smith,
> Yours very truly,
> GEORGE MACDONALD.[1]
>
> C.M. SMITH, ESQ.
> [Liverpool Terrace, Islington.]

But George MacDonald was little attracted to so-called *literary society.*

> The merely professional literary party was an abhorrence to him. He said it made him feel sick—he could not help it. He took more pleasure in smoking a pipe now and then with an old cobbler somewhere about the Theobald's Road than in an evening with the most delightful literary society that London could furnish.

This I quote from the unpublished novel; and, as the words are descriptive of Robert Falconer, who remained his author's type of what a man might be, we may presume that the words convey George MacDonald's own feelings. Describing a certain gathering of fashionable intellect which Falconer feels constrained to attend, the manuscript is very amusing:

> When he arrived he found the rooms quite up to the ordinary degree of crush and discomfort. Across the chaos of female cones and male obelisks, bowing and grinning, each with a veil of conventional fibre over

---

1 *Vide* an article of Max Müller's in the *Athenæum*, May 14, 1887.

the face, through which ever and anon a real thought and feeling peered and disappeared, he saw no one for some time that he knew...amusing himself with ludicrous suggestions and wishing the ladies would come in their nightgowns instead of in go-carts and colanders....

In spite, however, of George Murray Smith's hopes as to George MacDonald's future, he had not realized how far the latter's ideals stood in opposition to that sort of popularity which every publisher, however cultured he be, must look for. Smith, Elder & Co. found *David Elginbrod* hardly more attractive than *Seekers and Finders*. Their verdict coincided with every publisher's in London. Their rejection of the book, and the time wasted by their readers, largely account for my father's apparent tardy production. Had it not been for the daughter of a Manchester friend on the staff of the *Examiner*, she being then on a visit to Tudor Lodge,[1] the book might never have been published. But

> It chanced—eternal God that chance did guide— [2]

that this young lady, hearing of the book's unhappy wanderings, asked if she might show it to her friend, Miss Mulock, then living at Wildwood, Hampstead Heath. The authoress of *John Halifax, Gentleman*, at once realized the book's merits, took it to her own publishers, Hurst and Blackett, and told them they were fools to refuse it. "Are we?" they asked. "Then of course we will print it without delay." They gave its author £90 for it; and it still steadily sells. Never again had he difficulty in placing a book.[3]

David Elginbrod has been already and often mentioned. Its just and sensitive portraiture rather than its story—which yet is vigorous and profluent—its pictures of simple life in Highland cottage, of dull respectability in English Squire's home or suburban tradesman's, its imaginative treatment of

---

1 Miss Jessie Ballantyne, who married John Plumer, Esq., of Totnes.
2 A favourite quotation of my father from Spenser's *Faerie Queen*.
3 "Old Blackett offered me £800 once," wrote my father to his friend and Literary Agent, A.P. Watt, in 1890.

unfathomed possibilities in telepathy and suggestion, its advocacy of individualism in education, all contributed to the building of a novel unlike anything ever attempted before. But its chief claim upon those who study its author's own life will be the portraiture of his own father in David Elginbrod. It introduces us, moreover, to Robert Falconer, perhaps more definitely a creation than a facsimile or amplification of any one friend's temperament. In this book, too, there is an arresting sketch of Frederick Denison Maurice.

One of Ruskin's earliest letters to my father mentions *David Elginbrod*, though the story of their meeting has yet to be told. Ruskin nearly always found fault before he praised; indeed, he could be a ruthless critic even of those most tenderly dear to him.

John Ruskin to G.M.D.

June 30th, 1863.

DEAR MR. MACDONALD,

I hope to get over to tea to-morrow. Only—and we are to be by ourselves—you must keep the "kettle"—which I hope you are too great a poet to have discarded—hot till 7; for I can't get over sooner.

David E. is full of noble things and with beautiful little sentences.... It is a little too subtle in some places for a story, I think, but very beautiful everywhere. But I am most unhappily hard frozen just now and care only for stones and crocodiles. Being in your Hugh's pleasantest state of "awake in his coffin"—I only care for observations on the clay which I can scratch through the chinks in the lid—and hate to hear of grass and flowers—except fossil.

It's all nonsense about Everybody turning good. No one ever turns good who isn't.

Yours ever affectionately,

J. RUSKIN.

David Elginbrod was translated into German in 1873 by Julie Sutter, authoress of *England's Next War*, etc., etc., and published by Heuder und Zimmer, Frankfort, a/M.

The letters belonging to these earlier years of the sixties have many things of interest and show us very plainly that the increasing freedom from care, notwithstanding the incessant work of lecturing and teaching; the securer home and widening responsibilities; and, still more, the conviction that the world was so sorely in need of his message—these brought him, along with more happiness, freer utterance. Probably, too, new intimacies with men who could appreciate his fearless genius and eloquence gave him more confidence in his own powers. I have a strong suspicion, looking critically at his work, that, owing to his inherent modesty, he was slower than most great men in finding free play for his genius. Possibly his early training of submission to theological authority kept him in doubt of his own power; yet he never questioned the light given him, nor was he hampered by conventions and social orthodoxies. Now, however, with men and women of his own intellectual rank proud to be counted his friends, he grew more aware of his own power. Even if he never wrote better poetry than the sonnets, songs and ode in *Within and Without*, or blank verse more arresting than *A Hidden Life*, the conclusion cannot be avoided, when we compare *Seekers and Finders* with *David Elginbrod*, that his sense of art in fiction changed extraordinarily in those five years.

We found him, when at Huntly in 1857, collecting materials for a story he had in his mind; and already he may have seen that his early experiences and the vernacular of his own people were his proper vehicle. It must, however, have been quite in the early sixties that my father discovered his gift for lighter, imaginative narrative. For now and again, in place of a lecture he would read or recite a fairy-tale—particularly *The Light Princess*. All the fairy stories comprised in the little volume, *Dealings with the Fairies illustrated by Arthur Hughes* (1867), had been written before the end of 1863, and appeared first in the novel, *Adela Cathcart* (1864), as setting for them. *The Light Princess*, written on a long scroll, perhaps with some idea of making its form accord with vocal delivery, should be defined rather as a *jeu d'esprit*.

It hardly compares with the other fairy stories which were expressly written for the little people who rushed the platform of his knees and the arms of his chair, or transformed the lap of the mother and the footstool at her feet into front rows of his auditorium. *The Giant's Heart* remains to this day associated with my father's dramatic reading of it to us.

Early in 1860 my father was lecturing in Edinburgh before the Philosophical Institution on "The Poetical Literature of the Elizabethan Age." North of the Tweed people were already beginning to make much of him—indeed, gave him more social honouring than he cared for, his energies being all needed for his work. The next letter gives one news of this as well as of a point suggesting his willingness still to undertake any work that would bring grist to the mill. He had evidently been asked to lecture on Natural Philosophy at Bedford College in addition to his own subject, English Literature:

G.M.D. to his Wife.
EDINBURGH,
January 6, 1860.

Just a few lines, dearest Louie, for I have not time for more, as I am busy preparing for my lecture to-night. The evening before last I was a little annoyed by the presence of Lord B.—, a stuck-up Lord of Session—who is nothing but a Scotch lawyer and a bad one, and makes out that God is just a Lord of Session. To hear how the wretched creature lectured Mr. Erskine—the dear, good, humble, wise old man! His Stickship is one of the worst specimens of the worst phase of low Scotch—why they asked him I can't think—but certainly they want to give me the *best* society in one sense! I would rather take tea with an old washerwoman....Will you tell Mrs. Reid [Principal of Bedford College] that I will make the trial of the Natural Philosophy. I have very little doubt I shall succeed. I know plenty for them and know it well, too....

In the spring of 1862 my mother was at Hastings with her father and Mrs. Godwin, helping to nurse her youngest sister, dangerously ill with rheumatic fever; and the following deals with small matters, amusing and otherwise:

G.M.D. to his Wife.

DEAREST WIFE,

I got to London rather tired, hurried to Lime Street, swallowed a chop whole, which was providentially ready, gulped—(don't you see gulped and gulf are the same word?)—down two glasses of wine, darted off against probabilities, bounded through Fenchurch Street like an india-rubber ball, and got in time to the station—with one minute to spare....I was up and down before eight this morning to write some necessary letters....I read *Ulf* and several other stories. They are all very bad translations. As stories they just want the *one central spot of red*—the wonderful thing which, whether in a fairy story or a word or a human being, is the life and depth—whether of truth or humour or pathos—the eye to the face of it—the thing that shows the unshowable....How stupid I am, trying to be clever. *"That's damned fine!"* the sailor said to the horse that had just pitched him over a hedge. *"But how are you to get over?"* This is William's [Matheson] last find....I am now waiting for my pupils; I have two lessons of two hours before I see you to-morrow....

The next letter refers to the helpfulness of certain friends, and to his well-founded antipathy to the east wind. Mrs. Russell Gurney had taken care of some of us in our mother's absence.

G.M.D. to his Wife at Hastings.

DEAREST WIFE,

...My MSS. [*The Portent*] is in the publishers' hands. Mrs. Russell Gurney brought the children home [from 8 Palace Gardens] this afternoon. She is delighted with the upbringing of them. They look well. Winny so pretty. She would have no one but *Man*, as she calls Mr. Gurney [the Recorder of London] to carry her up to bed!...After leaving Court, Mr. R. G. had just time to go and get them some toys before they left....What a devil the East Wind is! Certainly there is not much of the divine in it except in the overruling. It takes all the hope out of a body—but not the faith. Good-night. Welcome the antechamber of death!

Do rest when you can, dear comfort. The children are very little trouble....Lily is just a little mother to them all—seeming to think of everyone before herself....

G.M.D. to his Wife.

March 7th, 1861.

Just a little chat before I go to bed....I have been talking, penwise, all this about my ugly self. Is it not strange that in the Christian law we can offer to God the most deformed and diseased thing we have got—ourselves?

I have had a most strange, delightful feeling lately—when disgusted with my own selfishness—of just giving away the *self* to God—throwing it off me up to heaven—to be forgotten and grow clean, without my smearing it all over with trying to wash out the spot.

This evening I could relish nothing but a poem of Chaucer's. We really have never surpassed him. He was a non-dramatic Shakespeare—not undramatic. There is no greater delight in Coleridge or Keats at hearing the nightingale than old Chaucer manifests.—The man of genius may not be a prophet but he is a prophecy: he forestalls what it will take ages to bring round for the many; but theirs it will be one day....You need not be uneasy about us. Lily is a host of Gideon—and as sweet as any *ordinary* angel. But it will be very jolly when you come back.

Here let me add that this eldest sister was always the same; mothering parents, brothers and sisters, guests hearty or dying, and refractory adoptions—even while, some years later, she was schooling her longings after outlet for her genius. My mother has told me how this eldest of the brood always instinctively knew of her parents' troubles, once, as has been already told, when she was but nine, feigning loss of appetite that the smaller ones might have more.

While my mother was now (Easter, 1862) kept at Hastings by her sister's illness, Dr. and Mrs. Hale arranged for two readings from my father. One was a Fairy-Tale of his own, the other Selections from Spenser's *Faerie Queen*. And their success made it possible for the whole family to get a change at the seaside.

But they returned to Tudor Lodge without their mother.

G.M.D. to his Wife.

...The children are very good indeed. Gracie most amusing in conversation with the rest. She was proving the superiority of her spoon both in material and manufacture over those of the lodgings, but saying how she would part with it for you, as you were very poor. They brought it in that you wanted a bonnet very much. This was amongst themselves. I generally listen in silence....I have but two lessons more. You see how uncertain teaching is....Emily has just come for me to kill a rat, and I have happily effected it—the largest I think I ever saw.... [1]

---

1 My father had a wonderful way of catching rats with his hand, thickly gloved.

CHAPTER II
JOHN RUSKIN

THE year 1863 must not be passed over without some further mention of John Ruskin and how he came into George MacDonald's life. With little hesitation—and judging from the big correspondence that passed between the men—I may add that my father was as much to him and did as much for him as he to and for my father. Yet the intimacy has been ignored in the Life of John Ruskin given in the Library Edition of his works. My parents perhaps knew more of Ruskin's tragical love affair— "almost the *Bride of Lammermoor* over again" he said to my father—than any others. Because there are still some living who slander the great man, the full story should some day be told. Much of it I had from my father, and numbers of documents in my hands bear upon it.

It was Mrs. La Touche, Rose's mother, who first introduced George MacDonald and John Ruskin, the occasion being the latter's attendance at one of the lectures at Tudor Lodge in 1863, and the acquaintance rapidly developed into a close intimacy.

Ruskin had just returned at the end of May from his visit to Talloires, hoping to forget the cruel reception of his economic articles in *Fraser's Magazine*, afterwards published as *Munera Pulveris*. The Editor had refused to continue their publication; and Ruskin's father, who died so soon after, had condemned them *in toto*. So that I think he was ready for developing a friendship so different from his other intimacies. Almost immediately begins the delightful series of letters, of which the following is a good specimen:

John Ruskin to G.M.D.

BADEN,
8*th* Nov., 1863.

MY DEAR MR. MACDONALD,
   I have your sweet letter, and the verses which are delightful, and I shall be so glad to see you again—and hear you talk. Though you can't do me any good in one way, I like to hear you. This is only to say I'm grateful to you for loving me—and that I hope to see more of your kind faces, yours and your wife's. What sort of a place am I in? It used to be prettier here than it is— (as every place in Switzerland) but it is still pretty—in a limestone valley—wooded with oak and pine. Hapsburg within a walk—the Alps within sight—the Rhine within an hour's rail-roll—every kind of thing within reach, except my old heart. Alas me—I've been born again with a vengeance—twofold more the child of darkness—not Hell; (for I'm heartily uncomfortable whenever I come near the hells they are making of their great towns with steam and avarice and cruelty and accursed labour) but of darkness—I'm so puzzled with everything, and so dead to everything. But I can't write more.

I quote this in particular because I cannot help thinking that the questions of industrialism touched upon began to assume in my father's mind a wider import. Ruskin compelled him, as he has the rest of the world, to look facts in the face, as regards machinery and industrialism; and a few years later I well remember the discussions on *Fors Clavigera* as each number appeared. Ruskin gave my father *Modern Painters* in their original green morocco binding in 1864.

Ruskin, like my father, had discarded all Calvinistic doctrine, though the latter was in Ruskin's eyes still orthodox. My father's unqualified optimism kept strong within him the faith that, when all is revealed, the ignominies of man's industrial progress may yet prove to be comprehended within the creative Will: that man may yet become a greater being than if the forbidden fruit had never been tasted.[1] Ruskin lacked the prophetic hope; his honesty *seemed* destructive to his faith.

Although I have space for only a very few of Ruskin's letters, it ought to be understood how strong was the two men's sympathy. Different in temperament and endowment, neither was afraid of speaking plainly of their disagreements. Thus while Ruskin freely criticized, sometimes scathingly, my father's writings and creed—though both he held in entire admiration—his friend upon at least one occasion upbraids him searchingly for inconsistent conduct. Nor was such fidelity qualified by the fact that Ruskin now and again helped my father in his financial difficulties; for it was done with a refinement of feeling seldom met with in those of blood-kinship. One little incident shows the generosity of the one and the scrupulous pride of the other. In 1866 Ruskin lent my father a sum of money. A few months later it was returned, but Ruskin refused it, saying he did not need it, and that my father must accept it as a gift. Again my father writes claiming the necessity of his own conscience. But Ruskin, having ascertained that my mother and sisters were in need of a new piano, insists upon giving one to my eldest sister, and so gets his way.

My own personal memory of Ruskin, especially in those days when he used to visit Rose La Touche in our house at Hammersmith, although forbidden by her parents to meet him, and when I had opportunities for doing trifling services both to the great man whom I just loved to shake

---

1 À *propos* of this, James A. Campbell of Barbreck writes thus: "Is this so? Does not George MacDonald rather feel that 'Industrialism' may be valuable because, like other oppressions, it may lead to repentance? And does he believe there is any 'Progress' for the soul through 'Evolution,' or indeed in any way, except through repentance?" I believe my friend is right and that his questions are not in disagreement with the observation expressed above, yet their implicit answers express better what my father would wish to be said. "Everything," my friend again asks, "assuredly for your father was *safe* in God's hands; but did he consider that man could grow and go forward at all until he 'came to the Father'?"

hands with, and to the frail, strangely beautiful, sweetly smiling girl, urges me to tell some day all I know of that wonderful love-story, if only that the world shall realize how honourable and pure-hearted the man was, and what a saintly person Rose La Touche had been all through childhood and girlhood, till she began to die of heartbreak—acute neurasthenia as, I think, the case would now be diagnosed. Thus I have a remarkable series of her mother's intimate letters to my mother, and of Rose's to my father, many of real literary value, apart from the glowing picture they give of the child, who, even in her earliest years while living in a home of great luxury, was a happy little saint.

From my father, too, I had the full story of Ruskin's relations with his wife, whose marriage with him was annulled. For my father had insisted upon knowing all about this event before he would help his friend to his heart's desire. The story reflects nothing but honour upon Ruskin—unless he lied to my father, or my father to me—one supposition as utterly incredible as the other. But it is impossible in this place to do more than suggest the story's bearing upon my father's and mother's life.

The next letter I reproduce suggests that Mrs. La Touche had been aware of some ill-success my father had encountered with publishers, and had spoken of it to Ruskin. He, as generous in defending his friends as he was ruthless in attacking his enemies, comes to the rescue with a rare sympathy and understanding. He at least seemed always incapable of even a suspicion that "people with naught are naughty."

John Ruskin to G.M.D.

6th Feb., 1865.

DEAR MACDONALD,

Mrs. L. told me of some unhappy little disappointment you had the other day. It is a shame that you can't come to me when any little matter of this sort comes wrong side up. I understand you perfectly—and shall be very grateful for all the love—and *expression* of it you can give me—only I've no love, to speak of, to give in return—but some sympathy, and, I really think, entire understanding; so that you need never shrink from saying you like me if you do—only you know I never believe anybody can possibly like me.

I hope the enclosed may be in time to be of some use—if you want any more tell me directly, or I'll be angry next time I find it out.

Ever affectionately yours,
J. RUSKIN.

Two days later comes another letter in similar strain. But it has this more particular interest in that, for the first time, Ruskin writes of Rose, and opens his heart in a way very few men do to another.

John Ruskin to G.M.D.

8th Feb., 1865.

DEAR MACDONALD,

I must get this out of my head please, to-day, for it's my birthday and I like having this to do for first business. Mind you're not to mind saying you love me, because of these tiresome things,—though I can't love anybody, except my mouse-pet in Ireland, who nibbles me to the very sick death with weariness to see her—and sends me bits of mignonette, forsooth—as if they were just as good as her own self, and makes me hate everybody else—but you ought to love her a little too—only I won't tell you why.

Ever your affectionate,
J. RUSKIN.

You know—I do think you would be happier in a country cottage—out of lecturing work and in peace. Only I *suspect*—there's wickedness for you!—that you can't do without London society.

Indeed, one often wonders if Ruskin was not right in thinking a country life would have opened to my father a freer way for his greater powers. But he was wrong in assuming that London was necessary. The thing that tied the author to town was the immediate and daily need to earn money by teaching.

Rose La Touche was now sixteen. My father and mother had met her at some dinner two years before, and the child had been attracted to them immediately. And now, it is clear from the letter of Ruskin's written five days later than the one last quoted, my parents were a little troubled about Ruskin's devotion to her, contrasted, likely enough, with her mother's assurance that his was but a sort of God-paternal affection for the wonderful maiden. Yet they saw also she was "too old to be made a pet of any more." Doubtless they realized that pathos of the next word in the letter that he "had never had any right people to care for"; and saw how deeply he needed the only thing that can make a home: they had theirs, and it meant all the world and more.

John Ruskin to G.M.D.

Feb. 13th, 1865.

My dear MacDonald,

I like you to ask questions sometimes, it is a relief to talk about things that prick one—but I wonder Mrs. L. never made you laugh at me a little about Rosie,—only she's too good to laugh at me except to my face. You know—the child's just like a fawn—and she likes me well enough—about as much as a nice squirrel would. She sends me orders every now and then—or a bit of mignonette—as I said—and thinks that "would be nice" for me. She sent me positive orders to Switzerland that I was to come to you the moment I came home—you were the only person, she thought, who could do me good—and you were "so nice." She is the only living thing—since my white dog died—that I care for—and I very nearly died myself when she got too old to be made a pet of any more—which was infinitely ridiculous; but I never had any right people to care for—and one can't get on with stones only—unless one shuts oneself right up at the Great St. Bernard. I tried that plan too last year—but it was too late—and I only disgusted myself with the mountains. I've got over the worst of it now and the stones will do, after this, I hope.

Ever affectionately yours,
J. Ruskin.

Although it involves anticipation, I reproduce here two other letters of Ruskin's to my father because they bring clearly before us their differing temperaments in regard to some questions that beset all men who think. What would I not give to have my father's replies! The occasion of the first was the death of A. J. Scott in 1866, with whom Ruskin was intimate.

John Ruskin to G.M.D.

DENMARK HILL, S.

DEAR MACDONALD,

I think there is indeed much for which you and all who loved Mr. Scott—among whom I earnestly count myself—may be deeply thankful in his tranquillity of faith, as the source of happiness to himself. What *any*body believes has long been a matter of absolutely no interest to me, as far as it bears on facts. For the wisest men can believe anything they like, and feebler persons, with less imagination, can believe nothing they like.

As far as I can see or have known anything of the Deity, He makes noble and beneficent laws, which if one keeps—it is fairly probable—not by any means certain—that one won't come to any terrific mischief,—but if one doesn't there's but one word for you. Fire is on the whole pleasantly warm—if you choose to burn your fingers with it—and then go to God for "comfort" He only laughs at you and says—"What did you do it for?" "I told you you had better not." It would be entirely undivine and against right order if He gave us then any comfort. I have never known any person whose mind was of any accurately trained strength who could get the slightest help out of such thoughts. In all your favourite Shakespeare—where is there an instance of a tragedy being softened off in that way? The best men simply mind their business—and what of others' business they have hand in—to the death. And "the rest is silence."
Ever affectionately yours,
J. RUSKIN.

Do not think I *dislike* what you say—or feel it unkind. But it is merely patting a tortoise's shell—or, as Sydney Smith puts it—"stroking the dome of St. Paul's to please the Dean and Chapter."

I suppose it is quite impossible for you dear good people, who think it your duty to believe whatever you like—and to expect always to get whatever is good for you, to enter into the minds of us poor, wicked people, who sternly think it our duty to believe nothing but what we know to be fact, and to expect nothing but what we've been used to get. Now—if it were possible for me to go to my Father in direct personal way—(which it is not) the very first thing I should say to him would be—"What have you been teasing me like this for?—Were there *no* toys in the cupboard you could have shown me,—but the one I can't have?" [1]

Then...

I must go and paint—or I shall spoil my day—and yours too.

Though my father's actual reply to this letter is not before us, his answers to the questions raised are constantly in his books; so that I, who knew the man better even than his books, and remember many talks with him—fearless, I do hope, on both sides—feel I must defend the ground on which he stood.

In that day's revulsion from dogmas impossible to honest minds, the tendency was to overvalue the fast-breeding facts of science, and Ruskin did not escape their lure.[2] I dare think my father would have countered Ruskin's scepticism in some such words as these: Since when have your devitalized facts, O Man of Science, found such paramount authority? Have you forgotten that Alpine revelation of which you would so often tell me? of "sanctity in the whole of Nature from the slightest thing to the vastest....no more explicable and definable than the feeling of love itself?" [3]

But the conflict was always waging for this passionate seeker for truth. There was no peace for him, even if he

---

1   À propos of this letter, my mother, to whom at Hastings it had been sent, writes thus: "How dreadfully sad it is. Can he be quite sure that God opened the cupboard door and showed him this best toy? Might he not have seen it through a chink or looking at it when the door was opened to others? Because the father has other children and he lets us look at each others' toys...."

2   The period in which these letters were written was one of a great darkness to Ruskin, when, owing to the influence of certain friends, his humility had led him to distrust the clear seeing of his youth and to listen to the arguments of Science. The story of his recovery is told in *Præterita*, in *Fors*, and in the preface to the last edition of *Modern Painters*. It came partly through the re-awakening of "Penetrative Imagination," partly and chiefly because of the evidence given to his senses at a certain Broadlands Conference that fitful gleams of a supernatural order, in which human affection holds its place, were indeed at times vouchsafed to men. Concerning this particular Conference, *vide infra*, p. 472. A friend tells me that Ruskin said to him concerning this spiritual communication: "I never could have recovered my faith in Christianity except for spiritualism."

3   Ruskin's feelings about the Alps I shall mention again, when telling of my father's visit to Switzerland.

was giving all his life and amazing energies to this something he could not utterly trust because *facts* would not uphold it, even though, now and rarely, a taste of its joy would overwhelm him. For against all simple acceptance of his undefined faith was the meek, wild Rose of adorable sweetness, of whom he wrote in 1872 that she had broken his heart much too thoroughly and finely for any such weeds as vain hopes to grow in the rifts; and yet again, five weeks later, when my parents had at last brought the two lovers together, that he had had three days of heaven which he would have bought with the rest of his life.

This reference to Ruskin's love-story—one of unwavering devotion to a lovely soul, in whose eyes he was Truth's champion against the wrong-headed world until calumny made her rank him among the outcast—bears, I do think, directly upon the tyranny of worldly wisdom which my father had set himself to oppose.

He was quite prepared for his friend's claim that our *minds* need believe nothing not demonstrable as fact. As he once said, "A dream may be full of truth, and a fact may be a mere shred for the winds of the limbo of vanities." [1] Or to use my own commoner words, he always claimed that faith transcends mind and fact; that its domain is the Kingdom of Love, Imagination and Creative Law—the verities which Science was then so busily and fussily discounting. I remember a milestone on my own journey that marked the parting of the ways. My father was listening with his keen and tender eyes to the young man's desire to be honest, I having then taken my M.D. degree. He was sitting at his desk, I standing. "Father," said I, tapping the table with a finger, "can you tell me that you *know* the God exists whom Jesus proclaimed? Can you tell it me with the same certainty that I can vouch for this table I am touching?" A look of spiritual indignation—almost of momentary anger

---

1 *Castle Warlock*, vol. iii, p. 314.

JOHN RUSKIN

at my stupidity—flashed across his face. "Of course not!" he exclaimed. "Do you think I could believe in a God demonstrated, proved by weight, resistance, inevitability?"[1] Or, as who should answer with Ruskin: Is that a God to worship who ordains that if a child plays with fire he shall burn his fingers—and there an end of it? Does ethical law take us any nearer Him than physical? "And what is the extent of our merely rational horizon? But for faith and imagination it were in truth a narrow one!"[2]

The truth is that if a man with the normal creative vitality strong in him, as in Ruskin beyond most men, have his love of children, his unsatisfied hunger for home-life, his adoration for women, all concentrated upon one frail image, and have that hunger and adoration constantly frustrated, it is small wonder that he cannot conform with creeds that deny the divinity of those gifts. "Better," said William Blake, "murder an infant in its cradle than nurse unacted desires."

In 1868 my father published the first series of his *Unspoken Sermons*; it brought the following letter from Ruskin, acknowledging the gift of the volume:

John Ruskin to G.M.D.
DENMARK HILL, S.
18*th Decr.*, 1868.

DEAR MACDONALD,

Thank you exceedingly for the book. They are the best sermons—beyond all compare—I have ever read, and if ever sermons did good, these will. Pages 23, 24 are very beautiful—unspeakably beautiful.[3] If they were but true—(I know someone who will like them so much.) But I feel so strongly that it is only the image of your own mind that you see in the sky! And you will say, "And who made the mind?" Well, the same hand that made the adder's ear—and the tiger's heart—and they shall be satisfied when they awake—with *their* likeness? It is a precious book though—God give you grace of it.

---

1 See also very apposite letter, p. 373.
2 *Castle Warlock*, vol. iii, p. 188.
3 The passage begins thus: "How terribly have the theologians misrepresented God in the measures of the low and showy, not the lofty and simple humanities...."

Ruskin, the prophet-artist, looked from without inwards; George MacDonald, the poet-novelist, looked from within outwards: that man's mission being the uplifting of work and its beauty, this man's the proving of the Divine Humanity. Ruskin's mind was the more scientific and aggressive, George MacDonald's imaginative and receptive—antithetic qualities that may be advantageously defined as male and female, though each of the two men was more of a man for his own special excellence.[1] The whole of Ruskin's mode of investigation and teaching was scientific: it depended upon the accurate collection of predictable facts, the arranging of them in order and class, and the deduction therefrom of the laws governing their nature, their history, their influence. Nor was he the less scientific that he repudiated the academic folly of those wise men who go to sea in a bowl and think their meagre equipment will carry them safely across the ocean. Ruskin's mind went beyond the "merely rational horizon," and by the vision of categorical truth thus got was guided to a deeper understanding of facts and their laws, than is possible to a Darwin, a Huxley, or a Metchnikoff. Indeed, so wide was his outlook that he learned the nature of man more from studying his relation to Art and Beauty, his duty towards his best possibilities in work, than from studying the facts of evolution. The tendency of Victorian science was to prove man a mechanism: whereas the whole of Ruskin's work went to show that this was precisely what he was not—and could not become, without disaster to soul and body, individual and race.

George MacDonald quite similarly fought against a doctrinal faith and a utilitarian duty that claim logical, mechanic efficiency. Yet he was quite as scientific as Ruskin in his fearless honesty and his refusal to believe anything

---

1 My use of these words has given some offence; yet I adhere to them. If I say my mother had beyond most women masculine courage, it is to name her the nobler woman; if I find my father gifted beyond most men with feminine pity, it proclaims him the greater man.

that was not inherently true. In both men it was imagination that informed them of the truth before they set about its analysis. Because of their vision which sees beyond the horizon of things, both were adventurers set out for an unknown yet to their eyes obvious land: "Not by reason sensible of deeming, but by reason imaginative," as Chaucer had it.[1] Ruskin declares that no great work "has been accomplished by human creatures in which instinct was not the principal mental agent, or in which the method of design could be defined by rule, or apprehended by reason. It is therefore that agency, through mechanism, destroys the powers of art and sentiments of religion together."[2] That instinct in my father was his exalted fairy vision, the light that in lighting every man reveals the secret of all.

Far from its being the image of his own mind, as Ruskin whimsically said, that my father saw in the sky, it was, I think he would answer, only when man is purified of faith in the material—"the cloak and cloud which shadows me from Thee"— [3] that he will see God.

Such vision is made possible in the fact presumed by all mystics that "Heaven lies about us in our infancy," and that we inherit some instinct, some memory-sense of that world of which, when our hearts are at their purest, we sometimes get visions through windows of starry flowers or chinks of bird-song —"bright shoots of everlastingness," never to be accounted for as subjective self-reflections.

I am constrained, as lover of both the men of whom I write, and a critic now laden with many more years of life and experience and perhaps of knowledge than either possessed in the year 1866, to bear witness to the purity of

---

1 Chaucer's translation of Boethius's *De Consolatione Philosophiæ*, p. 166. Early English Text Society.
2 *Fors Clavigera*, vol. v, p. 137. This recalls Anatole France's dictum: "La raison, la superbe raison est capricieuse et cruelle. La sainte ingénuité de l'instict ne trompe jamais." Pierre Nozière. Nelson, p. 132.
3 Henry Vaughan's "Cock-Crowing."

heart which they so truly impersonated, giving them power of vision, that "without deeming comprehendeth all things." That it was instant guide to conduct, their "principal mental agent," with both men, as surely as it was incentive to their every adventure, is made plain by two typical facts:

When in 1885 Oxford determined to endow experimental physiology, i.e. vivisection, Ruskin upon the very day that the decision was reached resigned his Slade Professorship. No arguments, such as we may be sure he was familiar with then as is every debating society now, counted as relevant; he saw, he knew the practice to be eternally opposed to that law which is supreme to mere ethical or scientific advantage. What if humanity gain all the secrets and remedies of the universe and lose its soul?—a remark which I may claim to epitomize my father's dealing with the question in *Paul Faber, Surgeon*.

Again, when my parents were in the States in 1873, a deputation waited upon my father to offer the pastorate of a certain fashionable church in New York at a salary equivalent to an English bishop's. Without hesitation or discussion, knowing too that my mother, in such a matter, as in almost all, would see eye to eye with himself, he refused it point blank: the serpent of worldly wisdom, however tempting the apple, could be no honest advocate. "He knew better than imagine duty determined by consequences, or take foresight for direction." [1]

"Things are in the saddle and ride mankind," wrote Emerson; but in both these instances it was purity of heart and divine vision that drove both men to their work without thought of its reward: the doing of which work always engenders an honesty above policy, a courage beyond that needed for fighting the Dragon. Such clear vision is surely the very ground and essence of religious faith; and in its illumination creeds count for little. If Ruskin "read his

---

[1] *Donal Grant*, vol. iii, p. 190. *Vide postea*, p. 492.

philosophy by the troubled light of wrong and suffering—not the light of the morning, but of a burning house" [1]—that was because he lacked perfect faith in the very imagination he was always upholding.

And yet both men were primarily and splendidly inductive. While Ruskin was charged to show mankind where socially they were wrong to-day, where they had been right yesterday and might be again tomorrow, my father's closer intensity made his concern the saving of the individual man. My father set himself to separate the true from the false in the old conceptions and dogmas concerning the saving of souls from their estrangement; Ruskin to prove what kind of faith and inspiration alone could rescue mankind and its world of loveliness from the "Dragon's claws" already fixed so firm in the social heart.[2] It was his intensity of love for the individual man and the belief in his intimacy with the divinely possible that ruled my father's genius; it was in the extensity of his greater knowledge, in the all-embracing adoration of the human dynamic that inspired Ruskin's. It is worth while enlarging upon this imaginative vision as the gift binding the two men together, because the lack of it among ourselves of the crowd accounts perhaps for our inability, personal and political, to accept as our guide in conduct the courage of our finer instincts, and to trust God for the consequences.

---

[1] *Paul Faber*, vol. i, p. 180.
[2] "Rich capitalists and landowners are only the claws of my Dragon." (*Fors Clavigera*, vol. v, p. 156.)

CHAPTER III
LEWIS CARROLL

MEANTIME our grandfather, now over eighty, had retired altogether from business, had grown a beard that softened much the austerity of his features, and had come to live at Elm Lodge, Hampstead.[1] It was now our privilege often to visit him and our Aunt Caroline, and in the summer of 1862, while they were at Aberystwith, we all had a happy holiday there. Thither Charles L. Dodgson (Lewis Carroll) came several times, and took many photographs, remarkable alike in permanence and beauty.

It was about this time, but at Tudor Lodge, that he asked my father's opinion upon a story he had written and named *Alice's Adventures Underground*, illustrated with pen-and-ink sketches by himself and minutely penned in printing characters. My father suggested that an experiment should be made upon his young family. Accordingly my mother read the story to us. When she came to the end I, being aged six, exclaimed that there ought to be sixty thousand volumes of it. Certainly it was our enthusiasm that persuaded our Uncle Dodgson, as we called him, to present the English-speaking world with one of its future classics, *Alice in Wonderland*. How happily could my father laugh over this loving humorist's impromptu drawings, full of the absurdities, mock-maxims and erratic logic so dear to the child-heart, young or old! While Dodgson, the shy, learned mathematician who hated

---

1 The old house still stands (in Elm Row). Then it had a good garden and stabling, but now is hedged round with meagre buildings.

inaccuracy, loved to question the very multiplication-table's veracity, my father, the poet, who hated any touch of irreverence, could laugh till tears ran at his friend's ridicule of smug formalism and copy-book maxims. What with Charles Dodgson, the versatile Mathesons, Alexander Strahan and his circle of witty Scots, or a little later the brilliant Canon Ainger, there was plenty of merriment along with sober talk in our home. Perhaps the discipline of the children was too constant; yet we had, if few physical games, enough amusement to leave us with joyous memories. One annual treat was Uncle Dodgson taking us to the Polytechnic for the entrancing "dissolving views" of fairy-tales, or to go down in the diving bell, or watch the mechanical athlete *Leotard*. There was also the Coliseum in Albany Street, with its storms by land and sea on a wonderful stage, and its great panorama of London. And there was Cremer's toy-shop in Regent Street—not to mention bath-buns and ginger-beer—all associated in my memory with the adorable writer of *Alice*.[1]

Nevertheless, and in spite of George MacDonald's delight in irresponsible gaity and fun, it must be apparent to any careful readers of his works, from *Within and Without* to *The Diary of an Old Soul*; from *Phantastes* to *Lilith*, but excluding all his fairy-tales for the young, that the atmosphere of sadness so prevalent in his youth was still often about him, yet never obscuring the snow-clad alps of his faith. Indeed,

---

1   I well remember leaning against him as he drew for me in my copybook—that pharisaical exponent of an impossibly perfect caligraphy—a picture that evoked from us shrieks of delight. In the far distance was a train steaming away from its station to negotiate a humpy railway bridge. In the fore-ground a very stout perspiring gentleman was mopping his head with one hand, while his wife, scraggy and grim, dragged him along by the other, and shouted at him, "It's puffing away fit to burst itself; we shall lose it John, if you don't run faster!" But out of his mouth soared a balloon of words: "I can't run no faster, and I won't go no furder!" Also do I remember the frame of a broken hand-mirror into which I pasted notepaper for him to draw reflections upon. A beautiful basket of apples he made under a wonderful tree with my sister Mary, not a bit like her, sitting beside it and the baby Ronald running with another apple to add to the pile.

a certain weariness of heart is very natural in spiritual pilgrims. "More of sorrowful than of joyful men are always standing about the everlasting doors that open into the presence of the Most High";[1] and all men whose imagination inspires them, in prophecy or art, in poetry or music, to the uplifting of their fellow-men, are at times heavy of heart, even while their optimism will never allow discouragement to assail them. So it is George MacDonald's very love of God that made the world's alienation from His Kingdom so full of sadness. Robert Falconer in Seekers and Finders exclaims, "Though one evil spirit may drive a woman out of Eden, all the devils in Hell cannot drive Heaven out of a woman!" Some seem able to forget the blight that has swept over humanity and so can talk smilingly of the Kingdom of Heaven within us. Some find in concrete beauty a sufficient joy to blot out the horror and ugliness of sin. But for George MacDonald no uttermost loveliness, not even the washing away of all sin, could make him free of the Kingdom—only perfect reunion with the creating, redeeming Love: till he had this in his very soul, he must often have some mystery of sorrowfulness about him. "Despondency," wrote F. D. Maurice, "is hardly a state of mind; it is the mind's forgetfulness of its own true state—which is a glorious state, as I need not tell you."[2] The sadness of the poet is only a shadow thrown by the light; of which he knows better than those who, having no vision, are content.

Here is a letter concerning the passing of David Matheson's little son:

G.M.D. to Mrs. David Matheson.

Tudor Lodge,
Jan 14, 1863.

My dear Mrs. Matheson,

Accept my best thanks for your kindness in writing to me about the dear child who bore my name. Perhaps he has already a new heavenly

---

1 *The Hope of the Gospel* (1892), p. 97.
2 *Life of Frederick Denison Maurice*, vol. i, p. 301.

name; but he will be to all eternity your own child. I know by thinking of anyone of my own, how dreadful the loss must be to you, but life at the longest is not so very long, and you will find him again by and by. He is only laid by for you—like a precious thought of God's goodness laid up in the mind, and known to be there, though you cannot call it up when you please and contemplate it. If God gave to take away again, he would not be the God that Jesus has taught us to know. [1] The loss of the body is not more to his being than the loss of the little curl of hair would have been to his body, had that yet been alive....

In the year 1862 the third son, Robert Falconer, was born, July 15th. Then, and again in 1863, my father visited Mr. Mark Sharman at Wellingborough—my mother's uncle; for the removal from Tudor Lodge to Earles Terrace, Kensington, was in progress, and my mother, with thoughts for his comfort always uppermost, wished to spare him the inevitable fatigue and worry. Portions of his letters home help intimacy with these days. Than such a change of air and scene, nothing could do him more good. My Great-Uncle-Mark was a real lover of horses, and on October 3rd my father joined in the first meet for cub-hunting. I do not doubt his mount was a certain mare he describes in *Adela Cathcart*, whose feat of crossing the railway cutting described in its chapter x was known locally as fact.

She was a thoroughgoing hunter; no beauty certainly, with her ewe-neck, drooping tail and white face and stocking; but she had an eye at once gentle and wild as that of a savage angel....Although not much of a hunting man, the motion of the creature gave me such a sense of power and joy, that I longed to be scouring the fields with her under me.[2]

How different were the ways of certain country gentlemen whom he met there from his own friends' we may judge from

---
1 *Vide* two poems, p. 485, and p. 536.
2 "He had an almost passionate love of horses...a very charming and convincing touch in their description," wrote Ronald MacDonald, in his article on our father published in a collection of Essays *From a Northern Window* (1911). "There are few of his novels where you will not find a horse; if only appearing as a property and not as a character, its presence will yet be touched with knowledge and tenderness."

a letter to my mother, wherein—after confessing that he had played whist for sixpenny points, he adds: "We had a pleasant little party there, but they were rather coarse for me. I hope there will be a woman next time to keep it nice...." Then he tells of the children's happiness about the farm and the admiration they won.

I do not know how long it was before my father set his face strongly against playing for money, however small the points or stakes. Money was the token of service rendered, and like all symbols must be treated reverently.[1] Wherever money was rightly used, both parties to its exchange were the gainers—in material and good-will; but in gambling, one man's gain was the other's loss. My father was always fond of a rubber, and when we were settled at Earles Terrace the whist parties were a regular institution.

The removal to 12 Earles Terrace, standing a little back from the Kensington High Road and opposite Holland House, was determined upon for three reasons: (i) it was on gravel soil, and so would suit my father's bronchial weakness better than the clay of Regent's Park; (ii) it would be more convenient for most people who attended his lectures and classes; and (iii) it had much more accommodation for the growing family, now seven in number, even though there was no room as large as the studio at Tudor Lodge.

Edwardes Square, in which so many artists and men of letters lived—and built for French officers, it is said, by an exiled Frenchman in anticipation of Napoleon's conquest of England—lay at the back of the Terrace; and we who lived there shared the right of entry to its unusually beautiful garden. Here the third son, Robert Falconer, was born.

---

1 *Vide* letter to Mrs. A. J. Scott, p. 400. See also *The Elect Lady* (1888), p. 190.

CHAPTER IV
SWITZERLAND

IN the summer of 1865 my father took a long desired and much needed holiday in Switzerland—and without my mother, she being hardly in fit health to go with him. Mr. Edward Charrington, in a charming letter to my mother, asks permission to be his *soi-disant* host, and encloses a cheque for £30, which he begs her not to allow him to refuse. The original plan had been to join A. J. Scott's family who were going up the Rhone to Les Plans near Bex; Ruskin, however, was urgent that my father should see the Bernese Oberland, but to avoid Geneva, "now one wilderness of accursed gambling and jewellers' shops," and go to Berne, where "there is some Swiss character left, and thence to Thun, Interlaken and Lauterbrunnen." So he joined William Matheson and another friend and left for Antwerp early in August.

What with intense heat, asthma, lumbago, toothache and sleeplessness, he was never well, and writing was difficult. But we realize from his letters how much he gained.

G.M.D. to his Wife.
Antwerp,
Sunday night.

...God be praised for that spire [Antwerp Cathedral]. I *would* go up though my head ached and I seemed worn out. 616 steps, 410 feet! I made the others go. I was on the point of crying several times with delight, only I didn't. But just think of a man being able to sit at a finger-and-pedal board—250 feet from the ground and play any tune he liked on 40 bells yet higher—play to the whole city spread below! Oh how I should delight to build a cathedral—towers if nothing else. *God be praised!* was all I could say—as the Arabs say when they see a beautiful woman. It has filled and glorified me, and I could go home contented if I didn't see an Alp....

ANTWERP,
Monday morning.

...If I hadn't climbed that tower and had a breath of divine air, I should have been ill to-day. I went up ill and came down well....Oh, for the mountains—God's church towers! But I have nothing in me to-day but weakness and hope. If I am ill again any time, that awful height, though I soon got over the feeling, will haunt me with yawning depth....But I thank God for that tower....

In Cologne the bad smells impressed him more than the cathedral, which, excepting "the grand roof of the unfinished tower," he did not find very imposing. But he was suffering badly from toothache.

...I did not sleep well, for there was thunder and lightning and a tremendous fire flaring away right in front of my windows at some distance, and tremendous bell-ringing through the night, and watchmen's rattles. But I believe they were only ringing the bells to please God or drive away the devil....Perhaps the best things we have seen since we left home were first the sight of the people pouring out of the cathedral at Antwerp as we entered, and then the congregation remaining or gathering afterwards. Many of the women had caps with lace-bound lappets like rams-horns....

BASEL, SWITZERLAND.

...The town at which we stopped [Weissenburg] is a French-German one in Alsace. We had seen nothing so interesting before. It lies off the railway. A policeman in a cocked hat and military clothes took us to a tavern, and took his share of a couple of bottles of wine with us...But the lovely old town! with the water running through it, and the fine old church and the pretty women and the quaintest houses with rows of windows one above another in every roof. *I must* take you there for a month some day. It is just the place to write a book in and could be reached easily without going all the way we did. Will you come, sweet wife? Then we went on to Strasburg. And here again we found a glory of a city. I never saw anything to compare to it, except the old town of Edinburgh, and that is squalid and vile—this rich and ancient and glorious—rather smelly, of course, like the other. At eight o'clock

SWITZERLAND

yesterday morning we sat drinking champagne in a street planted with trees all over. And I think it did us good. Then the cathedral—far beyond Cologne in every respect—built of red stone—no glass but stained in it throughout—dark and solemn—nay, very dark with wonderful galleries which I will explain to you when I see you. I never saw such a huge organ hung against the pillars as if it had been only a kitchen clock—a blaze of colour—a clock full of moving figures and fantasies as big as a house telling everything that a clock could know about, even to the feasts of the church with women and cherubs and men that walk one leg after the other, and Goddesses and old Death, and chariots and horses, etc., etc., more quaint than beautiful. Then I did what the others declared themselves unable for—I went up the tower and up the spire. Oh, my dear, what would you think of such climbing and such visions like out of a balloon!...I went up as far as they would let me without an order from the Mayor, and all my weariness and fatigue was gone. And, darling, I am sure the only cure for you and me and all of us is getting up, up—into the divine air. I for my part choose the steeple-cure for my weariness. How will it be when I get amongst God's steeples?

The roofs of Strasburg are dark with, some, as many as five tiers of windows! And the streets and the colours! Antwerp all white and same and tame compared with this....Then we came here and soon found the town was beautiful too. Here the roofs all brown, rich brown, like that picture of Beauty and the Beast and great queer dormer-windows in them. Our hotel is right over the Rhine—a great, broad stream of a bluish-green, purring and rushing down—the waters escaping in wild delight from the ice-prisons up there in the awful hills—a mighty deep stream as wide as the Thames at London Bridge. A long, wooden bridge close by constantly traversed by many feet puzzles you the first morning with its sounds....

SCHAFFHAUSEN.

...I like the look of this hotel better than any we have been in yet—perhaps partly because we have had a girl to bring us water, who talks broad, honest German and looks you full in the eyes. I hate hotels! I mean those great big brutes that only want to eat you, and lick your hands for what they can get out of you. Last night I could only bear the sheet over me and slept so all night, and there was a change towards morning and there was no watchful woman beside me to cover me up, and now [crippled with lumbago] I go about like an old man, and ashamed of being stared at. They will take me for a worn-out roué on his way to the baths. Yesterday I was twice up and down the upper half of Strasburg Cathedral-spire, and to-day the stairs at the hotel at Basle—three tremendous flights—seemed Alpine....But I must go to bed....There is a piano going downstairs. That sounds homely. And there is a round thing of white porcelain in a corner of this room, reaching to the ceiling and begirt with brass which is not homelike at all. It is the stove and is lighted from the passage outside—and I have a basin to wash in the shape and size of a pie-dish, and an eiderdown quilt on the bed, etc.—as you know....I shall be awake before the sun most likely—for I can't sleep—at least I have not slept well one night since I left. But I am very fairly well—all but my back and that's only a bother. Good-night, darling wife.

[THUN.]

[A portion missing]....giant shepherd-king sitting on the circle of the earth, the white-fleeced mountains, whose very calm looks like a frozen storm. And the highest of them is nearly twice as high as the highest in front.

And the little town below is gay as a doll's house. You never saw such decorations, for it is the time of an annual *Fest* which lasts for three days. What it means except that it is all for singing and that they give prizes, I don't know. We can't find out. The people come from all quarters of Switzerland....We went to a meadow in the evening where they meet. It was like a fair—with dancing-places surrounded and half-hidden by boughs. We wanted to go into one of these, but were told that we must dance if we did, against which in my case there were two impediments, ignorance and lumbago. They were all of the people, drinking wine and beer. One or two were a little elevated, but there was no sign of excess of any kind, nor a woman with other than a womanly good face to be seen....

MÜRREN.

I am much better, dear, and have been out a good part of the afternoon. And if I had seen nothing else, I could now go home content. Yet I am not sure whether amidst the lovely chaos of shifting clouds I have seen the highest peak of the Jungfrau. It is utterly useless to try to describe it....I hate the photographs, they convey *no* idea. The tints and the lines and the mass and the streams and the vapours, and the mingling, and the infinitude, and the loftiness, the glaciers and the slow crawling avalanches—they cannot be described.

Once to-day, looking through the mist, I said with just a slight reservation of doubt in my heart, "There that is as high as I want it to be," and straightway I saw a higher point grow out of the mist beyond. So I have found it with all the ways of God. And so will you too, dear love.

We have nice people, but I am *not* going to write about people....I said to them to-day that I should not lie still in my grave if I had not brought you to see it.

I have been into a cottage to-day to drink some milk and had a chat in German with the people....And perhaps I enjoyed the marvellous scene, not one instant the same, the more that I was alone. Sometimes in an instant the whole range is invisible from the mist which keeps boiling up almost constantly from the valley, and sweeps across the opposite mountains....I rather want to get home, for I have got all I wanted here—at least I have as much as I can take in now....I must bring you here next summer if I can.

My father's impressions gained from the trip bore fruit in his novel, *Wilfrid Cumbermede*, published in 1872, close following upon the grim ending to Ruskin's courtship of Rose La Touche. The book, I believe, was written while my parents were greatly troubled over Mrs. La Touche's conduct, trying to excuse her on the score of her narrow evangelicalism. The hero of the story, at any rate, has his life broken by misrepresentation of this sort. But it seems inconceivable that Mrs. La Touche, eagerly reading every book of my father's as soon as it appeared, and in close touch with the advanced thought of the day, could have been so narrow-minded. Anyhow, my parents had to choose between hers and Ruskin's friendship.

In this book the writer describes a wonderful walk up the bed and rocky barriers of a frozen stream, saying, "Its varied loveliness would take the soul of a Wordsworth or a Ruskin to comprehend or express"—a remark that taken with certain passages concerning the mystical influence of the Alps upon the soul, strengthens my assumption that Ruskin's suffering, his lavish giving of himself, and his starvation by her who alone could give him peace, were the incentive to the book's writing. Because of this, it is interesting to compare certain passages in *Præterita*, where Ruskin tells of his first knowledge of the Alps, with others in *Wilfrid Cumbermede*, descriptive of my father's own and similar impressions. But John Ruskin was a boy of fourteen, George MacDonald a man of forty-one when the transfiguration was vouchsafed to each.

It is his first sight of the snow-clad Alps from Schaffhausen of which Ruskin tells, and how throughout his life the vision "would associate itself with every just and noble sorrow, joy, or affection." Although there was no definite religious sentiment mingled with it, there was a continual perception of sanctity in the whole of nature from the slightest thing to the vastest; an instinctive awe, mingled with delight. And again, he speaks of it as a pleasure "infinitely greater than any which has since been possible to me in anything; comparable for intensity only to the joy of a lover in being near a noble and kind mistress, but no more explicable or definable than that feeling of love itself."[1]

My father's exaltation when he first beheld the Jungfrau results in a great word-picture:

> The mist yet rolled thick below, but far away and far up, yet as if close at hand, the clouds were broken into a mighty window through which looked in upon us a huge mountain peak swathed in snow. One great level band of darker cloud crossed its breast, above which rose the peak, triumphant in calmness, and stood unutterably solemn and grand, in clouds as white as its own whiteness. It had been there all the time!...With a sudden sweep the clouds curtained the mighty window and the Jungfrau withdrew into its Holy of Holies....But from the mind it glorified it has never vanished.... To have beheld a truth is an apotheosis. What the truth was I could not tell; but I had seen something which raised me above my former self and made me long to rise higher yet.... [2]

---

1 *Præterita*, vol. i., p. 133 *et seq.*
2 *Wilfrid Cumbermede*, vol. i, p. 244 *et seq.*

George MacDonald   J. A. Froude   Wilkie Collins   Anthony Trollope
W. M. Thackeray   Lord Macaulay   Bulwer Lytton   Thos. Carlyle   Charles Dickens
GROUP OF CONTEMPORARY WRITERS

CHAPTER V
THE EDINBURGH CHAIR

THE year 1865 was one of considerable events. It saw the publication of *Alec Forbes of Howglen*, a novel that fully justified George Smith's opinion as to his gifts in fiction: it is perhaps the most successful, *quâ* fiction, of all his efforts. It had so fine a reception that it encouraged the development of a book even nearer to his genius, *Robert Falconer*, though between these two came *Annals of a Quiet Neighbourhood*, running through a year of the Sunday Magazine. The latter story is based, as already related, upon his life at Arundel; his success with *Alec Forbes* having led him to write more definitely for the English reader. But not even in *Thomas Wingfold* or *Paul Faber*—which latter my father once told me he thought the best of all his novels, though emphatically it is not so—did he reach the level of his finest Scotch writing, even granting the possible inferiority of some later ones dealing with the North. His financial position was now easier, and remained easier—thanks largely to Alexander Strahan, the founder of *Good Words*, the *Sunday Magazine* and the *Contemporary Review*, and a most generous publisher. Yet the increasing demands of the young people vigorously outstripped the march of income. Maurice, with F. D. Maurice for his godfather, was born on February 7, 1864, and Bernard Powell, whose godmother was Mrs. La Touche, came on September 28, 1865.

Immediately on George MacDonald's return from

Switzerland his energies were all given to his candidature for the Edinburgh Chair of Rhetoric and Belles Lettres vacated by the poet and critic, W. E. Aytoun, who died in August of that year. The gift was in the hands of the Crown through the Home Secretary and Lord Advocate. In spite of having such men against him as David Masson, who was chosen, Daniel Wilson of Toronto, Professor Nicol of Glasgow, Dr. William Hanna, and other notable scholars, my father's reputation as a lecturer and the representative Scottish writer, as well as his popularity in Edinburgh society, would, many believed, have secured his election, had not *David Elginbrod* and its oft-quoted epitaph stood in his way. But he was not very sorry at his failure, though the salary was large: what event could he regret when all things were ordered from above? But I well remember my mother's relief at the disappointing news: she had grave doubts whether her husband's bronchial tubes could weather the Edinburgh winds.

On his way North he visited his friend of many years Thomas Constable, the publisher, at Grange, Borrowdale, where he spent a charming week, and got some shrewd suggestions concerning the coming contest. His host's daughter, Mary,[1] writes me of this visit:

> We all just loved him. One day he and I rode round Derwentwater together. I was a shy girl of about sixteen, but he talked so simply and interestingly, and just as if he liked all the things that I did, that I never forgot that ride. My father used to read out to us all his books as they came out.

During his candidature, he visited Thomas Erskine at Linlathen, where Thomas Carlyle and his brother Alexander, with Dr. John Brown (of *Rab and his Friends*), and Mrs. Batten, Mrs. Russell Gurney's mother, were fellow guests. He also stayed with Dr. Smeaton, of whose son Oliphant's reminiscences of my father mention has already been made.

---

[1] Mrs. Forsyth of Argyll.

THE EDINBURGH CHAIR

Generally, testimonials are worth little more than their face-value, viz. that of laudation, and perhaps even less in a biography than a council-chamber. Yet when such men as Maurice and Ruskin vouch for the guinea-stamp, they do surely indicate the man. The eulogies of Dean Stanley, Erasmus Darwin, F.R.S., Lord Houghton, John Stuart Blackie, Norman MacLeod, Charles Kingsley, Dean Plumptre, make a fine series; but I must be content with only two of the actual testimonials, and one letter concerning the candidature.

John Ruskin to G.M.D.

DENMARK HILL,
16th August, 1865.

MY DEAR MACDONALD,

I cannot offer testimonial to any one's fitness for a chair of rhetoric; for I do not know what rhetoric means. I should be very glad to think that there were simple people among us who could be talked into change of their opinions;—(generally, any change of opinion on the part of the British public would at present probably be for the better.) But I do not see that any rhetoric except the rattling of dice—in the wide sense of dice—has power over the multitude of to-day. The mellifluous expression of things which they suppose themselves to know, and like to have repeated energetically when they feel doubtful about them, is of course a popular kind of rhetoric in pulpit and senate, but *that* kind I don't think you'll teach anybody. The other set, [who] alone [represent] good art, of sensible people who say what they have got to say—and no more—cannot, I believe, be taught by anybody. I should think a sorrowful Ghost of all the murdered English in our sensation plays and operas might occupy the Rhetorical chair in a silently expressive manner—better than any poor human being in the midst of our Feast of Reason. But if keen and prophetic understanding of the emotional part of literature, and power of explaining clearly such understanding to others, fits for this Rhetorical position, that understanding and power you assuredly have: and I am sure no man would do his duty more conscientiously, or make the Professorship a means of more active good so far as way was open to its influence and authority. It would give me the sincerest pleasure to hear you had been successful, and especially in Edinburgh, for you are never so eloquent as when you are talking about Scotland.

Ever your affectionate Friend,
J. RUSKIN.

TESTIMONIAL FROM JOHN RUSKIN, ESQ., M.A., AUTHOR OF
Modern Painters, ETC., ETC.

My dear MacDonald,
    I am heartily glad you are trying for the Belles Lettres Scottish Professorship. Of all the literary men I know, I think you most love literature itself: the others love themselves and the expression of themselves; but you enjoy your own *art*, and the art of others when it is fine. I know you will do your duty earnestly and wholly, in any position: and perhaps the desire to make a Professorship real and useful is the first character which should be looked for in a candidate; being one often wanting even in the most able men. I am always glad to hear you lecture myself, and if I had a son, I would rather he took lessons in literary taste under you than under any person I know, for you would make him more than a scholar, a living and thoughtful reader.
    With every hope for your success, believe me faithfully and affectionately yours,

J. RUSKIN.

DENMARK HILL,
    August 18*th*, 1865.

Mr. A. S. McColl, my father's stepuncle, who was intimate with the intellect of Edinburgh, believed Ruskin's testimonial would make the election secure. He wrote that some who "thought *Within and Without* the greatest poem since Wordsworth," and yet were wavering because of *David Elginbrod's* free thinking, were so much impressed by Ruskin's praise, "knowing he has far too great a love of truth to say anything he does not fully believe," that they were now determined to do all they could to support my father.

TESTIMONIAL FROM THE REV. F.D. MAURICE, M.A.

I have known Mr. MacDonald for many years. I have been surprised, the longer I have been acquainted with him, by the extent and variety of his accomplishments. He appears to me to have as keen a delight in the literature of his own country and of other countries as any man I have ever met with; to study books as only a man does who really appreciates the authors of them; and to have a peculiar facility for communicating his thoughts to others, and for awakening in them an interest like his own. He is entirely free from pedantry; has great geniality in conversation as well as in lecturing; and must, I should think, be particularly acceptable as well as useful to young men. He would be a great acquisition to any university—to none, I should imagine, more than to that with which he has already the strongest patriotic sympathies. I only forbear to dwell upon his moral qualities, his great earnestness and high sense of duty, because I am sure that every one of his friends will bear testimony how these have been tested by severe trials during the whole of his life.

F.D. MAURICE.

August 18th, 1865.

Professor John Stuart Blackie's letter and testimonial are like his own personality, delightful, but lack perhaps something in weight—especially as he himself, though filling the Greek Chair, was such a heretic in convention. Indeed, with men like Maurice, Ruskin and Blackie as his chief supporters, it is not much wonder that the advisers of the Lord Advocate and the Home Secretary were nervous as to my father's soundness—even though they might have counted Dean Stanley, Norman MacLeod and Erasmus Darwin sufficiently respectable to balance any doubts. I presume A. J. Scott thought it would not help the candidate for him to give a testimonial.

I cannot close this period of keen anticipation without indicating the impossibility, as much now as in the Manchester days, for my parents to withhold from one another their sorrows and joys, their solaces and upliftings. My mother was now suffering in a manner not unusual with her when all her vitality was needed for an event of four or five weeks hence, its present distress hardly mitigated by the joy that would come in the morning. Yet her tender words to her husband, *à propos* of the invitation to visit Mr. Erskine, point yet again her perfect sharing with him in all his friendships:

Mrs G.M.D. to her Husband.

12 EARLES TERRACE.

I do hope you will go and see Mr. Erskine, dear Husband; it will do you some good. They will give you some strength, if I have been giving you weakness. It will be some comfort to me. Oh, do, I intreat you, go, and stay more than a day. That Christian Erskine and that Prophet Carlyle will give you something—you who are always giving out to others. I am doing very well. You can't think how strong I am. The last two nights I have slept all night, and am able to do a great deal in a quiet way in the day....

Then she tells of her father's kindness and tenderness to her, and of his keenness to hear all the news from Edinburgh; and she continues:

I am simply ashamed of having talked with you with all my insane changes of mood. They have been all true to me. But why have I troubled you with them? Because I have for fifteen years and more felt as if what I felt was yours and interesting to you, especially when shut up with hideous thoughts, ugly truths and the Devil. One night God spoke to me, and Heaven came. Oh, the sweetness of that rest and that sleep in him! That calm and trust in you! I can't tell you what it was like....I could have lain down then and been cut up or scoffed at or seen you carried away by all those who had pretended to love me, and yet could have loved you on and sung gentle songs of praise....I will make no promises any more, but will try your way of making each present time do its duty. So shall you teach me yet if you will.

G.M.D. to his Wife.

[Aug. 17, 1865.]

My darling, I shall love you more than ever. I can hardly be sorry for your sufferings, if they made you hear one word from Him which I do think you would hear. Thank you with all my heart for trusting me in sending me what you had thought in the night. Do not be in the least anxious about me. I feel very fairly well now....Simpson at Blackwood's says it is absurd to hear Mrs. Oliphant's worship (!) of me. "What is it for her to be writing novels when such a man, etc." Isn't it funny?...

CHAPTER VI
BUDE

IN 1866 A. J. Scott died, and George MacDonald had to face a sorrow he had not known the like of since his father died eight years before. The only mention of it among my father's papers is the letter he wrote to Mrs. Scott when the news reached him: nor do his healing words argue against the poignant realization of his loss:

G.M.D. to Mrs. A. J. Scott.

12 Earles Terrace, Kensington,
Feb. 9, 1866.

My very dear Friend,
...He who has left us was the best and greatest of our time. Those who know him best will say so most heartily. But we have no more lost him than the disciples lost their Lord when he went away that he might come closer to them than ever. Life is not very long in this place, dear Mrs. Scott. All we have to mind is to do our work, while the chariot of God's hours is bearing us to the higher life beyond.
He was—he is—my friend. He understood me, and gave me to understand him; and I think I did understand him to the measure of my inferior capacity. All my prosperity in literary life besides has come chiefly through him and you....How glad and quiet he must be now the struggle is over! My heart clings to him. How I could have served and waited on him, had that been in my power or his need! Who knows but he may help us all now in ways that we cannot understand. But the best is, we are all going to him. The one God be with him and us....

Words such as these are worth infinitely more as evidences of Truth transcending facts than the reasonings even of such men as Ruskin and my father. In which conviction I am constrained to set alongside this letter another written by my father (1878) to Mrs. Scott in reply to one of hers when my sister, Mary Josephine, died; for he again refers to his "beloved friend" A. J. Scott. After which no other word need be said about my father's loss:

G.M.D. to Mrs. A. J. Scott.

VILLA CATTANEO, NERVI,
May 12, 1878.

MY VERY DEAR MRS SCOTT,

I write for my wife and myself to thank you for your most kind letter. You could not have done better than send us a word from the "high countries," in the handwriting of our beloved friend. Ah! one day—we shall talk with him again. My faith in his Master and ours makes me bold to cling to such hopes. But for Him who conquered death by dying, how few and how feeble hopes of any kind should I have! and but for the Father of him and us, none at all.

My wife suffers still. I trust she will feel more by and by that death is but the shadow of life. But she sorely wants her child to talk to just for a little. I think we have all learned a little through the sorrow—and will more and more look forward....

Yours gratefully and lovingly,

GEORGE MACDONALD.

My father was now writing and producing his novels with great rapidity, though Mr. George Smith's prophecy that the publishers would be saving up to pay his price was hardly fulfilled. In 1866 *Annals of a Quiet Neighbourhood* was running through *The Sunday Magazine* anonymously, but appeared, with authorship proclaimed, in the usual three volumes in the following year, which also saw *Dealings With the Fairies*, illustrated by Arthur Hughes, and *Unspoken Sermons*. In 1867 also *Robert Falconer* was appearing as a serial in *The Argosy*, edited by Mrs. Henry Wood, and *Guild Court* in *Good Words* in the same year, both being published by Hurst and Blackett the following year. *Good Words for the Young* made its first appearance in 1869. Its publisher was Strahan, a man of amazing enterprise, who, whatever his misjudgments of men or his ruinous generosities, needed only, so some said, to sniff at an author's manuscript to realize its worth. But *Good Words for the Young* was too good to succeed, in spite of contributors such as Charles Kingsley, William Gilbert, W. R. S. Ralston, and George MacDonald. It reawakened, however, my father's surest gift of faerie-allegory, and produced *At the Back of the North Wind*, with like-inspired illustrations by Arthur Hughes. Of all my father's works, this remains the "best seller." Its secret here again lies in its two-world consciousness. A child no more grasps intellectually its exalted symbolism than he reflects upon Form's relation to its indwelling Idea when he runs to his mother with a primrose because of its beauty. Yet in both cases a lasting impression of the story's and the flower's place in the Divine Economy remains, consciously or not. One need not ask what the rose means if its sweetness pierces the veil and gives taste of the joy that "will never pass into nothingness." Nor need we commiserate Alexander Strahan on his failure.

The following year my father took over the editorship at a salary of £600 a year. Then appeared in its pages the second half of *At the Back of the North Wind* as well as *Ranald Bannerman's Boyhood*, so freely quoted in this Biography. But the magazine had to be discontinued, though my father volunteered and fulfilled its third and fourth years' editing without remuneration. Thereafter he declared he would do no more editing at any salary. It had lost us one delightful friend and brilliant writer who charged him with refusing his manuscript to find room for the editor's; while another was estranged for a while, and even revenged himself in a leading review by a bitter attack on *The Vicar's Daughter*. The names of both are well known and of honourable repute.

Good Words for the Young was as far in advance of those times as now, vulgarly speaking, it would be behind these. My father's knowledge as to what food children best thrive upon came from his own child-like faith in their celestial inheritance: being of the Spirit, their food must match their hunger; and he gathered for them manna from above.

But in the pedagogic teaching of the young, my father's theories were, some may think, less felicitous. Though my younger brothers and sisters fared better, as also my two eldest sisters, to whom my mother could give more time, I had no schooling till I was eleven, and could then barely read. But my father would from time to time give me and my sister Grace lessons in Latin and Euclid. They were not successful. In spite of wonderful patience, his theory—that we should be more interested in Æneas and Dido than in the five declensions, and ought to pick up a dead language as an infant learns speech without grammar and dictionary—had its limitations: Æneas and Dido remained less self-evident than Euclid's Axioms, more abstract even than his Definitions. My father's knowledge of his children's higher needs was surer than his ideas as to how the soil for them should be prepared: he knew the awakening of their imaginative sense was, after all, more important than academic grammar or coded moralities.

Take *At the Back of the North Wind*, however, as possibly the simplest of his prophetic utterances. All the strength of its teaching is allusive—an appeal to the imaginative seeing of a truth rather than a claim for its passive acceptance on the score of authority. Who, for instance, can logically accept the doctrine that, God having made the whole world, he being moreover all powerful and all good, everything in the world *must* be good, however much experiences and appearances deny the claim? But contrast North Wind's statement about the ship she has to sink:

I will tell you how I am able to bear it, Diamond: I am always hearing, through every noise, through all the noise I am making myself even, the sound of a far-off song. I do not exactly know where it is, or what it means; and I don't hear much of it, only the odour of its music, as it were, flitting across the great billows of the ocean outside this air in which I make such a storm; but what I do hear, is quite enough to make me able to bear the cry from the drowning ship. So it would you if you could hear it. [1]

True feeding of the child is more subtle a thing than psychologist can fathom. George MacDonald did fathom it—and in a way that was absolutely matchless. Magic and mystery, nonsense and fun—in no egregious fashions of the day, but in enduring forms of beauty—did more for us than moral precept or standardized education. *North Wind* is full of light, always renewing itself to this day: and so, for that matter, is Mother Hubbard and her doggiest of dogs. On the other hand, Dr. Watt's respectable discountenancing of the delight manifested by the canine tribe in barking and biting, left me quite as cold as Virgil's singing of *arms-and-the-man* because he was unkind enough to do it in Latin.

The child at his best is always imaginative and, in his games, his rimes, his dancing, his one thought is to get away from the things that restrain. So my father's irresponsible rimes, such as *Little Boy Blue,* just because their meaning is the wild harebell's rather than the economical bee's, may perhaps be given higher rank than his oft-quoted *Baby* poem, in which, however, older children do delight rapturously.

Then, again, my father was never willing to admit any time-urgency in education. Hamlet, he would say, went back to the University when over thirty; and it had been common to find men even older than that among the undergraduates in Aberdeen. Direct teaching was necessary for moral discipline, and this must be built upon the rock of the home, in order that mind-awakening might arise from obedience. Yet, I do think, in spite of our parents' love

---
1 *At the Back of the North Wind* (1871), p. 77.

and devotion, we became introspective, our consciences tied to the letter of the law. My father had no ambition for his children's ordinary success. Success or failure were but minor points: what mattered was conduct. Why need he be anxious for the morrow? We were worth to God and the world more than the lilies of the field whom He clothes in glory, or the sparrows none of whom fall without their Father. In all things he was consistent: he feared for us vulgar success and position.[1] My mother, however, was not equally unmindful of the world's criticism; and a trifling incident in my schooldays illustrates her sensitiveness to the social reproach of Nonconformity. Of this my father was quite regardless, even though his heresy had lost him the Chair in Edinburgh, and his frequent preaching from dissenting pulpits subjected him to condescensions from otherwise large-minded churchmen which my mother found hard to bear.

The master of the fourth form at my school has been immortalized by my schoolfellow, that kindly humorist, F. Antsey of *Vice Versa* renown, in his novel *The Giant's Robe*, who tells us the pedagogue's nicknames were "Prawn" and "Shellfish," though even more apposite was the one discovered by myself, viz. *The Reverend Billy Lobster*. One morning, in class, suddenly rang forth the command, "Stand up the boys whose fathers are clergymen!" Three responded, myself not of them. Then I was called up to the desk. "Isn't your father a clergyman." "No, Sir." "Didn't he write *Annals of a Quiet Neighbourhood*?" "Yes, Sir." "But it's written by a clergyman!" "No, Sir; *but my father was once a dissenting minister.*"

The Rev. B. Lobster turned scarlet with anger and screamed at me as if I was his first experience with boiling

---

1   Once he said he would make me a watchmaker, as my hands were better than my head; and he would have been quite as proud of a son if he proved a first-rate craftsman, I think, as a luminary in any profession. For his views on the value of handicrafts, see *There and Back* (1891), vol. i, pp. 58 *et seq.* Also *The Vicar's Daughter*, vol. ii, p. 123.

water, "Go back to your place!" Thereafter I, who had been growing in favour and expanding under the admirable teaching of this now irate cleric, could do nothing right for many a day; though I admit it was not long before he ceased to visit the sins of the father upon the child. All the masters of that school were in Holy Orders; and I do not doubt there had been some discussion in their common-room as to the integrity, social and doctrinal, of the much discussed novel's author. When I told my mother of the incident, her remark, that I was *not a man-of-the-world*, puzzled me.

George MacDonald's culture was no more tainted with nonconformist crudity than an Oxford polish or official sanctity. He feared no man, yet waited upon what was discoverable in everyone. This made him no less a keen and patient listener than a masterly, even prophetic, talker when any big subject was to the fore. He did not love debate, feeling always afraid lest the apparent need to justify one's own opinion should outbid zeal for truth. Yet his keen sense of logic made him shine in controversy, even if sometimes, in the strength of his convictions, his utterance was rather the inspired advocate's than the dispassionate judge's. He was Luther, not Erasmus.

Sir Henry Craik has recently written of my father thus:

> At the house of my eldest brother, the partner of Macmillan, and his wife, the authoress of *John Halifax*, I met many whose names were as familiar as household words. George MacDonald was often there—profuse in talk, often inspired by high imagination, but, I am inclined to think, rather uncertain about his own intellectual standing as compared with his fellows....[1]

I think this is probably true—although being so essentially unselfconscious, talking always with rare illumination, and standing so much above the average of

---
[1] "Sixty Years Ago," *Glasgow Herald*, December 2, 1922.

literary men and scholarly dons, it never occurred to him to appraise their inferiority. Ordinary people of culture dislike enthusiasm—can hardly tolerate "the face of a man glowing like an altar on which had descended the fire of heaven";[1] still more are they shy of, if not irritated by genius.

Exactly when my father first avowed himself a member of the Church of England I do not know. Presumably it was when he and my mother began to attend F. D. Maurice's church in Vere Street.[2]

I think it was in 1865 that my father became a lecturer in the evening classes at King's College, London. That noble institution, to which I myself owe everything, was the first modern champion for higher popular education; and these classes enabled many engaged in business to touch scholarship otherwise denied. I believe the students attending them were largely Dissenters; one at least, a bank clerk, William Carey Davies, son of a minister, became my father's devoted friend, keeping his bank-book and accounts in order for love's sake, correcting proofs and generally saving him much petty worry for many long years. But in 1866 my father got into hot water—or rather had a good deal splashed over him, quite tepid—for preaching in a conventicle. Professor E. H. Plumptre, afterwards Dean of Wells and one of his truest friends, was scandalized, as he had actually seen him a communicant at Vere Street. The Principal, Dr. Jelf, appears to have understood the position and honoured the latitudinarian for his candid explanation; at any rate he was content if the lecturer on English Literature undertook that in any public announcement of his engagements to preach he should refrain from mentioning his connection with King's

---

1 *Castle Warlock*, vol. i, p. 165.
2 I remember well going with them from Tudor Lodge in a four-wheeled cab; though more distinct in my memory than the great sermons remain the entrancing stable-staliness of the ancient vehicle and the fear lest the sounding-board suspended over the pulpit should fall and shut up for ever the preacher in his box.

College. This was easily conceded, as my father would never countenance any advertising of such occasions. So Dr. Jelf did not turn my father out as in 1856 he had ousted Professor Maurice.

À *propos* of this, the following undated letter illustrates my father's consistent antipathy to money-changers in the temple:

> G.M.D. *to the Secretary of a North London Congregational Church.*
>
> If you have a collection regularly every Sunday, I have nothing to say; but I will have nothing to do with any special services, or any extraordinary collection. I am a member of the Church of England, but care neither for that nor any other denomination as dividing or separating. It grates painfully on my ears to hear of services for the sake of reducing debt. Debts must be paid, and I will see to my own; but I will preach nowhere for the sake of anything but helping my fellows to be true and trusting. Pray leave me out of your scheme, and in the confidence that you will regard my wish in the matter, I will preach for your pastor on the evening of the 30th September.

But to revert to my father's ideas upon practical education. If his sons ever felt that education on more ordinary lines would have given them better opportunity for scholarly distinction at university or hospital, they do not forget the inestimable privileges of home-life and of contact with friends who, not only *suggestively* in the environment created by them, but sometimes by direct ministration, helped very early their emancipation. Shall I instance what I mean?

In 1867, one of these sons found himself at school for the first time, and a wretched ignoramus, in a class of thirty-two boys a year or two younger than himself. Two terms were hopelessly spent and no remove for him; to sing in the chapel choir, by which he earned his schooling, being his only joy. But then came his deliverance. The whole family spent that summer at Bude, where my father got material for *The Seaboard Parish*, transposing thence the church of Kilkhampton and naming the place Kilkhaven. Ruskin had suggested that his pupil, Octavia Hill,[1] should join us, and she became as truly a ministrant angel to that dull school-boy as later to city-degraded multitudes. For already was she carrying out Ruskin's ideas among the dilapidated houses and tenants he had bought for her in Paradise Row, Marylebone, and was worn out with her labours.[2] She spent a long holiday with us at Bude; and every morning she took that dreamy, indolent boy across the breakwater to the top of the Chapel-rock, and made him in love, if not with Æneas

---

[1] I read in a letter of Octavia Hill in 1863 to Madame Bodichon how the latter had asked her if she would allow a daughter of George MacDonald to join her drawing-class. Miss Hill says how much she owed to *David Elginbrod*, and how great the pleasure and duty would be if she might have this extra pupil without additional payment. She owed it also to Ruskin, whose pupil she had been for seven years, "to make all use of his teaching....I do always feel as if my life was the very happiest, the education given me the most wonderful...." But the actual meeting had taken place even earlier. Mrs C. Edmund Maurice thus writes of it to me (March 1922): "It must be sixty-one years since I first saw Dr. George MacDonald, and the impression made on me is still quite vivid. I had gone to the Working Men's College to help my sister Octavia, who was acting as Secretary for the Working Women's Classes held there in the afternoon and taught by ladies, friends of the Rev. F. D. Maurice. These ladies were most of them rather old-fashioned, prim and conservative. We heard that the Rev. F. D. Maurice had arranged for a lecture on poetry to be given to these ladies, and we asked leave to remain, little thinking what a treat we should have. I believe that Dr. MacDonald had not been long in London at the time (1859), and that he then had few London friends, and was feeling rather strange and lonely. His audience was not at all responsive, and after the lecture was over, he came up to Octavia and thanked her for the sympathy which her face had expressed, and the help it had been to him. He invited us to go and see him and his wife. We had been much impressed by the beauty of his reading and the noble expression of his face, and we were, of course, delighted at the opportunity of seeing more of him, and were surprised at the friendliness he showed to two young unknown girls, still in their teens. His invitation gave us the opportunity of seeing something of his beautiful home-life and the generous hospitality shown by him and Mrs. MacDonald. This impression was deepened more and more as the years passed on...."

[2] Ruskin, in *Fors Clavigera*, Letter 86, thus describes his relation to Miss Hill and the Marylebone houses: "...It is always to be remembered that she has acted as the administrator of this property, and paid me five per. cent upon it regularly—entirely without salary, and in pure kindness to the tenants. My own part in the work was in taking five instead of ten per cent., which the houses would have been made to pay to another landlord; and in pledging myself neither to sell the property nor raise the rents, thus enabling Miss Hill to assure the tenants of peace in their homes, and encourage every effort at the improvement of them.

and Dido, at least with the Latin Grammar, as well as—incidentally but quite permanently—with herself. Thereafter, in Latin at least, he generally held his place at the top of his class, the Rev. Billy Lobster intervening, however, for a spell. So that any charge against his parents of neglecting that boy's education is invalid.

But at Bude George MacDonald wrote hard and took but little pleasure. He made friends with Arthur Mills, then M.P. for Exeter; with the Rev. the Hon.—Thynne at Kilkhampton; and with the poet Hawker at Morwenstow. The breakwater was our joy, especially at high tides when the south-west wind brought furious, white-maned sea-horses scrambling over the sea-wall into the haven. My father, happy as his boys in dodging these drenching smotherers, would, with Maurice and Bernard, ages three and two, one under each arm, race across it to the Chapel-rock, and sometimes half up to his knees in the foamy water. The fascination of the sea's terror and loveliness must have been as strong as in his student days when he fought the winds by the bitter North Sea, though it could not now awaken the ecstatic melancholy of his boyhood.

We lived in two cottages, at the end of the quay, close to old Sir Thomas Acland's cottage built almost into the rocks. Once in a waggonette we drove to Morwenstow, and I remember the noble old poet, his young wife and baby, but especially the great slices of bread with clotted cream an inch thick and strawberry jam atop, trying to maintain a like altitude. Also I recall how the horses were too tired to get home, and how at the ascent from Coombe they refused to budge for any of their owner's persuading. So my father took the reins, when, at one word from him and no touch of whip, they blithely settled into their collars—another instance of the way creatures vied with one another, rich or poor, eloquent or dumb, in giving to this man what he needed: he was an hungered, and they gave him meat; a stranger, and they took him home.[1]

The Seaboard Parish is not one of the strong novels, neither story nor characters being very convincing. The incident of the drowned man was actually witnessed by us, and the incredible incident of a storm when two men leapt from the life-boat at the top of a wave to the main shrouds of a small schooner riding at anchor in the harbour, was told to my father by a coastguardsman with whom we hatched an invigorating intimacy. The description of the storm itself is worthy of Clark-Russell or Dickens in its detail and grandeur; but I do think my father's ingrain capacity for discovering the "spot of red" in every man he came in contact with tended to make him believe many a story that to others would be incredible. And yet few men, I think, would wilfully deceive him.

Those days at Bude remain in my mind as the happiest of all my childhood's holidays; and chiefly because our father, in spite of his indefatigable writing, took more share in our romps and pleasures than I ever remember. Then closer, because lighter-hearted, friendship with some of our parents' friends was possible, and certainly made for our happiness. Among these was Miss Frances Martin, whose attachment to my parents was second to none, I think. She practically founded and was, till her death in 1921, the mainstay of the Working Women's College in Fitzroy Street, to whose students my father often lectured.

---

[1] John Wesley and Father Ignatius are said to have had this gift of invigorating lower animals.

CHAPTER VII
VERBAL INSPIRATION

TO the years 1866-67 belong two letters that must have a place of their own, for they give us insight into George MacDonald's penetrating honesty when he accepts doubt itself as "the hammer that breaks the windows clouded with human fancies and lets in the pure light." They speak too of his great love to one who could not see with him, who thought his work unprofitable, yet whose piety was beyond question; and it is good to learn how he presented his faith to the old Calvinist uncle and the distrustful admirer.

The first is of importance also because, while incidentally touching certain of Dr. MacIntosh MacKay's objections to Shakespeare, it reveals a personal point in my father. His entire freedom from self-consciousness did not preclude that accurate understanding of himself in relation to his work, which he now claims to be his. A man who could write a novel like *Alec Forbes*; an exoteric poem of heavenly wisdom like "Better Things," or a humorous such as "The Deil's forhooit his ain"; such a fairy-tale as *The Golden Key*, or short story like *The Wow o' Rivven*—a master, moreover, of epigram and "celestial wit," as G. K. Chesterton names his felicitous figures; the author of these might, had he chosen—and he knew that he might—have fulfilled George Smith's prophecy that publishers would one day be saving up to pay his prices. Or again, one who could, from pulpit or platform, hold multitudes enthralled—and some there are who still remember his fierce denunciations of pharisaic iniquity, his power of touching the most secret sorrow with consolation and healing, or his appeals to imaginative feeling against the narrow-eyed denials of science—such an one could easily have got higher praise and richer emolument than George MacDonald ever desired.

G.M.D. to the Rev. Dr. MacIntosh MacKay at Harris.

12 Earles Terrace, Kensington, W.
May 6, 1866.

My dear Uncle,

Best thanks for your kind note. I think of the last visit you paid us with much pleasure, more than normally belongs to such meetings, from the strong and glad feeling produced in my mind that whatever might be the difference of opinion between us, I had an uncle whom I could love and honour. My hopes and expectations for the life to come are strong; and one of the great sources of its expected blessedness lies in the enlarged power we shall possess of seeing into each other's meanings, scopes and aims, and doing each other that *justice* which is the rarest virtue on earth. It is ever much easier to be kind than to be just....

...I am quite content that you should think my endeavours worthless, so long as you don't think *me* worthless, or a mere literary adventurer. Had I been capable of condescending merely to please, I might have been in very different circumstances now—better outwardly; inwardly, how much worse! But this may be mere boasting....I am glad you found some interest in my paper.[1] It is one result of much study of the poet. Indeed, I have studied him more than any book except the Gospels. As to his coarseness, one had only to read *any other* playwriter of his time, except perhaps John Lilly, who is of small account, to feel as if, compared with them, he must be an angel of purity. And there is much difference between the plays he wrote when first he began and the later ones, in this respect. Still, knowing the customs of the stage of his day, I suspect that some of the more objectionable passages—I could point to one in particular—were put in by the actor to make the vulgar laugh, and are not Shakespeare's at all. And mere coarseness put into the mouth of a coarse person is no more objectionable than the recording of Rabshakeh's nasty speech to the people of Jerusalem....

---

1 Either "The Art of Shakespeare, as revealed by Himself," 1863, reprinted in *A Dish of Orts*, 1893; or an article called "St. Georges' Day, 1564," published in 1864, and also reprinted in *A Dish of Orts*.

VERBAL INSPIRATION

The second letter is to a lady who had written my father asking if he had any of the old faith left. It defines his attitude towards "verbal inspiration."

...Have you really been reading my books, and at this time ask me what have I lost of the old faith? Much have I rejected of the new, but I have never rejected anything I could keep, and have never turned to gather again what I had once cast away. With the faith itself to be found in the old Scottish manse I trust I have a true sympathy. With many of the forms gathered around that faith and supposed by the faithful to set forth and explain their faith, I have none. At a very early age I had begun to cast them from me; but all the time my faith in Jesus as the Son of the Father of men and the Saviour of us all, has been growing. If it were not for the fear of it's sounding unkind, I would say that if you had been a disciple of his instead of mine, you would not have mistaken me so much. Do not suppose that I believe in Jesus because it is said so-and-so in a book. I believe in him because he is himself. The vision of him in that book, and, I trust, his own living power in me, have enabled me to understand him, to look him in the face, as it were, and accept him as my Master and Saviour, in following whom I shall come to the rest of the Father's peace. The Bible is to me the most precious *thing* in the world, because it tells me his story; and what good men thought about him who knew him and accepted him. *But the common theory of the inspiration of the words, instead of the breathing of God's truth into the hearts and souls of those who wrote it, and who then did their best with it, is degrading and evil*; and they who hold it are in danger of worshipping the letter instead of living in the Spirit, of being idolaters of the Bible instead of disciples of Jesus.... It is Jesus who is the Revelation of God, not the Bible; that is but a means to a mighty eternal end. The book is indeed sent us by God, but it nowhere claims to be his very word. If it were—and it would be no irreverence to say it—it would have been a good deal better written. Yet even its errors and blunders do not touch the truth, and are the merest trifles—dear as the little spot of earth on the whiteness of the snowdrop. Jesus alone is The Word of God.

With all sorts of doubts I am familiar, and the result of them is, has been, and will be, a widening of my heart and soul and mind to greater glories of the truth—the truth that is in Jesus—and not in Calvin or Luther or St. Paul or St. John, save as they got it from Him, from whom every simple heart may have it, and can alone get it. You cannot have such proof of the existence of God or the truth of the Gospel story as you can have of a proposition in Euclid or a chemical experiment. *But the man who will order his way by the word of the Master shall partake of his peace, and shall have in himself a growing conviction that in him are hid all the treasures of wisdom and knowledge....*

One thing more I must say: though the Bible contains many an utterance of the will of God, we do not need to go there to find how to begin to do his will. In every heart there is a consciousness of some duty or other required of it: that is the will of God. He who would be saved must get up and do that will—if it be but to sweep a room or make an apology, or pay a debt. It was he who had kept the commandments whom Jesus invited to be his follower in poverty and labour....

From your letter it seems that to be assured of my faith would be a help to you. I cannot say I never doubt, nor until I hold the very heart of good as my very own in Him, can I wish not to doubt. *For doubt is the hammer that breaks the windows clouded with human fancies, and lets in the pure light.*[1] But I do say that all my hope, all my joy, all my strength are in the Lord Christ and his Father; that all my theories of life and growth are rooted in him; that his truth is gradually clearing up the mysteries of this world...To Him I belong heart and soul and body, and he may do with me as he will—nay, nay—I pray him to do with me as he wills: for that is my only well-being and freedom.

Having read these letters, perhaps we shall understand the reason why many of George MacDonald's novels failed to hold the place once given them. For it was just this: from his point of view, it was impossible to paint true pictures if he ignored the source of all light and colour and joy; whereas the critics preferred to relegate the sun to astronomers, pigments to Academicians, and joy to young animals. Never has his method been attempted before or since; and, granted the truth of his premise, it is neither illogical nor inartistic. Even if his characters are sometimes too good or too wicked for credence, so were many authentic saints and kings. Even if his sense of the inseparability of the highest art from the highest truth necessitated a too frequent elucidation in didactic form, why, many writers—in his day and even now—offend in such wise, if with no inspiration or definite purpose, and yet are read largely. But where George MacDonald overstepped the canons of modern art—

---

1 The italics, I repeat, as in all the letters, are my own.

though not of ancient—lay in this alone, that he, the author, would sometimes, as if showman or chorus, take possession of his stage and stop the play's action to explain its characters' relation to Time and Eternity, or even to reproach his audience for their misplaced sympathies. Such interludes, however, used to be commoner than now. Thackeray adopted the mode mercilessly; but his harangues being mostly cynical—hardly the less troublesome for that—he was and still is forgiven. Tolstoy's novels, of course, are all tracts; but their lessons are nevertheless told with so strange an art, that we do not suspect he is uprooting and hurling to the winds our forests of deep-rooted prejudices. George MacDonald, however, believing in Man and the joy and peace he might find in life if he would but accept it, is dismissed by the ordinary novel-reader because he is "always preaching." "People," he once remarked, "find this great fault with me—that I turn my stories into sermons. They forget that I have a master to serve first before I can wait upon the public." Yet some who feel they owe all their understanding of life to George MacDonald, think he might have served no less faithfully if he had realized that his imaginative eloquence needed no pulpit. One thing was very clear to him. Seeing that Life and Religion were as inseparable as the thought of a rose from its beauty; seeing also how men and women who denied this in their modes of living felt more comfortable so long as they stigmatized all open expression of it as cant, he at least must be outspoken whenever, wherever he had opportunity. In better days it had not been only evangelicals and fanatics and martyrs who were fearless before social conventions; for in those days pictures were painted, cathedrals built and oratorios composed, to glorify God and inspire man. But things had changed.

Nevertheless, many who, though tossed in stormy doubts, refuse a Socratic anchorage eagerly grappled by other lovers of my father; those, whose spiritual instinct is more alert than their reasoning faculty, will soon and certainly get sight of some beacon of peace that outshines all their fears. His appeals to the imagination are *verbal inspiration* indeed, and in this gift he towers above any writer I know of. In some prophetic epigram or "celestial wit," he will reveal the truth suddenly, convincingly, like the drawing of a nebulous veil from the sky-piercing Jungfrau, his appeal a trumpet-call— "Awake thou that sleepest and rise from the dead!" As an instance of such utterance—in contrast with argument that perhaps hardly helps some of us—we light upon this—and then never forget it all through life's scourgings and "blank denials": *Freedom is the unclosing of the idea which lies at our root and is the vital power of our existence. The rose is the freedom of the rose-tree.*[1]

Yet again: of the many uplifting words with which George MacDonald gave hope to the sorrow-laden, is not this a "verbal inspiration," a burgeoning of "celestial wit"— *"The year's fruit must fall that the year's fruit may come, and the winter itself is the King's highway to the spring"?* [2]

Once more: let us look at an epigram, a magic torch, in narrative form—in fact, the instance of "celestial wit" quoted by Mr. Chesterton:

> Coming home with a great, grand purple fox-glove in his hand, he (Cupples) met some of the missionars returning from their chapel, and amongst the rest Robert Bruce, who stopped and spoke.
> "I'm surprised to see ye carryin' that thing o' the Lord's day, Mr. Cupples. Fowk'll think ill o' ye."
> "Weel, ye see, Mr. Bruce, it angert me sae to see the ill-faured thing positeevely growin' there upo' the Lord's day, that I pu'd it up 'maist by the reet. To think o' a weyd like that prankin' itsel' oot in its purple and its spots upo' the Sawbath day! It canna ken what it's about. I'm only feared I left eneuch o' 't to be up again afore lang." [3]

Or for a comparison between the efficiency of dialectic and celestial wit we may compare my father's essay on the

---

1 *Donal Grant*, vol. iii, p. 78.
2 *Castle Warlock*, vol. iii, p. 125.
3 *Alec Forbes*, vol. iii, p. 167

"Imagination: its Function and Culture,"[1] with certain passages in *The Princess and the Goblin*. The ancient grandmother is explaining why the moon-lamp in her beautiful room must never go out, though

> it does not happen above five times in a hundred years that anyone does see it....Besides—I will tell you a secret—if that light were to go out, you would fancy yourself lying in a bare garret on a heap of old straw, and would not see one of the pleasant things round about you all the time.[2]

Later the Princess Irene brings the miner-boy to see her grandmother; but instead of the palatial room and the beautiful woman to whose lap Irene is taken, he sees only the bare attic and the heap of musty straw and a ray of sunlight through a hole in the roof. The incident is told with such simplicity that it excites no arguing thoughts; yet inevitably, passively, do we accept it as a clear statement of the truth that only the pure in heart have imagination enough to see God.[3]

The modern artist is a failure because his ideal is "self-expression." Some of the old ones, who have welcomed my father above, did not fail, however imperfect their work may

---

1 First published 1867, and reprinted in *A Dish of Orts*, 1893.
2 *The Princess and the Goblin*, 1872, pp. 119 and 226-229.
3 Compare also *Paul Faber*, 1879, vol. iii, p. 24, containing a lucid passage, but, for some of us, inferior in upliftingness to the fairy-teaching above quoted.
 À propos of the way children accept this fairy-teaching all unconsciously—I will not say *subconsciously*, but rather *supraconsciously*—I am tempted to quote the words of a widely read friend of my own, who reveres my father's teaching as much as anyone living, Miss Rose Goodwin, and who has published a volume of lovely poems, *Verse for Little Children* (Charles and Dible). "Nothing could happen that could make my first introduction to him pass from my memory. Such a poignant ecstatic experience, at such an age (I was only six years old) was too profound, too thrilling for time to do other than deepen the impression. It chanced— 'Eternal God that chance did guide'—that I got hold of an old *Good Words for the Young*, the number containing that part of *The Princess and the Goblin* beginning with the chapter entitled "That Night Week." You will remember how it describes the little Princess, terrified by the goblin creature, running up the hill-side and finding heavenly refuge at last in her lovely grandmother's beautiful room. Those starry, vanishing walls! That fire of roses! The mysterious lamp that could shine through impenetrable stone! I had been reading steadily since I was four. I knew Grimm, Anderson, Lewis Carroll, etc., but never, never had I read *anything* approaching this!"

have been; for they forgot themselves and made their art just the revelation of God. As "the rose is the freedom of the rose-tree," so is gothic minster the freedom of the stone-mason, the Capella del Arena of the shepherd-boy, the North Wind of the philosopher-poet. George MacDonald's fairy stories are miraculous, prophetic for old and young: they will never lose their charm unless a prodigal world shall still content itself with swine's husks. His novels too, prove the fairy-faith to be quite consistent with elaborate plots no less than with character-delineation of, say, Sir Galahads in home-spun, aristocratic ogres wavering in their unrepentance, or infant tutelary saints groping in the town-kennels for lost treasure: all are something more than suggestive of the spiritual adventure, the romantic mysticism inspiring all that is quite real in life. These books will assuredly be read yet again when the world has grown wise enough to appreciate their writer's singleness of vision and the open road between him and God.

The rigidity of thought, the timidity, with which he had to contend fifty years ago, may be passing away; yet because men no longer believe in a punitive hell, they turn from an evangelist who offers, in place of its cherished miseries, a boundless hope. The new psychology is abolishing old theories of moral responsibility, even while it endorses in new-fangled terms the dogma of original sin. Truth is, we have grown weary of the goalless progression, have started aside into all sorts of tangential issues that take us only farther away from the heart of life, whence still comes the beat of our pulse. Yet, even granted some real progress during the past wonderful, and latterly most horrible, half-century, many believers in Man still wish that Carlyle and Ruskin, Emerson and Thoreau, Browning and Tennyson, Maurice, Newman and George MacDonald were among us again.

CHAPTER VIII
THE RETREAT

IN the autumn of 1867, on the return from Bude, we left Earles Terrace for The Retreat, Upper Mall, Hammersmith, the house afterwards occupied by William Morris, and renamed by him Kelmscott House. The eleventh and last of us, George MacKay, named after his great-uncle of Banff and god-mothered by the latter's daughter, Helen, Mrs. Alexander Powell, had been born in January; and once again the house proved too small. The new home was a great success. It was late Georgian, had a garden of nearly an acre, with roomy old stabling, a great walnut-tree in the stable yard, a tulip-tree, said to be the biggest but one in England, giving shade over the lawn, and a statue of Artemis with her stag leaping from the shrubbery. The roadway, bordered by ancient elms, ran between the house and river, widening into a semicircle opposite The Retreat; but there being no thoroughfare, the quiet was undisturbed, unless on holidays, such as the Oxford and Cambridge boat-race days.

The latter became occasions for entertaining on a larger scale than had been possible before. Relatives and friends would come from far and near for the great event. Literature was well represented—by Tennyson himself on one occasion. Yet there was no ostentation, and refreshments were, if lavish, quite simple. The serviceable children were worth double their number in servants; and once it was my glory to have rescued a cab from the human flood on the highroad half a mile away, and piloted it to the house for the Poet Laureate. What a great hand was his in its strong gentle grasp! What a deep, sad voice! I thought.

The following letter, although anticipating, refers to Tennyson coming to see the boat-race, and to his views about *Ossian*:

G.M.D. to Mrs. Alexander Powell.

THE RETREAT,
March 24, 1875.

MY DEAR HELEN,
...Tennyson seemed delighted with my little library which he did not think a little one: there seemed so many books he had never seen....What do you think he borrowed? A splendid copy of the Gaelic *Ossian*, which I bought at Uncle's [MacIntosh MacKay] sale, that he might read the prose Latin translation, which seems to be a literal one. He had never believed *Ossian* was a reality, but seemed a good deal more ready to believe in him when he had read a few lines, with which he was delighted....

But of more importance were the annual entertainments given to Octavia Hill's poor tenantry—varying between thirty and almost a hundred, I think. To these parties, friends, such as Ruskin, Mrs. Russell Gurney, the Cowper-Temples, the Charringtons, the Mathesons, Professor Maurice's son, C. Edmund Maurice (the well-known historian and consistent Radical, who married Miss Hill's sister, Emily), the Rev. Samuel Barnett (afterwards Canon of Bristol and founder of Toynbee Hall), the Rev. and Mrs. H. R. Haweis, the Revs. Garrett Horder and Henry Simon the ministers, Canon Ainger, the Burne-Joneses, George Masons, Arthur Hugheses, besides our own relatives, would come and help. We had a removable stage—"Brigham Young's four-poster," one Matheson named it—erected on the lawn; and the boys were efficient stage-carpenters. It was hung with curtains with such fine effect and economy as only our mother could have secured, and occasionally scenery was painted by E. R. Hughes,

THE RETREAT

Arthur Hughes's nephew. We acted plays for the people's entertainment, mostly written by our mother, and generally fairy-tales.[1] Some, however, were more ambitious, one being based upon Zola's *L'Assommoir*, and another, an adaptation from Dickens's *Haunted Man, The Tetterbys*. There was a midday dinner before and a tea after the play, the day ending with games and country dancing. I recall the first occasion in 1868, when Ruskin—who was much shocked at the people being so poorly dressed, the men without collars—led off the final Sir Roger with Octavia Hill as his partner.

The following letter refers to the first of these gatherings:

G.M.D. to John Ruskin.

THE RETREAT, HAMMERSMITH, W.,
June 24, 1868.

MY DEAR RUSKIN,

I do not know how to thank you for those beautiful books, so valuable and useful—if indeed that is not one and the same thing! And for the engravings from Turner—I do not deserve such exquisite things. But I am indeed delighted to possess them. I shall understand them, I fancy, so much better than any engravings of his I have seen before, simply from their perfectness. We shall all enjoy them greatly, and thank you often and often.[2]

My wife and I are troubled in our minds that in our anxiety to entertain the poor people, we neglected to make provision for our other guests. I believe you went home half dead with unfed fatigue. It was our first attempt, and we shall do better next time, I hope. We ought to have one room in the house provided with refreshments, but everything was sacrificed to the one end, which I hope was at least partially gained. But you will forgive us.

---

1 Some of these were published by Strahan in 1870, and named *Chamber Dramas for Children*, by Mrs. George MacDonald, with an exquisite frontispiece by Arthur Hughes, the very incarnation of Faerie, and now reproduced in the Centenary Edition of George MacDonald's *Fairy Tales* (George Allen & Unwin).

2 A set of proof steel plates after Turner's pictures. They were framed together in a series and hung in the study. My father would talk to us about them, so that as children we came to understand something of Turner's genius.

With glad recollections of your most kind visit, and love and thanks from both of us to you and Joan [Agnew, now Mrs. Arthur Severn] who was a perfect picture of goodness.

Yours most affectionately,
GEORGE MACDONALD.

In other ways my parents ministered to Octavia Hill's energies. It was not long before certain friends, chief among them Lord and Lady Ducie, purchased for her Barrett's Court, soon to be rebuilt and made a thoroughfare out of Wigmore Street into Barrett Street, and renamed St. Christopher's Place. If I remember aright, one or more of the disreputable houses had been rented by an undertaker, who found the custom his business secured from his sub-tenants so remunerative that it was not worth his while to collect rents. The first Saturday night after the property was conveyed to Miss Hill, there was as usual a free fight in the Court, with a line of policemen at its entrance in Wigmore Street, whose only hope was to keep the disturbance within its own limits; none dared enter the Court. Octavia Hill never knew fear—little woman that she was, scarcely taller than my mother. The police did their utmost to prevent her entering the Court; but she claimed her rights as owner, and, passing into the midst of the drunken furies, in half an hour had every one of them within doors and outward peace reigning. According to her principles not one of those tenants, disreputable though they were—thieves, drunkards, perhaps worse—was turned out unless they refused to pay their rents, the enforcement of which was the first step in their reform. Yet all rents for a long time were devoted to repairs and sanitation. She seldom gave money, but moved heaven and earth to find them work, and soon won their respect and obedience. Thus did she "raise the poor without gifts."[1] The basement of one house was

---

[1] "Consistent giving of work is what you are doing," wrote Ruskin in explanation of Octavia Hill's first report in 1870; "and succeeding, as you are sure by all the laws of

converted into an entertainment room, and there George MacDonald would gather round him the worst of characters; or rather Octavia Hill did so in the first place.

"Will you come and hear a friend of mine read something fine on Sunday?" she asked them one day.

"Parson, Miss?"

"No."

"White choker, Miss?"

"No, he generally wears a red tie."

"Done! I'll come!"

And hands were shaken on the bargain. So in that room in tweeds and a red tie my father would tell them stories and awaken keen and sympathetic interest; he would touch "the red spot." And when his stories were gradually understood to have originated in a man named Jesus Christ, the audience forgot any suspicion they might have had of a white choker; and many became constant attendants and helpers at such entertainments.

But, indeed, the MacDonald family all did their share and gave entertainments. Some played the piano well and all sang sweetly—one boy playing the violin; and so they gave little concerts—especially of carols at Christmas. Occasionally, too, they acted a play, such as their mother's *The Tetterbys* and, much later, her version of *The Pilgrim's Progress*.

My father's health during the first two years at The Retreat had improved, but with it came ever increasing demands upon his energies. Not only was the family growing more hungry, but the demands upon the house for hospitality were wonderful. "The more you give, the more you may," is a common argument against imprudence. An old oak cabinet with seventeenth-century carvings my mother bought

---

Nature and Heaven to succeed in doing. But that is not 'raising the poor without gifts.' It is raising by direct and continual gifts, granted to them on condition of their doing daily a certain quantity of useful work, to the systematizing of which you give far the richest of gifts, your own care, discipline, and personal sympathy."

has two panels, one representing Prudence taking counsel with herself in her hand-mirror, and the other, Charity, who before long would be holding a baby to her bosom in addition to the many children hanging on her skirts. Perhaps it helped us children to understand our mother. Anyhow, there was always someone to be taken in and befriended. One was an Oxford graduate, who came begging in rags and remained with us many weeks; but when at last my father found employment for his great abilities on the staff of a London newspaper, he decamped and was no more seen.[1] Then another drunkard was adopted for reformation, and his fiancée was made welcome to help the cure. He married and had more than one child, I believe, before he succumbed to a shattered constitution.

In these days also was fast developing my eldest sister's genius for acting. She had learned to read very young, and before she was eleven, I think, knew all Shakespeare intimately, and that with little or no help from her father. She mothered not only all the family, as has been told, but guests and servants also. A little stern with us perhaps in her younger days—something perhaps of her Scottish great-grandmother being in her blood—she became the tenderest, most devoted sister in our adolescence and manhood. The coachhouse was converted into a theatre with a gaslit stage, and the loose boxes served as green-room—though a cow for a time had lived in one and supplied the family with milk, daily drawn and watered by the gardener, whose eyes were so blue that the honest cow got all the blame for the milk's poverty, and he was forgiven. There we acted our plays; and friends came from afar, if only to see Lilia Scott MacDonald play Lady Macbeth to her father in the title-rôle. She was in close friendship with Kate Terry, the first and greatest of that gifted family, but who had left the stage and become Mrs. Arthur Lewis in,

---

[1] I remember him well, for my mother gave him my new overcoat by mistake, and I had to face another winter at school shabbier than ever.

THE RETREAT, HAMMERSMITH

I think, 1868. Phelps, the tragedian, came once, and was so profoundly impressed that he talked to my father of her gift as marvellous and vowed he would before long play Macbeth to her. Our old friend, Sir J. Forbes-Robertson, said to one of us not many years ago, "If your sister had gone on the stage, *So-and-so* would have had no career." But at Bude, Miss Cusham, the great American tragedienne, had told my parents such terrible things of the stage, and repeated them even more dismally when we met her again in the States in 1873, that they could not consent to their daughter becoming an actress. Mrs. Lewis too had had her share in this final decision that robbed the world of a genius—though she must have known of this girl that hell itself could not have smirched her whiteness.

These days were very happy, for we were fast developing a certain aptitude for music: my third sister, Grace, played Beethoven as I have never heard him rendered since. On Sunday evenings for tea and supper we kept open house, more particularly to the Matheson circle and the many young-men friends they introduced. The gatherings were often large, always happy. But no extra work was given to the servants, the family and guests together washing up the tea and supper things— "Your 'Day of Wash-up," Mrs. MacDonald!" said Canon Ainger, solemnly punning, his shirtsleeves rolled up and a teacloth in hand.

So, and although "genius least requires more than board-wages,"[1] there could be no relaxation for the master. Yet his work was in some ways happier than ever it had been. He had a house large enough not only for work but for play; his books were increasing in market-value; he was recognized as one of the first living writers; in 1868 his own University conferred upon him the degree of Doctor of Laws in consideration of his "high literary eminence as a poet and an author," to quote the official words; and last, not least, I think,

---
1 *There and Back*, vol. i, p. 55

he had a study after his own heart. His friend, the artist Cottier, who some years later attained much the same position in New York as William Morris in London, so far as his influence in decorative art was concerned, adorned the room for him in a sort of barbaric splendour: crimson-flock wall-paper with black fleurs-de-lis stencilled over, a dark blue ceiling with scattered stars in silver and gold, and a silver crescent moon; and specially designed brass-ball wall-brackets and chandeliers for the gas.

> Without are the shining river and white-sailed boats (as my father describes it in a letter), with the wind tossing the rosy hawthorn-bloom before my windows, and the magnolia trained up the wall looking in at one of them. It is rather a long room. The greater part has its walls filled with books, and I am sitting at one and quite surrounded by them. But when I lift my eyes, I look to the other end, and into the heart of a stage for acting upon, filling all the width and a third part of the length of the room. It is surrounded with curtains; but those in front of it are withdrawn, and there the space of it lies before me, a bare, empty hollow of green and blue and red, which to-morrow evening will be filled with group after group of moving, talking, shining, acting men and women, boys and girls. It looked to me like a human heart, waiting to be filled with the scenes of its own story—with this difference, that the heart itself will determine what sort those groups shall be....

For by that time the coach-house and stabling were needed for an equine adoption, and the stage was set up at the end of the study, obscuring for the time two of the five windows; and here in 1877 the *Pilgrim's Progress* was first acted.

And now is the time for recording one of those quiet gifts from above, of which the world, running as it reads, would take small note, and yet which in ministering to George MacDonald's needs was of first importance. I refer to the devoted friendship of William Carey Davies, than whom no knight had ever more loving squire, or rich man ever such a secretary. His son, George MacDonald Davies, the geologist, tells me how as a very young man his father had been nigh wrecked in prospects and faith, when he, one of a handful of earnest students, met my father at King's College.

Thereafter until his death in 1898 he was one of our closest friends.[1] For love's sake alone, he kept my father's accounts straight and relieved him of much drudgery in proof-reading, especially of such books as were set up in final form from their initial serial appearance.[2] He was widely read in English literature and a good German scholar.

In 1875, the small adjoining house, River Villa, was thrown into The Retreat. Besides giving us more room for ourselves, it enabled Miss Jane and Miss Anne Cobden (afterwards Mrs. Fisher Unwin and Mrs. Cobden-Sanderson), daughters of Richard Cobden, to join our house-party; and great was our privilege. Mrs. Cobden-Sanderson writes most truly that the life there was

full of excitement and interest. Meals were erratic; but no one complained, for self-forgetfulness was the rule of the house. The belief in Divine

---

[1] To show how the two men stood to each other I give this sonnet of W. C. Davies's:

"To GEORGE MACDONALD.

"Rich orange clouds float in the western sky
This afternoon; and through a smoky pane,
Blotted and streaked with drops of last night's rain,
I watch the glory gleam, and glow, and die.
Even now, across the broad stream flowing by,
Thy windows, thou art gazing where the train
Of Evening falls, and dyes with rosy stain
River and sky: thou seest more than I;
Believing this, with joy my heart doth fill.
And though, to my dull seeing, Truth's clear light
Shines faint, far off in heaven—star-like, by night,
Quenched in day's glare, or hid by fogs of ill—
Yet will I trust in this: To thine eyes still
Both earth and heaven with Truth's own beams are bright."

"January 25, 1868."

[2] How little printers' or publishers' readers could be relied upon for this is illustrated by a curious incident. The cheap edition of *David Elginbrod* was in the press. In the great demands upon its author, he had just decided to trust the printers without himself reading the proofs, when, taking up a galley-proof, he lit on an interpolation directly contradicting the sentence preceding it. Angry enough, he went straight to the printers and tackled the guilty compositor. It transpired that the publishers, having no copy of the first edition left on their shelves, had secured one from Mudie's, and that some stupid reader had pencilled an objectionable remark in the margin, which the compositor in perfect innocence had incorporated with the text!

Guidance carried us over the difficulties. *God mends all* was our faith.[1] ... With the MacDonalds' departure after eight years' residence there the days of Christian Socialism came to an end at Hammersmith, to be succeeded for a time in the same house by the more strenuous days of Marxian Socialism.

Those happy days were broken into by the visit to the United States in 1872, and the house was dismantled in 1877 for reasons that will presently be told.

---

[1] An anagram on the name *George MacDonald* reads: *"Corage; God mend al!"*, my father adopting it as a family motto.

CHAPTER IX
THE BLUE BELL

IN proof of George MacDonald's wonderful energy I have before me an itinerary of lectures he gave in Scotland. Beginning on January 5, 1869, he spoke during five weeks twenty-eight times, and never twice in the same town. Almost at the outset he was attacked with hæmoptysis, followed by bronchitis and asthma, of which he made light to my mother, though on the 17th, and in spite of his protestations, she joined him at Dumfries.

Consistently with my feeling that no man's portrait can be faithfully presented without showing also who and what were his friends, I may relate how he became acquainted with one of his most devoted admirers. Returning alone from the North, he was entertained by his friend Alex Stevenson, a wealthy mine-owner, an important member of whose bachelor household was the Bedlington terrier, Charlie. This latter personage immediately attached himself to my father with such ardour that he refused to sleep anywhere but on the mat outside his bedroom-door; and Mr. Stevenson insisted upon my father's accepting him as a gift. He became a real joy to us all at home, with his fine brains and loving heart. He was poisoned two years later by a neighbour whose field he would invade to chase the sheep.

My father's eczema, a life-long trouble, led to his trying a course of treatment at the Ilkley Hydropathic, but with little benefit. Even during the "cure" he could not rest, but must be giving big talks in little chapels, and little talks to fellow patients. Writing home he sends a message to Mary, now nearly sixteen, and having her doubts and despondencies, bright blackbird though she was. Her father writes to my mother:

> Give my love to Elfie and tell her that she is spoiling God's spring if she is one bit more gloomy than she can help with all her might.

Again to Elfie herself:

Where we are so often wrong is in letting the dull weather overcloud the fine. Until we are able to look up to God with as much peace and contentment in the gloomy mood as in the glad, although of course not with half the delight—perhaps with none of it—we are not in a downright *sensible* state. For why should we not be able to go on without feeling all right for a while, as long as he is, and we are his. Half ways won't do in anything....

The proposal to take my mother to Switzerland in the summer came very near fruition, and the cost would not now stand in the way. But an invitation came for my father to join a yachting trip, which would be a more bracing and restful holiday, and quite after his heart. My mother could not share it, of course, but she insisted upon his going. The yacht was *The Blue Bell*, schooner-rigged, of 120 tons, with a crew of fourteen men, and luxuriously appointed. It was owned by John Stevenson, a Glasgow merchant, and cousin of Alex Stevenson of Newcastle, and was bound for Norway.[1]

So my father joined the party, comprising the Rev. Dr. Robert Buchanan of Glasgow, the Rev.—Laughton, and the Rev. W. Ker, on June 10th at Wemyss Bay, and proceeded by steamer to Largs, where they joined *The Blue Bell*, and weighed anchor at noon. In the train my father wrote of feeling very tired and lame from a swollen knee, but apparently thought it of no importance. His first letter home is full of the yacht's beauty and his pleasure in his new experiences, but it is suggestive of coming trouble:

---

1 A brother of the owner was J.J. Stevenson, the well-known architect of the London Schoolboard—whose office my brother Robert Falconer entered in 1879.

THE BLUE BELL

G.M.D. to his Wife.

At anchor in Campbell Town Harbour,
Thursday night.

It was a delight to see, the moment I set foot on the deck of the yacht, the perfect trim, the whiteness of the deck and everything that was not varnished. You could lay yourself anywhere with perfect confidence of cleanness. While we sat at breakfast we got under way, and so smooth was it that we could tell by no motion that we had moved a yard. We just crept along as softly as in a dream. In a little while, getting from under the shelter of the greater Cumbray, the wind began to blow, and in a moment the deck was like a small precipice, so much did the yacht lie over. She was tearing through the water. So we held on for a while, and then got becalmed again. While we were just washing our hands before dinner, almost a squall struck us, and again she was off like a wild thing....It got so rough at last that Mr. Stevenson thought it more comfortable to make for this quiet harbour, where we got about sunset, and are now lying motionless. I have enjoyed it greatly. I have not looked at a book all day, and although my knee is very troublesome sometimes, I am much better. I have eaten heartily, and feel that I shall sleep sound. The three clergymen are very kind and agreeable, and we have got on very well. Ker is particularly attentive to me, doing everything he can for me....The Captain is such a good fellow, reminding me much of the coastguardsman at Bude, only he is much bigger and rather ugly....

I had a rather troubled night; indeed, I feared I should be ill, for I had a shivering-fit after I got into bed, but there is no fear of me to-night. To-morrow after the boat has gone ashore with our letters, we sail again round the Mull of Cantyre, and so northwards....It is cold to-night again. But you don't mind the cold so much at sea. I have a nice cabin for myself....

It is so fine to see the handling of the great sails—sometimes when they are reefing, you would think the men were fighting with a wild beast: the sail flaps and strains and cracks as if it *would* be off....

But on the 13th the knee was so much worse that at Lerwick a doctor was brought on board, who prescribed leeches and poulticing, diagnosing synovitis. He was now unable to move his leg for the pain. On the 15th he was given a larger cabin, one with the mast through it, but only a skylight instead of port-holes. Yet on the 16th he writes this bright letter to his eldest daughter, then visiting friends with her sister Grace—the James Campbells at Tullichewen Castle, Alexandria:

> Lerwick, Shetland.
> *Wednesday.*
>
> My darling Goose,
> Will you send me a letter to the Post Office, Trondhjem, Norway, to let me know how you and Gracie are. I am confined to bed with my knee. I have just had leeches on for the second time. Mr. Stevenson is *very* kind. I have not seen much, for there is no window or port-hole, though I have been moved into the best cabin—about as big as Irene's room—with the mast going through it. She is such a jolly yacht, and before my knee got so bad as to drive me to bed, I enjoyed it—sometimes greatly. Here comes a poultice. By and by I hope to be able to be lifted on deck, and see the coast of Norway, but I have not begun to get better quite yet. We are going to Unst, a neighbouring island first. Mr Stevenson has business about here with mines and ores, which will keep us a day or two....I hope you are getting on with your riding....

On the 17th at the Shetlands two doctors came to see him and decided that the sea-trip was the best treatment. But the suffering became every day more acute, and he could take nothing but Liebig's beef tea. To judge from my mother's description of the voyage, the other guests, all hale and jolly Scots, kind enough according to their lights, left him very much alone. My mother declared they were afraid of him, lest his horrible suffering should be a visitation for his heresies! Certainly he became a great anxiety to them all, and their host suggested leaving him at Trondhjem till they returned from the Loffoden Isles.

G.M.D. to his Wife.

> *Half-past three Monday morning,*
> *21st I think.*
>
> Oh these dreary nights of pain and sleeplessness. I have not slept half an hour since one o'clock. And I don't sleep much in the day either, though the day is better than the night. We have been since Saturday

morning crossing the North Sea, which has been wonderfully quiet—a good thing for my poor leg, though indeed the motion is not very irksome. We are approaching Christiansund on our way to Trondhjem, where we shall arrive I hope this morning, for it is better to lie still. That is all I can hope from it—except indeed I could get something I could eat. But I fear that is not likely. It was a week last night since I took to bed, and have seen neither sea nor sky since. Sometimes I have thought I *must* come home to you—but it would be an awful undertaking, with a leg which I can't draw up in bed, and no one to take care of me....But the days are going and will go. Probably from Trondhjem the rest will go on an excursion into the country, leaving me on board with John, the steward, which I shall like very much. There are good books on board, but I should have liked a novel, and there is nothing but that awful *Vanity Fair*. But I am keeping up pretty well, and try to sing sometimes, but don't make much of it....If I only were on the way home to you! It seems likely Mr. Stevenson will bring the yacht up the Thames—up to London—and then you can come and take me home—and that will be joyful, and I shall get some good out of it—perhaps I may have got some already—though the means is very nasty. It is quite doubtful if I shall be out of this cabin the whole time—whether I shall see the midnight sun or one aurora. But I don't mind that a bit—that is a sort of thing that will keep. How different it would be at home with you to take care of me and read to me! But I have only to get through it as patiently as I may....

Dr. Buchanan's entry in his Diary for June 22nd to 24th stands thus:

June 22nd (at Christiansund)....Got up at six this morning to cheer Mr. MacDonald, who was suffering a good deal: sat with him and rubbed his leg occasionally till eight. He is on the whole better to-day. He is very amiable and patient.

June 23rd (at Trondhjem)....We went ashore immediately to see the consul, Mr. Knodzen, and by his assistance to engage a doctor to come on board to see Mr. MacDonald....The doctor, evidently a judicious, careful man, thinks Mr. MacDonald has been allowing himself to get too low by refusing wine and nourishing food; and strongly insists on his using both. He may possibly lance the knee to-morrow.

Thursday, 24th June....The English steamer *Norway* arrived during the night, and is to sail to-morrow for the Tyne. Mr. MacDonald has resolved to return with her to England. Mr. Ker and I have been on board. She is a large steamer with good accommodation. They promise to give him a stateroom to himself and to pay him every attention—and expect to reach the Tyne by Monday night (28th)....He is so eager to be home. The doctor opened the abscess, and a great amount of matter was discharged. This will relieve the pain considerably.... [1]

At Trondhjem the skylight of his cabin was removed and he was hoisted up through it and carried to a fine stateroom on board the steamer. Dr. Buchanan stayed with him till they weighed anchor at 7 p.m. on the 24th.

The *Norway* reached the Tyne on the 28th, whence came the last and most memorable letter of the trip:

G.M.D. to his Wife.

NEWCASTLE-ON-TYNE,
Station Hotel.

Darling, I have been dozing when I ought to have been writing. To-morrow the first end of my prayers will come at last. I shall be with you. *Oh, I have gone through some of the folds of the shadow of death since I saw you, but the light has never ceased to shine.* The train arrives at 9.40 to-morrow evening, but I will telegraph again. Alec Stevenson has been a true brother. I am lying at the Station Hotel now, nursed by the quaintest, handsomest old lady! My knee is bad still—a large abscess.

No time for more. Love to all my chickens.

A. Stevenson will bring me to London to-morrow.

YOUR HUSBAND.

Tuesday evening. 3 weeks since I left home.

I well remember the emaciated look of my father as he was carried up to his bedroom. I thought he was dead. But the full misery and suffering involved in this pleasure-trip are best realized from a letter written by my mother to Mrs. A. S. MacColl, when the patient was almost convalescent and had been in Derbyshire a fortnight.

---

[1] These and fuller extracts from Mr. Buchanan's Diary were given me some years ago by my patient Mr. W. Hill Thornton, and I trust I am not wrong in quoting them. I have been unable to find Mr. Thornton and ask leave.

THE BLUE BELL

Mrs. G.M.D. to Mrs. A. S. MacColl.

The Peacock,
Rowsley, Derbyshire,
July 22nd [1869].

My very dear Mrs. MacColl,

...When George was away I am sure there was not a day that I did not mean to write and tell you about the delight, resuscitation and health we expected that he was going to get from this cruise to Norway with Mr. Stevenson. Though there were three church-ministers on board, he expected much communion with sea and sky, a new knowledge, new experience.

He had never been well since his lecturing tour; and he had been in bed for ten days with an attack of congestion of the lungs. Then this offer of five weeks of sea-life—the midnight sun, the fiords of Norway, etc., etc., no posts, no callers, no dinners—looked very health-giving, and we were both very hopeful about it. So he started.

His first letter from Glasgow said that he had not been able to sleep from pain in his knee....But then came another, after he had got on board, saying his knee was worse—and from Lerwick came worse news....The Doctors ordered leeches twice. Fancy *his* losing a lot of blood!....I heard no more after that, beyond that he had then been ten days in his cabin on his bed—no porthole even to look out at—sleepless nights, weary days—pain, pain, couldn't eat—could scarcely read, no woman near to attend him—not one face he had ever seen before about him—the most horrible noises incessantly going on about and around him. This was the last I heard for a week, when one morning I got a telegram to say our friend, Alexander Stevenson of Tynemouth, would bring him up to London; then another to say I was to meet him at King's Cross.

And oh! dear Mrs. MacColl, I shall never forget what I saw on arriving at the platform. There was an invalid carriage and in it a man propped up with pillows looking as if he were in the last stage of consumption, with a horrid cough. I could scarcely believe it was George. His eyes were sunken, his cheeks hollow, and he was so weak that his voice, as hollow as his cheeks, could not speak three words together from weakness. I was not the only one who thought he was a dying man. Mr. A. Stevenson told me he looked strong to what he did when they carried him strapped to a stretcher in an open boat from the steamer to land. And so he had been carried from the yacht—from his own berth up *through* the skylight of his cabin on to the steamer when they were off the town of Trondhjem. He said wherever they carried him people looked at him so—he looked like a hero coming from the wars, and "alas!" he said, "I had done nothing for anybody."

But he had suffered intensely, and who shall say those sufferings were not for other people—in what he may hereafter write. It seems to me evident enough that *this* was the only way in which he could be sent into the wilderness. He says himself that he had never had anything but the *luxury* of illness before, and it was well that he should know its real misery. Everybody was kind, you know; but they were all strong men and pious. You know this is only between ourselves, for it would be ungracious indeed not to acknowledge the kindness which they gave to their utmost. Well, I am forgetting my story. At Trondhjem I suppose he must have frightened them all. They got a Norwegian doctor—a delightful little man—really a lovable man. He pronounced it by that time to be an abscess and a very large one. It began about 4 inches up the side of the leg and spread all over the knee. It seemed like two. He lanced it and they got quite a large basinful of matter. Poulticings had to be continued and hot fomentations. On the steamer he got things more fit for an invalid. He was ordered wine, but couldn't take much. He had had nothing but Liebig's beef tea before that he could touch all that time. You may fancy how weak he must have grown....At N. Shields he sent to Alec Stevenson. No tender brother could have been more generous and lovely to him. He sent a first class doctor to remain with him till he came to him. He took him to his own "home and took care of him," then the next day took an invalid's carriage up to London, went with him himself, and never left him—wouldn't let him pay a penny. He helped the man to put him into the fly I had taken for him. Then the Doctor came, and he said it was all going on well. He wanted sleep and food—two necessaries which he had scarcely partaken of since he left home. Oh, it was wonderful to see him sleeping, sleeping, on and on like the stillest sleep of an infant. When we first laid him on his own bed he looked all round the room and cried with thankfulness. You see, I am telling you what I could only say to a dear Aunt-sister who knows him and loves him. He has been getting steadily better—at first it seemed fast. Then he got restless and wanted to be at work, then the doctor ordered change of air. He is engaged to write a novel—a very good engagement if he can fulfil it....The disappointment has been great. Fancy his hearing the men talk of the wonders of Nature and the foreign shores, and he never saw any of them! He says tho', it was nearly worth it all—the wonderful effect of the blue sky just above him as they laid him on the floor of his cabin when they took the skylight up. They lifted him up with cords. It was as if he looked out from his grave—the tall mast of the vessel rising from his cabin—that and the blue sky was all he saw—then he felt his Resurrection was come; but I should like you to hear him tell this. It was his one spot of joy....

CHAPTER X
FREDERICK DENISON MAURICE

THIS period of George MacDonald's life—one that brought him through apparent failure to the highest literary reputation throughout the English-speaking world—his pirated novels being read by the hundred-thousand in the United States, and ranking in popularity almost with Dickens' and Thackeray's—cannot be passed over without saying more of his friendship with Frederick Denison Maurice: the man whom Dr. Jelf turned out of King's College in 1853 for claiming the doctrine of eternal punishment to be rather a popular superstition than sanctioned by the strictest interpretation of the Thirty-nine Articles; to whom, moreover, the National Church owes more for defence and inspiration than it is likely ever to realize.

Professor Maurice was my father's senior by nineteen years, and it must have been largely his personality that attracted the latter to become a lay member of the Church of England. Even before his call to Arundel he had declared, as we have seen, that he would take Holy Orders but for the kind of men he found in the Church.[1] If he refrained from criticizing Maurice's adhesion to the Articles and the Athanasian Creed, it was because he would defend this passionately honest churchman from the charges of casuistry and "muddy mysticism." In *David Elginbrod* my father has drawn an unmistakable portrait of his friend, and

---

1 *Vide* letter from the Isle of Wight, p. 149.

summarized his defence of the Church and his repudiation of endless punishment. Yet to some it may seem a justification of the charge of casuistry.

> He looks upon the formulæ of the church as utterances of *living* truth—vital embodiments—to be regarded as one ought to regard human faces. In these human faces, others may see this or that inferior expression, may find out the mean and the small and the incomplete; he looks for and finds the ideal; the grand, sacred, God-meant meaning; and by that he holds as *the* meaning of the human countenances, for it is the meaning of him who made them. So with the confession of the Church of England; he believes that not man only, but God also, and God first and chief, had to do with the making of it; and therefore he looks in it for the Eternal and the Divine, and he finds what he seeks....He believes entirely that God loves, yea, *is* love; and, therefore, that hell itself must be subservient to that love, and but an embodiment of it; that the grand work of Justice is to make way for a Love which will give to every man that which is right and ten times more, even if it should be by means of awful suffering which the love of the Father will not shun, either for himself or his children....[1]

To this place belongs one verse of the manuscript of "A Thanksgiving for F. D. Maurice," quoted at some length at the close of this chapter—a verse omitted from the version published:

> He taught that hell itself is yet within
>   The confines of thy kingdom; and its fires
> The endless conflict of thy love with sin,
>   That even by horror works its pure desires.

The following letter gives us familiar touch with the great teacher, showing his belief in my father, and his characteristic humility. He is suggesting collaboration in a devotional work. The letter is undated. It probably belongs to the later sixties, while Professor Maurice was every Sunday bringing together at Vere Street a handful of fine intellects and devoted followers. The suggestion must

---

[1] *David Elginbrod*, vol. iii, pp. 197 *et seq*. I may add that following Professor Maurice, my father always claimed that the words *life eternal* in the New Testament bore no relation to time, though illimitable duration may follow as a consequence not of the word eternal, but of life itself: "This is life eternal, that they may know Thee, the only true God."

have given the purest joy to my parents, and was, I feel sure, eagerly responded to. But the fact that the book was never written—indeed there is no record of its being begun—suggests that the proposal came simultaneously with the failure in Professor Maurice's health—consequent largely upon the frequent journeys between Cambridge and London—which compelled his resignation of St. Peter's in 1869.

From F. D. Maurice to G. M. D.

Feb. 14.

Private.

MY DEAR MACDONALD,

I have been thinking much of the subject which has [been] filling my sermons for the last three months; I do not know that I think often of any other without coming back to that—the Unity of the Church, the expression of it in our two Sacraments, [and] the possibility of using them to bring men at least to some shame for their sectarian enmities, to some hope for their removal. The thought of publishing more sermons is to me rather painful and odious; yet if I could put forth a little of what I feel in some form or other it would be a relief. I have sometimes dreamed that I could write some prayers and meditations upon this topic, and that you might give us some hymns that would cheer men's hearts and kindle their hopes of something better to come. I could not speak of it to any one but you; the prayers and hymns must both be inspirations, or they will be good for nothing. But perhaps you will think of it. I would not interrupt any of your other pursuits, but if we might ever do this work together I should deem it a great honour to myself and I should feel I was not failing, as utterly as I have failed, in healing the wounds of the body politic. Will you turn it over in your mind?

Affectionately yours,

F.D. MAURICE.

On the occasion of Professor Maurice's leaving Vere Street, my father originated a testimonial to him, the sharing in which was strictly limited to those who felt themselves indebted to his teaching. I append the copy of the appeal sent to Mrs. A. J. Scott, seeing that it expresses some views of the writer's regarding money. As a matter of fact I believe the testimonial took form in the portrait in oils by Lowes Dickinson given to Queen's College.

GEORGE MACDONALD

G.M.D. to Mrs. A. J. Scott.

THE RETREAT, HAMMERSMITH, W.,
Nov. 3rd, 1869.

Some of us who honour and love Mr. Maurice as a teacher come from God, desire to minister to him of our earthly things, chiefly that he may be aware of our honour and love. Will you help us in this by making it known to those of your friends who would be glad to have a share in the offering? I beg, however, that no one may be asked to give who is not under personal obligation to Mr. Maurice. I should be most happy to receive the money and account for it.

I have such a sense of the sacredness of money, and such a conviction that it is only the vulgar mind which regards it as an unclean thing—because in secret it worships it—that I would gladly prevail on Mr. Maurice, should the amount be large enough, to accept our love in the form of the gold of God's making, that he might do with it as he would. But if he should for his own sacred reasons decline to accept it, in this form, I should turn it into that of such books as should make him feel rich in their possession....

In doctrine I do not think there was any sort of difference between F. D. Maurice and George MacDonald, and but little in opinion. What differences there might be, were not intellectual or doctrinal but such as mark the characteristics of two great minds. Maurice's scholarship was beyond question; my father always repudiated any claim to general scholarship, though none can deny that, in English literature at least, his studies were deep and wide. While the former always insisted upon the necessity of the historical element in theology, the latter, more typically the mystic, while also clinging to accepted evidence, would not have given it the same degree of importance. Yet in the celebrated controversy between Dean Mansel—that typical Tory, High Church Oxford Don—and Professor Maurice in 1848, the latter was the mystic and the Dean the agnostic. For Mansel claimed that God, being unconditioned, is unknowable and inconceivable; whereas the very points that made Maurice renounce his Unitarian faith were his sense of the urgent need, expressed by all the Old Testament Prophets, that man should and might have knowledge of the Creator, and the fact that this was given to him at last in the Incarnation.

All George MacDonald's writings tended in like direction, and it is precisely my father's poetical mysticism that will hold sway over human hopes and spiritual life long after the logical ecclesiasticism of his friend is forgotten. With due deliberation I make the claim, and for two reasons:

(1) Where Professor Maurice was concerned primarily with the Church's relation to God, my father's interest was with the individuals. Maurice, in his devotion to spiritual politics, found new hope for the world in Christian Socialism. Correspondingly his convictions demanded the rehabilitation of the Anglican Church as God's instrument and policy. He discovered in its articles and creeds truths hidden from wise and foolish alike, who see only the passing "inferior expression," rather than "the grand, God-meant meaning" of their lineaments. Correspondingly my father came to regard the Church of England—notwithstanding the defining of her faith in terms that must inevitably be misconstrued by the vast majority of her children—as allowing the individual a greater freedom in faith than any other Christian organization. Yet I am disposed to contrast briefly the two men's temperaments by affirming that while both were rebels against the old Tory Calvinism, the hope of one for the world's better living centred round Christian Socialism, and that of the other round a theocratic individualism. Both were equally radical in state politics. But Socialism may become as intolerant as autocracy, Ecclesiasticism as restrictive as Calvinism; and, so my father taught, a finer law will be found in an individualism conscious that liberty is won only in self-denial and the free sharing of all things. But while I do think that F. D. Maurice built more hopes than my father upon the rallying of state politics round the National Church and the development of Christian Socialism—which term,

by the way, he originated—he was hardly less a believer in individualism as foundational in the ideal state; he would have agreed with my father that, when all men are Christians, the state will inevitably be communist,[1] or perhaps cease to exist. In one word, however, F. D. Maurice had perhaps more hope in system and corporate charity as expedient and so incentive to religious faith than ever George MacDonald had. While I have rightly contrasted my father's *intent* of feeling with Ruskin's *extent* of knowledge, I do not feel that Maurice's extensiveness of mind in any way qualified his intensiveness of heart.

(2) The second reason for thinking that George MacDonald will still be influencing the people's faith, even when his friend is forgotten, is simply this, that he, more than any other teacher of his day, insisted that hope in a personal immortality with substantial body and glorified senses lies at the very root of our religious sense and longings. Maurice is said rather to have evaded discussion of the direct issue. My father realized that the ordinary presentment of this truth does little more than insist upon the *doctrine*, and so in a measure endangers the *faith*. Many orthodox Christians have, when all is told, this terrible fear: that they will not know or be known by their beloved ones; that they may have no memory of the life and beauty of the world they have left; and that they will be expected to find blissful contentment in the perfection of Christ risen and the forgiveness of their sins. George MacDonald always insisted that, if God was such as Christ taught, his Fatherhood must be infinitely greater than man's.

> What! (he wrote in 1867) shall God be the God of the families of the earth, and shall the love that he has thus created towards father and mother, brother and sister, wife and child, go moaning and longing to all eternity; or worse, far worse, die out of our bosoms? Shall God be God, and shall this be the end?[2]

---

1 Vide "A Shop in Heaven," *Thomas Wingfold*, vol. ii, p. 229.
2 *Unspoken Sermons*, 1st series, p. 242.

To be given a future existence with no memory or touch with the old; to begin again a new life, with new labours and joys and affections, could not be a resurrection of the dead, but a new creation having no reference to the old; it would not be continuation of life, but cessation; not a new birth, but just a creation of some other soul to take some unknown place. Nothing in all my father's writings is more beautiful than his letters of consolation to friends bereft; and the dominant note of them all is insisting upon the conscious continuity of life.

> Ane by ane they gang awa';
> The gatherer gathers great an' sma';
> Ane by ane makes ane an' a'.
>
> Aye, whan ane is ta'en frae ane,
> Ane on earth is left alane,
> Twa in heaven are knit again.
>
> Whan God's hairst [*harvest*] is in or lang [*before long*]
> Golden-heidit, ripe, and thrang,
> Syne [*then*] begins a better sang.[1]

If anyone interested as well in my father's character as in his work—and few men's, it will be allowed, have closer agreement with theirs than has his—will turn from this, one of his very early utterances on death, to *Lilith*, almost his latest, he will see how little the quality and substance of the poet's outlook changed, although he gained so much in extent of vision. If these simple verses, "Ane by ane they gang awa'," enlarge one's hope in a resurrection of the body, then the chapter in *Lilith*, called "The Cemetery," makes such hope more tranquil and sure than any doctrinal expression of it. As a matter of fact, all mere arguments in favour of the soul's immortality excite opposing argument, leaving many a man and woman in profoundly sceptical anguish; and perhaps this was why Maurice had so little to say about it. On the other hand, some "godly ballant" or imaginative

---
1 *Alec Forbes*, vol. iii, p. 195.

prose utterances concerning the better life, such as abound in *Lilith* and *Phantastes*, send an uprisen hope straight to the Gospels for invigoration into faith, and for realizing that the Kingdom of Heaven within us and Immortality are complemental conceptions.

"The Soul of man, says my father in the unpublished *Seekers and Finders*, "is the World turned outside in"; and in *Paul Faber* he speaks more poetically of a little child being a "mirrored universe"[1]—just interpretations, both, of the words of Ecclesiasticus, "He has placed the world in man's heart." Some people think to get into themselves a fuller measure of the Kingdom of Heaven by ignoring all evil, and so become sentimentalists; others, in shutting their eyes upon beauty and truth, get too much Kingdom of Hell into their consciousness, and so, without perhaps being made evil by it, become cynics. But George MacDonald, so great was his faith, so simple his heart, must get intimacy with both Kingdoms fearlessly. His soul held in it the whole world with all its heavens of light and hells of opacity. From his spiritual intrepidity came his discovery—one that every man must get for himself—that love is life eternal; that in the Kingdom of Heaven immortality is the one condition of its citizenship; so that he, the poet and mystic, gives us vision of a more glorious life than the fugitive glimpses granted to our intermittent sense of immortality, or than any church doctrines evoke. Some of us claim to be pantheists rather than Christians; but the more surely George MacDonald realized his Christ, the more surely did he behold God in primrose and lark and child, and know that all such little ones, being portions of the Heavenly Kingdom "turned outside in," are what they are because Love is immortal.

It is God who gives thee thy mirror of imagination,[2] and if thou keep it clean, it will give thee back no shadow but of the truth. Never a cry of

---

1 Vol. i, p. 18.
2 "God's imagination, which is at once the birth and the very truth of everything." (*Salted With Fire* (1897), p. 47.)

love went forth from human heart but it found some heavenly cord to fold it in. Be sure thy friend inhabits a day not out of harmony with this morning of earthly spring, with this sunlight, those rain-drops, that sweet wind that flows so softly over his grave.[1]

So once again we find the poet making us believe what the ecclesiastic so often fails in doing.

Perhaps no point in religious teaching has elicited so much sentimentalism as the subject of immortality; and perhaps this sentimentalism has, more than anything else, set honest thinkers to oppose doctrinal claims. I know no line of thought or imagining in which my father is so free from sentimentalism. "It is by no means a matter of the *first* importance," he wrote, "whether we live for ever or not":[2] as if he said even more bluntly: Of course there is no immortality for you, if you have no life in you, or at best "a life that flouts life with mop and mow!"[3] What you desire of continued existence would be worse than its cessation; to argue in favour of such an immortality is to argue against God's will concerning life, and is rather a plea for everlasting damnation. These are obviously not my father's words, or they would be better: they do but summarize certain passages upon the subject in *Thomas Wingfold, Curate*, where the whole argument is grandly presented in portions of an allegory dealing with *The Wandering Jew*.[4]

I need not ask my father's forgiveness for trying to formulate his faith in the resurrection—unless it be that I claim his utterances—not his faith—to be more confident than his greatest friend's. Lest there remain, however, any doubt as to George MacDonald's estimate of that friend, I quote here most of his "Thanksgiving for F. D. Maurice,"[5] written on his death in 1872.

---

1 *Paul Faber, Surgeon*, vol.i, p. 67.
2 *Thomas Wingfold, Curate*, vol. iii, p. 70.
3 *Lilith*, p. 202.
4 Loc. cit., vol. iii, chaps. x, xi, and xii.
5 *Poetical Works*, vol. i, p. 442.

A Thanksgiving for F.D. Maurice

Lord, for thy prophet's calm commanding voice,
    For his majestic innocence and truth,
For his unswerving purity of choice,
    For all his tender wrath and plenteous ruth;

For his obedient, wise, clear-listening care
    To hear for us what word The Word would say,
For all the trembling fervency of prayer
    With which he led our souls the prayerful way;

For all the heavenly glory of his face
    That caught the white Transfiguration's shine
And cast on us the reflex of thy grace—
    Of all thy men late left, the most divine;

For all his learning, and the thought of power
    That seized thy one Idea everywhere,
Brought the eternal down into the hour,
    And taught the dead thy life to claim and share;

For his humility, dove-clear of guile;—
    The sin denouncing, he, like thy great Paul,
Still claimed in it the greatest share, the while
    Our eyes, love-sharpened, saw him best of all!

For his high victories over sin and fear,
    The captive hope his words of truth set free,
For his abiding memory, holy, dear;
    Last, for his death and hiding now in thee,

We praise, we magnify thee, Lord of him:
    Thou hast him still; he ever was thine own;
Nor shall our tears prevail the path to dim
    That leads where, lowly still, he haunts thy throne.

BOOK VIII
AMERICA

CHAPTER I
THE INVITATION

PERHAPS the ten years from 1870 to 1880 were fuller of enterprise and hard work, of contest with sickness and sorrow, than any in George MacDonald's life. The industry of his pen was unremitting. In 1871 appeared an important contribution to the publishing world, namely his *Works of Fancy and Imagination,* in ten small 8vo. volumes. They contained most of his poetry and all the fairy-tales and short stories that had so far appeared, including *Phantastes* and *The Portent.* They were rapidly followed by *At the Back of the North Wind,* 1871; *Ranald Bannerman's Boyhood,* 1871; *The Princess and the Goblin,* 1872; *Wilfrid Cumbermede,* 1872; *The Vicar's Daughter,* 1872; *Gutta Percha Willie,* 1873; *Malcolm,* 1875; *The Wise Woman,* 1875; *Thomas Wingfold,* 1876; *St. George and St. Michael,* 1876; *Exotics,* etc.,1876; *The Marquis of Lossie,* 1877; *Sir Gibbie,* 1879; *Paul Faber,* 1879. Surely this was a good ten years' output. But when we realize his elaborate corrections and re-writing, we shall have truer sense of his patience, his devotion to his art, and his belief that nothing short of the best he could do was good enough.[1] Nor must we forget that he was constantly lecturing.

The increasing claims of family and friends made it now impossible for my mother to give as much critical help to the manuscripts; but I imagine there was many a discussion

---

[1] "God," he once said, "never gave man a thing to do concerning which it were irreverent to ponder how the Son of God would have done it."

of character, incident and narrative in those hours when the house was all sleeping; and perhaps even more of their children's idiosyncracies, physical, intellectual and moral. For now their individualities were demanding separate recognition and handling. Every family is unconsciously making for its disintegration, the while that the dearest bonds are strengthening always. The patriarchal ideal of government, and the Celtic clinging together of family units always strong in my father, encouraged a secret hope that the family, adding to and multiplying itself, would be always about them; and what mother ever was there who did not look to the prolongation of her own sway in her children's increase? "Life is propagation," wrote my father: "the perfect thing, from the spirit of God downwards, sends *itself* onward, not its work only, but its life."[1]

But the decade brought grievous changes, so that the disintegration began its sorrowful course by means that were not a natural consequence of youthful adventure with the world, or ordained by the sands of Time.

Our Grandfather Powell died in 1870 in his ninety-first year. He would still ride on horseback at eighty-six, and was as upright and alert, in spite of grave deafness, as in middle life. Once, I remember, when he came to see us at Hammersmith, my father offered him an easy-chair: "Which do you take me for," he asked curtly, "an invalid or an old man?" He loved us all dearly; and I carry his watch to this day, worn very thin—as he was—but neither invalided nor old in its time-keeping.

Before the ten years were run, two of the eleven—the rarest of her flock, I think, to the mother—were taken away. Mary, the elfish, sweet-singing Blackbird, died when twenty-four; and Maurice, so wonderfully fair—of whom his mother wrote after an illness when he was seven: "How good and lovely he is! He is more like an Angel than a mortal—only a most argufying angel certainly. He is made of such exquisitely fine

---

[1] *Castle Warlock*, vol. ii, p. 115.

clay. I think his soul must be like his skin"—died when fifteen. F. D. Maurice and Greville Matheson were also taken away.

On the other hand these years brought a few friends of rarest fidelity, multitudes of lovers and disciples, and widely extended experiences, largely the outcome of a visit to America in 1872. Chief among these friends, lovers and experiences stands Richard Watson Gilder whose romantic outlook and innocence, so like my father's, gave him the poetic vision and raciness of humour, that were the secret of his critical acumen and philanthropic labours.

During the first years of this period no great events occurred beyond book-production, though a few letters help us to realize the steady march of life.

The indifferent health of our family, one or more being generally ailing, and the increasing importunities of printers' devils upon the overwrought author, together with the fact that our mother, now nearing fifty, did not bear so well the many demands upon her, all made frequent change to the sea beneficial. In 1871 Halloway House,[1] in the Old London Road, Hastings, was taken and easily furnished out of superfluous chattels at The Retreat. The study was papered, painted and decorated with stars by my sisters' own hands. Thereafter much time was spent there. It had become increasingly doubtful whether The Retreat, so near the foggy river and evil-smelling black mud at low tide, was altogether wholesome.

Here is surprising news of *Good Words for the Young*:

G.M.D. to his Wife.

THE RETREAT, HAMMERSMITH, W.,
[*February* 25, 1871].

...I have a bit of bad news. The Magazine, which went up in the beginning of the volume, has fallen very much since. Strahan thinks it

---

[1] The Town Council of Hastings have set a memorial plaque on Halloway House, in which "the distinguished poet and novelist" lived.

is because there is too much of what he calls the fairy element. I have told him my story [*The Princess and the Goblin*] shall be finished in two months more....*I know it is as good work of the kind as I can do, and I think will be the most complete thing I have done*....Perhaps I could find a market for that kind of talent in America—I shouldn't wonder....

The letter is peculiarly informing. Evidently the ordinary parent was hardly better informed then than now concerning the child's diet. One is glad too to realize how true was the author's estimate of his own book—though the disappointment must have been great—as well as his surmise that America may be more appreciative.

My mother truly gloried in these fairy-tales that *Good Words for the Young* had elicited, and her astonishment that the public had no ear for them was great. But how glad my father was to relinquish the Editorial Chair—no one else ever sat in it—is told in the following extract. Mr. G—, I believe, had been invited to submit a story for the Magazine; but it proved quite unsuitable. He threatened legal proceedings, and told everyone how the Editor, having commissioned him to write a story, refused it because he had to make room for one of his own.

G.M.D. to his Wife at Hastings.

[*July 26, 1871.*]

...Mr. G—would have cut me yesterday in an omnibus, if I had let him. They say he thinks me just the devil. Poor man! He is always threatening his solicitor upon some one or other. I am more and more glad I am to be rid of the editing....

That summer Alex Stevenson commissioned George Lawson to make a terra-cotta bust, half life-size, of my father, and it was subsequently cast in bronze. But, in spite of its technical excellence, it missed the true ideal touch. At the same time my father, supported by Matthew Arnold, was writing to and calling upon all sorts of great people to get a Civil Pension annuity for Dr. MacIntosh MacKay; but the devoted old Calvinist died before the scheme bore fruit.

THE INVITATION

In the autumn of 1871 a project for seeing the Passion Play at Ammergau having fallen through, a trip to Holland was made. "But," wrote my father, "I don't care where it is so that I get some breath and something to wonder at a little."

Our parents and eldest sister, with George Reid, the artist—who the following year painted the portrait of George MacDonald, now in the National Portrait Gallery, and had already, in 1867, done the one for the Marischall College, Aberdeen,[1]—comprised the party. The young artist introduced them to Joseph Israels in Amsterdam, who gave my father a lovely sketch, entitled *Farewell!*—a woman with baby in arms looking out to sea at a distant fishing-boat.

Innumerable were the letters my father received from all sorts of people, religious, abusive. My mother always answered the worshipping or adoring young ladies who suffered from being "misunderstood." But he was very tender over young poets. Wherever he could give any real help he was lavish with his pen. My friend Ernest Rhys, the poet and critic, warmly testifies to this when he first met my father in 1877.

I am not quite sure from whom the suggestion first came of a lecturing tour in the United States. Dickens and Thackeray had already undergone the experience, and in the winter of 1872-73, J. A. Froude, Professor Tyndall, Edmund Yates, not to omit the flashy elocutionist Bellew, and "Professor" Pepper, the ghost illusionist, more or less dogged my father's footsteps. But it is clear that Richard Watson

---

[1] Mrs. Urquhart, a sister of the late Sir George Reid, P.R.S.A., tells me of a pretty incident concerning the painting of the Aberdeen portrait. A young lady, a Miss MacTaggart, had pressed the painter for an introduction, but was resolutely refused. One day, however, his studio fire getting low, he rang for coals. To his amazement the young lady answered it in cap and apron, unobtrusively made up the fire, swept the hearth and retired. Then my father remarked on her pretty figure and beautiful hands, and asked where she came from. So at the end of the sitting the importunate maid was introduced, and had a never forgotten interview. Mrs. Urquhart says she herself was very envious, all she was allowed being a peep out of window to see the writer of *Alec Forbes* come from his cab, though "all Aberdeen seemed to be crowded that night into the Mechanic's Institute to hear him speak."

Gilder had been in correspondence with my father on the subject.

G.M.D. to R. W. Gilder.

HALLOWAY HOUSE,
HASTINGS, ENGLAND,
Dec. 10, 1871.

DEAR MR. GILDER,

...I dare not believe that I deserve all that you and other kind American friends say of me; but in the sense of miserable demerit everyone may sometimes hope that he may be doing something beyond the reach of the fire, even as the saw and the plane did good work in the hands of the Son of the carpenter of Nazareth.

Till we meet, and I hope before long,

Yours very truly,
GEORGE MACDONALD.

So George and Louisa MacDonald became R. W. Gilder's very truly till Time failed them.

In the early part of the year 1872 everything was settled with Messrs. Redpath & Fall of Boston, the foremost lecture-bureau in America, for a tour to occupy the six or eight winter months. The emolument was tempting. In spite of desperately hard work, literature had failed to meet the demands on my father's purse. He was now forty-eight, and, although all suspicion of lung-disease was over, he still suffered frequently from bronchitis and quite terrible attacks of asthma. The letters of the spring in that year when he went lecturing in the North without my mother prove his unfitness. He was clearly feeling nearly exhausted. *Wilfrid Cumbermede*, which ran through *St. Paul's Magazine*, certainly suggests fatigue. Thus he writes to my mother on the eve of reaching home again:

> I shall be very glad to get home. *Oh the work undone that snarls at my heels—not to say the work unbegun.* But I think it is to teach me to trust and learn more and not be anxious.

So the invitation was accepted—the main condition being that he should not lecture more than five nights a week and that his fee should be £30 a lecture. But the beloved

THE INVITATION

man refused to send the agents any press-cuttings or friendly testimonials whereby they might gauge his ability to speak, of which they knew nothing. And, as will presently be seen, his modesty cost him dear.

But before America was adventured some dearest friends died. On April 1st came the saddest loss of all, in the death of Professor Maurice. I shall never forget the shock and grief it was to my mother when Strahan appeared at Halloway House and suddenly told her. But he had been ill for some weeks and the end was not unexpected. Only three months earlier, he had sent his little godson and namesake, then nearly eight years old, this letter:

> CAMBRIDGE,
> Jan. 3rd, 1872.
>
> MY DEAR GODSON,
> Thank you very much for remembering me and sending me such beautiful flowers on New Year's Day. They were put into water directly, and they look as fresh and bright as when they left you. God gave them their life and He renews it in them. So He does with you, my dear boy, and the life He gives you is a better one than the life of the flowers. I hope you will thank Him for it, and for that which He has given and still gives to your father and mother and brothers and sisters, more and more. May He always bless you and them in this year and every year.
> Your affectionate friend,
> F.D. MAURICE.

The blow was additionally hard for my mother to bear because it came only a few days before producing one of her plays in public for a Hastings charity: as witness these words to W. Carey Davies, who had written her very beautifully about the world's loss, and had sent her the two volumes of Maurice's *Mental and Moral Philosophy* just published.

> *Mrs. G.M.D. to W. C. Davies.*
> THE RETREAT,
> April 12, 1872.
> ...I don't know how to thank you and tell you of the comfort and help your note and the two books were to me. I was just so wretched when they came in. It has been a terribly trying time, so shut out as we were

from all the consolations of joining in the very last services connected with that most beloved name—and all that folly going on at Hastings! It was a nightmare to me, and would have been impossible had I not been able to raise the folly into a duty and so make it sacred, believing that, had he seen me behind those painted scenes, he would not have disowned me, nor scorned me as a friend—at least not for that reason. Ah! how life is altered! The sacramental glow is gone out of it....

Again, in July, Dr. Norman McLeod, H.M. Chaplain in Scotland, and Editor of *Good Words*, died. His long and affectionate friendship with my father was cemented by a mutual admiration which differences in certain doctrinal points could not shake. My father wrote thus to Mrs. McLeod:

G.M.D. to Mrs. Norman McLeod.
THE RETREAT, HAMMERSMITH,
July 7th, 1872.

MY DEAR MRS. MCLEOD,
I almost dread drawing near you with a letter. It seems as if all one could do, was to be silent and walk softly. Yet I would not have you think me heedless of you and your sorrow. And yet again, what is there to say? Comfort, all save what we can draw for ourselves from that eternal heart, is a phantom—a mere mockery. Either one must say and the other must believe that there is ground for everlasting exultation, or comfort is but the wiping of tears that for ever flow.

The sun shines, the wind blows soft, the summer is in the land; but your summer sun and your winter fire is gone, and the world is waste to you. So let it be. Your life is hid with Christ in God, at the heart of all summers—so "comfort thyself" that this world will look by and by a tearful dream fading away in the light of the morning. I do not know how I may bear it when similar sorrow come to myself, but it seems to me now as if the time was so short there was no need to bemoan ourselves, only to get our work done and be ready.

And, dear Mrs. McLeod, if you will not think me presuming, may I not say—do you not find your spirit drawing yet closer to the great heart that has *seemed* to leave you for a while? I ask this, because I think the law of the spirit is really the law of the universe; that as, when the Lord vanished from the sight of his friends, they found him in their hearts, far nearer then than before, so when any one like him departs, it is but, like him, to come nearer in the one spirit of truth and love....

THE INVITATION

Yet another bereavement was the death at Hastings on September 6th of Greville Ewing Matheson, my father's earliest of brother-like friends, of whom he wrote in 1891 as "the man whose literary judgment and sympathy I prized beyond that of the world beside." We had seen less of him of late years. His failing health increased his natural shyness, making him unwilling to face the many friends who flocked to our house. My father would have postponed the day of sailing for America had his friend's suffering been further prolonged. He and William Matheson were with him up to the last.

But before leaving England Ruskin's love-perplexities reached their culmination, and my parents, together with the Cowper-Temples—afterwards Lord and Lady Mount-Temple—made themselves responsible for supporting Rose La Touche against her mother. Their increasing intimacy with Ruskin had already lost them Mrs. La Touche's friendship, the reason for whose turning against Ruskin can never be certainly known. "When love itself is unkind, it is apt to be burning and bitter and malicious."[1] Terrible stories were told to wean the girl from her adoration of him. Once she wrote to my father for his sympathy: her love for Ruskin, she said, had been growing year by year since her childhood, "deepening in silence," until it had become an "intense spiritual power and suffering."

But she had not strength of mind or body to withstand her parents—she admitted it—and, her illness increasing, she died in May 1875. "She is only gone," said Ruskin, "where the hawthorn blossoms go." In August 1872 Rose La Touche had visited us at The Retreat, and Ruskin came home from Venice, after much corresponding with my parents, to see her; and he spoke of having had three days of heaven which he would have bought with all the rest of his life.

I have vivid memories of him and the frail girl in those days. I was but sixteen, and yet saw something of the heaven

---
1 *Salted With Fire* (1897), p. 205.

into which the sorrowful world was now changed for them. Also I remember very clearly Ruskin's strength of face, his searching blue eyes, and his trustful smile—his ultramarine blue cravat also!—and the joy it gave me to feel the grip of his hand, or to find a hansom-cab in the unfashionable streets of Hammersmith and bring it for him. I remember, too, the shadowy Rose, so amazingly thin, with her high colour and great eyes, and such a tender sad smile on her strangely red lips. They met once or twice more—at the Cowper-Temples it was, to whom she went after leaving us. But the remainder of her story is all darkness. She returned his last letter unopened, and Ruskin was never the same man again.

In May George MacDonald visited his old home, taking the little Maurice, age eight, with him for company. The special reason was to look up things at Cullen, which place, under the name of Portlossie, he was making the centre for his new novel, *Malcolm*. Yet *The Vicar's Daughter* was not yet out of his hands.

G.M.D. to his Wife.

Huntly,
May 20.

I must try to work on my proofs in the trains, or I don't know how I shall get through with the last of the *Vicar* which is now being lugged from me. I am going to preach here tomorrow evening. The sun is just breaking out of the stormy clouds in the west and shining through thin falling snow....A long letter from Rose [La Touche]...

In September my father and mother, with myself, sailed in the Cunard S.S. *Malta* for Boston, and were congratulated on the unusually short trip of twelve days. My mother's pluck in facing the sea was great; but she never left her berth the whole voyage, in spite of exceptionally good weather.

CHAPTER II
THE RECEPTION

THE lecture tour had seemed tempting enough from a pecuniary point of view. But I do not think my father brought home with him much over a thousand pounds; and he could perhaps have earned as much if the eight months had been spent in his study. But it gave his pen some rest, if not his mind; it provided him with new impressions even if they were not used directly as *copy*; and, his greatest reward for all the hardships of the tour, it brought him new friends who proved as fond and unchangeable as the nearest of old comrades.

Two among the latter, Russell Gurney and his wife, were gone a few weeks before to Washington, he having been appointed British representative on the Commission to settle British and American claims, other than the Alabama Claims, arising out of the Civil War. To have so well proved a friend already in the strange land was happy for my mother.

The material for writing this part of my parents' life is wonderfully rich, chiefly because of my mother's letters to her children. There are but few of my father's. Hers are characteristic—ardent, humorous, and, however astute in criticism, always kind. She fell in love with New England and New York—and not only because she saw her husband overwhelmed with the admiration and applause of an enthusiastic people. Just twenty-one years had they been married, the first ten of so much hardship, so much failure, so much ill-health, the second a period of quickly increasing powers and rising renown; and now at last the whole world seemed to be recognizing what she had known ever since the poor tutor first came to her father's house and opened the gates of Heaven to her.

Her letters alone would make a volume of warm human interest if only for the way they proclaim her courage and vigilant care of a husband in bad health all through the tour, and her solicitude for the children 3,000 miles away. He was the bear, she said, who must dance when his keeper, Mr. Redpath of the "Boston Lyceum Bureau," shook the chain; while she, to quote our delightful host in Boston, James T. Fields' more felicitous sobriquet was the "Drag-on" to St. George's intrepidity. For it was often her painful duty to forbid him the social functions ordained in his honour, thereby giving umbrage perhaps, until its absolute need was realized; or to cancel, on account of his illness, lectures long advertised, thereby incurring Redpath's anger. The latter did not trouble to understand either St. George or the "Drag-on." For, although it soon became evident that the work was too heavily planned, and with scarcely any consideration for the lecturer as regards the long daily journeys, my father would accept many invitations to preach, and always without fee: this being preposterous from Redpath's point of view, since it enabled the public to hear him gratuitously.

We reached Boston on September 30th, two days before our scheduled date, and yet were welcomed with open-arm hospitality by James T. Fields and his wife into their beautiful home, 148 Charles Street. Here the house-decorations were in the Morris style, the furniture genuinely old. The library had a wide range of first editions and manuscripts. There must be some who still remember our host and wife. He was devoted in his care for us, untiring too in his endeavours to ward off lion-hunters and autograph-albums: she was quite beautiful, with a tender stateliness that won our hearts immediately—and not least the boy's, I think. But even my mother's first letter shows how she gathered her little ones about her from 3,000 miles away.

Mrs. G.M.D. to Mary J. M. D.

BOSTON,
Thursday morning, Oct. 3rd, 1872.

MY DEAR ELFIE (AND ALL ANGELS),
 I can hardly believe we have been here three days—it seems like nearly as many weeks. Such a sense of newness and strangeness, clearness and brightness, all about and around us!....I'll try and fancy what questions you would ask me if I could get home to-night. Well, you'd want to know how I and Papa are—very well, thank you, dear; all of us flourishing apparently, both by the way we walk, talk, look, eat and sleep—though as to the latter I hope to improve in that function as we get used to not having anything substantial to eat after three o'clock, unless you call tea and thin wafer-biscuits and iced water substantialities! They are *very* charming people that we are with. You must not think they are not hospitable—quite the contrary—only they cram all their feed into two meals. Such breakfasts! and then dinner. Only we have not learnt to eat so much all at once. They have at eight o'clock breakfast fish and bird and meat and omelets and hominy or porridge and potatoes and beans and other vegetables, and four or five kinds of bread, and tea and coffee and iced water and Vichy water and wine if you like; and then a regular fruit dessert just like dinner with finger glasses and d'oyleys in due form. Mr. Fields is a polished, genial, kind, well-educated man. His wife a nature's lady—refined, delicate, largish and kind. He is, and evidently has been a lion-hunter, but it seems to me that this is because of his love of the lions more than for any reflected glory he gets by it. His autographs and letters and books, first editions, authors' own copies, presents of MS. copies, etc., etc., are really things to count oneself rich in possessing; but he only seems to rejoice in them as a schoolboy might dance with joy about his prizes for athletic sports. He is very simple-hearted and clever in his own way. He tells a story "*first-rate*," and has lots of most excellent ones to tell....She is really great and no end of kind. Her mind seems *full* of beautiful and best things—verse and prose....I meant to write much more to-day, but the callers and callers and callers—one after another, or rather in twos and threes after each other—have prevented me. Mr. Redpath says that Papa's popularity goes very much in strata—very much I think as it does at home. Those who care for him, care very much—others can't endure his writings. So they can't tell till they try whether he will *take*....The very first person we saw in Mrs. Fields' house was Mrs. B. Stowe! It was hard lines to be introduced

to her and have to shake hands with her before one had time to draw one's breath in the new country.[1] However, we had to be civil and so we were. We heard her read publicly last night....She is very amusing—not sweet, stern looking—not gracious, very humorous....

Mrs. G.M.D. to Lilia S. M. D.

BOSTON,
Saturday, Oct. 5th.

DEAR LILY,

...We had such a full day yesterday! Emerson, his wife and daughter came to lunch; after lunch we went to see Longfellow. He showed us his rooms and his pictures, and we saw one of his daughters. His house was Washington's headquarters—a hundred years old—which here is as wonderful as a three-hundred would be with us. Then in the evening we went to a severe tea and an elegant one—at the house of Mrs. Lowell's sister. (He is in England just now.) She is a very interesting person....One amusing chapter in the evening was my talking to a youth, a tremendous big boy with large open eyes who had travelled a good deal and talked charmingly, I thought, for so young and so big a fellow. I thought perhaps he was going into the Navy—thought he would make a jolly captain. I thought I was talking very kindly to him and encouraged him to speak his mind about things. When I heard afterwards he is *the* great preacher [Phillips Brooks] of the town—an Episcopalian clergyman, and is run after tremendously, I never was more flabbergasted....

148 CHARLES STREET, BOSTON,
Thursday, Oct. 10th.

...I have broken down rather with two horrid headaches. Yesterday we were to go out to spend the day at Manchester—their Hastings—not that it is like it—it is more like Oban, but it is the Fields' seaside summer house and it *is* a most charming place. We had a glorious day, such a day! the one in a thousand one gets in October....but when the sun shines here, how it shines!...the air is very exciting and of course all the kindness and praise Papa gets is very exciting, quite enough to account for to-day's headache....Mrs. Fields is a darling, giving you a new feeling of the divinity of grace and graciousness. I was too ill to go to a party last night, and she stayed with me and I had such a delightful evening with her alone....Next Saturday there is to be another reception and Miss Cushman is to come. I wore (this is according to your

---

1 Their feelings towards her could not be quite friendly because of her book *Lady Byron Vindicated*, first published in England in 1870.

orders, my dear Mademoiselle) my—your—black silk with the white lace. Mrs. Fields praised it and so did he—more than anything I have put on....She dresses very charmingly....Her hair is black and grizzly in the short bits, but goes into rich smooth coils in the long places. She never wears a scrap of lace or ribbon, pad or false hair, but morning and evening it always looks full dressed....He is just about our age.... She is perhaps 15 years younger. I wore my new black silk out of doors when we called on Longfellow. We are going there to tea—severe teas are the fashion here....Mr. Fields gave a lecture on Tuesday, and Papa to-night, so they have had great fun about hearing each other. They joke, too, about which shall wear the finest neckties and studs and rings.[1] Mr. Fields has some Dickens gave him. It is great fun to hear them. He is very droll and simple-hearted too—with a great appreciation of genius, and really is very clever himself....There is no end to their kindness....

Mrs. G.M.D. to L. S. M. D.

BOSTON,
Sunday, Oct. 13th.

DEAR LILY,
...Papa, Greville and I went to the Episcopalian church here, and heard a really lovely sermon from the Mr. Brooks whom I had talked to and been *so kind as to encourage to speak his mind*[2]. ....We had such a refreshing service, and he is a very powerful preacher. We stayed to the Communion....Mrs. Russell Gurney called on Friday with Mr. R. G....They had come to Boston for a week or ten days to be here the first time Papa lectures....It seemed so strange for us four—the Gurneys and us—to be driving together in this new world....I must say I don't think she looks

---

1   My father's rings were an intaglio antique of Psyche, given him by Ruskin as a perfect specimen of late Greek art, a blood-stone signet unengraved and a carbuncle. Only the intaglio was valuable, and this he lent me some years later. I lost it—to the horrible burdening of my conscience for the remainder of my days, notwithstanding a lavish, almost joyous, forgiveness, even more memorable. His shirt-studs were gold-filigree, and his watch-chain of the slenderest with its bunch of seal, watch-key and compass.
2   In 1877, this preacher, lecturing to the Divinity School of Yale College, incidentally referred to my father: "...Among the many sermons I have heard, I always remember one by Mr. George MacDonald, the English author....It had his brave and manly honesty. But over and through it all it had this quality: it was a message from God to these people by him....As I listened, I seemed to see how weak in contrast was the way in which other preachers had amused me and challenged my admiration for the working of their minds. Here was a gospel. Here were real tidings. And you listened and forgot the preacher. (*Lectures on Preaching*, by the Rt. Rev. Phillips Brooks, D.D., 1904, p. 16.)

quite altogether in her element, but she is very dear and quite as stiff and quite as *really* loving and kind as ever. Mr. Gurney looks as lovely and genial as ever....Mrs. Russell Gurney says I have not seen America at all yet. She says Boston and all the people we have met are so English and the town is so like a continental one. We think it exceedingly like the Hague. There is a very large public garden and walks through it, and trees and seats—so like Holland. In this Charles Street there are tall elms all down the street, and the houses are big and high, red brick, with flat and green shutters. I like Boston very much....

And even the youth found it all wonderful:

Greville M.D. to his Sister Winifred.

Boston,
Oct. 15.

...We are having such a gay time here that there is really very little time to do anything but go driving about the country watching the marvellous colours in the trees. It is so beautiful! Sometimes you see a tree just one blaze of carmine or rather blood-colour, then all this variety of foliage with the exquisitely graceful form of the American elms—a tree which we have nothing like. Tulip trees seem rather plentiful here; but they have hardly begun to change yet....

In such-like pleasures we spent a fortnight of rest before the work of the winter opened on October 10th in the Union Hall at Cambridgeport. This was his first lecture in America and his first anywhere on *Robert Burns*. But the second on the same subject was at the much larger Lyceum in Boston itself; and it was then that the public discovered one aspect of his genius—his power of inspired, uplifting criticism, in no way spoiled by his just facing of facts. Through his wise and weighty, poetic and passionate words, without notes or help other than a little volume of Burns's works, he set the man before them, the lover, the romantic ploughman, the poet, in true portraiture, while his sins and shortcomings were fully accredited to him. I must have heard him lecture on Burns over forty times, I think, in the States, and used to declare that on every occasion it was a different lecture. It was new to an American audience to hear such

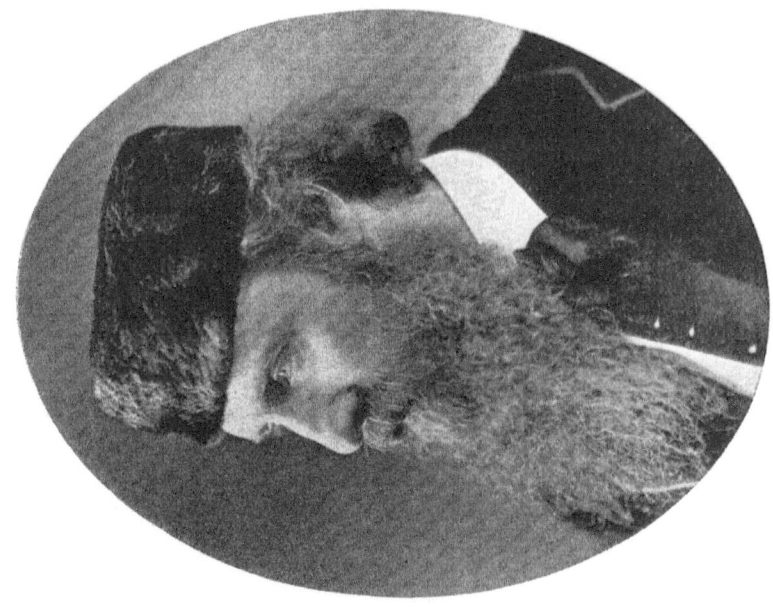

Photo by] [Sarony

GEORGE MACDONALD, 1873

Photo by] [Sarony

RICHARD WATSON GILDER, 1873

eloquence unbuttressed by academic elocution. Dr. Bellows likened him to Emerson, though when I heard that noble speaker, the fire of his soul did not flare up before his hearers quite as did George MacDonald's. Here is my mother's description of the *Burns* lecture; and in it we may easily read how proud a woman she was:

Mrs. G.M.D. to her Children.

MY DARLING IRENE, AND ALL CHILDREN,
...The people are so kind and glad to see Papa. I can't tell you how very happy it seems to make some people to look at him....It was very pleasant to hear different people tell of the way Papa's books had come to them, and the good and comfort they have been to them....Papa's lecture at Boston on Wednesday was the great event of the week to us....There were two thousand eight hundred and fifty ticket holders, besides a few that got in as friends. Such a hall! With two balconies all round it. They say Papa was heard in every corner of it. Was it not delightful for me? There I sat between Mr. and Mrs. Russell Gurney—and to sit there with them and see all those earnest, eager faces listening, almost breathlessly sometimes (we sat on the platform where we *could* see) was a sight I shan't forget....

My father's repertory included *Hamlet, Tom Hood,* the *Lyrics of Tennyson, King Lear, Macbeth* and *Milton*; but the favourite subject with American audiences was Robert Burns, and the choice for his first appearance in Boston. I remember how my father, after speaking for over a hundred minutes, dropped into a chair in the reception-room somewhat exhausted with the effort and the wonderful audience; how James T. Fields shook him by the hand, his eyes full of tears, and declared there had been nothing like it since Dickens; and how Redpath came rushing at him with this almost angry anti-climax, "See here, Mr. MacDonald, why didn't you *say* you could do this sort of thing? We'd have got 300 dollars a lecture for you! Guess the Lyceums all over the United States'll think they've *done* Redpath and Fall, sure! You make me sick! Yes, *Sir*."

And here I must interpose a word to tell how my mother won all hearts—except Redpath's! Her social charm, her beautiful yet inexpensive dressing, her wonderful eyes—in a land, moreover, where this feature was more generally notable than with us—and the fact that notwithstanding her grace of figure and sprightliness in manner, she was mother of eleven children, a number—"the *wrong* side of a dozen," my father said—quite as phenomenal in the States then as it would be here now, made her as popular as her husband. The photographic group of the family taken before leaving home was in great demand. At receptions I was so often sent upstairs to fetch it that I suggested to my mother that a good plan would be for her to wear it always like a sandwich board. But the amazement it caused, and the almost incredulous way ladies would look from it to the little sweet and satirical lady who was almost as much responsible for her husband as for her family, was delicious.

On October 30th my father visited Whittier, the Quaker poet at Amesbury, where he lectured.

> Mr. Whittier's house (my mother wrote) is a sweet, country-like cottage, wooden and low. We dined in the room that the roadside door opens on. Then through that was the little sacred study of one of the sweetest, most dignified, loving, humble and gentle of men. After the lecture, some of the Scotchmen made Papa a present of Whittier's poems. In the morning Mr. Whittier said that "Friend George must not be the only one to have presents," and he gave me his latest volume. He is a most lovable, holy man, but full of fire and enjoyment of all things good. He is very wide in his beliefs.

I remember the letter Whittier wrote to the local press speaking of the great work my father had done in the cause of religion and of his poetical worth, urging everybody not to miss this opportunity of hearing him lecture.

On November 2nd, after visiting Providence, R.I., he again lectured at the Boston Lyceum, this time on *Tom Hood*. On the 9th there was a great reception at the Fields'. But my father was kept to his bed with a bad gumboil and threats of a bronchitic attack, and before the reception was over we had news of a fire raging in the heart of Boston. It was a night of terrible anxiety, for the conflagration was spreading at an awful rate, and it seemed as if Charles Street itself might be involved. At any rate, Mr Fields set to work packing all valuables. Next morning nearly a hundred acres of that noble city, with its brick and iron, granite and marble palaces, stood in twisted rusty skeletons or lay low in smouldering ashes: $50,000,000, they said, vanished in smoke. Mr. Fields believed he was ruined, and walked about the Common most of the night with me and Mr. Robert Collyer, the renowned temperance preacher, a fellow guest at the Fields'. The flames from the raging furnace and the higher-flung masses of incandescent shreds and sparks and lurid smoke cast our shadow against the full moon, I remember.[1]

The fire began on a Saturday night. On Monday Mrs. Cunningham of Milton, eight miles away, came to fetch us. So open was she in heart, hand and hospitality that from that day she remained always a dearest friend.

Then came flying visits to New York, where we first met our future friends, Dr. J. G. Holland (the novelist and editor of *Scribner's Magazine*) and his family; and to Philadelphia. There our entertainers, the Lippincotts, rather overwhelmed us with their gold-brown-satin-lined carriages, their white marble palace for a home—"Grosvenor Square's almost cottages to it"—and their sedate and cold Quaker manners, giving the impression, at first only, that the City of William Penn could harbour no enthusiasms.

---

1 In the morning I explored the burning desert, and could not distinguish one street from another. But I noted particularly that the old brick buildings had behaved far better than the iron-framed stone-fronted palaces. Here and there a miserable Irish woman might be seen guarding her few chairs, a rickety table and such treasures as a Dutch clock or a plaster saint. But only a hundred or so of the poorest tenement houses, where the Irish lived, had perished; whatever the conditions now, there were then no poor Americans. They said, however, that the Irish were hurrying into Boston from all parts to get a share of the enormous relief-funds that were immediately raised.

"The ladies are more splendaciously attired in this house than any I have visited, all their dresses sent from London, every six months a fresh relay." The lecture was in the Opera House, packed full with 3,500 people. My father had never faced such an audience before, and he confessed it made him feel nervous at first. But, save for the occasional hesitation, common with him as he looked for a right word or phrase—which hesitation certain reporters noted as a blemish because foreign to their ideas of a highly cultivated elocution, though more discerning listeners found it added to the sense of his inspired spontaneity—he appeared perfectly at home. He held the attention of that mass of quiet people as easily as the dozen of ten years before in his little study at Tudor Lodge.

At Scotch Plains, N.J., we were truly ministered to by Dr. Abram Coles, who piloted him through an attack of "congestion of the lungs."

> ...Such a delightful man is our host. He fetched us from Jersey City, and at once Papa and I saw the most wonderful resemblance in his walk, his hurried, hesitating manner to whom do you think? F.D.M. [Maurice] the Good! He carried our bags for us from the cars. Then we talked with him, his eyes, his mouth, but most of all his manner and the dearest, loveliest, most humorous little laugh so wonderfully like him. The motions of his hands and the awfulness of his eye, so mingled with love, are all like....Papa says he *must* put them in a book some day....

Thence we travelled to Washington, where the Russell Gurneys welcomed us in their home, but had to give their guest a reception, at which great politicians abounded thick as thieves. Sharing the honours with my father was Professor Tyndall, some of whose entrancing lectures in Washington on *Light* it was my privilege to hear. A charming *débutante* being introduced to my father began telling him how much she had profited by his teaching. Some of his words on *Light* she'd never forget; they had opened her eyes to the truth pretty considerable and she guessed she'd now be a wiser girl all the time. "But," she rattled on, "your great work on *The Glaciers of the Alps*, well, I've *studied* that...." But here Mrs. Russell Gurney, with her quiet tact, came to my father's rescue, and the sweet impostor was led away by one of the private secretaries, perhaps to be presented to the most militant atheist of the day and to thank him for *Robert Falconer*.

Mrs. R. Gurney to Lilia S.M.D.

1512 H. St., Washington,
Nov. 25.

Dear Lily,

Yes, at 6 o'clock on Saturday evening we had the delight of welcoming your beloved Father and Mother, and do you know they were even dearer than ever! He was all muffled up in fur coat and handkerchief and alas! had a cold. She was in her nice black silk and seal-skin—with bright cheeks and beaming eyes, much better than at Boston! We did not have anyone at dinner to meet them, but at 9 o'clock they had to come down to be seen by a few whom we thought worthy: need I tell you how genial and pretty-behaved they were to every one, so that each guest went away only longing to know more of them? His cold, I grieve to say, was rather worse on Sunday, and he stayed in bed till one o'clock; but the dear mother came with us to Church, and it was a bright, sunshiny day to encourage us. At tea-time I was guilty of letting him talk too much—for I had let a young girl with a hungering and thirsting spirit come to see him, and the words he said were just suited to her need, and she went away refreshed and uplifted in spirit. I fear he suffered—but thought it *worth while*. We sang "Art thou weary?" and I heard the mother's rich contralto voice, and thought how much I had lost during all these 15 years in not having often enjoyed it, as I might and ought to have done.

This morning we have seen them off in a little compartment all to themselves in one of the huge cars. Your constant letters are their great joy and consolation....I must tell you that I thought the Mother quite masterly in her toilette—her thin black silk trimmed with Irish lace was the very thing for evening. Was it not good luck for us to be at his first lecture at Boston?...How many he has met with who feel they owe him unspeakable things! It seemed to me that I was seeing him reaping in joy and bringing his sheaves with him, after the sowing in tears of past years.

Ever lovingly yours,
Emelia Gurney.

After a visit to Baltimore—the only point remaining in the English boy's mind being the extraordinary beauty of every girl in church on a Sunday morning—we returned to Washington. There my father was struck down with a severe attack of bronchitis, and numbers of lectures were cancelled, as my mother relates:

Mrs. G.M.D. to Lilia S.M.D.

1512 H. STREET, WASHINGTON.
Dec. 3rd.

DEAREST LILY,
 ...I never saw him more prostrate except, of course, at the time of the Manchester illness. It is very serious this attack for him—we do not know yet whether he will be able to lecture again at all, and if he does he can scarcely make up all he has lost before the close of the lecture season. But if he can but get what will cover the debts that trouble him I do not think we ought to mind about more....We have given up Chicago. I wrote letters enough yesterday to put off lectures this side of Christmas to the value of over £300. Was it not trying for him? But he is so good—he lets me do just as I like and I write away to everybody....We must not mind that the large bottomless bag will have to have a division very high up near its mouth. But the Life is more than meat or money, and if you get Papa back alive and well we shall not mind that he could not make so many dollars as he intended. "I do so want to see Bobbie and Maurice," and he said it in such a sad tone. He longs to be home, and he seems to have little hope that he will be able to go on lecturing. But I hope—though my heart-strings are very near cracking in ten different places—that we may be able to go on....The dear Gurneys are so dear; Mrs. G. is lovely....

Your loving
MOTHER.

Next came two letters to my sisters from my father.

G.M.D. to Mary J.M.D.

MY DARLING ELFIE,
 ...I am much better, and have just written these verses to send to my chickens for the Little-Baby time [Christmas Day]. Would we were all the holy babies of our Father in heaven—out and out, I mean. My love to Lily and everyone. I have thought you all over.

Your loving
FATHER.

THE RECEPTION

A Song for Both Sides of the Atlantic.

Fur-footed, slow, for all thy gracious charms,
   We pray thee, dear December, to depart;
We kiss the Child thou bearest in thine arms,
   But all the year he dwelleth in our hearts.

Young January, with the wrinkled face,
   Follow thy sisters on their starry way;
Sweep on, we beg thee, with thy snowy train;
   When next thou com'st, we'll give thee leave to stay.

Make, February, few steps o'er the floor,
   Nor linger by the hearth when thou should'st cross;
Haste thee, nor turn to courtesy at the door;
   Pass through, and make us richer by thy loss.

Nor beat thy robes, O March, nor clutch the hair
   That hither, thither, all about thee flies;
O let thy dusty winds afar thee bear,
   That thy sweet sister come with smile and sighs.

And yet we care not whether sigh or smile
   Shall, April, on thy fair face win the day;
We love thee, girl, but thou hast not a wile
   To move a prayer except—oh, haste away!

Come then, dear May; lead o'er the sea-waves dull
   The eager ship, the angel of the boon;
And when our arms are as our full hearts full,
   Then go or linger, dear and perfect June.

But my father, with his faith and the wonderful resiliency it brought him, recovered quickly enough to justify a resumption of his task. Dr. Abram Coles came to see him at Washington and was astonished at my mother's daring in taking her patient out driving on her own responsibility and against his orders. She felt that he had no chance of recovery as long as he was confined to the artificially dried and overheated atmosphere of the house. And he immediately began to mend. We travelled very comfortably in a Pullman car to Elmira, New York, whence the following:

GEORGE MACDONALD

G.M.D. to Lilia S.M.D.

ELMIRA,
Dec. 22, 1872.

MY DARLING GOOSE,

This will hardly reach you on your birthday. Neither did I think of it for that but just for the sake of writing to you. But may you have as many happy birthdays in this world as will make you ready for a happier series of them afterwards, the first of which birthdays will be the one we call the day of death down here. But there is a better, grander birthday than that, which we may have every day—every hour that we turn away from ourselves to the living love that makes our love, and so are born again. And I think all these last birthdays will be summed up in one transcending birthday, far off it may be, but surely to come—the moment where we know in ourselves that we are one with God, are living by his life, and having neither thought nor wish but his—that is, desire nothing but what is perfectly lovely, and love everything in which there is anything to love.

I am greatly better. I thought as I lay in bed last Thursday night after a lecture that I should have to give up. My chest was so bad and I could not rest. The stove, which had been burning like a demon, and making us miserable with red-hot heat, for we could not control it much, went out, and the room grew cold. A great storm of wind, mixed with small snow, was roaring outside, and I felt it blowing on my face as I lay, and everything seemed against me. But what do you think? I grew easy and calm and restful, and fell fast asleep, and woke indescribably better, and have been better ever since. For there had come a change, and it was a great South wind that blew into the room and all about me. Like so many of God's messengers, it had *looked* fearful to my ignorance, when it was full of healing. Mamma, too, who had had such a frightful headache the day before, so bad that she had to let me go to the lecture alone, was so much better, that we got up and dressed in half an hour, put up our things, drank a cup of tea, and hurried off to the station for a five or six hours' journey here, and were nothing the worse, and in this house, belonging to the Mother-in-law of Mark Twain, we are revelling in *lapsury's luck*.

In a few days I will send you some more money. Mr. Davies will let you know when it arrives.

I have had your letter and those of all my darling chickens for my birthday [December 10th]. You must all take my thanks in a lump and divide it amongst you. I hope to write to you all before I return, but I have very little time....

Mamma has reminded me that it is your 21st birthday. I send you a little poem I wrote in the dark in one of our railway journeys a few days ago going to Buffalo.

Your loving
FATHER.

And then comes the poem:

TO MY GOOSE, ON HER TWNTY-FIRST BIRTHDAY.

Twenty-one, my darling child!
From thy girlhood all exiled!
Far behind, thy pattering feet
Tunes in memory's chambers beat,
But thy pondering childish face,
With its asking doubting grace,
Never more our eyes shall see—
Never to eternity.

Nay! nay! For, as atom oak
In acorn waits the sunny stroke,
And in oak that's broad and high,
Hid the little acorns lie,
Hidden in our holy child
Lay the woman, lonely isled;
And now, hidden in thy heart
Lies the child that still thou art;
And I have a subtle dream
That when things are what they seem,
Stubborn stuff no more a bar,
We may seem the thing we are.

And, when reasons I would find
In the cellars of my mind
For this wondrous father-love
To my first fair, wingless dove,
None I catch, to ease my thought,
Till in a sea I am afloat
Whose gentlest, softest ripples move
To the law of endless love.

So if I should die to-day—
Thou live to be old and gray,
And far outstrip me in the race
Toward the central splendour's grace,
Yet thou art eternally
Child to thy mother and to me.

GEORGE MACDONALD.

Obscure, I fear, my Goosie, but I am getting cold, and cannot do more with it now.

On Christmas Eve we travelled from Elmira to Jersey City. It was a terrible journey. We were constantly stopped by great snowdrifts in the cuttings. The stoves in the cars being dependent upon swift motion for their draught refused to burn. We were three hours late, half-frozen and famished. My father's asthma was bad and became alarming as we stepped out into the deep snow. No one met us, for we had crossed by the wrong ferry to a wrong depot, others being misled with us. Fortunately our hotel was not many yards away; but I thought we should never get him alive through the snow:

> ...He stood gasping in the street holding on to Greville's arm, tears rolling down his cheeks as if he would die then and there—and could not move for whole minutes, though it was only across the road he had to go to get to our inn. But the thermometer was five degrees below zero, and he said afterwards the air felt like strong acid cutting up his lungs. It was agony for him, and it was agony to see him...

But Richard Watson Gilder, having left his own Christmas party and gone to meet us at our right destination, had ascertained the blunder and came on to us. But by that time the remedial nitre-smoke had done its work.

In the morning our patient was well enough to proceed to the home of Gilder's mother at Newark, N.J., where we had rest and holiday. Mrs. Gilder was just the right, wholly lovable mother for the gay-hearted young poet,[1] already sub-Editor of *Scribner's*. He—poor man in pocket, rich in love and understanding—devoted himself with princely enthusiasm to us—even to the "lion's cub," who looks back upon him as the dearest of all his youthful friendships. But I cannot begin to write of him: there is no space. Let me, however, say that while America discovered George MacDonald as a new orator of strange gift in unselfconscious simplicity and valour, whom people almost worshipped for the uplift he gave them, Richard Watson Gilder seems

---

1 Author of *The New Day, The Poet and His Master, Reminiscences*.

to me first of the few among those fifty million warm-hearted souls who discovered the Man himself. And I affirm this, although in later years, when perhaps affairs and public life usurped too large a share of Gilder's rare genius—though, like R. L. Stevenson, nothing ever damped his youthful enthusiasms—he wrote in somewhat narrow criticism of my father's art. But his love never faltered.

Before proceeding, a word on the press notices will not be inopportune. For the most part the mere reporting of the lectures was full and accurate, better than English newspapers could afford. But the ridiculous fictions invented concerning my father's person, dress, and manners were the very opposite to a true picture of this man of prophetic passion and fearless honesty; and some press quotations will amuse people of literary taste as much in New York as in London. The Chicago reporter who wrote of "his diamond pins, jewelled shirt-studs, massive watch-chain, daintily shod feet and Christ-like countenance," could not once have looked at or listened with his heart to George MacDonald. In a New York religious paper we read of his "exquisitely white hands tapered and ringed with a signet, of which he makes the most eloquent use....The most engaging of lecturers, his language exact and copious comes from him with the dew of thought upon it, fresh as if just conceived. He walked into our hearts, etc., etc." Or again: "His gesture is, of all Englishmen we have ever listened to, the best, full of ease, grace and nature, while his hands and fingers are full of significance, pointed with meaning and dripping with emotion"! A few early notices declared that "he read execrably. We know of no public man more incapacitated for a platform speaker than Mr. MacDonald," etc., etc. But this last emanated, according to Redpath, from an opposition Lecture Bureau who had failed to get the agency for George MacDonald's tour.

It may seem to some almost like sacrilege that such foolish words should be set down, particularly if we have in our mind my mother's description of the reverent enthusiasm with which he was received everywhere by audiences keenly critical, save perhaps in certain unliterary places such as Cincinnati then was. Some must still be living who can recall his utter unselfconsciousness. Yet lest my citation of gushing stenographers seems bad in taste, I quote in addition two fairly average reports of my father's manner and style, one from a Boston weekly journal and the second from a New York religious paper.

There is something indescribable about the man which holds the audience till the last word. It is not eloquence or poetry, nor is there any straining for effect, but it is the man's soul that captivates. You love the man at once....

The deepest earnestness and reverence, mingled with great simplicity, and beautiful expressions alternated with homely ones, showed him a master of public speech to the mixed multitude. His voice is clear, musical, capable of much variety of expression, and adapted to all the changing moods of thought and feeling that marked the whole lecture. Looking his hearers full in the face, gesticulating with easy propriety, throwing his whole soul and body into his thought, and often adopting a familiar conversational manner, how could the people help listening to a man who thus brought his tribute to their hearts? It was a unique and characteristic effort, great in its very simplicity and originality, combined with exquisite touches of tenderness and keen searchings of human hearts.

CHAPTER III
NEW FRIENDS

LETTERS will best continue the story of my parents' fearsome and joyful experiences: and they need but little comment. One bit of happiness to my father is suggested by this note:

G.M.D. to Lilia S.M.D.

ORANGE, NEW JERSEY,
Jan. 3, 1873.

MY DEAR LILY,

This is a business letter. I am now sending home £400. When you hear from Mr. Davies that it has arrived, then write three cheques, as follows: Francis Sharman, Esq., £150; the Rt. Honble. William Cowper-Temple, £100; Stephen Ralli, Esq., £50; and enclose them with its accompanying letter, which I enclose to you, and which you may read to assure yourself that you understand the matter in hand.

This will leave £100 for your own use. I do not expect that to last you long; but my work has been so interrupted by my illness that I cannot well send you more just yet. I am not going to do much for a month. But the snow is now melting away under a steady thaw, and I hope to be better.

A happy new year to all my chickens. It *will* be a happy year when we come home to you....

Will you give five shillings all round to you girls, and half a crown to the boys each to buy something from Mama and me for the New Year. My love to you all.

Your
FATHER.

One of the most encouraging episodes was the visit to Orange Valley, N.J., where we made another lifelong friend, the Rev. George B. Bacon, D.D. [1]

---

[1] Son of the celebrated Leonard Bacon, and nephew of Delia Bacon who instituted the Shakespeare controversy and lost her reason over the cryptic system she discovered in the Plays and Sonnets.

GEORGE MACDONALD

Richard Watson Gilder to Lilia S.M.D.

Orange Valley, N.J., U.S.,
Jan. 5th '73.

My dear Miss MacDonald,

...I wish I could describe the situation so that in "your mind's eye" you could see it. The ground is covered with snow, and the woods, the hills, the valley, the village—are all one sheen of ice. For a rain has fallen, and then freezing, has encrusted every littlest twig, telegraph-wire, clothes-line, chimney, with crystal. A cloud has come down and rests along the top of the hills. It is Sunday afternoon—the day after your birthday. Your sweet mother has gone up with the parson and his family and Greville to [evening] communion service—and I remain here on guard—for the father is napping upstairs. In a minute I shall go up with a stick of wood and see if he wants anything beside. Does it seem possible to you that a three-thousand-miles-away man-boy—whom you have never seen—should delight in such little services to the man upstairs *almost* as much as you? Can you imagine that he feels as if he knew the whole ten at home, individually—and is as much interested in hearing about the breaking of the china-bowl that stood on the chest, the losing of the key, the making of Christmas presents—as the three wanderers are?

You might imagine that; but you can never know how the hearts of unknown multitudes are uplifted by the words that fall from the father's lips—you can never know how many here look upon him as a father indeed.

If the ten at home are a quarter as lovable as the three sent over to us—I should think you would have trouble in getting so much lovableness under one roof; and that you would have to build barns and sheds and spread yourselves a little....

I make bold to sign myself

Dick.

I remember well the walk home from the church. For a gentle wind had dispersed the mist, and the sun was setting in all possible glory; so that, though the trees' branches crashed noisily under the unaccustomed weight of ice, the little vitrified twigs not only danced, sparkled and flamed in ruddy prismatic colours, but tinkled bell-music in the breeze. It was fairyland.

NEW FRIENDS

Mrs G.M.D. to Mrs. Russell Gurney.

ORANGE VALLEY,
Jan. 6th.

DEAR, DEAR DOROTHEA,[1]
...Things are looking up and he is getting on bravely, though had you heard his feeble voice at the lecture and seen the night we had to be out in you would really wonder that he could have promised to preach. But if ever I wanted you to hear him when he was preaching it was yesterday morning— "One thing is needful." The lovely picture of those two [G.M.D. and George B. Bacon]—and the One Master—and the way he made you feel that he had sat at the Master's feet and that we were able to sit there—well....The service, too, was very sweet and simple. If it was not to be our dear, best beloved service—then it was the next best. Pretty chimes called the people from far—some come from such distances to this little church at the top of a hill looking over its charming valley.

When we went in, the organ was playing one of the loveliest voluntaries I ever heard. Pots of arum lilies were on the platform, and glasses of the loveliest flowers were arranged about the two desks. I felt as if I were in a grand cathedral for sound, and that the *Praise God* those lilies sang was one of the most beautiful thank-offerings I ever heard rise to Him. Then the people began to chant a Psalm; then another voluntary from the organ—during which most of the people knelt; then one verse of a hymn was sung, and then G.M.D. stood up and preached. It was a very blessed service altogether. The organist is the finest in America, and has been offered much money many times to go to New York to be organist; but he gives his services to this church and has for 14 years—Lowell Mason—you may have heard of him. I often have in England. He is a very devout man, and you could almost feel it in his playing. I tell you all this to show you that George is wonderfully better and that we are, after all our tempest-tossings, in a very delightful atmosphere....He [Dr. Bacon] says he saw us first at St. Peter's, Vere Street, 6 or 7 years ago and joined with us there in the communion service....I have been to-day to New York and taken lodgings for a fortnight, and I think we shall really enjoy "ganging our ain gait" a bit. There is a kind of ease in that we can't have any way else....

It was from no lack of proffered hospitality that the fortnight was spent in lodgings—indeed, my mother had to

---

[1] The name my mother gave Mrs. R. Gurney, she in response adopting Ruskin's name for my mother—"Mother-bird."

make a fight for it, and came near offending anxious friends. But they soon understood, and the young people, Dr. Holland's daughters, Miss Maria Oakey[1]—whom my mother almost, and her son quite worshipped as a very lovely specimen of American beauty and sweetness, who, with bewitching sedateness, hands folded in lap, would entrance us with droll and pathetic stories of Irish life; R. W. Gilder, Miss Helena De Kay, whom he married in 1874, and his sisters, flocked to our Bohemian *ménage*. The impromptu lunches, fetched from pastrycooks' and ice-cream stores, the English teas, were happy indeed; and not least in enjoyment of his brief respite was my father. We saw Edwin Booth play *Hamlet*, Sothern *Dundreary*, Wallack and Miss Cushman in *Guy Mannering*, heard Rubinstein's recitals, and the Jubilee Singers. We usually dined at a hotel on 4th Avenue, in the same block—never once at Delmonico's! Near at hand Miss Oakey and Miss De Kay shared a studio at the top of a Broadway house, greatly to their parents' dismay. But they painted delightfully; and I, being only a callow youth, with Richard W. Gilder ten years my senior, whom I chaperoned, were the only males ever admitted. The two ladies painted my portrait in oils—"The Music of the Future" it was called. Miss Oakey gave me a volume of Emerson's poems, which she would read aloud to me: it must have been the charm of her voice and blue eyes that made me oblivious to *The Sphinx's* mighty questionings. Once the Japanese screen was remiss in its duties, and the bright divinity, conscious only of her mirror on the wall, was recapturing her fallen locks and innocently ensnaring two adoring eyes—at least so the youth would rhapsodize in halting secret verse. Little lunches too were sometimes concocted in that studio on a gas ring by the ladies' white hands: Delmonico indeed!

---

1 Now the distinguished artist, Mrs. Maria Oakey Dewing.

NEW FRIENDS

Mrs G.M.D. to Mary and Lily M.D.

1256 Broadway, New York,
Jan. 10th, 1873.

My dearest Mary and Lily,

...We too give God thanks that He is helping our dears so graciously to bear their part of the burden—the burden of our separation. I have felt impatient, I fear, sometimes—it seems so long and so far—but when He helps us the impatience goes, and I know He does not need me to keep you all in the hollow of His hand, which is the only safety-place. In some ways it is surely true that absence brings nearer to each other. But precious to me will be the sight of the eyes when the time comes.

How dearly Lily must be doing for everybody. How beautifully kind you are being to her—all of you. Don't get weary of forbearing each other and *patiently* loving. I feel that Love wants patience more perhaps than anything—to keep it alive and flowering—to water its roots too. It won't grow without it. For even our dearest don't always fit into our notions of what we thought they would do, look or speak....

1256 Broadway,
January 17th.

Dearest dear Lily,

Such a budget of letters, the Christmas ones from our dear ten. We have had such a time of dissipation and rest that I have not been able to write and tell you of the different bits of pleasure we have had—but last night's was a pleasure too because it was Papa's work. He got through so well a 3-hours' journey [to Princetown, N.J., the Theological College] and lecture in the evening. At a Scotch Presbyterian minister's house—we stayed; very pleasant people, a beautiful white-headed man, with a very nice wife and some sweet Scotch lassie daughters....Papa gave such a glorious lecture on *Macbeth*. He is improving so wonderfully in dramatic power. Its lovely. He really sent us all into the cold shivers last night over the Ghost scene and the sleep walking scenes! He gets so eager and strong on what he has to say that it pours out with great flashes of eloquence that astonish even me. All the divines and the young men, 500 students, listened to him last night. Imagine Macbeth in a Presbyterian Church! This is quite the hot bed of the old Theology too, and yet they came out to hear him! And this old Dr. McCosh *asked Papa to preach!*

Callers—callers—callers—one man was a seal-skin hatter to whom I had sent for some caps for Father—my Christmas present to him. He does look such a dear old picture in it. I think I shall have him taken in it. It suits him, oh! ever so much better than those horrid felt things, and Greville in a beaver one I got him looks like an angel barbarian.... If I go on much longer with these headaches I shall have brains like a beaten steak when I come back. We are going again to-night to hear the nigger singers [Jubilee Singers]. They were slaves, and they sing songs of their religious experiences that used to comfort them in their bondage. I can't give you the least notion of what it was like. I never heard anything so droll and fervid, so touching, so pathetic, so true. Their voices are heavenly-ly musical. Their black and brown faces while they sing are ecstatic in earnestness. Papa sat with the tears rolling down his cheeks, and I was alternately and at the *same time* convulsed with laughter and choking tears—their chanting of the Lord's Prayer was equal to any cathedral music I ever heard. Yet how odd they looked!...

I remember, at our second hearing of them, how we remained in an ante-room after the audience had dispersed, and how, passing through the hall again, the gas lights were suddenly turned off, and how one of the singers we had been conversing with called out lustily, "All the same colour now!" My parents persuaded them to visit England, which they did, and very successfully, the following year.

One amusing incident deserves recording. Very soon after the lecturing tour had been determined upon—as early, I think, as February 1871—my father had had an invitation from the Burns Society in New York to be their guest at the annual dinner on the poet's birthday. He accepted, and asked whether these Scots in New York followed the custom set by the Caledonian Society in London—of appearing at the annual dinner in full dress kilt. The reply was that it was *de rigueur* for those who were Highlanders to wear their native costume. So my father of course took his kilt with him—even sword, dirk, and skian dubh. And to Delmonico's on January 24th he went in his MacDonald tartans—and was the only guest not in black swallow-tails and white tie! He was greeted with rapturous delight, and being the guest of the evening, had opportunity, in responding to the toast "Scottish Literature," for explanation and apology, and for vowing vengeance upon his most particular friend who had so misled him!

But the pilgrimage had to be resumed, and its progress involved the passage through valleys of humiliation and fighting with monsters not dreamed of by Bunyan.

Mrs G.M.D. to Mrs. Russell Gurney.

HENDRIE HOUSE,
WILLIAMSPORT, PENNS.,
Jan. 29th.

MY DEAREST DOROTHEA,

We are in the middle of another strange experience, nineteen hours on the cars [and only] 78 miles! I thought of you many times, and we said to each other "What would she say if she could see and hear?" We were at Elmira [entertained by Mrs Samuel L. Clemens] on Monday, and I decreed that we should stay here one night, and Harrisburg or Pittsburg the next. It was to be only 3 hours' journey. The snow was very thick—it snowed all the way. We went very slowly—there were no Palace cars to be had—an unusually rough set in the cars, with bad coughs [and wailing babies] and an unusual amount of tobacco being *exhausted* (forgive me, but *you* know how to pity us!). Within forty minutes of our goal, suddenly we were pulled up—and a man passing through the cars coolly said, "There's a wreck on in front—I guess we shall have to stay here all night!"...And there we were surely the whole night—our fires wouldn't burn, some of our lamps went out. When the line was cleared at last at half-past two we went on for two miles and suddenly were stopped again. The locomotive to the passenger train in advance of us had become frozen and waterless, and there we remained the whole of the cold, dark night with these wretched seats and wretcheder surroundings. We were not in motion again till nine in the morning, and it was nearly ten before we were let out of our pens at Williamsport. We shall now be obliged to spend another night on the cars before we reach Pittsburg...Can he stand all this?...He was very much better for the pleasant bit we had to ourselves in New York, and became quite vigorous—writing verse—correcting proofs—lecturing, visiting, and sleeping like a good-conscienced healthy man....

A further account of this infamous journey will be welcomed perhaps:

Mrs G.M.D. to L.S.M.D.

Pittsburg, Railway Hotel,
Thursday, January 30th, 1873.

A dirty, black, coalpitty sort of place with a black Manchester or Birmingham kind of sky.[1]

Dearest Lily,

...We left [Elmira] on Monday that we might make this long journey in easy stages, and we *have only* just arrived here....Carriages off the line detained us again, and in order to get there in time for the lecture we had to take a sleeping-car right on to here. At Harrisburg [we] hadn't time to get our luggage, which had Papa's coat and lecture books in it—and then the journey instead of being eleven hours was seventeen—and it was the *coldest night* known this winter! They couldn't keep the cars warm. Poor Papa—oh! if you had seen him at seven o'clock this morning you would all have cried. The conductor was very good to us, and had us into his little room where was a stove all to itself—he made up the stove and saved Papa's life—but not till he had been severely sick did his breathing get any better. When we arrived and came out into the cold air, it all came on again, and seemed as if he would suffocate. When we gave our names at the hotel the man, when I told him how ill Papa was, turned someone out of a room to give us a better one....*You'll* hear about *that* night when we come home, I guess. Greville is very eloquent upon it....

All our troubles have come in the last four journeys from freight trucks off the line—and there we have to wait and be thankful that we have not been telescoped by the next train after us, nor telescoped anybody else's train....I don't believe there is another man in the world that would go on so....

But the travelling was not always so unhappy, and often nothing but the fatigue to complain of. We three would play whist—either with dummy or a three-handed game invented by my father. Even merry we often were, and would write verses in competition on more ludicrous events, to send home to our dear ones. When a "palace-car" was available— and they were exceptional then—the comfort was great; and often a little compartment to ourselves was obtainable,

---

1 Richard W. Gilder had warned me that if we should see anyone around in Pittsburg with a clean face, it was because he wanted to pass incognito—more likely a criminal than a poet.

when possibly the windows might be practicable, and if we succeeded in opening one, with no complainings by conductor or passengers, as were invariable in an ordinary car. Often we had to stay at very bad hotels, the food being deplorable. Steaks were universal—veritable *pièces de resistance*. Their sole value was to the proprietor; for their defiance even of the knife made it possible to present the same slabs of leather at breakfast, dinner and supper again and again, until, possibly because of their damage to the cutlery, they were discarded to pave the side-walks. My mother liked the tomatoes, cranberries, and green corn on which she often dined; but my father could digest none of such things, and, but for the fact that good milk and eggs were always to be had, would have often done ill. If I ate the steaks, it was to spite the manager.

In the middle of February we visited Cincinnati, where my father had second cousins. My mother's account of these is good reading. The lectures, however, were not well received. But what could we expect when the population was chiefly pigs, and even driving a buggy through the snorting throngs that filled roadway and side-walks everywhere, scarcely roused them? Cincinnati was then known as Porkopolis.

Mrs G.M.D. to her Daughters.
En route from CINCINNATI, TO DELAWARE, OHIO.
Monday, Feb. 15th.

The days go, dears, but I get no letters and I grow sadly impatient. We have visited our relatives at Cincinnati. If variety, kindness and hospitality are charming, it certainly was a charming visit....Dr. Spence, our host, Papa's second cousin (his mother and Papa's father were first cousins) and his brother, James Spence, are tobacco manufacturers....They have two grown-up sons and three daughters. The second son, Charley, is 19. He has an organ in his bedroom, and plays the organ at the church they go to....It was a lesson to me that one cannot judge by looks, for I had set him down as a dull, over-grown lad in my mind; and after dinner I heard lovely church music that melted my soul into praise, mingled with longings for my home ones, and I discovered those sounds came from the raw-looking bear that had just left the room, taking Greville with him... On Sunday we went to dine with the other brother James. His house, his wife, his children and his grounds are pictures. I thought her the oddest woman we had met, but she fascinated me....She has an indescribable grace—wild kind of grace and taste—about her that was quite new to us. She is very pretty—30 years old she told us. She loves flowers and birds and fishes in such a human loving wild sort of way.[1] ....There's no sign of much money—the least grand house I've seen, but such an air of grace and sweetness about it. She is very blunt in her speech, but with a half comic, half shy and (if Maurice will let me have three halves) —half sweet look and tone. Her stories about birds and creatures and the pretty thoughts she has got from them were so fresh. Then her two little girls are the only quiet children I think that we have seen, sweet, bright, confiding, graceful, obedient children, and their dress was ravishing. Their black *Mammy* was quite part of the household, and we were introduced to her as such. It is the *only* house where we have seen people happily helped....

The lectures were not a success numerically considered, and the papers were more disagreeable than anywhere, I think....

Thence we proceeded to Delaware and Dayton, Ohio, and had fresh trials to face, though my parents accepted them with stoic endurance.

DELAWARE.

...At other towns before, we have nearly always been invited: no one but a feeble youth has met us here, and we are in a third or fourth-rate hotel. The chamber-towels are precisely like our knife-cloths at home, one for Papa and one for me. Unruly infants at table and idiotic-looking damsels staring their eyes out of their sockets at us, as if we had just escaped from Barnum's menageries. Did you hear all his show was burned up? The poor elephants, lions, two camels, roasted to death.

My loves—my loves—we think of you always and much. How we long to be back I think none of you can tell....

DAYTON, OHIO.
Sunday, Feb. 12, 1873.
2.30 p.m.

MY DEARS,

...But such journeys these are for weariness and length, and now in these days of snow there's always a truck or trucks or carriages off the line ahead. This is the fourth time within eight days that this has hindered us.

---

[1] She had a big aquarium, and the gold fish, I remember, would all come wagging their jaws close up against the glass when she sang to them!

I am on the sofa after having scoured myself and garments from the thick black of Pittsburg and cars. Pittsburg for blackness and darkness beats Manchester hollow. We left it yesterday morning at nine o'clock and were travelling all day—except when we were stopping. It was 12.30 before a ramshackle omnibus ejected us into this hotel—glad enough to escape from the coarseness and oaths of the men in the car, not to mention over again that daily trial to our commonest feelings of cleanliness and the fitness of things—their habit of ejecting streams of tobacco-juice all round you. The longer the journey the harder they spit; and the demon-like noises that precede the operation are quite as trying as the sight of the brown puddles all across the floor when you have to walk down the car and take your seat.[1] Don't we need pity?...

Monday. I didn't get on with my letter yesterday—I was so weak and faint all day; sometimes I tremble for fear that I shall give way....But I think it was only weakness....Papa is much better to-day. How much of recovery he does for himself in sleep....

A birthday letter follows. It is a good answer to those people who do not see how miraculous a mother's love is and that the number of her children cannot lessen her love for each individually; that it is a spring of living water, a grain of mustard seed. The letter too has this note of pathos: Maurice's god-father had died less than a year before, and my mother almost looked upon god-parentage as spiritually creative. He was nine years old now. He lived but six more, and was, next to our eldest sister, the most richly endowed of the family. Little did his mother dream how soon he would follow his god-father.

Mrs G.M.D. to Maurice M.D.

Altoona, Pennsylvania,
Feb. 16*th*, 1873.

My dearest Maurice,

I was very sorry I couldn't write to you on the 7th of February, my darling, precious little son—you are not forgotten by your Father and Mother...People that love each other can't be very far off each other, though

---

1   In visiting the States ten years later I saw nothing of these curious customs; and when I was last there in 1898, friends could hardly believe I had witnessed such. Indeed, the progress was as wonderful in provincial cities as in the great centres. Almost the only thing that had not changed was the American Heart and its amazing hospitality.

a great big sea comes in between the bodies of them. Love joins us, doesn't it, dear boy? When you are thinking about me you have got me, and when I think about you I know you are mine. I know God gave you to me and so you are mine; and I can think of your dear face and the loving little kiss and the loving little way you have of doing things for me; that brings you quite close to my mind, and then my heart holds you very tight when I get hold of you so!...But all your life God will be nearer to you than I can ever be, and He can help you more than Papa or I ever can. You are more His even than mine. We may often mistake you, or be so far away from you that we cannot look at you and speak to you just the minute you want something; but God the Great Father will never misunderstand you and He is always near you and helps every time you call to Him. Even when you only wish you could speak to Him, He will help you to speak—to Him. And every time you want to do what is right, He is *in* you making you want it. So, dear darling Boy, you must take care not to send Him away, but ask Him to come into you more and more....

The people that come to speak to Papa all say the same thing almost, in all the different cities hundreds of miles away from each other. They all say "that he seems like an old friend to them," or that they have known him so long and have spent so many pleasant hours with him; or often they say they have learnt so much from him that they want to "clasp him by the hand."...On Friday we went to Indiana, a small city, but it has a very large and handsome Court House, where the judges sit. When we passed this handsome building in the morning there was a large blue banner hanging out, and on it in silver letters I saw, "*George MacDonald, England. Eminent Scotch Orator. Subject, Robert Burns.*" Yet at such a rich place no one asked us to tea or dinner and we had to go to the sort of Inn that you couldn't help fancying all night that robbers might be in the next room; and the master of the Inn looked as if he might be the greatest villain of all. I thought Robert would have made up lots of robber and murder stories out of that horrid, dirty house and dark passages....One gentleman we met invited us to stay at Altoona before the next lecture; so we would not stay an hour more than we need in *that* hole. We got up and had our breakfast and walked down to the station. The only light we had was the moon which shone very brightly on the new fallen snow—and how it sparkled! The reflection of the moon on the fresh snow gemmed all the road with crystals. You have had some snow, have you not, lately? But I scarcely think you have had to walk out by moonlight in it....We got to a junction at 8.30, where there was only a shed, and they told us we must wait there till 11.30—such a wretched place! and snow still thick on the ground. But we sent Greville (our courier you know) to go and look if there was anything of a town: he came back in about five minutes and said there was a little hotel near. Oh, Maurice, I *was* so glad! For Papa had begun to be asthmatic, and though there was a stove in the shed all the poor men and rough farmers' boys were round it and spitting out their tobacco juice all round it. Gladly we followed Greville, and in three minutes we went into the daintiest toylike hotel—Glen Hotel, it was called—I ever saw. A man took us into a pretty, little parlour with Brussels carpet and a couch and a stove fire and a Bible and a hymn-book and *Pilgrim's Progress* and a volume of sermons. He soon made it nice and bright, and said we should soon have some breakfast. So though we had had a nasty breakfast at 5.30 at Indiana, we were quite ready for the nicest breakfast we had had for many days at 8.30. The man's wife cooked it and his little son—Ronald's age, I should think—waited on us. Papa really enjoyed the meal of eggs and tea and hot cakes and nice rolls and cheese and butter and milk. The country about was so lovely with hills and river and trees that I daresay people go there in the summer....We had nearly three hours very comfortable there. Papa and I slept, Greville read us to sleep—not the sermons but a story of Miss Thackeray's. When we came away the landlord shook hands with us. He had been so kind and charged so little....

Your own
MOTHER.

I am glad to hear you have had daisies already in your grass. They sell them sometimes in pots here.

Reverting for a moment to the Burns dinner in New York and linking it in my mind with my young brothers, I recall a passage in my brother Ronald, the playwright and novelist's mention of the joy we all took in seeing our father in his kilt:

To childish eyes—perhaps to others—George MacDonald was a very splendid sight in full Highland costume; and carried himself in it, upon his rare occasions, with the port that will make the best of a good thing. And yet, whether it were the kilt at a familiar festivity, a new jewel, or some specially gorgeous smoking-jacket or cap, his was always the pleasant pride of perennial childhood; it was, "Please look at my new shoes," rather than, "Look at me because my shoes are new."[1]

---

1 *From a Northern Window*, p. 78.

CHAPTER IV

FAREWELL

THE duration of the tour was extended to compensate the disappointments incurred through illness; but the local lecture bureaus sometimes refused to pay the full fee on the score of the lecturer having broken his engagement. Chicago, St. Louis, Buffalo, Detriot, Ann Arbor had yet to be visited, besides Canada. On the whole, he grew fitter for his work in spite of the long journeys, the irregular feeding and the great receptions. I think my mother now suffered more, though, whenever her husband began to flag, she always got the better of her excruciating headaches and fatigue. But some rest and recreation were found at Mrs. Cunningham's.

Mrs G.M.D. to her Children.

MILTON, MASS.,
March 5th, 1873.

DEAREST ONES,

This is the second morning in this paradise of peace and goodness. Father is certainly better for the rest and quiet to work in, for he has the most enchanting room for writing with books all round him, and odours of delicious flowers, and to-day sunshine enough to content anyone's heart. The snow is still as thick and glittering as ever, though the sun is so hot and bright. Yesterday Mrs. Cunningham drove Greville and me out in the wee-est little sleigh and, turning a curve, over we went on to a high bank of snow—I first, and we were so fastened in that there we lay. I could not move, and if the horse had persisted in going on, my arm would have been torn out of the socket; but he was very good and only dragged us a very few steps. Greville extricated himself, and went to the horse's head and we were soon picked out of the snow; and shaking it off with our laughter, we were soon packed in again and went smoothly enough for the rest of the way....

March 8th, being their twenty-second wedding-day, brought this letter:

Richard W. Gilder to Mr. and Mrs. G.M.D.

EDITORIAL ROOMS OF *Scribner's Monthly,*
March 8th, 1873.

DEAR MOMMY AND PAPA,

Here's your good health, and your family—and may they all live long and prosper! including the twelfth infant [himself]. We all drank to you at Dr. Holland's this wedding-day morning amid the clink of goblets (of water) and crinkle of buck-wheat cakes.

I've curdled and groaned and wept over *The Haunted House*; and now we shall see what effect it has upon the printer.

"Outside, forsaken, in the dim
Phantom-haunted chaos grim
He stands with the deed going on in him!"

is the stunningest thing I can think of. It twists one's heart up into hard knots and sends the blood into one's boots with a bound. G. MacD. has almost out-done himself this time!...I am very fond of you, so are a great many thousand other people—but not so much.

For ever and a day thine,
R. WATSON GILDER, ALIAS THE BOY DICK.

The poem *The Haunted House*[1] appeared in *Scribner's*. It was inspired by a picture of Thomas Moran, who had leaped into instant fame because of his wonderful pictures of the Yellowstone Country—of which he had already given my father some sketches.

The second week in March we visited in Boston Mrs. Payne, sister of Mrs. Oliver Wendell Holmes. Like everyone else, it seemed as if she could not do enough for our comfort.

---

1 *Poetical Works*, vol. ii, p. 203. Of this poem my brother Ronald writes thus: "For the ghastliness of initial terror Poe might have run Thomas Moran's interpreter close—perhaps equalled him. But hardly, I think, could even Poe, in this the mere mechanism of George MacDonald's idea, have excelled him; for the lurking truth of the horror's spiritual source would have slipped between Poe's fingers; or, perceived, would have been drowned in 'damnable iteration,'" (*From a Northern Window*, p. 111.)

Mrs G.M.D. to her Daughter Mary.

BOSTON,
March 16.

DEAREST MY OWN MARY,

...Oh, my darlings, I can hardly bear to think about you all, it sets me longing so painfully. I am getting so disagreeable, so sick of talk and people, and I am afraid I have been very cross to-day. I am very thankful to God for one thing—that I am nearly sure there is not one of my daughters but would behave better than I do to people I can't like. That is a comfort and a thing they have to thank their earthly father for; primarily, of course, that the Heavenly Father gave them *such* an earthly one. Papa is better, he lectures splendidly....

Then we saw a new actress, Mlle Jananschek, with wonderful versatility, play the dual rôle of Lady Dedlock and Hortense in a play called *Chesney Wold*, adapted from *Bleak House*. On another night she played Lady Macbeth so indifferently that it set my parents thinking: and soon, partly also because of my father's new discovered dramatic power in his readings of *Macbeth*, they had a new idea for the development of Lilia's genius.

G.M.D. to his Daughter Lilia.

BOSTON, U.S.A.,
March 20th, 1873.

...Seriously I am inclined to try how it feels to be a murderer. I find I can learn Macbeth's part very easily for me, and before we come home expect to be complete in it, as far as the words go. Whether I can act it is another thing, but if you will be Lady Macbeth I will try. What made me think of it, and Mamma too—was seeing the latter done pretty well and the former very ludicrously the other night....

From Boston, Redpath and Fall danced their bear to New York again. Nor were we sorry, for it meant Dick Gilder, Maria Oakey, George B. Bacon and his wife and Dr. Holland's daughters.

Thence, *en route* for Chicago, my mother writes about our home-coming and the house-cleaning at The Retreat, insisting upon my sisters getting every possible help and good regular meals:

FAREWELL

Mrs G.M.D. to Mary J.M.D.

WYOMING VALLEY HOTEL,
WILKESBARRE, PA.,
March 25th.

...We hope to spend Sunday at Niagara. Won't that be grand? Tell my Ronald boy I am always seeing books I want to buy him—but the bags of gold have failed us, and our little dreams have waked up into gray morning realities. Still a great many beautiful things and thoughts and loves have come to us here, and I think on the whole the father will go back to you reinvigorated—though *not to rest.* Oh! I'm such a bad traveller, I wish I were strong. But here followeth a list for the present future.... Friday, Buffalo —no lecture till Niagara either Saty. Or Sunday. Monday, Hamilton, Canada—shall like to be in our own dominions. Tues., April 1st, Toronto, Can. Wed., Ann Arbor, Mich.—where the Spences' mother lives. Friday, Chicago, Ill., about 900 miles from New York....April 23rd, Montreal; April 26, Boston! Then to New York, and Hurray! a few more lectures and on the 24th May the torture of the sea, and then my Heaven if we get to our Haven. So no more just now, dear Molly....

We were splendidly entertained at Chicago by the Rev. Robert Laird Collier, a Unitarian well known a few years later in this country as a fearless and eloquent preacher. He would talk to me like an intellectual equal, and told me his creed and his doctrine for many years had been just *Robert Falconer*—"Yes, sir, no more, no less." My father, finding himself in much sympathy with American as with English Unitarians, preached for him. I remember how in Boston, James T. Fields once arranged for a special meeting of him and Dr. Bellows, the greatest Unitarian preacher in the States, so that they should thrash out their divergences. At the end of it, my father, avowing himself confirmed more strongly than ever, if this were possible, in his Trinitarian faith, felt at the same time bound to admit that the difference between his own and Dr. Bellow's creed could hardly be defined.

"Oh, pshaw!" exclaimed Mr. Fields, as if in annoyance at the result, though himself a Unitarian. "But all *I* can add is 'Bellows be....blowed!'"

We cannot do without my mother's long and lovely letter from Chicago; for again she gives us sense of her longing for home, besides describing Niagara and our tremendous host.

> *Mrs. G.M.D. to Lilia S.M.D.*
>
> CHICAGO, 847, INDIANA AVENUE,
> *Sunday, April 6th, 1873.*

DEAREST MY DEAR LILY,

Here we are ever so many miles further away from you and yet nearer in time, and nearer and dearer in soul as we get older and want more of each other....Sometimes I break down a little, and then your and the others' dear letters build me up again. I had a feast yesterday in yours... you toiling away like a mother bee to send your sisters to their enjoyments and profit, you darling love. You are all darling loves—as I think you all round, I feel so rejoicing and happy. I don't know how to keep my cup from running over.

No, I don't keep it—its always running over and filling up faster than ever—like those tremendous outpourings of those big lakes down into the Niagara rapids and basins which we saw last Sunday. It is almost unbelievable that it is only a week since we tramped about in the snow and ice on to Goat Island up the tower—on to the brink of those great Falls; and now we are so oppressed with heat—obliged to leave off clothing and sleep with our window wide open!...Papa lectured during a tremendous thunderstorm....I hope to-morrow will be finer for *R. Burns*....To-morrow's will be the fortieth lecture I have heard on that poor but talented genius! The long and short of which is that "he did as well as he could, but he might have done better"—like the French master's verdict on his scholars leaving school....

Niagara was our greatest and only treat of the kind since we came. The standing on the top of that Terrapin Tower and feeling borne up and away from everything and seeing those mighty waves rolling and dashing beneath us, brought the idea of infinity and majesty more *intent* upon me than anything in my life—anything material, I mean, that ever I saw. I felt as if I might be, and behold yet not be, of the earth or on it. I imagine that I knew more certainly then than ever before what it would be to have a spiritual body and belong to Creation—not merely to this little earth-bit of it....

We are in the house of a Unitarian clergyman. This the parsonage is a very fine house. He is a most interesting man. He just adores your father and Frederick Robertson and Tennyson and M. Arnold....He is a widower, has four children, two boys, two girls—a little precious, sweet baby of two years old. His wife died only in September last and must have been a lovely woman. He talks of her as easily as if she were only in the country—and believes he "has her around always." He *knows* she is here. He is immensely enthusiastic, but the most curious man altogether that we have met;...and yet the good and earnest and spiritually minded are all alike here—as they are all the world over....

I cannot refrain from giving here a letter from R. W. Gilder: it shows how he stood to us. My mother would often send him one of the home letters.

April 15th, '73.

MY DEAR MOMMY,

How glad I was to get your, and father's and the children's letters. How much more interesting these overseas letters are than most novels—to me. It is like reading a continuation of one of G.M.D.'s books—written by the characters themselves....

I enjoyed these home letters more than I can tell you—every word and line. You can have no idea what a thing to me it is—to say that just in a little home-near ramble you walk past the "Castle walls" [Hastings Castle]. O my—when can I do that? Some time in the flesh I hope—and in the intoxication of youth. But if life goes well with me—I shall never be old, no matter what the birthdays say!...Just put Dick in some of your off-hand little heaven-going petitions and continue always to love him....Amen....

But an incident more notable even than Chicago and Niagara was the visit to the little University town of Ann Arbor, its country around still glorious with fruit-blossoms, its city wonderful in the splendour of its residences and gardens, considering its small population, then barely 10,000. We were entertained by the Rev.—Fisk, the son-in-law of old Mrs. Spence, who was first cousin of my grandfather MacDonald, and mother of our Spence relatives in Cincinnati.[1] It was delightful to see her and my father talking over old times and places together. She told him many things about his family he had not known.

Perhaps this fresh touch with his boyhood, and the re-memorizing of his father's love, had something to do with

---

1 Her mother was sister to Isobel Robertson, Mrs. C. E. MacDonald.

his preaching there; for my mother writes of its extraordinary eloquence and how nearly all the churches were closed so that ministers and people might hear him.

Mrs. G.M.D. to Lilia S.M.D.

ANN ARBOR,
Sunday morning, April 19th, 1873.

DEAREST LILY,

We came here on Thursday. Your dear letter came in like an unexpected jewel among beach stones....I was undressed. The eldest son came to our door with it. Father and I read it in bed together holding a candle.... The old lady is a very sweet old lady, and she is very kind to me....

After service, Sunday night. Father has been preaching so divinely, so simply, so powerfully. All the other places in the town, except the Episcopalians, shut their churches that their ministers and their congregations might have the opportunity of hearing him. If ever, dear, he was truly eloquent, it was to-night; if ever he was speaking the truth as if by the power of the Spirit within him, it was to-night. I hung on every word as an utterance from the voice of the Father speaking through him....The effect was tremendous, the listening was silence itself. He was so overcome afterwards that I was afraid for him—and he has to lecture to-morrow. So I went out and got a coat to put on before he left the church—he was in such a heat. Then I smuggled him into the vestry and got Mr. Duffield to lock the door and prevent people from coming in; for I saw signs of many intending to come in and have a "good time." Mr. D. is the minister....He is very energetic, very clever....Greville heard him preach this morning, and liked him very much indeed. I told him this in as inoffensive a way as I could. He seemed delighted and said, "Well, I guess it was about as good as I'd got. I've had that sermon melted down and soaked in pickle for a great while, and it was bound to come out to somebody, and so it came out this morning." It seemed so strange to me to be talking like that just after the grand, heart-searching, soul-purifying words we had been hearing. I wondered he could dare speak at all just then!—There seemed such a Presence there—and after such a prayer as we had after the sermon! It was a more intense prayer than any I ever heard....He's in bed now—the dear saint, the preacher, the Man of God....I begin to think he ought to manage to preach always—but how? God knows best. I'm sure we don't—he or I. How people do love him, Lily! It's wonderful and yet it's not, either—when they tell you what his writing has done for them....

The remaining facts of the lecturing tour can be told in very few words. A visit to Toronto and Montreal and a few more lectures in Massachusetts and Vermont, and then a farewell visit to Boston, with a benefit matinée lecture. It was then that a dinner party came, ineffaceable in my memory. For Emerson and Oliver Wendell Holmes, Sothern, the actor, and Dr. Bellows were among the guests to bid farewell to my father, with the brilliant James T. Fields for host. Yet not the talk of wisdom and wit, nor the inimitable stories of our host, not the conjuring of the popular actor with corks and forks, wineglasses and napkins, dominate the recollection, but rather the beautiful face and exalted look of the New England Prophet, and the charm with which the Autocrat of the Breakfast-table singled out the still shy youth for conversation.

A most generous and understanding thing was done at that time by friends in Boston. Inaugurated by Mrs. Whitney, author of the then celebrated *Gayworthys*, they presented what they called a "Copyright Testimonial" to my father, raising over $1500 in recognition, by a few among the tens of thousands indebted to him, of the fact that his books in America had brought him practically no remuneration. I do not think any of the piratical publishers contributed to the fund; but at least two items were of $500 each.

À propos of international copyright, I may incidentally quote from a letter of Mark Twain's to my father nine years afterwards. The two writers were very intimate and had discussed co-operation in a novel together, so as to secure copyright on both sides of the Atlantic. But there were many difficulties in the way—not chiefly those of motive and style. So deeply religious a man, however, was the great humourist that his father-in-law, Mr. Langdon, had been urgent that he should write a Life of Christ, believing that his keen observation and knowledge of men, coupled with his real religious fervour, would startle many into a truer fidelity:

ELMIRA, N.Y.,
Sept. 19/82

DEAR MR. MACDONALD,

I'll send you the book, with name in it, sure, as soon as it issues from the press, which will not be before the Spring....Since I may choose, I will take the *Back of the North Wind* in return, for our children's sake; they have read and re-read their own copy so many times that it looks as if it had been through the wars.

I thank you ever so much for remembering me in the agency matter, though it comes a year too late. Osgood, in Boston,[1] and Chatto in London, take care of all my literary business now in America, England and the Continent, and I am having a delightful rest in consequence. A book of mine used to pay me nothing in England—pays me two to three thousand pounds now. Osgood sells my occasional magazine rubbish at figures which make me blush, they are so atrocious. I perceive, now, after all these wasted years, that an author ought always to be connected with a highwayman.

Yours sincerely,
S.L. CLEMENS.

Here I must also mention a letter of Mark Twain to W. D. Howells in 1899:

All these things might move and interest one. But how desperately more I have been moved to-night by the thought of a little old copy in the nursery of *At the Back of the North Wind*. Oh, what happy days they were when that book was read, and how Susy [died in 1896] loved it!....Death is so kind, benignant, to whom he loves, but he goes by us others and will not look our way.[2]

Our last days in New York were spent at Dr. J. G. Holland's house on Park Avenue. Numbers of farewell dinners and receptions had to be faced and enjoyed. One incident has been already referred to, but now has peculiar interest in view of my mother's home-letter from Ann Arbor, in which, speaking of my father's preaching— "I hung on every word as an utterance from the voice of the Father through

---

1 The firm is now Messrs. Houghton, Mifflin & Co.
2 *Mark Twain*. A Biography by Albert Bigelow Paine, 1912, vol. ii, p. 1074.

FAREWELL

him"—she adds, "I begin to think he ought to manage to preach always—but how?" A deputation of deacons from a church on Fifth Avenue waited upon my father to ascertain whether he would accept its pastorate at a stipend of $20,000 per annum. As already related, my father declined the offer without discussion or delay.[1]

In May some fifty of the more prominent literary friends invited him, in token of public gratitude,[2] to give a farewell lecture. The subject asked for was *Hamlet*, the place chosen was the huge Association Hall, and the lecturer was to receive the gross proceeds. May 19th was the day fixed. Every corner was packed, though, to quote *The Tribune*: "If everyone in New York who had been made better and gentler by his teachings had gone to this lecture, no house ever built would have held them." William Cullen Bryant was in the chair, supported by Dr. J. G. Holland, R. W. Gilder, Mark Twain, Charles Dudley Warner, Bret Harte, Whitelaw Reid, George W. Curtis, Dr. Abram Coles, Thomas Moran; and Dr. Henry Bellows delivered to the lecturer the farewell greetings of his American friends. My father's concluding words were these:

> For the kindness I have received in America I am very grateful. We came loving you, and knowing that we should love you yet more; and instead of being disappointed, our hearts are larger and fuller for the love of so many more friends than we had before. If word of mine could be of any value, the love between the countries will surely be at least a little strengthened by your goodness, which, if only in honesty, but yet more in happiness, we are compelled to carry back with us. Your big hearts, huge

---

1   *Vide antea*, p. 340. I well remember the incident, seeing that, had the offer been accepted, I should have been enabled, so I thought, to go to Oxford.
2   Here is an instance of private gratitude. A few days before sailing a young Boston gentleman, unknown to him, writes thus: "I would like to hear your voice more, and in order to win the right to hear it in the order of Nature, I hereby offer to serve you in any manual employment which a man can do who has been so idly educated that he has been qualified for no kind of work. I should pay my passage and should expect just the position of a hired servant. This offer will hold good some while." I do not know what reply my father sent; but of course he could not accept the offer.

in hospitality and welcome, have been very tender with me and mine—so patient with my failures and shortcomings. And as you and I, whate'er befall, will never find misunderstanding possible, so may it be with our fellow countrymen, yours and mine. Never let us misunderstand each other, whatever we do. Let there be no lies between us. Let us know that, whatever vain rumours of dislike and annoyance and ill-natured criticism come to us, they arise only among the triflers on both sides; let us know that the thinking and honest men of both sides are just like each other, that they care for each other and believe in each other....I trust and hope that we in England and you in America, who have the same blood, and the same language, and the same literature, the same Shakespeare, not to speak of the same Bible, will only be the better friends for everything that compels us to explain what we mean to each other.

Nothing need be said of the farewells. There was real grief too—and much on our side, though there was unspeakable joy ahead for those two parents. Richard Watson Gilder, no worshipper of wealth or the spread wings of the mighty Eagle, was to us an epitome of the United States. So I give two letters he wrote when the parting was over—the longer, because I think his and Helena de Kay's grandchildren will love it; and the other because George MacDonald's grandchildren will be made happy in reading such true words of their wonderful grandmother.

From R. W. Gilder to Mr. and Mrs. G.M.D.

NEWARK, N.J., U.S.,
May 25th, '73.

DEAR SOULS,

My heart is so full that I can hardly say anything at all—this day. Early in the morning, before I was out of bed Ma and Jean came into my room to see the little box opened, and there were your two dear, blessed faces. O that was too much—and my garnet ring and my purse—and the ever living, lovely memory of you three people. "Words are poor things" indeed. How can I ever tell you what you have been to me—but you shall see it in the life of me, where, with other true and blessed things, it shall quicken some worthy flower and fruit, I trust. Now really I do feel as if you had let me creep into your hearts and curl up in a little corner— your *hearts*—I say, but it is all one heart. I cannot think of you two as separate—I don't know which I am writing to—rather I am writing to the One that is both....O, you who only have my secret in keeping—how I love you for that too—love you for loving Her. It is not love's blindness—or yet love's clear vision merely with me, in that matter. *Every one who knows her well—stands in a sort of loving awe of her—it is a cathedral indeed "full of a most lovely light."*...

From R. W. Gilder to Lilia S.M.D.

Scribner's
654 Broadway, N. York, U.S.,
June 6th, '73.

My dear Miss Lily,

As I consider your mother and father and Greville three very full and interesting letters from *me* to the rest of the family, I rather feel as if *you* owed *me* a letter, instead of my owing you. But I must tell you how very glad I was to get that nice family letter from you—while your parents were still here. I wish you could find time, in little intervals of your home happiness, or in little episodes of it, to keep me informed as to the general tenor of your lives. I think no English friend or relations can be much more interested than your American brother in all that happens to the entire thirteen of you....Tell the mother that—but I will write to her myself. *You don't know how she carried all hearts by storm here! We expected that of the father—but the mother took America by surprise,* you see.

Very truly and brotherly yours,
R. Watson Gilder.

BOOK IX
THE VALLEY OF THE SHADOW

FAMILY OF GEORGE AND LOUISA MACDONALD, WITH E. R. HUGHES, 1876

CHAPTER I
PALAZZO CATTANEO

SO the home-life was resumed. To have read of the parents' hunger for their children during those long months, to have witnessed the reading of their letters behind drawn curtains, one candle held between, are enough to picture the home-coming, the shouting and dancing of the ten, the embraces that could scarce ever again let go eldest or youngest.

But harder partings than the wide ocean's lay in store for George and Louisa MacDonald.

The years 1873 and 1874 were amongst the happiest spent at The Retreat. *Malcolm* gave news of the mental strength its writer regained from the rest to his pen and the temporary alleviation of his debts. That these did weigh sorely upon him one cannot doubt. As the wounded flesh still must suffer, however sure the patient's belief that healing will come, so must the honest mind ache with obligations overdue, however strong the faith that the morrow will take thought for yesterday even before itself.

Visits of American friends brought new delights, though the house was much put to it to match trans-Atlantic hospitalities. Indeed, it could not attempt such lavish entertaining if only because my father dared not set work aside and devote himself to his guests as is done in Canada and the States. Laird Collier and his two sons; Mrs. Whitney with her deaf husband and her daughter; Mark Twain; Mary

Mapes Dodge, author of *The Silver Skates*, with her son; and Antoinette Sterling, attended by her lover and future husband, paid us longer or shorter, single or frequent, visits.¹

In the autumn of 1873 my father and mother with two sisters again visited Cullen and Huntly, chiefly in reference to the needs of *Malcolm*, a story whose matchless characterization of the piper, Miss Horn, Barbara Catanach, Phemy Mair, and the fisher-lad heir to the marquisate, sets it among his best Scotch novels. The Portlossie of that book is Cullen, and the original of the blind piper, though the idea came from that ancestor who escaped from Culloden, was, I am advised, a certain Farquhar McGillanders.

Then came a great happiness—the engagement of Mary Josephine to Edward R. Hughes, a young artist, rapidly acquiring renown for the purity of his ideals and his technical excellence. Nephew to our friend Arthur Hughes, he was "an Apollo in looks," people said, affectionate, industrious and sensitive to all fine influences. My mother was hardly less happy over it than her child.

The following winter was passed chiefly at Halloway House, though it was given up in 1875. That year Mary contracted scarlet fever, and, from having been the most muscular of the family—Lewis Carroll's brother, Wilfred Dodgson, who taught her to box, used to call her the "Kensington Chicken"—she now rapidly lost weight, and her lungs became affected. My father had been thinking of another lecturing tour in the States, but this illness would have made it impossible for my mother to go, and he could not go alone.

So convinced were my parents now that the riverside home did not suit my father and must be blamed for my sister's illness, that they decided to leave it. My father had

---

1 There was another whom we had not met in the States. He avowed devotion to the negro cause, brought an uneducated coloured wife with him, and, in return for unbounded hospitality and money, as well as literary help, swindled and insulted my father.

been ill there more or less all through the winter of 1874-5, although his energy was amazing.[1] Besides *Malcolm*, published in 1875; *Gutta Percha Willie: the Working Genius*, which had run through the final year of *Good Words for the Young*, appeared in book-form in 1873; this same year *St. George and St. Michael*, illustrated by Sydney P. Hall, was running through the *Graphic*; and *The Wise Woman: a Parable*, appeared the same year, simultaneously in the States under the title of *The Double Story*.[2]

In 1874 also was published *England's Antiphon*, illustrated by Arthur Hughes. It traces "the course of our religious poetry—the cream of a people's thought—from an early period of our literary history."

In the spring of 1875 the old farmhouse of Great Tangley Manor, between Guildford and Wonersh, was taken furnished for six months. It was a great delight to all of us, my father rejoicing in the fact that "it was built when Shakespeare was a boy—in 1582—of great oak beams within and without." But the parents were not there together very often, as Mary had to be at the sea and was not mending. My father now had a horse of his own to ride—the gift of my mother, who since her father died had had a small income of her own. His own experience had long convinced him that "there is nothing so good for the inside of a man as the outside of a horse." Kind and anxious relatives expostulated; and our Uncle Joshua Sing,[3] a dear and single-hearted although wealthy man, called to chide, yet on his return home sent a cheque for the mare's first year's keep. She had given work and play to the boys at The Retreat, who groomed and baited her, allowing her an occasional frolic on the lawn. Her setting a fore-foot upon my shoulder in token of affection is still remembered in the family.

---

1   In October 1874 he delivered the inaugural address at the first opening of the Working Women's College in Fitzroy Street.
2   Now published under the name of *The Lost Princess*.
3   The family have now reverted to the older spelling of their name and write it *Synge*.

Mrs. G.M.D. to her Husband.

TANGLEY MANOR,
Sunday afternoon, 2 o'clock,
April 17th, 1875.

We have just come in from a morning on the hills through the lanes. We sat down in the sun for more than an hour. I read over one of your sermons given in Renshaw Street,[1] to them—it was so appropriate for the occasion—the season, the situation. It made me know—reading it there—how it was that you lived through all that time and how I managed to hang on by the eyelids—yes, your eyelids....It is truly a pretty picture I am living in. I never felt more like an old mother hen—all the boys and girls are so good to me and yet so independent and happy. We have been reading the *Blithesdale Romance* in the afternoons and evenings, a book easily realized in this house of really seven gables—and so completely shut away from all life but our own....Charming lanes and sloping hills, and woods—abound all round us—I feel as if it were almost too good to be true that such a place is ours for 6 months. I am always looking at things with your eyes; and I do think, blue as they are, you will see the sky heavenly blue and the air deliciously balmy and quiet....

G.M.D. to R. W. Gilder

THE RETREAT,
HAMMERSMITH, LONDON.
May 15, 1875.

MY DEAR BOY,

I have been more or less ill all the winter, now in bed, now hard at work. It is summer weather at last, and although I can yet bear no fatigue, I am much better and working hard at my story....As soon as I get it finished I shall bethink myself about your story—on whose tail, when I have once caught sight of it, I shall not be long in casting salt. I lean to a wild one, into which one can put so much more, but I cannot tell yet....

Is your volume ready yet? I wish I had time to write verses! Perhaps I shall have when I am too old to write stupid prose—and feel the husk splitting away to let out the leaves of the new life....[2]

Next in point of date comes an instance of the sort of letter he would write to us when very young. The younger boys were at Tangley with an admirable tutor.

---

1 Some of these sermons had been taken down in shorthand and transcribed for my mother by Henry Septimus Sutton.
2 "The rose is the freedom of the rose-tree," *vide antea*, p. 357.

PALAZZO CATTANEO

From G.M.D. to his Son Robert Falconer, age thirteen.

THE RETREAT,
July 15, 1875.

MY DEAR DOGGIE,

They tell me this is your birthday. I hope you will have a happy one, although neither your mother nor I, nor any of your sisters, are with you. You know people are not far from each other because their bodies are not near; and people may be together all day long and be awful miles apart because they do not love each other....

G.M.D. to his Wife at Hastings.

TANGLEY,
August 1875.

...I am not yet much better, but I have done better work to-day—and before dinner, I walked the mare up to Blackheath, and have had the first real enjoyment of country that I have had for many a day....I found it nearly perfect—the day warm without being too hot up there—the finest heather perhaps that I ever saw, and a thousand dainty interminglings of wildness and culture....I almost think it is the very place for a story I am thinking of....I have about £8 in the bank and five in my pocket....

At the end of the summer some permanent home other than The Retreat had to be found. Bournemouth was then at the height of its reputation for lung troubles, its pine forests not yet being demolished, and it had already proved helpful to my sister. A very pretty newly built house, almost hidden among the aromatic trees, was taken at Boscombe, and named Corage, the first word in our father's anagram, "*Corage! God mend al!*" Henry Cecil lived near by with his consumptive wife and their family. When she died he gave her two Shetland ponies, their chaise and harness to my mother, and for a while the little creatures had come to The Retreat. Then a little stable was built for them at Corage, and our mother would herself drive the comical shaggy things. She admitted that she had no control over them, but vowed they knew the rules of the road: for, to her astonishment, they always took her safely to the destination she set out for. The Retreat was shut up, though its annexe, River Villa, was still occupied, and now by three Misses Cobden.

Certainly our father was greatly helped by the winter at Boscombe. He had the mare to ride, and my mother the ponies to drive. Indeed, but for the sick *lammie*, as my father so often wrote of Mary, those days would have been very happy and peaceful.

Yet still the master had to fight ill-health and printers' devils, if he was to provide for all, including the medical student in London. While at Halloway House my mother had taken a brave step to relieve him: she put her children's talents to some use. Greatly to the dismay of all our relatives, and of many long-tried friends, she produced in public some of the family theatrical successes. A public representation of *The Tetterbys* had already been given at Hastings for Miss Kingsbury's Convalescent Home. Its success, artistically and financially, was so great that my mother presented her little company there professionally; and the local press gave unequivocal praise to the completeness of the production, but especially to Miss MacDonald's remarkable powers in character delineation. Thereafter my mother's genius in organization was turned to practical use; and, still to relieve her husband's burdens, for many years she devoted herself not only to her sick children—four of whom succumbed to tubercular disease[1] —but to *The Pilgrim's Progress*, the second part of which she dramatized for her family. Its first public performance was given at Christchurch, Hants, on March 8, 1877, the twenty-sixth anniversary of their wedding-day.

If the gifts of God were sometimes bestowed upon this brave and open-handed man and wife in such wise that prosperous relatives took them for extravagance rather

---

1 Which, later, my father wrote of, grimly for him, as "the family attendant."

than divine favour; if it appeared to some who loved them best that these gifts, their divine source notwithstanding, had to be paid for by toil not less cheerful for its drudgery, and, after all, relieved the father scarcely at all, I for one dare not join in such comments. Yet because I would record a certain talk with my father on the subject, I must first confess to some anguish that mother and sisters should have to do these things, and that brothers should have their education interrupted. It never distressed me to see my eldest sister play in public—and precisely because her own person vanished in her art; whereas the fact that the others could not conceal their identity made it inexpressibly painful. I told my father all I felt, and I do not forget his sympathy with me—nor the admission that himself had felt much as I did, but that, my mother being so sure this work was given her to do, he must bow to her interpretation of God's will—more particularly indeed that it was all to relieve him from his at times intolerable weariness. He took it as a humbling of his worldly pride; and he would have me realize better my mother's singleness of heart, her devotion to her darlings' interests—she being no less concerned than myself for her little sons' education. "You have no conception, my boy," I remember him saying, "how deep and passionate is your mother's love for you—for you and for your brothers and sisters, *as if you were each her only chick.*" And then I recalled to myself how once, a few years before, she had sat on the floor beside one of these sons for half the night, as he lay in anguish till his sin was confessed, and how she re-created the sunrise for him.

But if, in spite of all such help, my father's work became yet more urgent and its interruptions more frequent, there were wonderful solaces. So often do I find in the letters to my mother words like these:

...This illness compels me to change my plan and finish one volume before I write the whole [three]. If it pleases God that I do that, it must be the best way, though I can't quite see that it is.¹ ...I am very stupid. My windows are darkened—*all but the sky-lights*.² But I think I shall soon be all right again....Love to my two darlings....

Living now so much at Boscombe, visits to the Cowper-Temples at their seat, Broadlands, Romsey, were easy. Lord Mount-Temple has written thus of his first meeting with George MacDonald in 1867:

> A young tutor in our family lay in a dying state in our house in Curzon Street. Mr Davies [Rev. J. Llewellyn Davies] came and administered the Communion to him, and brought also to the young sick man a fellow-countryman (for he was Scotch) to read *Saul* to him. It was George MacDonald; and from that time he has been one of our dearest friends and teachers.³

Occasionally my father would spend a night or two at Broadlands, whence, on December 21, 1875, came to my mother words that have interest to us:

> ...I have had a little chat with Ruskin....There is a Mrs. A. [a society spiritualistic medium] here. I don't take to her much, but Ruskin is very much interested....She has seen and described, without ever having seen her, Rose [La Touche] whispering to Mr. Ruskin. He is convinced....⁴

In 1877 one of the Cowper-Temples' religious conferences was in full swing, and had my father's support.

---

1   A few years later the risk of such a plan became evident. My father was writing a novel for a certain periodical, the agreement having been duly executed. But the publisher was dissatisfied, and the author, rather than modify his methods or have any dispute, refunded the £100 paid him in advance, though he had to borrow it, at 5 per cent. and did it in spite of his agent, Mr. A. P. Watt's protests. Nor would he accept a refunding of the latter's commission.
2   I think he is recalling the skylight of the *Blue Bell*, when they lifted his starved and tormented body through it up into the blue sky, and he felt his resurrection was come. *Vide antea*, p. 394. "A prayin' hert was nae reef (*roof*) till 't. *Sir Gibbie*, vol. ii, p. 188.
3   *Memorials of Lord Mount-Temple*, privately printed.
4   *Vide antea*, p. 335.

PALAZZO CATTANEO

Mrs. G.M.D. to her Husband at Broadlands.

CORAGE, BOSCOMBE,
[*Aug.* 2, 1877].

I keep picturing you to myself under the beeches, comforting and inspiring other people—and I am not to hear your winged words.[1]... Our darling little sick lamb is better certainly....The sea and the pines are making such a sweet noise—I am at the open door-window after tea, Mary on the sofa behind it. Ted [Hughes] is mending some braid on her jacket....If it were not for that dreadful fever! and the tearing cough!...Lily is well and very beautiful—as nearly perfect a woman as lives anywhere I think "here below."...

Then this comes in reply:

G.M.D. to his Wife at Corage.

BROADLANDS, ROMSEY,
[*Aug.* 4, 1877].

Thanks, dearest, for your letter. You would have liked to see the angel's [Mrs. Cowper-Temple] face as she gave it me back after reading it—for I did what I never did before, I think, gave one of my wife's letters to another to read. She said "What a wife she is to you!" or something more lovely....They are all so sweet about Mary, and they all prayed for her under the beeches yesterday....But *might* you not come? Just for Sunday.... Probably Mr. Russell Gurney is coming down to-morrow. And do you know, I quite like Lord Radstock, and I have learned a good deal; and much this afternoon about St. John's Gospel from Mr. Duglass the Jew.... Love to Elfie. I hope to nurse her a bit on Monday....

The following poem, scribbled and scored and amended, I find on a half sheet of Broadlands notepaper; and I presume it belongs here. So careful was my father of his verses' polish, that it is necessary to indicate that he had apparently discarded these.

> Give me thy peace,
> My heart is aching with unquietness:
> O, let its inharmonious beating cease,
> Thy hand upon it press.

---

1 The title page of *Unspoken Sermons* carries in red the legend ἔπεα Ἄπτερα, i.e. *wingless words*.

> My Sun! my Day!
> Swift night and day betwixt, my world doth reel:
> Potter, take not thy hand from off the clay
> That whirls upon thy wheel.
>
> A darksome cloud
> Lo! From the shadowy place doth sweep;
> But to the earth my heart shall not be bowed—
> In thee we wake and sleep.
>
> I am a bubble
> Upon thy ever moving, restless sea:
> Send me not only tossing, trespass, trouble—
> Take me down into thee!

In the autumn of 1877 it was decided that the sick daughter must go to Italy. A childless and wealthy old relative of my mother's—not a brother, or a brother-in-law, by the way—was appealed to for the loan of £300 to help this young cousin of his—especially beloved by him and his wife—to recover her health. But he refused, writing a very affectionate letter with some conventionally religious jargon. He died intestate three months before the young cousin he would not help; but, fine man of business though he was, he found this world's currency so gravely depreciated that he could not negotiate in the other his £100,000, and had to leave it all behind him. Nevertheless, what was right must be, money or no money, and the journey was undertaken. The party comprised Mother, Lily, Mary, Irene and Ronald. They stayed at Mentone and Genoa, and then were drawn to Nervi by an advertisement of its Palazzo Cattaneo, which, the rent being very moderate, they took for the winter.

My father's letters to my mother tell of the several obstacles to his joining them—though all along he believed it would be arranged—chiefly an attack of bronchitis and pleurisy while The Retreat was in process of dismemberment prior to letting,[1] and anxiety concerning the sale of his new book, *Paul Faber, Surgeon*. Strahan, having separated from

---

[1] It was taken over by William Morris the following year.

his partners, was unable to offer such prices as he used to give for a new book, even before it was finished; and now declined *Paul Faber* as unsuitable for his newly launched *Day of Rest*. Everything seemed to militate against his hope—"Hope the nimbus of life," he once said—that he would go to Italy. But meantime his illness gave him greater touch with one son and his daughter Winifred, as they, rejoicing in the opportunity for such service, nursed him; and that, I think, went for some happiness. While in bed he pencilled his letters.

G.M.D. at The Retreat to his Wife at Nervi.

...You would like to hear the way G. talks. He is a boy no longer however. One thing he sees plainly—the elevating power of suffering even on these poor women....I have once or twice been tempted to feel abandoned—in this messy and struggling house....But it is only a touch of the Valley of Humiliation—of the Hill of Difficulty rather....My love to my little sick dove. Tell her to keep a big heart for God to fill for her. When I was a boy my desire was to be loved; but now my prayer is to be made able to love....What a little we know yet! And how much is to be known....Don't be anxious about me. I shall soon be well....How comfortable I am compared with the last time when I didn't have you—on board the *Blue Bell*!...

I dare not attempt to pay for the horses' keep while we are away. [1]

Then comes an admission that may surprise some who have not beheld the rock of my father's faith. My mother had been telling how vicious the mosquitoes were in Genoa:

G.M.D. to his Wife.

...Never had I so many worldly mosquitoes about me, but they don't get within my curtains much. I grow surer and surer. Winnie nurses me so sweetly, and [the boy] too, and I don't think I shall be long ill. I have seldom been quieter in mind than this day—but *I am sometimes hard put to it with the Apollyon of unbelief*....

I think some true believers in my father may get a shock from this confession—which he knew he might make to

---

1 The ponies being a gift, could not be sold, and they were taken charge of by Mr. Cowper-Temple; the mare was sold for £50—my father offering to take less if that proved beyond her value.

that all-understanding wife without saddening her. Some, less sure of him, may wonder if even his great faith was but a reed to bend or break in stress of circumstance. But these have never touched the clue to his sufficing faith. The whole difficulty lies in the word *doubt*, in the handling of which my father is always and nothing less than prophetic. With him the word was purely intellectual—never spiritual. My father never doubted the shining of the Light: even if the hell we have turned the world into might obscure with its smoke sometimes—perhaps when he was considering the money-difficulty—his clarity of vision. And not even my father could always see through such a veil—although he never doubted the Light and the Life that shone behind it and made a glory of life in spite of all present anguish. 'Twas his utter honesty in league with his supreme belief that made him sometimes cry out—

> Have pity on us for the look of things
> When blank denial stares us in the face.
> Although the serpent-mask have lied before,
> It fascinates the bird that darkling sings,
> And numbs the little prayer-bird's beating wings;[1]

and then—

> Through all the fog, through all earth's wintery sighs,
> I scent Thy spring, I feel the eternal air,
> Warm, soft, and dewy, filled with flowery eyes,
> And gentle, murmuring motions everywhere—
> Of life in heart, and tree, and brook, and moss;
> Thy breath wakes beauty, love, and bliss, and prayer,
> And strength to hang with nails upon thy cross.[2]

---

1 *Diary of an Old Soul*, November 3rd. And compare this: "Every common day, he who would be a live child of the living has to fight the God-denying look of things, to believe that, in spite of their look, they are God's and God is in them, and working his saving will in them." (*Castle Warlock*, vol. ii. p. 296.)

2 *Diary of an Old Soul*, May 6th. See also *Unspoken Sermons*, Series 2, 1885, p. 242: "A man may be haunted with doubts, and only grow thereby in faith. Doubts are the messengers of the Living One to rouse the honest. They are the first to knock at our door of

Christ himself suffered this "blank denial," this obscuration as He hung upon the Cross: else He had not suffered the worst that man can suffer.

But to resume the story of my father's present difficulty and its solution. As soon as he was better enough to move, Mrs. Cowper-Temple fetched him from the dismantled house to Great Stanhope Street.

G.M.D. to his Wife.

15 Gt. Stanhope Street, W.,
Oct. 18, 1877.

...To-morrow surely I shall hear something of my affairs. Dear love, trust hard in God, for he is our rest and our peace and our love....I want to be able to say—and not only mean it but be able to stand to it—"though he slay me yet will I trust in him!"...Surely I shall be allowed to come to you....Love to "all my pretty chickens and their dam, at one *sweet* swoop."...

Strahan, though he adhered to his refusal of *Paul Faber's* serial production, bought the rights for a first three-volume edition and offered my father a bill for £400, at three months. It was accepted, though less than half the sort of price he had of late secured for his novels. The bill was endorsed by Mr. Cowper-Temple and discounted. But when all the home debts were paid, it left but £50 in hand. And yet my father still felt sure that he was to spend Christmas in Italy.

15 Stanhope Street.

...Mr. Temple is away at his quarries—went last night and will be back on Friday. Fancy these quarries with the little railway are all his! I am getting better—my appetite a little improving, I think....Oh, your last letter is so good. It looks as if you had been seeing into my difficulties about coming and saying the best, the right thing....Of course I cannot think I am not to come to you. But neither can I bear the thought of leaving any behind me, and the expense and the little that will be left

---

things that are not yet, but have to be, understood: and theirs in general is the inhospitable reception of angels that do not come in their own likeness. Doubt must precede every deeper assurance; for uncertainties are what we first see when we look into a region hitherto unknown, unexplored, unannexed...." *Vide antea*, p. 374.

frightens me out and out sometimes. But I am hoping to see my way. And such good news of the darling!

Oct. 22, 1877.

...I have had such a curious letter from an Italian in Calcutta who had been brought, he says, from being an atheist to believe—by my books....

Certainly we could live on much less [in Italy]. I should be content with macaroni....Even if I should not come to you—only, please God, I shall—every happy thought you have, and every sense of delight in what you have about you, is something for me too....I enclose you a letter from Joshua [Sing], whom I had asked, if I should need it some time, if he would lend me £100. I would rather not if I can do without it, but you see how good and hearty he is. How gladdening your news about Mary is!...

Enclosed is this sacredly playful poem to the sick daughter:

TO MY ELFIE.

Lammie, lying and sighing
   Under the Orange-tree,
With brother and sisters round thee trying
   To shelter and comfort thee—

Mother giving thee clover,
   Mother giving thee milk,
Longing to cover thee up and over
   With love as fine as silk—

Father sends thee a bleat
   Over mountain and flat;
He would give thee his wool and eyes and feet,
   If only you would grow fat.

But all is well, my blossom—
   The lovely strong *I AM*,
He who carries the lamb in his bosom,
   Is carrying thee, my lamb.

G.M.D.

And now we are again privileged to see how prayer may be answered:

PALAZZO CATTANEO

G.M.D. to his Wife.

15 Gt. Stanhope Street, W.,
Oct. 29, 1877.

...I am so glad you like the little Song. It was only meant to be like the baby-verses I wrote for Lily when she was a wee, white thing....Dearest, here came a gap, and I read your letter to the angel-sister. Then William the brother came in, and she went out. He said he wanted me to do him a favour: I was so pleased, thinking he really wanted me to do something for him. Then I cannot tell you how sweetly he begged me to take "a few of his slates"—which were represented by a cheque for £200. I tried to refuse it—but it wouldn't do. Then she came in and kissed me, and laughed at me. So here is the cheque, and I shall be with you soon now, my love....This ought to make me gooder....

> If to myself—"God sometimes interferes"—
> I said, my faith at once would be struck blind.
> I see him all in all, the lifing mind,
> Or nowhere in the vacant miles and years.
> A love he is that watches and that hears,
> Or but a mist fumed up from minds of men,
> Whose fear and hope reach out beyond their ken. [1]

But immediately came another surprise: my father was given a Civil List Pension:

G.M.D. to his Wife.

Corage,
Nov. 2, 1877.

...We are now getting ready to start, though we cannot be out by your birthday. My love and thanks to you for being what you are and have been to me. May your birthday be hopeful, for hope is sure to come right if only we go on hoping long enough. My love to Mary on her mother's birthday [November 5th]. I never forget the lark's nest I found the morning she was born....[Here comes a letter] from Lord Beaconsfield's secretary, telling me that the Queen has given me £100 a year. Isn't it nice? I must send you the news for your birthday....Mrs. Temple *thinks* it is the Princess Alice's[2] doing, but Mr. Russell Gurney rather thinks it is Lord Beaconsfield's, moved by late reviews....

---

[1] *Diary of an Old Soul*, January 9th.
[2] A year before he had been taken by Dean Stanley to Buckingham Palace to be presented to H.R.H. Princess Alice, whom he found very simple and charming.

So my father with his chicks joined my mother with hers at the Villa Cattaneo— "a great house," he wrote to Carey Davies, "surrounded with orange trees, some full of fruit. We look straight South, nearly right down on the Mediterranean which delights us with colour." The following stanzas describe it; they exist only in roughest script, scored and altered with inter-breaking lines and alternative rimes, as though they had never quite pleased their writer. Yet they give a vivid picture of the great bare house, with its shabby mural paintings and quiet oratory:

PALAZZO CATTANEO.

The house is dingy, hard and bare,
    Save foolish fancies on the walls;
Cold iron guards the wide stone stair;
    Through empty ways the loud wind calls.

Few curtains cloud the windows wide,
    Few carpets warm the spaces great;
On marble floors the footsteps slide,
    Or stalk on tiles and slabs of slate.

Yet house we never yet have found
    So fitted to our loves and works—
Though scarce it has from roof to ground,
    A spot where simple beauty lurks.

The cause is plain, nor hard to say—
    Here we have room for all our clan:
An ample hall for food or play,
    Or song to cheer the inner man;

And rooms enough for day and night,
    And some for welcome friends' repose:
Room, room, blest room, in width and height,
    For verse to burgeon out of prose.

And, last and sweetest, down below,
    A hidden, lowly silent room,
Where any hour the heart may go
    To gather light amid its gloom.

> The Virgin on the altar-stone
>   Nor yet has troubled any prayer;
> She stands there silent and alone,
>   Nor grudges that we the place should share.
>
> And so the house, with room for guest,
>   With lofty hall, and stairways wide,
> With quiet cell for hoping rest,
>   Thank God! has all our need supplied.

At Christmas he wrote this greeting:

WRITTEN FOR MY FRIENDS, CHRISTMAS, 1877, NERVI.

> They all were looking for a king
>   To slay their foes, and lift them high:
> He came a little baby thing
>   That made a woman cry.
>
> O Son of Man, to right my lot
>   Nought but thy presence can avail;
> Yet on the road thy wheels are not,
>   Nor on the sea thy sail.
>
> My why or when thou wilt not heed,
>   But come down thine own secret stair,
> That thou may'st answer all my need,
>   Yea, every by-gone prayer.
>
>   GEORGE MACDONALD[1]

A recurrent interest to students of my father is his love for stairways. We find them in *Donal Grant*, *Lilith*, *The Princess and the Goblin*, and *At the Back of the North Wind*; we have seen, too, how the tower-stairs of Antwerp and Cologne affected him. In a letter to Carey Davies he says, "I have a passion for stairs."[2] Indeed, a full essay might be written on his symbolic utterance, so close akin is it to transcendental mysticism, and, I more than suspect, to the Celtic second-sight. To him a symbol was far more than an arbitrary outward and visible sign of an abstract conception:

---

1 Printed with slight variation in *Paul Faber, Surgeon*, vol. iii, p. 203; and with still more variation in *The Poetical Works*, vol. ii, p. 323.
2 *Vide* p. 530.

its high virtue lay in a common *substance* with the idea presented. Perhaps this accounts for certain Roman Catholics claiming that he was never really outside the pale of the Church. Compare these lines:

> Oh, present Christ! make my eyes as keen as stings
> To see thee at their heart, the glory even of things;

and—

> Thou goest too. From every clod
> Into thy foot-print flows the indwelling wine;
> And in my daily bread, keen-eyed I greet
> Its being's heart, the very body of God.[1]

Once, forty years ago, I held conversation with my father on the laws of symbolism. He would allow that the algebraic symbol, which concerns only the three-dimensioned, has no *substantial* relation to the unknown quantity; nor the "tree where it falleth" to the man unredeemed, the comparison being false. But the rose, when it gives some glimmer of the freedom for which a man hungers, does so because of its *substantial* unity with the man, each in degree being a signature of God's immanence. To a spiritual pilgrim the flower no longer seems a mere pretty design on the veil, "the cloak and cloud that shadows me from Thee"; for see! she opens her wicket into the land of poetic reality, and he, passing through and looking gratefully back, then knows her for his sister the Rose, of spiritual substance one with himself. So may even a gem, giving from its heart reflections of heavenly glory, awaken like memory in ourselves and send our eyes upwards. So also may we find co-substance between the stairs of a cathedral-spire and our own "secret stair" up to the wider vision—the faculty of defying the "plumb-line of gravity"[2] being the common and imaginative heritage. I do not claim to remember more than the trend of the argument; and I have to present it in my own halting words.

---
1 *Diary of an Old Soul*, February 5th and 7th.
2 *Lilith*, p. 33.

CHAPTER II
PORTO FINO

> Be welcome, years! With your rich harvests come;
> Wither the body, and make rich the heart;
> For who that bears the golden corn-sheaves home
> Will heed the paint rubbed from his groaning cart? [1]
>
> G.M.D.

L.P.M.D.

New Year, 1878.

THUS opened, perhaps, the heaviest burdened of all the twenty-seven years, with sunshine and blue sea, palms and oranges all about them. The quatrain was written for my mother's greeting and with full sense that before long Mary Josephine must be taken from them. She died at Nervi on April 27th. "She was born into the other world the same day," my mother wrote me, "that my mother was born into this." She was two months less than twenty-five, and had been engaged over four years. The sweetest of their golden sheaves was exacted by the over-Lord. Although they had nursed my Uncles Alec and John in their rapid consumptions, though my father had watched and tended my little Aunt Bella in the latter days of her illness, perhaps for the first time the full tragedy of death assailed them. Perhaps, I dare suggest, they did not find it easier to face than do those whose faith fails them utterly in striving to penetrate the veil. In Mary Josephine's case the desire for life, the full sense of its worth, remained almost till the last, strong in her emaciated, cough-

---

[1] Cf. "The New Year," *Poetical Works*, vol. ii, p. 210

racked body, clinging to parents and lover and the beauty of the earth. Yet she knew all about it, and her soul was at peace. Ted Hughes came out at news of her imminent danger and stayed till they buried her body.

G.M.D. to Henry Cecil.

Villa Cattaneo, Nervi,
May 12, 1878.

My dear Cecil,

...Ah, my dear friend, we better understand your mental condition and feelings than we did before. Our child is gone from us, but we are following after, and I shall hold her yet again to my soul....The dreadful thing would be that some died and others did not. The only cure for everything is Christ in us. If he be our Saviour, then why should even my own faults and miserable parvitude render me at all hopeless, or even cast down; for these are but the skins that the ever newborn eternal serpent is casting from her; and there is in me the everlasting will, the living thing that hates these and prays against them, and will one day emerge pure and clean and loving entirely....

We do not return to England this year. We live cheaper here, and another winter of Italy will do much for me and perhaps make me able to encounter another in America....

To my mother, with the solace of nursing taken away, the world for a while seemed awful and meaningless. Shaken to the very foundations of her soul, death gave little rest from his terror. For a while, as is common till eyes and hands get accustomed to their grim uselessness, all sense of her daughter's nearness was denied her; and nothing short of this could make life tolerable. Each love of that brave woman's heart was a whole world placed in it. Yet when the most urgent of these duties was torn from her, the loss was not less terrible that ten other darling worlds remained hungry for her care, nor that their father was still needing her support and comforting. So that in reading the following poem, written upon her ensuing birthday, it will be seen how absolutely it was for my mother alone and only for the present aspect of her grief:

PORTO FINO

Porto Fino, November 5, 1878.

> To tell thee that our blessed child
> Is watching thee from somewhere nigh,
>   Mourns with thee when thy agony grows wild,
> Sits sometimes by thy bed while slow the hours go by,
>
>   Were but to mock thy weary pain
> With pleasant fancies of a half-held creed,
>   To gather up and offer thee again
> What thou hadst cast away as nothing to thy need.
>
>   But when the Shepherd great was dead
> Death did but let the Shepherd's glory out:
>   She heard his voice and followed where he led—
> He were no Shepherd now, not leading her about.
>
>   Take courage fresh, my Wife, this day
> Step out with me to find her new abode;
>   We go together, cannot lose the way,
> The wearier our feet, the shorter still the road.
>
>   Let us go on. We do not care
> For aught but life that is all one with love:
>   We seek not death, but still we climb the stair
> Where death is one wide landing to the rooms above.

Is this too intimate a word between a father and mother over their loss, too passionate an epitome of their six-months' tears, to give an unheeding public? Surely not for those who have read thus far. These I would beg to turn, while the sense and sound of it are still in their hearts, and read once more *Love me, Beloved*, the marriage gift of George MacDonald to Louisa Powell. For, having done so, they will know, if perchance never before, what a divinely joyful, blessedly responsible gift may be this of marriage and child-bearing—poverty and hardship and bitter losses notwithstanding. As my father and mother gave this token of their rejoicing bondage to the world, so do I think they will approve my giving for them this token of the tears that came of that same bonding together.

But my father had had, since March, six weeks of invalidism himself, though under the Italian sun the attack was very different from those usual with him.

Octavia Hill, worn out with work, and suffering from Ruskin's unjust criticism of her in *Fors*, had been visiting them, though, just before Mary Josephine's death, she had gone to Rapallo *en route* for Rome. Concerning Miss Hill, my father had written on March 3rd to Carey Davies:

> She is very far from well, too anxious to get back to work, I think, to favour recovery. Ruskin has not been fair to her, I am sorry to have to allow. I have seen that *Fors*[1]. ....Altogether it is a hard time, but I have to learn that God, and not his channels of gift, is the Source of all I have and receive. I am not forsaken.....If I can get over this summer—but of course *I cannot*—but he can get me over life itself into more life—all is right—all is well.

Only a few days later had come the news from Mrs. Arthur Severn of Ruskin's mental breakdown.

So restorative had the climate proved to my father, and so keen was the feeling for seclusion and rest, that on the termination of the Palazzo Cattaneo's tenancy they took for a twelvemonth the Villa Barratta at Porto Fino—a romantic situation over-looking the little bay of the town, and across to Rapallo. It is about a third of the way between Genoa and Spezzia, its station being Sta. Margherita, three miles along a good road closed at both ends, so that the journey was done by row-boat.

> Here (wrote my eldest sister to Carey Davies) we have such a domestic, secluded, delicious life and see three times as much of Papa as we used to at home. He is hard at work as ever. The country all about us is lovely even in winter.

---

[1] Ruskin's words were, of course, prognostic of his mental breakdown, the subconscious brain being irritated into upheavals of suspicion and vituperation. The correspondence will be found in vol. xxix of the Library Edition of Ruskin's Works, Letter 86. The great man was certainly very cruel. Instance these two sentences: "...For this particular opinion, that I trust the wrong people, I wish you to give me *two* sufficient examples of the error you have imagined. You yourself will be a notable third, etc., etc." Miss Hill's letters in this correspondence are beautiful in self-possession, temperate utterance and gratitude to him.

PORTO FINO

Barely settled in the huge Villa Barratta,[1] came news of Russell Gurney's death. He was seventy-four.

G.M.D. to Mrs. Russell Gurney.

PORTO FINO,
June 5, 1878.

DEAR SISTER EMELIA,

You have been a happy wife, and now you will be a patient widow. The noble man is gone to his kind, and may we all come near him again some blessed day of the eternal age.

The world will be like a dream to you after this, a constant waiting for something at hand. Your dearest are nearly all out of sight now; but it is not visible proximity but love that is the bond, the oneness. Well as you knew him, greatly as you loved him, you will know him better, love him better now. Be sure of this, the grandest thing in England, the justice of her administration of the laws, is a purer, grander thing yet, because Russell Gurney has had a share in it. And the Lord who loves justice as his own being will know how many cities to set him over.

Age was drawing near him here, but he has escaped from it to the land of youth. All *there* is impenetrably hidden from us for a time, lest we should by the glory of it miss the door into it....And there is your old warrior gone after our young maiden....

G.M.D. to W. C. Davies.

June 19, 1878.

...Yes, I have never known such a time. Friend after friend going—more than one not dead, but more or less deranged. But our hope is in heaven. God comes nearer and nearer. If only we went as fast as he was drawing us....If we would but understand that we are pilgrims and strangers! It is no use trying to nestle down.

Things look much better for me now, I thank God, in money ways. He will keep me short, I daresay, as will probably always be best for me, but he will enable me to die without debt, I do think. Mr. Russell Gurney has left me £500, which will go far to clear me off, I hope—would almost, if I were not straitened for present cash. But I do not want this talked about....*Paul Faber* will be out in 3 volumes in October, and a new story [*Sir Gibbie*] begun in the *Glasgow* [*Weekly*] *Mail* in September, which is more than half done....

The summer of 1878 I was enabled to rejoin my people at Porto Fino. I had never seen my father in such good health:

---

1 Now enlarged and named Hotel Splendide.

the great heat was tonic to him. But my mother was very frail, and scarcely able to move from the house save in her Bath-chair. We spent much of every day in the sea, so delightful was the little bay for swimming across to the peninsula standing across it. We had our own boat, and our father would take an oar upon occasion and pull with his boys. Well I remember one thunderstorm that rose in sudden black majesty while we were rowing home from Sta. Margherita. The thunder was less awful than in our latitudes, but the lightning much finer, splitting the firmament in slashing coruscations.[1]

Not the least of my own pleasures was a new intimacy with my fourteen-year-old brother, Maurice, whom I was never to see again. We would have long talks about chemistry, physics and evolution, and I wondered at his instant and imaginative understanding.

Paul Faber was finished here. *Sir Gibbie* too, appearing in *Lippincott's Magazine* in the States simultaneously with its serial issue at home, was mostly done here, and marked a renewal of my father's powers. In some ways it is the most picturesque of his Scottish stories, full of his belief in the peasantry and their power of seeing deep truths in common things.

So the year 1879 opened with renewed hopes. My eldest sister's birthday brought her this:

>FOR MY LILY.
>Child, I would give thee gifts untold,
>   If power did equal will,
>Not merely things to have and hold,
>   But joys thy heart to fill.

---

[1] It was on this occasion, I think, that my father would say he first grasped the realism of Coleridge's lines:

>"Like waters shot from some high crag,
>The lightning fell with never a jag,
>A river steep and wide."

And these in their turn recall the description of lightning in *The Flight of the Shadow* (1891), p. 68. "...It was the burst of a ball-headed torrent of fire from a dark cloud, like water sudden from a mountain's heart, which went rushing down a rugged channel, as if the cloud were indeed a mountain, and the fire one of its cataracts...."

> I would not give my child a stone,
>   But bread whereby to live:
> Thy God sees nothing not his own,
>   And only has to give.
>
> But human billows swell and dip,
>   Winds blow from every part;
> Then wonder not, although God's ship
>   Take long to reach thy heart.
>
> GEORGE MACDONALD.

The truth of my father's renewed health and mental power was not lost upon my mother. She was determined that, if it was anyway possible, he should winter abroad for some years at least; and she got her way—seemingly God's also. Nor did she waver even when fresh grief overwhelmed her in the death of my brother Maurice, after an eighteen days' pneumonia—a malady generally fatal in Italy. But probably there was already tuberculosis disease at work, the abscess in the leg two years before suggesting the possibility.

The two following letters tell something of how Death took the child for whom, so great was his mind, so blameless his soul, his parents had cherished more aspiring hopes than for any other of their boys; while the second, my mother's, also formulates her intentions to make secure my father's improvement in health:

G.M.D. to W. C. Davies.

PORTO FINO,
March 19, 1879.

MY DEAR DAVIES,

...He was quite a child by himself—in the eyes of his brothers and sisters as well as ours. Though not so strong as his elder brothers, he was the most active, and the best swimmer and diver of them all. He had been weakly and had what seemed a cold for part of the winter, but was better, when one Sunday morning about 3 o'clock he was seized with severe hæmorrhage. That ceased but was followed by inflammation of the lungs, and on the 18th day he died. We had hoped almost to the last hour. He was just over fifteen. It is a sore affliction, but though cast down we are not destroyed. Jesus rose again glorious, and to that I cleave fast. My boy is of course dearer to me than before, and we shall find him again, with his love as fresh as the life that cannot die. Not a murmur escaped him. His contentment was lovely and his soul strong to the end—his obedience perfect—and his rest in God marvellous.

Mrs. G.M.D. to W. C. Davies.

PORTO FINO,
April 10th, 1879.

MY DEAR MR. DAVIES,

Alas, that we should be such complaining, difficult children to bear the gifts and the discipline of the Father! He has, as it were, given stronger and better life back into the hands of my husband, and yet he has taken to himself that strong young life that seemed to be preparing so vigorously, so manfully for the soldiership to which he was called when in Frederick Maurice's arms on his baptismal day. Ah! dear friend, it is so wrenching: and yet why strive with the Giver because He cares *more* for his lovely gift than we did or can? We love to think the sweet daughter and son are together—she helping him with her always wise and tender motherliness in his new surroundings. Surely some day, even here, I shall be able to thank the Father for taking him to himself: at present I cannot get further than asking, as I heard Maurice himself in a whisper doing, for "all to be taken away that now makes it hard to say *Thy will be done.*" The fervency and sweet submission of the tones in which those last words were uttered are still as heavenly music in memory's ears.

But I did not intend to write so, though I know I am not speaking into an unsympathetic heart. I wish you had heard us talking about you the other evening. Lily looked up and said—"I *do* love Mr. Davies. What a faithful dear he is!" I only tell you this to show you your love and beautiful kindness to my husband, your devoted service to him, have not been lost even on his children.

I wonder whether you will be surprised to hear that we are intending to act our Bunyan's *Pilgrim's Progress* wherever we can. We have already made four engagements, the results of which will pay—and more—our journey home. But then we must have some more in order to pay our journey back. It is so wonderful to have Mr. MacDonald writing away without cough or asthma—day after day....*The Pilgrims* has [become] such a reality to us that it seems a *duty* to do it—from the multitude of *testimonies* we have had to the moral and good of the play....

Perhaps a point in connection with my brother's death should be mentioned because it explains a letter significant of one characteristic essentially my parents'—that of casting aside as irrelevant all worldly prudence when set against a spiritual obligation. Their friend, Dr. Schetilig of Nervi, a highly qualified graduate of Berlin, full of resource and kindness, was in constant attendance. When at last he could give them no hope of Maurice's recovery, they telegraphed for me. I could not feel it right to go.[1]

G.M.D. to his Son G.M.M.D.

Monday, half-past two.
...Our Maurice is alive, but that is nearly all I can say....He has been sleeping a good deal to-day, and it seems as if he was gently gliding into the land where all is well. He is angelic—a poor word, but at least not too strong to express his patience and sweetness; and for his intellect, that is as marvellous as the disease. Yesterday he played a good game of draughts—and a long one, with Ronald.

I fear your mother will have a terrible illness when it is over; the fatigue is great, great, and she never goes to bed now, but gets a nod or two when she can't help it....His brothers and sisters are just like strong angels tending a weak one; and for his mother, one can't say more than that she is a perfect mother to him. God is with us and will help us to hope on and on beyond all sights and sounds....

Tuesday morning.
...The doctor says there is just the smallest star of hope. His lungs are as bad as they can be. He is a wonderful boy, with an energy incredible—moving about in the bed in a way you could hardly believe, and now and then making us all laugh in the midst of his terrible restlessness, and much misery, though no unhappiness. His smile is still to be had, like the sun breaking out in the winter....That telegram was sent in a time of much dread, and although there is as much doubt still, we are not in such distress. Then we naturally cried out for your help, and, as I said, I am very glad to know you were only prevented by a doubt of your duty. But take

---

1 A word of explanation may perhaps be allowed, even if, in this case at least, love ought to have been the only mentor, *ruat cælum*. I was to stand in April for my final M.R.C.S. examination, and had been thrown back so much by illness that it was a question whether I could pass. If I failed, it would postpone my qualifying for six months; and I was naturally keen to relieve my father of my own necessities. But the account of my brother's sigh and turning of his face to the wall when he heard I would not come, has never left me.

care, my boy, lest you should ever lend ear to the advice of any with whom *prudence*, so-called, is the first thing. We have had a letter on the subject from...which is just as worldly as it is prudent, as careful for the life it would save as careless for the life it would ruin. Fancy telling our boys and girls not to nurse their withering brother for fear they should develop the same fell disease hidden in themselves! She is most kind, however, and does not know better. Oh, these wise people that look down on the simple. [1]

I am glad to say your mother had an hour and a half's sleep this evening while I nursed, with plenty of needful help. This morning she was beginning to talk nonsense to herself from fatigue, but then got a mouthful of rest, enough to restore her senses. God grant the "little star of hope," which Schetilig confessed to this evening, may grow a sun—and, if not, give us strength to help the darling to die.

The cemetery of Porto Fino stands on a promontory embracing the bay, so that its chapel looks on one side on to the busy little quay and on the other away over the blue Mediterranean. For any heretics that yet must be given earth's dues, a portion of land among rocks washed by the sea in storm is left unconsecrated. There Maurice's body was buried; and, in Rome's despite, it has consecrated those rocks for all time.

In the midst of the worst anxiety had come news of Mrs. Smart's death, the lady who, twenty-three years before at Kingswear, had tended my father and mother so lovingly when they were poor strangers, and he was at death's door:

G.M.D. to the Rev. John Smart.

Porto Fino,
March 11, 1879.

Dear and honoured Friend,

You know why I have not written to you before—that while you were mourning the loss of the much loved lady who had so long helped you to live, we were watching our boy, and helping him to die. Life looks very short to me now—or rather I should say—Life is drawing very near....

Dear to me is the memory of your sweet, generous, hospitable, gracious

---

1 Nothing is so unintelligible to the children of the world as the ways of the children of light—to themselves simple enough. (*Castle Warlock*, vol. i, p. 133.)

"The care of the prudent wise is as fumes of sulphur to the red rose of life." (*The Flight of the Shadow*, p. 96.)

wife—a pattern of Christian ministering. Great has been the kindness of both her and you to me and mine, and it shall never be forgotten....

And now, very soon after the burial of Maurice's body, came help all unawares. Before this fresh tragedy was upon them a letter had come telling of Richard Watson Gilder's break-down in health and his intended visit to Europe. So he, his wife and little son were earnestly desired at Villa Barratta, and arrived at a moment of their deepest weariness of heart. The visit was all too short, though the baby, Rodman, was left at the Villa Barratta while his parents went to Pisa and Rome. Of the little one—Rodboy, as they called him—my mother thus writes:

Mrs. G.M.D. to Richard and Helena Gilder.

PORTO FINO,
May 2, 1879.

I wish you could see how dear and bright and golden-haired and clever-eyed and happy-mouthed your darling boy is looking—so sweet and obedient. The Angels might rejoice in him for a playmate; indeed they must be rejoicing even now, if they are allowed to see him. He is a darling of darlings, and we are all blessed in having his sweet face and being kissed by his dear little mouth....We are full of business—packing and theatrical. You should see Rodboy at our rehearsals! It is simply delicious—his solemnity, his joy, his sighs, his thoughtful gaze; when they sang, he laughed aloud and sang too.

* * * * *

Thus ends the story of the double tragedy; for so, if we forget, it must look to us: but

> Death, like high faith levelling, lifteth all.
> When I awake, my daughter and my son,
> Grown sister and brother, in my arms shall fall,
> Tenfold my girl and boy.[1]

For my mother the desolation was framed in this golden hope, that, in spite of all, God had brought them to Italy as

---
1 *Diary of an Old Soul*, January 4th

a land of promise where her prophet was to find rest for his tired brain, health for his constantly ailing body, air for his spiritual wings. Quite sure to my mother was this; and she never doubted that now her chief duty was its fulfilling: she knew that for some years at least her husband was not to winter in England.

If faith ever needed ordeal to prove its worth, surely we find it in this last twelvemonth. Fearlessly may we recall my father's every word, whether in his books or his letters, that bears upon the rightness of honest, unquerulous doubt. For my own part, I shall always remember with worshipping and grateful heart the confession to my mother, almost on the eve of his departure to join her at Nervi, that he had been fighting "the Apollyon of Unbelief"; and along with it will remain his birthday-poem to her six months after Mary Josephine had left them. Then it was he took to himself the mother's own misery, namely, that the old conventional forms of religion's comforting were failing her utterly. In this present renewal of "Death's terror" [1] we find the victory over it.

Just as death's denial is forced upon us by its fearsome evidences—

> Have pity on us for the look of things
> When blank denial stares us in the face—

and declares our utter dependence, so is life's triumphant affirmation of its immortality, independently of any evidences, the essence and truth of all religion. Death and its trappings we may *know of,* Life and its resurrection we *believe in.* Just as we will not, cannot put our trust, our belief, in Death, so we cannot *know*—in the way we know the beloved body lies there dead in the box—that the darling life has realized Love's own immortality. Small wonder—with battalions of braggart facts ranged before our senses and souls in denial of Him who is the Resurrection and the

---

[1] In the letter to his stepmother, quoted in the following chapter, he speaks of "Death's Terror."

Life—small wonder that, in the days of this poor mortality, we have always, day by day, year by year, to fight "the Apollyon of Unbelief." For us to doubt that my father and mother did in the spring of 1879 triumph over the enemy, while still they must remain in the fighting line, is to throw down our arms and turn traitors. Yet proof of immortal life, as proof is counted by the scientist, can never be given. Nor shall we ask for it when at the last we are delivered from the body of this death; for we shall understand that such faith as George MacDonald's was not other than divine knowledge. This he puts very definitely:

> To make things real to us is the end and battle-cause of life. We often think we believe what we are only presenting to our imaginations. The least thing can overthrow that kind of faith. The imagination is an endless help towards faith, but it is no more faith than a dream of food will make us strong for the next day's work. To know God as the beginning and end, the root and cause, the giver, the enabler, the love and joy and perfect good, the present one existence in all things and degrees and conditions, is life; and faith, in its simplest, truest, mightiest form is—to do his will.[1]
>
> Do you ask (again writes my father) why no intellectual proof is to be had? I tell you that such would but delay, perhaps altogether impair for you, that better, that best, that only vision, which by its own radiance will sweep away doubt for ever. Being then in the light and knowing it, the lack of intellectual proof will trouble you no more than would your inability to silence a metaphysician who declared that you had no real existence....The mists and the storms and the cold will pass—the sun and the sky are for evermore.[2]

Yet one more book belongs to these days. Although not published till 1880, it was the Valley of the Shadow that inspired its pages with a revelation not only of victory won while still the fight must be maintained, but of my father's passionate tranquillity—a characteristic perennial in him, and seen no less in my mother whenever instant wisdom and courage were demanded of her. I refer to the little volume named *A Book of Strife in the form of The Diary*

---

1 *Donal Grant*, 1883, vol. i, p. 14.
2 *Paul Faber, Surgeon*, 1879, vol. ii, p. 217.

of an Old Soul—to give its full name. Besides one stanza of dedication to *Sweet Friends*, and signed *Your Old Soul*,

> It consists of a chain of stanzas, of which the links number three hundred and sixty-six, being one for each possible day of the year. Each link is a stanza of seven verses of rhymed five-accent iambic measure, with a wealth of variation in the arrangement of the rhymes, which is extraordinarily effective in averting monotony. The whole is a record of a life's rather than a year's religious thought. So personal, so single-minded, so intense, at once so exalted and profound is this remarkable poem, that criticism of it is only for friends with a common appreciation. [1]

And yet he gave it willingly to the world. Looking thus deep into the heart of one empowered with a message, some of us may get surer conviction of that message's source and truth. The book has been quoted here so often that further examples of its writer's inexhaustible art, of the piety that alone could grant is visions of transfiguration, are unnecessary. To some it seems the most inspired of all his utterances. During my father's lifetime it interested only his exceptionally understanding readers, but now has a steady and increasing circulation. Ruskin, in his Oxford Lectures on "The Pleasures of England," spoke thus of it: "The generation which has seen *Hiawatha* and George MacDonald's *Soul's Diary*, and Keble's Hymns might fairly claim to be an age not destitute of religious poetry." [2]

Though it is anticipating, it will be interesting here to mention the vicissitudes of this little *Diary of an Old Soul*, out of whose sale, my father, having had it printed at first at his own expense, probably made no money at all.

To judge from the next letter, Ruskin had evidently said something more positive than the above; moreover Sir Edward Cook's words are taken only from his précis of

---

[1] Ronald MacDonald's Essay on George MacDonald, *From a Northern Window*, p. 110.
[2] *Studies in Ruskin*, by Edward T. Cook, 1890, p. 228

the Oxford Lectures. Now, however, we can quote a correspondent who heard the lecture:

> Mr. Ruskin instanced Mr. George MacDonald's *Diary of an Old Soul* as a proof that Faith and Poetry were still united— "quaint, full of devotion, high in tone, the best example of the survival of faith in this sceptical age." Everybody is asking to-day what that *Diary* is. Nobody seems to have heard of it until Mr. Ruskin mentioned it. I believe it has not been advertised, indeed is sold almost privately. It is a volume full of sonnets, more in the style of George Herbert than of any other English poet, and full of beauties.[1]

When a certain publisher in 1884 was considering its re-publication, my father referred to Ruskin's lectures. Writing to his friend and literary agent, A. P. Watt, he says:

> BORDIGHERA,
> *Nov.* 7, 1884.
>
> ...I cannot but think I could get it [my price] easily after what Ruskin has been so late saying about me....Business people are not quite within the scope of my understanding and I should be very sorry to misjudge them—only *what* I have been told about them! At the same time people say worse things of myself which I know to be false. Let God judge between me and any I have a quarrel with....So if the information as to Mr. Ruskin's speech concerning me at Oxford does not influence Mr.—to go farther, I will take what you can get for me from him. *But it must be put in the agreement that no copies are to be sent for review*....I cannot and will not have those cuttings used for advertisement. I did not send them for any purpose but to encourage Mr.—to venture....Besides, the description is false: there is not one sonnet in the book. If I would *use* such, why should I not supply my own critics?...

He gave his most sacred musings and converse with God to us, his followers; but he would not submit them to common-minded reviewers.

---

1 *Liverpool Mercury*, October 28, 1884.

BOOK X
CORAGGIO

CHAPTER I
MR. GREATHEART

THIS last book of George and Louisa MacDonald's pilgrimage covers over twenty years, reaching to their golden wedding-day, and a little beyond to the final accomplishment of their warfare. Greater happiness was theirs, I think, during this period, even if the multifold sadness of migrating hopes kept their eyes increasingly upon the horizon. Although material comfort was added in more than one beautiful home of their own, and much quiet joy came from my father's increasing influence in the thoughts and faiths of men, yet the anguish of fresh losses and certain misunderstandings—once with one so dear that for a spell it looked worse than death—was not hid from their children and best loved friends.

Till 1887 the yearly flitting of the large household to and from Italy was a matter of difficulty in many ways, and had been hardly possible without the help of *The Pilgrim's Progress* and one or two other plays, e.g. the *Polyeuctus* of Corneille and *Macbeth*. These were given in the summers between 1879 and 1887 all over England and even in Scotland. The company was large and some members needed constant nursing. In 1881 my mother adopted two little girls and subsequently their consumptive mother, presumably at death's door, but who lived for seven years as one of the family at Casa Coraggio. She had been abandoned by a French husband and was penniless. The two children were educated by my sisters. Then in The Retreat days a poor little patient had been taken in, nursed and educated. Thanks to my sister Winifred's years of devoted teaching he was with further training able to qualify at the College of Organists, and afterwards to hold good posts. To add four to the family looked like lack of common sense, though hardly from the poor orphans' point of view. Such extra demands upon my sisters would have been intolerable to any less unselfish. So it can be easily understood what a venturesome business was this—my mother's crusade against the Paynim who stood between her husband and the holy land of health and lengthened days. The pen that could write its story should be plucked from a bird-of-Paradise wing, pointed by humour, and dipped in ink as red as love itself. Then perhaps some hand among

> Men with eyes opened by the second birth,
> To whom the seen, husk of the unseen is,[1]

might find the right words for its failures and triumphs, its pathos and joy, its visible and invisible beauty.

In the first place the Lord Chamberlain refused to license a religious play; yet, being above the law, my mother always found means for circumventing it! Wherever the family appeared, among rich or poor, in public hall or private house, the *Pilgrim's Progress* awakened deep enthusiasm and spiritual uplifting; indeed, it did very much more than secure sunny winters for my father. In place of scenery, curtains, some in appliqué designs of birds and flowers, made by the mother and her daughters, served for setting. For music, there was a piano beyond with the actors' singing, and sometimes a violin. The change of occupation may have been good for my father; yet he wrote as much as ever, frequently correcting proofs as he waited the call for Mr. Greatheart. And by that name he became generally known thereafter to many of his most intimate friends, old and new—the Mount-Temples,

---

1 *Diary of an Old Soul*, February 6th

Mrs. Russell Gurney, Octavia Hill, Prebendary Carlile, Edward Clifford, the artist, the Burne-Joneses, Arthur Hughes and W. Carey Davies, all of whom came to look upon the *Pilgrim's Progress* as part of my father's mission in the world. In 1882 Ronald became an undergraduate at Trinity College, Oxford, and Robert Falconer entered the architect's office in London, both joining the family in the summers and taking chief part in the "fit-ups," the advance-agency work, etc., thus developing in boyhood their later aptitude for managing boys and men. For my own part, being now able to earn my own living, and so taking no share in the dramatic representations, I could never rejoice in the work if only because the old peace and rest in the home was thenceforward, till 1887, made impossible by the exigencies of the drama. Although it was hardly successful economically, it certainly made more possible the half-yearly journeys to Italy. Physically the work seemed too much for my sisters, and was in danger of interfering with my brothers' prospects. My sister Grace's lungs gave way, but, in spite of it, she was married to the Rev. Kingsbury Jameson in April 1881, and the following year her little Octavia was born. Grace died in May 1884; and the little one, who brought joy to whomever she touched, and renewed her grandmother's youth,[1] was stricken with tuberculosis meningitis, and followed her mother in February 1891.

As I have said already, many friends were sad about the enterprise, in spite of my father's wholehearted endorsement of it, and the fact that it gave a little outlet for my eldest sister's genius: she played Christiana—a near presentment of her own person and character. They doubted its necessity, talked of the social disqualification it entailed and of its spoiling the children's prospects; while they covered up their dismay by claiming that things of such

---

1 In 1882 my mother wrote to W. Carey Davies: "Baby Octavia, the most wonderful and beautiful that ever was created, is well and lovely."

sanctity were out of place on the stage. As to the prudential aspect of it, neither of our parents regarded it at all; while the suggestion that religion belonged to one place rather than another was to my father heathenish. Something of his attitude is shown in a letter to his stepmother. It came from Bromsgrove, while my mother was being treated at Droitwich for her hands' rheumatoid arthritis:

From G.M.D. to his Stepmother.
Bromsgrove,
Aug. 18, 1879.

...If I did not hope in the risen Christ, where should my life be now? But I desire to hasten on my way that I may find my children again—and all my dear ones who have gone before me. Neither Louisa nor I knew much about death till those two were taken from us within the year—and now we know its terror and its comfort.

You know we have been acting with considerable success in London and other places. We have gained friends by it and lost not one. Now we have a little rest till near the end of September, when we have a month or five weeks of acting and lecturing before we set out again for Italy, where we are still hoping to buy a house before the winter....I am wonderfully well....No bronchitis for nearly two years now....And so Jeanie is married also! [1]...

But I dare not let any criticism of my own—I being perforce external to the heart of the enterprise—detract from the truth that my mother's interpretation of the *Pilgrim's Progress* created a profound impression upon everyone susceptible to such spiritual art. Dean Stanley was high in praise of its sanctity, Burne-Jones of its beauty. A daughter of the then Bishop of Carlisle, Miss Mary M. Goodwin, tells me how in 1881, when she was a girl, she had a bitter disappointment in being prevented by illness from seeing the play, and how our friend, Mrs. George Moore, told my father of it. "So George MacDonald quietly took up a bit of paper, wrote on it, folded it, and gave it to my

---

1 To Mr. Crawford Noble of Aberdeen.

THE BIG ROOM AT CASA CORAGGIO
From an oil painting by Irene MacDonald (Mrs. Cecil Brewer)

sister, saying, 'Give her that with my love.' The disappointment was healed by the message, which was this poem:

> 'Pain and sorrow,
> Plough and harrow,
> For the seed its place to find;
> For the growing
> Still the blowing
> Of the Spirit's thinking wind;
> For the corn that it will bear,
> Love eternal everywhere.'"

Miss Goodwin tells how a few years later she saw the performance at Carlisle and took them a dog-cartful of flowers for the Land of Beulah. "No one," she adds, "who ever saw it could forget Mr. Greatheart, or the beauty and reverence of the whole thing."

But always the hard and lovable work was rewarded by the Italian winters beneath gorgeous blue skies, amidst the olive woods, palms and roses, and the contentment of home. Drives were often taken up into the Maritime Alps with their wonderful villages, that seemed

to have climbed up to look over the heads of other things....each with its church standing highest, the guardian of the flock of houses beneath it, whence were seen many a water-course, mostly dry, with lovely oleanders growing in the middle of it; over multitudinous oliveyards and vineyards; over mills with great wheels, and little ribbons of water to drive them—running sometimes along the tops of walls to get at their work; over rugged pines, and ugly, verdureless, raw hillsides—away to the sea, lying in the heat like a heavenly vat in which all the tails of all the peacocks God was making, lay steeped in their proper dye.[1]

The peace and joy that these things stood for gave strong support in work for which not one of the company was physically fit. A home at Bordighera, in large part given by friends, was now theirs; and it quickly became the centre of life for a rapidly growing colony of intellectual Scots and English. In 1877 a plan had been organized for giving my

---
1 *A Rough Shaking* (1891), p. 41.

parents a freehold house of their own, to which H.R.H. the Princess Alice of Hesse, the Earl and Countess of Ducie, Lord and Lady Darnley, the Cowper-Temples, Russell Gurneys, Lord Lawrence, the Charringtons, Mathesons, the Baroness Paul Ralli, the Miss Hills, Mr. and Mrs. C. Edmund Maurice, and a host of relatives and other friends, even old servants, contributed. To this a further sum raised by mortgage was added; and if the house, planned by my father himself and named Casa Coraggio, resulted in more accommodation than the family needed, it "enlarged the place of their tent," gave my father a study after his desires,[1] and made possible a great living room, measuring 52 feet by 26 feet by 13 feet, a third part of which, curtained off, enshrined a fine two-manual pipe-organ,[2] and served as dining-room, the whole room being readily set free for social and family gatherings. The highest property, Dante tells us, increases to each by the sharing of it with others; and the room was often thrown open to any friends and their friends who liked to join the family on their Sunday assembling or at the *At-Homes* on Wednesday afternoons, when my father would read and expound his favourite literature, during some winters giving courses on Dante or Shakespeare. On Sundays, perhaps a hundred or more would come, and everyone, friends or strangers, were deeply touched by the personal welcome and thought for their comfort. The sweet organ, played by my mother, and some of the church choir, trained by her, would sing anthem, psalms and hymns simply and upliftingly. The whole room with its

---

[1] Prebendary Carlile thus writes me (December 12, 1922): "The picture of your great father sitting in his study is still fresh in my mind, though it is thirty years ago. His splendid hospitality with an almost empty pocket amazed me. His keen eye could see beauty and reveal it even when all around seemed ugly and repelling. He radiated Divine Love....He often drew me to him and wanted to know the best I had recently seen in the worst criminals that were always passing through my hands and whose lives, so changed by God, shamed by their devotion the easy-going passivity of many religious people."

[2] But not built till 1891. It was the bequest of my Uncle George Powell, who died in October of the preceding year.

quietly coloured draperies and old furniture was dim-lit by candles. At eight o'clock my father took his seat by the open fire, where the mantel supported two ancient wooden figures of St. Christopher and St. Elizabeth of Hungary.

One friend wrote that it was worth a journey from London to hear my father read the forty-third chapter of Isaiah:

> The Divine Voice itself seemed to come to us as he finished by saying, "Take it to yourself personally: what He said to Jacob, He says to you."

He then tells how my father spoke of Christ's talk with Peter at the Sea of Tiberius, and ended thus:

> This is the common experience of man: in youth, joy, freedom, activity; in old age, slavery and compulsion. Is this what man was made for, then? But note the context, "When thou shalt be old thou shalt stretch forth thy hands." It is for us to stretch forth our hands, and say "Thy will be done." The young man, arrogant as young men are wont to be, seeks his own way; he grows old, gives himself to God, and then only becomes free. The moment he can say "Thy will is mine, Thy law my liberty, Thy love my life," then, at first or at last, he becomes free.

Another[1] sends me notes of one Coraggio reading of Tennyson's *Two Voices*. They are eminently characteristic of my father's fire-side manner, and may set us comparing to-day's psycho-analysis with his:

> ...It is very easy to put it [depression] all down to physical causes, the liver or the nerves, and so on. But—saving the presence of our friend the Doctor—I do not believe in that: if *he* could make us really *good*, we should not need very many medicines. Remember, we carry about with us all we have inherited from our ancestors in body and in mind.[2] Of course medical remedies may aid. But in the long run there is only one cure, and that is a spiritual one.
>
> Since this poem was written there has been a tremendous wave of unbelief over the world. One result has been that there is more real faith abroad now than there ever has been in the world before. But doubt and questioning must now affect every thinking mind, and this in some

---

1 The Rev. W. F. Curtoys (Cromhall Rectory, Charfield.)
2 In the matter of submerged inheritances, *vide The Elect Lady* (1888), p. 35.

cases leads to the suggestions of this Tempting Voice. Well, if there be no God, the Tempting Voice is right. All human life would be a sham. Man is befooled. But yet there is another way. *Go and do God's will and you will know. That is the remedy to the gloomy doubts and the terrible depression of this age.* And remember what so many forget, the Christian duty of joy.... You say: "it is not in my power to rejoice now." Well, I deny it. You have the power, if only you will exert the will. And don't let slip the youthful dreams. Such things will help you against that false self which comes with the Tempting Voice to despair. And don't let gloomy pictures of results keep coming before you. "To-morrow" has no existence till it actually comes. Let it take care of itself.

I have many vivid pictures of my father hung in the long gallery of my life. They glow in colour, and not one, whatever of reawakening of sorrows they may bring, would I turn to the wall. This, however, has a niche and illumination all its own: the old man with his white head and beard, his searching blue eyes, his crimson velvet cap, seated in low armchair by the fire, two candles on a little gate-legged table before him, the red glow of the olive logs occasionally breaking into flame and lighting up the green and red tiles, just as his words of fire leapt into flaming life and drove out the dark shadows from our souls. I recall no other light in the great room, and its contrast with the listeners so still and rapt. At last my father would, perhaps quite unexpectedly, rise and kneel, so that all, needy or critical, whatever their creed or hope, must feel their hearts opening out to God, for once perhaps if never again, like the red rose finding its freedom in the root-idea of the divine will. And then came a blessing, wonderful in its quiet, deeply penetrating, almost tremulous words, recalling the tones, still lingering in my heart from childhood's days, of Frederick Denison Maurice's benedictions; then a deep silence, and perhaps the organ softly rolling forth Handel's Largo from the far Jerusalem. Still and quiet even now, the guests would at last rise and go down the wide stone stair and out beneath the flashing stars of the huge Italian sky.

MR. GREATHEART

If ever room more than justified the idea of its planning, it was that room. It was home-place or concert-room, theatre or dancing room, oratory or dining-room, the heart of every occasion being our father's and mother's. Only the other day C. Edmund Maurice wrote me of a little incident that is a ray of sunlight over the world placed in George MacDonald's heart. He begins by quoting a trenchant word of his friend:

> I think one of his sayings that most impressed me was, "If anyone tells me it is an easy thing to speak the truth, I should tell him that he had never tried it." [1]

Then he continues:

> I remember a lecture of his on Shakespeare's *Julius Cæsar* in which he compared Cæsar to the more bragging kind of Irishman. Unfortunately there was an Irishman present; but he was quite pacified at the end by the lecturer saying he himself was a Highlander and therefore liable to the same Celtic temptation.

Mr. Maurice further refers to another day when my father was lecturing on Shakespeare's Sonnets.

> When he had finished, a man in the audience rose and held forth on the very questionable meanings which he believed were to be found in the Sonnets, and complaining bitterly of MacDonald for not mentioning them. Most of the audience were aghast at the bad taste of the attack. But MacDonald heard him out quietly, then went to him and laying his hand on his shoulder, said, "There, you shall have the last word!"

One of the loveliest uses to which the room was put was the representation of mediæval pictures in *tableaux vivants* at Christmas. The beauty of these was, I do affirm, extraordinary—almost incredible to professional stage-craft—so small was the cost, so simple the lighting, so exquisite and gorgeous the effects attained. It was my mother's genius that managed all these things, showing yet again how much the true artist can do with the poorest material. To these entertainments the Italian children of

---

[1] This is interesting as particularly recalled by a historian distinguished for his meticulous accuracy. The remark was often made by my father.

the town would joyfully come, a circumstance that gave some offence to certain English. But they had to be even more disturbed on another occasion when a concert was given, the admission to which was only by payment, and the entire proceeds were given towards wiping off the debt on the new Catholic Church in the town. Naturally the love for my parents extended beyond the English colony, and Padre Giacomo, when he met my father on the high road, would embrace him.

Christmas too, the season at which myself was oftenest able to join the home, was made gay with itinerant carol-singing, and a Christmas tree for intimate friends, Italian children coming too. Even the Christmas day of 1880, when the furniture from England, for which a small schooner had been chartered,[1] had not yet arrived, must not pass without its entertainment. Thus my sister Lilia writes:

L.S.M.D. to Miss Jane E. Cobden.

CASA CORAGGIO,
Jan. 9, 1881.

...If you don't mind a house guiltless of furniture [except hired necessities] we hope you will come and stay with us; we shall be so disappointed it you don't....I am quite sure you would like our new abode.... Everyone is quite happy. We are all steeped to our elbows in black paint and coloured stains for wood. Mamma and Grace are doing the walls of Mamma's little sitting-room, a dull red with eucalyptus leaves all over it. I have been upholsterer all the week, and out of boxes and Turkey-red have turned out some very neat things in chairs and ottomans, and have nearly lost the use of the tips of my fingers thanks to hammer and nails....We had some Christmas tableaux last week—the Annunciation, the Visit of Elizabeth, the Shepherds' Visit, the Mother and Child and St. John. We had all the English one day, and about one hundred of the Italians the next, the people about, anyone that happened....The [adopted] babies flourish and their mother is no worse. They made a lovely Christ Child and St. John the other night and were quite good....

---

1   Its passage was attended by some anxiety, for my father would never insure either his life or his property, and its arrival was much delayed by bad weather.

MR. GREATHEART

One recalls the first Christmas at The Tackleway, Hastings, with its penny toys and books, its half-oranges and story-telling by the young father. Nor at Casa Corragio was the simplicity less, even if the beauty and extent of hospitality were greater. A description of such doings is given by Lord Mount-Temple, and printed in his *Memorials* already referred to:

...On Christmas Eve, we were dining in our little room looking on the olive wood, and we heard the sound of many voices, and looking out, lamps glimmered among the trees, and figures carrying lanterns and sheets of music. Who should they be but the dear MacDonald family visiting the houses of all the invalids in the place, to sing them carols and bring them the glad tidings of Christmas. The next day they had beautiful tableaux of the Annunciation, the Stable, the Angels, and the Shepherds, ending up with the San Sisto Madonna, in their wonderful room in the Coraggio, and they had invited the peasants to come and enjoy this, for them, novel representation of the event of the blessed Christmas-tide.[1] That house, Coraggio, is the very heart of Bordighera, the rich core of it, always raying out to all around, and gathering them to itself.

We had weekly poetry readings there, enriched by the thoughts and the voice of the reader. Sometimes there were concerts and theatricals for our amusement or for some charity, and this winter there was a concert for the completion of the Church for the poor of the Marina. This delighted the good Father Giacomo, the village priest, as a mark of true Christian feeling and catholicity. And how can I describe the Sunday evenings!...

Casa Coraggio was full of guests at those Christmas times, cousins and old friends, and always some who contributed their share to the house-keeping expenses. Indeed, without these, and none were ever admitted to this privilege except

---

[1] Novel indeed from the point of view of modern Catholic Art among the Latin races. I well remember a crêche in the church of Old Bordighera at one of these Christmas-tides. The holy Mother was clad in a white satin costume, low-necked, long-trained and trimmed with pearls. St. Joseph was in to-day's full evening dress and white tie. The angelic choir, dressed like ballet-girls—to make them more homelike, I presume—were ranged on the ruined roof supported by ricketty Roman columns, and the Christ Child was almost invisible for the lace that decked his person and manger. The wonder is the cattle were not in trousers and the ass in motley! Of course in fashionable churches the crêche would be realistic enough, if still gaudy, but for the ignorant peasantry it must be less literal, more idealistic!

friends, or at least those who were closely connected with such, the heavy expenses of the big house with its four adoptions could hardly have been met. But the house-keeping was so wonderful that some of us visitors found the only explanation in a miraculous intervention of saints or heavenly brownies. Truth is my sisters had all the gifts of their mother in facing rebellious odds and tempting them into helpfulness.

My mother, besides her domestic surprises and enterprises, played the organ in church and, as already said, trained the choir: only those who have been involved in such work can realize the constant patience and strain it entailed.

Another fine instance is before me of my mother's resource in entertainment. If the idea was my mother's, the verses of invitation were my father's; and these explain the whole thing:

> Please come on Monday
> The day after Sunday,
> And mind that you start with
> Something to part with;
> A fire shall be ready
> Glowing and steady
> To receive it and burn it
> And never return it.
> Books that are silly,
> Clothes outworn and chilly,
> Hats, umbrellas or bonnets,
> Dull letters, bad sonnets,
> Whate'er to the furnace
> By nature calls "Burn us!"
> An ancient, bad temper
> Will be noted no damper—
> The fire will not scorn it
> But glory to burn it!
> Here every bad picture
> Finds refuge from stricture;
> Or any old grudge
> That refuses to budge,
>
> We'll make it the tomb
> For all sorts of gloom,
> The out-of-door path
> For every man's wrath.
> All lying and hinting,
> All jealous squinting,
> All unkind talking
> And each other balking,
> Let the fire's holy actions
> Turn to ghostly abstractions.
> All antimacassars,
> All moth-egg amassers,
> Old gloves and old feathers,
> Old shoes and old leathers,
> Greasy or tar-ry,
> Bring all you can carry!
> We would not deceive you:
> The fire shall relieve you,
> The world will feel better
> And so be your debtor.
> Be welcome then—very—
> And come and be merry!
>
> GEORGE AND LOUISA MACDONALD.

CASA CORAGGIO,
    Dec. 31st, 1885.

Bonfire at 7 p.m.
Dancing at 8.

Photo by] GEORGE MACDONALD, 1884 [R. F. MacDonald

MR. GREATHEART

Before relating the innermost story of these days, apart from the social aspects of family life, an incident showing the whole family's physical courage and unshakable hospitality must not be missed.

At 5.30 in the morning of February 23, 1887, the terrible earthquake began, lasting till 9. a.m., and beginning again in less severity the next morning. Its centre was Nice, and it extended from Milan to Marseilles; so that Bordighera, distant from Nice only a little more than twenty miles, was entrapped in its fellest grip.

Mrs. G.M.D. to Miss Anna Leigh Smith.

CASA CORAGGIO,
February 24th, 1887.

MY DEAREST NANNIE,

...Have you had tidings of the great trouble that has fallen upon Bordighera in the last two days? An earthquake yesterday morning, about six o'clock, surprised us out of our beds. I remember some slight ones we had at Algiers, but I never knew the real terror of one before. The poor people have suffered the most—their houses came tumbling about their ears, some buried in the ruins. Our plaster cracked and ceilings and vases and jugs broken—but our walls, so well built, stood firm—the only danger to us is from the stupid stucco tower that I dare say you remember vexed us so—George having ordered the tower to be of the same stone as the rest of the house. However, it received such a shock yesterday that it will have to be taken down. Yesterday there was such a panic that no one would do anything—besides it was Ash Wednesday and no one would lift a finger to work. So the night was spent by all the poor camping out, and some terrified women from the cracked hotels would not accept any shelter and sat all night in carriages on the high road, or under the olives all day. We had one family to meals, their kitchen and roof having fallen in, and another came to camp out in our big room for the night; but we had also to pack all the top story into the ground floor, and away from the unsafe tower. So an immense amount of packing and coaxing and a little manœvring had to be exercised to keep our large household in good spirits and to keep off faints and hysterics, besides being very tired and sick with the motion and alarm....

I remain ever and always your loving friend,

LOUISA POWELL MACDONALD.

GEORGE MACDONALD

G.M.D. to W. Carey Davies.

BORDIGHERA,
March 8, 1887.
Our wedding day 36 years ago.

...We have had the most extraordinary time—terrible indeed in its awfulness. That one shock was worth having lived to know what power may be. You knew it must be none other than God. No lesser power could hold the earth like that, as if it were "A very little thing," and shake you as if your big house were a doll's fly....Don't be anxious about us. We are all right....

Mrs. G.M.D. to W. Carey Davies.

CASA CORAGGIO,
March 20, 1887.

...I am so surprised to hear that your parson was so alarmed by the earthquake that he ran away in an expensive carriage. It was only the old fogies that did that here, and the poor nerveless creatures—but I suppose when a man sees every one else running he runs too, if he does not know better. Well, I hope he is better now....Such will be as frightened and try to rush off when they are told they are going to die....

But these letters tell nothing of the splendid behaviour of my mother and sisters, every one of whom did marvels, as I heard from many sources, to allay the abject fear possessing visitors and natives alike. Casa Coraggio, and the next house, Kingsbury Jameson's, my sister Grace's husband, he being assistant chaplain, fared better than some of the villas, though those built by the English escaped serious hurt. On the following morning, i.e. the 24th, my mother was in the English church close by sitting at the organ for a few moments' refreshment, when a second fierce earthquake occurred. "The whole bulk of the building began to shudder, just like the skin of a horse determined to get rid of a gad-fly";[1] and then such was the swaying and shaking that she felt sure it was going to collapse and bury them. My mother never failed the

---

1 *A Rough Shaking*, p. 45. The description in this book of the earthquake instances my father's realistic power.

moment's need: she pulled out all her stops and played the Hallelujah Chorus.

The shocks continued in lessening degree and increasing interval for a fortnight. Ruin upon ruin was left on mountain and by seashore. In the sky above were then begun a series of the most glorious sunsets ever beheld, night after night, week after week, till Easter passed into summer.

Within doors at Coraggio the havoc was great, and everyone was taxed to supply and comfort the household and visitors, most of whom spent the worst days under the olives, while my father stayed in his study and wrote.[1] His books had been flung in a heap on the floor: it was just as though, he said, a titan terrier had mistaken the house for a rat and tried to shake the life out of it. To me one remarkable fact about the earthquake is that it left no signs of shock upon my parents or sisters:

The earth shall quake 'neath them that trust the solid ground.[2]

Lilia S.M.D. to Miss Jane Cobden.

C. C. B.
March 2, 1887.

...Household arrangements have been a good deal upset, but its nerves have kept wondrous steady. The English about us have suffered not at all, and in some cases have behaved disgracefully. Mentone must be in a dreadful state—and places towards Genoa. We are in the thick of sewing parties for people whose every rag is buried....

---

1   My sister Irene, Mrs. Cecil Brewer, reminds me thus: "There was a little figure of Christ at the top of one book-case. When all its books were flung on to the floor, this figure still stood, though it had not been fixed in any way."
2   *Diary of an Old Soul*, September 13th.

CHAPTER II
THE PASSING OF CHRISTIANA

OF Lilia Scott MacDonald's many admirers and lovers, for her there was but one. She lost him because, to repudiate her art even for his sake had been like sitting with Peter by the fire in the midst of the hall: as much a denying of her faith as if she had gone on the stage against her parents' decision. Her genius and her duty reigned together on one throne. The young man, refined in heart and brain and beloved by us all, lacked courage. He was prospectively wealthy; but the relative whose probable heir he was, and who also loved my sister, refused to sanction their marriage unless she undertook never to act in public again. Such a condition was an insult to her own gifts and art. Moreover, it was foolishly tyrannical, seeing that, as he had no profession or other guarantee of future independence, my sister might be compelled to earn money. He had not the courage to face possible poverty, though my sister would have married him penniless: she *knew* that with a husband to stand by her, she could bring the world to her feet. He urged her to acquiesce, and she had no alternative but to send him away, though it should break her heart. Then she erected defences of utter sweetness and resignation, giving her life more than ever to others. She made light of it to her best friend, Miss Jane Cobden: "I suppose you know I haven't got a young man any more. It feels very strange—as if I had never been without him all my life before. I shall get used to it in time—it couldn't be helped...." (November 1880). And again, a little later: "You are quite right. Things must have been for the best with me—and not me only—that is my comfort. And God gives me a light heart. I thank Him." (January 1881.)

My brother Ronald married in 1888. Being a schoolmaster, having taken high place in the History Schools at Oxford, he went with his wife to the United States, and for the sake of her health accepted the headmastership of an episcopal school for boys at Asheville, N.C. There his wife died, and in 1890 my sister Lilia joined him to keep house and help him to such consolation as was possible.

G.M.D. to Miss Lilia S.M.D. at Asheville, U.S.A.

C. C. B.
Jan 4, 1891 [*her birthday*].

DEAREST CHILD,

I could say so much to you, and yet I am constantly surrounded by a sort of cactus-hedge that seems to make adequate utterance impossible. It is so much easier to write romances where you cannot easily lie, than to say the commonest things where you may go wrong any moment....I can only tell you I love you with true heart fervently, and love you far more because you are God's child than because you are mine.—I don't thank you for coming to us, for you could not help it, but the whole universe is "tented" with love, and you hold one of the corners of the great love-canopy for your mother and me. I don't think I am very ambitious, except the strong desire "to go where I am" be ambition; and I know I take small satisfaction in looking on my past; but I do live expecting great things in the life that is ripening for me and all mine—when we shall all have the universe for our own, and be good merry helpful children in the great house of our Father. I think then we shall be able to pass into and through each other's very souls as we please, knowing each other's thought and being, along with our own, and so being like God. When we are all just as loving and unselfish as Jesus; when like him, our one thought of delight is that God is, and is what he is; when the fact that a being is just another person from ourselves is enough to make that being precious[1] —then, darling, you

---

1 So making it impossible to return a blow. This epitomizes my father's pacifism—he so instinctively a fighter! *Vide A Rough Shaking*, p. 79: "To Clare another boy was another of himself."

and I and all will have the grand liberty wherewith Christ makes free—opening his hand to send us out like white doves to range the Universe.

Have I now shown that the attempt to speak what I mean is the same kind of failure that walking is—a mere, constantly recurring recovery from falling?...

I have still one *great* poem in my mind, but it will never be written, I think, except we have a fortune left us, so that I need not write any more stories—of which I am beginning to be tired....

My dear love to Ronald. I could not bear you to leave him any more than you could yourself. Tell him from me that Novalis says: "This world is not a dream, but it may, and perhaps ought to become one." Anyhow it will pass—to make way for the world God has hidden in our hearts.

Darling, I wish you life eternal. I daresay the birthdays will still be sparks in its glory. May I one day see that mould in God out of which you came.

Your loving
FATHER.

Here I insert a letter to C. Edmund Maurice, who had given my father a copy of his book *Richard de Lacy, a Tale of the Later Lollards*, then just published:

G.M.D. to C.E. Maurice.

CASA CORAGGIO, BORDIGHERA,
March 1, 1891.

MY DEAR EDMUND,

...Your work as usual is good, though I did mark a passage or two I could have found a little fault with—merely in composition. I fear I am something of a martinet. But as to the substance of the book I do not feel justified, in my ignorance to criticise. I read it with pleasure, and with, I hope, some real enlightenment....The moral lesson is one we are always needing —that the divergence from rectitude for the sake of a more important rectitude is not only dangerous but ruinous. I wish I knew half you do about the conditions of former generations, but neither my tastes nor opportunities have ever led me into those regions—except where they bordered on the interests of literature and the history of religious development. My son Ronald seems to send his main contemplative energy in that direction, though I daresay you and he would have a fight now and then!

We are a house of mourning afresh at present, though by no means crushed, for we live and are saved by the sure hope of what is to come. Our little Octavia has gone to her mother. She was the young light of her

Grannie's eyes....She had had a sort of intermittent fever, for several weeks, but there seemed no immediate danger when she was seized with convulsions and died in half an hour....

A friend to whom my sister became devotedly attached, and who spent the winters at Casa Coraggio, she having disease of her lungs fairly advanced, now became so much worse that, as Ronald, already in better health himself, was bringing his school into fine condition, and had an elderly cousin keeping house for him, Lilia came home again to nurse her friend. Though by this time everyone was fully aware of the infectiousness of tuberculosis disease, my sister's devotion and day-and-night waiting upon her friend increased as the mischief and danger advanced. The dying woman would often refuse food and medicine save from Lilia's hand, so that now one may fancy she was feeding with her own life the starved fire that would yet win the day.

Because of this friend's illness [she is spoken of as E. in this chapter's letters], my father, who had a lengthy lecturing engagement, must leave Bordighera before the rest of the family, and he came to his son's house in Harley Street.

Then came news to him of E.'s death, her latter days more terrible than any my mother had to bear in her own children's. She died at Boulogne, still nursed by Lilia, as well as a brother and sister of her own. Lilia's devotion was such that one could only expect her own infection: and the signs of it were immediate. My people came to England, having rented Stock Rectory, Billericay, for the summer, most of which time my father was away on his last lecturing-tour.

Throughout the relatively short illness my sister's self-control and sweetness were wonderful, even if sometimes her sense of humour or some histrionic compulsion would possess her. She was the most perfect woman her parents, her sisters and brothers, had ever known. My parents' letters are filled with fears and anguish, hope and courage, all dealing with her variations in symptoms, the consultations of doctors, the little drives, her great suffering. Fortunately my father, now sixty-seven, was wonderfully well, seeming quite fit for his work. My mother always got new vigour from some fountain of youth whenever impossible demands were made upon her.

While in the North my father spent a few days at Huntly, where his cousin, James MacDonald, a Celtic scholar and antiquarian, was in possession of The Farm.

G.M.D. to his Wife.

HUNTLY,
July 13*th*, 1891.

DEAREST,
...I have just returned with James from the churchyard where the bodies of all my people are laid—a grassy place, and very quiet, in the middle of undulatory fields and with bare hills all about. But I see the country more beautiful than I used to see it. The air is delicious, and full of sweet odours, mostly white clover, and there is over it much sky. I get little bits of dreamy pleasure sometimes, but none without the future to set things right. "What is it all for?" I should constantly be saying with Tolstoi, but for the hope of the glory of God....

Mrs. G.M.D. to her Husband.

STOCK RECTORY,
July 15. *Bob's birthday*. [1891.]

So very many thanks to you, my dearest, for your lovely letter this morning with bits in it about your country and the white clover (we have a good deal of it here—Irene put out a little vase full of it yesterday) and the words and thoughts about the Glory of the Lord—being the end of all—made Handel's "And the Glory of the Lord" go in my head right gloriously and preach lovely to me with your having shot it to me from your bow. Lily advances, though slowly....Indeed it *must* come all right some day....MacKay[1] is very sweet and helpful and combs Lily's hair or plays picquet with her and helps me with Orange Jelly and reads in your study and is generally good and slow and dull and funny and kind as his head allows him....I think it is quite delightful your having this quiet bit of old world time, Dearest and Beautifullest. Yes I feel too very strongly what you say about its all being so futile *if*...

---

1 Then a medical student at Christ's College, Cambridge.

LILIA SCOTT MACDONALD AS *CHRISTIANA*

THE PASSING OF CHRISTIANA

G.M.D. to his Wife.

HUNTLY.

I have been out for a few miles' drive—to the old church of Ruthven, of which only the gable and belfry remain, with a beautiful old bell, looking quite new, though I think the date on it is 250 years ago, with the legend in Latin "Every kingdom against itself [shall] be laid waste." Right at the foot of the belfry the fool of my story [1] is buried, with a gravestone set up by the people of Huntly telling about him, and how he thought that bell, now above his body, always said "Come hame, come hame." Close to him, in a place chosen by himself lies the Dr. Grant whose violin I bought. They are the only two lying there. I had never been there before. James made his man and another go up and take a rubbing of the legend on the bell. They could climb up the edge of the gable on the corbel-steps of it....

HUNTLY,
Sunday night, July 19th, 1891.

I have just come home from preaching in that great old church, in which I think I was only once in my life before, and am not sure of that. I think it would hold 2,000 if crammed. They had no service in the congregational place....Here is a little poem I wrote for the O'Neills' little boy [in Belfast] who is dying of disease of the hip-joint....

> I want to go, like other boys,
>   Out in the shining day;
> Dear Lord, I want to make a noise,
>   And run about and play.
>
> My weakness makes my mother sad;
>   Oh, set me on my feet!
> It would make father very glad
>   To meet me in the street!
>
> Ah, wilt thou not appear one day,
>   And smile, and say to me,
> "Rise up, my child, and come and play"?
>   And I shall go with thee.
>
> Thou wilt at last, whate'er befall,
>   Come out to find thy boy;
> And then my heart will be too small
>   For half of its great joy.

---

1 *The Wow o' Rivven*, in *The Portent and Other Stories*. Fisher Unwin's reprint.

...We had such a lovely sky last night of purest gold and blue clouds, a sort of Japanese blue, such as I seemed never to have seen before—in long streaks in the north. There is no night in clear weather at this time of year....

Mrs. G.M.D. to her Husband.

Sep. (?) 1891.

..."I feel all the while that it is someone else inside me making me do it"—and while she said it, she had such an absolutely absurd look of E. on her that I could not but believe she was right, and that E.'s spirit was actually *upon her*. What if she is helping us to get her well?...

The following little word of sympathy I introduce to keep touch with one friend who was herself ill:

Mrs. Russell Gurney to Mrs. G.M.D.

Sept. 8, 1891.

...And you, dear Mother-Bird, I wonder how the daily watch tells on you—I guess what it must be now the supporting Greatheart is away on another mission. Adieu, adieu. I've had a little less torment the last 3 nights and days.

Ever with tenderest love thy time-worn friend, ever blest in the MacDonald stronghold!

E. R. G.

And now Lady Caroline Charteris[1] died, a deeply loved friend since, I think, 1865 or earlier. She had made known her generosity to my father long before her person and name. Every Christmas for many years had come "To the children of George MacDonald" a great hamper full of Scottish fare and heavenly cheer, but never with any hint of the donor. At last she, herself being away from home, instructed some tradesman to pack the hamper and despatch it, but forgot to warn him against giving any clue to her name. So that when a card was found bearing the legend "With the Lady Caroline Charteris's compts." other joy than the shortbread and Scotch-bun and preserves was ours; and there was no more hiding of her light under a Christmas hamper.

---

1 Daughter of the 7th Earl of Wemyss and March, born 1816.

THE PASSING OF CHRISTIANA

Lady Caroline left my father a repeater watch, for which, in bequeathing it to a son, he wrote the following poem, now engraved inside the case and uniting in one memory the father and his friend:

To My Watch

Tiny, absolute machine,
Meting out with click so clean,
Every thread of Spider-Time,
To whose measure God sets rime,
Weaving garment for my life,
And weaving the shroud for ended strife,
Be my friend till, all undrest,
God shall clothe me in his best.

Gift of lady gone away,
Where they do not time the day;
Beating like her golden heart,
Faultless tuned by Love's own art;
Wisdom-toy, exhort me ever,
Till I leave thee for the giver.

Son, like-minded, take it next,
Compass on Time's ocean vext;
Be thy soul, though stars unseen,
Time eternally serene,
Whate'er befall,
Full of *Corage!*
God mend al!

Almost in the same week came news of a loss of a different nature, that gave no sense of grief or even a word of reproach to the trustee responsible for the investment. It was the disappearance of what to my mother was a large part of her father's legacy.

Mrs. G.M.D. to her Husband.

Stock Rectory,
Tuesday.

...Have you seen that the Eng. Bank of the River Plate is done up? Perhaps you may remember there was £2,000 of ours, yours and mine, in it. There's a nut for us to crack without any kernel....It doesn't seem very hard except for the children...

But to return. There was never the least hope of even temporary betterment in my sister's case; and they were compelled to hurry back to Bordighera without waiting for her father, lest she should be too ill to travel.

G.M.D. to his Wife.

85 Harley Street, W.
Oct. 13, 1891.

...My memory gets so troublesome—I suppose by my brain being tired. I have things to tell you, and then by the time I sit down to write, I cannot remember them....For Lily, it seems just the old story of ups and downs. But we must remember that we are only in a sort of passing vision here, and that the real life lies beyond us. If Lily goes now, how much the sooner you and I may find her again! Life is waiting us. We have to awake—or die—which you will—to reach it. Only let us believe the great way, and trust altogether. When I come, I shall be able to help you....We have had a nice talk, Greville and I, at and after lunch....

"Has he been overworking himself," he asked a patient concerning her husband who had gone out of his mind. "Oh, dear, no! We belong to the landed gentry," was her reply!...

G.M.D. to his Wife.

Glyndyl, Bangor, N.W.,
Oct. 27, 1891.

...She [Lilia] has never taken care of herself, and now we must take care of her. If it should please God to leave her, we shall all take care of her; if not, we shall find her soon at the farthest. The great creative love which has closed us in these heavy bodies will open the doors of our cages and let us fly free in his high liberty....Oh dear, what a mere inn of a place the world is! And thank God! we must widen and widen our thoughts and hearts. A great good is coming to us all—too big for this world to hold....

A heart-rending letter then tells of my mother's journey with Lilia and the two other girls, and of the patient's self-control in the train, sitting bolt upright, showing no fatigue, and coughing, to my mother's amazement, not at all; but my mother adds words fraught with sadness for us who owe her everything we are and have, yet so often have failed and hurt her:

THE PASSING OF CHRISTIANA

Mrs. G.M.D. to her Husband.

C.C.B,
Oct. 30, 1891.

...But oh! she did suffer!—and indeed all her life she has been an intensely suffering soul. Knowing all I do now of what unintentional agonies we have made our children suffer, all the while having a heart full of love and intended good-will to them, I could not *dare*, of my choice, have over again such a lovely family as was given to us to rear and teach and guide. Well, thank God, with all our mistakes and come-shortnesses, the children are and have been all trying to do their duty, and in their measure serving their God....

G.M.D. to his Wife.

85 HARLEY STREET, W.,
Nov. 5, 1891.

...This is your birthday, dearest. I hope you are full of hope in it. Though the outer decay, the inner, the thing that trusts in the perfect creative life, grows stronger—does it not? God will be better to us than we think, however expectant we be....

Dearest, my love to you on this your birthday—a good day for me. I thank God for you.

Your loving
HUSBAND.

G.M.D. to his Wife.

85 HARLEY STREET,
Nov. 6, 1891.

...I may as well use this paper which wrapt my last lecture-fee to write my next to last letter to you....My work is done[1] and I am better now than when I began it—48 lectures in 58 days....I hope I shall be able to help you in the nursing. I think I might manage to feed her fire for her in the night for one thing. Greville says neither of the girls is strong enough to bear being disturbed in her sleep....

...On Sunday afternoon Mr. William Nichol[2] came to sing to me....He sang *Comfort ye*, and I have not heard it anything like so well rendered since you.

G. says I have 15 or 20 years' work in me yet. The doctors say a man's age is the age of his arteries, and there is no decay, no age in mine. He says there is not an unsound spot in me....

---

1 This lecture was literally the last: he never spoke again in public for any fee.
2 One of my own staunchest friends, a professor at the R.A.M., and the most exquisite tenor I ever heard in the tenderness of his art.

The following day my father paid his last visit to William Matheson, than whom no friend was ever in all the world's history more faithful. He died on the 21st. He had loved my eldest sister from childhood upwards, but knowing himself unacceptable—being but ten years younger than her parents—he never spoke a word of it, save to my mother, and so remained the same devoted "uncle" to us all.

My father reached Coraggio on November 8th. Though his drooping "White Lily" had revived a little in the sunshine, even going out in her bath-chair four days before the end, the hope awakened proved fallacious. So little had her imminent danger been realized that, the Wednesday before, my father gave the first of his readings to some sixty or seventy guests. She died in his arms on Sunday, November 22nd, and was buried on the 25th, her age being thirty-nine.

So the Post from the Celestial City presented her with a letter. When he had read this letter to her, he gave her therewith a sure token that he was a true messenger, and was come to bid her make haste to be gone. The token was, an arrow with a point sharpened with love, let easily into her heart, which by degrees wrought so effectually with her, that at the time appointed she must be gone....She called for Mr. Greatheart, her guide, and told him how matters were. So he told her he was heartily glad of the news, and could have been glad had the post come for him, saying, "Thus and thus it must be; and we that survive will accompany you to the river side."

When the coffin was carried into the church the congregation joined in the singing, "My God, my Father, while I stray." The tremulous, subdued voices showed how deeply everyone was mourning the loss of a cherished friend, that woman who, from her very childhood, had been a mother to old and young. Her father could hardly leave the grave: he came back twice after all others had left, and it was with difficulty he was at last led away. The day was terribly wet: all nature was lamenting.

But Christiana answered, "Come wet, come dry, I long to be gone: for however the weather is in my journey, I shall have time enough when I come there to sit down and rest, and dry me."...The last words she was heard to say were, "I come,

Lord, to be with thee, and bless thee!" So her children and friends returned to their place, for those that waited for Christiana had carried her out of their sight. At her departure her children wept.

Only one picture of Mr. Greatheart hangs in my gallery. I see him clad from shoulders to feet in chainmail and camail, with the white, red-crossed surcoat and his great two-handed sword. He has seen Christiana disappear in the Dark River, and then comes down to the listeners who wait upon his every word, saying, "Thanks be to God who has given us the victory!"

> Thy great deliverance is a greater thing
> Than purest imagination can foregrasp;
> A thing beyond all conscious hungering,
> Beyond all hope that makes the poet sing.
> It takes the clinging world, undoes its clasp,
> Floats it afar upon a mighty sea,
> And leaves us quiet with love and liberty and thee.[1]

---

[1] *Diary of an Old Soul*, May 5th.

CHAPTER III
A SHEAF OF LETTERS

THIS and the next chapter cover the years from 1881 to 1897, and hold little but letters belonging to the closing years, together with some words of elucidation and some relative to significant incidents.

G.M.D. to George Rolleston, M.D., F.R.S., Linacre Professor of Anatomy and Physiology, Oxford.[1]

Casa Coraggio, Bordighera,
June 16th, 1881.
[Written the day he died.]

Beloved Friend,

Do not start at the warmth of my address, for brief as was our opportunity of knowing each other, it was more than long enough to make me love you. I write because I hear you are very ill. I know not a little about illness, and my heart is with you in yours. Be of good courage; there is a live heart at the centre of the lovely order of the Universe—a heart to which all the rest is but a clothing form,—a heart that bears every truthful thought, every help-needing cry of each of its children, and must deliver them.

All my life, I might nearly say, I have been trying to find that one Being, and to know him consciously present; hope grows and grows with the years that lead me nearer to the end of my earthly life; and in my best moods it seems ever that the only thing worth desiring is that his will be done; that there lies before me a fulness of life, sufficient to content the giving of a perfect Father, and that the part of his child is to yield all and see that he does not himself stand in the way of the mighty design.

But why do I write thus to you who may know all this, tenfold better than I? Just because I want to come near to you in your illness....Christ speaks of the world's goods as not ours—as things that cannot be ours, but are in their nature foreign to power of possession. Our own things

---

1 *Vide* the poem "George Rolleston," *Poetical Works*, vol. i, p. 443.

are the riches towards God. What I may have in this kind I offer you, in love and sympathy with you and yours.

May the great life whose creating power is Love be with you and make you strong and comfort you. One moment's contact between his heart and his child's makes of that child a young God. "I said ye are Gods."

May he make you triumph over pain and doubt and dread, and restore you to perfect, divine health....

G.M.D. to W. C. Davies

CASA CORAGGIO,
Jan. 19, 1883.

DEAR DAVIES,

...In my illnesses I sometimes make verses. These times I have taken to Rondels and Triolets. Here are three of the latter—

> I'm a poor man, I grant,
> But I am well neighboured;
> And none shall me daunt,
> Though a poor man, I grant,
> For I shall not want—
> The Lord is my shepherd!
> I am a poor man, I grant,
> But I am well neighboured.[1]
>
> ---------------
>
> When I awake from sleep,
> Lord, I am still with thee;
> For while I slumbered deep,
> Nor could awake from sleep,
> 'Twas thy storm waves did sweep
> So softly over me;
> And when I wake from sleep,
> Lord, I am still with thee.
>
> ---------------
>
> Lord, what is man
> That thou art mindful of him?
> Though in creation's van,
> Lord, what is man,
> Who wills less than he can,
> Lets his ideal scoff him!
> Lord, what is man
> That thou art mindful of him?[2]

All King David's, you see!...

---

1 *Poetical Works*, vol. ii, p. 410
2 *Ibid*, vol. ii, p. 331. The second of these three seems to have escaped publication.

G.M.D. to his Son G.M.M.D.

BORDIGHERA,
April 6, 1884.

MY DEARLY LOVED SON,

It puzzles me a little that you, to whom God has given more insight than many have into the necessities of the spiritual relations, should be so changeable and troubled by the appearances of things. "In quietness and confidence shall be your strength." "Wait on the Lord." You are so impatient! You will hardly give him time to do anything for you! As you are so easily troubled, as your faith in him seems so much in the abstract, and when it comes to the matter of next month or next year you are full of doubt—as if what the day was to bring forth must be evil and not good, notwithstanding that perfect goodness is at the head of your affairs—this being the case, I see why you should be troubled and tossed about as you are. Do not be always speculating on your future and thinking what you shall do. You are not a bit nearer knowing for that; and it is a great waste of brain tissue, to say nothing of spiritual energy left dormant.... *There is more action in dismissing a useless care than in a month's brooding over the possible or the probable.* When the hour for decision arrives, one moment's clear untroubled thought will do what weeks and weeks of brooding beforehand will only make more uncertain and difficult....

G.M.D. to W. Carey Davies.

Feb 17, 1885.

MY DEAR DAVIES,

Thank you for the newspaper cutting [re Fyvie Castle]. I wish I had read it before Donal Grant....

I knew it was a grand stair; I have a passion for stairs; for I have a photograph of an engraving of it given me by the widow of the last owner but one [Mrs. Cosmo Gordon]—with whom we are intimate. But I have never been there, and the stair is evidently much grander than I knew.

I am told there is a disused avenue at Glamis like the one I have in the book. Of that I had not a glimmer of an idea. All I knew of it was the story of the devil and the card-players which I had heard as a child. Oddly, too, since inventing the æolian harp on the roof, I came on the same idea in a French novel....

I think I would rather not hear that Gordon was alive. But if he is, it is best. He *may* be, but I do not think it....

Khartoum fell January 26, 1885. My father had met General Gordon several times, and it was inevitable that they should love one another. That greatest among military evangelists had given my father the chain mail of a Crusader he had himself found in the Sudan.[1]

It seems almost unintelligible that my father should still be constantly harassed for want of money. "How is it," he asks of A. P. Watt, *à propos* of a certain negotiation, "that while I have ten times the number of readers I had ten years ago, I cannot get nearly such good prices for my books?" The answer is not forthcoming. The following letter may make us ask again whether in spite of my father's indomitable belief that his needs would be supplied, he did not inevitably suffer more than the world, more perhaps than even his wife knew, from frictional workings of the temporal wheels.

G.M.D. to A. P. Watt.

BORDIGHERA,
Jan 10, 1885.

MY DEAR WATT,
...I don't know that ever I *seemed* worse off. I say *seemed* because I do not acknowledge the *look* of things. I am spending borrowed money now, and *see* no way but to borrow more. If I had a good offer for my house I would sell it....You see I have only one son off my hands yet—that makes it so heavy with two of them away from home. However, they cause me no other burden whatever—thank God, as I hope you will find with yours.... What do you think? It is very odd how those who have plenty seem to stick to their money when others are most in want of it. But business is a strange country to me....

I think it [*The Elect Lady*] will turn out well. It is a Scotch story without any Scotch and *touches* on Highland affairs not in detail but in principle...I am very glad you have got another place for the story. What should I do without you!...

It was about this time that my father had to write to a warm friend and admirer refusing a gift from her, and with a sternness that must have hurt him sorely. I quote but a few words of the very long letter, and then follow it with one from Lord Mount-Temple refusing my father's

---

1 Vide "To Gordon Leaving Khartoum," *Poetical Works*, vol. i, p. 444, and "General Gordon," *Poetical Works*, vol. i, p. 264.

repayment of a loan. The two incidents have nothing to do with each other, but fall together well in the text. The second has interest because indicating the big heart of its writer, though we do not yet find the world prepared for his prophetic hope.

G.M.D. to Mrs. X—

...I thank you heartily and lovingly for your kind thoughts of us....I am not ashamed of taking money; if I were I would not take it; neither do I wish the fact concealed that I have often accepted money with grateful and unending obligation. But I could not take it in circumstances where the world around would be sure to misunderstand....I have to confess that I should have found another great obstacle in the way—this, that I could not have been sure that, at some time before long, when you were dissatisfied with something I had done, you would not have said something, in still continuing kindness I would not doubt, which would have made me sorry that I had ever been laid under obligation to you. For an obligation ought to be a sweet thing, like a scent of old rose-leaves, to be carried in one's soul to all eternity—a bond of ever-growing union—not a burden which one keeps ever hitching on the other shoulder because he cannot to all Eternity get rid of it....Can I accept anything of earthly value from one who so judges me—rightly or wrongly? Would it not be a mean thing, and confirm such a judgement? I say *earthly* value, because yet I must take whatever heavenly gift you had to give me—of which, of course, what love you could give would be the first. If you say, "the heavenly given and accepted, why refuse the earthly"? I should answer, "There is not yet quite enough of the heavenly to embalm the earthly, not to say redeem, and raise it from the dead....

      Verily your friend,
        George MacDonald.

Lord Mount-Temple to G.M.D.

      15 Great Stanhope Street,
       Feb 1, 1886.

My dear Friend and Teacher,

I have received your honourable conscientious fulfilment of your engagement, but my affection and sympathy for you prompts me to treat it as waste paper and to leave for your own use this produce of your brain. Pray forgive me for taking this liberty with your handwriting and reducing it to ashes....

We are going to change from this house to the bank of the river at Chelsea, where we shall have a delightfully rural position.

Politics are very difficult and the Irish problem impossible to solve satisfactorily. All Europe is being influenced by the rising wave of democracy and socialism—in preparation, I hope, for the manifested dispensation of the Holy Ghost. The Pentecostal blessing was poured on the whole multitude, and now the Banks of Privilege and Superiorities are being overwhelmed by the claims and combined force of the masses. I think I perceive the preparation for that 2nd coming which has been the hope and comfort of so many devout hearts....

The new house on the Embankment was "dedicated" in a religious service on July 2, 1887, and for it my father wrote this poem:

For the Dedication of Shelley House.

Lord, this earth so high and great,
    All its floors and stairs and towers,
All its splendours and its state,
    Is thy Father's house and ours.

But like birds in sheltering wood,
    Nests we build of warmer stuff,
Lest thy strong house-angels should
    All unwittingly be rough.

Lord, this house is all Thine own,
    All and whole and every part;
Let the guard around it thrown
    Be Thy presence in its heart.

Thine is every bed and chair,
    Every table, every book:—
Meet us up and down the stair;
    Talk with us in every nook.

Thine is every servant-hand,
    Thine each foot upon the floor;
Never shall the Master stand
    Waiting at un-opened door.[1]

G.M.D. to W. Carey Davies.

Bordighera,
March 20, 1886.

My dear Davies,

...I wonder what Gladstone is going to do about Ireland. I must say I do not look for much good at hand from it. I fear things will have to be a good deal worse before they begin to be better. And where lies the

---

[1] The poem was first published in *The Vineyard*, April 1912, vol. iv.

blame, if it be not on those who have drawn their pay without doing their work? —I mean the landlords who have not been the heads of the people in some reciprocative sense. I cannot tell. But you will see from my book[1] how I feel about these things.

...I find one of my great failings is being angry with the stupidity of people—I mean of course such stupidity as seems to have moral roots. With merely intellectual stupidity no one has a right to be angry at all—and perhaps not with any sort. If I felt as much as I ought how miserable it is not to carry an open mind toward all that is living and true, surely I should pity rather than be angry....

To pay you for your trouble, in earthly things, here is a small return in spiritual things:

> When I look back upon my life nigh spent,
> Nigh spent although the feeble stream flows on,
> I more of follies than of sins repent,
> Less for offence than Love's shortcomings moan.
> With self, O Father, leave me not alone,
> Leave not with the beguiler the beguiled;
> Besmirched and ragged, Lord, take back thy own;
> A fool I bring thee to be made a child.[2]

The next four letters are typical of those he would write to his sons.

G.M.D. to his Son Robert Falconer, age twenty-four.

C. C. B.,
Aug. 29th, 1886.

...We have no boys with us at present; perhaps we may never all meet again together in this world. God knows: but I have all my life, I think, been attended (I would call it *haunted*, were it not that the word has the atmosphere about it of the undesired) by the feeling of a meeting at hand. It must come one day—the hour when our hearts, all of them, will come together as they have never come before—when, knowing God, we shall know each other in a way infinitely beyond any way we have now. But the new way will fold up the old way in it. The Kingdom of Heaven has come near us that we may enter into it, and be all at home together. Kingdom and home are one....Lily has just taken me on the loggia to see two broad, faint-red rays shooting up into the blue from the far-down sun, while all the mountains and the towering clouds are a misty gray. They say this is the hottest day there has been....

---

1 *What's Mine's Mine*, 1886.
2 *Poetical Works*, vol i, p. 321.

G.M.D. to his Son G.M.M.D.

Christmas 1886.

When a man comes to feel quiet confidence and hope, even when the life he *feels* is indeed not worth living, then he is getting ready fast. When one in a dream can welcome the thought of the sun and the active day, he is worth waking. But many of us will not consent to leave our coffins till we have made them tidy. I don't think Jesus folded his death garments: the angels did that after he had gone out of his three days' chamber. This is not quite coherent, but it may make *thinks* in you. May you have a divinely good Christmas.

Jan. 19, 1887.

...Many good birthdays be yours, as many will surely be, if only we let our Lord have his way for and with us. More and more I see and feel that what the Father is thinking is my whole treasure and well being. To be one with him seems the only common sense, as well as the only peace. Let him do with you, my beloved son, as he wills. Be hearty with his will. *Submission is not the right feeling when we say "Thy will be done." His will is the only good....*

BORDIGHERA,
Jan. 20, 1889.

This is your Sunday birthday. My love to you, and the desire which is sure to come true, that you may have all the good that may be gathered in the world to which the Lord of souls sent you through us. That existence is a splendid thing I am more and more convinced, while, at the same time, but for my hope in God, I should have no wish for its continuance, and should feel it but a phantasmagoria. But Jesus Christ *did* come, for no man could have invented him; and he thought our being worth giving himself for; and he was perfectly satisfied with his God and Father. And so I am content in God. Rather than believe in the popular God, I would believe in none, with the agnostics....

In September 1890, the fifth of the sons, the only one of the family besides the eldest daughter who had marked dramatic gifts, was married after seven years of happy betrothal—an occasion for much rejoicing.[1]

---

[1] Bernard MacDonald, M.A. Cantab., is now Professor of Elocution at Queen's College, London, and Lecturer on Voice Production at Mansfield College, Oxford.

G.M.D. to Henry Cecil at Bournemouth (on the occasion of the tragical death of his eldest son.)

BORDIGHERA,
March 3, 1890.

DEAR OLD FRIEND,

What can I say to you, for the hand of the Lord is heavy upon you. But it is his hand, and the very heaviness of it is good. ...There is but one thought that can comfort, and that is that God is immeasurably more the father of our children than we are. It is all because he is our father that we are fathers....It is all well—even in the face of such pain as yours—or the world goes to pieces for me.

It is well to say "The Lord gave and the Lord hath taken away," but it is not enough. We must add, And the Lord will give again: "The gifts of God are without repentance." He takes that he may give more closely—make *more ours*....The bond is henceforth closer between you and your son....

> To give a thing and take again
> Is counted meanness among men;
> Still less to take what once is given
> Can be the royal way of heaven!
>
> But human hearts are crumbly stuff,
> And never, never love enough;
> And so God takes and, with a smile,
> Puts our best things away awhile.
>
> Some therefore weep, some rave, some scorn;
> Some wish they never had been born;
> Some humble grow at last and still,
> And then God gives them what they will. [1]

I close this sheaf of letters with a quotation from the article by Sir William D. Geddes on "George MacDonald as a Poet," in *Blackwood's Magazine*, March 1891:

> ...We even make bold to say that in native gift of poetic insight he was born with a richer dower than has fallen to any of our age since Alfred Tennyson saw the light of day. To have the dews of one's youth retained under the browner shades of life or beneath the snows of age, to be one of those whose heart has kept pure the holy forms of young imagination, is the prerogative of genius: and to none has this special phase of that prerogative been given in our age more largely than to George MacDonald....

---

1 "The Giver," *Poetical Works*, vol. ii, p. 128. The original form as above, some may think the better.

GEORGE MACDONALD, 1880

MRS. GEORGE MACDONALD, 1885

Photo by [*Elliott & Fry*

CHAPTER IV
LAST WORDS

A STAR shining in one man's soul may, like a lantern, shed light for many a wayfarer. If we had not yet realized George MacDonald's faculty of deep listening to another man speaking from the depths of his soul, or his rare gift in assaying gold hid in the dross of perplexities, we should get striking light upon these points from a communication I recently had from the Rev. John Rooker, later Rector of Sevenoaks and Rural Dean.

When curate of St. Michael's, Chester Square, some thirty-five years ago, he first met my father, being invited to St. John Lea, Brondesbury, where my people were spending the summer of 1888, and where my brother Ronald was married.

> I went (writes Mr. Rooker) with no little nervousness, but his reception put me at ease at once. I was struck by his appearance, of course—that beautiful kindly shrewd face....It seemed to me (if I may reverently say so) as if I were talking to S. John the Apostle. I never think of Dr. MacDonald without instinctively thinking of S. John. There was in him that gentleness and humanity and strength—a depth of fire below the surface in spite of all his sweetness—that I fancy were characteristics of the disciple Jesus loved.
> Well, we sat in the library—where boxes were being packed and books lying about the room, prior to departure for Bordighera. And then I opened my heart to him as I had hardly ever opened it to any stranger before. Doubts and fears—sore burdens just then—were bluntly put before him, and he sat and listened with the utmost patience. It was strange—and yet it was not strange—to find myself talking to him so freely. I saw, I felt, his holiness and nearness to God, and yet I should

not have been afraid to confess to him most secret sins. There was a humanity about him, and a searching honesty, which, along with his sympathy, made me feel that he would understand me. He would not cast me out.

I suppose men and women felt like this when they talked with our Lord. His holiness attracted them, and His love and pity encouraged them to come and open up their hearts, sure that He would not drive them away....

I forget much of his reply, but I remember this: "I should not be surprised," he said, "if God has not some special work for you to do." I cannot describe the comfort those simple words gave me. Then this tension of mind was a discipline, and meant good. I could bear it, and perhaps one day thank God for it.

Then just before I left he said—and I can hear him now—"But after all, whatever help or comfort any one may try to give you, it is but to follow the advice of Jesus. 'Enter into thy closet, and shut to thy door, and pray to thy Father in secret'—pour out your heart to God—get down on your knees—He will help you as no one else can, and will give you an answer of peace."

I left him with "uplifted head," and thankful heart—but only years unfolded to me the depth of his words.

In 1896 my parents spent the summer months at Holmbury St. Mary, a village in Surrey. Mr. Rooker was then Vicar of Coldharbour, an adjoining parish on the flank of Leith Hill, and he tells us further:

He came with one of his daughters [Irene] to tea, and sat out on the terrace looking at the glorious view with much enjoyment. I remember what a picturesque figure he made. The following Sunday morning he came over to our little church. I see him now among the congregation, and I see him with regret. I was a young Vicar then, and I should act differently now. There was a prophet among us, and I never asked him to give us a message. I think the incongruity struck me—that he should be there and anyone else preaching—but I was not sure whether I dare ask him or ought to ask him, and I let the opportunity slip. I have never forgiven myself.

...On another occasion when I was at tea with Dr. MacDonald at Holmbury a grandchild was in the room. Mrs. MacDonald was on the sofa, as I do not think she was very strong. I noticed the tender affection of the grandparents, and laughingly remarked to Dr. MacDonald—"Why is it that grandparents often spoil their grandchildren? Perhaps as parents they were strict disciplinarians, but as grandparents they are not." Dr. MacDonald looked across at Mrs. MacDonald and smiled—

"What do you say?" he asked. "Perhaps it is because as we grow older we have more faith," she said. "When we were young we thought everything depended on ourselves—and on our training. Now we see that God has a hand in the education, and we leave matters more to Him."

...His last letter to me was arranging another visit to Coldharbour. "My wife and I," he wrote, "are somewhat tired now *by* life, but not tired *of* it." I do not think I ever saw him again, but I never cease to thank God for him, and I hope one day I may be permitted to tell him so.

Instead of coming home, they spent the summer of 1892 in Switzerland, at Arth. My mother was failing much, and scarcely took the air save in her bath-chair. She never quite recovered from the loss of her eldest child the year before, though she was still the life of choir and organ in the little Bordighera church. My father was seeing through the press the two volumes of his *Poetical Works*.

G.M.D. to W. Carey Davies.

BORDIGHERA,
June 15, 1892.

...I have no impulse toward public work this year. I do not think I should feel at all sorry if I were told I should never preach or lecture again. Somehow I have very little feeling of doing good that way. But let everything always be as our Father wills. I hope, with you, I shall not have to change much in my new edition of Poems. It is very troublesome, but one cannot let wrongness of any kind willingly pass. It will be in two volumes and complete—all except the Diary, Translations, and the Poems in *Phantastes*....I have just finished a story called *Heather and Snow*....

I have already remarked on my father's devotion to accuracy in form and polish. Though closely related to his honesty and precision in everything he did, it may seem remarkable in one whom less intelligent readers used to accuse of "vagueness" and "nebulosity." The point of view of a craftsman intent upon polishing his work is necessarily different from that when its first inspiration dominated his design. So the critic is often misguided, and not least, perhaps, when judging his own work; his humbleness in the face of great ideas then makes him question his own powers. I think we find many earlier versions of my father's poems not improved in the collected *Poetical Works*,[1] the polish actually sometimes veiling the brilliancy of the inherent light. Yet we could not do without these volumes, and only regret that they do not include much of his finest verse scattered through novels and fairy-tales.

While on this point, I would add one more word. My father was never what mere schoolmen consider a first-rate academic critic, perhaps just because he was so very much more. In his *Essays*[2] we sometimes even miss his genius—particularly, perhaps, in that on the *Imagination*, for, as already suggested, it falls short of his other references to the subject, both in prose and verse. But none the less we may well claim his gift of criticism to be profound and enthusiastic. All who remember his minutely learned critique on Hamlet—"the noblest character in all fiction"—or any of his lectures, must admit this: they were unlike anything else ever given to the world. I believe that his *Hamlet* will yet be recognized as the most important interpretation of the play ever written. But the writer's power lay rather in the consanguinity of his mind with Shakespeare's and every other poet's. It is his intuitive understanding—like a mother's of her children, a son's of his father—rather than learned analysis—of which there is yet overwhelming evidence—that makes it so splendid. It is his special pleading for the play's revelations, rather than his criticism, that gives his *Hamlet* a place quite apart from all other writings on this subject. The honestly passionate advocate is a greater man than the most honest judge: what the former must have, namely *fire*, the latter must do without.

---

[1] My father was fully aware that a poet's emendations were not always satisfactory. He would enlarge upon this when lecturing on *The Ancient Mariner*, and insist upon our comparing the first and final versions.

[2] *A Dish of Orts*, 1893.

LAST WORDS

G.M.D. to A. P. Watt.

BORDIGHERA,
Feb. 26, 1885.

...As I expected, the critics are down on my *Hamlet* on all sides. Of course! They are just of the class which I say cannot understand him or his inventor. How should there be anything in common between me and the ——*Review*, for instance—a paper I have looked upon with literal repugnance almost since its first appearance!...I am not in the least surprised. It shows me the more how desirable it was that the coming generations should have what help I could give them to start with, some notion of what Shakespeare meant in his *Hamlet*; for the interpretation commonly given makes a very poor thing of it compared with what I see in it. But how should the commonplace understand the best that the highest intellect of the country could produce? But the truth will stand....

Tennyson died October 6, 1892, and my father refers thus to the nation's loss:

G.M.D. to W. Carey Davies.

BORDIGHERA,
Oct. 15, 1892.

MY DEAR DAVIES,

Tennyson is gone to his peers, and I do not mourn much for any of the dead. God be with us here and there—that is all. We shall soon join them....I feel as if I should never lecture more. I have no impulse to do so. If I am willed to do it, the impulse will wake....I am certain I have greatly improved many of my poems. I was much displeased with them. But the first way of a thing sticks to you against reason somehow....

I like your taking Renan's part, but really the chatter of the world, that is the newspapers, is not worth minding. They, the newspapers, are becoming more and more impudent....

When speaking of Tennyson, my father used to say that all men are poets; for, though perhaps they cannot write poetry, they can listen to it, hunger for it and love it. So that a poet is just more of a man than most. He can listen to Nature, though others cannot understand her words because they do not love her enough; more, he can translate them so that all who are not overfed with self-esteem can understand. Tennyson stood greatest among all the lyrical poets, and my father ranked *In Memoriam* as peerless in the century.

The next letter hints at how faith may give youthful happiness to a man, though time loads him with burdens. I do not omit one personal point, for it surely concerns my father's happiness.

G.M.D. to W. Carey Davies.

BORDIGHERA,
Jan. 22, 1893.

I gather from your last letter that you are now fifty years of age. I am nearly twenty years your senior—not very far from 70 now, but if I do not in all things, I do in all essential things feel younger than when I was a child. Certainly I am happier and more hopeful, though I think I always had a large gift of hope. It has been the one constitutional power of life in me—none of my making surely!

...Have you seen that Greville is made a Physician to King's College Hospital. We are all very much pleased. You have known him ever since he went to school at King's—a choir boy....

I am rather driven with work, I think sometimes; but if my faith were stronger, as I hope it is on the way to being, I should never feel that.

G.M.D. to A. P. Watt

HAXTED HOUSE,
EDENBRIDGE,
June 11, 1893.

DEAR WATT,

I can't do it, even to oblige you....I never have and never will consent to be interviewed. I will do *nothing* to bring my personality before the public in any way farther than my work in itself necessitates. Pardon my brevity. I have begun again to work, but writing takes all the strength I have to spend....My memory plays me sad tricks now. It comes of the frosty invasion of old age—preparing me to go home, thank God. Till then I must work, and that is good....

VILLETTA DEMIDOFF,
PRATOLINO, ITALY,
June 18, 1894.

...I am a little better, I think, and begin to imagine it possible I should one day begin another book. But I continue very weak mentally. I am only able to read and understand books worth reading, mixed with a good story now and then....We are in a most lovely place with a big park all about us and fine weather, not at all too hot to enjoy it in....

LAST WORDS

I am buried in Villari's *Life and Times of Savonarola*, and that wants so much thinking that the fact of its being in Italian hardly makes me longer in reading it....

Among the many happy influences that held him to youthfulness in thought and feeling, was the friendship of Miss Violet and Hyacinth Cavendish Bentinck and their mother Mrs. Scott. They owned a villa in Florence and visited Bordighera from time to time. The little incident of their giving him a big opal full of fire brought them a letter that Miss Violet has cherished always. My father's delight in gems was wonderful. They were to him symbolic of course—"the glory even of things"—though their significance altogether transcended mere poetical use. When held by their beauty, his mind journeyed perhaps into subconscious memories of ancient race-feelings; he was transformed into the pure mystic, his own logical mind becoming subordinate.

Nor did his love of the colour, glimmer and star-shine of jewels lessen as the years filled up his treasury with things that cannot rust or be stolen.

In precious stones he took a delight almost barbaric, but enriched by the knowledge of the amateur.[1] There is a passage in chapter lxi of *Castle Warlock* that describes the pouring out, into a patch of evening sunlight upon a bare floor, of a great treasure-trove of unset precious stones. "Into the pool began to tumble a small cataract of shredded rainbows, flashing all the colours visible to the human eye—and more." When the receptacle is empty, "The stream that flowed from it...lay where it fell, a silent motionless tempest of conflicting yet utterly harmonious hues, with a foamy spray of spikey flashes and spots that ate into the eyes with their fierce colours....There pulsed the mystical glowing red—heart and lord of colours; there the jubilant yellow—light crowned to ethereal gold; there the wide-eyed, spirit blue—the truth unfathomable; there the green that haunts the brain—storeland of Nature's boundless secrets.... All the gems were there—sapphires, emeralds, and rubies; but they were scarce to be noted in the glorious mass of new-born, ever dying colour that gushed from the fountains of the light-dividing diamonds...."

---

1 *From a Northern Window*, p. 79.

Since 1883, my father had always worn a blue star-sapphire ring. He mentions it in *Lilith*, and always saw in its mobile six-rayed centre of light, its blue sky and clouds, some mystical wonder. So the following letter anent the opal is not surprising.

G.M.D. to Mrs. Scott and the Misses Cavendish Bentinck.

May 11, 1896.

What can I say to you for your loving gift! It is lovely, it is glorious. It has such wonderful ways with it! I could give a lecture upon its changeful beauties....It is just a bit of huddled rainbow. I had never dreamed of having such a lovely thing. I must make haste and grow better, lest I should be sorry to die and leave it behind me. Thank you, thank you, for the beautiful infinitude of its change. My wife and the girls are equally delighted with it.

In the end we shall find that God has taken away our bits of coloured glass, and give us all opals instead. Oh how we shall love him at last! And that we may love him truly, infinitely, let us trust him now, when we find it most difficult! Good-night, dears.

May your lovely gift melt into my dreams.

Follows a birthday letter to Lady Mount-Temple, and, after the above imaginative outburst, very apposite in its desire for "the fulness of the Real."

Lord Mount-Temple, it must be remembered, had died in 1888 in perfect peace and eagerly looking for the first step out into the wider world of life. He would playfully complain that his dear one's prayers had to be answered though they delayed his longed-for deliverance. Once he opened his heart to me concerning his faith: "I have had no great troubles or afflictions, no hardships to face, no terrible griefs. I don't know why. It could not have been that I did not need them; perhaps I shall be given them yet in the new life."

G.M.D. to Lady Mount-Temple.

Allerton, Totnes, S. Devon,
Oct 7th, 1897.

For myself and my wife I write to meet your birthday to-morrow, with old and new, the old ever reviving into the new, and taking fresh hold. What a long time you have been setting fresh lights to the wood that has long been laid in order, and which must at length burst out in the perfect sacrifice of conscious love and adoration to God who is at the root of all increase and all gladness and contentment. He it is who checks and admonishes and turns us into the right way. I have felt both his bit in my mouth and his spur in my flank and desire that he may take and have his own strange and *therefore* perfect way with me, whatever may be my foolish way of judging it. Would that my being were consciously filled with the gladness of his obedience! Nothing less can content me. May you, dear loving sister, have it in the very fulness of God! May you and we be *real*, and so grow into the fulness of the Real! That which is in God alone exists, and alone can become ours.

The letters end with one following W. Carey Davies's death after a short illness.

G.M.D. to Mrs. W. C. Davies.
CASA CORAGGIO,
BORDIGHERA, ITALY,
Good Friday, 1898.

DEAR MRS. DAVIES,
...I have been indeed unable to think, and still more to know what I was thinking. Indeed I feel sometimes as if I were about to lose all power of thought. But when I find Carey again, he will help to set me right. Ah, you will be glad when you go to him, and find him all right and well and happy! Surely our Lord meant no less for us! He is in joy and peace with Him.

I am drawing nearer to the time I shall have to go. I do not think it will be just yet, and it is a good thing we should not know when the call will come, but may He give me what readiness he pleases. I should like to be as ready as your husband. I do not think I can ever be more ready than he.

Write to me again although I do not deserve it....

This, I think, is the last letter actually written by my father. It strikes the deeper note of sadness that rang through the remaining years. Yet he kept his last vigil in a serenity of hope untouched by his great sufferings.

CHAPTER V

THE LONG VIGIL

A MAN'S life is his work, and not less so if it be a mission—work done not primarily for livelihood. So George MacDonald's books must tell us more of his life than could any biography; and we shall look to the most notable of his last works for the crowning expressions of himself and his faith.

Indeed, the final years of his active life gave the world some of his greatest writing. If, to some, certain books suggest waning powers, as much might be said of several written in his prime. *The Elect Lady* (1888), with its captivating church—of three children and a broken-legged chicken—in contrast with a repellant miser, perhaps did not reach the highest level; but *There and Back* (1891), the last of his novels published in three volumes, was fresh and strong; some friends, among them conspicuously Carey Davies, thought it the best of the English novels. In another, *The Flight of the Shadow* (1891), the author dismisses his didactic and returns to the simple narrative style of *The Portent*, in a surprising and fantastic tale.

Lilith, the greatest, some think, of all his purely imaginative books, appeared in 1895, and was followed two years later by his last book of all, *Salted With Fire*,[1] where he once more handles Scottish material and shows us the grim conscience of an erring minister.

Among prose writings, *Phantastes* (1858) was the first essentially imaginative message, and *Lilith* the last. *Phantastes* was quite simple. It dealt with the eclipse of

---

1 Its original title was *Salted with Fire: a Minister's Story*.

truth by the Shadow, whom yet the sun may set speeding away into nothingness. *Lilith* is more complex in its superb, if odd imagery; and it tells of a viler Shadow more awful, who had "himself within him," and, from the selfish use of celestial gifts, became so Satanic that only Hell Fire could drive "himself" out.

Even the greatest poets may not find right and best word for the visions granted in their declining years. However young-eyed they be, the brain may grow old:

> But when I am quite old, and words are slow,
> Like dying things that keep their holes for woe,
> And memory's withering tendrils clasp with effort vain—[1]

Lilith, however, even if it looks for too quick a grasp of its symbolic allusiveness, gives no hint of waning power. Yet it attracted little notice. Even George MacDonald's multitude of followers and disciples, though he beyond all had fought for their mental freedom, hardly cared or dared to listen to his messengers, however arresting, when they appeared in unexpected habiliments. It is the same, of course, in every walk of life: a man is valued for his idiosyncratic work; any departure from it that proves him greater than a specialist is disapproved, if not condemned: "let the cobbler stick to his last!" they say. When, for an earlier instance, my father produced his *Hamlet* (1885), that masterly example of scholarly and inspired criticism, it was condemned and passed by.[2] And now—after many years' use of fiction as a vehicle for re-stating the Gospel in its original beauty—when he went back to fairy-tale as one way to give truth her liberty, they doubted, and set *Lilith's* strange splendour and horror aside.

Apart from its workmanship, which is often of his best, the new book was remarkable for a curious reason. Whereas

---
1 *Diary of an Old Soul*, October 19th.
2 If his *England's Antiphon* (1874), a survey of our national religious poetry, had a better reception, it was due, I almost think, to its issue by Macmillan as one in a series "for Sunday reading": from its label the flock suspected that it would suit their digestions.

a common complaint against most of my father's novels is that he over-loads his profound thought with ratiocination hardly needed by intelligent readers, here he accredits them, as I have suggested, with unusually alert perception. *Lilith*, indeed, needs reading and re-reading before the heart of its magic is reached; and even then much may be missed by those who are not already intimate with its writer's spirit and style. My mother, though I do not think her mind had lost any of its elasticity, was troubled by the book's strange imagery; her distress gave my father real heartache, so that he began to question his ability to utter his last urgent message. They agreed to submit its script to one of us—that one, in fact, to whom two years later he said, "You are the only one left to me who quite understands me." That reader found it so enthralling, that, when it was described by him as "the Revelation of St. George," husband and wife were made happy and the book was published. Many, if not all, who best understand my father, agree, I do think, with this verdict; but the book never got its dues.

The way in which my father first wrote *Lilith* in 1890 is important. He was possessed by a feeling—he would hardly let me call it a conviction, I think—that it was a mandate direct from God, for which he himself was to find form and clothing; and he set about its transcription in tranquillity. Its first writing is unlike anything else he ever did. It runs from page to page, with few breaks into new paragraphs, with little punctuation, with scarcely a word altered, and in a handwriting freer perhaps than most of his, yet with the same beautiful legibility. The mandate thus embodied in symbolic forms, over which he did not ponder, he then gave it more correct array: he re-wrote it, allowing the typewriter its help, but adding his usual and profuse pen-emendations.

Comparing carefully the two versions, some will think the earlier a better and simpler narrative. Five years intervened

THE LONG VIGIL

between the initial writing and the final book; but in both the same note of present sadness echoes throughout—a note, however, in no way out of harmony with the far-calling chimes of an unfathomable faith.

In this place a few words may be said of the story's motive, so as to give readers some clue. Like *Phantastes*, *Lilith* is an allegory of two worlds—

> Ah! the two worlds! So strangely are they one,
> And yet so measurelessly wide apart!—[1]

each revealing truths of the other not even dreamed of so long as only one is frequented.

> Yet hints come to me from the realm unknown;
> Airs drift across the twilight border-land,
> Odoured with life; and, as from some far strand
> Sea-murmured, whispers to my heart are blown
> That fill me with a joy I cannot speak.[2]

It both binds in one and unfolds the world of concrete Beauty and the realm of abstract Truth. Necessarily also it treats of their condition in dimensions—of which there be seven in all, three concrete, as I take it, and four abstract interblending but more positively vital. These four compose an inseparable unity commonly spoken of as the much debated *fourth dimension*—that concept of existence which, being spiritual, is not indeed independent of the concrete, but contains and controls the concrete three dimensions in creative manifestation.

One of *Lilith's* typical bits of symbolism is that of an ancient book, diagonally bisected, and fixed among dummy volumes in dummy shelves; which book, when the searcher has partially escaped his own concrete dimensions, is removable in its entirety and its message is revealed.

All the imageries are interwoven in masterly workmanship,

---

[1] *Lilith*, Centenary edition, 1924 (G. Allen & Unwin), with frontispiece by F. D. Bedford, and Introduction, together with paraphrase of and extracts from the discarded first manuscript, p. 204.
[2] *Diary of an Old Soul*, May 29th.

each strengthening the other in elucidation of the spiritual life. Thus, illustrating the interdependence of the material and spiritual dimensions:

> "You see that large tree to your left, about thirty yards away?" [asked the Raven]. "It stands on the hearth of your kitchen, and grows nearly straight up its chimney. That rose-bush is close to the lady at the piano. If you could but hear the music! Those great long heads of wild hyacinth are inside the piano, among the strings of it, and give that peculiar sweetness to her playing! Pardon me: I forgot your deafness!"
> "Two objects," I said, "cannot exist in the same place at the same time!"
> "Can they not? I did not know. I remember now they do teach that with you. It is a great mistake—one of the greatest wiseacre ever made! No man of the universe, only a man of the world could have said so!" [1]

It is only in a seven-fold vision that we get possessed by the truth in Beauty, and only in like comprehension realize the evil where Beauty is degraded. It is to my father's teaching upon the conundrum of sin that I venture to offer a clue—the one, indeed, any reader should yet perhaps find better for himself. If in this offer I seem presumptuous, I claim that as no knight will repudiate his squire's help, so no good father will reject his son's—however haltingly he runs beside.

It will perhaps be admitted that God is not conceived in the abstract but only through His works, which, including man, and chief among them the Incarnate Christ, are His manifestation—the outward and visible signs of Him who perpetually creates and inspires, reconciles and redeems the whole world. So, by how much an individual's capacity for seeing, hearing, feeling Beauty and Loveliness, and for recognizing them as symbolic, is increased, by so much does the living God become real to him, and not abstract. It is because of such truth that we are able to believe in the Kingdom of Heaven within us, although the crude attempts to

---

[1] *Lilith*, p. 26.

materialize apocalyptic vision in second-rate literature and art have left us cold and sceptical. Because of such truth also we can believe that

> All places shall be hell that are not heaven, [1]

and yet find ourselves unable to credit the unending flames.

So the immanence of God is the secret of all Beauty, and God is knowable to us only through Beauty. Human fatherhood invites the imagining of the Divine Fatherhood; man's power over the world and its forces implies a personal power, immeasurably mighty, in the Creator; Man's love, faithful to the death, makes possible the belief in that Spirit Who so loved the world that, through vicarious suffering, He is saving it.

But, granted Man's divisiveness in love, in passion—"What is a true passion but a heavenly hunger?" [2]—in sacrifice, we are then brought face to face with the eternal enigma. For all these gifts to Man lie in danger of terrible misuse until he gets above the law of his mortality, overcomes death and rises from the grave of his three dimensions. This misuse, originating in the divorce of the concrete dimensions from the spiritual; and because life is yet and always a portion of the infinite power; may result in disaster of utmost horror. It is a physical law that the greater the altitude, the greater the fall's momentum: it is no less a spiritual law. "The higher ye rise, ye come into the waur danger, till ance ye're fairly intil the ane safe place, the hert o' th' Father." [3] Such fall from Grace—to use the old and lovely phrase—would be irremediable, save that life still spells God and immortal Love.

The book was written, I do think, in view of the increasingly easy tendencies in universalists, who, because

---

1 Marlowe's *Faust*, quoted in *Salted with Fire*, p. 123.
2 *Weighed and Wanting* (1882), vol. i, p. 63.
3 *Salted With Fire*, p. 61.

they had now discarded everlasting retribution as a popular superstition, were dismissing hell-fire altogether, and with it the need for repentance as the way back into the Kingdom. With hell incarnate in ugliness and falsehood all about and within, we are prone to find comfort in declaring that Evil is but shadow cast by the Light, the devil but an imagined symbol of the distress caused by darkness; and to find Hell a tolerably comfortable caravanserai. But George MacDonald must descend with his Master into its precincts, and, out of love for his fellow-travellers, raise their souls from out the deadly euphoric smoke till they are able once more to cry out at the scorch of the flames. "On the other hand, how tenderly does he bring help and comfort to those lost, not in Hell but in the dark streets; how clearly he shows them that poverty, sickness and distress may cut roads into the Land of Life, never discovered by prosperity." [1]

In 1885 my father had written the preface to a book that attracted more notice than *Lilith*, the authorship of which was commonly attributed to him. We see at once why he gave support to its Danish writer:

> ...When I say the book is full of Truth, I do not mean truth of theory or truth in art, but something far deeper and higher—the realities of our relations to God and man and duty—all, in short, that belongs to the conscience. Prominent among these is the awful verity, that we make our fate in unmaking ourselves; that men, in defacing the image of God in themselves, construct for themselves a world of horror and dismay.... [2]

But though these *Letters from Hell* are imaginative, their pictures are too concrete—like, indeed, the pre-Raphaelite frescos in Pisa's Campo Santo—to have been inspired by George MacDonald, and therefore to many do not appeal as, I believe, *Lilith* will yet do.

William Blake has said: "God is within and without, even in the depths of Hell"; [3] and *Lilith* tackles the eternal

---

1 I quote my friend James A. Campbell of Barbreck.
2 *Letters from Hell*, Preface (1885), p. vi.
3 *Jerusalem*, p. 12, line 15.

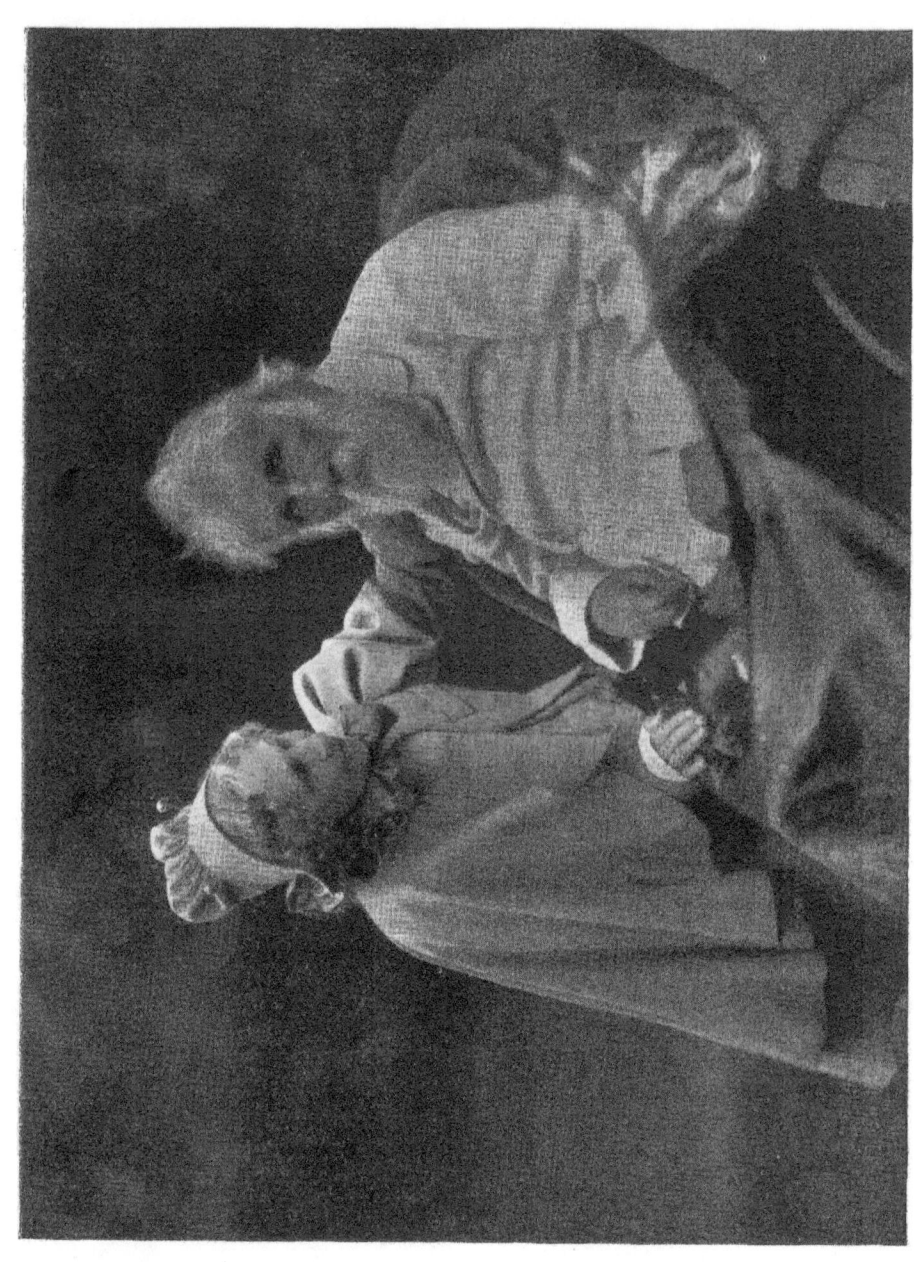

THE LONG VIGIL

paradox of, on the one hand, Beauty, inspiring in power, evoking man's worship; and, on the other, its profanation, persuasive in equal power, but to man's utter undoing: the paradox of passion, which is but "heavenly hunger" and its prostitution to greed; of the god-like becoming devil-incarnate.

It is in the boldness of this paradox that the book's note of prophecy rings. It spells for the reader, as mutually revealing, the wrath and the pity of God enshrined together in that creation which was once the most lovely but becomes most accursed of all—Lilith, the Angel-vampire. In it we perhaps seem to understand how it comes to pass that, though man is created to uphold the Kingdom of Heaven within him, he generates Hell in his heart and belches its flames to scorch the Heavens beyond him. We find too, symbolic suggestion of a word uttered at the close of the noblest sermon of my father that I remember, "Who, then, shall ever dare to say, 'God has done all He can'"?

Blake insists that "Everything that lives is holy." Something in Lilith's soul still lives in divine and potential loveliness, in spite of her beauty's foul desires. Not even the lowest of courtesans is ever robbed of this innermost jewel—her "virginity that can never be defiled," as Blake has it; or my father—

> A gutter-child, a thief, a girl who never in this world had even a notion of purity, may lie smiling in the arms of the Eternal, while the head of a lordly house that still flourishes like a green bay-tree, may be wandering about with the dogs beyond the walls of the city.[1]

Towards the end of *Lilith*, some are congregated in the Cemetery.

> "What is that flapping of wings I hear?" I asked.
> "The Shadow is hovering," replied Adam; "there is one here [Lilith] whom he counts his own! But ours once, never more can she be his!"[2]

---

1 *Salted with Fire*, p. 161. Vide antea, p. 344.
2 *Lilith*, pp. 332 *et seq*.

I have no reason for thinking that my father made any study of Blake's prophetic books. Indeed, there is nothing new in any prophecy—only the eternally ancient; and every prophet must be given his own vision, must find his own mode and metaphor for its proclamation. But my father did unquestionably get help from Blake in his need to tell us the truth about the Grave. Every man has to rise from it, get quit of its three-dimensioned imprisonment; but he will gather strength for the growth of his four-dimensioned wings and for breaking the crysalid bonds only by happy acceptance of sleep in God's cemetery, whose exquisite cold is death to all evil.

For as long as I can remember there hung in my father's study four of Blake's illustrations to Blair's *Grave*—the good man dead on his tomb-like bed, the bad man fiercely escaping with evil spirits, the Spirit of Man with the candle of the Lord searching all the Grave's inward parts,[1] and the old man driven—the North Wind blowing where it listeth—into his tomb, to find himself reborn into the fulness of youth, with head uplifted to the risen sun:

> And the man through Death's door going
> Leaves old Death behind.[2]

I cannot doubt that my father, though he knew little of Blake beyond his lyrics, lit upon through him the idea of the Cemetery in *Lilith*. There we are shown the old man lying in his tomb and nearing the end of his long vigil; there alongside, a woman in sleep less happy than his, but waiting for the healing of some sore that still mars her beauty a little. The writing of this strange chapter will give many a reader some sense of that infinite hope which may burgeon into faith; it is an utterance in art that transcends all creeds or rhetorical arguments.

The only books of William Blake that my father had

---

1 Proverbs xx. 27.
2 "Autumn Song," *Poetical Works*, vol. i, p. 341.

in his library were a facsimile of the original *Jerusalem* and an early hand-coloured reproduction of *The Marriage of Heaven and Hell*, besides *Gilchrist's Life*, which last I remember my parents reading and discussing. As a youth I would dip into and puzzle over the two former; but I do not remember my father ever making comment upon them. Yet if I wanted to indicate a comparison between Blake's and George MacDonald's teaching, I should choose the description in *Lilith* [1] of Mr. Raven plunging his beak in the sod, drawing out a wriggling worm, tossing it into the air, when "it spread great wings, gorgeous in red and black, and soared aloft," and couple it with two other quotations:

> I think of death as the first pulse of the new strength shaking itself free from the old mouldy remnants of earth-garments, that it may begin in freedom the new life that grows out of the old. The caterpillar dies into the butterfly....[2]

> O Life, burn at this feeble shell of me,
> Till I the sore garment off shall push,
> Flap out my Psyche wings, and to thee rush.[3]

Then I should quote one of Blake's many words concerning "the dark and intricate caves of the *Mundane Shell*—hardened shadow of Heaven and Hell"—which "finishes where the lark mounts"—

> Mounting with wings of light into the Great Expanse
> His little throat bursts with inspiration,
> With eyes of soft humility and wonder, love and awe.[4]

I lay all this stress upon the importance of *Lilith* because I am writing my father's life; for it was not only the majestic thought of his old age, but portion also of the suffering that, mercifully near the end, led him up to his long and last vigil. And here I append the closing words of his final book:

---

1 P. 23.   2 *David Elginbrod*, vol. iii, p. 136.
3 *Diary of an Old Soul*, March 10th.
4 Blake's *Milton*, Book II, p. 31.

God is deeper in us than our own life; yes, God's life is the very centre and creative cause of that life which we call *ours*; therefore is the Life in us stronger than the Death, in as much as the creating Good is stronger than the created Evil.[1]

*   *   *   *   *

For many years—indeed, for as long as I can remember—my father had suffered from eczema, now better, now worse, and liable to aggravation by an East Wind. His digestion was seldom at fault. Diet and various courses of treatment from time to time—sulphur baths, homœopathy, hydropathic systems, or the remedies and regimen of renowned specialists—scarcely helped him. He was a great sleeper always, and could almost at any moment—perhaps because of his beautiful innocency—lie down and sleep. My mother believed always that he owed his life to this sleeping and the healing it brought to mind and skin and bronchial tubes.

But though his tendency to bronchitis and asthma steadily diminished since he had wintered in Italy, the eczema was not relieved. Indeed it slowly became more troublesome, and towards the middle of the nineties it began to interfere with his sleep. He had for years almost given up alcohol, and though Chianti was always on the table, he seldom touched it. Smoking he had long abandoned. But exercise, of late years never a happy pursuit, became increasingly difficult. In the early days of cycling he tried more than one form of tricycle—but never with enjoyment or regularity, so that he gained little from it. Nor was he fond of driving, though he always enjoyed excursions up the Vallecrosia or Roja Valleys, or to the mountain towns of Dolceaqua and Pigna, or by San Remo to La Colla, or even San Romolo at the foot of the Bignone, or to La Mortola. Then there were visits to Mrs. Scott and her daughters at Florence, and to Pisa. Once the summer months were spent at the villa Demidoff in the rich-wooded Pratolino, and gave recreation and

---

1   *Salted With Fire*, 1897, p. 325.

change. But his books were his chief solace, and at Casa Coraggio he taught himself Spanish; later, Dutch also, with the idea, I think, of getting nearer understanding with Jacob Böhme, whose works he had some early knowledge of—if we may judge from *David Elginbrod*—and to which in later years we have some evidence of his returning. Law's quarto edition of *Böhme's Complete Works*, and a very early Dutch edition of the *Forty Questions* were on his shelves. Certainly in *Lilith*, as in many other books, we may often suspect an understanding of "The Teutonic Philosopher's" thoughts, even if my father was not deeply versed in his works. What more like his faith than that inspired cobbler's teaching that, however deep a man may be in Hell, he can never be outside God?[1]

In the winter of 1896-7 an incident occurred that stirred the best and deepest feelings of the English colony at Bordighera. Dr. John A. Goodchild, the family's medical adviser and much beloved by my father as a man of unusual poetical gift and strange mystical mind, was infamously attacked in an Italian court of law on the false charge of libelling a practitioner of other nationality, who was scarcely a rival. One after another of my people were subpœnaed, one as witness for the prosecution. My father was deeply moved, and spoke in court with such fiery indignation in defence of his friend that his evidence probably had much to do with the withdrawal of the case. James A. Campbell of Barbreck, also beloved of my father, was watching it with keen interest. He writes of it to myself:

> Endowed with a keenly sensitive temperament, pitiful of all sorrow, he did not perhaps recognize the Fire of Charity in his own soul when it flamed forth in defence of others. On the occasion when he was summoned as a witness before the court, he spoke in chivalrous and strong defence of his friend. But afterwards he was much troubled that he should

---

1 Compare stanza on p. 398.

have spoken "inadvisedly"; while to those who heard him it seemed that he had only obeyed the orders of his Master, in reference to such occurrences, by taking no anxious thought, and saying what was given him to say.

But I believe my father did not quickly relinquish the blaming of his swift and splendid anger.

The vigour indeed of his mind at this time in relation to his immediate world was still as positive as his imaginative vision was alert. The friend last quoted is witness to this also. In illustration of my father's delight in colour, he writes me:

> I remember one day at Casa Coraggio, when conversation turned upon the wonderful colouring of Southern skies and seas, he said, "Yes, they are splendid! But I have only to close my eyes and I see a bit of grey rock and great clouds in a deep blue sky, and the wind blowing over the golden whins that the English call gorse."

Yet in spite of his youthful spirituality, my father would often feel the oppressiveness of an admiration-atmosphere, so to speak, in Bordighera's stifling, chattering little colony, with its constantly flitting additions from pleasure-seeking, wealthy trippers. My friend refers to this point also:

> My sister tells me how she was talking once with him quietly in a corner of the great room on a reception day. A number of people came in together, and he said, "I want to go on talking to you, but I can't stand this!" He got up and went away for a short time, returning afterwards to welcome them.

But early in that year (1897) my father, being then seventy-three, the eczema became alarming, so gravely did it interfere with sleep. It was a constant torture—no less—and my father's sadness increased. He realized that his brain sometimes would not respond to his imagination, though he set himself a course of reading as if to discipline his fatigue into some renewal of life. Then even this became difficult. But my mother's devotion to him, her indomitable hope for his recovery, were as apparent in the letters she wrote to me, giving instances of his wit and humour suddenly breaking through his increasing taciturnity, as to my sister Irene, who alone of the eleven was now left at home. Once his breakfast egg was unusually large, and he quietly remarked, as my mother opened it for him, "It must have taken two hens to lay that one." Little messages he would send in her letters as "Yes; give him my interminable love," sometimes adding a sentence in his own now very shaky hand. He soon needed more nursing than my mother and sisters could give. He had a devoted and trained man and woman to help, and his gratitude for simplest services was in a way heart-rending. The suffering, I say, was terrible. It looked as though for a spell Satan, the sceptic and materialist, still in doubt if the faith of even a saint could survive his testing of it, was allowed to try his hand once again. To the earlier days of this sleep-forbidding torture belong, I think, these lines, which, with their many erasures and substituted words, are not quite easy to disentangle: it must be remembered also that such odds and ends of unpolished verse were no more intended for publication than his letters. My only addition is the punctuation.

"O that thou wouldst rend the heavens and come down!"

>Come through the gloom of clouded skies,
> The slow dim rain and fog athwart,
>Through East winds keen and wrong and lies,
> Come and make strong my hopeless heart.
>
>Come through the sickness and the pain,
> The sore unrest that tosses still,
>The aching dark that hides the gain—
> Come and arouse my fainting will.
>
>Come through the prate of foolish words,
> The Science with no Lord behind,
>Through all the pangs of untuned chords
> Speak wisdom to my shaken mind.
>
>Through all the fears—that spirits bow—
> Of what hath been or may befall,
>Come down and talk with me, for thou
> Canst tell me all about them all.

> Come, Lord of Life—here is thy seat,
>   Heart of all joy below, above—
> One minute let me kiss thy feet
>   And name the names of those I love.
>
> For, when thou comest, well I know
>   Thou wast not all the time away;
> And strong I rise, when thou dost go,
>   To meet the dark another day.

My father's dejection was akin to Job's; and if at his worst, just before his deliverance from the evil thing came, he even echoed the words of his Master that God had forsaken him, his spirit was thereupon commended to God.

Then came upon him his long vigil—"a constant waiting for something at hand." [1] With the peace of it, his skin became clear of blemish like a child's, and his old power of sleep came back to him. Yet for five years he scarcely spoke one word, accepting all services with gentle gratitude, obeying all injunctions. Nor to the last, though the heart-rending air of waiting for something—far off or near by—never left him, had he any other look than his old one of wistful enquiry; while his eyes, still blue as a child's—"those blue eyes that seemed rather made for other people to look into them than for himself to look out of"[2] —with no sign of old age in or about them, lost none of their celestial intelligence. "All the night long the morning is at hand." [3]

In 1900 a house at Haslemere, planned by my architect brother, was built for my parents, and given to my mother for her life-time. It was named "St. George's Wood," had lovely gardens and three acres of woodland with superb beeches that overspread the road. Here in the summer my father was well known by sight, as he took his daily drives. In his red cloak and white serge suit, with grey felt hat, he looked most beautiful. A young friend, who did not know him

---

1 *Vide* G.M.D. to Mrs. Russell Gurney, p. 487.
2 *At the Back of the North Wind*, p. 345.
3 *Lilith*, p. 332.

personally, would run up and down the road on his bicycle that he might see yet again, and never too often, "the grand old saint." Here too they celebrated their golden wedding in 1901, though the actual day was March 8th, and now it was June. To my mother, looking so bright and young-eyed, with children, nephews, nieces and grandchildren about her, and the few old friends left, such as Octavia Hill, Mr. and Mrs. C. E. Maurice, it was a blissful day; and my father, though he spoke never a word, took heart from her. Yet one closely observant might see that whenever she left the room his gaze would follow her and remain on the door till she came back again; and then he would sigh contentedly.

But a time came when my mother, worn out with clinging to hopes which increasingly failed her, and herself ailing with an internal affection, at last realized two things: one that he would never recover his power of speech, and the other that skilful and kind nurses could do more for him than she in her waning strength. She turned her face to the wall. Her own suffering and waywardness were great, and the devoted nursing of her one daughter, Irene, was their only mitigation.[1] Yet to the last she sent me tender notes and encouragements about my father. She died in January, 1902, three years before him. For some days my two sisters, both of whom were with her at the last, dared not tell my father, almost afraid that he would not grasp it. But when they did so, he wept bitterly.

> Many a wrong and its curing song;
> Many a road, and many an inn;
> Room to roam, but only one home
> For all the world to win![2]

---

[1] My sister Winifred had married C. E. Troup, now Sir Edward Troup, K.C.B., in January, 1897. My sister Irene married Cecil Brewer, the celebrated architect, in May, 1904.
[2] "Eve, the eternal Mother's Song," *Lilith*, p. 316; given also in *Phantastes*, 1st ed., p. 286.

During the years that followed, my sister Irene till her marriage scarcely left him, tending him with constant and sunny watchfulness. He spent much of his time in bed. But whether there or sitting dressed, he was always waiting, always beautiful to behold, in spite of the cloud upon the snow-clad mountain. If anyone came to the door for entry, he would turn and look with a moment's quiet expectation, and then, seeing it was not my mother, would sigh deeply and begin his waiting again. He was keeping the long vigil till she came for him.

* * * * *

George MacDonald died at Ashtead, Surrey, on September 18, 1905, after some months of perfect love and cherishing from his youngest daughter, Winifred Louisa Troup. His body was cremated at Woking, and the ashes buried at Bordighera beside the body of his wife.

* * * * *

> And when grim Death doth take me by the throat,
> Thou wilt have pity on thy handiwork;
> Thou wilt not let him on my suffering gloat,
> But draw my soul out—gladder than man or boy
> When thy saved creatures from the narrow ark
> Rushed out, and leaped and laughed and cried for joy,
> And the great rainbow strode across the dark.[1]

---

1 *Diary of an Old Soul*, October 21st.

BIBLIOGRAPHY

"IN a literary life of some forty-two years George MacDonald produced some fifty-two volumes, of which twenty-five may be classed as novels, three as prose fantasies, eight as tales and allegories for children, five as sermons, three as literary and miscellaneous critical essays, and three as collections of short stories; and five volumes of verse, the greater part of which, with many poems gathered from the pages of the prose works, arranged in two volumes and finally revised by his own hand, was reissued in 1893."[1]

The following list includes all the above with the dates of publication. In many cases, especially where the author had sold the copyright, the publishers were changed more than once. Some of the books ran to five or six editions. A large number ran through periodicals before publication, and one short story, *Far Above Rubies*, appeared in the Christmas number of *The Sketch*, 1898, and did not appear in book form.

Within and Without, a Poem	1855	Longmans, Brown, Green.
Poems	1857	Longmans, Brown, Green.
Phantastes : a Faerie Romance for Men and Women	1858	Smith, Elder.
A new edition, illustrated by Arthur Hughes	1905	A.C. Fifield.
Everyman edition	n.d.	Messrs. J.M. Dent.
David Elginbrod. 3 vols.	1863	Hurst & Blackett.
New edition 1 vol.	n.d.	Hurst & Blackett.
Adela Cathcart. 3 vols.	1864	Hurst & Blackett.
The Portent: a story of the Inner Vision of the Highlanders commonly called the *Second Sight*	1864	Smith Elder.
Alec Forbes of Howglen. 3 vols.	1865	Hurst & Blackett.
Cheap edition 1 vol.	n.d.	Hurst & Blackett.
Annals of a Quiet Neighbourhood. 3 vols.	1867	Hurst & Blackett.
Cheap edition 1 vol.	1882	Kegan Paul.

---

1 Ronald MacDonald's Essay in *From a Northern Window*, p. 68.

GEORGE MACDONALD

Dealings with the Fairies	1867	Strahan.
The Disciple and other Poems	1867	Strahan.
Unspoken Sermons. 1st Series	1867	Strahan.
2nd Series	1885	Longmans, Green.
3rd Series	1889	Longmans, Green.
Guild Court 3 vols.	1868	Hurst & Blackett.
Cheap edition 1 vol.	1905	George Newnes.
Robert Falconer. 3 vols.	1868	Hurst & Blackett.
Cheap edition 1 vol.	n.d.	Hurst & Blackett.
The Seaboard Parish. 3 vols.	1868	Tinsley Bros.
Cheap edition 1 vol.	1892	Kegan Paul
The Miracles of our Lord. 1 vol.	1870	Strahan.
At the Back of the North Wind	1871	Strahan.
New edition	1886	Blackie & Sons.
Ranald Bannerman's Boyhood	1871	Strahan.
New edition	1886	Blackie & Sons.
Works of Fancy and Imagination (chiefly reprints) sm. 8vo. 10 vols.	1871	Chatto & Windus.
The Princess and the Goblin	1872	Strahan.
New edition	1886	Blackie & Sons.
The Vicar's Daughter 3 vols.	1872	Tinsley Bros.
New edition 1 vol.	n.d.	Sampson Low
Wilfrid Cumbermede. 3 vols.	1872	Hurst & Blackett.
New edition 1 vol.	1893	Kegan Paul
Gutta Percha Willie: the Working Genius	1873	Henry S. King
New edition	1886	Blackie & Sons.
England's Antiphon	1874	Macmillan.
Malcolm. 3 vols.	1875	Henry S. King
New edition 1 vol.	1879	Kegan Paul
The Wise Woman, a Parable	1875	Strahan.
New edition, renamed The Lost Princess or	n.d.	Cassell.
The Wise Woman	1895	Wells, Gardner, Darton.
Thomas Wingfold, Curate. 3 vols.	1876	Hurst & Blackett.
New edition. 1 vol.	1886	Kegan Paul
St. George and St. Michael. 3 vols.	1876	Henry S. King
New edition. 1 vol.	n.d.	Kegan Paul
Exotics: a Transition (in verse) of the Spiritual Songs of Novalis, the Hymn Book of Luther and other Poems from the German and Italian.	1876	Strahan.
The Marquis of Lossie. 3 vols.	1877	Hurst & Blackett.
New edition. 1 vol.	1878	Kegan Paul

BIBLIOGRAPHY

Sir Gibbie. 3 vols.	1879	Hurst & Blackett.
New edition. 1 vol.	n.d.	Hurst & Blackett.
Everyman edition.	1914	J.M. Dent & Sons.
Paul Faber, Surgeon. 3 vols.	1879	Hurst & Blackett.
New edition. 1 vol.	1883	Kegan Paul & Co.
A Book of Strife, in the form of the Diary of an Old Soul	1880	Printed privately.
	1909	A.C. Fifield
New edition.	1913	J.M. Dent & Sons.
New edition.		
Mary Marston. 3 vols.	1881	Sampson Low.
Castle Warlock, a homely romance. 3 vols.	1882	Sampson Low.
New edition. 1 vol.	1883	Kegan Paul
Weighed and Wanting. 3 vols.	1882	Sampson Low.
New edition. 1 vol.	n.d.	H.S. King
The Gifts of the Christ Child, and other Tales. 2 vols.	1882	Sampson Low.
Afterwards published with title of *Stephen Archer and Other Tales*. 1 vol.	n.d.	Richard Edward King.
Orts	1882	Sampson Low.
A Dish of Orts. Enlarged edition of Orts.	1893	Sampson Low.
Donal Grant. 3 vols.	1883	Kegan Paul.
New edition. 1 vol.	1883	Kegan Paul.
A Threefold Cord. Poems by Three Friends, edited by George MacDonald.	1883	Printed privately.
The Princess and Curdie.	1883	Chatto & Windus.
New edition.	n.d.	Blackie & Sons.
The Tragedie of Hamlet--with a study of the text of the Folio of 1623.	1885	Longmans, Green.
Centenary edition.	1924	George Allen & Unwin.
What's Mine's Mine. 3 vols.	1886	Kegan Paul.
New edition. 1 vol.	1886	Kegan Paul.
Home Again, a Tale. 1 vol.	1887	Kegan Paul.
The Elect Lady. 1 vol.	1888	Kegan Paul.
Cross Purposes, and The Shadows : Two Fairy Stories (reprinted from Dealings With the Fairies).	1886	Blackie & Sons.
A Rough Shaking, a Tale.	1890	Blackie & Sons.
The Light Princess and other Fairy Stories (reprinted from Dealings with the Fairies).	1890	Blackie & Sons.
There and Back. 3 vols.	1891	Kegan Paul.
New edition. 1 vol.	1891	Kegan Paul.
The Flight of the Shadow. 1 vol.	1891	Kegan Paul.

A Cabinet of Gems, cut and polished by Sir Philip Sidney, now for their more radiance presented without their setting by George MacDonald.	1891	Ellit Stock.
The Hope of the Gospel.	1892	Ward, Lock, Bowden.
Heather and Snow. 2 vols.	1893	Chatto & Windus.
New edition. 1 vol.	n.d.	Chatto & Windus.
Lilith, a Romance. 1 vol.	1895	Chatto & Windus.
Centenary edition.	1924	George Allen & Unwin.
Rampolli : Growths from a Long-planted Root, being translations chiefly from the German, along with A Year's Diary of an Old Soul (Poems).	1897	Longmans, Green.
Salted With Fire, a Tale. 1 vol.	1897	Hurst & Blackett.
Poetical Works of George MacDonald. 2 vols.	1893	Chatto & Windus.
New edition.	1915	Chatto & Windus.
The Portent and Other Stories (reprints).	n.d.	T. Fisher Unwin.
Fairy Tales of George MacDonald (reprints).	1904	A.C. Fifield
Centenary edition.	1924	George Allen & Unwin.
Scotch Songs and Ballads (reprints).	1893	John Roe Smith (Aberdeen).

INDEX

Aberdeen—
  its standard of education, 68
  its poverty, 69
Adela Cathcart, 324, 345
Adoptions, G.M.D. and Wife's, 501
"Æsthetics of Public Worship," 114
Ailments, all mental, 201
Ainger, Canon, 385
Alderly Cross, 208
Alec Forbes of Howglen, 19 (quoted), 21, 54, 59, 376, 403
Algiers, 267, 268, 270
Alice, H.R.H. Princess, G.M.D. presented to, 479, 506
Alice in Wonderland, 342
Allegory, 297, 405
"Almost a Providence," 209
Alps, Maritime, excursions into, 556
Anagram, G.M.D.'s, 388, 469
Animals, G.M.D.'s hope for their future, 177
Annals of a Quiet Neighbourhood, 155, 353 (quoted), 154
Ann Arbor, sermon at, 455
Anstey, F. (quoted), 364
"Apollyon of Unbelief," 475, 494
Arnold, Matthew, 115, 300, 412
Arth, Switzerland, 539
Arundel—
  description of, 136, 137
  the call to, 138
At-homes at Casa Coraggio, 506
At the Back of the North Wind, 361
  Mark Twain's admiration of, 458 (quoted), 363, 560
Aytoun, W.E., 354

Bacon, Rev. G. B., D. D., 437
  his church, 439
Bagpipes, 40
Ballads, 299
Baltimore, 430
Bards, the MacDonald, 39
Beauty—
  of Nature, 122
  of religion, 108
  in women, 126
Bedford College, 304
Beecher Stowe, Mrs., 306, 309, 421
Bellows, Rev. H., D. D., 453, 459
Betrothal, G.M.D.'s, 116
Blackie, J.S. Professor, 301, 357
Blake, William, 216, 310
  his illustrations to Blair's *Grave*, 554
Bleachfields of Huntly, 26, 30
Blue Bell, The, 390
Bodichon, Madame, 269, 300
Boehme, Jacob, 557
Bogie, River, 20

Bolton, 250
Bolton Chapel, 252
  generosity of its congregation, 254
Bordighera, 505, 513
Boscombe, 469
Boston—
  its reception of G.M.D., 425
  its great fire, 427
Box-beds at The Farm, 34
Broadlands, conferences, 472
Broken Swords, The, 214
Brooks, Philipps, Rt. Rev., D.D., 422
  his criticism of G.M.D., 423
Brother-love, G.M.D.'s views on, 168
Brown, J., M.D., meeting with G.M.D., 354
Browne, Maddox, 302
Browning's *Christmas Eve*, G.M.D.'s article on, 185
Buchanan, Rev. R. D.D., 393
Bude, 367
Burial, Scottish, 172
Burne-Jones, Sir E., 380, 503
Burns, Robert, lectures on, in U.S.A., 424
Burns Society, N.Y., dinner at, 442
Butler, Mrs. Josephine, 300
Byron, Lady, 194, 249, 266, 278, 300
  first meeting with G.M.D., 275
  her hospitality, 304
  described in *The Vicar's Daughter*, 306
  on borrowing, 310
  her death, 313
Byron, Lady, and Mrs. H. B. Stowe, 309

Cabinet of Gems, A, 220
Cabrach, the, 251
Calvinism, 19, 85, 309
Campbell, J. A., of Barbreck (quoted), 40, 75, 330, 557
Campbell, Rev. J. MacLeod, 70, 193
Candle-fir, 22
Carlile, Rev. Prebendary (quoted), 506
Carlyle, Thomas, 192, 206, 222
  meeting with G.M.D., 354
Carroll, Lewis (C.L. Dodgson), 301
  submits *Alice in Wonderland* to G.M.D.'s children, 342
Casa Coraggio—
  described, 506
  tableaux vivants at, 509
  concert for Italian church, 510
  behaviour during earthquake, 513
Castle Warlock, 115, 146, 147 (quoted), 186, 200, 209, 336, 337, 366, 376, 410, 476, 492
Catechism, Shorter, G.M.D. on, 53, 59, 91
Cattaneo, Palazzo, 474
Cavendish-Bentinck, the Misses, 542, 543

567

Cecil, Henry, 173, 469, 484
  translates song of G.M.D., 250
  letter to, 536
"Celestial Wit," G.M.D.'s, 376
Celt, the, 77
Chair of Belles Lettres, Edinburgh, 354
Channing, Rev. Dr., 185
Chanter-kist, 28
Charades—
  in Aberdeen, 74
  at The Limes, 119
Charteris, Lady Caroline, 522
"Chaucer a non-dramatic Shakespeare," 327
Chemistry—
  at Aberdeen, 70
  at Highbury, 115, 129
  at Manchester, 216
Chesterton, G.K., on G.M.D.'s "Celestial Wit," 371
Children—
  discipline of, 237
  education of, 367
Christ's Mission, sketch of, 222
Christie, Tibbie, G.M.D. visits her, 113
Christmas—
  at Hastings, 286
  at Casa Coraggio, 511
Cincinnati, 445
Clan, its system, discipline and freedom, 44
Clifford, Rev. John, D.D., on *David Elginbrod*, 234
Cobden, the Misses, 388
Cobden, L.S.M.D.'s letters to Miss Jane (Mrs. Fisher Unwin), 510, 515, 516
Cobden-Sanderson, Mrs., words on The Retreat, 388
Coleridge, S.T., on reading the Scriptures, 137
Collier, Rev. R. Laird, 453
Constable, Thomas, 354
Copyright, international, 457
Cork, 118, 124
Corncraik, 56
Cowper-Temple, *vide* Mount-Temple
Craik, Sir H.P.C., M.P. (quoted), 365
Crofters, G.M.D.'s study of, 57
Culloden, 39
Curtoys, Rev. W.F. (quoted), 507
Cushman, Miss, tragedienne, 385, 422

Darwin, Erasmus, 355
David Elginbrod (quoted), 318, 322, 323, 398
  epitaph in (quoted), 45, 234, 251, 320, 555
Davies, W.C., 366, 387, 490
  his death, 544
Deacons at Arundel, 178
Death, G.M.D.'s fearlessness of, 200, 253
De Kay, Miss H. (Mrs. R.W. Gilder), 440
De Morgan, William, 304
Diary of an Old Soul, The (quoted), 110, 234, 253, 260, 299, 476, 479, 482, 494, 496, 502, 515, 527, 547, 549, 553, 554, 555, 562
Dimension, The Fourth, 549
Disciple, The—
  autobiographical, 85
  eulogized in the *Scotsman*, 88
Dish of Orts, A, 71, 308, 372, 377
Doctrine, G.M.D. on, 155
Dodgson, Rev. C.L., *see* Carroll, Lewis

Dodgson, Wilfred, 466
Dominie, the Huntly, 60
Donal Grant (quoted), 26, 57, 340, 376, 495
Doubt, 198
  almost necessary in real earnestness, 198
  G.M.D.'s views on, 475
  "The hammer to break clouded windows," 374

Earles Terrace, removal to, 346
Earthquake of 1887 at Bordighera, 513
Edinburgh, description of, 228
Elect Lady, The, 546
"Electro-Biology," 302
Elfie, Little, verses, 243
Elmira, U.S.A., 432
Emerson, R.W., 425, 457
England's Antiphon, 467, 547
Epistles, the, compared with the Gospels, 184
Erskine, T., of Linlathen, 192, 194, 325, 354, 358
  on *Within and Without*, 292
Eternal punishment, 398, 405, 551

Fairyland and Kingdom of Heaven, 299
Fairy Tales, G.M.D.'s, 378—
  Princess and the Goblin, The, 9, 123, 377, 411
  Phantastes, 288, 294
  The Light Princess, 324
  The Giant's Heart, 325
  At the Back of the North Wind, 10, 361, 363, 458, 560
  Lilith, 547
Faith, enthusiastic, 255
Fall of Man, the, 551
Family life, 111, 410
Famine, the Highland, 30
Farewell lecture on *Hamlet* in U.S.A., 459
Farm, The, Huntly, 26
  its vicissitudes, 30
Fear of death, none in G.M.D., 200, 253
Fields, J.T., 457
  his humour, 420, 453
Fir-candles, 23
Flight of the Shadow, The, 488, 492, 546
Forbes-Robertson, Sir J., 312, 385
Forgiveness, 221
France, Anatole (quoted), 339
Francis, A.M., 202
Freedom, 376
Free will, 507, 535
Fyvie Castle, 530

Geddes, Sir W.D., 57
  on G.M.D.'s student days, 75, 78, 80
  ranks G.M.D. second only to Tennyson, 536
Genius, 385
"Getting on," 185, 194, 195
Ghosts, G.M.D.'s belief in (footnote), 115
Giacomo, Padre, 510
Giant's Heart, The, 325
Gilder, Richard Watson, 410, 434, 444, 451, 455, 460, 468
  letters to L.S.M.D., 438
  visit to Porto Fino, 493
Glencoe described, 42
"God—just a Lord of Session," 325

INDEX   569

God not conceived in abstract, 400, 550
God's will and man's, 292
Godwin, Rev. J.H., 99, 119, 157
   letter on the duty of being successful, 114, 183
   says G.M.D. does not make himself understood, 185
Golden Pot, Hoffmann's, 259, 297
Golden wedding, 561
Goodchild, Dr. J.A., G.M.D.'s defence of, in libel action, 557
Goodwin, Rose, 377
Good Words for the Young—
   G.M.D.'s editorship, 361
   its failure, 411
Gordon, fifth Duke of, and his crofter tenants, 21
   his funeral witnessed by G.M.D., 52
Gordon, General, 531
Gordon, house of, 20
Gospel, summary of Jesus Christ's work, 185
"Greatheart, Mr.," 502
Green, Rev. Charles, 114
Greenwood, James, 320
Gurney, Russell, 300
   in U.S.A., 419
   death of, 487
Gurney, Mrs. Russell, 424, 522
Gutta Percha Willie, 409

Hæmorrhage from lungs, 144, 252
Halloway House, Hastings, 411
Hamlet, The Tragedie of, 540, 547
Harrison, Dr., 217
Haslemere, St. George's Wood, 560
Hastings, 280
   Christmas at, 285
Haunted House, The, 451
Hawker, Rev. R.S., 369
Heather and Snow, 75
Heresy hunt, the, 177
Hidden Life, A (quoted), 56, 57, 61, 70, 111, 170, 277, 292
Highbury College—
   its staff, 113
   its training, 118
Hill, Octavia—
   G.M.D.'s first meeting with, 368
   entertainments of her tenantry by G.M.D., 380
   early work, her, 382
   and Ruskin, 486
Hoffmann, A.E.T., his possible help to G.M.D., 73, 259
Holland, Dr. J.G., 427
Holmes, O.W., 457
Home-coming, the, 466
Hope of the Gospel, The, 344
Housekeeping in Manchester, 227
Hughes, Arthur, 302, 312, 361
Hughes, E.R., 466, 473, 484
Hunt, James, Ph.D., 301
Huntly—
   market-day at, 22, 57
   G.M.D. and family at The Farm, 264
Huntly News, The, for 1937 (sic), 242
Hymn, A Mother's, 199

Ice-storm, 438
"Idol of Chance" repudiated, 147
Immanence, God's, 201, 482, 551

Industrialism, 191, 329
Inheritance of good and evil, 507
In Memoriam, G.M.D.'s opinion on, 541
Instinct, spiritual, 339 *et seq.*
Intemperance in Scotland, 62
Israels, Joseph, 413

Jameson, Rev. K., 503
Jelf, Rev. R.W., D.D., Principal of King's College, 397
Joy, duty of, 508
Jubilee Singers, 442

Kelpies, 20, 54
Kennedy, Rev. John, D.D., 68, 69, 74
   his orthodoxy, 79
King's College, London, G.M.D.'s lectureship at, 366
Kingsley, Charles, 300, 355
Kingswear, 259
Kite, The, 166

Ladies' College, Manchester, 216, 218
La Touche, Mrs., 328, 353
La Touche, Rose, 328
   her character, 331
   describes her feelings for Ruskin, 417
   at The Retreat, 417
Lawson, George, his bust of G.M.D., 412
Leigh-Smith, Miss Anna, 269, 513
Leith, Mrs. D., *vide* MacDonald, Louisa
Letters from Hell, its preface by G.M.D., 552
Librarian, Owen's College, G.M.D. seeks post of, 201, 207
Library at "castle in the far North," 72
Light Princess, The, 324
Lilith, 403, 405, 546, 550, 553, 560, 561
Limes, The—
   Upper Clapton, home of Powell family, 98
   seat in oak-tree at, 127
"Literary Society" described, 321
Longman, C.J., 224
Longmans, publishers, 240
   generosity of, 221
Love me Beloved, 152
Lynch, Thomas, 159, 201, 311

Macbeth, 452
MacColl, A. Stewart, 52
   Mrs. A.S., letter to, 394
MacColl, Duncan, M.D., R.N., 53
   Margaret, G.M.D.'s stepmother, 53, 129
   Norman, editor of *Athenæum*, 52
MacDonald, the three brothers, 160
   their faiths compared, 175
MacDonald, Alec—
   his enterprise, 161
   his love-story, 169
   his boyhood, 186
   his death, 172
MacDonald, Bella, 55, 245
   her death, 251
MacDonald, Bernard P., birth, 353, 535
MacDonald, Caroline Grace (Mrs. Kingsbury Jameson)—
   birth, 215
   death, 503
MacDonald, C.E., G.M.D.'s grandfather, 25, 39

MacDonald, Mrs. C.E., née Isabella
    Robertston (grandmother of G.M.D.),
    26
  her burning of family papers, 27
  her diary, 64
MacDonald, Charles F., 129, 272, 291
MacDonald, George—
  earliest memory, 21, 52
  early intimacy with peasantry, 24
  fortitude, 32
  prose is broken-down poetry, 44
  horsemanship, 54, 55, 120, 345, 369
  sisters, 55
  machinery, 58
  requisitions washstand for pulpit, 59
  humour, 59, 130, 326, 327, 478, 559
  first President of Juvenile Temperance
    Society, 63
  high spirits, 65, 271, 343, 369
  leadership in games, 65
  love of the sea, 65, 67, 369, 488
  wins Bursary at King's College, 67
  meets Chartists and Fergus O'Connor,
    69
  love of chemistry, 70
  lectures on chemistry, 115, 129, 216
  love of stairways, 71, 347, 349, 481, 485
  catalogues library, its educational value
    to him, 72
  tartan coat, 75
  dress, 76, 423, 449
  grows a beard, 234
  a black sheep, 79
  early poetry, 80
  intimacy with Helen MacKay, 83
  optimism, 84, 198, 476
  a man of action, 91
  earliest declaration of his teaching, 93
  industry, 94, 317, 418, 502
  tutorship at Fulham, 107
  eschews smoking, 108
  writes of his unfitness for ministry, 108
  athleticism, 112
  enters Highbury College, 113
  debates on "Æsthetics of Public
    Worship" and "Ghosts," 114
  betrothal, 116
  reproached for unconventionality, 118
  "supply" duties at Cork, 118, 124
  love for G.E. Matheson, 119, 157, 417
  musical, if ungifted, 126
  student life and pleasures in London,
    120
  woman's beauty, 126
  as preacher unacceptable to some,
    129, 138
  Aberdeen note-books, 140
  first attack of hæmorrhage, 144
  second attack of hæmorrhage, 252
  would take Holy Orders but for the
    ministers the Church admits, 149
  his library, 150, 380, 386, 515
  marriage, 151
  "neither Arminian nor Calvinist," 155
  the Pastor, 155
  on riches, 156
  the young much attracted to him, 156
  first child born, 159
  on brother-love, 168
  his hopes for the lower animals, 177
  his orthodoxy questioned at Arundel,
    177

MacDonald, George (continued)—
  asked to resign pastorate, 178
  address to critics at Arundel, 179
  stipend reduced, 179
  the Epistles compared with the Gospels,
    184
  his passionate tranquillity, 185
  his attitude towards Unitarians, 185
  his tenderness of heart, 186
  understands Bible better for recreation,
    187
  Manchester described, 191
  has no love for any sects, 197
  humbleness of mind, 198, 208
  refuses compromise, 200
  refuses to turn stones into bread, 201
  applies for post of librarian, 201, 207
  first disappointment in publishing, 204
  his mission, 213
  revisits Huntly, 233, 264, 293, 418
  his poverty, 243, 244, 273
  his fearlessness of death, 253
  relinquishes style of Rev., 263
  explains acceptance of gifts, 272
  his Pantheism defined, 278, 311
  his gift in story-telling, 286
  as handy-man, 288
  on God's Will, 292, 507, 535
  his ballads, 299
  medallion by Munro, 301
  secures Lectureship at Bedford College,
    304
  his portraiture, 306
  as playwright, 307, 309, 311
  first novel, 307
  writes for *Encyclopædia Britannica*, 307
  study at Tudor Lodge, 312
  study at The Retreat, 386
  study at Casa Coraggio, 506, 515
  renunciation of self, 326, 327
  intimacy with his children, 327, 370
  on Chaucer, 327
  as sportsman, 327
  attitude towards industrialism, 330
  repudiation of physical evidences, 336
  attitude towards vivisection, 340
  refuses pastorate in New York, 124, 340,
    459
  his gaiety and love of fun, 343
  his sadness, 201, 344
  on gambling, 346
  genius unmatched as writer for
    children, 363
  on money, 346, 400
  refuses gift of money, 513
  his love of mountains, "God's church
    towers," 348, 350, 352
  Chair of Rhetoric and Belles Lettres, 354
  his debt to A.J. Scott, 359
  edits *Good Words for the Young*, and
    loses friends, 361
  education of his children, 362
  his views on education, 363
  cares nothing for success and position,
    364
  his gift for listening, 365, 538
  his place as poet, 14, 88, 536
  Lecturer at King's College, 366
  on Church collections, 367
  visits the poet Hawker, 369
  "celestial wit," 371
  verbal inspiration, 373

INDEX

MacDonald, George (*continued*)—
his dialectic compared with his celestial wit, 377
entertains poor, 380
befriends derelicts, 384
L.L.D., conferred, 385
his energy, 389, 409
yachting trip, 390
abscess on knee, 393
eternal punishment, 398, 405
asked to collaborate with F.D. Maurice, 399
raises testimonial to F.D. Maurice, 399
compared with F.D. Maurice, 401
doctrine and faith, 402
on immortality, 402
the Kingdom of Heaven, 404
thanksgiving for F.D. Maurice, 406
troubles as editor, 412
portraits painted, 413
sails for U.S.A., 418
his eloquence, 423
enthusiastic reception in Boston, 425
reception in Philadelphia, 428
confused with Professor Tyndal, 429
dramatic power, 441
appears in kilt at Burns dinner, 442
snowed up, 443
visits Niagara, 454
America's gratitude, 459
his daily riding, 466
publishers' difficulties, 477
at Broadlands Conference, 472
intellectual and spiritual doubt, 475
Civil List pension, 479
symbol and substance, 482
improved health in Italy, 489
adopted children, 501
as Mr. Greatheart, 502
free will, 507, 535
his psycho-analysis, 507
joy, duty of, 508
memory portrait of him, 508, 527
friendliness with village priest, 510
invitation verses, 512
appreciation of A.P. Watt, his literary agent, 531
his tranquillity, 515, 523, 545
his pacifism, 517
brain-fatigue, 524
faith stronger for bodily decay, 525
one moment's thought worth months of brooding, 530
popularity increases, but money earned diminishes, 531
intellectual and moral stupidity, 533
views on Ireland, 533
submission to God's will not the right feeling, 535
would rather be atheist than believe in the popular God, 535
God takes that He may give more closely, 536
likened to St. John, 538
spends summer of 1892 at Arth, 539
polishing of his verse, 539
as critic, 539
his critique of *Hamlet*, 540
opinion of *In Memoriam* and Tennyson, 541
the poet more a man than most, 541

MacDonald, George (*continued*)—
refuses to be interviewed, 542
symbols, 543
his love of precious stones, 543
God the root of all increase, 545
physical sufferings, 556
faculty for sleep, 556
his chivalry and defence of friend in Italian court, 557
his swift and splendid anger, 558
the long vigil, 560
death, 562
for Fairy Tales, *see* under Fairy Tales
for Novels, *see* under Novels
for Unpublished Poems, *see* under Poems, Unpublished
for Tales for the Young, *see* under Young, Tales for the
MacDonald, Mrs. George, 94, 98
her originality and charm, 102
her characteristic letters, 106
her prophetic dream, 125
questions her fitness, 126
her "wonderful eyes" and personality, 139
her humour, 141, 181, 182, 469
her fortitude, 144, 195, 210, 514, 523
her vigilance, 226, 357, 561
contribution to *Adela Cathcart*, 261
her suffering, 141, 227, 233, 483, 561
description of Christmas Day at Hastings, 286
artistry in entertaining, 272, 313
how accepted in U.S.A., 426
her contralto voice, 429
inexhaustible affection, 447
her Shetland ponies, 469
her adoptions, 501
her tenderness, 505
her fountain of youth, 520
explains grandparents' leniency to grandchildren, 539
last illness and death, 561
MacDonald, George, Senior, 30
his financial burdens, 29
his generosity, 35, 234, 248
his humour, 36, 59, 130, 146, 149, 158, 191 (footnote), 209, 235
"a kind of chief of the clan," 37
his love of nature, 131
on schism, 132
his concern for his sons' ill success, 195
his tenderness, 207, 241
death, 293
MacDonald, G. Mackay, birth, 379, 520
MacDonald, Greville, letters to, 491, 530, 534, 535
MacDonald, Helen, mother of G.M.D., 30, 32
MacDonald, Irene (Mrs. Cecil Brewer)—
birth, 281, 515
marriage, 561
MacDonald, James (Senior), 242
MacDonald, James (Junior), 520
MacDonald, Jane (Mrs. Crawford Noble), 9, 55, 93, 146, 504
MacDonald John—
his enthusiasm, 161
his *wanderlust*, 161
compared with G.M.D., 162
his love of philosophy and logic, 162
his humour, 163

MacDonald, John (*continued*)—
    identified with *Eric Ericson*, 164
    his dreaminess, 165
    his portrait in *What's Mine's Mine*, 166
    narrowly escapes assassination in
        Russia, 167
    his poetry compared with G.M.D.'s,
        173
    his opinion of Goethe, 175
    lungs attacked, 290
    death, 292
MacDonald, Lilia Scott—
    birth, 159
    her deep quiet, 202
    the child-mother, 326
    her sweetness, 327
    as Lady MacBeth, 385
    her genius, 503
    her artistry, 510
    ruled by her art and her duty, 516
    goes to U.S.A., 517
    as sister, daughter, friend, 517, 519
    her illness, 521
    death of, 526
MacDonald, Louisa (Mrs. David Leith),
    55, 313
MacDonald, Mary, 226, 236
    engagement, 466
    death, 483
MacDonald, Maurice, 410
    birth, 353
    death, 489
MacDonald, Robert F., birth, 345
    letters to, 469, 313
MacDonald, Ronald—
    birth, 313
    (quoted, footnote), 213, 345, 449, 451,
        496, 543, 563
    takes mastership in U.S.A., 517
MacDonald, William, the piper fugitive
    from Culloden, 39, 41
MacDonald, Winifred L. (Lady Troup)—
    birth, 296, 475
    marriage, 561
Machinery, G.M.D.'s view on, 58
MacIntosh, cousins of G.M.D., 49
MacIntosh, Charles, F.R.S., inventor of
    hot air blast and rubber cloth, 49
MacIntosh, John, builds Longwood House,
    49
MacIntosh, William, 49
MacKay, Lieutenant George, 46
MacKay, Helen McL., 61, 75, 82 (*vide*
    also Powell, Mrs. Alec)
    her beauty and accomplishments, 97
MacKay, General Hugh of Killiecrankie,
    49
MacKay, Rev. MacIntosh, LL.D., 43, 47,
    48, 215, 372, 412
MacLeod, Rev. Norman, D.D., 301, 355
    G.M.'s letter on his death, 416
Malcolm, 40, 465
Manchester, 191
Manuscripts, G.M.D.'s minute revisions,
    218, 539, 548
Maritime Alps, villages of, described, 505
Martin, Miss F., 370
Mary Marston (quoted), 126
Matheson, Annie, 115
Matheson, Greville E., 119, 157, 158
    G.M.D.'s estimate of, 417
    death of, 417

Matheson, Greville E. (Junior), 150
Matheson, Rev. James, 115
Matheson, Leonard, 115
Matheson, William, 120, 347
    death of, 526
Matthews, Mrs. Charles, 289
Maud, Tennyson's, 247
Maurice, C. E.—
    letter from G.M.D., 518
    on G.M.D.'s tact, 509
Maurice, Mrs. C. E., on first meeting
    G.M.D., 368
Maurice, Rev. F. D., 192, 194, 218, 290,
    397
    described in *David Elginbrod*, 323, 398
    testimonial to G.M.D., 356
    his views of eternal punishment, 398
    proposes collaboration with G.M.D.,
        399
    compared with G.M.D., 401
    G.M.D.'s thanksgiving for, 406
    death of, 415
    (quoted), 509
Mavor, Bell, servant at The Farm, 59
Millar, Rev. A., 63
Missie, G.M.D.'s horse, 54, 235
Mission, G.M.D.'s, 213
Money, sacredness of, 400
Morison, Rev. John, D.D., 91
Morris, Caleb, Rev., 148
Mosquitoes, spiritual and other, 475
Mount-Temple, Lord—
    first meets G.M.D., 472
    at Casa Coraggio, 511
    letter to G.M.D., 532
    his death, 543
Mount-Temple, Lady—
    praises Mrs. G.M.D., 473
    letter to, 543
Mulock, Miss, 300, 322
Munro, Alex, 301
Music, G.M.D.'s love of, 126

Nature—
    beauty of, 122
    understanding of, 124
New York, apartments in, 440
Niagara, described by Mrs. G.M.D., 454
Nichol, William, 525
Noble, Mrs. Crawford, *vide* MacDonald,
    Jane
Note-books, G.M.D.'s, of student days,
    140
Novalis, spiritual songs of, translated by
    G.M.D., 159
Novels and Stories, G.M.D.'s—
    Alec Forbes (quoted), 19, 21, 54, 59, 376,
        403
    Castle Warlock (quoted), 115, 146, 147,
        186, 200, 209, 336, 337, 366, 376,
        410, 476, 492
    Donal Grant (quoted), 26, 57, 340, 376,
        495
    Robert Falconer (quoted), 29, 39, 67,
        166, 242, 321
    David Elginbrod (quoted), 45, 234, 251,
        318, 320, 322, 323, 398, 555
    What's Mine's Mine (quoted), 38, 49,
        123, 126, 163, 166, 168
    Malcolm, 40, 465
    Heather and Snow, 75
    Weighed and Wanting (quote), 85, 551

INDEX 573

Novels and Stories, G.M.D.'s—*(continued)*—
  Mary Marston (footnote), 126
  Annals of a Quiet Neighbourhood (quoted), 154, 155, 353
  St. George and St. Michael (quoted), 209, 247, 280
  Broken Swords, The, 214
  Thomas Wingfold, Curate, (quoted), 277, 405
  The Vicar's Daughter (quoted), 306
  Seekers and Finders (unpublished novel), 307, 319
    (quoted), 321, 404
  Adela Cathcart, 324
    (quoted), 345
  Paul Faber, Surgeon, 474, 477, 488
    (quoted), 340, 405, 496
  Wilfrid Cumbermede (quoted), 351 *et seq.*
  Salted With Fire, 546
    (quoted), 404, 417, 551, 553, 556
  Sir Gibbie, 488
    (quoted), 472
  Flight of the Shadow, The, 546
    (quoted), 488, 492
  Wow o' Rivven, 521
  Elect Lady, The, 546
  There and Back, 546
    (quoted), 386

Oakey, Miss M. (Mrs. T. W. Dewing), 440
Old Gravel Pits Meeting House, 151
Oliphant, Mrs. (novelist), 300
  her "worship" of G.M.D., 358
Ordination—
  G.M.D.'s, 157
  G.M.D.'s views on, 142
  G.M.D. senior's views on, 142
Original sin, G.M.D. on, 507

Painted Table, the, 231
Palazzo Cattaneo, poem, 480
Pantheism, G.M.D.'s, 278, 311
Parkes, Miss Bessie Rayner, 271
Party spirit, danger in, 204
Passion, true, "a heavenly hunger," 551
Paul Faber, Surgeon, 474, 477, 488
  (quoted), 340, 405, 496
Paul, St., cared little about orthodoxy, 197
Pension, Civil List, granted to G.M.D., 479
Phantastes, 15, 288, 294
  compared with *Lilith*, 547, 561
Phelps, S., tragedian, 385
Philadelphia, G.M.D.'s reception in, 428
Pilgrim's Progress, The, 490, 501
  its first acting, 386
  first public presentment of, 470
Pittsburg, 444
Plumptre, Dean E.H., 366
Poem by G.E. Matheson, "*Lighter and Sweeter*," 157
Poems published, G.M.D.'s, quoted in text—
  Hidden Life, A., 56, 57, 61, 70, 111, 170, 277, 292
  Disciple, The, 85 *et seq.*
  Spring Song, 96
  "*Were I a skilful painter*," 106
  Diary of an Old Soul, 110, 234, 253, 260, 299, 476, 479, 482, 494, 502, 527, 562
  Within and Without (see under W)

Poems published, G.M.D.'s *(continued)*—
  Manchester Poem, A, 191
  Love Me, Beloved, 152
  Mother's Hymn, A, 199
  Little Elfie, 243
  To A.I.N.B., 266
  Better Things, 276
  Sangreal, The, 311
  Ane by ane they gang awa', 403
  Thanksgiving to F.D. Maurice, 406
  The Haunted House, 451
  "*They all were looking for a king*," 481
  The New Year, 483
  George Rolleston, 528
  "*I'm a poor man, I grant*," 529
  "*Lord, what is man?*" 529
  To Gordon leaving Khartoum, 531
  "*When I look back upon my life nigh spent*," 535
  The Giver, 536
Poems, G.M.D.'s, unpublished elsewhere—
  "*Bury me deep*," 81
  Spirit of Havoc, 81
  "*Time dieth ever*," 95
  "*Mysterious night*," 95
  Nähe der Geliebten, 122
  "*He taught that Hell itself*," 398
  Both sides of the Atlantic, 431
  To L.S.M.D., 433
  "*Give me thy peace*," 473
  To my Elfie, 478
  Palazzo Cattaneo, 480
  "*To tell thee that our blessed child*," 484
  "*Child, I would give thee*," 488
  "*Pain and Sorrow*," 505
  Invitation verses, 512
  "*I want to go like other boys*," 521
  To my watch, 523
  "*When I awake from sleep*," 529
  "*O that Thou wouldst rend the heavens*," 559
  For the Dedication of Shelley House, 532
Poems unpublished elsewhere—
  By J.H. MacDonald, Twenty-one, 164
  By W.C. Davies, 387
  By H. Cecil (translation), 250
Poetical Works, 539
Popularity not expected by G.M.D., 214
Portent, The (quoted), 73
Porto Fino described, 486
Portraits by Sir G. Reid, 413
Possessions not ours, 528
Powell, Alexander, 83
  his humorous courtship, 100
Powell, Alec and Helen, their hospitality, 206
Powell, Mrs. Alec (Helen MacKay), 136, 140
  her fascination, 139, 245
Powell, Angela, wife of A.M. Francis, 103
  describes G.M.D.'s first coming to The Limes, 98, 105
Powell, Caroline Chase, 104
Powell, Charlotte (wife of Professor J.H. Godwin), 99
Powell, Florentia (wife of Joshua Sing), 104
Powell, George H., 103, 506
Powell, James, family of, 96
  his quartette parties, 104
  friendship with Coleridge, 137
  sets G.M.D.'s Psalm 116 to music, 148
  death of, 410

Powell, Mrs. James, 116
  death of, 135
Powell, Sir Leonard, 96
Powell, Louisa, 94, 95, 98 (see MacDonald, Mrs. George)
Powell, Phœbe (Mrs. Joseph King), her genius for philanthropy, 101
Powell, T.J. and T., leather factors, 97
Prayer—
  answered, 312, 313, 479
  public and private, 250
Preaching room, the, 212
"Preliminary Exercises," 118
Presumption, G.M.D. accused of, 196
Princess and the Goblin, The, 123
  G.M.D.'s own opinion of, 411
  (quoted), 377
Providence, special, G.M.D.'s views on, 109
Psycho-analysis, G.M.D.'s, 507
Publishing vicissitudes, G.M.D.'s, 477
Punishment, everlasting, 398
Pye-Smith, Rev. J., D.D., 151

Queen's Square, 305

Ranald Bannerman's Boyhood (quoted), 55 *et seq.* 77, 361
Recreation, 187
Reformation always first rejected, 197
Reid, Sir G., P.R.S.A., 413
Reid, Mrs., Principal of Bedford College, 300, 325
Rent, incident of, forgotten, 202
Reporters in U.S.A., 435, 436
Retreat, The, 379
  its theatre, 384
  dismantling of, and G.M.D.'s illness, 475
"Revelation of St. George," 548
Revenge not a Gaelic trait, 40
Rhys, Ernest, 9, 413
Robert Falconer—
  gives offence, 242; (quoted), 29, 39, 67, 166
  in *Seekers and Finders*, 321
Robertston, Rev. F.W., death of, 203
Robinson, Henry Crabb, 300, 310
Rolleston, George M.D., 528
Rooker, Rev. J., describes meeting G.M.D., 537
Rossettis, the, 302
Rough Shaking, A, 505, 514
  (quoted), 517
Rumour, "the greatest liar under the sun," 197
Ruskin, John, 194
  introduction to G.M.D., 328
  compared with G.M.D., 329, *et seq.*, 338, 341
  his gifts, 330
  his pathetic intimacy with G.M.D., 333
  on death of A.J. Scott, 334
  controverts G.M.D.'s faith, 334
  his indebtedness to spiritualism, 335
  testimonial to G.M.D., 355
  dances with O. Hill, 381
  on death of Rose La Touche, 417
  at Broadlands, 472
  his breakdown, 486
  on *The Diary of an Old Soul*, 497
Rutherford, Mark, 114

Sabbath, the Scotch, 14
  little difference between it and English Dissenters', 177
Sadness, woman's and man's, 201
Saffi, Count A., 254
St. George and St. Michael (quoted), 209, 247, 280
Salaries of ministers, 124, 131
Salted With Fire, 546
  (quoted), 551, 553, 556
  (footnote), 404, 417
School-games, 65
Science and poetry, conflict between, 71
Schism, 132
Scotsman's critique of poems, 277
Scotsman's critique of *The Disciple*, 88
Scott, A.J., 191
  first mention of, 121
  Louisa Powell's admiration of, 125
  his encouragement of G.M.D., 194
  his close friendship for G.M.D., death of, 359
Scott, Mrs. A.J., letters to, 359, 360, 400
Scott, Sir Walter, friendship with Dr. M. MacKay, 43
Second sight, 293
Seekers and Finders, 307, 319, 321, 404
Shelley, article by G.M.D. in *Encyclopædia Britannica*, 308
Shetland ponies, 469
Sin—
  the conundrum of, 550
  not a negation, 552
Sing (or Synge), Joshua, 467, 478
Sir Gibbie, 488
  (quoted), 472
Slates, a few, in answer to prayer, 479
Sleep, 247
  "the antechamber of death," 326
  G.M.D.'s capacity for, 556
Smallpox, 200
Smart, the Rev. J., 262
  death of, 493
Smeaton, Rev. Dr., 354
Smeaton, Oliphant, 286
Smith, Alphæus, 156
Smith, George M., publisher, his prophecy of G.M.D.'s work, 318
Smith-Williams, W., 319
Society—
  a "rag-stuffed idol," 200
  in Manchester, 210
Spectator, The Christian, G.M.D.'s work for, 212
Spence, Mrs. Mary, 146
Spence families in Cincinnati, 445
Spence, Mrs., at Ann Arbor, 455
Spinning factory at Huntly, 22
Stairways, G.M.D.'s love of, 71, 347, 349, 481, 485
Stanley, Dean, 504
  (footnote), 479
Step-mother, G.M.D.'s, *vide* MacColl
Stevenson, Alex, 390, 412
Stevenson, J.J., the architect, 390
Stipend at Arundel reduced, 179
Stowe, Mrs. Beecher, see Beecher Stowe
Studies, G.M.D.'s, 312, 386, 411, 506, 515
Strahan, A., 353, 415, 477
Strathbogie, 20, 65

INDEX

Success, 214, 280
   martyrdom nobler than, 198
Superstitions, Irish, 128
Sutter, Julie, 323
Sutton, H.S., 217, 236, 468
Switzerland, 347
Symbolism, 396, 482
Synge, *see* Sing

Tackleway, The, Hastings, 274, 279
Tangley Manor, 468
Temperance Society, Huntly Juvenile, 63
Tennyson, Lord—
   visits The Retreat, 380
   Two Voices, address by G.M.D., 507
   his death, 541
Terry, Kate (Mrs. Arthur Lewis), 383
Testimonial, copyright to G.M.D., 457
Tetterbys, The, 470
There and Back, 386, 546
Thomas Wingfold, Curate, 405
   (quoted), 277
Three brothers, the, 160
   their fine manners as boys, 53
   their unity in heart and purse, 168
   their faiths compared, 175
Thunderstorms, 488
"Too good to be true," 172
Tradesmen, 227
Training, theological, at Highbury College, 118
Troup, Rev. Robert G., 34, 60, 72, 198, 226, 244
Troup, Lady, *see* MacDonald, Winifred L.
Troup, Sir E., K.C.B., 561
Truth, 204
   change in its forms inevitable, 197
Tuberculosis, 34, 146, 519
Tudor Lodge, 312
Twain, Mark, 457
Twenty-one, John H. MacDonald's poem, 164

Unhappiness, cause of, in non-believers 110
Unitarianism, 185, 453
Unity of England and the United States, 460
Unspoken Sermons, (quoted), 402, 473, 476
Urquhart, Mrs., 413

Verbal inspiration (footnote), 114, 373
Vicar's Daughter, The (quoted), 306
Vigilance, Mrs. G.M.D.'s constant, 226, 357, 561
Vision, imaginative, to-day's lack of, 341
Vivisection, 340

Wandering Jew, The, 405
War, G.M.D.'s views on, 215, 517
Washington, G.M.D.'s illness in, 430
Watt, A.P. (footnote), 472
   letters to, 497, 541, 542, 531
Weighed and Wanting (quoted), 85, 551
What's Mine's Mine (quoted), 38, 49, 123 *et seq.*, 126, 168
   John MacDonald drawn in, 163, 166
Whitney, Mrs., 457
Whittier, J.G., 426
Wilfrid Cumbermede and Ruskin, 351, *et seq.*
Wilkinson, Garth, M.R.C.S., 260, 271
Williams, Dr. C.J.B., consulted by G.M.D., 145
Within and Without, 152, 209, 218, 220, 221, 223, 230, 246, 252
   G.M.D.'s own analysis of, 224
Wool-work slippers, the, 94
Works of Fancy and Imagination, 409
Wow o' Rivven, The, 371, 521

Young, Tales for the, G.M.D.'s—
   Ranald Bannerman's Boyhood, 55 *et seq.*, 77, 361
   Gutta Percha Willie, 409
   A Rough Shaking, 505, 514, 517

www.ingramcontent.com/pod-product-compliance
Lightning Source LLC
Chambersburg PA
CBHW020108240426
43661CB00002B/73